Lecture Notes in Computer Science 3579

Commenced Publication in 1973
Founding and Former Series Editors:
Gerhard Goos, Juris Hartmanis, and Jan van Leeuwen

David Lowe   Martin Gaedke (Eds.)

Web Engineering

5th International Conference, ICWE 2005
Sydney, Australia, July 27-29, 2005
Proceedings

 Springer

Volume Editors

David Lowe
University of Technology, Sydney
PO Box 123, Broadway NSW 2007, Australia
E-mail: david.lowe@uts.edu.au

Martin Gaedke
University of Karlsruhe, Institute of Telematics
Department of Computer Science
Zirkel 2, 76128 Karlsruhe, Germany
E-mail: gaedke@tm.uni-karlsruhe.de

Library of Congress Control Number: 2005929289

CR Subject Classification (1998): D.2, C.2, I.2.11, H.4, H.2, H.3, H.5, K.4, K.6

ISSN   0302-9743
ISBN-10   3-540-27996-2 Springer Berlin Heidelberg New York
ISBN-13   978-3-540-27996-9 Springer Berlin Heidelberg New York

Springer is a part of Springer Science+Business Media

springeronline.com

© Springer-Verlag Berlin Heidelberg 2005
Printed in Germany

Typesetting: Camera-ready by author, data conversion by Olgun Computergrafik
Printed on acid-free paper   SPIN: 11531371   06/3142   5 4 3 2 1 0

Preface

Over the last few years Web Engineering has begun to gain mainstream acceptance within the software engineering, IT and related disciplines. In particular, both researchers and practitioners are increasingly recognising the unique characteristics of Web systems, and what these characteristics imply in terms of the approaches we take to Web systems development and deployment in practice.

A scan of the publications in related conference proceedings and journals highlights the diversity of the discipline areas which contribute to both the richness and the complexity of Web Engineering.

The 5th International Conference on Web Engineering (ICWE2005), held in Sydney, Australia, extends the traditions established by the earlier conferences in the series: ICWE2004 in Munich, Germany; ICWE2003 in Oviedo, Spain; ICWE2002 in Santa Fe, Argentina; and ICWE2001 in Cáceres, Spain. Not only have these conferences helped disseminate cutting edge research within the field of Web Engineering, but they also have helped define and shape the discipline itself. The program we have put together for ICWE 2005 continues this evolution. Indeed, we can now begin to see the maturing of the field.

For possibly the first time, there was very little debate within the Program Committee about which papers were in and out of scope, and much more debate around the contributions which papers were actually making to the field.

We have started reaching a point where we are gaining a common understanding of the nature of our own discipline!

The ICWE 2005 conference received a total of approximately 180 submissions, with authors from 32 countries and 6 continents. It was particularly pleasing to see a much greater representation of papers from South East Asia compared to previous conferences. All submitted papers were rigorously reviewed by the excellent program committee, and 33 were eventually selected as full papers (18% acceptance), 36 as short papers (20%), and 17 posters and demos. The selected papers cover a broad spectrum, including: modelling and frameworks, architectures, content and media, testing, web services and ontologies, security, design, querying, measurement, users and usability, and tools and environments. The conference will also be host to an excellent suite of tutorials and workshops over 2 days.

And to enrich the program even further, we have had four outstanding speakers agree to give keynotes. Virgilio Almeida provides a view from within the discipline, highlighting several key areas which must be addressed within the design of Web systems. Al Davis provides a view from outside the discipline looking in, giving considerable insight into the context which drives Web development. Craig Errey brings a fascinating commercial perspective, illustrating what we can learn from other discipline areas (in this case psychology). And Lars Rasmussen discusses issues that affect the integration of new functionality into existing systems, particularly within the context of extraordinarily 'high-load' systems.

We wish to express our gratitude to all those who have contributed to making ICWE 2005 a success. We are particularly grateful to the core members of our organising committee and program committee: Yogesh Deshpande, Steve Hansen, Ka-Kit Fung, Athula Ginige, Aditya Ghose, Daniel Schwabe, Bebo White, Emilia Mendes, Gustavo Rossi, Rafael Calvo, and Xiaoying Kong, as well as several other key contributors, particularly Rosa Tay, and Richard van de Stadt.

We would also like to thank the workshop and tutorial organisers. Particular thanks go to the Program Committee members and reviewers, who with enormous care and insight, provided reviews which helped us build an excellent program.

Finally, enormous thanks go to the authors of the papers which were submitted to the conference. It is really their work which is at the core of the ICWE conference series, and which has helped shaped our discipline. Thank you!

We hope you find the papers presented in this volume useful and that they help in further advancing Web Engineering through research, education and practice.

May 2005

David Lowe
San Murugesan
Martin Gaedke

Organisation

Organising Committee

General Chair
>San Murugesan, Southern Cross University, Australia

Program Co-Chairs
>David Lowe, University of Technology, Sydney, Australia
>Martin Gaedke, University of Karlsruhe, Germany

Local Arrangements
>Steve Hansen, University of Western Sydney, Australia

Promotion
>Yogesh Deshpande, University of Western Sydney, Australia

Finance
>Ka-Kit Fung, University of Technology, Sydney, Australia

Additional Members
>Athula Ginige, University of Western Sydney, Australia
>Aditya Ghose, University of Wollongong, Australia

Core Program Committee

Program Co-Chairs
>David Lowe, University of Technology, Sydney, Australia
>Martin Gaedke, University of Karlsruhe, Germany

Tutorials/Workshops Chair
>Aditya Ghose, University of Wollongong, Australia

Panels Chair
>Daniel Schwabe, PUC Rio de Janeiro, Brazil

Keynotes Chair
>Bebo White, Stanford Linear Accelerator Center, USA

Posters/Demos Chair
>Emilia Mendes, University of Auckland, New Zealand

Doctoral Consortium Chair
>Gustavo Rossi, Universidad Nacional de la Plata, Argentina

Industry Briefing Chair
>Rafael Calvo, University of Sydney, Australia

Systems
>Xiaoying Kong, University of Technology, Sydney, Australia

Extended Program Committee

Jesus Aguilar-Ruiz	Universidad Pontificia de Salamanca, Spain
Grigoris Antoniou	University of Crete, Greece
Luciano Baresi	Politecnico di Milano, Italy
Michael Bieber	NJIT, USA
Christoph Bussler	Oracle Corporation, USA
Leslie Carr	University of Southampton, UK
Fabio Casati	HP Labs, USA
Sara Comai	Politecnico di Milano, Italy
Ernesto Damiani	Universita' di Milano, Italy
Paul Dantzig	IBM T. J. Watson Research Center, USA
Susan Dart	IT Strategy Consultant, Australia
Olga De Troyer	Vrije Universiteit Brussel, Belgium
Yogesh Deshpande	Univ of Western Sydney, Australia
Gill Dobbie	University of Auckland, New Zealand
Asuman Dogac	Middle East T. U. Ankara, Turkey
Schahram Dustdar	Vienna University of Technology, Austria
John Eklund	Access Testing Centre P/L, Australia
Deiter Fensel	Innsbruck, Austria
Cameron Ferstat	IBM Systems Group, Australia
Piero Fraternali	Politecnico di Milano, Italy
Ka-Kit Fung	Univ of Technology, Sydney, Australia
Athula Ginige	Univ of Western Sydney, Australia
Angela Goh	NTU, Singapore
Jaime Gómez	Universidad de Alicante, Spain
Wook-Shin Han	Kyung-Pook National University, Korea
Steve Hansen	University of Western Sydney, Australia
Frank van Harmelen	Vrije Universiteit, Amsterdam, The Netherlands
Manfred Hauswirth	EPFL Lausanne, Switzerland
Geert-Jan Houben	Eindhoven University, The Netherlands
Arun Iyengar	IBM, USA
Martti Jeenicke	University of Hamburg, Germany
David Kearney	University of South Australia, Australia
Hiroyuki Kitagawa	University of Tsukuba, Japan
Carlos Delgado Kloos	Universidad Carlos III de Madrid, Spain
Nora Koch	Ludwig-Maximilians-Universität München, Germany
Nara Kulathuramaiyer	Universiti Malaysia Sarawak, Malaysia
Jose Labra	Universidad de Oviedo, Spain
Frank Leymann	IBM Software Group, Germany
Xiaoming Li	Peking University, China
Qing Li	City University of Hong Kong, China

Sponsorship

Primary Organising Sponsor

University of Technology, Sydney

Additional Organising Sponsors

University of Western Sydney
Bringing knowledge to life

Southern Cross UNIVERSITY
A new way to think

Industry Silver Sponsor

SAP RESEARCH

Endorsement

IW³C² Endorsed Conference

Workshops

Web Information Systems Modelling

Flavius Frasincar
  Eindhoven University of Technology, The Netherlands
Geert-Jan Houben
  Eindhoven University of Technology, The Netherlands
Richard Vdovjak
  Eindhoven University of Technology, The Netherlands

Agent-Based Web Engineering

Aneesh Krishna
  University of Wollongong, Australia
Chattrakul Sambattheera
  Mahasarakham University, Thailand, and
  University of Wollongong, Australia

Web Metrics and Measurement

Emilia Mendes
  The University of Auckland, New Zealand
Luciano Baresi
  Politecnico di Milano, Italy
Sandro Morasca
  Università degli Studi dell'Insubria, Italy

Model-Driven Web Engineering

Nora Koch
  Institut für Informatik, Ludwig-Maximilians-Universität München, and
  FAST GmbH, Germany
Gustavo Rossi
  LIFIA, Facultad de Informática Universidad Nacional de La Plata, Argentina
Antonio Vallecillo
  ETSI Informática, University of Málaga, Spain

Device Indpendent Web Engineering

Markus Lauff
  SAP AG - SAP Research, Germany
Thomas Ziegert
  SAP AG - SAP Research, Germany

Tutorials

Semantic Web Services
Christoph Bussler
   National University of Ireland
Liliana Cabral
   The Open University, United Kingdom
John Domingue
   The Open University, United Kingdom
Matthew Moran
   National University of Ireland
Dumitru Roman
   Leopold-Franzens Universität Innsbruck, Austria
Michael Stollberg
   Leopold-Franzens Universität Innsbruck, Austria
Michal Zaremba
   National University of Ireland

Measuring and Evaluating Web Quality
Luis Antonio Olsina
   National University of La Pampa, Argentina

Web Cost Estimation
Emilia Mendes
   University of Auckland, New Zealand

Pragmatic Reuse: Building Web App Product Lines
Stanislaw Jarzabek
   National University of Singapore
Damith Chatura Rajapakse
   National University of Singapore

Web Engineering: Managing Complexity
Athula Ginige
   University of Western Sydney, Australia
Jeewani Anupama Ginige
   University of Western Sydney, Australia

Engineering Web Information Systems
Klaus-Dieter Schewe
   Massey University, New Zealand
Bernhard Thalheim
   Christian Albrechts University Kiel, Germany

Referees

Juan Jose Garcia Adeva
Bugrahan Akcay
Veli Bicer
David Benavides
Veli Bicer
Razvan Stefan Bot
Sven Casteleyn
Vicente Luque Centeno
Paolo Ceravolo
Raquel M. Crespo
Amador Durán
Pablo Fernández
Norberto Fernández-García
Jesus Arias Fisteus
Cristiano Fugazza
Gabriel Pui Cheong Fung
Irene Garrigos
Cagdas Evren Gerede
Nicola Gessa
Michael Grossniklaus
Yavuz Gurcan
Armin Haller
Jan Henke
Kathleen M. Higginbotham
Il Im
Angelo Di Iorio
Yoshiharu Ishikawa
Roland Kaschek
Markus Kirchberg
Sebastian Kloeckner
Xiaoying Kong
Jacek Kopecky
Reto Krummenacher
Holger Lausen
Michael Lee
Xiang Li
Maria de los Angeles Martin

Andrea Maurino
Johannes Meinecke
Santiago Meliá
Matthew Moran
Nathalie Moreno
Javier Muñoz
Tuncay Namli
Nkechi Nnadi
Martin Nussbaumer
Alper Okcan
Mehmet Olduz
Eyal Oren
Mario Munoz Organero
Janaka Pitadeniya
Peter Plessers
Maria Plummer
Robin Privman
Antonia Reina
Manuel Resinas
Gonzalo Rojas
Brahmananda Sapkota
Roshan Sembacuttiaratchy
Zenga Z. Shan
Zhongnan Shen
Norihide Shinagawa
Gleb Skolbetsyn
Puay Siew Tan
Bernhard Thalheim
Giovanni Toffetti
Ioan Toma
Alexei Tretiakov
Pablo Trinidad
Albert Weichselbraun
Paul Y. Yang
Norazlin Yusop
Anna V. Zhdanova

XIV   Organisation

Table of Contents

Keynotes

Keynote: Just Enough Requirements Management for Web Engineering ... 1
  Al Davis

Keynote: Performance, Availability and Security in Web Design 3
  Virgilio A.F. Almeida

Keynote: Bridging the Gap Between Requirements and Design 5
  Craig Errey

Keynote: Google Maps and Browser Support for Rich Web Applications .. 7
  Lars Rasmussen

Web Engineering Milieu

Web Service Engineering –
Advancing a New Software Engineering Discipline 8
  Ruth Breu, Michael Breu, Michael Hafner, and Andrea Nowak

Toward a Comprehension View of Web Engineering 19
  Semia Sonia Selmi, Naoufel Kraiem, and Henda Ben Ghezala

A Need-Oriented Assessment of Technological Trends in Web Engineering . 30
  Damith C. Rajapakse and Stan Jarzabek

Adding Usability to Web Engineering Models and Tools 36
  Richard Atterer and Albrecht Schmidt

Evaluation and Verification

Organization-Oriented Measurement and Evaluation Framework
for Software and Web Engineering Projects 42
  Luis Olsina, Fernanda Papa, and Hernán Molina

Web Usability Measurement: Comparing Logic Scoring Preference
to Subjective Assessment 53
  Michael Chun Long Yip and Emilia Mendes

Effectively Capturing User Navigation Paths in the Web
Using Web Server Logs 63
  Amithalal Caldera and Yogesh Deshpande

Design Verification of Web Applications Using Symbolic Model Checking . 69
  Eugenio Di Sciascio, Francesco M. Donini, Marina Mongiello,
  Rodolfo Totaro, and Daniela Castelluccia

Non-functional Requirements / Testing

Towards Model-Driven Testing of a Web Application Generator 75
  Luciano Baresi, Piero Fraternali, Massimo Tisi, and Sandro Morasca

WIT: A Framework for In-container Testing of Web-Portal Applications . . 87
  Wenliang Xiong, Harpreet Bajwa, and Frank Maurer

How to Deal with Non-functional Properties in Web Service Development . 98
  Guadalupe Ortiz, Juan Hernández, and Pedro J. Clemente

Use Constraint Hierarchy for Non-functional Requirements Analysis 104
  Ying Guan and Aditya K. Ghose

Miscellaneous 1

Towards a Taxonomy of Hypermedia and Web Application Size Metrics . . . 110
  Emilia Mendes, Steve Counsell, and Nile Mosley

Identifying Websites with Flow Simulation 124
  Pierre Senellart

An Increase Web Services Performance Method 130
  Whe Dar Lin

A System of Patterns for Web Navigation 136
  Mohammed Abul Khayes Akanda and Daniel M. German

Query / Retrieval

A Design of Spatial XQuery for Mobile and Location-Based Applications . . 142
  Soon-Young Park, Jae-Dong Lee, and Hae-Young Bae

An Article Language Model for BBS Search 152
  Jingfang Xu, Yangbo Zhu, and Xing Li

Conqueries: An Agent That Supports Query Expansion 161
  Jean-Yves Delort

Ubiquitous Information Retrieval Using Multi-level Characteristics 167
  Joonhee Kwon and Sungrim Kim

Applications 1

First-Order Patterns for Information Integration 173
  Mark A. Cameron and Kerry Taylor

Web Application Development: Java, .Net and Lamp at the Same Time . . . 185
  Jaime Navón and Pablo Bustos

A Security Acceleration Using XML Signcryption Scheme
in Mobile Grid Web Services 191
  *Namje Park, Kiyoung Moon, Kyoil Chung, Dongho Won,
  and Yuliang Zheng*

Light-Weight Distributed Web Interfaces:
Preparing the Web for Heterogeneous Environments 197
  *Chris Vandervelpen, Geert Vanderhulst, Kris Luyten,
  and Karin Coninx*

Building Blocks for Identity Federations 203
  Johannes Meinecke, Martin Nussbaumer, and Martin Gaedke

Applications 2

Level of Detail Concepts in Data-Intensive Web Applications 209
  Sara Comai

Separation of Navigation Routing Code in J2EE Web Applications 221
  Minmin Han and Christine Hofmeister

Video-Based Sign Language Content Annotation
by Incorporation of MPEG-7 Standard 232
  Rashad Aouf and Steve Hansen

E-Legislative Services: Issues and Architecture 237
  Elena Sánchez-Nielsen and Francisco Chávez-Gutiérrez

Applications 3

An Application Framework for Collaborative Learning 243
  Aiman Turani, Rafael A. Calvo, and Peter Goodyear

An Investigation of Cloning in Web Applications 252
  Damith C. Rajapakse and Stan Jarzabek

Intelligent Web Information Service Model
for Minimizing Information Gap Among People in E-Government 263
  *Gye Hang Hong, Jang Hee Lee, Tae Hyun Kim, Sang Chan Park,
  Hyung Min Rho, and Dong Sik Jang*

Intelligent Website Evolution of Public Sector
Based on Data Mining Tools 267
    Jang Hee Lee and Gye Hang Hong

Ontologies / XML

An Experiment on the Matching and Reuse of XML Schemas 273
    Jianguo Lu, Shengrui Wang, and Ju Wang

Aggregation in Ontologies: Practical Implementations in OWL 285
    Csaba Veres

Recursive Application of Structural Templates
to Efficiently Compress Parsed XML 296
    *Akira Kinno, Hideki Yukitomo, Takehiro Nakayama,
    and Atsushi Takeshita*

Matching Semantic Web Services Using Different Ontologies 302
    Le Duy Ngan and Angela Goh

Semantics / Web Services

Improving Semantic Consistency of Web Sites
by Quantifying User Intent 308
    *Carsten Stolz, Maximilian Viermetz, Michal Skubacz,
    and Ralph Neuneier*

A Framework to Support QoS-Aware Usage of Web Services 318
    *Eunjoo Lee, Woosung Jung, Wookjin Lee, Youngjoo Park,
    Byungjeong Lee, Heechern Kim, and Chisu Wu*

Integrating Web Applications and Web Services 328
    Nicholas L. Carroll and Rafael A. Calvo

The Semantic Web Services Tetrahedron: Achieving Integration
with Semantic Web Services 334
    *Juan Miguel Gómez, Mariano Rico, Francisco García-Sánchez,
    and César J. Acuña*

Security

Secure Web Forms with Client-Side Signatures 340
    Mikko Honkala and Petri Vuorimaa

Robust and Simple Authentication Protocol
for Secure Communication on the Web 352
    Eun-Jun Yoon, Woo-Hun Kim, and Kee-Young Yoo

Offline Expansion of XACML Policies Based on P3P Metadata 363
    Claudio Ardagna, Ernesto Damiani, Sabrina De Capitani di Vimercati,
    Cristiano Fugazza, and Pierangela Samarati

Miscellaneous 2

Automatic Optimization of Web Recommendations
Using Feedback and Ontology Graphs 375
    Nick Golovin and Erhard Rahm

Recommender Systems Using Support Vector Machines 387
    Sung-Hwan Min and Ingoo Han

Multi-channel Publication of Interactive Media Content
for Web Information Systems 394
    Nico Oorts, Filip Hendrickx, Tom Beckers, and Rik Van De Walle

Classification of RSS-Formatted Documents
Using Full Text Similarity Measures 400
    Katarzyna Wegrzyn-Wolska and Piotr S. Szczepaniak

Design 1 (Adaptation / User-Awareness)

Modelling Adaptivity with Aspects 406
    Hubert Baumeister, Alexander Knapp, Nora Koch, and Gefei Zhang

An Approach to User-Behavior-Aware Web Applications 417
    Stefano Ceri, Florian Daniel, Vera Demaldé, and Federico M. Facca

A Component-Based Reflective Middleware Approach
to Context-Aware Adaptive Systems 429
    Zhang Kuo, Wu Yanni, Zheng Zhenkun, Wang Xiaoge, and Chen Yu

Adaptation of Web Pages for Hand-Held Devices...................... 435
    Balasubramanian Appiah Venkatakrishnan and San Murugesan

Design 2 (Model-Based Approaches)

A Model-Based Approach for Integrating Third Party Systems
with Web Applications 441
    Nathalie Moreno and Antonio Vallecillo

A Model-Driven Approach
for Designing Distributed Web Information Systems 453
    Richard Vdovjak and Geert-Jan Houben

MDA Transformations Applied to Web Application Development 465
Santiago Meliá, Andreas Kraus, and Nora Koch

Higher-Level Information Aspects of Web Systems:
Addressing the Problem of Disconnection 472
Farooque Azam, Zhang Li, and Rashid Ahmad

Design 3 (End-Users / Requirements)

As Easy as "Click": End-User Web Engineering 478
*Jochen Rode, Yogita Bhardwaj, Manuel A. Pérez-Quiñones,
Mary Beth Rosson, and Jonathan Howarth*

Towards End User Development of Web Applications for SMEs:
A Component Based Approach 489
Jeewani A. Ginige, Buddhima De Silva, and Athula Ginige

Web Applications: A Simple Pluggable Architecture
for Business Rich Clients 500
Duncan Mac-Vicar and Jaime Navón

From Web Requirements to Navigational Design –
A Transformational Approach 506
Pedro Valderas, Joan Fons, and Vicente Pelechano

Design 4 (Frameworks / Commercial Experience)

Web Applications Design with a Multi-process Approach 512
Semia Sonia Selmi, Naoufel Kraiem, and Henda Ben Ghezala

"Designing for the Web" Revisited:
A Survey of Informal and Experienced Web Developers 522
Mary Beth Rosson, Julie F. Ballin, Jochen Rode, and Brooke Toward

Web OPEN-Integrated: Proposed Framework for Web Development 533
Rashid Ahmad, Zhang Li, and Farooque Azam

Framework for Collaborative Web Applications 539
Ioakim Makis Marmaridis and Athula Ginige

Design 5

Discovering Re-usable Design Solutions in Web Conceptual Schemas:
Metrics and Methodology 545
*Yannis Panagis, Evangelos Sakkopoulos, Spiros Sirmakessis,
Athanasios Tsakalidis, and Giannis Tzimas*

The Role of Visual Tools in a Web Application Design
and Verification Framework: A Visual Notation for LTL Formulae 557
    Marco Brambilla, Alin Deutsch, Liying Sui, and Victor Vianu

OOHDMDA – An MDA Approach for OOHDM 569
    Hans Albrecht Schmid and Oliver Donnerhak

A Service-Centric Architecture for Web Applications 575
    Hans Albrecht Schmid

Posters

NavOptim: On the Possibility of Minimising Navigation Effort 581
    Xiaoying Kong and David Lowe

A First Step Towards the Web Engineering Body of Knowledge 585
    Antonio Navarro, José Luis Sierra, Alfredo Fernández-Valmayor,
    and Baltasar Fernández-Manjón

Design Considerations for Web-Based Interactive TV Services 588
    Meng-Huang Lee and He-Rong Zhong

Web Service Based Integration of Biological Interaction Databases 591
    Seong Joon Yoo, Min Kyung Kim, and Seon Hee Park

Integrating Process Management and Content Management
for Service Industries 594
    Young Gil Kim, Chul Young Kim, and Sang Chan Park

Service Publishing and Discovering Model
in a Web Services Oriented Peer-to-Peer System 597
    Ruixuan Li, Zhi Zhang, Wei Song, Feng Ke, and Zhengding Lu

A Web Services Method on Embedded Systems 600
    Whe Dar Lin

Evaluating Current Testing Processes of Web-Portal Applications 603
    Harpreet Bajwa, Wenliang Xiong, and Frank Maurer

XML Approach to Communication Design of WebGIS 606
    Yingwei Luo, Xinpeng Liu, Xiaolin Wang, and Zhuoqun Xu

Automatic Generation of Client-Server Collaborative Web Applications
from Diagrams 609
    Mitsuhisa Taguchi and Takehiro Tokuda

Web Operational Analysis Through Performance-Related Ontologies
in OWL for Intelligent Applications 612
    Isaac Lera, Carlos Juiz, and Ramon Puigjaner

WCAG Formalization with W3C Techniques 615
    *Vicente Luque Centeno, Carlos Delgado Kloos, Martin Gaedke,
    and Martin Nussbaumer*

Analyzing Time-to-Market and Reliability Trade-Offs
with Bayesian Belief Networks 618
    Jianyun Zhou and Tor Stålhane

A UI-Driven Lightweight Framework for Developing Web Applications 621
    *Keeyoull Lee, Sanghyun Park, Chunwoo Lee, Woosung Jung,
    Wookjin Lee, Byungjeong Lee, Heechern Kim, and Chisu Wu*

Demos

Modelling the Behaviour of Web Applications with ArgoUWE 624
    Alexander Knapp, Nora Koch, and Gefei Zhang

Simulating Web Applications Design Models 627
    Pedro Peixoto

Author Index 631

Keynote: Just Enough Requirements Management for Web Engineering

Al Davis

College of Business
University of Colorado at Colorado Springs
Colorado Springs, CO 80933-7150 USA
adavis@uccs.edu

1 Brief Bio

Al Davis is professor of information systems at the University of Colorado at Colorado Springs. He was a member of the board of directors of Requisite, Inc., acquired by Rational Software Corporation in February 1997, and subsequently acquired by IBM in 2003. He has consulted for many corporations over the past twenty-seven years, including Boeing, Cigna Insurance, Federal Express, Front-Range Solutions, Fujitsu, General Electric, Great Plains Software, IBM, Loral, MCI, Mitsubishi Electric, NEC, NTT, Rational Software, Rockwell, Schlumberger, Sharp, Software Productivity Consortium, Storage Tek, and Sumitomo. Previously, he was

- Chairman and CEO of Omni-Vista, Inc., a software company in Colorado Springs;
- Vice President of Engineering Services at BTG, Inc., a Virginia-based company that went public in 1995, and was acquired by Titan in 2001;
- a Director of R&D at GTE Communication Systems in Phoenix, Arizona. GTE was acquired by Verizon in 1999;
- Director of the Software Technology Center at GTE Laboratories in Waltham, Massachusetts.

He has held academic positions at George Mason University, University of Tennessee, and University of Illinois at Champaign-Urbana. He was Editor-in-Chief of IEEE Software from 1994 to 1998. He is an editor for the Journal of Systems and Software (1987-present) and was an editor for Communications of the ACM (1981-1991). He is the author of

- Software Requirements: Objects, Functions and States (Prentice Hall, 1st edition 1990; 2nd edition 1993);
- the best-selling 201 Principles of Software Development (McGraw Hill, 1995);
- Great Software Debates (Wiley and IEEE CS Press, 2004), and
- Just Enough Requirements Management (Dorset House, 2005).

Dr. Davis has published 100+ articles in journals, conferences and trade press, and lectured 500+ times in over 20 countries. Much of his current research

D. Lowe and M. Gaedke (Eds.): ICWE 2005, LNCS 3579, pp. 1–2, 2005.
© Springer-Verlag Berlin Heidelberg 2005

centers around discovering "just enough" ways of performing requirements engineering, specifically "the largely unexplored middle ground between the requirements purists and the requirements cowboys." [Tom DeMarco] He maintains the most extensive bibliography on the web for requirements-related subjects (http://web.uccs.edu/adavis/reqbib.htm). He is the founder of the *IEEE International Conferences of Requirements Engineering*, and served as general chair of its first conference in 1994. He has been a fellow of the IEEE since 1994, and earned his Ph.D. in Computer Science from the University of Illinois in 1975. Find out more about Al Davis at http://web.uccs.edu/adavis.

2   Talk Abstract

When building web applications, strong temptation exists to "just build it." After all, the tools available today for web engineering are just so easy to use. The operational environment is so tolerant of implementation problems. And the expectations of the user community allow for constant evolution. On the other hand, almost every type of application, including those that are highly financial-critical and life-critical, is migrating to the web. This trend works against the attitude of "just build it." So, the answer cannot be "forget about requirements; we'll figure them out later." And the answer cannot be "write a formal requirements specification for all parties to approve prior to system implementation." Requirements management exists to reduce risk, but it also needs to be made simpler, not more complex. And in today's competitive world we need to find ways to accelerate system development dramatically; modern requirements management must thus reduce, not extend, the effort.

The Capability Maturity Model (CMM) movement has tended to cause companies to over-methodize, while the agile programming movement has tended to cause companies to under-methodize. The result is that requirements are either over-analyzed and over-specified, or are totally ignored. This common-sense talk addresses the "right" level at which requirements should be addressed, with emphasis on recognizing that the "right" level is different for every project.

The talk will cover all three major areas of requirements management: elicitation, triage, and specification. Each will be described, its goals will be made clear, common practices will be described, and recommendations for doing it in a "just enough" manner for web engineering will be explored. The talk will also discuss the factors that would cause you to want to alter the "just enough" prescription for your own needs.

Keynote: Performance, Availability and Security in Web Design

Virgilio A.F. Almeida

Federal University of Minas Gerais - UFMG
Brazil
virgilio@dcc.ufmg.br

1 Brief Bio

Virgilio A.F. Almeida is a Professor and former Chair of the Computer Science Department at the Federal University of Minas Gerais (UFMG), Brazil. He received a Ph.D. degree in Computer Science from Vanderbilt University, an MS in Computer Science from the Pontifical Catholic University in Rio de Janeiro (PUC-RIO), and BSEE from UFMG. His research interests include analysis, modeling, and evaluation of the behavior of large scale distributed systems, capacity planning, IT security, Internet and WWW technologies. He was a Visiting Professor at Boston University (1996) and Polytechnic University of Catalonia in Barcelona (2003) and held visiting appointments at Xerox PARC (1997) and Hewlett-Packard Research Laboratory in Palo Alto (2001 and 2004).

He has published over 100 technical papers and was co-author of five books, including "Performance by Design: computer capacity planning by example" "Capacity Planning for Web Services: metrics, models, and methods," "Scaling for E-business: technologies, models, performance, and capacity planning," and "Capacity Planning and Performance Modeling: from mainframes to client-server systems", published by Prentice Hall in 2004, 2002, 2000, and 1994, respectively. He is also a frequent reviewer for a variety of international journals covering Internet and distributed systems issues, and served on the programme committees of various international conferences (including the WWW Conference, ACM-SIGMETRICS, and Performance 2005). He was the program co-chair of the ACM-WOSP'2004 Conference and will be the general co-chair of ACM-USENIX IMC 2006 Conference. Almeida serves on the Editorial Board of First Monday, a multidisciplinary journal on the Internet (www.firstmonday.org).

His research has been funded by the Brazilian Research Council (CNPq), Brazilian Ministry of Science and Technology, and HP Brazil. Almeida was the recipient of various prizes, teaching awards, and best paper awards including an award from Compaq/Brazil for the paper "Characterizing Reference Locality in the WWW" (with Mark Crovella and Azer Bestavros). He served as the chairman of the National Board on Graduate Education in Computer Science in Brazil and as a member of the Computer Science Committee in the Brazilian Research Council.

D. Lowe and M. Gaedke (Eds.): ICWE 2005, LNCS 3579, pp. 3–4, 2005.

2   Talk Abstract

Performance, around-the-clock availability, and security are the most common indicators of quality of service on the Web. Management faces a twofold challenge. On the one hand, it has to meet customer expectations in terms of quality of service. On the other hand, companies have to keep IT costs under control to stay competitive. Planning the infrastructure of Web services requires more than just adding extra hardware or software. It requires more than intuition, ad-hoc procedures, or rules of thumb. Many possible alternative solutions can be used to implement a Web service; one has to be able to determine the most cost-effective system solution. This is where Web Engineering and Capacity Planning techniques come into play. This presentation introduces quantitative capacity planning techniques and examples for different Web scenarios, showing precisely how to identify and address performance, availability and security-related problems.

Keynote: Bridging the Gap Between Requirements and Design

Craig Errey

The Performance Technologies Group Pty Ltd
Sydney, Australia
`craige@ptg-global.com`

1 Brief Bio

Craig is the Managing Director of The Performance Technologies Group (PTG). PTG specialises in requirements modelling, high performance user interface design, usability and accessibility. PTG improves customer experience and business performance with all technologies – websites, intranets, business applications, speech recognition systems, interactive voice response, interactive television and hardware.

PTG placed 64th in the 2004 BRW Fast 100, with an average of 50% growth per annum, since starting in 1999. PTG currently employs over 20 people with backgrounds ranging from psychology, computer science, information environment, marketing, business strategy and human computer interaction.

Craig's primary role is the research, development and implementation of the company's IP and methodologies. His credentials and experience encompass the disciplines of psychology, HR consulting, change management, and technology. By aligning business, marketing and customer strategies to website and application design, he helps organisations create real and measurable value for people and business. As a psychologist, he understands the way people think and is therefore able to create systems that are simple, user-friendly and effective.

Craig has consulted in usability and user interface design for Commonwealth Bank, Qantas, Vodafone, NSW Department of Commerce, ANZ, Defence, Department of Health and Ageing, IBM, Motorola, National Bank, QBE MM, Hutchison Telecoms / Orange / 3, NSW RTA, Tourism Australia, Tourism NSW, Zurich, Telstra, E*trade and Citibank.

Craig holds a Master's Degree in Organisational Psychology from UNSW, is a member of the APS and the APS College of Organisational Psychologists, and is a Registered Psychologist in NSW.

2 Talk Abstract

Despite billions of dollars being spent on IT around the world each year on business applications, Excel spread sheets continue to be the corporate chewing gum of choice.

D. Lowe and M. Gaedke (Eds.): ICWE 2005, LNCS 3579, pp. 5–6, 2005.

IT has failed to consistently and predictably produce the results required of business. IT has focussed on technical aspects – efficiency, response times, data base optimisation, network performance, architectures, interoperability and so on.

The majority of IT projects have experienced one more of the following:

- The technology solution is chosen before the requirements are know,
- The requirements change throughout the project,
- They're late,
- They don't deliver what was expected,
- They cost more that expected,
- They don't work the way people work.

What is needed is a bridge between business, requirements and IT. IT lacks this 'blueprint' to build an application the right way, the first time.

But it's not just IT's problem. Craig's own fields of user interface design and usability also have significant problems in their methods. There are various standards, like ISO 9241 (part 11) and ISO 13407:1999) that ultimately describe what usability is and how to measure it, but there is no systematic process to move from requirements to design. There is not even an agreed operational definition of usability, other than that used to measure it (efficiency, effectiveness and satisfaction). This means that if two designers approach the same user interface design process, independently, they will come up with markedly different designs. This is not what is expected from a 'quality' process.

Craig will be presenting a basis for a new framework for business IT that integrates business and user requirements using a blend software engineering, psychology and design principles to create a precise blueprint that IT can build from that bridges requirements to design – that is, getting IT right the first time.

Keynote: Google Maps and Browser Support for Rich Web Applications

Lars Rasmussen

Google
lars@google.com

1   Brief Bio

Lars Eilstrup Rasmussen is a member of Google's technical staff and the lead engineer of the team that created Google Maps. He currently works out of Google's Sydney office and is actively working to expand Google's engineering presence in Australia.

Lars holds a Ph.D. in theoretical computer science from the University of California at Berkeley, which nominated his thesis on approximate counting for the ACM Doctoral Dissertation Award.

In early 2003, Lars co-founded with his brother Jens Eilstrup Rasmussen a mapping-related startup, Where 2 Technologies, which was acquired by Google in October of 2004.

2   Talk Abstract

Lars designed and built the original prototype of Google Maps, which launched this January as a Google Labs experiment. He will discuss why his team chose a javascript-heavy approach, the challenges of doing so, and how browsers might develop in the future to better support rich web applications such as Google Maps.

D. Lowe and M. Gaedke (Eds.): ICWE 2005, LNCS 3579, p. 7, 2005.
© Springer-Verlag Berlin Heidelberg 2005

Web Service Engineering –
Advancing a New Software Engineering Discipline

Ruth Breu[1], Michael Breu[1], Michael Hafner[1], and Andrea Nowak[2]

[1] Universität Innsbruck, Institut für Informatik, Techniker Straße 21a, A – 6020 Innsbruck
{ruth.breu,michael.breu,m.hafner}@uibk.ac.at
[2] ARC Seibersdorf Research, Kramergasse 1, A–1010 Wien
andrea.nowak@arcs.ac.at

Abstract. In this paper we present SECTET, a tool-based framework for the design, implementation and quality assurance of web service based applications. Main focus in SECTET is put on the design of inter-organizational workflows, the model driven realization of security aspects and testing of workflows. We present an overview of the model views, the design activities and the underlying architecture.

1 Introduction

Component-based software development has been one of the hot topics in software engineering for at least the last decade. The idea of constructing IT systems in the same modular way as cars or washing machines is appealing and has led many people to think about new markets and business models for software components.

While platform dependence was a great obstacle for bringing such scenarios into practice some years ago, web service technology now opens a plethora of new possibilities ranging from the realization of inter-organizational workflows, new flexible ways of cooperation between business partners and virtual web service market places. Not every today´s vision will find its way into practice, but in any case composing web services to new applications is an upcoming important paradigm of software development.

What we will address in this paper is the question how techniques and methods of software engineering apply to this new style of programming. More precisely, we will focus on *modelling* and *testing* web service based systems.

In a web service based application there are always at least two types of stakeholders – the supplier of some service and the client using the service. In this paper we will only take the client view and assume that the web services to be used are already given. We will not deal with the steps to deploy some web service and the steps to find web services of interest.

In the subsequent sections we will present the tool-based method SECTET for web service engineering. SECTET is developed by our research group Quality Engineering in a cluster of cooperation projects with our project partners ARC Seibersdorf research (project SECTINO) and world-direct/Telekom Austria (project FLOWTEST).

SECTET is targeted towards the high-level development of inter-organizational workflows based on web service technology. From the technological side the basic constituents of our framework are the atomic web services and a web service orchestration language like BPEL4WS [8] together with the related tools [9]. From the

D. Lowe and M. Gaedke (Eds.): ICWE 2005, LNCS 3579, pp. 8–18, 2005.

methodological side we deal with aspects how to specify the interface of a web service, how to design an inter-organizational workflow step by step and how to test such an application.

We put a special focus on the aspect of security playing a crucial role in most inter-organizational workflows. Our goal is to assess security requirements at a high level of abstraction and to provide pattern-based solutions. Due to the background of our project partners we concentrate on applications in e-government and e-business, though the general approach is application-independent.

The backbone of our method are UML models. We use class diagrams and the predicative language OCL [19] for describing (XML-)data and interfaces, and activity diagrams for describing workflows. We use these models from two perspectives. The first is the requirements specification perspective supporting a step by step development of inter-organizational systems. In the second perspective we pursue a model-driven approach in which code is generated based on specific models.

Since all standards and languages in web services technology are based on low-level XML structures in our conviction such a model-driven approach is of primary choice to achieve an adequate level of abstraction for the development of web services based applications.

Our approach is novel in many respects. We contribute substantially to requirements specification, model-based specification of security requirements and testing of inter-organizational workflows in the context of web services. Related approaches which however focus on different technologies can be found in the areas of workflow management (e.g. [3, 10, 11, 13]), authorization models (e.g. [5, 15, 22]) and testing [21]. To our knowledge the term *Web Service Engineering* has been first used by Starke [20], however in a very unspecific way.

In the sequel we present an overview of the core concepts of our framework. In the SECTINO project we have developed a set of basic models and views of an inter-organizational application. We distinguish two basic classifications, the component vs. workflow view and the global vs. local view which are presented in section 2. Section 3 deals with the aspects of model-driven software development in SECTINO, while Section 4 is devoted to the step by step development of inter-organizational systems. Section 5 sketches the requirements to a testing environment for inter-organizational workflows and, finally, we draw some conclusions in Section 6.

For a more detailed presentation of single aspects of our approach we refer to a series of accompanying papers, in particular [2, 6, 12].

2 Views and Models

We conceive an inter-organizational application as a network of partners communicating by calling (web) services and exchanging (XML) data. Within the design of such an application we distinguish two orthogonal classifications and views of the system: the *global* or *local view* on the one hand side and the *component* or *workflow view* on the other side.

The *global view* conceives the inter-organizational system as a whole, the *local view* focuses on the behavior and structure of one partner within the network.

In the *component view* each partner is conceived as a node offering a set of services with given properties. The component view is independent of the context in which the services are used. In the *workflow view* the orchestration of the partners´ services is defined.

Within this classification schema we distinguish the *interface model* (local component view), the *global workflow model* describing the business protocol of the cooperating partners, and the *local workflow model* describing the behaviour of each partner node (cf. Fig. 1).

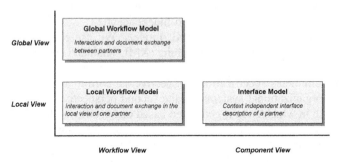

Fig. 1. Models and Views

This orthogonal perspective allows us to combine the design of components offering services that different types of partners may call in different contexts with the design of workflows that focus on particular usage scenarios. In many applications the component view of (some or all) partners is already given when the interorganizational workflow is developed.

As running example we will use the interaction between a business agent (the Tax Advisor) and a public service provider (the Municipality) for submitting and processing annual statements concerning the municipal tax of companies. Table 1 shows a portion of the informal textual description of the workflow.

2.1 Interface Model

The interface model describes the set of services a partner node offers to the outside. The interface model consists of the following submodels.

- The *document model* is a UML class diagram describing the data type view of the partner. We talk of documents in order to stress that we do not interpret this class diagram in the usual object oriented setting but in the context of XML schema [23].
- The *interface* contains a set of abstract (UML-)operations representing services the component offers to its clients. The types of the parameters are either basic types or classes in the document model. Additionally, pre- and postconditions (in OCL style) specify the behavior of the abstract services.
- The *role model* describes the roles having access to the services. An example of a role within the municipality component is the tax advisor (e.g. calling the web service sendProcessedAnnualStatement of the municipality).
- The *access model* describes the conditions under which a certain role has the permission to call a given service. We use the predicative approach of [7] to specify the access model. This approach uses an OCL dialect to specify conditions under

which a given role has the permission to call an operation. This permission may depend on the parameters, the state of the calling subject (e.g. its geographical location) and on the internal representation of the subject.

Table 1. Informal Description of the *Workflow Process Annual Statement*

Workflow Process Annual Statement
Partners Tax Advisor, Municipality
Main Steps
1. The Tax Advisor prepares the annual statement of his client
2. The Tax Advisor sends the annual statement to the Municipality.
3. The Municipality checks the incoming statement for validity.
4. The Municipality stipulates the communal taxes based on the incoming annual statement and the received payments during the year and prepares the notification.
5. The Municipality sends the notification back to the Tax Advisor.
6. The Tax Advisor receives the notification and checks it according to expected results.
Variants
...
Security Requirements
2. The annual statement is confidential and has to be signed by the tax advisor.
5. The notification is confidential and is signed by the Municipality.
2./5. The reception of the annual statement and the notification have to be non-repudiable.

Example

The tax advisor has the right to call the web service sendProcessedAnnualStatement of the municipality component if the town of the applicant´s annual statement is the same as the town of the municipality. We assume that **AnnualStatement** is a class in the document model describing the structure of annual statements; one of the attributes of **AnnualStatement** is town. Moreover, getLocation() is a service that returns the town of the municipality.

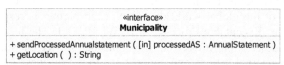

context Municipality: sendProcessedAnnualStatement (processedAS: AnnualStatement)
perm[tax advisor]:   processedAS.town = Municipality.getLocation()

2.2   Global Workflow Model

The *global workflow model* describes an abstract view of the business protocol between partners in autonomous organizations. The global workflow is abstract in the sense that it describes the interaction of partners at a level that contains neither internal steps nor the connection to the business logic. The global workflow model consists of the following submodels.

- The *global workflow* is described by a UML activity diagram enhanced by security requirements concerning the communication between the partners The actions in this workflow diagram refer to the services offered by the respective partner.
- The *document model* and the *role model* describe the data exchanged by the partners in the workflow and the partner roles, respectively. Both models are class diagrams.

As an example, Fig. 2 depicts a portion of the global workflow between the Tax Advisor and the Municipality. The notes attached with the objects processedAS and notification, are security requirements explained in more detail in the subsequent section. In the complete model the workflow comprises additional partners (e.g. the health insurance for checking employees registered).

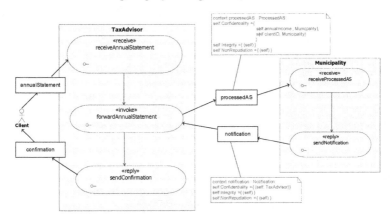

Fig. 2. Portion of the global workflow *Process Annual Statement*

The global workflow model is typically designed by the consortium of partners involved in the workflow. Many applications include strong legal requirements for the workflow or document model.

2.3 Local Workflow Model

A *local workflow model* is developed for each partner type. The local workflow defines the portion of the global workflow which each partner is responsible for and corresponds to the "Executable Process" in BPWL4WS1.1. The local workflow is a concrete process description. It does not only consider service calls from the outside but also contains internal actions and connections to the business logic. A complete local workflow model is direct input for a local workflow management system. The local models are typically developed by representatives of the partners involved.

Similarly to the global workflow model, the local workflow model consists of an activity diagram modeling the local workflow, document models and role models.

3 Model-Driven Development of Inter-organizational Applications

In our method we use models both for requirements elicitation and for code generation. The backbone of the inter-organizational application are the web services provided by the partners together with the local workflow engines controlling the workflow instances at each partner´s side[1].

---

[1] We conceive a centrally managed workflow as special case in which only one central partner is provided with such a workflow engine

The local workflow model of each partner type is the input to the local workflow engine. The target architecture does not provide an own workflow engine but uses a BPEL4WS-based workflow engine and a related UML front-end [16], other workflow engines and modelling front-ends are equally possible.

What SECTINO focuses on is the model-based generation of security components. While there are plenty of standards for web service security allowing security requirements like confidentiality and integrity to be implemented at XML and SOAP level (e.g. [18]), our claim is that a broad application of these standards requires a high-level development environment. With our approach we pursue model-based development of security components. The related core security architecture for each partner node is depicted in Fig. 3. This architecture wraps the basic web service components and the local workflow engine by a security gateway supporting the following services in the current version.

- Authentication of the requestor
- Decryption/encryption of messages
- Signing messages (with a system generated signature)
- Checking authorization of web service calls

More details about this reference architecture can be found in [12]. Fig. 4 illustrates the core inputs and outputs of the code generation.

- We specify security requirements concerning message exchange between partners in the global workflow model (cf. the notes in Fig. 2 requiring the confidentiality, integrity and non-repudiation of the documents exchanged) and generate the configuration files of the security gateway.
- The role and access model of the interface model are transformed into policies in the Policy Repository. The policy enforcement is based on the OASIS standard XACML [17].

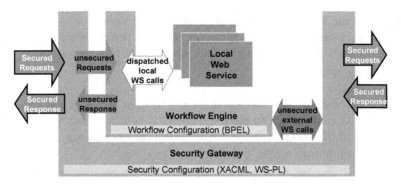

Fig. 3. SECTINO Schematic Reference Architecture

4 Requirements Elicitation

The models allowing code generation which have been discussed in the previous section are at a high though programmatic level of abstraction. Thus, our goal in SECTET is to integrate these models in a method that guides developers step by step to realize security-critical inter-organizational applications.

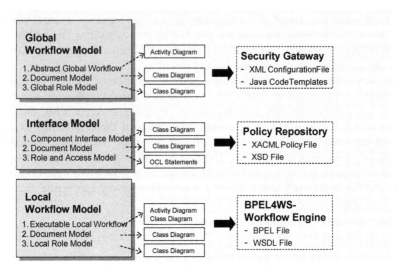

Fig. 4. Model-Driven Security in SECTET

For developing the local workflow models and the security-related annotations we proceed in the three basic steps of Fig. 5.

S1	Describe the business protocol informally in a global view
S2	Develop the global workflow model
S3	Develop the local workflow models for the partner nodes

Fig. 5. The three basic design steps of inter-organizational workflows

S1 – Describe the Workflow Informally in the Global View

Table 1 shows a small portion of such an informal description. We suggest a format close to an informal use case description [14] including the following parts.

– Name of the workflow
– Partner types
– Roles within the partner types (e.g. there may be roles *Secretary* and *Tax Advisor* within the partner type **Tax Advisor**)
– Main steps of the workflow together with variants and exceptions
– Security requirements on the workflow

The informal description is typically developed in cooperation with domain experts. This is particularly important for the security aspects which in many cases refer to legal requirements such as data protection or signature act. In non-standard cases a detailed threat and risk analysis of the security requirements is advisable (cf. [4]).

S2 – Develop the Global Workflow Model

The next step is to transform the textual description of the workflow into the formal representation of the global workflow model. Main activities within this step are the following.

- Identify the actions within the workflow taking into account the interface view of the partners and the primitives of the web service orchestration language (e.g. invoking web services, sending replies)
- Define the whole process including variants, loops and concurrently executed actions
- Model the security requirements in a formal way based on the annotation language
- Define the Document and the Role Model

It is important to note that not all informal security requirements can be transformed into formal ones in the model. Indeed, our language offers a set of patterns expressing standard security requirements. Security requirements that cannot be mapped onto the patterns have to be implemented programmatically in the security components.

S3 – Develop the Local Workflows for the Partner Nodes

In the last step the executable local workflows are developed. This comprises the following tasks.

- Divide the global workflow into local portions for each partner type
- Refine this local workflow based on the primitives of the chosen web service orchestration language by adding local actions and calls to the business logic
- Develop the document and the role model based on the respective models of the global workflow model

In general, the first task is non-straightforward and a problem that is subject of intensive research in a more formal setting [1, 3].

We follow a pragmatic approach and map the global workflow to a number of local workflow stubs. In this setting it is in the responsibility of the local partners to implement behavior that conforms to the global workflow. Rather than proving the correctness of the local executable workflows with respect to the abstract global workflow we provide a testing environment (cf. Section 5).

5 Testing Inter-organizational Workflows

Though developed at a high level of abstraction the resulting inter-organizational application in general will contain bugs. This both concerns the web service calls and the flow itself. In the cooperation project FLOWTEST we currently work on a model-based test environment for inter-organizational workflows.

Three major building blocks for such a test environment can be identified as follows.

| T1 Local and global testing |
| T2 Specification of test conditions |
| T3 Test management and test data generation |

Fig. 6. Basic building blocks of a test environment for inter-organizational workflows

T1 – Local and Global Testing

According to the model views and the executable artefacts we can distinguish three levels for testing inter-organizational applications. Each of these levels focuses on specific aspects of the execution.

- Testing the atomic web services – these tests are performed by the provider of the web service and the user of the web service. Client tests refer to the externally visible behaviour of the underlying business logic, while provider tests refer to the internal behaviour.
- Testing the local workflows – these tests are performed by each local partner. Local workflow tests focus on the orchestration of web services from the view of the partner. In order to support local testability the web services of the partner nodes (that may be called from the local flow) should be replaceable by local stubs.
- Testing the global workflow – these tests are performed by the responsible for the global workflow. Global workflow tests focus on the interplay of the local workflows. Similar to local workflow testing the availability of local stubs is a crucial requirement for global workflow testing.

T2 – Specification of Test Conditions
Our goal is to provide a test environment which works at the same level of abstraction as the design and implementation environment based on models. To this purpose we need a language for expressing test conditions.

Similarly to the specification of permissions we provide an OCL dialect for expressing properties over the document model. The test properties may be defined as conditions that have to be fulfilled independently of the input or as conditions that have to be fulfilled by specific test data.

As an example, Fig. 7 contains a simple postcondition requiring returned person data to fulfil an obvious constraint and a specific test condition for the test input string "012345".

```
getEnrollmentData (passportId: String): Person
post result.dateOfBirth.year <= 2005

sampleTestcond::
getEnrollmentData ("012345")
post result.name = "Erika Mustermann"
```

Fig. 7. Sample Test Conditions

Taking into account the test levels described in T1 the test conditions may be associated with the following model elements.

- Conditions on the execution of atomic web services
- Conditions on the execution of local workflows or on single steps within these workflows
- Conditions on the execution of global workflows or on single steps within these workflows

T3 – Test Management and Test Data Generation
The last aspect is concerned with the generation of (XML-)test data and the management of tests. Since the executable artefacts are programs including branches, loops and sequential and parallel composition well-known techniques of test data generation and test management can be applied at this place. This includes equivalence classes or random value tests.

6   Conclusion

In the preceding sections we have presented SECTET, a tool-based method for the development of security-critical inter-organizational applications. SECTET provides many novel aspects ranging from model-based development of security requirements to requirements elicitation and testing of inter-organizational workflows.

Future work has to be done in several directions. First, we will extend the set of supported security requirements. Primary candidates for such an extension are the support of qualified signatures and rights delegation. Second, we currently define the development method in more detail in the application area of e-government work-flows. Moreover, the proposed requirements for the testing environment have to be elaborated and realized. A further aspect we will work out in detail is change management of the workflows.

First positive results in pilot applications with our industrial cooperation partners encourage us to further steps.

References

1. Van der Aalst, W.M.P. 2000. Loosely Coupled Interorganizational Workflows: Modeling and Analyzing Workflows Crossing Organizational Boundaries. In: Information and Management 37 (2000) 2, pp. 67-75.
2. M. Alam, R. Breu, M. Breu. Model-Driven Security for Web Services (MDS4WS), Proc. INMIC 2004, 2004.
3. W.M.P. van der Aalst and M. Weske. The P2P appraoch to Interorganizational Workflows. In: Proc. CAiSE 01, Springer Lecture Notes in Computer Science vol. 2068, pp. 140-156. Springer-Verlag, Berlin, 2001.
4. R. Breu, K. Burger, M. Hafner, G. Popp. Towards a Systematic Development of Secure Systems. Special Issue of the Information Systems Security Journal, Auerbach, 2004.
5. E. Bertino, S. Castano, E. Ferrari: Securing XML Documents with Author X. In: IEEE Internet Computing, vol. 5,no. 3, May/June 2001.
6. R. Breu, M. Hafner, B. Weber, A. Nowak: Model Driven Security for Inter-Organizational Workflows in e-Government. Accepted for TCGOV 2005.
7. R. Breu, G. Popp: Actor-Centric Modeling of User Rights. In: M.Wermelinger, T. Margaria-Steffen (Eds.): Proc. FASE 2004, Springer LNCS Vol. 2984,p. 165-179, 2004.
8. IBM, Microsoft, BEA Systems, SAP AG, Siebel Systems, "Specification: Business Process Execution Language for Web Services Version 1.1". See
   http://www-128.ibm.com/developerworks/library/ws-bpel/
9. IBM, "Business Process Execution Language for Web Services Java™ Run Time (BPWS4J)". See: http://www.alphaworks.ibm.com/tech/bpws4j
10. F. Casati and M. Shan. Event-based Interaction Management for Composite E-Services in eFlow. Information Systems Frontiers 4(2), 2002.
11. P. Grefen, K. Aberer, Y. Hoffner, H. Ludwig: CrossFlow: cross-organizational workflow management in dynamic virtual enterprises. In: International Journal of Computer Systems Science & Engineering 15 (2000) 5, pp. 277-290.
12. M. Hafner, R. Breu, M. Breu: A Security Architecure For Inter-organizational Workflows - Putting Web Service Security Standards Together. Accepted for ICEIS 2005.
13. W.K. Huang, V. Atluri. SecureFlow: A secure Web-enabled Workflow Management System. ACM Workshop on Role-Based Access Control, 1999.
14. I. Jacobson, G. Booch, J. Rumbaugh. The Unified Software Development Process. Addison-Wesley, 1999.

15. T. Lodderstedt, D. Basin, J. Doser. Secureuml: A uml-based modeling language for model-driven security. In: J.-M. Jézéquel, H. Hussmann, S. Cook (eds.): UML 2002. Lecture Notes in Computer Science, vol. 2460, Springer, 2002.

16. K. Mantell, "From UML to BPEL", IBM-developerWorks, 2003. See: http://www-106.ibm.com/developerworks/webservices/library/ws-uml2bpel/

17. T. Moses (ed.), et al., "XACML Profile for Web-Services", XACML TC Working draft, Version 04. September 29, 2003.

18. A. Nadalin, C. Kaler, P. Hallam-Baker, R. Monzillo, 2004. Web Services Security: SOAP Message Security 1.0 (WS Security 2004), OASIS Standard 200401, March 2004. See: http://docs.oasis-open.org/wss/2004/01/oasis-200401-wss-soap-message-security-1.0.pdf

19. UML 2.0 OCL Final Adopted specification. http://www.omg.org/cgi-bin/doc?ptc/2003-10-14

20. G. Starke. Web Service Engineering. Objekt-Spektrum 01/2002, SIGS DATACOM

21. I. Schieferdecker, B. Stepien. Automated Testing of XML/SOAP based Web Services. 13. Fachkonferenz der Gesellschaft für Informatik (GI) Fachgruppe "Kommunikation in verteilten Systemen", Leipzig, 2003.

22. J. Wainer, P. Barthelmess and A. Kumar: W-RBAC – A Workflow Security Model Incorporating Controlled Overriding of Constraints In International Journal of Cooperative Information Systems. Vol. 12, No 4 (2003) 455-485.

23. W3C Recommendation XML Schema Part 2: Datatypes. 02 May 2001

Toward a Comprehension View of Web Engineering

Semia Sonia Selmi, Naoufel Kraiem, and Henda Ben Ghezala

ENSI, National School of Computer Science, 2010 Manouba, Tunisia
Semiasonia.selmi@riadi.rnu.tn
Naoufel.kraiem@ensi.rnu.tn
Henda.BG@cck.rnu.tn

Abstract. The paper is an attempt to explore some of the issues underlying Web applications development through the use of disciplined approaches. We first present the proposed Web engineering framework which suggests considering web engineering along four different views. Each view is capturing a particular relevant aspect of Web engineering. Motivations for developing the framework are three fold: (a) to help understand and clarify the Web engineering domain, (b) to guide in classifying and comparing both web applications and approaches and (c) to help researchers to identify new research axes. Next, we briefly present evaluation of 7 different Web-based approaches according to the Web engineering framework.

1 Introduction

The technological evolution of the last decade has made the World Wide Web the ideal platform for the development of Web-based hypermedia applications and the primary support for their delivery. Indeed, an enormous number of applications have been developed and their widespread acceptance points to the effectiveness of Web design approaches. However, current applications often fail since their development is often on an ad-hoc basis, without the support of appropriate methodologies able to manage the high complexity of information.

Obviously, we have little understanding about how web applications should be developed. For example, there is no consensus on which approach to be used for development. There is also little evidence about their effectiveness and even less idea about how they are.

Consequently, considerable attention has been given to Web engineering, a new discipline proposed to provide a systematic and disciplined approach for developing, documenting and maintaining Web/hypermedia applications.

Web engineering is a rather a new research area, so, studying and understanding deeply this discipline need a web engineering framework. We propose a framework in which we consider web engineering through four different view-points each one capturing a particular aspect of this discipline.

Motivations for developing the framework are three fold: (a) to help understand and clarify the web engineering domain, (b) to guide in classifying and comparing both Web applications and approaches and (c) to help researchers identify new research axes. The latter is an important issue since the whole Web engineering field is relying on the two fundamental concepts namely *Web applications* and *Web-based hypermedia design approaches*.

D. Lowe and M. Gaedke (Eds.): ICWE 2005, LNCS 3579, pp. 19–29, 2005.

This paper is an attempt to explore some of the issues underlying Web applications development and to propose a framework. The remainder of this paper is organized as follow. Section 2 is an overview of the framework which is further detailed in section 3. Section 4 reviews 7 current web development approaches evaluated according to the framework. Finally, conclusions are drawn in section 5.

2   Framework Overview

The development of a Web application is a multi-faceted activity, involving not only technical but also organisational, managerial and even social and artistic issues [11]. Web application development refers to a set of activities applied in order to develop a web application of high quality having awaited characteristics, and to carry out this development efficiently and coherently. Obviously, goals of Web application development introduce two basic concepts namely Web application as a product and the used Web approach as a process.

The proposed Web engineering framework is based on both concepts and implies considering them along four different views, each view captures a particular relevant aspect of Web engineering.

As shown in Fig. 1, framework is composed of:

- *Nature* view deals with the classification of both web applications and web-based hypermedia methods applied for the design and the development of web applications.
- *Form* view includes representations of methods at different levels of detail.
- *Purpose* view deals with intentional aspects. It concerns goals which we attempt to reach in the web engineering field.
- *Development Cycle* view deals with the web applications development process and their enactment.

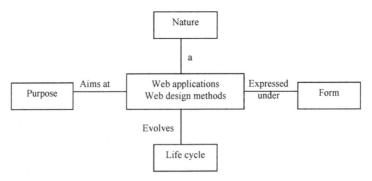

Fig. 1. Web Engineering Framework

We have adopted a faceted classification approach similar to the one proposed by [27] in Requirements Engineering. Each view is associated with a set of facets which are considered as viewpoints or dimensions suitable to characterize and classify approaches and/or applications according to this view.

A metric is attached to each facet which is measured by a set of relevant attributes. Both web applications and methods are positioned in the framework by affecting values to the attributes of each facet. Attribute values are defined within a domain which may be a predefined type (Integer, Boolean, etc), an enumerated type (ENUM{x, y, z}), or a structured type (SET or TUPLE).

The multi-facet and multi-view approach adopted makes it possible to look at web engineering in a comprehensive way. Facets provide an in-depth description of each aspect of Web engineering whereas aspects give a view of Web engineering in all its diversity.

3 The proposed Framework

3.1 The Nature View

The Nature view is characterized by two facets namely the *application nature* facet and the *method nature* facet.

Application Nature Facet

Many classifications of web applications are referenced in literature. For instance, classifications proposed in [14] [13] and [1] are generally based on functionality criteria and are, consequently, considered as specific classifications.

A more general classification is proposed by both [7] and [9]. According to [7], a distinction can be made between a *Web application* and a *Web site.* The web application uses a web site as the front end to a more back office application.

[9] proposes a similar distinction by identifying the *kiosk type* and the *application type*. A kiosk web site mainly provides information and allows users to navigate through that information. Whereas, an application web site is an information system where users process data, communicate and collaborate with other users.

As classification in [9] is largely referenced in literature such as in [17] [31] and [9], we keep this classification and define the following application nature attribute having the same name of the facet:

Application nature: ENUM {kiosk type, application type}

Method Nature Facet

Some researchers have attempted to classify web design approaches such [32] in which approaches are classified into 4 categories: *Resource-oriented* approaches, *Site-oriented* approaches, *Design-oriented* approaches, *Model-based* approaches.

[9] proposed another classification of web design approaches based on three categories: *Data-driven* approaches, *User-centered* approaches, *User-driven* approaches.

A web design approach can be classified in only one category according to the second classification. As the latter is the most referenced in literature, we define the following attribute having same name with the facet:

Method nature: ENUM {data-driven, user-driven, user-centered}

3.2 Form View

The form view is composed of the three following facets: Models facet, Notation facet and Abstraction facet.

Models Facet

The model facet is concerned with the content of a web design approach.

With the rapid increase of web applications complexity it becomes increasingly important for web design approaches to provide different modelling artefacts that support various viewpoints. When designing complex web applications, designers can look at the application from different but inter-related perspectives. They can break down applications into manageable pieces. Indeed, approaches consider design process in terms of process phases and their deliverables, often models.

The following models[1]: *Conceptual model, Navigation model* and *Presentation model* are commonly delivered. Besides, and due to the evolution of the web and web applications, other phases are recognized delivering the following design models: *Requirements analysis model, User model, Adaptation model* and *Business process mode and Business model* (required especially for e-commerce applications).

Thus, in order to capture aspects considered during web applications design, the Models facet introduces the following attribute with the same name:

Models: SET (ENUM {Requirements analysis model, Conceptual model, Navigation model, presentation model, User model, Adaptation model, Business process model, Business model})

Notation Facet

In order to support the representation of application features during development lifecycle, notations with different levels of formality and abstraction are used.

To express structural features, the best-known conceptual data models, like E-R Model and various objects models [29] are mostly used. Various approaches belonging to the hypermedia field are proposed to enrich traditional conceptual models with new concepts.

For modelling the navigation, most approaches employ notations and techniques proposed for the more general problem of human-computer interaction specification [10] and extend data models with navigation primitives.

For presentation modelling, most of methods, except methods based entirely on UML, use principally proprietary formalisms and notations combined sometimes with standard notations.

The domain of the attribute Notation captures the notation used in a method.

Notation: ENUM {Standard, Proper, Mixture}.

Abstraction Facet

The Abstraction facet allows capturing abstraction levels in which methods are described. Depending on its level of abstraction, the method component will be reused as such or will be instantiated before being assembled in the method under construction. Approaches based on meta-modeling mechanism are at the meta-type level. The abstraction facet has one attribute *level* having values in the following enumerated domain:

Level: SET (ENUM {type, meta-type}).

---

[1] Models mentioned are deliverables of the three common design phases referenced in [11]

3.3 Purpose View

The purpose view deals with goals assigned to web application methods. This issue is associated with the *purpose* facet. As applications change and evolve continuously in time, a method should support this evolution. This aspect is captured by the facet named *Method management policy*. These two facets are described in the following.

Purpose Facet

Synthesis of studies in the Software Engineering [20], [8] and Information Systems communities [3],[22] and [25] have shown two main aims of web application design methods:

- Prescriptive: they prescribe how the process should be accomplished.
- Descriptive: they study existing processes and describe how the process is carried out.

However, some approaches mix descriptive and prescriptive strategies [22]. A web application design approach can be classified according to the role that plays in the Purpose facet:

Purpose: SET (ENUM {descriptive, prescriptive})

Method Management Policy Facet

Given the rapid changes in context and in user requirements when considering the Web, an environment where change in both technology and user requirements is a standard part of life, applications should have the ability to evolve. This evolution should be supported during their development. Design evolution should be supported with automatic propagation of the modifications from one step to another during development process. The use of structured techniques and the product of a process tracings and separation between the following aspects of design constitute a solid base to method evolution.

As in Software Engineering, reuse is also an aspect of this view. Reuse is a strategic tool for reducing the cost and improving the quality of hypermedia design and development. It consists in taking advantage of any of the efforts done for previous works to reduce the needed effort to achieve a new one [19]. Reuse can occur at any level of hypermedia development. It may concern data, software components conceptual schemas, design schemas, content and physical application pages as well as design experience. The most common form of reuse on the web is content reuse.

Thus, a web design method might be positioned within the Method Management Policy facet with the two following attributes *Evolution* and *Reuse* which allow to determine respectively even the method supports evolution and reuse or not.

Evolution: Boolean
Reuse: Boolean

3.4 The Development Cycle View

Lifecycle Coverage Facet

Several lifecycle models of a web application have been proposed in the literature such as in [30], [2], and [11]. However, typical activities involved in the construction of a web application can be partially obtained from the lifecycle models of traditional Information Systems and enriched with specific activities. The lifecycle model used as a reference in this paper was proposed in [11].

Note that defining the lifecycle coverage facet allows one to determine activities considered during the development of a web application.

Life cycle Coverage: SET (ENUM {Requirement Analysis, Conceptualisation, Proto-typing & validation, Implementation, Evolution & Maintenance})

Construction Technique Facet

In the web development context, we find the construction techniques of traditional Information Systems domain, exploring the meta-modelling aspect and using languages. Meta-modelling consists in identifying common and generic characteristics to different applications and representing them by a system of generic concepts. It uses two principal techniques: instantiation and assembling. It is to note that most of web applications are developed based on developer's experience, we can that they are the result of an ad-hoc technique of construction.

Technique: ENUM {Instantiation, Assembly, language, ad-hoc}

Interaction Facet

Compared with traditional software applications, web applications tend to provide much more sophisticated interactions with users.

Dynamic description and transformations occurred when users interact with application should be supported by the web design approach. Thus, an approach needs to provide the ability to model these different interactions in a complete way so that users' interactions can be captured, designed and implemented.

We introduce a Boolean attribute *Interaction* which allow determining if method considers interaction of users with application or not do.

Interaction: Boolean

Enactment Support Facet

Besides the construction process of web applications, the development view deals also with their enactment.

CAWE category (Computer Aided Web Engineering) provides best development lifecycle coverage by applying design modelling and code generation techniques. We find all basic principles of software engineering. Benefits are comparable to those of CASE tools, we cite for instance reduction of effort and reuse. Efforts have been conducted in last years to the design and the development of prototype of hypermedia and web design tools.

Consequently, this facet has an attribute *tool support* that allows knowing the tool used.

Tool support: text

Dynamic Generation Facet

Information content of web applications is stored in pages and users can request a page by its name or can access through path.

In some situations, page content is assembled at run time from information stored in the data base or a repository. It can also be generated from loaded modules e.g. CGI. Web sites using this strategy are dynamic web sites. These have the advantage to keep the content up to date and synchronised with the data of the data bases. All these aspects should be taken into account by the design method when developing applications.

According to this facet, methods are classified into those that consider dynamic content generation and those that not do. This facet is described by a Boolean attribute.

Dynamic generation: Boolean

Adaptation Facet

Many researches have been focused on adaptation forms such as [4] [6] [19]. [33] completes these adaptation dimensions by namely adaptation based on functionality and adaptation based on management of material conditions of exploitation. Summarizing, adaptive dimensions are following: adaptive content, adaptive navigation, adaptive presentation, Adaptive functionality, Management of Material conditions of exploitation.

Adaptation: SET (ENUM {content, navigation, presentation, functionality, material condition of exploitation})

4   Review of 7 Web Design Approaches According to the Framework

We propose, in this section, to illustrate the use of the web engineering framework through the evaluation of the 7 following web-based hypermedia design approaches: Relationship Management Methodology (RMM) [17], Object-Oriented Hypermedia Design Model (OOHDM) [30] [15], Hypermedia Flexible Process Model (HFPM) [22], UML-based Web Engineering (UWE) [19], the method proposed by Takahashi [31], Web Sites Design Method (WSDM) [9] and WebML [6].

We aim to get a large picture of the web engineering area and to help understand currently developed web-based hypermedia approaches.

Table 1, Table 2 and Table 3 provide instantiation of the 7 approaches according to the four views of the proposed web engineering framework namely: Nature, Form, Purpose and Development Cycle.

Several conclusions can be obtained from we can get both strength points and limitations of evaluated approaches.

Each of these proposed approaches has its strength points. We can notice, for instance, that except WSDM all approaches are proposed for the development of complex web applications and cover the whole life cycle of web applications. They support reuse and are able to evolve when application environment change. This is made possible since approaches consider the different design steps separately.

Although proposed approaches have strength, some limitations can be identified such as:

The Inability to Model Business Processes: Most existing modeling approaches do not address the modeling of functionality or business processes. Except WSDM,

Table 1. Instantiation of 7 web-based hypermedia approaches according to Nature view and Form view of the Web Engineering Framework

	Nature View		Form View		
	Application Nature	**Method Nature**	**Models**	**Notation**	**Abstraction**
RMM	applications	Data-driven	Conceptual M. Navigational M. Presentation M.	Mix	Type
OOHDM	applications	User-driven	Req. Analysis M. Conceptual M. Navigational M. Presentation M.	Mix	Type
Takahashi M.	applications	User-driven	Req. Analysis M. Conceptual M.	Mix	Type
HFPM	applications	User-driven	Req. Analysis M. Conceptual M. Navigational M. Presentation M.	Mix	Type
UWE	kiosques	User-centred	Req. Analysis M. Conceptual M. Navigational M. Presentation M. User Model Adaptation M.	Standard	Type
WSDM	kiosques	User-centred	Req. Analysis M. Conceptual M. Navigational M. User M. Business process M.	Mix	Type
WebML	applications	Data-driven	Conceptual M. Navigational M. Presentation M. User Model Adaptation M.	Mix	Type

Table 2. Instantiation of 7 web-based hypermedia approaches according to Purpose view of the Web Engineering Framework

	Purpose View		
	Purpose	**Method management Policy**	
		Evolution	**Reuse**
RMM	Presc.	Yes	Yes
OOHDM	Presc.	Yes	Yes
Takahashi M.	Presc.	Yes	Yes
HFPM	Presc. + Desc.	Yes	Yes
UWE	Presc.	Yes	Yes
WSDM	Presc.	Yes	Yes
WebML	Presc.	Yes	Yes

approaches focus has been on the organization aspects, navigation and presentation modalities. Some others approaches are user-centered and then consider moreover user viewpoint. However, none has addressed Business processes viewpoint which has been consistently overlooked.

Table 3. Instantiation of 7 web-based hypermedia approaches according to Development cycle view of the Web Engineering Framework

	Development Cycle View					
			Enact-ment Support			
	Life cycle Coverage	Techni-que	Tool support	Dynamic Generation	Interaction	Adaptation
RMM	Conceptualization Design Prototyping & validation Implementation	/	RMCase	No	No	No
OOHDM	Req. analysis Conceptualization Design Implementation	/	OOHDM-Web	Yes	Yes	Yes (relatively)
Takahashi M.	Req. analysis Conceptualization Design Implementation Maintenance	/	WebArchi-tect PilotBoat	No	No	No
HFPM	Req. analysis Conceptualization Design Implementation Maintenance	/	/	No	No	No
UWE	Req. analysis Conceptualization Design Implementation Maintenance	/	/	No	Yes	Yes
WSDM	Req. analysis Conceptualization Design Implementation	/	/	No	No	Yes (relatively)
WebML	Req. analysis Conceptualization Design	language	WebRatio Site devel-opment studio 24	No	Yes	Yes

The Inability to Support Various Abstraction Levels: Modeling approaches need to provide modeling artifacts at different abstraction levels. The need for various abstraction levels is reflected in the importance to be guided from high to low abstraction level.

The Not Use of Standard Notation: Except UWE, existing modelling approaches address main design phases through the use of different notations in most cases proprietary. However, it desirable to adopt known and standard notations. This facilitates both communication between involved people in design and maintenance phase. The latter plays an increasingly important role in comparison with conventional software systems.

Inability to Model Interaction Aspects: Not all existing modelling techniques support interaction aspect during web design. However, modelling techniques need to provide ability to model users' interactions with web applications. They should specify transformations occurred when user interacts with application, objects behaviour after external events and dynamic descriptions.

Inability to Support Dynamic Generation Content: Major web applications are becoming complex in term of information and then need to be dynamic, that is content is assembled at run time from information stored. Information sources to which a web application can connect may include databases, file servers, document repositories, etc. Consequently, modelling approaches need to support dynamic generation of content.

5 Conclusion and Further Work

More recently, the web engineering community advocates and emphasizes the use of disciplined approaches for the development of web applications.

Our study has shown that both web design approaches and web applications can not be treated adequately with simple predicate-based classification techniques. However, here is a need for a four-dimensional framework to well describe web engineering discipline. Through the notion of dimensions and facets, we are able to successfully capture the global view and the more detailed view of web engineering respectively.

References

1. Amitay, A., Carmel, D., Darlow, A., Lempel, A., Soffer, A.: The Connectivity Sonar: Detecting Site Functionality by Structural Patterns. J. Digit. Information. 4 (2003) Issue 3
2. Atzeni, P., Mecca, G., Merialdo, P.: To Weave the Web. 23rd Conference on Very Large Data Bases (VLDB'97), pp. 206-215, Athens, Greece, August 26-29
3. Brinkkemper, S.: Formalisation of information systems modeling. Ph. D. Thesis (1990), University of Nijmegen, Thesis Publishers
4. Brusilovsky, P.: Methods and Techniques of Adaptive Hypermedia. Int. J. of User Modeling and User-Adapted Interaction (1996). Kluwer Academic Publishers 6, 2-3, 87-129
5. Chen, P.P.: The entity-relationship model: toward a unified view of data. ACM TODS (1976) 1, 1, 9-36
6. Ceri, S., Fraternali, P., Bongio, A.: Web Modeling Language (WebML): a modeling language for designing Web sites. 9th International World Wide Web Conference (Www9), Amsterdam, Netherlands, May 15-19, 2000
7. Conallen, J.: Modeling web Application Architectures with UML. Communications of the ACM. 42 (1999) N°.10, pp.63-70
8. Curtis, B., Kellner, M. I., Over, J.: Process Modeling. Communications of the ACM. 35 (1992) N° 9, pp 75-90
9. De Troyer, O.M.F., Leune, C.J.: WSDM: a User Centered Design Method for Web Sites. WWW7 Conference (1998), Brisbane
10. Fraternali, P., Paolini, P.: A conceptual model and a tool environment for developing more scalable and dynamic Web applications. EDBT'98. 421-435, Valencia, Spain
11. Fraternali, P.: Tools and Approaches for Developing Data-Intensive web Applications: a Survey. ACM Computing Surveys (1999)
12. Garzotto, F., Paolini, P., Schwabe, D.: HDM. A model-based approach to hypertext application design. ACM Transactions on Information Systems 11(1993), N°1 1-26
13. Ginige, A.: Web Engineering: An Introduction. IEEE Multimedia (2001)

14. Gnaho, C.: Définition d'un Cadre Méthodologique pour l'Ingénierie des Systèmes d'Information Web Adaptatifs. Ph. D. Thesis (2000) Paris1 University
15. Güell, N., Schwabe, D., Vilain, P.: Modeling Interactions and navigation in Web Applications. World Wide Web and Conceptual Modeling Workshop, ER'00 Conference, LNCS 1921, Springer, Salt Lake City (2000).
16. Halasz, F., Schwartz, M.: The Dexter Reference Model. Hypertext Standardization workshop 95-133, Gaithersburg, Maryland: National Institute of Standards and Technology Publication 500-178 (1990)
17. Isakowitz, T., Stohr, E.A., Balasubramanian, P.: RMM: a Methodology for Structured Hypermedia Design. Communications of the ACM, Vol. 38, N°.8, pp. 34-44, (1995)
18. Jones, D., T. lynch: A Model for the design of web-based systems that supports Adoption, Appropriation and Evolution. 1st ICSE Workshop on Web Engineering, Murugesan, S., Deshpande, Y. (eds), Los Angeles, pp 47-56.
19. N. Koch: Software Engineering for Adaptive Hypermedia Systems-Reference Model, Modelling Techniques and Development Process. Ph.D Thesis (2001), Fakultät der Mathematik und Informatik, Ludwig-Maximilians-Universität München, December .
20. Lonchamp, J.: A structured Conceptual and Terminological Framework for Software Process Engineering. International Conference on Software Process (1993)
21. J. Nanard and M. Nanard: Toward an Hypermedia Design Pattern Space. Hypertext'99 Workshop on Design Pattern in Hypermedia
22. Olsina, L.: Building a Web-based information system applying the hypermedia flexible process modeling strategy. 1st International Workshop on Hypermedia development, Hypertext'98
23. Papazoglou, M.P., Yang, J.: The Role of services and Transactions for Integrated value chains. chapter IX, Idea Group Publishing, (2002)
24. Paterno, P., Mancini, C.: Designing Web User Interfaces for Museum Applications to Support different Types of Users. International Conference about Museums and the Web, March 12-14, New Orleans, LA, 1999, pp. 75-86
25. Rolland, C., Plihon, V.: Using generic chunks to generate process models fragments. 2nd IEEE Int. Conf. on Requirements Engineering, ICRE'96
26. Rolland, C., Prakash, N.: A proposal for context-specific method engineering. IFIP WG 8.1 Conference on Method Engineering, Chapman and Hall, pp 191-208, Colorado Spring, 1996
27. Rolland, C., Ben Achour, C., Cauvet, C., Ralyté, J., Sutcliffe, A., Maiden, N.A.M., Jarke, M., Haumer, P., Pohl, K., Dubois, Heymans, P.: A proposal for a scenario classification framework. Requirements Engineering Journal, 3, 1, 1998
28. Rossi, G., Schwabe, D., Garrido, A.: Design reuse in hypermedia applications development. 8th ACM conference on Hypertext (1997), ACM press,, pp. 57-66
29. Rumbaugh, J., Blaha, M., Premerlani, W., Eddy, F., Loresen, W.: Object-oriented modeling and design. Prentice Hall international, (1991)
30. Schwabe, D., Rossi, G., Barbosa, S.: Systematic Hypermedia Application Design with OOHDM. ACM-Hypertext96 (1996)
31. Takahashi, K., Lang, E.: Analysis and Design of Web based Information Systems. Sixth International World Wide Web Conference, (1997)
32. Vigna, G., Coda, F., Garzotto, F., Ghezzi, C.: A Generative World Wide Web object-oriented Model. Politecnico di Milano, Technical Report (1997)
33. Villanova-Olivier, M.:Adaptabilité dans les systèmes d'information sur le Web: Modélisation et mise en oeuvre de l'accès progressif. Ph. D. Thesis (2002), Grenoble, France

A Need-Oriented Assessment of Technological Trends in Web Engineering

Damith C. Rajapakse and Stan Jarzabek

Department of Computer Science, School of Computing
National University of Singapore
{damithch,stan}@comp.nus.edu.sg

Abstract. As Web technologies change and multiply fast, their comprehension, assessment, selection and adoption are likely to be increasingly difficult, accidental and sub-optimal. Most often, needs are both important elements in technology assessment/selection and drivers of technology proliferation and evolution. We believe a need-oriented organization of Web technologies, as presented in this paper, is a useful starting point for comprehending the multitude of existing and emerging Web technologies from an essential and stable perspective. We identify important technological needs in relation to a reference architecture for Web Applications, and show how different technological trends address each need. We hope the paper will be of interest to those who want to get a grasp of the Web technology landscape and understand major trends.

1 Introduction

Web technologies change and multiply fast. For the practitioner and the researcher alike, a single summary of the state of the art in Web technologies could be invaluable in quickly grasping the current state of the art. To be useful, such a summary needs to be concrete enough to give sufficient details about the technologies, yet abstract enough to withstand rapid changes to concrete details. In this paper we attempt to present such a summary, organized around "Technology needs". Technology needs are both important elements in technology assessment/selection and drivers of technology proliferation and evolution. Hence, we believe that such an organization provides a perspective that is more user-oriented, fundamental and stable than the technologies themselves. Starting with a reference architecture for WAs, we identify important technology needs of the tiers and workflows of a typical WA, and then organize the technologies into different trends that has emerged to serve these needs.

Ours is not the first attempt to ease the difficulty of comprehending Web Engineering Resources (WER). Christodoulou et al [4][5], for example, proposed a reference model [4] for organizing knowledge about WERs, with a framework [5] for comparative evaluation of WERs. While the goal of Christodoulou's work and ours is the same, the methods are different, and the results – complementary to each other. Christodoulou's framework is more abstract; it does not concentrate on needs or specific technologies. Our framework is specific about concrete details of technologies, and their relation to needs and trends. It does not require the reader to discover and assemble concrete details on their own, as is the case with [5]. Therefore, we believe our paper could be of immediate benefit to those seeking a quick overview of the Web technology landscape. We consider integrating concepts from Christodoulou's framework into ours, as an interesting future project.

D. Lowe and M. Gaedke (Eds.): ICWE 2005, LNCS 3579, pp. 30–35, 2005.

2 Needs, Trends and Technologies

As shown in Fig. 1, WAs typically follow a multi-tier client-server architecture. The client-side of a WA consists of users accessing the WA using a *User agent* (E.g., Web browser) running on a *User device* (e.g., PC). In this paper, we focus on the most common User agent configuration: Web browser running on a PC. The server-side of the WA may be organized into multiple tiers and run on a Web server, possibly augmented by Application servers, Transaction monitors or Message servers. In this section, we discuss most important *WA-specific* needs of the tiers and workflows of a WA, and trends in Web technologies that address those needs. For each trend, we briefly mention the *implementation related* technologies (languages, standards, protocols, tools and techniques) that typify each trend.

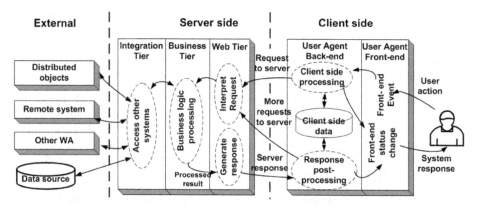

Fig. 1. Web Application Reference Architecture

The Need for Better Front-End Languages. Client-side of a WAs is primarily driven by HTML, a non-proprietary language standardized by World Wide Web Consortium (W3C) [18]. However, HTML syntax lacks the strictness of a programming language. The resulting difficulties in validating and processing HTML documents have led to a trend towards XML syntax. Extensible HTML (XHTML), the successor of HTML, is a family of document types and modules that reproduce, subset, and extend HTML, reformulated in XML [18]. Reduced authoring costs, an improved match to database and workflow applications, and clean integration with other XML applications are some of the cited benefits of XHTML [18]. Furthermore, HTML's lack of support for specialized contents has led to a number of specialized markup languages (e.g., MathML [18] – for mathematical content).

The Need to Separate Content, Structure, and Presentation. A typical HTML document is a mixture of content, structure, and presentational information. Keeping these three aspects as separate as possible is beneficial for development, maintenance (as different experts could develop/maintain each separately), and reuse (as each could be reused separately). *Styles* [18] were added to HTML as a way to separate out presentational information. Styles describe how documents are presented on a User agent. Cascading Style Sheets (CSS) [18] is one such style mechanism that is gaining wide use. Another related technology is XSL (Extensible Style Sheets) [18], a family of recommendations for defining XML document transformation and presentation. Included in XSL is XSL Transformations (XSLT). An XSL style sheet can change the presentational as well as structural information of a document. It can be used on any XML document. XSL and CSS can be used together in a complementary manner.

The Need for a Better UI. Pure HTML UIs are static, and limited in functionality. The need to make WA UIs as sophisticated as traditional GUI applications has resulted in several trends. The first trend is to embed client-side scripts in HTML pages. JavaScript and VBScript are two languages commonly used for client-side scripting. Jscript [1] (succeeded by Jscript.NET [1]) is the Microsoft variant of JavaScript. ECMAScript [7] is a public domain specification that attempts to standardize client-side scripting. The second trend is embedding lightweight applications/components in HTML pages. Java applets and ActiveX controls are two technologies used for this purpose. A Java applet is a Java program that can be downloaded and executed by a browser. ActiveX controls can be run by a COM (Component Object Model) [1] aware browser and can be written in a variety of languages. The third trend is the use of plug-ins to enable using different objects inside the browser (e.g., Adobe Acrobat plug-in allows viewing PDF documents from within browsers).

The Need for Client-Side Processing. Although WAs follow "thin client" paradigm (minimal functionality client, more processing on server), performing some processing on the client-side (e.g., input validation on forms) can significantly reduce network traffic and improve response time. The trends for client-side processing are similar to that of the previous section, i.e., embedded client-side scripts (JavaScript, VBScript, etc.), embedded small applications (Applets, ActiveX), and plug-ins.

The Need to Use Mainstream Languages for Business Logic Processing. The bulk of the business logic processing of a typical WA happens on the server-side. Common Gateway Interface (CGI) is one standard for using mainstream programming languages to implement business logic. CGI defines how data is passed from a server to a CGI-compliant program. Two popular CGI programming languages are Perl and Python. Java is another popular language used for developing WAs. For example, Java Servlets [11] are modules of Java code that run in a server application and respond to client requests by interpreting the request, doing business logic processing, and generating dynamic content. Component technologies such as Enterprise Java Beans (EJB [11]) can further simplify server-side programming. They facilitate reuse of common services, allowing a developer to focus on the business logic of a WA, rather than on the "plumbing" code.

The Need to Separate Response from Response Generation Code. Generating the response involves generating text of one language (e.g., HTML) using another language (e.g., Perl or Java). The simplest solution is to write the server response directly to the output stream (e.g. using print() function). Java Servlets follow this method. However, this approach requires encoding each piece of the server response as a string literal, obviously a cumbersome task. Embedding scripts to represent dynamic content in otherwise static text files, commonly called "Server pages", tries to separate server response from the code generating that response (scripts). The web server processes the server page and sends the generated text output to the client-side. In Server-side Includes (SSI) technique – a limited form of server pages – scripting commands embedded within a web page are parsed by the web server to generate dynamic content. SSI functionality is limited to adding small pieces of dynamic information (e.g, common footer). PHP (Hypertext Preprocessor), ASP (Active Server Pages – succeeded by ASP.NET), and JSP (Java Server Pages) are Server page technologies that are more capable than SSI. Several extensions with similar capabilities exist for Perl (e.g. Mason [9]) and Python (e.g., Spyce [15]). A further improvement is to separate the server response and scripts into separate files. Java Beans (in conjunction with JSP) and ASP.NET's *Code-behind* feature are some technologies that push in this direction. A successful separation of server response from code gives us *Templates* – representative documents one can create and edit using ordinary Web authoring tools while preserving the hooks to scripts. Freemarker [8] and Velocity [17] for Java, HTML::Template and Text::Template for Perl, Smarty [14] for PHP, DTML for Python, are examples of templating mechanisms. Macromedia's CFML (Cold Fusion Markup Language) [3] is another proprietary templating language.

The Need for Rapid UI Building. Unlike a traditional application where UI and the event handling code form one cohesive unit, UI of a WA needs to run on a diverse set of thin clients while communicating with the server-based event handling logic via the stateless HTTP protocol. Server-side UI component technologies are an effort to hide this complexities from the developer. They include a set of APIs for representing UI components against which it is easy to write code for managing their state, handling events, input validation etc. ASP.NET Web Forms [1] and JSF (Java Server Faces) [12] are two such server-side UI component technologies.

The Need for Integration. There are three types of integration that we can think of: intra-WA integration, inter-WA integration, and integration between WA and other external systems. The trend in intra-WA integration (integration of the remotely located parts of a WA) is to use general purpose distributed application technologies (e.g., CORBA [6], DCOM [1], .NET remoting technology [1], and Java RMI [11]) In inter-WA integration we can also use WA-specific technologies. For example, JSR-168 [12] Portlet specification defines a common API for Portlets in Web Portals. Even more sophisticated integration could be achieved using *Web services* [18] – programmatic interfaces made available by a WA for communication with other WAs. Web services could be combined to create WAs, regardless of where they reside or how they were implemented. When WAs need to integrate with external non-WAs (e.g. Mail servers) the integration method depends on the mutual availability of an integration technology and a communication protocol.

The Need for End-to-End Solutions. The need for end-to-end technology solutions is based on two desires: the desire to start with a set of compatible technologies, to avoid interoperability issues, and the desire to have much of the common infrastructure ready-made and well integrated, to minimize the development effort. Platforms (underlying technological environments or architectures) and frameworks (collections of software containing specialized APIs, services, and tools) serve this need. The J2EE (Java 2 Platform, Enterprise Edition) [11] defines the standard for developing multi-tier enterprise applications (not limited to WAs) using Java. It provides containers for client applications, web components based on Servlets and JSP technologies, and EJB components. The J2EE Connector Architecture defines a standard architecture for connecting the J2EE platform to heterogeneous Enterprise Information Systems (EIS). From the Microsoft camp, the .NET [1] umbrella includes a similar set of WA building technologies. It is integrated with Windows platform and has a heavy emphasis on web services. A major part of .NET is the .NET framework, which consists of the Common Language Runtime (CLR) and the .NET Framework class library. CLR provides common services for .NET Framework applications written in a variety of languages, including C, C++, C#, and Visual Basic. The NET Framework class library includes ASP.NET, ADO.NET, and support for Web services. Microsoft Host Integration Server and Microsoft BizTalk Server aid in integration of .NET WAs and other EIS. In addition, numerous other less sophisticated frameworks exist (e.g., Seagull [13] for PHP, Mason [9] for Perl, Albatross [2] for Python, Jakarta Struts [10] and Turbine [16] for Java).

3 Concluding Remarks

We hope our need-oriented perspective helps one to grasp essential trends in Web technology landscape, independently of the many specific technological solutions that have emerged in response to various needs. Space limitations prevented us from a detailed discussion of a number of needs (e.g., the need for device independence, the need to make WAs secure, the need to "internationalize", need for "accessibility", the need for server-side/client-side data persistence). In the future work, we plan to extend our Web technology assessment framework with concepts introduced by others [4]. We also plan to continuously refine our need/trend/technology taxonomy. For the ease of reference, given next is a tabulated summary of the needs, trends, and technologies discussed in this paper.

Need	Trends → Technologies
Better front-end languages	Incorporate XML → XHTML
	Markup for specialized contents → MathML, SVG, etc.
Separate content, structure, presentation	Styles → CSS, XSL
	Transformations → XSLT (part of XSL)
Better UI, Client-side processing	Embed client-side scripts → JavaScript, Jscript, VBScript
	Embed light weight applications → Java Applets, ActiveX
	User agent plug-ins → e.g., Adobe plug-in for pdf
Use mainstream languages	Standards (e.g., CGI with Perl, Python, etc.)
	Components → E.g, Java Servlets, EJB, COM+
Separate response from response generation code	Write to output stream → Java Servlets
	Server pages → SSI, ASP/ASP.NET, JSP, PHP, Mason, Spyce
	Server pages (with hooks) → JSP+Java Beans, ASP.NET Code behind
	Templates → Freemarker, Velocity, Smarty, HTML::Template, DTML, CFML
Rapid UI building	Server-side UI components → ASP.NET Web forms, JSF
Integration	Regular → CORBA, RMI, DCOM, .NET Remoting
	Web specific → Portlets, Web services
End-to-end solutions	Platforms/ Frameworks → J2EE, .NET Struts, Turbine, Seagull, Mason, Albatross

References

1. ASP, ASP.NET, COM, JScript, VBScript and .NET at, http://www.microsoft.com/
2. Albatross home page, http://www.object-craft.com.au/projects/albatross/
3. CFML home page, http://www.macromedia.com/devnet/mx/coldfusion/cfml.html
4. Christodoulou, S. P., and Papatheodorou, T. S., "WEP: A Reference Model and the Portal of Web Engineering Resources", *Proc. Intl Workshop on Web Engineering*, 2004
5. Christodoulou, S. P., Tzimou D. G., and Papatheodorou, T. S., "An Evaluation Support Framework for Internet Technologies and Tools", *Proc. IASTED conference on Communications, Internet and Information Technology*, 2003
6. CORBA home page, http://www.corba.org/
7. ECMA home page, http://www.ecma-international.org
8. Freemarker home page, http://freemarker.sourceforge.net/
9. HTML::Mason home page, http://www.masonhq.com
10. Jakarta Struts project home page, http://struts.apache.org/
11. Java Servlets, JSP, J2EE, RMI home pages at http://java.sun.com/
12. JSR documentation at http://www.jcp.org
13. Seagull home page, http://seagull.phpkitchen.com/
14. Smarty home page, http://smarty.php.net
15. Spyce home page, http://spyce.sourceforge.net/
16. Turbine project home page, http://jakarta.apache.org/turbine/
17. Velocity home page, http://jakarta.apache.org/velocity/
18. World Wide Web Consortium Web site (containing home pages for CSS, HTML, XHTML, MathML, Styles, WebServices, XForms, XSL), http://www.w3.org

Adding Usability
to Web Engineering Models and Tools

Richard Atterer[1] and Albrecht Schmidt[2]

[1] Media Informatics Group
Ludwig-Maximilians-University Munich, Germany
`richard.atterer@ifi.lmu.de`
[2] Embedded Interaction Research Group
Ludwig-Maximilians-University Munich, Germany
`albrecht.schmidt@acm.org`

Abstract. In this paper, we examine how the task of creating usable websites can be made more efficient. Models and generation of websites have been a central issue for Web Engineering over recent years. However, usability tool integration has not been a primary focus – few usability validators take advantage of models which describe the website. After a look at existing tools, we examine how information stored in models can help to improve validation. Furthermore, we highlight additional properties which, if present in models, would improve validation quality. We present the prototype of a model-based usability validator. Given the presentation model of an existing web page, it verifies a set of guidelines. Web Engineering methods need to take usability into account at many levels. Beyond the extension of models, this requires further semi-automated and manual steps for user testing.

1   Introduction

A basic demand of any website is that its *web application must work* in the sense that it must be possible to use the website for its intended purpose – this is addressed by research into Web Engineering methods, models and tools. However, there is also the equally important demand that the *web application must be usable* by the visitors of the website. Usability research includes work on sets of guidelines which help to improve website usability. Additionally, established procedures like user tests provide information about issues which make a site difficult to use. In this paper, we build upon existing research results in both of the above areas. We have analysed state-of-the-art Web Engineering solutions in previous work [2] and concluded that usability has not been their primary focus so far. Regarding usability, we have looked at a variety of different sources, including the W3C's Web Accessibility Initiative (WAI) and related documents [9], the Yale Web Style Guide [8] and Jakob Nielsen's alertbox series [7].

So far, research effort has concentrated *either* on development of Web Engineering models (and associated page generation tools) *or* on usability/accessibility validators, despite the fact that the information stored in Web

D. Lowe and M. Gaedke (Eds.): ICWE 2005, LNCS 3579, pp. 36–41, 2005.

Engineering models could be very useful to these validators. The main contribution of this work is the analysis of how usability validation of websites can be improved when abstract information from models is available.

Section 2 of this paper examines the limits inherent in validating HTML pages without having a model which describes certain properties of these pages. Section 3 highlights the benefits of model-based usability validation in a systematic approach, taking into account presentational, navigational and functional aspects, and section 4 lists a number of proposed model extensions. After the presentation of the prototype validator in section 5, section 6 discusses the benefits of combining knowledge from the fields of Web Engineering and usability research, and presents some areas which should be addressed in future research.

2   Current Usability Validation Approaches

There exists a large number of usability and accessibility guidelines which is validated by current tools just by analysing the HTML pages, CSS (cascading style sheets) and other content that can be retrieved from a website.

However, the implementation of checks for these guidelines often suffers from the problem that no model is available, i.e. no abstract description of certain properties of the web page (or its parts). This way, the validator either fails to find certain usability problems in the pages or it outputs too many general warning messages. For instance, it is straightforward to check given HTML code for high colour contrast [4] and the use of a limited number of different font faces, but it is not possible to do this reliably for images which contain a rendered version of some text, unless a model provides information regarding the text contained in the image.

As part of our research, we have looked at the following usability and accessibility validators:

- A-Prompt (`http://aprompt.snow.utoronto.ca`)
- Bobby (`http://bobby.watchfire.com`)
- EvalIris [1]
- Kwaresmi (`http://www.isys.ucl.ac.be/bchi/research/Kwaresmi.htm`)
- LIFT (`http://www.usablenet.com`)
- NAUTICUS (`http://giove.cnuce.cnr.it/nauticus/nauticus.html`)
- WAVE (`http://wave.webaim.org`)
- WebTango [5]

None of these tools works with a presentational or navigational model taken from a Web Engineering solution like UWE [6] or OO-H [3]. Furthermore, none allows interactive "reverse-engineering" of models from existing web pages, or annotating them with abstract information like the tool prototype we present in section 5. Looking at the output of the tools, it becomes clear that the lack of additional, more abstract information about the pages is a problem: Many tools output messages which tell the user to perform manual checks for some of the page content.

3   Automatic Usability Checking Based on Models

The quality of automated usability tool support can be increased significantly by taking advantage of the models which are available in current Web Engineering solutions. For instance, UWE and OO-H both feature navigational models which provide details on the ways the site is intended to be traversed, and presentational models which define abstract properties of the page layout – for example, they allow us to assign meaning to parts of the page layout, like "this is advertisement". Due to space constraints, this section only gives a few examples of possible improvements.

3.1   Presentational Aspects

Standard Page Layout.   With a model which describes the different page areas, we can check whether the page design follows one out of a number of de-facto standards, for example "three columns with header, site name at top, navigation at left, advertisement at right". Related to this, it is possible to check whether the layout of content is consistent across all pages.

Liquid Layout.   Using the model, we can easily say which part of the page has the main content. Consequently, the rule that a page's width should adjust to the browser window width can be made more accurate: It is desirable that the *main content's width* increase with the browser window width.

Essential Content.   Finally, a tool can alert the user if page areas with certain content are missing. Content which should normally be present on every page includes the page creator's identity, a "last changed" note and a link to the site's entry page. Additionally, a complex site's main page will benefit from the presence of a search facility, a "news"-style list of recently updated site content, and other similar items.

3.2   Navigational and Functional Aspects

Navigation Paths.   A model-based tool can analyse the possible navigation paths of the site in a variety of ways. For instance, the click distance between arbitrary pages can be calculated. The web developer can subsequently specify e.g. "there should only be 3 clicks from the product view to the final 'thank you for buying' message".

Interaction Patterns.   The models of current Web Engineering solutions feature support for certain patterns, such as a "guided tour", i.e. a series of pages connected with "previous" and "next" buttons. It is possible to offer tool support for automatic recognition of such patterns, e.g. by looking for sequential steps in the model's activity diagrams. This way, it is ensured that typical ways of interacting with a site use appropriate, established interaction patterns.

Intended Audience.   The model for a website could specify properties of the site's intended audience. For instance, the audience can be assigned a "literacy" value, ranging from "children" to "academic person". An automated check can subsequently warn about site content which exceeds the target audience's vocabulary. Another example is the audience's type of Internet access – if it is slow, the pages must not contain too many large graphics.

4 Extending Web Engineering Models

If attributes related to usability are included in the Web Engineering models, this will allow tools to increase usability automatically or to warn the developer when certain guidelines are violated. We recommend that the following selection of attributes be included in Web Engineering models:

- Timing
  - Overall contact time of a user with the site?
  - Contact time per visit?
  - How long will the user need for the main tasks?
  - What is the maximum time for delivery of a page?
- Purpose of the site
  - What is the main objective of the web site?
  - What information and navigation complexity is desired?
  - Is the page mainly sensational, educational, or informational?
- Target group, anticipated user
  - What is the main user group?
  - Age distribution of the anticipated users.
  - Computer related skill level of potential users?
  - What infrastructure (e.g. computer type, connection speed) do potential users have?

Timing, site purpose and target group are central to many of the usability issues raised. The concrete attributes in these categories may vary depending on the models and Web Engineering system.

5 Prototype of a Model-Based Usability Validator

The implemented prototype of a model-based usability validator demonstrates some of the ideas presented in this paper. The most obvious difference from other validators is that the input to the program does not solely consist of a web page (or its URL), but that additional information about the page needs to be provided.

Like the majority of the other available validators, the tool is a server-side program with a web interface. The tool illustrates two concepts: The reverse-engineering of a (simplified) presentation model from a finished web page, and automated usability validation using that page model.

After the user has supplied the URL of a web page, she or he is presented with a version of the page with some added controls (shown in figure 1). These

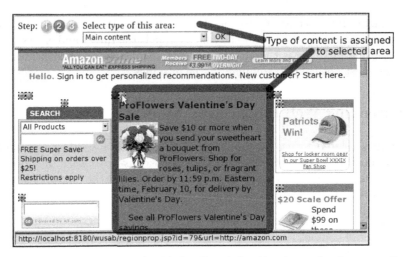

Fig. 1. Selection of a page area (highlighted) and classification as "main content" using the prototype usability validation tool

controls allow the selection of regions of the page layout if it is based on HTML tables. Having selected a region, the user can assign a content type to it, for instance "main content", "navigation" or "advertising". After some or all parts of the page have been annotated, the tool can perform a number of tests and output a result screen which alerts the user to problems with the web page.

6   Discussion and Conclusion

How Usability Can Benefit from Web Engineering. It may be argued that automatic checks are not equivalent to what a suitably trained expert could achieve. Replacing the usability expert in the process is not the aim of our research. However, we believe that the addition of "usability support" to Web Engineering solutions would lead to improved usability for websites because otherwise, in practice *no* measures which improve usability would be employed.

Today, general interest by web developers in usability is not as high as it should be. However, if the tools used by a developer "get it right" by default and require specific actions to override these defaults, the quality of the results will be significantly enhanced – an effect which has already been observed with GUI editors.

With support built into the tools, the resulting web pages are consistent by default, and the automatic checks inherent in the process provide feedback about usability-related problems, with only little extra effort by the developer.

How Web Engineering Can Benefit from Usability Methods. For the architects of Web Engineering solutions, the models are one of the most important aspects in their work: On one hand, the more properties the models define for web pages and entire websites, the more powerful the respective tool support can be. On the other hand, more detailed models also result in more work for the web developer who needs to create them. It tends to be difficult to find the right balance between automatability and simple modelling.

With our work, we hope to provide a basis for further enhancements to Web Engineering tools and models. We show that additional information in the models will lead to better usability in the final website. This way, we hope that this paper will assist Web Engineering architects in deciding where extensions to their models make sense.

All in all, the bar for Web Engineering is raised not only to allow the creation of *functional* websites, but also the creation of *easy-to-use* ones.

Further Work. In our current and future work, we concentrate on tool support for improving usability in the context of Web Engineering, and investigate how a user centred design process can be combined with a Web Engineering process. This includes extensions to models and requires new steps in the development process. This paper is only one of the first steps in this direction; apart from implementing prototypes for model-supported usability validation, it must be evaluated in practice whether the proposed solutions result in better usability.

Acknowledgement

This work was funded by the BMBF (intermedia project) and by the DFG (Embedded Interaction Research Group).

References

1. J. Abascal, M. Arrue, N. Garay, J. Tomás: EvalIris – A Web Service for Web Accessibility Evaluation. In *Proceedings of the 12th International World Wide Web Conference*, Budapest, Hungary, 20–24 May 2003.
2. R. Atterer: Where Web Engineering Tool Support Ends: Building Usable Websites. In *Proc. of the 20th Annual ACM Symposium on Applied Computing*, USA, 2005
3. C. Cachero, J. Gómez, O. Pastor: Object-Oriented Conceptual Modeling of Web Application Interfaces: the OO-HMethod Abstract Presentation Model. In *Proceedings of the 1st International Conference on Electronic Commerce and Web Technologies EC-Web 2000*, UK, pages 206–215, Springer LNCS 1875, 2000
4. F. H. Imai, N. Tsumura, Y. Miyake: Perceptual color difference metric for complex images based on Mahalanobis distance. Journal of Electronic Imaging – April 2001 – Volume 10, Issue 2, pages 385–393
5. M. Y. Ivory, R. R. Sinha, M. A. Hearst: Empirically Validated Web Page Design Metrics. In *Proceedings of the SIG-CHI on Human factors in computing systems*, March 31 – April 5, 2001, Seattle, WA, USA. ACM, 2001
6. A. Knapp, N. Koch, G. Zhang, H.-M. Hassler: Modeling Business Processes in Web Applications with ArgoUWE. In *Proceedings of the 7th International Conference on the Unified Modeling Language (UML2004)*. Springer Verlag, October 2004
7. J. Nielsen: Alertbox: Current Issues in Web Usability. http://useit.com/alertbox/, accessed 10 Feb 2004.
8. Web Style Guide http://www.webstyleguide.com/, accessed 5 November 2004.
9. World Wide Web Commitee (W3C): Web Accessibility Initiative (WAI), http://www.w3.org/WAI/, accessed 5 Feb 2005.

Organization-Oriented Measurement and Evaluation Framework for Software and Web Engineering Projects

Luis Olsina, Fernanda Papa, and Hernán Molina

GIDIS_Web, Department of Informatics,
Engineering School at Universidad Nacional de La Pampa,
Calle 9 y 110, (6360) General Pico, La Pampa, Argentina
{olsinal,pmfer,hmolina}@ing.unlpam.edu.ar

Abstract. A common challenge faced by many software and Web organizations is to have sound specifications of metrics and indicators metadata, and a clear establishment of measurement and evaluation frameworks and programs. In addition, organizations can succeed in this endeavour if resulting measurements and evaluations are tailored to their information needs for specific purposes, contexts, and user viewpoints. In previous works an ontology for software metrics and indicators was specified based as much as possible on the concepts of specific ISO standards. In this paper, we discuss a measurement and evaluation framework so-called INCAMI (*Information Need, Concept model, Attribute, Metric* and *Indicator*), which is based on that ontology. We argue this framework can be more robust and well-established than the GQM (Goal-Question-Metric) paradigm for measurement and evaluation purposes. Finally, an example is presented and the strengths and weaknesses of this framework compared with others are analysed as well.

1 Introduction

Without sound specifications of metrics and indicators metadata, and a clear establishment of measurement and evaluation frameworks and programs, organization's projects are less repeatable and controllable, and therefore more prone to fail. While many useful approaches for and successful practical examples of software measurement programs exist, the inability to specify clearly and consistently about measurement and evaluation concepts (i.e. the metadata) hampers unfortunately the progress of the software and Web engineering as a whole, and hinders their widespread adoption. For instance, the GQM paradigm is a useful, simple, purpose-oriented measurement approach that has been used in different measurement projects and organizations [1]. However, as Kitchenham *et al* pointed out [8], GQM is not intended to define metrics at a level of detail suitable to ensure that they are trustworthy, in particular, whether or not they are repeatable. Nor is GQM a robust framework for evaluation purposes as we will discuss later on.

Software and Web organizations introducing a measurement and evaluation program need to establish a set of activities and procedures to specify, collect, store, and use trustworthy metrics and indicators metadata and data. Without appropiate definitions of metrics and indicators it is difficult to ensure measure and indicator values are repeatable and comparable among projects.

D. Lowe and M. Gaedke (Eds.): ICWE 2005, LNCS 3579, pp. 42–52, 2005.

In order to bridge this gap, we have built a sound and explicit specification of metrics and indicators metadata, i.e., an ontology for this domain. Thus, the main domain concepts, properties, relationships, and axioms were explicitally specified [9, 12]. The sources of knowledge for the ontology stemmed from our own experience backed up by previous works about metrics and evaluation processes and methods [11], from different software-related ISO standards [4, 5, 7], and recognized research articles and books [2, 8, 14], among others.

In this paper, we discuss an organization-oriented measurement and evaluation framework so-called INCAMI – that stands for *Information Need, Concept model, Attribute, Metric* and *Indicator.* The metrics and indicators ontology and the cataloging system [10] are the rationale for our INCAMI framework. It is made up of four main components, namely: The measurement and evaluation project definition itself; the nonfunctional requirements definition and specification; the measurement design and execution, and; the evaluation design and execution. In addition, the present work also aims to bring the attention about the usefulness of this framework and strategy as well as to introduce why INCAMI can be a more robust and engineered framework than others. INCAMI_Tool, which is a prototype tool to support this framework, allows saving consistently not only metadata of metrics and indicators but also measure and indicator values for specific measurement and evaluation projects. Inter and intra-project analyses and comparisons can be now performed in a consistent way.

The rest of this article proceeds as follows. In Section 2, we discuss the main components of the INCAMI framework. In Section 3, a quality in use example for an e-learning application as proof of concepts is presented. In Section 4, related works and the strengths and weaknesses of the INCAMI framework compared with others are analysed as well. Finally, concluding remarks are drawn.

2   Framework for Measuring and Evaluating Information Needs

The approach behind the INCAMI framework is based upon the assumption that for an organization to measure and evaluate in a purpose-oriented way it must first specify the information need for a measurement and evaluation project, then it must design and select the specific set of useful metrics for measurement purposes, and lastly interpret the metrics values by means of contextual indicators with the aim of evaluating the degree the stated information need has been achieved. The strength of INCAMI resides in which not only permit recording the metrics and indicators values but also the metrics and indicators metadata (and related project metadata) in order to allow drawing consistent and traceable analyses, conclusions, and recommendations.

The conceptual framework is made up of four main components, namely: The nonfunctional requirements definition and specification; the measurement design and execution; the evaluation design and execution, and; the measurement and evaluation project definition itself. Each component is supported by many of the ontological concepts, properties, and relationships defined in [9, 12]. For instance, in the aforementioned requirement definition component, concepts such as *Information Need, Calculable Concept, Concept Model, Entity, Entity Category,* and *Attribute* intervene. Some other concepts were added to the INCAMI_Tool for design and implementation reasons. In the sequel, the first three components are illustrated.

2.1 Information Need, Concept Model, and Attributes

For the non-functional requirement specification component (i.e., the *INCAMI.requirement* package), key concepts such as *Information Need, Calculable Concept, Concept Model,* and *Attribute,* among others, intervene as shown in Fig. 1.

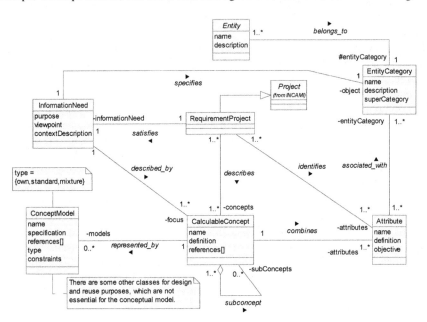

Fig. 1. Key concepts and relationships that intervene in the INCAMI.requirement package for the definition and specification of non-functional requirements

First of all, the *Information Need* for a measurement and evaluation *Project* must be agreed. Information need is defined as the insight necessary to manage objectives, goals, risks, and problems [9]. Usually, information needs come from two organizational/project sources: goals that decision-makers seek to achieve, or obstacles that hinder reaching the goals – e.g. obstacles involve basically risks and problems. The *InformationNeed* class has three properties (i.e. the *purpose*, the user *viewpoint*, and the *contextDescription*), and two main relationships with the *CalcuableConcept* and the *EntityCategory* classes respectively (as seen in Fig. 1).

A calculable concept can be defined as an abstract relationship between attributes of entities' categories and information needs [9]; in fact, quality, quality in use, cost, etc. are instances of a calculable concept. For instance, a common practice is to assess quality by means of the quantification of lower abstraction concepts such as attributes of entities' categories. The attribute can be shortly defined as a measurable property of an entity category (e.g. categories of entities of interest to Software and Web Engineering are resource, process, product, product in use, service, and project as a whole). An entity category may have many attributes, though only some of them may be useful to a given measurement and evaluation project's purpose.

To illustrate the above concepts let us consider the following example that will be expanded in section 3. A basic information need for an organization's project within a quality assurance program may be *"understand the quality in use of the X e-learning application that supports courses tasks for pre-enrolled students"*. Therefore, given the *entity category* (i.e., an e-learning application, which its *superCategory* is a product) it allows evaluators to specify an *information need*, that is to say, the *purpose* (i.e. understand), the *user viewpoint* (i.e. a novice student), in a given *context* of use (e.g. as support to a math preparatory course for pre-enrolled students, the software is installed in the Engineering School server with known bandwidth constraints), with the *focus* on a *calculable concept* (quality in use) and *subconcepts* (effectiveness, productivity, and satisfaction), which can be *represented by* a *concept model* (e.g. the ISO quality-in-use model [5]) and associated *attributes* as shown in Fig. 2.

1.Quality in Use
    1.1. Effectiveness
        1.1.1. *Task Effectiveness* (TE)
        1.1.2. *Task Completeness* (TC)
    1.2. Productivity
        1.2.1. *Efficiency related to Task Effectiveness* (ETE)
        1.2.2. *Efficiency related to Task Completeness* (ETC)
    1.3. Satisfaction

Fig. 2. Specifying an instance of the Quality in Use model.

In summary, the *INCAMI.requirement* package allows the definition and specification of non-functional requirements in a sound and well-established way. Its underlying strategy is organization and purpose-oriented by information needs; evaluator-driven by domain experts, and; concept model-centred where the concept model type can be whether a standard-based model, an organization own-defined model, or a mixture of both. The INCAMI_Tool currently implements concept models in the form of requirement trees. In addition to save the measurement and evaluation project data and metadata, it also allows importing partially or totally a previously-edited requirement tree for a new project.

2.2 Metrics and Measurement

For the measurement design and execution component (i.e., the *INCAMI.measurement* package in the framework) purposeful metrics should be selected. In general, each attribute can be quantified by one or more metrics, but in practice just one metric should be selected for each attribute of the requirement tree, given a specific measurement project.

The *Metric* contains the definition of the selected *Measurement* and/or *Calculation Method* and *Scale*. For instance, the measurement method is defined as the particular logical sequence of operations and possible heuristics specified for allowing the realisation of a metric description by a measurement; while the scale is defined as a set of values with defined properties [9]. Therefore, the metric m represents a mapping m: $A \rightarrow X$, where A is an empirical attribute of an entity category (the empirical world), X the variable to which categorical or numerical values can be assigned (the formal world), and the arrow denotes a mapping.

In order to perform this mapping a sound and precise measurement activity definition is needed by specifying explicitly the metric's method and scale (see Fig. 3). We

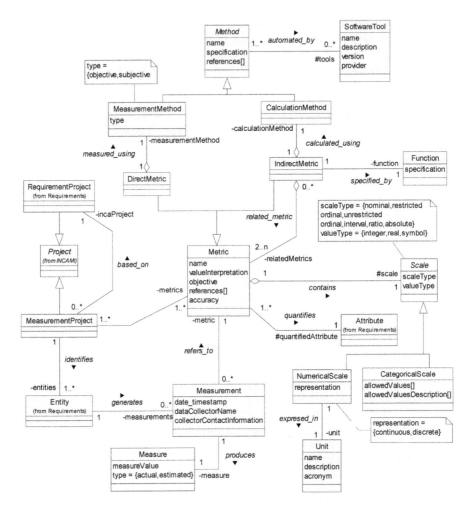

Fig. 3. Key terms and relationships that intervene in the INCAMI.measurement package for the definition of metric and measurement concepts

can apply an *objective* or *subjective* measurement method for *Direct Metrics*; conversely, we can perform a calculation method for *Indirect Metrics*, that is, when a formula intervenes. A direct metric is defined as a metric of an attribute that does not depend upon a metric of any other attribute [9].

To illustrate the above concepts, let's consider an attribute of the effectiveness characteristic from Fig. 2. Effectiveness assesses whether the tasks performed by users achieve specified goals with accuracy and completeness in a specified context of use [5]. Particularly, for the *Task Completeness* attribute, we can design a metric that specifies what proportion of the tasks is completed by a given user. The indirect metric's name is *Task Completeness Ratio*; the formula is TCR= #CT / #PT, where #CT is the number of completed tasks, and #PT is the number of proposed tasks [6]. The scale type of the indirect metric is ratio represented by a numerical scale with a real value type. The unit description is completed tasks per proposed tasks by a user. In the formula intervenes two direct metrics with objective measurement methods (we further can specify thoroughly the metadata for each direct metric).

Once the metric was defined and selected, we can perform the measurement process, i.e., the activity that uses a metric definition in order to produce a measure's value. *Measurement* class allows to record the date/time stamp, the owner information in charge of the measurement activity, and the actual or estimated yielded value.

However, because the value of a particular metric will not represent the elementary requirement's satisfaction level, we need to define a new mapping that will produce an elementary indicator value. One fact worth mentioning is that the selected metrics are useful for a measurement process as long as the selected indicators are useful for an evaluation process.

2.3 Indicators and Evaluation

For the evaluation design and execution component (i.e., the *INCAMI.evaluation* package) contextual indicators should be selected. Indicators are ultimately the foundation for interpretation of information needs and decision-making. There are two types of indicators: *Elementary* and *Global Indicators* (see Fig. 4).

In [9] the indicator term is stated as "*the defined calculation method and scale in addition to the model and decision criteria in order to provide an estimate or evaluation of a calculable concept with respect to defined information needs*". Particularly, we define an elementary indicator as that which does not depend upon other indicators to evaluate or estimate a concept at lower level of abstraction (i.e., for associated attributes to a concept model). On the other side, we define a partial or global indicator as that which is derived from other indicators to evaluate or estimate a concept at higher level of abstraction (i.e., for subconcepts and concepts). Therefore, the elementary indicator represents a new mapping coming from the interpretation of the metric's value of an attribute (the formal world) into the new variable to which categorical or numerical values can be assigned (the new formal world). In order to perform this mapping, an *Elementary* and *Global Model* and *Decision Criteria* for a specific user information need must be considered.

Thus, an elementary indicator for each attribute of the concept model can be defined. For instance, to the 1.1.2 attribute in Fig. 2, the name of the elementary indicator can be *Task Completeness Performance Level* (TC_PL). The *specification* of the elementary model can look like this:

TC_PL = 100% if TCR = 1; TC_PL = 0% if TCR <= $X_{min;}$ where X_{min} is some agreed lower threshold as 0.45; otherwise TC_PL = TCR * 100 if X_{min} < TCR < 1

The decision criteria that a model of an indicator may have are the agreed acceptability levels in a given scale; for instance, it is *unsatisfactory* if the range is 0 to 45 percent; *marginal*, if it is greater than 45 and less or equal than 70; otherwise, *satisfactory*. Notice that a score within a marginal range indicates a need for improvement actions. An unsatisfactory rating means change actions must take high priority.

Regarding partial and global indicators, an aggregation and scoring model and decision criteria must be selected. The quantitative aggregation and scoring models aim at making the evaluation process well structured, objective, and comprehensible to evaluators. For example, if our procedure is based on a linear additive scoring model,

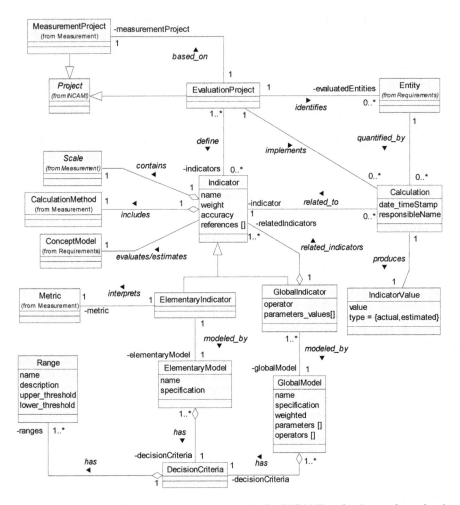

Fig. 4. Key terms and relationships that intervene in the INCAMI.evaluation package for the definition of indicators and evaluation concepts

the aggregation and computing of partial/global indicators (P/GI), considering relatives weights (W) is based on the following formula:

$$P/GI = (W_1 \ EI_1 + W_2 \ EI_2 + ... + W_m \ EI_m); \tag{1}$$

such that if the elementary indicator (EI) is in the percentage scale the following holds:

$$0 <= EI_i <= 100; \quad \text{and the sum of weights for an aggregation block must fulfil,}$$
$$(W_1 + W_2 + ... + W_m) = 1; \quad \text{if } W_i > 0; \text{ to } i = 1 ... m;$$

where m is the number of subconcepts at the same level in the tree aggregation block.

The basic arithmetic aggregation operator for inputs is the plus (+) connector. We can not use Eq. 1 to model input simultaneity or replaceability, among other limitations (see [11, 13] for a broader discussion).

Therefore, once we have selected a scoring model, the aggregation process follows the hierarchical structure as defined in the quality in use requirement tree (Fig 2), from bottom to top. Applying a stepwise aggregation mechanism, we obtain a global schema. This model let's compute partial and global indicators in the execution stage. The quality-in-use global indicator's value ultimately represents the global degree of satisfaction in meeting the stated requirements for a user viewpoint.

3   A Quality in Use Example for an e-Learning Application

Quality in use is the combined effect of the internal and external quality subconcepts (e.g., usability, functionality, reliability, and efficiency characteristics [5]) for the end user. It can be measured and evaluated by the extent to which specified users can achieve specified goals with *effectiveness*, *productivity*, *safety*, and *satisfaction* in specified contexts of use. When designing and documenting quality in use requirement, measurement and evaluation processes, at least the following information is needed:

a) Descriptions of the components of the context of use including user type, equipment, environment, and application tasks (i.e., tasks are the steps or sub-goals undertaken to reach an intended goal by a user group type), and;
b) Quality in use metrics and indicators for the intended purpose and information need.

The INCAMI_Tool allows recording all this information.

Notice that one important difference between evaluating external quality and evaluating quality in use is that the former generally involves no real users but rather experts as long as the latter always involves real end users. It is unthinkable to conduct a task testing in a real context of use without the end user participation [13].

Recently, we have conducted an e-learning case study from the quality in use perspective. The information need was established in section 2.1 in addition to the requirement tree shown in Fig. 2. Given the "*Qplus Virtual Campus*" Web application (www.qplus.com.ar/productos.htm), which since 2003 is being employed as support to a math preparatory course in the Engineering School, four tasks and six pre-enrolled students were chosen for testing purpose. Experimental design issues were considered as well, such as randomisation of the user list, among other issues.

On the other hand, in the design of the measurement process, for each attribute of the requirement tree a metric was selected. In section 2.2, the *Task Completeness Ratio* metric for the *Task Completeness* attribute was illustrated. This indirect metric specifies what proportion of the proposed tasks is fully completed by a given user. The final metric we used is the average for the six selected users; similar considerations were taken into account for designing almost all the other metrics. The exception was to the *Satisfaction* concept. For this, we designed a closed questionnaire with subcategories (as for example content, navigation, aesthetics, functions, etc), where items and scales were considered. The questionnaire's items were designed to represent attributes. Thus, we considered a direct metric for each item, and then we specified a formula to compute the indirect metric value; this formula computes the whole score for a questionnaire complete response (this procedure will be discussed in a follow-up article).

Lastly, in the design of the evaluation process, for each leaf of the requirement tree an elementary indicator is selected; it interprets the metric's value of the attribute.

In section 2.3, we illustrated the specification of the *Task Completeness Performance Level* elementary indicator (Table 1 shows the final indicators values both to elementary and partial/global ones). Likewise in other case studies [11, 13], we used a weighted, non-linear, multi-criteria scoring model for the aggregation and enactment processes.

Table 1. Global, partial and elementary indicators' values to the quality in use case study

Code	Global/Partial Indicator Name	Elementary Indicator Name	Weight	Actual Value
1.	Quality in Use Level			57.43
1.1	Effectiveness Level		0.33	59.67
1.1.1		*Task Effectiveness Performance Level*	0.5	54.17
1.1.2		*Task Completeness Performance Level*	0.5	65.58
1.2	Productivity Level		0.33	51.87
1.2.1		*Efficiency Level related to Task Effectiveness*	0.5	49.76
1.2.2		*Efficiency Level related to Task Completeness*	0.5	54.04
1.3	Satisfaction Level		0.33	87.08
1.3.1		*Calculated Satisfaction Level*	1	87.08

As a final remark, when the execution of the measurement and evaluation activities were performed for a given project, decision-makers can analyse the results and draw conclusions and recommendations with regard to the established information need. For instance, the global indicator value for the quality-in-use study (see Table 1) fell into the marginal acceptability level (i.e., a 57.43 percent of the whole requirements has been reached); this outcome means that improvement actions need to be planned. Lastly, the INCAMI_Tool allows saving consistently not only metadata for requirements, metrics and indicators but also actual or estimated values for specific projects.

4   Discussion and Related Works

To make quality assurance a useful support process to software and Web development and maintenance projects, organizations must have sound specifications of metrics and indicators metadata associated consistently to data sets, as well as a clear establishment of measurement and evaluation frameworks and programs. In addition, organizations will not willingly waste their resources if resulting measurements and evaluations are not tailored to their information needs for specific purposes, contexts, and user viewpoints.

The proposed INCAMI approach is based upon the assumption that, for an organization to measure and evaluate in a purpose-oriented way it must first specify nonfunctional requirements starting from information needs, then it must design and select the specific set of useful metrics for measurement purpose, and lastly interpret the metrics values by means of contextual indicators with the aim of evaluating or estimating the degree the stated requirements have been met. The INCAMI's strength resides in which not only allow recording actual or estimated values for metrics and indicators but also recording associated metadata. In this way, consistent and traceable analyses, conclusions, and recommendations can be drawn.

However, contrary to our approach that is based on an ontological conceptualisa-tion of metrics and indicators, GQM [1] lacks this conceptual base so that it could not assure that measure values (and the associated metadata like scale, unit, measurement method, and so forth) are trustworthy and consistent for ulterior analysis among pro-jects. Besides, GQM lacks specific concepts for evaluation in order to interpret meas-ures. For instance, elementary and global indicators and related terms are essential for evaluation as shown above. The interpretation of measures is a weak point in GQM. Conversely, GQM is more flexible that INCAMI in the sense that it is not always necessary to have a concept model specification in order to perform a measurement project.

On the other hand, it is worthy of mention the efforts carried out by Kitchenham *et al.* [8] in the definition of a conceptual framework and infrastructure (based on the ER model) to specify entities, attributes and relationships for measuring and instantiating projects, with the purpose of analysing metrics and datasets in a consistent way. This last framework is the closest one to our research, which we tried to strengthen not only from the conceptual modeling point of view (using O-O approaches), but also from the ontological point of view including a broader set of concepts. Particularly, we deal with evaluation concepts that Kitchenham *et al.* did not.

Finally, it is also worthy of mention that there are a pair of useful ISO standards re-lated to software measurement [7], and evaluation processes [4]. The primary aim of these standards was to reach a consensus about the issued models and processes; however, they do not constitute themselves a formal nor a semiformal ontology. Moreover, in [12] we highlighted some lack of consensus about the used terminology among these ISO documents. Despite this, in [7] there is a basic measurement infor-mation model that was also useful as a source of knowledge for our approach.

5 Concluding Remarks

Developing successful Web sites and applications with economic and quality issues in mind requires broader perspectives and the incorporation of a number of principles, models and methods from diverse disciplines. Web Engineering has a very short his-tory compared with other engineering disciplines, but is rapidly evolving [3]. Like any other engineering science, Web Engineering is concerned with the establishment and use of sound scientific, engineering and management principles, and disciplined and systematic approaches to the successful development, deployment, maintenance and evolution of Web sites and applications within budgetary, calendar, and quality constraints. The measurement and evaluation framework discussed here can contrib-ute by making a humble progress to the state of the art of Software and Web Engi-neering quality assurance processes and tools.

As a matter of fact, the INCAMI framework has also its roots in our previous researches such as the Web Quality Evaluation Methodology (WebQEM) [12], and the ontology of metrics and indicators. The underlying conceptual ground of WebQEM is now materialized by the INCAMI framework in a systematic and rigorous way. WebQEM has been used in different case studies [12, 13], and in some industrial Web quality evaluation processes.

Due to the importance of managing the acquired organizational knowledge during quality assurance projects, a semantic infrastructure that embraces organizational memory is being considered. This can be integrated to the INAMI_Tool and framework, regarding that ontologies and Semantic Web are enabling technologies for our current research aim.

Finally, architectural and navigational design aspects of the Web-based INCAMI_Tool will be illustrated in a follow-up manuscript.

Acknowledgments

This research is supported by the UNLPam-09/F022, and the PICT 11-13623 research projects. Thanks to Guillermo Covella who was in charge of conducting the e-learning case study.

References

1. Basili V., Rombach H.D. (1989) "The TAME Project: Towards Improvement-Oriented Software Environments", *IEEE Trans. on Software Engineering*, 14(6), pp. 758-773.
2. Briand L., Morasca S. and Basili V. (2002) "An Operational Process for Goal-driven Definition of Measures", *IEEE Trans. on Software Engineering*, 28(12), pp. 1106-1125.
3. Deshpande Y., Murugesan S., Ginige A., Hansen S., Schwabe D., Gaedke M., White B (2002) "Web Engineering", *Journal of Web Engineering, Rinton Press* US, 1(1), pp. 61-73.
4. ISO/IEC 14598-1:1999 "International Standard, Information technology - Software product evaluation - Part 1: General Overview".
5. ISO/IEC 9126-1 (2001) "International Standard, Software Engineering - Product Quality - Part 1: Quality Model".
6. ISO/IEC DTR 9126-4 (2001) "Software Engineering - Software Product Quality - Part 4: Quality in Use Metrics".
7. ISO/IEC 15939 (2002) "Software Engineering - Software Measurement Process".
8. Kitchenham B.A., Hughes R.T., Linkman S.G. (2001) "Modelling Software Measurement Data", *IEEE Transactions on Software Engineering*, 27(9), pp. 788-804.
9. Martín M., Olsina L. (2003) "Towards an Ontology for Software Metrics and Indicators as the Foundation for a Cataloging Web System", *In proceed. of IEEE Computer Society (1st Latin American Web Congress)*, Santiago de Chile, pp 103-113, ISBN 0-7695-2058-8.
10. Molina H., Papa F., Martín M. de los A., Olsina L. (2004) "Semantic Capabilities for the Metrics and Indicators Cataloging Web System". In: *Engineering Advanced Web Applications*, Matera M. Comai S. (Eds.), Rinton Press Inc., US, pp. 97-109, ISBN 1-58949-046-0.
11. Olsina L., Rossi G. (2002) "Measuring Web Application Quality with WebQEM", *IEEE Multimedia*, 9(4), pp. 20-29.
12. Olsina L., Martín M. (2004) Ontology for Software Metrics and Indicators, *Journal of Web Engineering, Rinton Press*, US, Vol 2 N° 4, pp. 262-281, ISSN 1540-9589.
13. Olsina L., Covella G., Rossi G. (2005) "Web Quality" Chapter to appear in a Springer Book titled *Web Engineering: Theory and Practice of Metrics and Measurement for Web Development*, Emilia Mendes and Nile Mosley Eds.
14. Zuse H. (1998) *A Framework of Software Measurement*, Walter de Gruyter, Berlín-NY.

Web Usability Measurement: Comparing Logic Scoring Preference to Subjective Assessment

Michael Chun Long Yip and Emilia Mendes

Computer Science Department, The University of Auckland, Auckland, New Zealand
myip005@ec.auckland.ac.nz
emilia@cs.auckland.ac.nz

Abstract. This paper investigates one of the existing methods for measuring usability – Logic Scoring Preference (LSP), and discusses the results of two formal experiments carried out to assess the extent to which LSP embodies the subjective perception of users in regards to Web usability. The two experiments used Computer Science students as experimental subjects. Our results suggest that scores obtained via LSP are significantly different from scores obtained via subjective opinion. In addition, we obtained contradictory results when investigating the consistency of LSP scores across subjects.

1 Introduction

There are many reasons for why usability should be considered in a software development process [4]:

- Ensuring that the product best suits its target users will make it the product of choice among competitors.
- Having a superior product can justify a slightly higher price, since people would not mind paying more for a product that they trust.
- More money can be made through the ability to sell a product that is easier to use
- Even if the end users are not customers, but employees, a more usable product increases productivity among workers.
- A more intuitive product would also mean that less time is spent learning how to perform a new task. Better productivity means more work is done, and therefore usability saves time, which in turn saves money.
- A formal usability test provides evidence that the product is not defective and lives up to expectations. This can be important for lawful purposes.
- Besides monetary gains, a more usable product contributes to better quality resulting in a better relationship between developers and consumers, which in turn ensures patronage.
- In addition, a usable product gives comfort to the user, making them less stressed and allowing them to enjoy using the software, even if the product is not meant for entertainment purposes.

There are several methods proposed in the literature that can be employed for assessing usability [4]. One such method, which is the focus of this research, is Feature Analysis. This method encompasses the evaluation of an application by considering key features, their importance and their effect on usability. This is generally accomplished using some score calculation. Such method is useful not only for measuring

D. Lowe and M. Gaedke (Eds.): ICWE 2005, LNCS 3579, pp. 53–62, 2005.

usability and for comparison with other systems, but also to provide detailed results indicating which areas or features need further improvement.

Feature analysis within a Web engineering context was first used by Olsina and Rossi [6]. They propose a Website quality evaluation method (WebQEM), which uses a feature analysis technique to calculate a score that measures the quality of a Website. The feature analysis technique employed is called Logic Scoring Preference (LSP), and will be detailed in Section 2. WebQEM bases its feature list on the ISO 9126 quality model [5], with the highest-level features as Usability, Functionality, Reliability, and Efficiency.

Unlike Olsina and Rossi [6], this research focuses only on a subset of Web quality measurement, that is, Web usability measurement. We conducted two formal experiments to investigate the following:

- To what extent the LSP method captures the subjective views of users regarding Web usability.
- To what extent the usability scores obtained using LSP are consistent across subjects with similar experience using the Web, for the same Website.

The results obtained from both experiments did find a significant difference between the scores obtained using LSP and those based on subjective opinion. However, we obtained contradictory results when investigating the consistency of LSP scores across subjects.

The remainder of this paper is organised as follows: Sect. 2 introduces the LSP method. Sect. 3 presents our research method and the hypotheses we investigated. The data analysis is described in Sect. 4, followed by a summary and discussion of the results in Sect. 5. Finally, our conclusions and comments on future work are presented in Sect. 6.

2   Logic Scoring Preference

The Logic Scoring Preference method, or LSP, was proposed in 1996 by Dujmovic, who used it to evaluate and select complex hardware and software systems. The purpose of LSP is to evaluate features quantitatively (by means of logic scoring) for the comparison of different entities (e.g. software systems, applications) [1],[2],[3].

In LSP, the features are decomposed into aggregation blocks. This decomposition continues within each block until all the lowest level features are directly measurable. This is illustrated in Fig. 1:

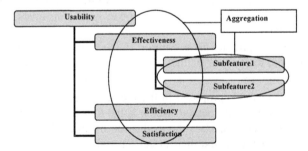

Fig. 1. Aggregation Blocks

Thus, a tree of decomposed features at one level will have a number of aggregation blocks, each resulting in a higher-level feature going up the tree right through to the highest-level features (see Fig. 1).

Next, for each feature, an elementary criterion is defined. For this, the elementary preference E_i needs to be determined by calculating a percentage from the feature score X_i. This relationship is represented in the following equation:

$$E_i = G_i(X_i) \tag{1}$$

Where E is the elementary preference.

G is the function for calculating E.

X is the score of a feature.

i is the number of a particular feature.

One way to evaluate the elementary criterion is by use of a preference scale. In this scale, a cut-off point needs to be defined on either side of the scale. For example a scale related to response time may use as cut-off points a response time of 1 second or less for a score of 100%, and 6 seconds or over for a score of 0% [3].

The elementary preferences for each measurable feature in one aggregation block are used to calculate the preference score of the higher feature. This in turn is used with the preferences scores of an even higher feature, continuing right up until a global preference is reached. The global preference is defined as:

$$E = L(E_1, \dots, E_n) \tag{2}$$

Where E is the global preference.

L is the function for evaluating E.

E_n is the elementary preference of feature n.

n is the number of features in the aggregation block.

The function L yields an output preference e_0, for the global preference E, or any subfeature E_i. Its formula is:

$$e_0 = (W_1 E_1^r + \dots + W_k E_k^r)^{1/r}, W_1 + \dots + W_k = 1 \tag{3}$$

Where e_0 is the output preference.

W is the weight of the particular feature.

E is the elementary preference of a feature.

k is the number of features in the aggregation block.

r is a conjunctive/disjunctive coefficient of the aggregation block.

For each E_i a weight W is defined for the corresponding feature. The weight is a fraction of 1 and signifies the importance of a particular feature within the aggregation block.

To illustrate the use of LSP we provide an example [3]:

Assuming an aggregation block consisting of 3 inputs, x, y, and z. Their weights are 0.5, 0.3, and 0.2 respectively, and their elementary scores are 0.7, 0.9, and 0.6 respectively.

The chosen conjunction value for this aggregation block is C-+, with which the r-value is -0.208. For details on how the r-values are calculated please refer to [2],[3].

The equation is therefore:

$$(0.5 \times 0.7^{-0.208} + 0.3 \times 0.9^{-0.208} + 0.2 \times 0.6^{-0.208})^{(-1/0.208)} = 0.730255 \tag{4}$$

The parent feature of this aggregation block now has the score of 0.730255, which will be used for evaluating the score of the aggregation block in which the parent feature belongs to.

The r coefficient represents the degree of simultaneity for a group of features within an aggregation block. This is described in terms of conjunction and disjunction. Conjunction refers to how desirable it is that the features within an aggregation block should exist together, while disjunction is the antonym of conjunction. The formula for e_0 represents certain types of mathematical means when certain values for r are used. For example, when $r=1$, the formula is the same as that of a regular arithmetic mean, and when $r=2$ the formula yields the square mean. The other two means mentioned are the geometric and harmonic means. Dujmovic presents 20 such functions [3] and an abridged list of 9 generalised functions [2].

3   Research Method and Hypotheses

The overall research question in our study was to assess the usefulness of using LSP for Web usability measurement. To address this question we have compared LSP scores to scores obtained from subject opinion, and also looked specifically at how similar LSP scores were from one another, given the same Website and users with similar experience.

We refined our research question in two null hypotheses, which are as follows:

H_{A0} – The usability scores obtained using LSP for the same Website are similar across subjects with similar experience in using the Web.

H_{B0} – Usability scores obtained using LSP are not significantly different from usability scores obtained via subjective opinion for the same Website, for subjects with similar experience in using the Web.

Our alternative hypotheses, i.e., what we expected to occur, were then stated as:

H_{A1} – The usability scores obtained using LSP for the same Website are not consistent across subjects with similar experience in using the Web.

H_{B1} – Usability scores obtained using LSP are significantly different from usability scores obtained via subjective opinion for the same Website, for subjects with similar experience in using the Web.

The dependent variable in both experiments was the final score given to a Website. The independent variables were: subjects' experience in usability assessment and usability measurement technique (LSP or subjective opinion).

There were also several confounding factors that we had to take into account, some of which we were able to control, which were as follows:

- Subjects' understanding of the method
- Subjects' computing skills level
- Subjects' previous experience using the Web
- Subjects' understanding of English
- Type of Website (e.g. e-commerce, academic)
- Server load
- Internet speed
- Environment, Location
- Time, instance, date of evaluation
- Computers used (e.g. processor speed, display unit, input methods)

A confounding factor is a variable that can hide a genuine association or incorrectly suggest the existence of an association between variables. If not taken into account, confounding factors can bias the results of a study.

Except for 'type of website', we were able to control on both experiments all the confounding factors we identified. Table 1 provides details on the methods used to control the confounding variables.

We had planned to use a single type of Website in both experiments to control one of the confounding factors (Type of Website). Our choice was to use a Website of a New Zealand tertiary Institution (Otago University). Unfortunately, due to technical problems beyond our control, we had to use the University of Auckland's Website on our first experiment, since this was the only website we had access to since we were restricted to access only our intranet. Further discussion on this issue is provided in Section 5.

In terms of both experiments' design, we used a one-factor, two-treatment design. The factor was represented by subjects' previous experience using the Web. The two treatments were the two usability assessment techniques: LSP versus subjective opinion. It was not possible to have a control object in any of our experiments since we did not have a real 'placebo' treatment, similar to what is used in medical experiments. A control represents 'absense of', however even a subjective opinion still affects the outcome, which is the final website score. Our experimental objects were the Websites assessed, and the experimental subjects were the students who volunteered to participate.

For each of the experiments data was gathered using two questionnaires, one for LSP and another for subjective assessment. The LSP questionnaire was organised in three parts, as follows:

- Part I asked subjects about the relationship between features. These features are the same as the usability features suggested in [6]. Information received from the first part includes features' weights, and their simultaneity between groups.
- Part II asked subjects to identify upper and lower thresholds for each feature. These would identify cut-off points for each feature, which represent acceptable and unacceptable values.
- Part III asked subjects to evaluate a given website based on the measurable features from the first two parts, using the scales that they have defined in part two.

The subjective assessment questionnaire asked subjects to rate a given website's usability using a 100-point scale (0% means completely useless; 100% means absolute best).

Both questionnaires were implemented as Web forms and the data was stored on a relational database. This was done to facilitate data analysis. Two pilot studies were carried out beforehand to validate these questionnaires and to make sure subjects would use no more than 20 to 30 minutes to assess the website(s) and fill-out the questionnaires.

Regarding the size of our samples, we had 10 subjects in our first experiment and 12 in the second. We emailed out invitations to our third-year and postgraduate computer science students and 22 subjects in total volunteered to participate. We are aware that our samples were self-selected rather than random, however this was the only way to obtain participants to both experiments.

Table 1. Confounding factors which were controlled on both experiments

Confounding Factors	Method
Subjects' understanding of the method	Questionnaires that did not require previous knowledge of either LSP or subjective assessment.
Subjects' computing skill levels	Sample included only third-year and postgraduate computer science students.
Subjects' previous experience using the Web	Sample included only third-year and postgraduate computer science students.
Subjects' understanding of English	Previous to the experiments subjects had to rate themselves on their understanding of English. All rated themselves high, later confirmed by one of the authors.
Server load	A single server hosting the questionnaire, single servers hosting the websites.
Internet speed	Internet speed was the same for all computers.
Environment, Location	A single laboratory was used
Time, instance, date of evaluation	All subjects participated in the experiment at the same time and place.
Computers used (e.g. processor speed, display unit, input methods)	All computers had the same configuration and speed.

Both experiments were conducted using the same laboratory, however within a few weeks from each other. One of the authors managed the execution of both experiments.

4   Data Analysis

All the statistical results were obtained using SPSS v.10.1. Statistical tests were selected based on the type and distribution of the data. Our dependent variable was measured on a ratio scale however to decide on which test to use we also had to determine if the distribution of scores was normally or non-normally distributed. We employed the Kolmogorov-Smirnov nonparametric test to test for normality. All significance levels were set at 0.05. A significance level is used as a cut-off point to determine if a null hypothesis should be rejected or not. Generally significance levels are set at 0.1, 0.05 and 0.01.

Other statistical tests used were the two-independent samples t-test (2-TT) and the Mann-Whitney test for independent samples (2-MW). Both are used to compare two independent samples to see if there are significant differences between their values distribution. If there is then we reject the null hypothesis.

4.1   First Hypothesis – H_{A0}

Our first hypothesis was solely related to the LSP scores obtained. This hypothesis is as follows:

H_{A0} – The usability scores obtained using LSP for the same Website are similar across subjects with similar experience in using the Web.

We employed the Mann-Whitney test to compare the 10 scores obtained from experiment 1 to the sample's mean of 8.12 (see Fig. 2).

Fig. 2 shows that the both significances were below the 0.05 threshold, indicating that LSP scores could not come from the same distribution as the mean-based values. What this means is that LSP scores were not in fact similar across subjects for a given Website. These results provide evidence to reject the null hypothesis H_{A0} for experiment 1.

We repeated the same procedure for experiment 2, however this time we used the two-independent samples t-test to test our hypothesis since the LSP scores were normally distributed. Here the mean was 10.94 and we had 12 LSP scores.

Fig. 3 shows different results to those shown in Fig. 2, indicating that for experiment 2 LSP scores were similar across subjects for a given Website. These results did not provide evidence to reject the null hypothesis H_{a0}.

Our first experiment rejected the null hypothesis and our second experiment did not. The difference between these two experiments, apart from the subjects who volunteered to participate, is the Website evaluated. Experiment 1 used the University of Auckland's website, which was already well known to all participants. However experiment 2 used a website from another tertiary Institution, which was unknown to most participants. We believe that one possible explanation for the largely different LSP scores for experiment 1 may be a previous opinion towards the Website, which may have biased the results.

Test Statistics [b]

	LSPEXP1
Mann-Whitney U	20.000
Wilcoxon W	75.000
Z	-2.515
Asymp. Sig. (2-tailed)	.012
Exact Sig. [2*(1-tailed Sig.)]	.023 [a]

    a.   Not corrected for ties.

    b.   Grouping Variable: VAR00001

Fig. 2. Results for Mann-Whitney U test for Experiment 1 for H_{A0}

Independent Samples Test

		Levene's Test for Equality of Variances		t-test for Equality of Means						
									95% Confidence Interval of the Difference	
		F	Sig.	t	df	Sig. (2-tailed)	Mean Difference	Std. Error Difference	Lower	Upper
LSPEXP2	Equal variances assumed	5.831	.025	.001	22	.999	.0059	7.54079	-15.63269	15.64458
	Equal variances not assumed			.001	11.000	.999	.0059	7.54079	-16.59121	16.60310

Fig. 3. Results for T-test for Experiment 2 for H_{A0}

4.2 Second Hypothesis – H_{B0}

Our second hypothesis was related to the LSP and subjective scores. This hypothesis is as follows:

H_{B0} – Usability scores obtained using LSP are not significantly different from usability scores obtained via subjective opinion for the same Website, for subjects with similar experience in using the Web.

To test this hypothesis we had to compare LSP scores to the subjective scores. For the first experiment we used the Mann-Whitney test to compare the 10 LSP scores to another 10 subjective scores since LSP scores were not normally distributed (see Fig. 4).

Fig. 4 shows that the both significances were below the 0.05 threshold, indicating that LSP scores could not come from the same distribution as the subjective scores. The subjective scores were in fact much greater than LSP scores. What this result suggests is that LSP scores were significantly different from subjective scores, thus providing evidence to reject the null hypothesis H_{B0} for experiment 1.

We repeated the same procedure for experiment 2, however this time we used the two-independent samples t-test to test our hypothesis since the LSP and subjective scores were normally distributed (see Fig. 5).

Test Statistics [b]

	LSPEXP1
Mann-Whitney U	2.000
Wilcoxon W	57.000
Z	-3.804
Asymp. Sig. (2-tailed)	.000
Exact Sig. [2*(1-tailed Sig.)]	.000 [a]

a. Not corrected for ties.

b. Grouping Variable: VAR00001

Fig. 4. Results for Mann-Whitney U test for Experiment 1 for H_{B0}

Independent Samples Test

		Levene's Test for Equality of Variances		t-test for Equality of Means						
									95% Confidence Interval of the Difference	
		F	Sig.	t	df	Sig. (2-tailed)	Mean Difference	Std. Error Difference	Lower	Upper
LSPEXP2	Equal variances assumed	.838	.370	-8.433	22	.000	-69.9707	8.29699	-87.17763	-52.76381
	Equal variances not assumed			-8.433	15.437	.000	-69.9707	8.29699	-87.61186	-52.32959

Fig. 5. Results for T-test for Experiment 2 for H_{B0}

Fig. 5 shows similar trends to those shown in Fig. 4, i.e., that LSP scores were significantly different from subjective scores. This result also provides evidence to reject the null hypothesis H_{B0} for experiment 2.

Both experiments provided evidence to reject the null hypothesis H_{B0} and to support the alternative hypothesis H_{B1}, thus showing that usability scores obtained using LSP are significantly different from usability scores obtained via subjective opinion for the same Website, for subjects with similar experience in using the Web.

5 Summary and Discussion of Results

There are three types of validity that may influence the outcomes of an experiment: internal, external, and construct validity. Internal validity represents to what extent conclusions can be drawn about the causal effect of the independent variables on the dependent variables. Except for type of Website, we have controlled all confounding factors. In addition, we have assigned subjects to treatments randomly. However. We are aware that using a website in experiment 1 which was well-known to the participants may have biased the results we obtained for that experiment. Unfortunately, we were unable to do anything about that since it was a technical problem that was outside our control.

Construct validity represents to what extent the variables precisely measure the concepts they claim to measure. Usability was measured using final scores from applying LSP or subjective assessment. However the set of usability features we used to calculate LSP was a subset of all usability features we had identified. We did not use the full set otherwise it would take subjects too long to carry out the evaluation, reducing even more our sample sizes.

External validity represents the domain to which a study's findings can be generalised. We used self-selected samples of students that not necessarily are representative of real users. However this was the only choice we had given the circumstances.

The results obtained for experiments 1 and 2 regarding hypothesis H_{A0} were contradictory. However given that experiment 2 used an unfamiliar website we believe that results obtained by this experiment be more representative, i.e., LSP scores are similar given the same website and subjects with similar experiences.

As for H_{B0} both experiments rejected the null hypothesis, suggesting that the usability scores obtained via LSP do not correspond to users' subjective perception of usability. Our results however provide no means of measuring which technique truly measures the usability of a website. The subjective scores tended to be a lot closer to the mean, and thus more likely to yield a repeatable result with a smaller range of values. However, this does not mean that the subjective scores accurately represent the true usability of the website.

6   Conclusions and Future Work

This paper has presented the results of two formal experiments that investigated Web usability measurement. Both experiments tested the same hypotheses. The first hypotheses tested to what extent LSP scores varied broadly given the same website and subjects with similar experience. The second hypothesis tested to what extent the scores obtained using LSP represent the subjective opinion users have regarding the usability of a website.

Our experiments rejected the second hypothesis, however presented contradictory results for the first hypothesis. Further replications of this experiment are necessary in order to validate further our findings. This will be the subject of future work.

References

1. Dujmovic, J. J. Criteria for computer performance analysis. Procs. ACM SIGMETRICS, Boulder, Colorado, United States, (1979).
2. Dujmovic, J. J. A cost-benefit decision model: analysis, comparison and selection of data management. ACM TODS, 12(3), (1987), 472-520.

3. Dujmovic, J. J. A Method for Evaluation and Selection of Complex Hardware and Software Systems. Procs. 22nd International Conference for the Resource Management and Performance Evaluation of Enterprise Computer Systems, Turnersville, New Jersey, (1996).
4. Faulkner, X. Usability Engineering (1st ed.). Houndmills, Basingstoke, Hamphshire, London: Macmillan Press LTD, (2000).
5. ISO. Software Engineering - Product Quality, 9126-1 (pp. 25): International Organisation for Standardisation, (2001).
6. Olsina, L. A., & Rossi, G. Measuring Web application quality with WebQEM. IEEE Multimedia, 9(4), (2002), 20-29.

Effectively Capturing User Navigation Paths in the Web Using Web Server Logs

Amithalal Caldera and Yogesh Deshpande

School of Computing and Information Technology, College of Science
Technology and Engineering, University of Western Sydney
PO Box 1797, Penrith South DC, NSW 1797, Australia
{h.caldera,y.deshpande}@uws.edu.au

Abstract. Most of the approaches to analyse the Web server logs to capture user access patterns are heuristic based and affected by the use of proxy servers, caching and stateless service model of the HTTP protocol. No heuristic has addressed all of these problems. In this paper, we propose a new heuristic to overcome this limitation. The heuristic exploits the background knowledge of user navigational behaviour recorded in the server logs without requiring additional information through cookies, logins and session ids. The heuristic is evaluated by analysing the logs of a university Web server that records user ids for administrative reasons, which allows us to compare it against the concrete knowledge of user sessions. We also evaluate our heuristic against some of the existing heuristics. The evaluation has shown very satisfactory result.

1 Introduction

A Web server log explicitly records the browsing behaviour of site visitors and consists of details about file requests to a Web server and the server responses to those requests. A typical Web server log contains information such as the IP address of the machine that made the request, the date and time a request was made, the request method that the client used (GET, POST), the protocol used, the URL of the requested page, the status code of the response message, the size of the document transferred, the URL of the referrer page from which the request was initiated and the user agent, which is the application software used to browse the Web.

A sequence of requests to a server from a single user within a certain time window is called *a user session*. The powerful user tracking techniques such as requiring authentication [9], storing cookies [4] or generating session IDs [7] have been used in capturing the user sessions on the Web. To protect the privacy of users, Web server logs in general do not record such information unless an application, such as in e-commerce, requires it. In the absence of explicit knowledge of user identities, most of the approaches used to capture user sessions through the Web server logs are heuristic. The heuristic strategy only exploits the background knowledge on user navigational behaviour to assess whether requests registered by the Web server can belong to the same individual and whether these requests were performed during the same or subsequent visits of the individual to the site. However, the computations are affected by the use of one or more proxy servers, caching and stateless service model of the HTTP protocol [2,6]. None of the several existing heuristics addresses all of these problems. We propose a new heuristic to overcome these limitations.

D. Lowe and M. Gaedke (Eds.): ICWE 2005, LNCS 3579, pp. 63–68, 2005.

2 Related Works

Cooley et al [2,3] propose four heuristics for the attribution of requests to different users. We denote them as **h1**, **h2**, **h3** and **h4**. Heuristic **h1** states that *each different user-agent type for an IP address represents a different user.* A user-agent identifies the browser version and the operating system. The rationale here is that a user rarely employs more than one browser when navigating the Web. Hence, a user session is defined by aggregating accesses on unique user agents for an IP address. However, the algorithm ignores the possibility of the accesses representing more than one active session, for example through multiple browser windows, for a specific user over time. Heuristic **h2** states that *If a Web page is requested and this page is not reachable from previously visited pages, then the request should be attributed to a different user. A new session is also suspected if the referrer is undefined.* A referrer is the URL of the page the client was on before requesting the current page. The rationale behind this heuristic is that users generally follow links to reach a page. However, this overlooks the use of bookmarks or explicit typing of URL to reach pages not connected via links in which case the referrer is not available. So, this heuristic might misclassify these accesses as requests from different users. Heuristic **h3** states that *the duration of a session must not exceed a pre-specified threshold.* The threshold is an upper bound on the time spent in the site during a visit. Heuristic **h4** states that *a new session is suspected if the time spent on a page exceeds a pre-specified time threshold.* Users who do not request pages within a certain time limit are assumed to have left the site. Researchers have used some or all of the above heuristics to identify user sessions. In [8], IP and user agent are used to identify unique users and a time period of 6 hours is used as an upper bound for a session. In [1], IP addresses are used to identify users and their consecutive page requests are grouped by using both a session upper bound and a page upper bound.

3 Issues in Heuristic Based Approaches

The identification of user sessions directly from the server logs using heuristics is also affected by the use of proxy server(s), caching and statelessness of HTTP protocol.

The process of user session identification is usually performed mostly based on the IP address [1]. When a user's browser makes a request, the request is routed through a proxy at the ISP. The IP address that is then seen at the Web site is the IP address of the ISP's proxy, not the user's machine. Further complicating the matter, the ISP may have a number of proxies and user requests may go through different proxies. Thus, requests made by a single user (in a single visit) may have multiple IP addresses and one IP address may 'hide' multiple users.

Web browsers and proxy servers frequently cache the pages that have recently been accessed and meet the subsequent requests to these pages from the caches. There are no corresponding log entries for those accesses to the cached pages. Estimating their effect on capturing user sessions from the server logs is non-trivial.

The HTTP protocol is stateless as every request from the client to the server is treated independently and information from previous connections to the server is not maintained for use in future connection [5]. Thus, it does not allow support for establishing long-term connections between the Web server and the client. Therefore, the requests of a single user are recorded in the server logs nested with the requests of other users. As such, clustering of server log entries into its sessions is also non- trivial.

4   A New Heuristic

A new heuristic proposed in this paper is a combination of four heuristics. The four heuristics are termed as H1, H2, H3 and h4. The first three heuristics are the results of our own analysis of Web server logs and introduced here. The last is the existing heuristic described in section 2.

H1: Each different user agent for a domain of the IP addresses represents a different user sessions.

In general, an IP address represents a domain and a server. As described above, an ISP may have one or more proxy servers but they will all belong to a single domain. A single IP address may appear in multiple sessions in which case different user agents identify separate sessions. The heuristic h1 described in section 2 is similar to this and the IP address itself may be used instead of the domain. When multiple IP addresses appear in a single session but belong to the same ISP, they are assumed to share the same domain and, again, different user agents identify distinct user sessions.

H2: Let p and q be two consecutive page requests in a session S identified by heuristic H1. Let also r(q) and ip(q) be the referrer and IP address of q respectively. The membership of q in S is confirmed if one of the following three conditions is satisfied.

1. If r(q) is equal to r(p) or p, or r(q) was previously invoked within S
2. If r(q) is undefined and q was previously invoked within S
3. If r(q) is undefined and ip(q) does not represent a common proxy server
Otherwise, q belongs to a new session.

Heuristic H1 ensures that pages requested by the same user are not separated into different sessions provided that s/he uses only one browser and one operating system. As the market for both browsers and operating systems gets ever more consolidated, it is highly likely that different users coming behind the same ISP will have the same user agent. H1 is unable to decipher this situation. Heuristic H2 further checks each session identified by H1 for the validity of the membership of its entries within itself.

Assuming that users follow hyperlinks to reach a page, each access pair of the referrer page and the requested page constitute a connected traversal path. That is, if none of the pages is brought from the cache, $r(q)$ should be equal to p. Otherwise, we assume that the user must have accessed a cached page connecting p and q. These hits are missed in the server log. But these missing cache hits must have accessed the server in the recent past. Hence, heuristic H2 does not need the requested page to be accessible from the page immediately accessed before it to confirm the memberships.

When $r(q)$ is undefined, the heuristic assures the membership of q in the session depending on whether q was previously invoked or $ip(q)$ does not represent a common proxy server. Users use bookmarks or type URLs to request pages in which case the referrer is undefined. It can be argued that the request page of this type might have been previously visited in the recent history. A proxy server is said to be common if numerous overlapping requests from multiple users come behind it. If $ip(q)$ does not represent such a common proxy server, it is assumed that q should be part of *S* as each of the requests of *S* carries the same user agent and IP address.

H3: *All consecutive requests that are invoked within a small time interval belong to the same session.*

User requests for one URL frequently result in multiple entries in the server logs representing requests for the hyperlinked elements, such as images, style sheets and so on. As they are automatically downloaded due to the HTML tags, the time spans between them is very small and it is possible for a log to reflect an inaccurate ordering of them that the request for the referrer page follows the requested page. H2 will identify them into separate user sessions although the user agent and IP address remain the same. Hence, it is reasonable to group all the consecutive requests invoked within a small time interval as part of the same session. Two different time thresholds are used for common and non-common proxy servers as the numerous overlapping requests can come behind the common proxy servers in very short time intervals.

5   Experimental Environments and Set Up

The Web logs used in this investigation came from the server for a student lab used exclusively to teach two Internet-related subjects. The students have to create a Web site each and then learn scripting for both client-side and server-side processing. Each student is given an id and Web space. The server runs Microsoft Internet Information Server 5.0 on Windows 2000 advanced server platform. The lab has 20 workstations, each with a unique, hard-wired IP address. These machines primarily run Windows 2000 professional. Students access the server from the special lab, other labs or from outside, using either the university dial-up lines or some ISP. The university routes its traffic through two proxies. The university semester runs for 16 weeks during which time the students typically complete two assignments, some quizzes and a mini-project each. The lab has been running for almost seven years. We chose the first semester of 2003, viz. March-June 2003 that was the latest semester when we launched our experiments. Approximately 500 students enrolled in the two subjects. We examined the Web server logs of the entire semester. The server logs are created daily, starting at 10.00 AM and go on for the next 24 hours and the size of the log files ranged from over 1 MB to more than 77 MB.

Web server logs, in general, easily reach tens of megabytes per day, which causes the session identification process to be really slow and inefficient without an initial cleaning task. The cleaning process employed here performs the following tasks. First, the log entries referring to images are removed, based on the suffixes such as gif, jpg, jpeg, and png. Second, log entries with server response codes 4xx and 5xx are removed since they are client and server errors respectively. Third, robot accesses in the server logs are removed. Finally, the entries for the system administrator and tutors who mark the student assignments are eliminated, since we want to analyse only student sessions. The cleaned data is the base to which the heuristic is applied.

6   Results

The performance of the new heuristic is first evaluated by comparing the number of sessions produced by it to the 'exact' number of sessions, derived from a combination of explicit user id and heuristic h4, defined above, to split the students' activities. This combination is assumed to be the best approximation for the exact sessions as user id uniquely identifies every user. The 'exact' method is called M1 and the method of constructing sessions using the new heuristic M2. Then, the new heuristic is compared with two combinations of existing heuristics, (h1, h4) and (h1, h2, h4), similarly. These are called methods M3 and M4 respectively. The time thresholds of 15 minutes and 3 and 16 seconds have been taken as the specified thresholds in h4 and the new heuristic respectively. Table 1 shows the statistics of sessions produced by each method and log entries (Hits). The percentages of differences between total sessions identified by M1=19694 and those of M2, M3 and M4 defined by $Si=((M1-Mi)/M1)\times100$, where $i=1,3$ are recorded as $S1=-11.68$, $S2=-14.72$ and $S3=-491.30$. According to Table 1, the new heuristic overestimates the exact method with the minimum average and percentage difference than the other three methods.

Table 1. Number of Sessions Produced and Statistics

Item	Hits	M1	M2	M3	M4
Total	2,201,304.00	19,694.00	21,995.00	22,592.00	116,451.00
Average per day	20,195.45	180.68	201.79	207.27	1,068.36
Maximum per day	2,73,677.00	1,583.00	1,789.00	1,827.00	15,713.00
Minimum per day	420.00	5.00	5.00	5.00	15.00

7 Chi-Squared Tests

The chi-squared test is used here to investigate the significance of three methods M2, M3 and M4 shown on Table 1 to the exact method M1. We take the null hypothesis as H_0: Two samples are from same distribution and alternative hypothesis as H_1: Two samples are not from same distribution. χ^2 values calculated over 109 observations for each test method are recorded in Table 2. Of methods M2 and M3, which are not significantly different to the exact method, M2 gives the smallest χ^2 value (largest P-value) concluding that the new heuristic best approximates the exact method.

Table 2. Chi-squared Test Results

Control	Test method	d.f	Observed χ^2 values	P-value	Significance at 5%
M1	M2	108	68.154	0.999	Insignificant
M1	M3	108	106.076	0.534	Insignificant
M1	M4	108	4144.802	0.001	Significant

8 Conclusions and Further Work

This paper has proposed a new heuristic that can be used to capture user navigation paths in the Web by exploring Web server logs and reported on the investigation into the efficiency of it. The investigation has confirmed that the new heuristic outperforms the existing heuristics and best approximates the exact method. However, this analysis is based on the daily logs that start at 10 am, when a good number of students are already at work. When a student starts his/her session before 10 am and continues after 10 am, that session is split into two logs. The latter log is short of some initial accesses of many users and the referrer heuristic H2 is adversely affected by this. M2 may exhibit lesser deviation than here if we merged all the log files together and ran the analysis again. Our future work includes the evaluating the heuristic as a user-oriented log analysis tool.

References

1. Berendit, B. and M. Spiliopoulou, *Analysis of Navigation Behaviour in Web Sites Integrating Multiple Information Systems*, VLDB Journal, **9**(1): p. 56-75, 2000,
2. Cooley, R., B. Mobasher, and J. Srivastava, *Data preparation for mining world wide web browsing patterns*, In Journal of Knowledge and Information Systems, **1**(1): p. 5-32, February, 1999,
3. Cooley, R., B. Mobasher, and J. Srivastava, *Grouping web page references into transactions for mining world wide web browsing patterns*, In Knowledge and Data Engineering workshop: p. 2-9, 1997,
4. Elo-Dean, S. and M. Videros, *Data mining the IBM Official 1996 Olympics Web Site*, Workshop on Research Issues in data Engineering, 1997,
5. Iyengar, A., *Dynamic Argument Embedding: Preserving State on the World Wide Web*, IEEE Internet Computing, **1**(2): p. 50-56, March-April, 1997,
6. Pitkow, J., *In Search of Reliable Usage Data on the WWW*, In Ths Sixth International World Wide Web Conference, 1997,
7. Yan, T.W., M. Jacobsen, H. Garcia-Molina, and U. Dayal, *From User Access Patterns to Dynamic Hypertext Linking*, In Fifth International World Wide Web Conference, 1996,
8. Yao, Y.Y., H.J. Hamilton, and X. Wang, *PagePrompter: An Intelligent Agent for Web Navigation Created Using Data Mining Techniques*, Technical Report CS-2000-08, Department of Computer Science, University of Regina, 2000,
9. Zaiane, O.R., M. Xin, and J. Han, *Discovering Web Access Patterns and Trends by Applying OLAP and Data Mining Technology on Web Logs*, In Advances in Digital Libraries: p. 19-29, 1998,

Design Verification of Web Applications
Using Symbolic Model Checking

Eugenio Di Sciascio[1], Francesco M. Donini[2], Marina Mongiello[1],
Rodolfo Totaro[1], and Daniela Castelluccia[1]

[1] Dipartimento di Elettrotecnica ed Elettronica
Politecnico di Bari, Italy
{disciascio,mongiello,r.totaro}@poliba.it
[2] Università della Tuscia Viterbo, Italy
donini@unitus.it

Abstract. Fast and reliable development of Web Applications (WA) calls for methods that address systematic design, and tools that cover all the aspects of the design process and complement the current implementation technologies. To ensure the reliability of WA it is important that they be validated and verified at early design phase. We focus on black-box, automated verification of the UML design of a WA using Model Checking techniques.

1 Introduction

Web Applications (WA) are a class of software systems that support a wide range of important activities, ranging from business functions to scientific and medical applications. The evolution speed of such applications makes Web Engineering a complex activity whose strategies are still being developed. The development of WA needs both methods and formalisms that address systematic design, and tools that can cover all the aspects of the design process and complement the current implementation technologies. Given the relevance of the activities performed by WA, it is important to ensure their reliability through a validation and verification process. Particularly, we consider the design phase and propose a method for checking the correctness of the UML design.

We choose for our purpose the Model Checking method [1] a technique for sound and complete reasoning about finite-state transition systems, that performs an automated verification of a system model with respect to its specification. Specifications are expressed in a logical formalism, generally a logic within a temporal framework.

The main advantage of model checking is that it can be performed automatically unlike test and other formal methods that need user interaction.

Several verification tools have been developed for system analysis based on different formal models. In our proposal we use Symbolic Model Verifier (SMV)[10].

First of all, we propose a mathematical model of a WA partitioning the usual Kripke structure into windows, links, pages and actions. Then we specify properties to be checked in a temporal logic, Computation Tree Logic (CTL). Verification is performed adapting the SMV model checker to our formalism.

An implemented system embeds a parser to perform the automated parsing of the XMI output of the UML tool and to automatically build the SMV model to be verified

D. Lowe and M. Gaedke (Eds.): ICWE 2005, LNCS 3579, pp. 69–74, 2005.

with respect to specifications. The remaining of the paper is organized as follows: in Section 2 we describe the model we propose for web applications and the properties to be verified. Section 3 describes the evaluation environment and the implemented system. In the last Section we describe some related works and the conclusion.

2 Proposed Model

The complexity of the hypertextual structure of the Web cannot be modelled using a simple graph structure in which nodes represent pages and arcs represent hyperlinks. In fact, the widespread use of frames, while controversial, makes a window be composed by several pages. Moreover, new implementation technologies such as scripts, servlets, applets add dynamic properties to web pages. Hence, links can lead to a new window or start an action inside a dynamic page. It is required a more compact and powerful model to convey the complexity of the linked page, the hierarchy of windows, the type of different media linked to web pages, the actions that can be performed.

We propose a mathematical model of a WA based on an extension of the simple graph generally adopted to model the pages and the links between pages. The main advantage of the model is that it is also a support for the formal verification of a WA properties. In previous papers [13], [12] we proposed a model for automatic check of web applications. Here we extend the model with the possibility to represent actions performed in a page.

More specifically, we propose an extension of the Kripke structure generally used to convey the semantics of CTL . The model is translated in a proper CTL model. States in the model are windows, pages, links and actions since a state in the model represents everything is visible in an observation.

Definition 1. *A Web Application Graph (WAG) is a graph $G = (N, C)$ where nodes N are divided as $N = W \cup P \cup L \cup A$ (Windows, Pages, Links and Actions), such that*

1. *W, P, L, A are pairwise disjoint, i.e. $W \cap P = \emptyset$, $W \cap L = \emptyset$ $W \cap A = \emptyset$ $L \cap P = \emptyset$ $L \cap A = \emptyset$ $P \cap A = \emptyset$ and*
2. *arcs connect only windows with pages, pages with links or actions, links with windows and actions with windows, i.e. $C \subseteq (W \times P) \cup (P \times (L \cup A)) \cup ((L \cup A) \times W)$;*
3. *$\forall w \in W \exists p \in P : (w, p) \in C$ "Every window contains at least one page";*
4. *$\forall x \in (L \cup A) \exists w \in W : (x, w) \in C$ "Every link points to a window and every action creates a window".*

Definition 2. *A navigation path is a sequence $w_1 w_2 \ldots w_n$ where $\forall 1 < i < n - 1$*

$$\exists p \in P \exists x \in (L \cup A) : w_i \rightarrow p \land p \rightarrow x \land x \rightarrow w_{i+1}$$

Modeling a WAG in CTL Computation Tree Logic can be used to express and verify properties of the above Web Application Graph, if nodes of the graph are taken as states and arcs as state transitions. It is sufficient to reserve four propositional letters w, p, l, a to distinguish nodes modeling windows, pages, links and actions respectively. Then a correct translator will assign exactly one letter among w, p, l, a to each state, and enforce that transitions occur only from windows to pages they contain, from pages to links they contain or actions they perform, and from links or actions to the next window. Incidentally, we note that such conditions could also be verified in the WAG by checking the following CTL formulas (where numbers correspond with those in Definition 1):

- $AG((w \vee p \vee l \vee a) \wedge (\neg w \vee \neg p) \wedge (\neg w \vee \neg l) \wedge (\neg w \vee \neg a) \wedge (\neg p \vee \neg a) \wedge$
  $\wedge (\neg p \vee \neg l) \wedge (\neg p \vee \neg a) \wedge (\neg l \vee \neg a))$
- $AG(w \Rightarrow AXp \wedge p \Rightarrow AX(l \vee a) \wedge l \Rightarrow AXw \wedge a \Rightarrow AXw)$

We stress the fact that the original transitions in the WA are from a window to another window, and these transitions are kept in our state model. The transitions from a window to pages they contain, and from pages to links and actions pages contain, are only a technical way to model frames and security properties.

Many interesting properties can be checked if other propositional letters are used to capture the relevant content of windows, pages, links or action. For instance we can introduce the following letters: 1) *private* denotes that a window or a page contains private information; 2) *login, logout* denote that an action is a login or a logout action; 3) *error* denotes that a page contains an error message.

In our model we have to check that these letters are used correctly with the following CTL specification:

1. *private* is applicable only to pages or windows, so it is not applicable to links or actions: $AG(l \vee a \Rightarrow \neg private)$
2. *login* and *logout* are applicable only to actions: $AG(w \vee p \vee l \Rightarrow \neg login \wedge \neg logout)$
3. *error* is applicable only to pages: $AG(w \vee l \vee a \Rightarrow \neg error)$
4. a *private* window must contain at least one *private* page:
   $AG(w \wedge private \Rightarrow EX(private))$
5. a *not private* window must not contain *private* pages:
   $AG(w \wedge \neg private \Rightarrow AX(\neg private))$

Using these propositions we can check some interesting properties of a web application design. For example we can check whether the access to private page occurs through a login, hence whether it is correct:

6. we must find some *private* information after a *login* action:
   $AG(login \Rightarrow EF(private))$
7. after a *login* action we can make a *logout* action in the future or the application must manage a *login error* and it must be possible to make a *login* again: $AG(login \Rightarrow AG(w \Rightarrow EX((EXlogout) \vee error) \vee EFlogin)$
8. after a *logout* action we can load only *not private* pages before a new login:
   $AG(logout \Rightarrow A(\neg privateUlogin))$
9. the homepage must verify the following property: $A(\neg privateUlogin)$

Another property of web application design concerns the error management; we can check the web application behavior when an error occurs. For instance:

10. for every *not logout* action the web application must manage eventually an *error* page: $AG(a \wedge \neg logout \Rightarrow EXEXerror))$
11. the user must repeat the *login* action when an *error* occurs:
    $AG(error \Rightarrow A(\neg privateUlogin))$

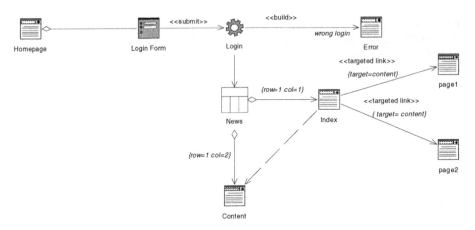

Fig. 1. UML model of the checked web application design

Definition 3 (Verifying a Web Application). *Given a WAG G modeling a web application, an initial state s and a property p, the web application verifies p iff p holds for s in G.*

A deployed implementation of our approach will embed inside an automatic verifier for CTL ; however, for building a prototype showing the feasibility of the approach, the verification phase may be also performed using an available tool, such as SMV . In this case, the verification process consists in expressing the Web Application Graph in the SMV input language – also with the help of parametric modules – and then launch the verification.

3   Evaluation Environment

The method we propose is made up of two phases: the fist one is the check of a web application during the design phase based on its UML model. In a second step the check will be extended to the web application implementation.

In the first step, we use the UML design of the application developed according to the methodologies proposed by Conallen [2]. In the UML diagram, the components of an application are labelled with the proper properties, *e.g.* login, logout, private, error in order to perform the translation in the SMV model. An implemented system embeds the SMV verifier to check the model with respect to the specifications described in Section 2.

Our system automatically translates the output (in XMI format) of the UML tool used for the design in the SMV code that models the corresponding WAG. To show the rationale of the approach, let us consider the UML design model in Figure 1. Figure 2 shows the corresponding WAG, in which the dotted lines represent the modifications on the model after verification.

The model was checked against the specifications described in Section 2. Verification found several faults in the model. First of all, in the WAG did not exist a state

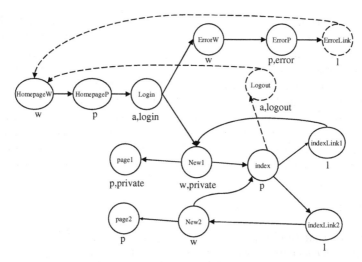

Fig. 2. WAG corresponding to the UML model shown in Figure 1

labelled with the private property, hence the property 6 in previous section was not satisfied. Besides, after a *login* it should be possible to perform a *logout* action, the model checker verified the absence of a *logout* state in the WAG, through the specification 7 that was not verified. To solve the encountered problem, it was necessary to introduce a logout action linked to a page. Other specifications were not verified as, for example the specification concerning the *login* action (property 8 in the previous section) because of the absence of a link to the *HomepageW* that could enable to follow a link to a login action. Finally, the model had to be modified in order to satisfy the properties 4 and 11 concerning the error management. After a logout it must be possible to login again, so the model checker system found the absence of an arc to connect the logout state to the *HomepageW*.

4   Related Work

To the best of our knowledge only few works have considered web application analysis; anyway most of them are not based on a formal method approach. We briefly describe the more relevant proposals. Some approaches consider the web similar to a database, hence propose conceptual models of its structure; more recent approaches focus on web applications under a web engineering point of view. A complete review of all the modeling techniques is in [8]. HDM [6] is one of the first model-driven design of hypermedia applications; successive proposals are RMM[15], Strudel [9], Araneus[11] they all build on the HDM model, and support specific navigation constructs. Conallen [2] proposes a UML-based methodology. The main advantage of the method is the possibility to represent all the component of a web application using standard UML notations. The method proposed in [7] is based on a UML model of WA and considers the testing and validation of the developed web system. In [5] the method proposes web application analysis based on queue models. Finally, in [4] the proposed method aims to verify the correct use of duplicated pages inside a web constructed using HTML language and ASP code. Once again the method does not consider a formal approach. On the other hand, model checking based on a $\mu - calculus$ language has been used in [3]. The approach does not consider the analysis of dynamic pages. Anyway the model of the web they consider is a graph in which states are pages and transitions between states are hyperlinks in the pages, hence hyperlinks cannot be qualified by properties as we do. Previous approaches considered in [14] propose automata to describe the structure of the links in a hypertext and define a branching temporal logic (hypertext logic) HTL to describe the sequence of transitions between states in the automata. The logic is used to verify the propositions of the temporal logic, but again dynamic pages are not considered.

References

1. E.M. Clarke, O.M. Grumberg, and D.A. Peled. *Model Checking*. 1999.
2. J. Conallen. *Building Web applications with UML*. 2002.
3. L. de Alfaro. Model checking the World Wide Web. pages 77–85, 2001.
4. G. Di Lucca and M. Di Penta. An approach to identify duplicated web pages. In *26th Annual International Computer Software and Applications Conference*, pages 481 – 486, Oxford, England, 2002.
5. M. Di Penta, G. Antoniol, G. Casazza, and E. Merlo. Modeling web maintenance centers through queue models. In *Fifth European Conference on Software Maintenance and Reengineering*, pages 131 – 139, Lisbon, Portugal, 2001.
6. D. Schwabe F. Garzotto, P. Paolini. Hdm - a model-based approach to hypertext application design. *ACM TOIS*, 11(1):1–26, 1993.
7. P. Tonella F. Ricca. Testing processes of web applications. *Annals of software engineering*, 14(1):93–114, 2002.
8. P. Fraternali. Tools and approaches for developing data-intensive web applications: a survey. *ACM Computing Survey*, 31(3):227–263, 1999.
9. J. Kang A.Y. Levy M. F. Fernandez, D. Florescu and D. Suciu. Catching the boat with strudel: experiences with a web-site management system. In *ACM - SIGMOD*, pages 414–425, 1998.
10. K. L. McMillan. The SMV system, February 1992. http://www.cs.cmu.edu/ modelcheck/smv/smvmanual.r2.2.ps.
11. G. Mecca P.Atzeni and P.Meriado. Design and maintenance of data-intensive web sites. In *Proc. of EDBT-98*, pages 436–450, 1998.
12. E. Di Sciascio, F M. Donini, M. Mongiello, and G. Piscitelli. Anweb: a system for automatic support to web application verification. In *Proc. of SEKE '02*, pages 609–616, July 2002.
13. E. Di Sciascio, F.M. Donini, M. Mongiello, and G. Piscitelli. Web Applications Design and Maintenance using Symbolic Model Checking. In *Proc. of CSMR '03*, pages 63–72, Benevento, Italy, March 26–28 2003. IEEE.
14. P.D. Stotts and J.C. Furuta. Hyperdocuments as automata: verification of trace-based browsing properties by model checking. *TOIS*, 16(1):1–30, 1998.
15. E. Stohr T. Isakowitz and P. Balasubramanian. Rmm : a methodology for structured hypermedia design. *Comm. ACM*, 38(8):34–44, 1995.

Towards Model-Driven Testing
of a Web Application Generator

Luciano Baresi[1], Piero Fraternali[1], Massimo Tisi[1], and Sandro Morasca[2]

[1] Dipartimento di Elettronica e Informazione
Politecnico di Milano, Milano, Italy
{baresi,fraterna,tisi}@elet.polimi.it
[2] Dipartimento di Scienze della Cultura, Politiche e dell'Informazione
Università dell'Insubria, Como, Italy
sandro.morasca@uninsubria.it

Abstract. Conceptual modelling is a promising approach for Web application development, thanks to innovative CASE tools that can transform high-level specifications into executable code. So far, the impact of conceptual modelling has been evaluated mostly on analysis and design. This paper addresses its influence on testing, one of the most important and effort-consuming phases, by investigating how the traditional notions of testing carry over to the problem of verifying the correctness of Web applications produced by model-driven code generators. The paper examines an industrial case study carried out in a software factory where code generators are produced for a commercial Web CASE tool.

1 Introduction

Web application testing is a challenging but scarcely investigated subject in the Web Engineering community. In the state of the practice, Web application developers still use a "code and fix" approach to software verification, rather than a systematic and tool-supported method. This situation is the combined result of many factors: Web applications are multi-tiered systems and testing requires different procedures for each tier; developers use multiple languages (e.g., SQL, Java, XSLT, HTML), which hampers a unified testing paradigm; the runtime environment (e.g., the browser) cannot be fully controlled and often behaves differently in different products.

In recent years, *conceptual modelling* has been used to tackle such a complexity. The core idea is that applications are specified by using a high-level visual notation and the implementation code is automatically generated from design models. The benefits of conceptual modelling have been extensively studied in the upper phases of the development process. Little is known on the impact of conceptual modelling on the testing phase.

This paper tries to overcome this limitation and investigates the relationship between conceptual modelling and testing. As automatic code generation substitutes manual coding, the focus of testing shifts from verifying individual Web applications to testing the Web code generator; the latter objective lends itself

D. Lowe and M. Gaedke (Eds.): ICWE 2005, LNCS 3579, pp. 75–86, 2005.

to systematic treatment and potentially yields far-reaching benefits, because the results of testing the code generator affect the development of multiple applications.

With model-driven development, the activity of testing a specific Web application splits into two sub-tasks: *schema validation* and *code generator validation*. The former assesses whether the application's conceptual schema[1] is correct with respect to the application requirements and adheres to the syntax and semantics of the chosen Web modelling language. The latter aims at evaluating whether the code generator maps all correct conceptual schemas into correct implementations on all platforms[2]. While the former activity must be performed for every individual application, the latter can be done only once for each deployment platform.

Schema validation requires non-trivial human expertise. However, various techniques, like rapid prototyping [1], model verification [2], and usage analysis [3], may alleviate such a task. Furthermore, schema validation is technology-independent and thus can be addressed also by domain experts.

The validation of the code generator is the novel problem addressed in this paper. The intuition behind our work is that if one could ensure that the code generator produces a correct implementation for all legal and meaningful conceptual schemas (i.e., combinations of modelling constructs), then testing Web applications would reduce to the more treatable problem of schema validation.

The contribution of the paper is twofold. On the theoretical side, we propose a novel formalization of the problem of testing Web code generators as an instance of ordinary black-box testing where test data generation is based on the grammar of a graphical conceptual modeling language (WebML). Testing confidence is expressed by a notion of syntactic coverage, and is characterized by three different classes of coverage (rule, edge, and path) with increasing power and complexity.

From the practical standpoint, the theoretical results were applied to a real scenario. We analyzed the testing process of the code generator produced by the WebRatio CASE tool company (http://www.webratio.com), which maps specifications in the WebML language [1] into code for the J2EE architecture. In the WebRatio software factory, each release of the code generator is tested by automatically running 38 test cases constructed manually by developers in the last four years. Such tests are repeated for all the platforms on which WebRatio applications are certified. We analyzed the empirical test cases used by WebRatio, quantified the associated testing confidence, and identified the minimal test set under the three formal notions of coverage. We also considered 46 conceptual schemas of real applications developed by WebRatio and its partners and recomputed coverage measures with respect to the fragment of WebML that is actually used in real-world applications. This re-evaluation reinforced the testing confidence in the empirically developed test cases.

---

[1] From now on, we use the more precise term *schema* to denote the design specification of a particular application encoded in a given Web modelling language

[2] By platform we mean a specific mix of products for running a Web application at all the involved tiers

All the described experiments were conducted using a prototype visual coverage tool developed in Java.

Although applied to WebML, it is important to stress that all the results are independent of the chosen modelling language and technological setting. Any Web modelling language expressible by means of a formal grammar and equipped with a code generator could be used.

2 Background on WebML and Testing

WebML [1] is a conceptual language originally conceived for specifying Web applications developed on top of database content described using the E-R model.

A WebML schema consists of one or more hypertexts (called *site views*), expressing the Web interface used to publish or manipulate the data specified in the underlying E-R schema.

A site view is a graph of *pages* to be presented on the Web. Pages enclose *content units*, representing components for publishing content in the page (e.g., indexes listing items from which the user may select a particular object, details of a single object, entry forms, and so on); content units may have a *selector*, which is a predicate identifying the entity instances to be extracted from the underlying database and displayed by the unit. Pages and units can be connected with *links* to express a variety of navigation effects and to provide the necessary parameters passing from one unit to another one. Figure 1 shows a WebML hypertext specification and its possible rendition in HTML.

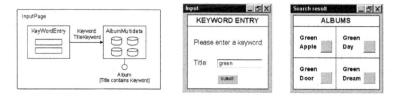

Fig. 1. Example of WebML hypertext and a possible rendition in HTML

The hypertext contains one page (called Input Page), with two units. An entry unit (KeyWordEntry) represents a data entry form and a multidata unit (AlbumMultidata) displays all the instances of entity Album whose titles contain the submitted keyword. The link from the entry unit to the multidata unit is rendered as the submit button, which transports the string inserted by the user as a parameter to be used in the computation of the selector condition ([Title contains Keyword]) of the multidata unit.

In addition to content publishing, WebML allows the specification of operations, like Web Service invocation or the update of content, possibly wrapped inside atomic transactions. Basic data update operations are: the creation, modification and deletion of instances of an entity, or the creation and deletion of

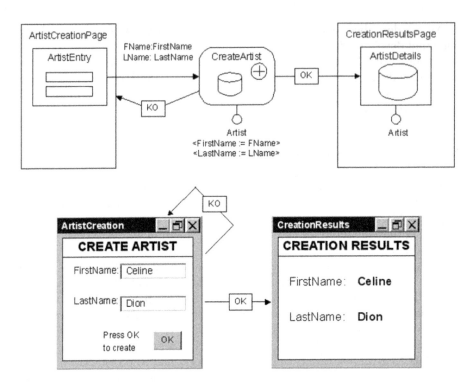

Fig. 2. Example of WebML hypertext with operations and a possible rendition in HTML

instances of a relationship. Operations do not display data and are placed outside the pages; user-defined operations can be specified, such as sending an e-mail, logging in and out, e-paying for something, and so on. Figure 2 shows a WebML hypertext specification including operation units and its possible rendition.

The hypertext contains one page (ArtistCreation) with an entry unit (ArtistEntry), whereby the user can enter the details of a new artist. Navigating the output link of the entry unit triggers a create operation (CreateArtist) unit, which inserts a new artist into the database. If the operation succeeds, its output link OK is followed, which displays a page (CreationResults) with the details of the new artist. Otherwise, page ArtistCreation is redisplayed.

In addition to the visual notation, WebML has a formal syntax, encoded in XML. As an example, the following fragment of the WebML DTD shows the syntactical structure of a site view construct.

```
<!ELEMENT SITEVIEW (OPERATIONUNITS, TRANSACTION*, AREA*, PAGE*,
GLOBALPARAMETER*, PROPERTY*, COMMENT?)>
<!ATTLIST SITEVIEW
        id                      ID          #REQUIRED
        name                    CDATA       #IMPLIED
        homePage                IDREF       #IMPLIED
```

```
protected                      (yes|no)    "no"
secure                         (yes|no)    "no"
localize                       (yes|no)    "no"
presentation:style-sheet       CDATA       #IMPLIED
presentation:page-layout       CDATA       #IMPLIED
graphmetadata:go               IDREF       #IMPLIED
>
```

The expressive power of WebML stems primarily from its capability of combining a few elementary concepts in multiple ways to obtain a variety of effects. As we will see, assessing the coverage of testing with respect to all the "meaningful" combinations of concepts is an essential goal of our work.

WebML is implemented in WebRatio, a commercial CASE tool for designing data-centric Web applications.

The architecture of WebRatio (shown in Figure 3) consists of two layers: a WebML Design Layer, providing functions for the visual editing of specifications, and a Runtime Support Layer, implementing the basic services for executing WebML units on top of a standard Web application framework.

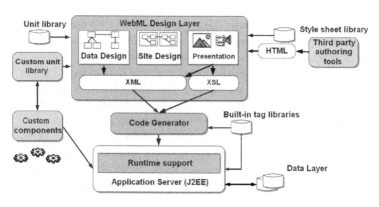

Fig. 3. Architecture of WebRatio

The design layer includes graphical user interfaces for data and hypertext design, which produce an internal representation in XML of the WebML schemas; a second module (called Data Mapping Module) maps the entities and relationships of the conceptual data schema to one or more physical data sources, which can be either created by the tool or pre-existing. A third module for Presentation Design allows the designer to create XSL style sheets from XHTML mockups, associate XSL styles with WebML pages, and organize page layout by arranging the relative positions of content units in each page.

The architecture is completed by the **WebRatio Code Generator**, which exploits XSL transformations to translate the XML specifications visually edited in the design layer into application code executable on top of any platform conforming to the J2EE specifications.

2.1 Software Testing

Testing a program [4] entails running it with a number of input data and checking whether it behaves as expected. Formally, if P denotes a program under test and D its input domain (i.e., the set of all data that can be supplied to P), given a particular $d \in D$, P is *correct* for d if its corresponding output, $P(d)$, satisfies P's specifications. Each element $d \in D$ is said to be a *test case*[3] and a *test set* is a finite set of test data. In general, the only way to achieve absolute certainty about the correctness of P is *exhaustive testing*, that is testing $\forall d \in D$. Obviously, such testing is almost never possible in practice, due to the unwieldy (if not infinite) number of possible inputs, and thus the selection of the actual test set becomes fundamental to assess the correctness of the program. To this end, one can envisage different *testing criteria*, for generating the test set $S \subseteq D$ and probing the correctness of P, and *coverage measures*, for evaluating how thoroughly S can test P. Coverage can be taken as a quantitative measure of testing confidence: the broader the coverage, the more extensive the testing process and thus the confidence on the tested program.

In test data selection, *white-box testing* uses information about the internal structure of the program for selecting test cases, whereas *black-box testing* (also called *functional testing*) only considers the program's functionality and tries to exercise it. In this latter case, test data generation can be facilitated, and even automated, if it is possible to represent the program's behavior – or at least its inputs – in a formal way. This is the case of *syntax-driven testing* [5], which uses the grammar that describes the input domain D to select the test data. A complete coverage of the program input is reached if the test data cover all the grammar's productions, i.e., if the creation of the test data through the grammar requires that each production be applied at least once.

The number of *used* productions is captured by the concept of *rule coverage* [6], which defines the *percentage of grammar productions (rules) applied for deriving the test data*. However, rule coverage is insufficient to characterize the quality of the selected test set, because all test data that contain a given type of input elements are considered equivalent, irrespective of the *context* in which the element appears. Lämmel [6] overcomes this limitations by introducing a subtler coverage measure, called *context-dependent rule coverage*, which takes into account the *context* in which a rule is covered. Intuitively, two input data are *not* considered equivalent if they exercise the same production, but in different combinations with the other rules of the grammar.

Besides selecting "smart" test data, testing also needs a means to evaluate the correctness of program executions. The so-called *oracle* defines a mechanism for verifying that the outputs obtained by executing the program with the test data actually comply with the program specification. Implementing the oracle is often one of the most demanding tasks of the whole testing process.

---

[3] In this paper, we do not distinguish between test case and test datum and we use them as synonyms

3   Testing the Web Application Generator

In this section, we bind the concepts of testing theory to their counterparts in the realm of testing Web code generators, using the WebRatio code generator as running case. We propose a black-box approach based on the formal grammar of WebML. We did not start with a white-box approach because of its intrinsic costs and the need for suitable tools to instrument the different parts of the generator. White-box techniques are the natural complement to our approach and are part of our future work.

The program under test P corresponds to the WebRatio code generator and its input domain D is the set of all possible application schemas, i.e., the set of all valid sentences in the WebML syntax exemplified in Section 2.

An input datum d is a specific WebML schema (an XML file, that comes from the translation of the graphical representation of the model). For example, the following fragment of XML code is a simplified version of the ArtistCreation test case and shows the typical structure of our input data.

```
<SITEVIEW id="sv1" [...]>
  <PAGE id="page1" name="ArtistCreationPage">
    <ENTRYUNIT id="enu1" name="ArtistEntry">
      <LINK id="ln1" to="cru1">
        <LINKPARAMETER id="par1" source="fld1" target="cru1.att2"/>
        <LINKPARAMETER id="par2" source="fld2" target="cru1.att3"/>
      </LINK>
      <FIELD id="fld1" name="FName"/> <FIELD id="fld2" name="LName"/>
    </ENTRYUNIT>
  </PAGE>
  <OPERATIONUNITS>
    <CREATEUNIT entity="ent1" id="cru1" name="CreateArtist">
      <KO-LINK id="kln1" to="page1"/> <OK-LINK id="oln1" to="dau1"/>
    </CREATEUNIT>
  </OPERATIONUNITS>
  <PAGE id="page2" name="CreationResultsPage">
    <DATAUNIT entity="ent1" id="dau1" name="ArtistDetail"/>
  </PAGE>
</SITEVIEW>
```

A test set S is a set of such schemas. In the experimentation, the test set comprises the 38 WebML schemas used in the WebRatio factory. To give an idea, the first group of test schemas contains cases developed to verify the core features of WebML. Other test schemas derive from the addition of new features to the tool or to the language. Finally, the verification of some bug introduced a number of ad-hoc test cases.

The output of the tested program P is a Web application $a = P(d)$, and the oracle used to verify the output is any program capable of deciding whether the application a conforms to P, that is, whether it implements the schema d correctly. In the experimentation, the output is a Web application for the J2EE platform automatically produced by the WebRatio code generator from a WebML schema; for testing purposes, such an application is associated with a fixed-content data source. The oracle is a program that runs an input script representing a significant user navigation of the generated application; the oracle checks XPath logical expressions on the HTML code returned by the Web server. If any XPath expression evaluates to false, the test succeeds, otherwise the code generator is considered to behave correctly with respect to the supplied test schema[4]. Intuitively, each oracle navigates the Web application and verifies whether the displayed pages comprise the expected content. The investigation of the oracle problem is well beyond the scope of the paper.

3.1   Setting Up the Experimentation

In the ideal world, testing the code generator would require inventing all possible conceptual schemas, generating the corresponding applications, and checking them with the oracle. Since an exhaustive testing is inherently infeasible, the testing problem has been reformulated as that of quantitatively assessing the degree of confidence with respect to a given test set S by following a syntax-driven approach. In this scenario, the testing problem can be summarized by the following questions:

- What fraction of the WebML language is covered by the test set?
- What is the minimal subset of the test set sufficient for achieving the same coverage as the whole set?
- How does the coverage change if one considers only the fragment of the WebML language "used in practice"?

Syntax-driven testing applied to Web code generation requires that each non-terminal symbol in the WebML grammar (i.e. each possible WebML primitive) be used at least once by some test in the test set. The WebML grammar is context-free and each rule (production) models a single WebML construct (e.g., page, unit, link). The grammar is rendered graphically by means of a *Direct Occurrence Graph (DOG)* to highlight the dependencies between rules (explained later) and the usages by the different test cases.

The DOG is a graph built by representing grammar productions as nodes and their relations as edges. For example, two productions $p_1 := A \rightarrow B$ and $p_2 := B \rightarrow C$ are connected by a directed edge from p_1 to p_2 because the right-hand side of p_1 contains an occurrence of the non terminal symbol expanded by p_2. Direct occurrence relationships generate possibly cyclic graphs.

When applied to the WebML grammar, the DOG shows all the possible uses of each WebML construct with respect to the other primitives of the language. For example, Figure 4 shows the representation of the SITEVIEW element, displayed in the Java tool developed for supporting coverage analysis. We report, as example, the grammar production for element SITEVIEW (generated from element SITEVIEW of the DTD fragment shown above).

---

[4] In testing theory, a test succeeds *if it reveals a failure*

```
SITEVIEW -> OPERATIONUNITS, TRANSACTION*, AREA*, PAGE*,
  GLOBALPARAMETER*, PROPERTY*, COMMENT?, <SITEVIEW@id>, <SITEVIEW@name>?,
  <SITEVIEW@homePage>?, <SITEVIEW@protected>, <SITEVIEW@secure>,
  <SITEVIEW@localize>, <SITEVIEW@presentation:style-sheet>?,
  <SITEVIEW@presentation:page-layout>?, <SITEVIEW@graphmetadata:go>?
```

The upper part of the graph shows two *incoming* edges: the SITEVIEW can be contained in a NAVIGATION element or be referenced by the siteView attribute of a LOGOUTUNIT. The lower part of the graph shows outgoing edges, i.e., the elements "used" by the SITEVIEW construct. Proceeding counterclockwise, we encounter the DTD elements nested inside the SITEVIEW element (in white), the homePage attribute (referencing a PAGE element), the textual attributes (in grey), and the enumeration attributes (in light gray). The DOG visualization tool is used to visually present the coverage of the WebML grammar provided by a given test set by decorating and annotating the nodes and edges of the graph. The three kinds of coverage measures that we are going to introduce (and that our tool calculates) mirror the concepts of statement, branch and path coverage, usually used in testing source code.

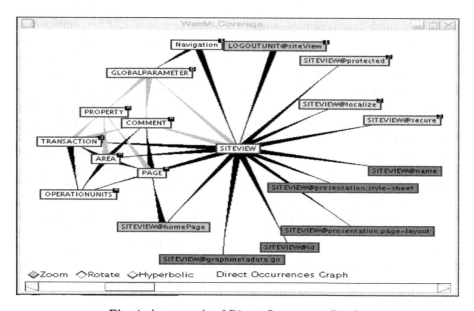

Fig. 4. An example of Direct Occurrence Graph

Rule Coverage. The simplest measure of the confidence provided by a test set can be obtained by assessing the percentage of the WebML grammar rules covered by the WebML schemas in the test cases. We call this measure *rule coverage*. Despite its simplicity, rule coverage analysis can already return important information, i.e., the set of elements of the conceptual model that are never used during the testing session, thus giving the first guidelines for improving the completeness of the test set. The processing of the WebML syntax led to a DOG with 528 nodes. The WebRatio test set induced a node coverage of 89.2%, thus highlighting the presence of 58 untested nodes (6 constructs and 52 attribute values). By manually inspecting the uncovered nodes with the DOG navigator, the WebRatio staff recognized the absence of test cases for a few, scarcely used, features of the WebML language. Minimality analysis revealed that a subset composed of 9 out of 38 test cases would provide the same rule coverage percentage. This result conflicted with the empirical evidence of the usefulness of the remaining 29 test cases, which prompted us to define more precise coverage measures.

Edge Coverage. To make coverage more precise, we took into account the context in which a WebML construct is used, by considering not only the nodes of the DOG, but also its edges. Intuitively, an edge from construct A to construct B represents the usage of B in the context of A. Therefore, a different edge (say $C \rightarrow B$) may represent a different usage of the same construct B in another context. For instance, the WebML construct PAGE can be used in a variety of ways: nested in a site view, in an area, or as a sub-page of a page. All these situations correspond to different DOG edges. This notion of context is crucial in any real modelling language, where the same primitive can be combined in multiple ways. We call the percentage of covered edges in the DOG *edge coverage*. Covering each edge means building a test set that uses each pair of language constructs in all legal combinations (i.e. combinations permitted by the WebML DTD specification). This criterion is nearly equivalent to Lämmel's context-dependent rule coverage. The DOG used in our experiment had 984 edges. The complete test set induces an edge coverage of 76.93%, thus showing the intrinsic significance of the empirical test set, which was designed without any systematic method for quantitatively assessing confidence. Minimality analysis showed that there are 4 equivalent test sets that provide the same 76.93% coverage measure. Each minimal set contains 16 Web applications. Thus, regardless of the specific minimal set chosen, edge coverage is not sufficient to justify the remaining 22 test applications, which prompted us for further investigation. Edge coverage analysis also pointed out a significant overlap of test cases because several test schemas, taken alone, cover about 500 edges out of 984. Furthermore, the results of the analysis supported the systematic addition of new test cases. The edge coverage percentage was easily improved by designing a few test cases for the uncovered edges, also reducing the overlaps among test schemas.

Path Coverage. As a final evaluation, we considered an additional coverage measure to investigate not only relations between pairs of concepts, but also possible combinations of groups of WebML constructs, because the designers' experience suggested that the subtlest errors originate from unexpected complex interactions of multiple language concepts. The *path coverage* measure addresses this issue. It is defined as the percentage of *paths* covered in the DOG. Covering all paths intuitively means that the test set exercises each construct in all its legal combinations with all the other constructs. 100% path coverage is clearly an infeasible requirement in most practical cases, even after breaking cycles. Nevertheless we discovered interesting information on the effectiveness of the test set. In the experimentation, our tool calculated more than 12 million legal paths, of which the test set exercises less than 1%. Minimality analysis was more revealing. With the help of our software tool, we identified one redundant test schema, which could be removed from the test set safely, and 6 test schemas that contribute a very low number of new paths to the coverage. Although theoretically speaking the latter test cases cannot be removed from the test set in a totally safe way, their contribution is marginal, as they are almost totally overlapping with other cases. This is an example of the optimization guidelines provided by the path coverage analysis to the developers of the testing set. It is much more important to evaluate the inadequacy of a given test case, rather than demonstrating its adequacy.

3.2 Baseline Definition with Real Web Applications

To improve the coverage figures, we evaluated the hypothesis that only a subset of all possible WebML paths is exercised by real developers. We focused on 46 real-world Web applications generated with WebRatio and performed the analysis on a reduced DOG comprising only the paths actually included in such applications. This path coverage measurement over the reduced DOG better assesses the impact of testing on real-world Web development. Path coverage jumped to a reasonable 33.43% on the reduced DOG, which strongly increases the confidence on the test set manually crafted by WebRatio developers, who probably know well which parts of the language are actually used in practice. We also determined that each real-world Web application was covered by the test cases for an average of 50.08%, with values ranging from 41.51% to 54.74%.

Real-world path coverage can also be used for assessing the necessity of each test case. We found that 3 of the 6 test cases with low path coverage contribution do not exercise any new path in the real-world subset, so they appear superfluous also with respect to the real-world usage of WebML.

3.3 Limits of Grammar-Based Systematic Testing

The experimentation also revealed some interesting limits of grammar-based testing. The evaluation cannot be applied to lexical errors, e.g., those errors that depend on particular formats of string values. For example, grammar-based testing does not uncover bugs caused by character encoding, multi-word fields, or the interpretation of special characters. Such lexical errors must be addressed by a specific group of tests.

4   Conclusions and Future Work

In this paper we have addressed the problem of systematically testing Web applications in the model-driven scenario, where testing splits into schema verification and code generator verification. We have provided both the formal underpinning of code generator testing and the results of an in-depth experimentation.

To the best of our knowledge, our study is the first formal investigation of testing in a *model&generate* Web development environment. Systematic testing has already been applied to schema validation by Ricca and Tonella [7] by representing the structure of the single Web application with an ad-hoc UML schema. Others [8] follow the same approach with different representations. Further experimental work is ongoing, to reach complete path coverage for the core paths of WebML and for the paths statistically more significant in real-world applications. Slight extensions of the implemented tools will enable the quantitative assessment of the testing confidence of individual Web applications, starting from their conceptual model and test sets defined during requirements analysis.

From the theoretical viewpoint, a promising research direction is the quantitative evaluation of the relation between the generator's correctness measures and other Web application quality metrics (e.g., usability). Finally, a further direction involves the connection of grammar-based testing with white-box testing in the field of Web applications, a study that could bridge two of the most promising approaches in software testing.

References

1. S. Ceri, P. Fraternali, et al.: Designing Data-Intensive Web Application. Morgan Kauffman (2003)
2. Lanzi, P., Matera, M., Maurino, A.: A framework for exploiting conceptual modeling in the evaluation of web application quality. In: Proc. ICWE 2004. Volume 3140 of LNCS., Springer Verlag (2004) 50–54
3. Masand, B.M., Spiliopoulou, M., eds.: Web Usage Analysis and User Profiling, WEBKDD'99, San Diego, CA, August 15, 1999. In Masand, B.M., Spiliopoulou, M., eds.: WEBKDD. Volume 1836 of LNCS., Springer (2000)
4. Myers, G.J., Sandler, C.: The Art of Software Testing. John Wiley & Sons (2004)
5. Beizer, B.: Black-box Testing: Techniques for Functional Testing of Software and Systems. John Wiley & Sons, Inc. (1995)
6. Lämmel, R.: Grammar testing. In: FASE '01: Proc. 4th Int. Conf. on Fundamental Approaches to Software Engineering. (2001) 201–216
7. Ricca, F., Tonella, P.: Analysis and testing of web applications. In: ICSE '01: Proceedings of the 23rd International Conference on Software Engineering, IEEE Computer Society (2001) 25–34
8. Liu, C.H., Kung, D.C., Hsia, P., Hsu, C.T.: Structural testing of web applications. In: ISSRE '00: Proc. 11th Int. Symp. on Software Reliability Engineering (ISSRE'00). (2000) 84

WIT: A Framework for In-container Testing of Web-Portal Applications

Wenliang Xiong, Harpreet Bajwa, and Frank Maurer

University of Calgary, Department of Computer Science, Calgary, Alberta, Canada T2N 1N4
Tel. +1 (403) 220-7140
{xiongw,bajwa,maurer}@cpsc.ucalgary.ca

Abstract. In this paper we describe a novel approach that allows for in-container testing of web portal applications. Concretely, our approach helps in locating and debugging (a) Deployment environment related problems, (b) Security: role based testing of resource access and (c) Problems arising from the interaction between the container and the application code in the form of request and response objects and other application environment objects. Our approach allows developers to write automated in-container test cases for web portal applications. Using Aspect technology, the test code is injected into the application code allowing the tests to run in the same environment as the portal application. WIT, our testing framework, provides the developers the ability to control the portal server environment by setting up an initial environment state before the execution of the application code. After the application code is executed, the environment state can be validated and cleaned up to prevent any traces or side effects. A test failure is reported if the results of executing the original code are incorrect. In this paper, we present the overall testing approach, design & implementation of WIT as well as a usage scenario.

1 Introduction

Container-based web technologies ease the burden on developers by providing underlying services such as persistence, security etc so that developers can concentrate on implementing the business logic. By providing robust and fine-tuned services to the application code the reliability, maintainability and performance of websites is improved considerably. The container further provides added value by managing the life cycle of the application code. While the advantages of container-based technologies are obvious, a container acts as a black box from the application developer's point of view and is only accessible via the API. Thus, automated testing of container-based application is challenging.

When an error occurs on the client side, it is difficult to predict the precise origin of the error. One of the reasons of the error may come from the container interacting incorrectly with the application code. Also, unpredictable changes in the container environment are often caused when the application code is deployed in the container. Although the application code runs correctly in the testing development container environment, developers cannot be guaranteed success of the application in the production environment.

Testing an application for such errors that surface only at deployment time requires an approach for executing the test code inside the container environment and the

D. Lowe and M. Gaedke (Eds.): ICWE 2005, LNCS 3579, pp. 87–97, 2005.
© Springer-Verlag Berlin Heidelberg 2005

ability to access and control the environment specific objects. We refer to this approach henceforth as in-container testing (ICT). Existing tools for front-end GUI or back-end business logic testing cannot test the deployment-related problems such as those mentioned above because the tests run outside of the container. A high-level report of the problems provided by them cannot be used to narrow down the scope of problems.

The motivation for our work comes from one of our industry partners that are building enterprise java based web portal applications [1]. The company reported 1) unknown deployment related errors and 2) lack of an automated way to test access to sensitive portal resources[1]. This paper addresses the problems discussed above by proposing a novel approach for performing automated ICT using the WIT framework for JSR [2] compliant portals.

The rest of the paper is organized as follows. Section 2 explains in detail the deployment related problems needed to be addressed by ICT. A detailed explanation of the architecture of web portal applications is provided in Section3. Section 4 provides a description of the design of WIT. Then some example usage scenarios and details on how tests can be implemented and run using WIT is provided in Section 5. Section 6 compares related work and approaches that currently exist for in-container testing of web-applications. Finally, section 7 discusses the future work and concludes our paper.

2   Problems Needed to Be Addressed by ICT

Unpredictable changes in the container environment are often caused when the application code is deployed in the production environment. Testing an application for such errors that surface only at deployment time requires an approach for executing the test code inside the container environment. In the following section we briefly discuss some of the problems encountered when a web-application is deployed in the production environment.

a) Deployment related problems: Certain environment attributes are set within the container at deployment time for e.g. descriptor files are read at deployment time and the environment is configured accordingly. That might, for example, mean that certain database resources are different in the test and the deployment environment or that some security roles do not match. Another possible difference between the test and the production container environment may be due to the fact that a different version of a library file is being referenced by the application code. All these subtle differences may introduce an error. For example, a portlet configured with the connection string to database A in the testing environment, for some reason, is assigned a connection string to database B when deployed to the production environment. Portlet code executing successfully in the test environment may fail because of the changed connection string. Another example: The version of a specific jar library is different in the test and production environment, e.g. a newer version is deployed in the test environment and referred by the portlet code

---

[1] A more comprehensive analysis of portal test practices and the results of our case study are published concurrently in ICWE 2005 [16]

directly or indirectly. The above examples highlight that the successful execution of the portlet code in test environment cannot guarantee its success in the production environment.

b) Security: role based testing of resource access. Access to sensitive resources for e.g. portlets [3] is controlled by assigning permissions to individual users or user groups granting the appropriate access. Without automated testing tool support the administrator setting the permissions must log in as a user with a specific role and test manually each time the applications are deployed in the production environment to verify whether the permissions have been correctly assigned.

c) Problems arising from the interaction between the container and the application code in the form of request, response objects and other application environment objects. In container-based web application, data submitted by the browser is assembled by the container as a request object. The data is then forwarded to the application code through access to certain environment objects. After the execution of the application code, results are sent back to the browser as a response object assembled by the container. The request and response objects are primarily responsible for carrying the data exchanged between the container and the application code. The application code can use all accessible objects as part of its business logic. Changing the values of some environment objects might create side effects on other parts of the application. Automatically testing the application code that relies on these objects requires a mechanism that allows developers to manipulate all these objects.

3 Portlet-Based Web-Portal Application Architecture

Web Portals are an example of container-based web application providing a single integrated point of access to information by aggregating multiple streams of dynamic content rendered as portlet windows. Technically, a portlet is a piece of code that runs within the portlet container [3] and provides content fragments to be embedded into the portal pages.

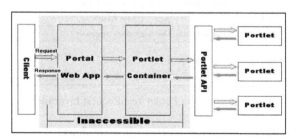

Fig. 1. Portal Server Component-Interactions

A client request as shown in Fig. 1 for a portal page interacts with multiple interfaces defined by the portal server components. The portal server completes the client request for the portal page by retrieving the portlets written by the developer for the current page. Thereafter the portal server invokes the portlet container for each portlet. The final portal page presented to the client represents the aggregated content generated by several portlets. With commercial portal servers, the source code of the portal server components as highlighted in Fig. 1 is inaccessible to the developer.

Because of the complexity of web portals, automated in-container testing presents four unique challenges. Firstly, the portlet API layer depicted in Fig. 1 is the only way that portlets can 'talk' to the inaccessible components. Thus, we need to find a way to intercept calls from the container to the portlets and vice versa so that testers can access and manipulate the calls generated by the container. Secondly, testing portlets involves invoking a series of inaccessible interactions in the portal server as seen in the Fig. 1. Thirdly, since the tests run in the container we need to collect individual test results of executing each portlet and then send back the aggregated results to the test client. Lastly, while the test code runs with the original application code, portal clients still should receive the correct response from the portlets. Thus, minimizing the side effects of the test code on the original portlet code becomes imperative. In the next section, we describe how our approach addresses these issues.

4 WIT: Web Portal Application In-container Testing Framework

4.1 Design Overview

The WIT system consists of following modules: Converter, Weaver, Invoker, Controller, and Repository.

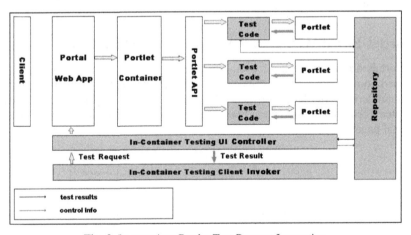

Fig. 2. In-container Portlet Test Request Invocation

The tests are initiated by the testing client Invoker depicted in Fig.2. This starts a process whereby the test Controller assembles and sends the request for the portlet under test and simultaneously, writes the test control instruct to the Repository. Before the request reaches the portlet under test, a check is made to ensure that the test control instruct allows the test code to execute. If the check is successful, the test code 1) intercepts the calls between the application code and the portlet API and 2) sets up the initial state to execute the portlet code. After the portlet code is executed, the results of the tests get stored in the Repository and then reported to developers by the Controller.

4.2 Invoker and Controller

The Invoker is the starting point of the in-container testing process. The responsibilities of the Invoker are twofold. First, it calls the Converter & Weaver as explained in section 4.3 to generate portlet code together with the test code and then deploys the generated code into the target portal server. Secondly, it sends a test request to the Controller and reports the test results returned by the Controller. The Controller is a servlet that accepts the test request from the Invoker. It then simulates the invocation of the portlet from a browser and assembles the portlet request. Meanwhile, it writes a control instruct into the Repository to indicate which portlet is going to be tested. The Controller is also responsible for querying the test results saved in the Repository and then sending them back to the Invoker.

4.3 Converter and Weaver

We utilized AspectJ technology [4, 5] in order to intercept calls to the portlet code by injecting the test code into the portlet code.

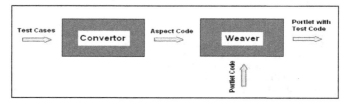

Fig. 3. Injecting the test code into Portlets

As shown in Fig. 3 test cases written for in-container testing are fed into the Converter first to generate Aspect code. This code is in turn compiled with the original portlet code by the AspectJ Weaver. As a result of this, the portlet binary class files are weaved in with the test code. During this phase, information like the location of the Repository is compiled into the portlet code as well. The final output of this converting & weaving phase is deployable portlet code together with the testing code.

4.4 Repository

Multiple Portlets run simultaneously within the portlet container and so does the test code. Writing the test results into a central location makes it possible to collect all the test results asynchronously. In order to provide better performance by avoiding I/O disk operations, we have chosen an in-memory database as our repository. Besides, the test results Repository also contains control information indicating which portlets are going to be tested. Only test code in Portlets indicated by the control information is executed. In this way, we avoid the side-effect from our tests on other portlets. Furthermore, if we clear such control information in Repository, no test code will be executed and thus, portlets are restored to the normal state to accept requests from users.

5 Usage Scenario of WIT

After providing an overview on the WIT architecture, we will now describe how a tester can write the in-container test cases for WIT. Further, three main usage scenarios of WIT will be discussed in detail with reference to an Accounts portlet example. Fig. 4 shows an example of an Accounts portlet class containing a method called doView[2] [2] which is invoked by the container. The portlet accesses the database connection string to connect to the backend database. The corresponding account id is retrieved from the PortletSession object [2], which is sent to the back-end database system to get the detail account information, which is in turn returned to client.

```
1)  public class AccountsPortlet{
2)  public void doView(PortletRequest request, PortletResponse re-
    sponse){
3)  try {
4)  PortletSettings portletSettings = request.getPortletSettings();
5)  String dbConnStr = portletSettings.getAttribute("AccountDB");
6)  //Now the AccountsPortlet can persist information to the back-end
    Account database
    ...........
7)  String acctId =
8)  (String)request.getPortletSession().getAttribute("acctId");
9)  AccountDetail ad = AccountDB.getAccountDetail(acctId);
10) Request.setAttribute("AcctDtl", ad);
11) PrintWriter out = response.getWriter();
12) //following pseudo code prints out the AccountDetail object
13) response.setContentType("text/html");
14) out.println(......);
15) }
```

Fig. 4. doView Method – AccountsPortlet Class

5.1 In-container Test Case Naming Conventions

Our in-container test case classes follow a specific naming convention.

Name of test case class: = Name of portlet class + "Test"

The name of each test case starts exactly with the name of the portlet being tested and ends with the string *"Test"*. For each portlet method being tested, there is a pair of test methods in the test case. The access modifier of these methods must be public, and the return type must be void. The name of these methods consists of three parts. The first part is either *"before"* or *"after"*, and the second part is the name of methods being tested, and the third part is any valid string to make the test methods more meaningful.

Name of test methods: = (before | after) +
"_" + name of methods under testing +
"_" + additional string

---

[2] doView is the core method in which a portlet developer implements the business logic

5.2 Testing Deployment Related Problems

The test scenario presented in this section allows testing for deployment related problems (see Section 2 – (a)). The PortletSettings [2] object contains configuration parameters accessed by the portlet code at runtime. These parameters are initially defined in the portlet descriptor file called portlet.xml. The portal administrator uses the administrative interface to configure individual portlet by editing the configuration parameters before deploying the application into the production environment.

For instance the accounts portlet as shown in Fig. 4 (line 4, 5, 6) accesses the database connection string by reading the configuration parameter from the portlet descriptor file (refer Fig. 5).

```
<concrete-portlet href="#Accounts">
  <portlet-name>Accounts</portlet-name>
    ......
  <config-param>
    <param-name>AccountDB</param-name>
    <param-value>jdbc:db2://localhost:50000/AccountDB</param-value>
  </config-param>
</concrete-portlet>
```

Fig. 5. A snippet of portlet.xml showing configuration parameters

The AccountsPortletTest code in Fig. 6 checks for the valid database connection string in the production environment. An incorrect value read by the portlet at runtime on the production environment will cause the AccountsPortletTest to fail.

```
public class AccountsPortletTest extends TestCase {
  private final String AccountDBConnStr =
                    "jdbc:db2://DB2BOX:50000/AccountDB";

  public void after_doView_ testGetAcctDBConnStr
  (PortletRequest request, PortletResponse response) {
      PortletSettings portletSettings = re
      quest.getPortletSettings();
      String dbConnStr = portletSettings.getAttribute("AccountDB");
      assertEquals("AccountDB Connection String is incorrect",
              dbConnStr, AccountDBConnStr);
  }
}
```

Fig. 6. doView() – AccountsPortlet Test Case For Database Connection String

5.3 Automated Testing Security: Role Based Testing of Resource Access

The test scenario presented in this section tests security privileges. We first highlight how the In-container security test case classes differ in naming convention from other test classes. A specific naming convention described below is used.

Name of security test case class: = Name of portlet class + "SecurityTest"
Name of security test case: ="test"+ (View|Edit|Config) + "Security"

Next, we discuss an example scenario below whereby a portal user called David is trying to access a sensitive resource which ideally he should not have access to.

WIT, will first weave the security test case testViewSecurity () code in Fig. 7 into the doView() of the account portlet class, and then login to the portal application with the specified user name and password, and then send a request to view AccountsPortlet. If the request is successful for some reason the doView() method in AccountsPortlet will be executed – which should have been prevented by the security system. Thus, the execution of the doView method means that the security test has failed and, thus, the testViewSecurity method triggers a "fail". This in turn reports a test failure to the developer.

```
public class AccountsPortletSecurityTest
                extends SecurityTestCase {
    public String getAuthenUrl() { return "http://ict5/login"; }
    public String getAuthenUser() {return "david"; }
    public String getAuthenPwd() { return "pass"; }
    public String getPortletInvokeUrl() {
        return "http://ict5/Acct";
    }
    public String testViewSecurity() {
        fail("the user:"+getAuthenUser()+" should not be
                    able to view the AccountPortlet");
    }
```

Fig. 7. doView() – AccountsPortlet Test Case For Security

5.4 Testing Problems Arising from the Interaction Between the Container and the Application Code

The test scenario presented in this section tests problems arising from the interaction between the container and the application code in the form of request, response objects and other application environment objects.

The AccountsPortlet depicted in Fig. 4 displays account detail information according to the account id number submitted by the user (line 7-14). In Fig. 8, developers set up the initial testing environment in the **before_doView**test_GetAcctDetail method by adding an account id into session object, and check the environment in the **after_doView**test_GetAcctDetail method by comparing the outBalance with the expected number 10. If the account outbalance is not what we expected, then a failure is fired.

```
public class AccountsPortletTest extends TestCase {
  public void before_doView_testGetAcctDetail
    (PortletRequest request, PortletResponse response) {
        session.setAttribute("acctId", "123");
  }

  public void after_doView_testGetAcctDetail
    (PortletRequest request, PortletResponse response) {
    AccountDetail ad =
                (AccountDetail) request.getAttribute("AcctDtl");
    double outBalance = ad.getOutstandingBalance();
    assertEquals("outstanding balance is incorrect", outBalance, 10);
  }
}
```

Fig. 8. doView () Test Case – AccountsPortletTest Class

5.5 Using WIT to Run Tests

After a tester has written automated portlet tests, he/she is able to compile, deploy and invoke all of them using a custom ANT [6] command that we developed. At the end of the script run, test results are displayed in the script window and the browser. The Ant based script can be integrated with the regular build process and promotes regression testing. The ICT accounts portlet tests for demo usage scenario were deployed and run in the IBM Websphere Portal Server [11] environment.

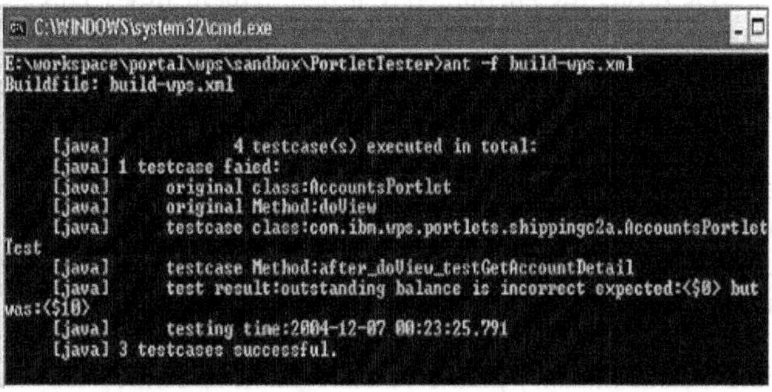

Fig. 9. Results of Test Execution of AccountsPortletTest Cases

6 Related Work

To our best knowledge, WIT is the only framework at this time that supports in-container testing of portlet-based applications. Other alternate approaches such as those provided by Cactus [7] can test Servlets [12], EJBs [13] and JSPs [14], etc. Portlets cannot be tested using the Cactus framework.

Further, the in-container testing approach used by the Cactus framework is more restricted than ours. Components, like Servlets, tested using Cactus are instantiated as normal classes in the test code versus using the real container to manage the component's lifecycle. Thus, they actually do now run in the same environment as when they are deployed. The limitation of this approach is that although the tests run in a real container, some in-container methods and its interactions with the real container cannot be completely tested as the services provided by the real container are being in-completely used. Thus Cactus tests may not be able to adequately detect deployment related errors as well as security issues (refer Section2 – (a), (b)) which can be tested effectively using our approach.

Client side testing frameworks such as httpUnit [8] and jWebUnit [9] support is more geared towards black box testing in a web environment. It can easily query the server externally and analyze the responses received. The frameworks, however, do not give a detailed control over the environment and constructing an initial state for the test is time consuming and often involves multiple http requests.

The Mock Objects approach [10] is another complimentary strategy to in-container testing of methods. In essence, it fakes implementation of the services provided by the container by using simulated objects. The main goal of mock objects is to unit test a method in isolation of domain objects by using simulated copies instead of real objects. Mock Objects suffer from the drawback that they do not assure that the in-container methods will run correctly when deployed on the chosen container. They only allow for a fine grained testing of business logic of in-container methods independent of the real context in which they run.

7 Conclusions and Future Work

Within this paper, we first presented the need for automated testing support in areas where portal applications currently cannot be tested automatically. We then elaborated on the various problems encountered at deployment time. This established the requirement that the tests must execute in the real container in order to test application code using the services provided by the container. To address these problems we have provided automated testing support through the WIT framework. The paper discusses the design and implementation of the WIT framework followed by examples of its usage scenarios. The framework allows in-container testing of web portal applications and provides a way of detecting and debugging deployment and security related problems associated with portlets. Using WIT, some manual testing can be replaced by automated tests.

We developed the ICT testing approach using WIT for portlets due to the scale of problem reported by our industry partner. Future versions of the WIT framework will be provided with configurable settings to perform in-container testing of other container-based web components such as servlets, EJBs, Struts [15] etc. The results of our ongoing empirical studies validating the usability and usefulness of WIT shall be presented in the future.

References

1. Christian Wege, DaimerChrysler. Portal Server Technology. IEEE Internet Computing 2002.
2. JSR-000168 Portlet Specification.
   http://www.jcp.org/aboutJava/communityprocess/review/jsr168/ (Last Visited: February 11, 2005).
3. Portal Introduction-IBM.
   http://www-106.ibm.com/developerworks/ibm/library/i-portletintro (Last Visited: February 7, 2005).
4. Aspect Oriented Programming Gregor Kiczales, John Lamping, Anurag Mendhekar, Chris Maeda, Cristina Lopes, Jean-Marc Loingtier and John Irwin Xerox Palo Alto Research Center; European Conference on Object-Oriented Programming(ECOOP),Finland June 1997.
5. AspectJ Eclipse Project http://eclipse.org/aspectj/ (Last Visited: February 7, 2005).
6. Apache ANT http://ant.apache.org/ (Last Visited: February 7, 2005).
7. Cactus Apache Jakarta Project http://jakarta.apache.org/cactus/ (Last Visited: January 29,2005)
8. Client Side Testing using HttpUnit. http://httpunit.sourceforge.net/ (Last Visited: February 7,2005)
9. Client Side Testing of web-applications using jWebUnit http://jwebunit.sourceforge.net/ (Last Visited: February 7,2005).
10. Mocks Objects. http://c2.com/cgi/wiki?MockObject (Last Visited: January 25,2005).
11. IBM Websphere Portal Zone http://www7b.software.ibm.com/wsdd/zones/portal/ (Last Visited: February 7, 2005).

12. JSR-000154 Java Servlet 2.4 Specification.
    http://www.jcp.org/aboutJava/communityprocess/final/jsr154/ (Last Visited: February 11, 2005)
13. EJB Specification. http://java.sun.com/products/ejb/docs.html (Last Visited: February 11, 2005)
14. JSR-000152 JavaServer Pages 2.0 Specification.
    http://www.jcp.org/aboutJava/communityprocess/final/jsr152/ (Last Visited: February 11, 2005)
15. The Apache Struts Web Application Framework. http://struts.apache.org/ (Last Visited: February 11, 2005)
16. Harpreet Bajwa, Wenliang Xiong, Frank Maurer: Evaluating Current Testing Processes of Web-Portal Applications. Proc of ICWE 2005.

How to Deal with Non-functional Properties
in Web Service Development*

Guadalupe Ortiz, Juan Hernández, and Pedro J. Clemente

University of Extremadura, Quercus Software Engineering Group
{gobellot,juanher,jclemente}@unex.es
http://quercuseg.unex.es

Abstract. Web Service technologies offer a successful way for interoperability among web applications. However, current approaches do not propose an acceptable method to decouple non-functional properties from Web Service implementations, leaving as a result a large amount of code scattered and tangled all over the application, thus raising problems at design, implementation, maintenance and evolution. It is the aim of this paper to describe how aspect-oriented techniques allow these properties to be easily modularized and reused. We will also analyse how information about properties can be added in the WSDL file, in order to keep clients informed of the characteristics of the service they are going to use. Finally, we will demonstrate how the client will be able to choose which optional properties have to be applied in his invocation in a transparent way, automatically generating the necessary changes in his code in a modularized and decoupled way.

1 Introduction

Web Services convey one step further in the long way that object-oriented technologies and distributed platforms have walked. However, due to the juvenility of this technology, some important points, such as non-functional property addition to the services, have not been faced yet, in spite of their being essential, considering their fast evolution to bigger and more complex services.

The addition of non-functional properties to Web Services leads to implementation changes, as these properties can actually affect various modules in the application. That is not very appropriate, since we would then have many lines of code repeated along our application with its consequent loss of time on development and maintenance. Furthermore, there are properties such as *logging*, *timing* and *security* amongst others, which are normally required in plenty of different applications; therefore, it would be desirable to be able to reuse them should they be necessary.

This problem was already faced in component-based programming [8]. Containers deal with non-functional properties [3], and there are also approaches where *Aspect-Oriented Programming* (AOP) [6] is used to deal with such properties [1] [9]. Regardless of the fact that the concept of container is not contemplated by Web Service technologies in the sense of component programming, the main contribution of this

---

* This work has been developed with the support of CICYT under contract TIC2002-04309-C02-01

D. Lowe and M. Gaedke (Eds.): ICWE 2005, LNCS 3579, pp. 98–103, 2005.

paper is our claim that aspect-oriented techniques may be used for adding non-functional properties to Web Services. This way, we could abstract our deployment from these properties in the implementation to deal with them later. In addition, we will show how WSDL files may be modified, appending information on the properties added. In this sense, some properties are service-exclusive, that is, they do not affect the clients. However, other properties in the service, which do affect the client in the operation result or involving changes to his code, can be used by them optionally.

The rest of the paper is organized as follows: in Section 2, a case study is presented to identify the said problems. Section 3 outlines how AOP can help to solve this problem, and how AspectJ has been used and applied in Web Service development, allowing the addition of different kinds of non-functional properties in a modularized way. In Section 4, we discuss our proposal, whereas other related approaches are examined in Section 5, and the main conclusions are presented in Section 6.

2   Crosscutting Concerns in Web Services

Consider a simple example of a travel agent service, which offers four different operations: *countryAirportInformation* provides information about all the airports in a particular country; *nameAirportInformation* provides information on a given airport, *weatherAirportInformation* provides information about the weather in the airport in question; finally, *buyAirlineFlight* allows the user to buy a pre-booked flight.

The non-functional *timing* property could be added in order to calculate the time of use of two of our operations: *countryAirportInformation* and *nameAirportInformation*. This addition would cause code to be repeated and scattered all over the application, which implies not only a bad design, but also problems in maintenance and evolution. Furthermore, if we now wished to add the same property to the other operations, we would have no chance of reusability.

AOP is the answer to the problem, since it was created to design and code crosscutting concerns. AOP deals with elements that are scattered all over an implementation. As a result, we can modify these properties without influencing the rest of the code in the application. AOP is also successfully used in the Web Service domain for implementing orchestrations and reusing their interaction patterns [7].

3   Adding Non-functional Properties to Web Services

In this section we are going to show how aspect-oriented techniques may be used in order to solve the difficulties presented above. AOP describes five kinds of elements to modularize crosscutting concerns: firstly, we have to define the *join point* model which indicates the points where new behaviours could be included. Secondly, we have to define a way to indicate the *join points* in question to specify in which points of the implementation we wish to insert the new code. Next, we ought to determine how we are going to specify the new behaviour. We would then encapsulate the specified join points and their corresponding behaviours into independent units. Finally, a method to weave the new code with the original one has to be applied [4].

Non-functional properties are always added in the service. However, property additions to the service can sometimes affect the client, not only on the result of the invocation, but also involving changes in his code. In this sense three different alternatives will be studied: properties which do not affect the client, properties which affect the client on the result, and those which affect the client in his codification.

3.1 Properties Which Do Not Affect the Client

The *timing* property can be modelled as an *AspectJ* aspect. This property only affects the service, as the client obtains the same information from the operation whether the time of use is being monitored or not. For our example, the property would be implemented as depicted in *Figure 1*, where we highlight *pointcut Information()*, which injects code in the execution of methods *countryAirportInformation* and *nameAirportInformation*. The corresponding *advice* shows the code to be injected.

```
public aspect TimingAspect {
pointcut Information(): execution(public * *.countryAirportInformation(..))  || execution (public *.* nameAirportInformation(..));
around (): Information(){   long T1 = System.currentTimeMillis();
                            proceed();
                            long T2 = System.currentTimeMillis();
                            long timeTaken= T2-T1;// timeTaken used for its requirements}
```

Fig. 1. Operations offered by *TravelAgentService* with an aspect modeling the *timing* property

The WSDL document is composed of different tags related to the interface, operations, parameters, ports..., of the service. The information appended, as shown, has the duty to communicate new added properties to the client. This information facilitates the properties description, the operations affected and whether they are optional or not, as depicted in *Figure 2*. The WSDL file follows the W3C standard. This is the reason why we have included that information in the *documentation* tag; consequently, any client who does not know its function will not be affected at all.

```
<documentation>    <property name="Timing">
                        <description=" Timing property : Measures the operations execution time/>
                        <optional="no">
                        <applied to>    <operation name="countryAirportInformation></operation>
                                        <operation name="nameAirportInformation></operation>      </applied to>
                    </property>
</documentation>
```

Fig. 2. WSDL documentation tag with the timing property added

With the intention of making property addition with *AspectJ* transparent to the developer, apart from replacing the *Java* compilation by the *AspectJ* weaving, we have created some additional compilation targets and a code generation process which will be invoked during service building. Therefore, the developer chooses which property he wants to apply and, in a totally transparent way, the aspect is generated and the information added to the WSDL file at compilation time. This way, the developer, when designing the application, can focus on its main functionality, adding the properties from a pool at a later stage.

3.2 Properties Chosen by the Client

We can also use the information added in the WSDL file to offer the client the possibility of choosing which properties he wants to be applied during his invocation. In order to enable this to happen, two new processes have been included: one in the client which intercepts the outgoing SOAP message to add the information about which properties should be applied; the other one will be in the service, which intercepts the incoming SOAP message to determine which properties have been chosen by the client. On the other hand, we are going to differentiate between two cases: firstly, those properties which can be chosen without the need of modifying the client code, and secondly, those which do imply changes in the client code. Both processes are represented in *Figures 3a)* and *3b)*, respectively.

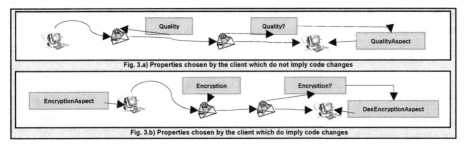

Fig. 3.a) Properties chosen by the client which do not imply code changes

Fig. 3.b) Properties chosen by the client which do imply code changes

Fig. 3. Processes for the addition of non-functional properties chosen by the client

3.2.1 Properties Which Do Not Imply Changes in the Client Code

Let us consider we have a service which offers stock market quotations. The service can offer the same operation with real time or delayed quotations depending on the kind of client. The client does not need to make changes to the code, but the result may be different. Currently, the operation returns the delayed result (for regular clients), but with the *Real Time* property application, it returns the real time result (for advanced clients). The advanced client developer will include the new target related to the *Real Time* property at compilation. This target will modify the class which intercepts the outgoing message for this property to be applied. Otherwise, the class which intercepts the incoming message is included at service side to determine which properties are requested, thus the aspects will implement one behaviour or the other.

In our case study we could apply one property of this type to the operation *airportWeatherInformation,* as represented in *Figure 3a)*. The operation returns the temperature when requested by ordinary clients; however, advanced clients receive a larger amount of weather information. The implementation at client side is the same, but the developer includes the *Quality* property so as to get more information.

3.2.2 Properties Which Imply Changes in the Client Code

Consider we want to provide security to our service. The *Encryption* property would imply changes in the client codification. The service currently offers its operations without encryption, but those clients who wish to have their invocations encrypted can do so. The process, shown in *Figure 3b)*, is as follows: The developer will include the encryption target at compilation time so the class which intercepts the outgoing message will include this property and the *encryption* aspect will be added. Similarly, the same changes that took place in the previous case are implemented in the service: the incoming message will be intercepted, and if *encryption* was included, the parameters will be desencrypted by the aspect at destination.

4 Discussion: Attributes and Shortcomings

The benefits provided by the use of aspect-oriented techniques are twofold. Firstly, it avoids crosscutting concerns, so service maintenance is kept simpler and the application structure well modularized. On top of that, aspects may be reused to build other services, thus diminishing developing costs and efforts, while improving the flexibility, reliability, and reusability of the application. In addition, the client is notified of the non-functional properties that affect the Web Service through the WSDL documentation. In this sense, the client can choose from the battery of properties offered by the service which ones should be applied during his invocation, and all the necessary code will be generated automatically in a totally transparent way.

Table 1. Performance measurements for the addition of non-functional properties

Metrics	Timing		Quality		Encryption	
	O	AOP	O	AOP	O	AOP
ART (ms)	5142,5	5393,3	2225,571	24880,5	848,75	886,5
ACN	0	1	0	2	1	1
PMM (%)	45	0	60	0	30	0
EIN	1	0	0	0	1	0

Finally, *Table 1* shows the performance metrics we have measured on the example implemented with (AOP) and without (O) AOP techniques. To start with, the *average response time* (ART) is quite similar in both implementations, although the AOP time is slightly longer, it is not a big price to pay for the improvements. Secondly, the *number of classes added* (ACN) is bigger when using AOP, as we implement the properties in aspects. Besides, no *method* has *to be modified* at all when using aspects (PMM), whereas, when no aspects are used, every method which will be offered as a new operation will undergo modification, with a high *percentage* of lines to be added. Finally, new *external invocations* (EIN) have to be added if we do not use AOP. For all these reasons, our proposal proves to be rather efficient at performance as response time is not wasted while improving modularity, reusability and maintenance.

5 Related Work

Although there are undoubtedly important infrastructural issues concerning Web Services, there seems to be little discussion on how to add non-functional properties to them.

Firstly, we can distinguish one contribution from S. Göbel *et al.*, where non functional properties, such as security, accuracy or other service quality-related ones, are specified in component models by using aspects [5]; we walk one step ahead using this technology along with Web Services.

Secondly, MB. Verheecke et al. suggest the use of a dynamic aspect-oriented language called *JAsCo* for decoupling services from the application that invokes them [10]. They focus mainly on the client side; in contrast, our proposal uses a general use aspect-oriented language and is mainly centred on the server side.

Finally, we can also mention a paper that concentrates on a new language based on XML, AO4BPPEL, being one aspect-oriented extension for BPEL [2]. In contrast with our proposal based on languages with wide applications support, they need a new weaver for the proposed language, which is not available on the Web nowadays.

6 Conclusions

The results obtained in this study show how AOP is really useful in order to avoid crosscutting in Web Service development. In particular, AspectJ has been used for dealing with concerns which crosscut Web Service implementation, while improving the reusability of non-functional properties in the development of different services.

One of the main advantages of our proposal is the possibility of adding these properties without modifying the service code, as well as adding some information about them in the WSDL file, without hindering the client who disclaims the use of aspects tags. The client who is aware of the usefulness of this information can choose the properties which will be applied during his invocation. The necessary code would be generated in a totally transparent way both in the service and in the client's side.

References

1. Bonér, J. What are the key issues for commercial AOP use: how does AspectWerkz address them? Proc. 3rd Int. Conf. AOSD, ACM Press, Lancaster, UK, 2004
2. Charfi, A., Mezini, M. *Aspect-Oriented Web Service Composition*, Proc. 2004 European Conference on Web Services (ECOWS 2004), Erfurt, Germany, September, 2004.
3. Duclos, F, Estublier, J, Morat, P: Describing and using non functional aspects in component based applications. Proc 1st Int. Conf. AOSD, ACM Press, Enschede, The Netherlands, 2002
4. Elrad, T., Aksit, M., Kitzales, G., Lieberherr, K., Ossher, H.: *Discussing Aspects of AOP*. Communications of the ACM, Vol.44, No. 10, October 2001.
5. Göbel, S., Pohl Cristoph, Röttger, S., Zschaler, S. The COMQUAD Component Model: Enabling Dynamic Selection of Implementations by Weaving Non-functional Aspects. Proc. 3rd Int. Conf. AOSD, ACM Press, Lancaster, UK, 2004
6. Kiczales, G. *Aspect-Oriented Programming*, Proc. ECOOP, Jyväskylä, Finland, June 1997.
7. Ortiz G., Hernández J., Clemente, P.J: *Web Service Orchestration and Interaction Patterns: an Aspect-Oriented Approach*, Proc. 2nd. ICSOC. New York, USA, November 2004.
8. Szyperski, C.: Component Software. Beyond Object-Oriented Programming. Addison-Wesley (1997).
9. Tal Chen, Joseph (Yossi) Gil. AspectJ2EE=AOP+J2EE: Towards an Aspect Based, Programmable and Extensible Middleware FrameWork. Proc. ECOOP, Oslo, 2004
10. Verheecke, B., Cibrán, M.A.: AOP for Dynamic Configuration and Management of Web Services. Proc. Int. Conf. on Web Services, (ICWS-Europe'03) Erfurt, Germany, (2003)

Use Constraint Hierarchy
for Non-functional Requirements Analysis

Ying Guan and Aditya K. Ghose

Decision Systems Lab, School of IT and Computer Science
University of Wollongong, NSW 2522, Australia
{yg32,aditya}@uow.edu.au

Abstract. Non-functional requirements are critical in web engineering applications, but often ignored. Usually, these are articulated as statements of objectives, as opposed to prepositional assertions. A key challenge in dealing with objectives is that there is no obvious means of deciding when they are satisfied. In effect, these objectives are never fully satisfied, but *satisficed* to varying degrees. Alternative design decisions need to trade-off varying degrees of satisfaction of potentially mutually contradictory non-functional requirements. The key contribution of this paper is the use of the hierarchical constraint logic programming framework [3, 6] in dealing with non-functional requirements. We show how NFRs can be formulated as soft constraints and how the machinery associated with constraint hierarchies can be used to evaluate the alternative trade-offs involved in seeking to satisfy a set of non-functional requirements that might pull in different directions.

1 Introduction

Non-functional requirements [2] are concerned about the quality characteristics of a software system. NFRs are extremely important for the design of a system. Any errors, omissions, inaccuracies to take NFRs into account may cause unexpected failures of systems. Non-functional requirements are specially important in *web engineering* applications, but often ignored. Usually, NFRs are articulated as statements of objectives, as opposed to prepositional assertions (that evaluate to true or false). For example, the stakeholders may want the security levels of the system to be high, the performance be also high, and the cost be maintained as low as possible, etc. A key challenge in dealing with objectives is that there is no obvious means of deciding when they are satisfied. In effect, these objectives are never fully satisfied, but *satisficed* to varying degrees. Alternative design decisions need to trade-off varying degrees of satisfaction of potentially mutually contradictory non-functional requirements.

The key contribution of this paper is the use of the hierarchical constraint logic programming framework [3, 6] in dealing with non-functional requirements. Constraint logic programming was developed to extend the ability of traditional logic programming to deal with knowledge (facts and rules) expressed as Horn clauses with specially designated *constraint predicates*. The resulting systems were more efficient than standard logic programming systems because of their ability to use to special-purpose *constraint solvers,* which, in effect, understood the "meaning" of the constraint predicates, and dealt with them in more efficient ways than the resolution proof procedure that most logic programming systems relied on. Constraint logic programming also offered better expressivity. Hierarchical constraint logic programming (HCLP)

D. Lowe and M. Gaedke (Eds.): ICWE 2005, LNCS 3579, pp. 104–109, 2005.

was developed to deal with the fact that many of the constraints articulated by users in real-life problems are *soft constraints,* i.e., these were constraints that one would ideally seek to satisfy, but which could be violated (or satisfied to a lesser degree) if absolutely necessary. Soft constraints typically have varying degrees of priority, hence the HCLP framework permits the specification of *constraint hierarchies,* i.e., sets of soft constraints labelled with varying degrees of priority. Our larger project seeks to deploy the full capability of the HCLP framework in dealing with non-functional requirements. In the current paper, for the sake of brevity, we only focus on the constraint hierarchy component of framework. Our focus is on showing how NFRs can be formulated as soft constraints and how the machinery associated with constraint hierarchies can be used to evaluate the alternative trade-offs involved in seeking to satisfy a set of non-functional requirements that might pull in different directions.

The rest of this document is organized in the following manner. In Section 2, we give an overview of non-functional requirement. In section 3, we detail the constraint hierarchy level. In section 4, an example is given to illustrate how to apply our proposed method to solve conflicts among NFRs of software requirements and section 6 is the conclusion.

2   Non-functional Requirements

A key challenge in dealing with NFRs is articulating them in terms of metrics, on which one could then apply thresholds or seek to maximize or minimize. In Table1, we list possible measures for some NFRs, along the lines of the proposal in [1]. Those possible metrics would permit us to formulate constraint-style representations of NFRs. In this table, we only list part of those attributes that are easy to be specified using numbers, while there still exist other attributes that are difficult to be expressed in explicit numeric way, for instance, reliability, portability, etc. We believe that quantitative metrics for these can also be developed in the future, adding strength to our proposal.

The purpose of the NFRs level in our approach is to capture and represent non functional requirements. The structure for this level is defined below:

Definition 1. Non-functional requirement level is described as a tuple:

NFRL = < Q, A> where:

- Q is set of non-functional requirements,
- A is set of quality factors associated with each non-functional requirements in Q.

3   Constraint Hierarchy Level

After requirement elicitation, designers usually need to express preferences on each non-functional requirements of this system as well as on functional requirements. Preferences on non-functional requirements can be specified as soft constraints and the functional requirements can be expressed as hard constraints. In this level we need to formalize soft constraints for quality factors specified in NFRs level. In order to make those constraints computable, we choose a proposed mechanism hierarchical constraint hierarchy [3,6]. Constraint hierarchies (CHs) belong to traditional frameworks for handling of over-constrained problems. They allow expressing hard constraints which have to be satisfied and several preference levels of soft constraints which violations are minimized level by level subsequently [5].

Table 1. Possible Measures of some quality attributes

Quality Attribute	Possible Measures
Security	Time/effort/resources required, probability of detecting attack, percentage of services still available under denial-of-services attack; restore data/services; extent to which data/services damaged and/or legitimate access denied; resources needed for satisfying these demands; cost to satisfying these demands.
Efficiency	response time, miss rate, data loss, concurrent transaction number,
Availability	time interval when the system must be available, available time, time interval in which system can be in degraded mode, repair time, task time, number of problems solved
Cost	cost in terms of elements affected,effort,money;extent to which this affects other functions or quality attributes
Maintainability	cost in terms of number of elements afftected,effort,money
Accuracy	number of error ,rate of fail or successful operations to total operation, amount of time/data lost
Usability	use system efficiently, minimize impact of errors

Firstly, let us have a brief review of the hierarchical constraint logical programming. To introduce the constraint hierarchies, we use the definition of constraint hierarchies in [6]. A *constraint* is a relation over some domain D. A constraint is thus an expression of the form $p(t_1,...t_n)$ where p is an n-ary symbol in domain D and each t_i is a term. A *labeled constraint* is a constraint labeled with a strength, written lc where c is a constraint and l is a strength. In a constraint hierarchy, the stronger a constraint is, the more it influences the solution of the hierarchy. A *constraint hierarchy* is a finite set of labeled constraints. And in the same level, weight can be used to determine which constraint is more important. A *valuation* for a set of constraints is a function that maps free variables in the constraints to elements in domain D over which the constraints are defined. A *solution* to a constraint hierarchy is such a set of valuations for the free variables in the hierarchy that any valuation in the solution set satisfies at least the required constraints. An error function $e(c\theta)$ is used to indicate how nearly constraint c is satisfied for a valuation θ. CHs define the so called comparators aimed to select solutions (the best assignment of values to particular variables) via minimizing errors of violated constraints. Currently, there three groups of comparators: global, local and regional comparators. For a local comparator, each constraint is considered individually, for a global comparator, the errors for all constraints at a given level are aggregated using combining function g. For a regional comparator, each constraint at a given level is considered individually. There are a number of comparators by defining the combining function g and the relations <>g and <g for each (the symbol <> means equal). Global comparator includes weighted-sum-better, worse-case-better and least-squares-better.

After the quick review about CH, now we can introduce constraint hierarchy level. NFR level states quality factors of the system, while not all variables relating to quality factors can be assigned values. So the variables of constraint hierarchy is a projection on the whole set of quality factors. In table 1, we have listed some possible measures for those quality attributes that are easy to be measured using hard numbers. Then for each non-functional requirement, they have a set of quality factors that have been assigned with values. And each non-functional requirement has its label assigned manually by stakeholders. Therefore, all NFRs and quality factors associated to them could compose a constraint hierarchy.

Before comparing valuations, we need to identify a prefer solution in constraint form. For example, we may set the prefer cost to be 0 and response time to be 0, although they cannot be satisfied. This solution can be used as a method to compare the proposed solutions after the computation of the hierarchical model, usually, solution with the smallest distance from this predefined solution is set as the best solution.

Now we can give the comparison process for constraint hierarchy: 1) For each quality factor, choose the value from a constraint about it in the highest label level; 2) if cannot find the solution after step1, then choose the value from a constraint about it with the highest weight; 3) if cannot find the solution after step2, then use comparator to choose the value from a constraint about it which has the smallest error sequence; 4) I if cannot find the solution after step3, then compare values from constraints with the value of this quality factor from prefer solution, choose the value with shortest distance.

4   Case Study

This section briefly illustrates how the approach we proposed can be applied, through a case study of the analysis and design of a web-based financial trading system, Financial bundle trading system (FBTS) [5].

FBTS is a web-based continuous electronic market that traders can use to execute bundle orders. With a bundle order, a trader can order a combination of stocks or assets. FBTS is an automated, continuous auction market that executes bundle orders to buy and sell.

The main non-functional requirements for FBTS could be elicited as: *Security, Efficiency, Cost, Maintainability, Usability* and *Accuracy*. The structures for each non-functional requirement are listed in table 2; CH is listed in table 3.

Table 2. Non-functional Level of FBTS

Q	A
Security	Response time, resources needed for satisfying these demands; cost in terms of elements affected.
Efficiency	response time, error rate, transaction speed, number of possible concurrent transaction, cost in terms of elements affected
Accuracy	rate of fail or successful operations to total operation, rate of data lost, cost in terms of elements affected
Usability	rate of impact errors
Cost	budget cost
Maintainability	recovery time, repair time, cost in terms of elements affected

A prefer solution for this constraint hierarchy is the values of cost, response time, error rate, recovery time, repair time and rate of fail operations are 0 respectively, and transaction speed and concurrent transaction are 5000 respectively. Based constraint hierarchy stated in table 2, a simpler form of constraint hierarchy can be generated.

Table 3. Constraint hierarchy for FBTS

Q	Label	Weight	A	Constraint
Security	Strong	1	Response time (rt), resources needed for satisfying these demands; cost in terms of elements affected (c).	$rt = 1s$ $c > 21,000$
Efficiency	Strong	1	response time (rt), error rate(er), transaction speed(ts), number of possible concurrent transaction (ct), cost in terms of elements affected (c)	$rt= 0.5s$ $er < 0.01\%$ $ts > 1000/min$ $ct > 1000$ $c > 25,000$
Accuracy	Strong	0.8	rate of fail or successful operations to total operation(fr), rate of data lost(rdl), cost in terms of elements affected(c)	$fr < 0.01\%$ $rdl < 0.01\%$ $c > 22,000$
Cost	Medium	1	budget cost(c)	$c < 20,000$
Maintain-ability	Weak	1	recovery time(ryt), repair time(rpt), cost in terms of elements affected(c)	$ryt < 1$ min $rpt < 2$min $c > 15,000$

> *Strong*   *rt=1, c>21,000*
> *Strong*   *rt=0.5, ts>1000, ct>1000, c>25,000, er<0.0001*
> *Strong*   *fr<0.0001, c>22,000, rdl<0.0001*
> *Medium*   *c<20,000*
> *Weak*   *c>15,000, ryt<1, rpt<2*

From the above constraint hierarchy, we can see that there exist conflicts for *cost (c)* in *Strong* level and *Medium* level and for attribute *response time (rt)* in *Strong* level. In this constraint hierarchy, there is no *required* constraint, so *Strong* is the biggest strength. Correspondingly, for attribute cost, we only consider the value in the *Strong* constraints. At *Strong* level, there is still the *response time* conflict. The weights for these two constraints are equal; we cannot depend on weight to select the solution. So, we choose comparator to compare these two solutions. If we choose response time greater than 1 second, the error sequence is [[0],[0.5]], while if we choose response time being 0.5 second, the error sequence is [[0.5],[0]]. We still cannot get the better solution. Finally, we compare the distance between these two solutions and the prefer solution predefined, and the solution with response time has the shorter distance, so *rt* 0.5 is chosen. The best solution is *rt < 0.5, ts > 1000, ct > 1000, c> 25,000, ryt< 1, rpt < 2, er < 0.0001, fr < 0.0001.*

5   Conclusions

In this paper we have proposed a meta-level framework that can be used to detect and solve potential conflicts among non-functional requirements by constructing constraint hierarchy based on all possible quality factors relate to the prospective system. With the constraint hierarchy and the selection steps stated in section 3, possible solutions can be generated after the comparisons among constraints. Our proposed approach only focuses on conflicts that might arise among the cooperation between different non-functional requirements with the assumption that conflicts among stakeholders have already been eliminated after negotiation. In this paper, we only focus on those non-functional requirements that are easy to be specified using hard numbers, while there are still many other non-functional requirements, such as, reliability, portability, etc., which are not mentioned in this paper. These will be remained as future work.

References

1. Bass Len, Paul Clements, Rick Kazman: Software architecture in practice, Boston, Addison-Wesley, c2003
2. Chung, L., Nixon, B., Yu, E., and Mylopoulos, J.: Non-Functional Requirements in Software Engineering, Kluwer Academic Publishing, 2000.
3. Molly Wilson, Alan Boring: Hierarchical Constraint Logical Programming, Journal of logic programming,1993
4. Ming Fan, Jan Stallaert, Andrew B. Whinston: A Web-Based Financial Trading System, Computer archive, Volume 32, Issue 4 (April 1999), Pages: 64 - 70, 1999
5. Hana Rudová,: Constraint Satisfaction with Preferences, Ph.D. Thesis,2001
6. Molly Wilson: Hierarchical Constraint Logic Programming, Technical Report 93-05-01, University of Washington, May 1993. (PhD Dissertation)

Towards a Taxonomy of Hypermedia
and Web Application Size Metrics

Emilia Mendes[1], Steve Counsell[2], and Nile Mosley[3]

[1] The University of Auckland, Private bag 92019, Auckland, NZ
emilia@cs.auckland.ac.nz
[2] Brunel University, Uxbridge UB8 3PH, Middlesex, UK
steve.counsell@brunel.ac.uk
[3] MetriQ (NZ) Limited, 19A Clairville Crescent, Wai-O-Taiki Bay, Auckland, NZ
nile@metriq.biz

Abstract. Surveying and classifying previous work on a particular field have several benefits, which are: i) to help organise a given body of knowledge; ii) to provide results that can help identify gaps that need to be filled; iii) to provide a categorization that can also be applied or adapted to other surveys; iv) to provide a classification and summary of results that may benefit researchers who wish to carry out meta-analyses. This paper presents a survey literature of hypermedia and Web size metrics published within the last 12 years and classifies the surveyed studies according to a proposed taxonomy. In addition, we also discuss the changes, mainly in the motivation for size metrics, that have occurred during our review period.

1 Introduction

Within the last 12 years several hypermedia and Web size metrics have been proposed, mainly motivated to help the authoring process of applications or to be used for Web cost estimation. Despite their importance for Web practitioners and those investigating Web cost estimation there is no single reference to date that classifies and compares such metrics.

We are aware of two previous surveys on Web metrics [4],[9] however none looked specifically into hypermedia and Web size metrics or metrics for authoring and cost estimation.

Dhyani et al. [4] concentrates on metrics that belong to one of the following six categories:

- *Web Graph Properties* – Metrics that measure structural properties of the Web on both macroscopic and microscopic scales.
- *Web Page Significance* – Metrics used to assess candidate pages in response to a search query and have a bearing on the quality of search and retrieval on the Web.
- *Usage Characterization* – Metrics that measure user behavior aiming at improving the content, organization and presentation of Web sites.
- *Web Page Similarity* – Metrics that measure the extent of association between Web pages.
- *Web Page Search and Retrieval* – Metrics for evaluating and comparing the performance of Web search and retrieval services.

D. Lowe and M. Gaedke (Eds.): ICWE 2005, LNCS 3579, pp. 110–123, 2005.

- *Information Theoretic* – Metrics that capture properties related to information needs, production and consumption.

Calero et al. [9] provides a survey where Web metrics are classified into three dimensions, all related to Web quality:

- *Web Features Dimension* – Incorporates Content, Navigation and Presentation metrics.
- *Quality Characteristics Dimension* – Incorporates Functionality, Reliability, Efficiency, Portability and Maintainability metrics.
- *Life Cycle Processes Dimension* – Process metrics related to a Web development life cycle.

In addition to the above classification they also assess their surveyed metrics according to a second criteria:

- *Granularity Level* – Whether the metric's scope is a "Web page" or "Web site".
- *Theoretical Validation* – Whether or not a metric has been validated theoretically.
- *Empirical Validation* – Whether or not a metric has been empirically validated.
- *Automated Support* – Whether or not there is a support tool that facilitates the calculation of the metric.

The contribution of this paper is twofold: first, to provide a survey on hypermedia and Web size metrics based on literature published within the last 12 years; second, to provide a taxonomy of size metrics that helps classify this existing body of knowledge. A taxonomy represents a model that is used to classify and understand a body of knowledge [13].

The classification used by our taxonomy was based on basic concepts of software measurement [10], [14],[3].

The remainder of this paper is organised as follows: Section 2 introduces our taxonomy, explaining terms and definitions that are part of this classification. Section 3 presents our literature review, which was based on 15 papers. Section 4 applies the proposed taxonomy to classify each of the papers from our literature review. In Section 5 we discuss the change in trends that have occurred in the area of hypermedia and Web metrics within the last 12 years. Finally, conclusions are presented in Section 6.

2 Size Metrics Taxonomy

The basis for the taxonomy we propose consists of software measurement concepts [10], [14] and literature in software size metrics and measurement [3].

Motivation: Describes the rationale for proposing a given size metric. Examples of motivation can be "to help author hypermedia applications", or "to estimate effort".

Harvesting Time: Describes when in the development life cycle the metric should be measured or estimated. This category can be simply "Early size metric" or "Late size metric", however a longer description can also be given whenever necessary (e.g. "Late size metric to be measured after the implementation is finished").

Metric Foundation: Describes whether the size metric is a Problem-orientated metric or a Solution-orientated metric [3].

- *Problem-Orientated Metric*: A problem-orientated metric assumes that an application size corresponds directly to the size of the problem to be solved in order to deliver a corresponding application. So, the greater the problem, the greater the size. In this context, the problem to be solved is denoted by the functionality of the application to be developed. Problem-orientated size metrics generally take the form of surrogate metrics of functionality. These metrics can be extracted from the specification or design documents. An example of a common problem-orientated metric is Function Points, which aims to measure the size of an application in terms of the amount of functionality within the application, as described by its proposed specification.
- *Solution-Orientated Metric*: In contrast, a solution-orientated metric assumes that an application's size corresponds to the actual delivered size of an application (e.g. Lines of code).

Class: Allows for the organisation of size metrics into either of three possible classes: Length, Complexity, and Functionality [10].

- *Length:* Measures the physical size of a hypermedia or Web application;
- *Functionality:* Measures the functions supplied by the application to the user;
- *Complexity:* Measures the structural complexity of a hyperdocument, where the structure of a hyperdocument is represented by the way nodes are interconnected by links.

According to the descriptions given above, we can say that the foundation for both length and complexity metrics is "solution-orientated", whereas the foundation for a functionality size metric is "problem-orientated".

Entity: Represents the product to which the size metric is associated. Possible values are "Web hypermedia application", "Web software application", "Web application", "Hypermedia application", "Hypertext application", "Media", "Program/Script".

- *Web Hypermedia Application [5]:* A non-conventional software application where chunks of information are generally text/images/video and the structure is static.
- *Web Software Application [5]:* A conventional software application that depends on the Web or uses the Web's infrastructure for execution (e.g. legacy information systems, e-commerce).
- *Web Application:* An application that combines characteristics of both Web software and Web hypermedia applications.
- *Media:* A multimedia component, e.g. graphic, audio, video, animation, photograph.
- *Program/Script:* Code employed to add functionality to an application (e.g. Perl scripts, javasrcipt).

Measurement Scale: Describes the nature of the mapping M from the empirical system to the numerical/symbolic system and determines what sort of manipulations we can apply to a metric. The five scales are Nominal, Ordinal, Interval, Ratio and Absolute [10], as follows:

- *Nominal:* Defines classes or categories, and places entities in a particular class or category, based on the value of the attribute.

- *Ordinal:* Augments the nominal scale with information about an ordering of classes or categories.
- *Interval:* Augments the ordinal scale with information about the size of the intervals that separate the classes.
- *Ratio:* Preserves ordering, the size of intervals between classes, and ratios between classes. Can have one or more associated unit(s) of measurement.
- *Absolute:* The metric always takes the form "number of occurrences of x in the entity E". Has associated only one unit of measurement.

Computation: Describes whether a size metric can be measured Directly or Indirectly [10]. Indirect measurement means that the metric is computed based on other metrics. Conversely, Direct measurement means that the size metric does not rely on other metrics in order to be measured.

Validation: Describes whether a size metric has been validated. Possible values are "validated Empirically", "validated Theoretically", "Both", and "None". This is similar to one of the criterion suggested by Calero et al. [4].

Model Dependency: Represents whether a size metric requires the use of a specific Web methodology or model in order to be measures. Possible values are "Specific", and "Nonspecific".

3 Literature Review of Hypermedia and Web Size Metrics

This Section presents a literature review of hypermedia and Web size metrics proposed within the past 12 years, described in chronological order. We have not detailed too much these metrics due to shortage of space.

3.1 1992 – Size Metrics by Botafogo et al.

Botafogo et al. [1] proposed size metrics to be used to help identify problems with the hyperdocument being created. Their focus was on the hyperdocument's navigation rather than on its content.

- *Compactness:* Measures how well connected (by links) a hyperdocument is. Its value varies between zero (completely disconnected) and one (completely connected).
- *Stratum:* Measures to what degree the hyperdocument is organised into a single reading path. Its value varies between zero (no imposed reading order) and one (single path).

3.2 1995 – Size Metrics by Yamada et al.

Yamada et al. [21] proposed size metrics to measure authoring and maintenance problems.

- *Interface Shallowness:* Cognitive load on users. Assumes that applications are structured hierarchically, each level corresponds to a cognitive "layer", and moving from one layer to another increases the cognitive load on users.

- *Downward Compactness:* Structural complexity of reaching the nth node from the root.
- *Downward Navigability:* Measures hypermedia navigability, where an easily navigable hypermedia application (1) has a shallow interface layer from the root to the nth node and (2) is compact from the root (that is, it is structurally simple to reach the nth node from the root).

3.3 1995 – Size Metrics by Hatzimanikatis et al.

Hatzimanikatis et al. [12] proposed size metrics to measure the readability and maintainability of hypermedia applications.

- *Path Complexity:* The number of different paths or cycles that can be found in a hyperdocument, assuming it to be a graph. The *path complexity* of a linear hyperdocument is minimal.
- *Tree Impurity:* The extent to which a graph deviates from being a tree.
- *Modularity:* Measures if the nodes are self-contained and independent.
- *Individual Node Complexity:* Complexity that a single node imposes on the overall structure.

3.4 1996 – Size Metrics by Bray

Bray [2] proposed size metrics to measure the size of Web applications.

- *Page Size:* Measured in three different ways:
  1. The sum of space used (Kbytes) by its Web pages (PS1);
  2. The sum of the number of words in its Web pages (PS2);
  3. The sum of the number of image references in its Web pages (PS3).
- *Outbound Connection:* Number of links that point to another Web application/site.
- *Inbound Connection:* Number of links from other applications pointing to application w.

3.5 1997 – Size Metrics by Fletcher et al.

Fletcher et al. [11] proposed size metrics to predict effort to develop multimedia applications[1].

- *Media Type:* Number of graphics, audio, video, animations, photographs.
- *Media Source:* If media is original or reused.
- *Component Duration:* Duration of an animation, sound or video.
- *Number of Objects* (including sounds): Number of objects on the screen.
- *Screen Connectivity:* Number of links between a screen and other screens.
- *Screen Events:* Number of events on a screen.
- *Actions per Event:* Average number of actions per event.

---

[1] Although this work targets at multimedia applications, the strong similarities allow for the same assessment to be applied to hypermedia applications

3.6 1998; 2000 – Size Metrics by Cowderoy

Cowderoy [7],[8] proposed size metrics to predict effort to develop Web applications.

Web application

- *Web Pages:* Number of Web pages in an application.
- *Home Pages:* Number of major entry points to the Web application.
- *Leaf Nodes:* Number of Web pages in an application that have no siblings.
- *Hidden Nodes:* Number of Web pages excluded from the main navigation buttons.
- *Depth:* Number of Web pages on the second level that have siblings.
- *Application Paragraph Count:* Number of PPC for all Web pages in an application.
- *Delivered Images:* Number of unique images used by the Web application.
- *Audio Files:* Number of unique audio files used in a Web application.
- *Application Movies:* Number of PMs for all the Web pages in an application.
- *3d Objects:* Number of files (inc;. 3D objects) used in a Web application.
- *Virtual Worlds:* Number of files (incl. virtual worlds) used in a Web application.
- *External Hyperlinks:* Number of unique URLs in the Web application.

Web page

- *Actions:* Number of independent actions by use of Javascript, Active X etc.
- *Page Paragraph Count (PPC):* Number of paragraphs in a Web page.
- *Word Count:* Number of words in a Web page.
- *Navigational Structures:* Number of different structures in a Web page.
- *Page Movies (PM):* Number of movie files used in a Web page.
- *Interconnectivity:* Number of URLs that link to other pages in the same application.

Media

- *Image Size (IS):* Computed as width * height.
- *Image Composites:* Number of layers from which the final image was created.
- *Language Versions:* Number of image versions that must be produced to accommodate different languages or different cultural priorities.
- *Duration:* Summed duration of all sequences within an audio file.
- *Audio Sequences:* Number of sequences within the audio file.
- *Imported Images:* Number of graphics images imported into an audio file.

Program

- *Lines of Source Code:* The number of lines of code in a program/script.
- *McCabe Ciclomatic Complexity:* The structural complexity of a program/script.

3.7 1999; 2000; 2001 – Size Metrics by Mendes et al.

Mendes et al. [16]-[18] proposed size metrics initially to estimate effort to develop Hypermedia applications [17] and later to estimate effort for Web applications [16],[18].

Hypermedia application

- *Hyperdocument Size:* Number of files (e.g. HTML files).
- Complexity
- *Connectivity:* Number of non-dynamically generated links within a hypermedia application.
- *Compactness:* Measures how inter-connected the nodes are.
- Stratum: Measures to what degree the application is organised for directed reading.
- *Link Generality:* Measures if the link applies to a single or multiple instances.

Web application

- *Page Count:* Number of HTML or SHTML files .
- *Media Count:* Number of unique media files.
- *Program Count:* The number of CGI scripts, JavaScript files, and Java applets.
- *Total Page Allocation:* Space (Mbytes) allocated for all HTML or SHTML pages.
- *Total Media Allocation:* Space (Mbytes) allocated for all media files.
- *Total Code Length:* Number of lines of code for all programs.
- *Reused Media Count:* Number of reused or modified media files.
- *Reused Program Count:* Number of reused or modified programs.
- *Total Reused Media Allocation:* Space (Mbytes).allocated for all reused media files.
- *Total Reused Code Length:* Number of lines of code for all reused programs.
- *Code Comment Length:* Number of comment lines in all programs.
- *Reused Code Length:* Number of reused lines of code in all programs.
- *Reused Comment Length:* Number of reused comment lines in all programs.
- *Total Page Complexity:* Average number of different types of media used, excluding text.
- *Connectivity:* Number of internal links, not including dynamically generated links.
- *Connectivity Density:* Computed as *Connectivity* divided by *page count*.
- *Cyclomatic Complexity:* Computed as *Connectivity -page count*) + 2.

Web page

- *Page Allocation:* Allocated space (Kbytes) of a HTML or SHTML file.
- *Page Complexity:* Number of different types of media used on a page, not including text.
- *Graphic Complexity:* Number of graphics media.
- *Audio Complexity:* Number of audio media.
- *Video Complexity:* Number of video media.
- *Animation Complexity:* Number of animations.
- *Scanned Image Complexity:* Number of scanned images.
- Complexity
- *Page Linking Complexity:* Number of links.

Media

- *Media Duration:* Duration (minutes).of audio, video, and animation
- *Media Allocation:* Size (Kbytes) of a media file.

Program

- *Program Code Length:* Number of lines of code in program.

3.8 2000 – Size Metrics by Rollo

Rollo [21] did not suggest any new size metrics. However, he was the first, as far as we know, to investigate the issues of measuring functionality of Web applications aiming at cost estimation, using numerous function point analysis methods.

- *Functional Size:* Number of function points associated with a Web application. Function points were measures using COSMIC-FFP[2], Mark II and Albrecht [21].

3.9 2000 – Size Metrics by Cleary

Cleary [6] proposed size metrics to estimate effort to develop Web applications.

Web hypermedia application

- *Non-textual Elements:* Number of unique non-textual elements within an application.
- *Externally Sourced Elements:* Number of externally sourced elements.
- *Customised Infra-structure Components:* Number of customised infra-structure components.
- *Total Web Points:* Size of a Web hypermedia application in Web points.

Web software application

- *Function Points:* Functionality of a Web software application.

Web page

- *Non-textual Elements Page:* Number of non-textual elements.
- *Words Page:* Number of words.
- *Web Points:* Length of a Web page. Scale points are "Low", "Medium" and "High". Each point is attributed a number of Web points, previously calibrated to a specific dataset.
- Complexity
- *Number of Links into a Web Page:* Number of incoming links (internal or external links).
- *Number of Links out of a Web Page:* Number of outgoing links (internal or external links).
- *Web Page Complexity:* Complexity of a Web page based upon its *number of words*, and combined *number of incoming* and *outgoing links*, plus the *number of non-textual elements*.

---

[2] COSMIC-FFP = COmmon Software Measurement International Consortium-Full Function Points

3.10   2000 – Size Metrics by Reifer

Reifer [20] proposed size metrics to be used to estimate effort to develop Web applications.

- *Web Objects:* The number of Web Objects in a Web application using Halstead's equation for volume, tuned for Web applications. The equation is as follows:

$$V = N \log_2(n) = (N_1 + N_2) \log_2 (n_1 + n_2) \tag{1}$$

where:

N = number of total occurrences of operands and operators
n = number of distinct operands and operators
N_1 = total occurrences of operand estimator
N_2 = total occurrences of operator estimators
n_1 = number of unique operands estimator
n_2 = number of unique operators estimators
V = volume of work involved represented as Web Objects

Operands are comprised of the following metrics:

- *Number of Building Blocks:* Number of components, e.g., Active X, DCOM, OLE.
- *Number of COTS:* Number of COTS components (including any wrapper code).
- *Number of Multimedia Files:* Number of multimedia files, except graphics files.
- *Number of Object or Application Points [7],[8]:* Number of object/application points etc.
- *Number of Lines:* Number of xml, sgml, html and query language lines.
- *Number of Web Components:* Number of applets, agents etc.
- *Number of Graphics Files:* Number of templates, images, pictures etc.
- *Number of Scripts:* Number of scripts for visual language, audio, motion etc.

3.11   2003 – Size Metrics by Mangia and Paiano

Mangia and Paiano proposed size metrics to estimate effort to develop Web applications modelled using the W2000 methodology [15].

Web application

- *Macro:* Macro-functions required by the user.
- *DEI:* Input data for each operation.
- *DEO:* Output data for each operation.
- *Entities:* Information entities which conceptually model the database.
- *AppLimit:* Application limit of each operation.
- *LInteraction:* Level of interaction various users of the application have in each operation.
- *Compatibility:* Compatibility between each operation and application's delivery devices.
- *TypeNodes:* Types of nodes which constitute the navigational structure.
- *Acessibility:* Accessibility associations and pattern of navigation between node types.

- *NavCluster:* Navigation cluster.
- *ClassVisibility:* Visibility that classes of users have of the navigational structure.
- *DeviceVisibility:* Visibility that delivery devices have of the navigational structure.

3.12 2003 – Size Metrics by Mendes et al.

Mendes et al. [19] proposed size metrics to estimate effort to develop Web applications.

- *Web Pages:* Number of Web pages in a Web application.
- *New Web Pages:* Number of Web pages created from scratch.
- *Customer Web Pages:* Number of Web pages provided by the customer.
- *Outsourced Web pages:* Number of outsourced Web pages.
- *Text Pages:* Number of text pages (A4 size) that had to be typed.
- *Electronic Text Pages:* Number of reused text pages in electronic format.
- *Scanned Text Pages:* Number of reused text pages that had to be scanned with OCR
- *New Images:* Number of new images/photos/icons/buttons created.
- *Electronic Images:* Number of reused images/photos in electronic format.
- *Scanned Images:* Number of reused images/photos that need to be scanned.
- *External Images:* Number of images obtained from an image/photo library or outsourced.
- *New Animations:* Number of new animations (Flash/gif/3D etc) created from scratch.
- *External Animations:* Number of reused animations (Flash/gif/3D etc).
- *New Audio:* Number of new audio/video clips created.
- *External Audio:* Number of reused audio/video clips.
- *High Fots:* Number of High-effort[3] features off-the-shelf (FOTS), i.e., reused as is.
- *High FotsA:* Number of High-effort FOTS adapted to local circumstances.
- *High New:* Number of new High-effort Feature/ Functionality developed from scratch.
- *Fots:* Number of Low-effort FOTS, i.e., reused as is.
- *FotsA:* Number of Low-effort FOTS adapted to local circumstances.
- *New:* Number of new Low-effort Feature/ Functionality developed from scratch.

4 Application of Taxonomy to Surveyed Size Metrics

This Section discusses the literature review presented in Section 3 in light of the taxonomy proposed in Section 2. In order to provide a more effective discussion, we have summarised the main findings from the literature review, presented as Table 1. The literature review was based on 15 studies, where 133 metrics were proposed in

---

[3] High effort means that a single feature used at least 12 person hours to be created from scratch or four person hours to be adapted

total. The detailed results for the application of the taxonomy to the size metrics can be downloaded from http://www.cs.auckland.ac.nz/~emilia/detailedtable.pdf.

Eleven studies (73%) proposed size metrics motivated by their use to estimate effort for developing applications. This suggests that, at least for the studies motivated towards effort estimation, size metrics should be harvested early in the development cycle to be of use for estimating effort and costs. However, out of the 109 metrics proposed for effort estimation, only 33 metrics (30%) are *Early* metrics, all of which were proposed by only two studies [19], [15]. Most of the proposed metrics are solution-orientated (83%) and length (62%) metrics. Thirteen (64%) metrics, out of a total of 19 functionality metrics, measure functionality using some of the function points analysis methods, and the remaining six base their measurement on a list of features/functions to be provided to customers at the start of the development [19].

Table 1. Summary of Literature review findings

Category	Values	studies	%
Motivation	Help author hypermedia applications	1	6.6%
	To give feedback on possible improvements that will lead to better authoring and maintenance	1	6.6%
	Measure readability and maintainability	1	6.6%
	to measure the size of Web applications	1	6.6%
	estimate effort to develop multimedia applications	1	6.6%
	to estimate effort to develop Web applications	9	60%
	to estimate effort to develop hypermedia applications	1	6.6%

Category	Values	metrics	%
Harvesting Time	Early	33	25%
	Late	100	75%
Metric foundation	Problem-orientated	23	17%
	Solution-orientated	110	83%
Class	Length	82	62%
	Functionality	19	14%
	Complexity	32	24%
Entity	Web software application	1	1%
	Web hypermedia application	4	3%
	Web application	76	57%
	Hypermedia application	14	11%
	Hypertext application	0	0%
	Web page	22	16%
	Media	11	8%
	Program/Script	5	4%
Measurement Scale	Nominal	4	3%
	Ordinal	4	3%
	Interval	0	0%
	Ratio	118	89%
	Absolute	7	5%
Computation	Direct	103	77%
	Indirect	30	23%
Validation	Empirically	69	52%
	Theoretically	0	0%
	Both	5	4%
	None	59	44%

Slightly more than half of proposed size metrics (57%) relate to the entity Web application, which suggests they can be used for static as well as dynamic Web applications. Only 38 size metrics (28%) are bottom-up metrics, allowing for the measurement of "parts" of an application (e.g. Web page, media). The remaining 72% target at the whole application, where application can either be hypermedia (11%), Web hypermedia (3%), Web software (1%), or Web (57%). The majority of metrics are measured on a ratio scale (89%), not surprising given that most metrics are solution-orientated. This is also reflected on the number of metrics that can be computed directly (77%), as opposed to indirectly (23%). A comparatively high number of metrics have been proposed without either empirical or theoretical validation (44%), which unfortunately makes their corresponding studies "advocacy research". Empirical and/or theoretical validation are fundamental to building our scientific knowledge [10]. Despite the small number of size metrics measured using either the nominal (3%) or ordinal scale (3%), researchers and practitioners alike should take care when applying these metrics since their measures cannot be employed arithmetically, without being in violation of the Representational Theory of measurement, a fundamental concept which is often ignored (e.g. [6], [20]).

5 Change in Trends

In the years 1992 to 1996 size was measured solely using complexity size metrics. In 1997 came the first publication that demonstrated the use of hypermedia/multimedia size metrics for cost estimation. From 1998 to 2000 more work was devoted to size metrics applicable to cost estimation; three of these were by industry practitioners [7],[8],[6],[20] who proposed metrics and exemplified their use with very small data sets or development practices from just one Web company for each practitioner. Regrettably, their findings may not be applicable to other Web companies work and practices and cannot be considered an empirical validation, so hampering the external and internal validity of their findings, respectively.

Except for [19] and [15], all size metrics proposed for cost estimation presented in Section 3 have been related to implemented Web applications, represented predominantly by solution-orientated size metrics. Even when targeted at measuring functionality based on function point analysis, researchers only considered the final Web application, rather than requirements documentation generated using existing Web development methods. This makes their usefulness as early effort predictors questionable. Except for Rollo [21], all literature cited in Section 3 employed at least one Solution-Orientated type of metric. This may be explained by the difficulty in using early size metrics, gathered at the start of the Web development life cycle.

Length and complexity metrics are classes used respectively by 62% and 24% of the 133 size metrics presented in Section 3. Functionality was used as a class of only 14% of the size metrics. The small amount of previous work using functionality size metrics may be explained by the fact that until recently the highest volume of Web applications developed used solely static pages, written in HTML, with graphics and Javascript. Therefore both researchers and practitioners would have focused on size metrics that were adequate for this type of Web application.

6 Conclusions

This paper presented a survey literature of hypermedia and Web size metrics published in the literature within the last 12 years, and classified the surveyed studies according to a proposed taxonomy.

Eleven studies proposed a total of 133 size metrics to be used for effort estimation. However, only 33 can be harvested early in development cycle, necessary criterion for estimating effort and costs. 83% and 68% of the metrics are solution-orientated and length metrics, respectively. Close to two-thirds of the functionality size metrics measure functionality using function points analysis methods. The other third uses a list of features/functions to be provided to customers at the start of the development. 89% of the metrics are measured on a ratio scale and 77% can be computed directly. 44% of the metrics have not been validated empirically or theoretically.

Regarding the change in trends we have observed that from 1996 onwards, the majority of size metrics were geared towards Web applications, rather than hypermedia applications, illustrating a shift in the focus not only from the research community but also by practitioners. Most size metrics were aimed at cost estimation, except for those proposed between 1992 and 1996.

Recent work [19],[20] showed that complexity size metrics do not seem to be as important as functionality and length size metrics. This may be due to the motivation behind the proposition of such metrics. However, it may also point towards a change in the characteristics of Web applications developed in the past, compared to those developed today. Many Web applications are moving to be "dynamic" applications, where pages are generated "on-the-fly". This may indicate that looking at an application's structure, represented by its links, ceases to be as important as in the past. This also explains the gradual exclusion of complexity size metrics from recent literature.

References

1. Botafogo, R., Rivlin, A.E. and Shneiderman, B. Structural Analysis of Hypertexts: Identifying Hierarchies and Useful Metrics, ACM TOIS,10(2), (1992), 143–179.
2. Bray, T. Measuring the Web. Proc. Fifth WWW Conference, May 6-10, Paris, France, (1996) http://www5conf.inria.fr/fich_html/papers/P9/Overview.html.
3. Briand, L.C., and Wieczorek, I. Software Resource Estimation. Encyclopedia of Sw. Eng., 2, P-Z (2nd ed.), Marciniak, John J. (ed.) NY: John Wiley & Sons, (2002),1160–1196.
4. Calero, C., Ruiz, J., and Piattini, M. A Web Metrics Survey Using WQM, Proceedings ICWE04, LNCS 3140, Springer-Verlag Heidelberg, (July 2004), (2004), 147–160.
5. Christodoulou, S. P., Zafiris, P. A., Papatheodorou, T. S. WWW2000: The Developer's view and a practitioner's approach to Web Engineering, Proc. 2nd ICSE Workshop Web Eng. (2000), 75–92.
6. Cleary, DWeb-based development and functional size measurement. Proc. IFPUG 2000 Conference, (2000).
7. Cowderoy, A.J.C., Donaldson, A.J.M., Jenkins, J.O. A Metrics framework for multimedia creation, Proc. 5th IEEE Metrics Symposium, Maryland, USA, (1998).
8. Cowderoy, A.J.C., Measures of size and complexity for web-site content, Proc. 11th ESCOM Conference, Munich, Germany, (2000), 423–431.
9. Dhyani, D., Ng, W.K., and Bhowmick, S.S. A survey of Web metrics, ACM Computing Surveys, 34(4), (December 2002), (2002), 469–503.
10. Fenton, N. E. and Pfleeger, S. L., Software Metrics, A Rigorous & Practical Approach, 2nd edition, PWS Publishing Company and International Thomson Computer Press, (1997).
11. Fletcher, T., MacDonell, S. G., and Wong, W. B. L. Early experiences in Measuring Multimedia Systems Development Effort. In: Multimedia Technology and Applications, Hong Kong: Springer-Verlag, (1997), 211–220.

12. Hatzimanikatis, A. E., Tsalidis, C. T., and Chistodoulakis, D. Measuring the Readability and Maintainability of Hyperdocuments, J. of Software Maintenance, Research and Practice, 7, (1995), 77–90.
13. IEEE, Standard Taxonomy for Software Engineering Standards (ANSI). The Institute of Electrical and Electronics Engineers Inc., (1986).
14. Kitchenham, B.A., Hughes, R.T., and Linkman, S.G. Modeling software measurement data, IEEE TSE, 27, 9, (Sept. 2001), (2001), 788–804.
15. Mangia, L., and Paiano, R. MMWA: A Software Sizing Model for Web Applications, Proc. WISE'03, (2003).
16. Mendes, E., and Mosley, N.. Web Metrics and Development Effort Prediction, Proc. ACOSM 2000, (2000).
17. Mendes, E., Hall, W., Harrison, R. Applying measurement principles to improve hypermedia authoring, NRHM, 5, Taylor Graham Publishers, (1999),105–132.
18. Mendes, E., Mosley, N., and Counsell, S. Web Metrics – Estimating Design and Authoring Effort. IEEE Multimedia, Special Issue on Web Engineering, Jan.-Mar., (2001), 50–57.
19. Mendes, E., Mosley, N., and Counsell, S. Investigating Early Web Size Measures for Web Costimation, Proc. EASE'2003 Conference, Keele University, (2003).
20. Reifer, D.J. Web development: estimating quick-to-market software. IEEE Software, (Nov/Dec), (2000), 57–64.
21. Rollo, T. Sizing e-commerce. Proc. ACOSM 2000, Sydney, Australia, (2000).
22. Yamada, S., Hong, J., and Sugita, S. Development and Evaluation of Hypermedia for Museum Education: Validation of Metrics, ACM Transactions on Computer-Human Interaction, 2(4), (1995), 284–307.

Identifying Websites with Flow Simulation

Pierre Senellart[1,2]

[1] École normale supérieure, 45 rue d'Ulm, F-75230 Paris Cedex 05, France
[2] INRIA Futurs, 10 rue Jacques Monod, F-91893 Orsay Cedex, France
pierre@senellart.com

Abstract. We present in this paper a method to discover the set of webpages contained in a logical website, based on the link structure of the Web graph. Such a method is useful in the context of Web archiving and website importance computation. To identify the boundaries of a website, we combine the use of an online version of the preflow-push algorithm, an algorithm for the maximum flow problem in traffic networks, and of the Markov CLuster (MCL) algorithm. The latter is used on a crawled portion of the Web graph in order to build a seed of initial webpages, a seed which is extended using the former. An experiment on a subsite of the INRIA Website is described.

1 Introduction

Though the notion of *website* is commonly understood, there is no simple formal definition of it. The most obvious idea would be to define a *logical website* as the set of pages hosted by a given server. Though correct for many websites, it does not reflect their intuitive notion since some may span over several servers, and servers may host various sites.

The problem of discovering the boundaries between logical websites occurs in the topic of automatic Web archiving, that some instituions (e.g. national libraries) want to perform [1]: once webpages are selected to be archived, what is the boundary of the corresponding websites? To be able to define websites could also lead to *website importance* computation: to devise a *SiteRank* for websites, as *PageRank* [2] is defined for webpages.

The method for website identification we present in this paper heavily relies on the (directed) graph structure of the Web, with webpages as nodes and hyperlinks as edges. The fundamental assumption is that webpages in the same website are much more connected between them than webpages from different websites. We use an adaptation and combination of two algorithms related to flow simulation in traffic networks: a *preflow-push* algorithm by Goldberg [3] which solves the maximum flow problem and the *Markov CLuster algorithm* (abbreviated as *MCL*) by van Dongen [4], a graph clustering algorithm. MCL is used to cluster a part of the Web in order to build *seeds* of websites which are extended to complete logical websites with the preflow-push algorithm. The techniques used are not based on the concept of webservers, domain names or other heuristics, like traditional website recognition methods, but on the link structure of the Web graph and, secondarily, on the global form of the URLs.

D. Lowe and M. Gaedke (Eds.): ICWE 2005, LNCS 3579, pp. 124–129, 2005.

We show in Section 2 how flow simulation and the maximum flow problem may be used to identify websites in the Web graph. We notice that in many cases, the seed of webpages the simulation starts from needs to be extended; we present thus a way to use MCL for that purpose. An experiment is presented in Section 3. Finally, we discuss related works in Section 4. **An extended version of this paper is available in [5].**

2   Website Identification Process

In this section, we present an algorithm to solve the *maximum flow/ minimum cut* problem, namely the preflow-push algorithm, and its online adaptation to the Web. This algorithm is applied to extend a seed of webpages into a complete logical website. Then we briefly introduce MCL, a graph clustering algorithm, which is used to grow the initial seed of webpages. We finally describe our complete website identification process.

Preflow-Push Algorithm. We assume that the reader is familiar with the *maximum flow/minimum cut* problem. An introduction to this topic can be found in [6]. Let $T = (S, c, s, t)$ be a traffic network, where S is the set of nodes, $c : S^2 \rightarrow \mathbb{R}_+$ the capacity function, s the source node and t the sink node. The preflow-push algorithm is based on the notion of *preflow*: a *preflow* in T is a function $f : S^2 \rightarrow \mathbb{R}$ which satisfies:

(i)   (*Symmetry*) $\forall (u, v) \in S^2, f(u, v) = -f(v, u)$
(ii) (*Capacity constraint*) $\forall (u, v) \in S^2, f(u, v) \leq c(u, v)$
(iii) (*Relaxed flow conservation*) $\forall u \in S \setminus \{s, t\}, \sum_{v \in S} f(u, v) \leq 0$

This definition means that, in a preflow, a node u can have some *overflow* $o(u) = -\sum_{v \in S} f(u, v)$: it can receive more from the nodes it is pointed by than it sends to the nodes it points to. The preflow-push algorithm, as well as other algorithms working with preflows, maintains at each step a preflow in T, converging finally toward a flow in T which is maximal, thus solving the *maximum flow/minimum cut* problem.

All nodes are assigned a height (0 in the beginning for all nodes except the source). At each iteration, the preflow is *pushed* from a node with overflow to a lower node. If there are no lower nodes to unload a node with overflow, this node is *raised*. The algorithm ends when there are no nodes with overflow any longer. This algorithm can be demonstrated to converge toward a maximum flow in T (cf [3]), with a complexity of $O(|S|^2|A|)$ ($|A|$ is the number of edges with non-zero capacity), whatever the strategy for selecting nodes with overflow.

Adaptation to the Web. The fundamental assumption of website identification based on the graph structure of the Web is that webpages in the same website are much more connected between them than webpages from different websites. If the Web is seen as a traffic network in which some fluid flows from a set of source nodes in the same website, the bottleneck of the flow should not be inside the website, where there are many internal connections (and thus, a large capacity), but between the website and the rest of the Web, where the connections are much more sparse.

The idea behind using flow simulation to identify websites is that a clear cut should be visible between a "source of seed webpages" of a site and a "sink for the remaining part of the Web", a cut which would match the borders of the website. This cut is computed as a minimum cut in a traffic network whose underlying graph is the Web graph. More formally, let $Seed$ be a set of seed webpages, characteristic of the website we would like to compute the borders of, and sim a similarity function over webpages. We consider the traffic network $T_{Seed} = (S, c, s, t)$ where:

- S is the set of webpages in the World Wide Web, along with two virtual nodes s (a virtual source) and t (a virtual sink).
- (i) For all $(u, v) \in (S \setminus \{s, t\})^2$, $c(u, v) = sim(u, v)$ if there is a link from u to v, $c(u, v) = 0$ otherwise.
  (ii) For all $u \in Seed$, $c(s, u) = +\infty$
  (iii) For all $u \in S \setminus \{s, t\}$, $c(u, t) = \varepsilon$ ($\varepsilon << 1$)

The choice of the similarity function is important. The most simple choice would be to use a constant function. In this case, however, a cut separating the seed webpages from the rest would be most likely minimal. We chose to use a function of the edit distance between the URLs of the webpages: even if a website span over several webservers, the URLs of the pages tend to look similar.

On-line Preflow-Push. Classical graph and network algorithms are *off-line*: they require that the entire matrix is stored, so that computations can be made on it. In the context of the Web, *on-line* algorithms are more interesting. An on-line algorithm on the Web graph is an algorithm which does not require the storage of the entire matrix of the graph, and in which computations are made progressively, at the same time webpages are crawled. The preflow-push algorithm can be made on-line in a straightforward way: webpages with overflow are progressively crawled and dealt with (pushed or raised). Several strategies adapted to crawling can be chosen. We decided to use a greedy one: the node with maximum overflow is selected at each step.

Seed Extension with Graph Clustering. Applying this version of the preflow-push algorithm on a seed of characteristic webpages of a website gives quite good results on small or medium-sized, well-organized, websites. When the website is very large or not well organized, however, the algorithm only retrieves a small proportion of the webpages of the real website (cf Table 1). The problem is that a small seed is not sufficient to discover the entire website.

MCL is a graph clustering algorithm by van Dongen [4]: given an undirected graph as input, MCL will output a set of densely connected *clusters* of nodes. Based on an alternation of *expansion* and *inflation* of the graph matrix, MCL does not require any strong condition on the graph. The reader is advised to refer to [4] or [5] for a more detailed description. MCL is used to extend the seed the on-line preflow-push starts from. The entire process is shown below.

Process for Identifying a Website W

1. Find a superset S of a large part of W (S may be, for instance, the set of webpages hosted by the main webserver for W); crawl and build the corresponding subgraph G_S of the Web graph.
2. Cluster G_S using MCL on the underlying undirected graph G'_S (there is an edge (u, v) in G'_S if and only if either (u, v) or (v, u) is in G_S).
3. Find the obtained cluster K which is the most relevant to W. It may be identified by finding the cluster which contains the largest number of URLs containing some given keyword.
4. Use the on-line preflow-push algorithm with K as a seed. The resulting set of pages is the logical website for W found by the process.

---

3   Experiment

Our main experiment was on the website of our research team, GEMO (other experiments are described in [5]). Its entry point is http://www-rocq.inria.fr/verso/ (VERSO is the former name for GEMO) and it spans over several webservers, of the inria.fr domain and of other domains.

A large part of the webpages hosted on webservers of the inria.fr domain was crawled. Following the process described in Section 2, a MCL clustering was performed on the underlying undirected graph. The most relevant cluster was identified as the one with the largest number of URLs containing "verso". Finally, flow simulation with preflow-push gave the resulting logical GEMO website.

Table 1 shows some data about the website found by the algorithm, along with results of other simpler methods[1]:

- **Flow Simulation**: direct on-line preflow-push, starting from the website entry page.
- **MCL**: clusters from MCL, without flow simulation
- **MCL + Flow Simulation**: process described above
- http://www-rocq.inria.fr/verso/*: "naive" recursive crawl of the hierarchy of URLs starting from the website entry page.

As noted in Section 2, flow simulation alone retrieves a very small portion of the relevant webpages, whereas MCL effectively retrieves many more webpages, which are nearly all relevant (that is, the precision is very high). The recall for MCL clusters is still low, however; this is why the online preflow-push is applied afterwards. The complete process gives a good precision (over 90%) and especially gives a high recall, much higher than all the other methods. This shows the

---

[1] Precision and recall are defined as follows: the precision of a set of webpages W is the ratio of relevant webpages in W over the size of W; the recall of a set of webpages W is the ratio of relevant webpages in W over the total number of relevant webpages

Table 1. GEMO website, according to different methods

	Number of Pages	Precision	Recall
Flow Simulation	8	87.5%	1.3%
MCL	320	99.7%	33.0%
MCL + Flow Simulation	788	90.4%	86.4%
`http://www-rocq.inria.fr/verso/*`	221	100%	44.4%

interest of the combination of flow simulation and graph clustering techniques, over each technique alone. The naive technique naturally has a perfect precision but a rather low recall: there is indeed a need for more elaborate website identification methods, such as the one we used.

The results of our experiment on the GEMO cluster are thus very satisfactory. It is to be noted, though, that this does not represent the relative performance of the different techniques on every website. On smaller or more organized ones, the online preflow-push algorithm alone may be sufficient. On many websites, the naive recursive crawl of the hierarchy of URLs may even be perfect. Still, a large part of the Web is composed of not-so-well organized websites, spanning over several webservers, like the GEMO website.

4   Related Work

In most works where the notion of website appears, it is taken to be the pages hosted by a given webserver, or a lexical hierarchy of URLs (e.g. the set of URLs that share a common prefix), in addition to heuristics such as the recognition of /~user/ part in an URL. Links between pages are usually only taken into account in an elementary way, such as in [7] where *clan graphs* are introduced to find closely connected pages. In that paper, websites are still assumed to be on a single webserver and much importance is given in the form of the URLs. In [8], Mathieu proposes a way to partition the Web by using the fact that the matrix of the Web graph in which URLs are lexically ordered is nearly block diagonal. Each block seems to correspond to a logical website, heavily connected inside and sparsely connected with other webpages.

The maximum flow problem in traffic networks is a classical and much studied algorithmic problem. Karzanov developed the notion of *preflow* [9] and Goldberg invented the preflow-push algorithm [3]. Flake et al [10] use a modified version of the preflow-push algorithm on the Web graph in a similar way as we do, for identifying Web communities. Beside the purpose, our approach differs in the on-line adaptation of the preflow-push algorithm, in the choice of the capacity of the edges and in the use of an extended seed.

5   Conclusion

We presented in this paper a website identification process, based on a combination of flow simulation and graph clustering. The preflow-push algorithm, which solves the maximum flow problem in a traffic network, was adapted to the case of the World Wide Web. Logical websites are discovered by computing the minimum cut between a set of seed webpages and the rest of the Web, a seed which is computed using the Markov CLuster algorithm.

The first obvious perspective on this topic would be to improve the performance of the process, both in its execution time and in the quality of its results. Currently, the graph clustering needs to be computed on an off-line, crawled, subgraph of the Web, which can take a few days for a large graph, in order not to overload the corresponding webservers. It would thus be very useful to be able to realize an on-line computation of MCL. The adaptation is not obvious, especially because of the behavior of the inflation operator, which cannot be easily expressed in terms of classical linear algebra operators. Other improvements could be made on the online preflow-push algorithm, in particular with the choice of an efficient crawling strategy. Finally, a semi-automatic method, with the possibility of splitting and merging selected MCL clusters, would allow a more precise selection of the website to identify.

We would like to acknowledge Serge Abiteboul and Grégory Cobéna for their advice on this research topic.

References

1. Abiteboul, S., Cobéna, G., Massanes, J., Sadrati, G.: A first experience in archiving the French Web. In: Proceedings of the European Conference on Digital Libraries. (2002)
2. Page, L., Brin, S., Motwani, R., Winograd, T.: The pagerank citation ranking: Bringing order to the web. Technical report, Stanford Digital Library Technologies Project (1998)
3. Goldberg, A.V., Tarjan, R.E.: A new approach to the maximum-flow problem. Journal of the ACM **35** (1988) 921–940
4. van Dongen, S.M.: Graph Clustering by Flow Simulation. PhD thesis, University of Utrecht (2000)
5. Senellart, P.: Identifying websites with flow simulation. Technical Report 387, Gemo, INRIA Futurs, Orsay, France (2005)
   `ftp://ftp.inria.fr/INRIA/Projects/gemo/gemo/GemoReport-387.ps.gz`.
6. Cormen, T.H., Leiserson, C.E., Rivest, R.L.: Introduction to Algorithms. The MIT Electrical Engineering and Computer Science Series. The MIT Press / McGraw-Hill Book Company (1990)
7. Terveen, L., Hill, W., Amento, B.: Constructing, organizing, and visualizing collections of topically related Web resources. ACM Transactions on Computer-Human Interaction **6** (1999) 67–94
8. Mathieu, F.: Mesures d'Importance à la PageRank. PhD thesis, Université Montpellier II (2004)
9. Karzanov, A.V.: Determing the maximal flow in a network by the method of preflows. Soviet Mathematics Doklady **15** (1974) 434–437
10. Flake, G., Lawrence, S., Giles, C.L.: Efficient identification of Web communities. In: Sixth ACM SIGKDD International Conference on Knowledge Discovery and Data Mining, Boston, MA (2000) 150–160

An Increase Web Services Performance Method

Whe Dar Lin

The Overseas Chinese Institute of Technology, Dept of Information Management,
No. 100, Chiao Kwang Road, Taichung 40721, Taiwan
darlin@ocit.edu.tw

Abstract. In this paper, our loading balance processes electronic commerce transactions to increase Web services performance. Our method includes a loading balance value to resolve the concurrent data problem among EC services databases Web systems. In the new algorithm proposed here, a loading evaluation is introduced and utilized to make the efficiency of the result. The simulation results show that our system outperforms existing schedulers such as branch and bound algorithm, and the shifting bottleneck heuristic when an application requires an EC transaction model. We have analyzed a variety of transaction schemes compatible with other kinds of protocol standards and developed a modeling framework on which we can selectively extract the merits of these schemes while maintaining good consistency. Simulation results show that our system outperforms existing schedulers such as throughput and commit time when an application requires an EC transaction model. The electronic commerce transactions hype has barely subsided, the media, venture capitalists, and stock markets have already moved on to the mobile Internet. Knowing a change is coming is loading balance, predicting its shape and form for electronic commerce transactions to increase Web services performance on PC-centric models to mobile and person-centric techniques.

1 Introduction

The structure of computing is changing. EC Web systems rely increasingly on the coupling of local applications with applications running on remote Web servers. Assisted with low-power, low-cost, and portable computing Web systems such as laptops and personal digital assistants (PDAs), real-time agents can now work anywhere at any time. Mobility and portability do pose challenges to database management and EC transactions on EC Web systems, for they require the use of real-time information services designed to provide coherent and reliable information access to wide varieties of data originating from separate information sources in order to support greater workgroups and achieve better organizational productivity. In the EC era, there is a general trend towards the partnership in between EC Web systems so as to ensure better EC transaction application efficacy and efficiency [1, 3, 7, 11, 16].

The ultimate goal is to provide a richer and more user-friendly environment of information by integrating the user's desktop facilities with information exchange and collaboration infrastructures including groupware Web systems and shared database servers. In a business setting, these information services are typically part of a real-time database management system [2, 4, 6, 8, 11, 12].

The multi-channel customer revolution coupled with the development of mobile technology in its to have a profound effect. A commercial deal usually involves sev-

D. Lowe and M. Gaedke (Eds.): ICWE 2005, LNCS 3579, pp. 130–135, 2005.

eral transactions including the transfer of contract documents, billing, and settlement of payment. Sometimes several transactions need to be integrated, as when billing and settlement are to be processed at the same time [13, 14, 15, 16].

Where the uncertainty lies is in precisely when and how loading will be imposed and which will emerge as EC transactions. Evolutionary methods have been applied to a variety of different problems. In this paper, an algorithm for EC transaction management based on an evolutionary model is proposed. This novel algorithm generates a loading balance value for the purpose of improving the responsiveness to EC transactions on the Internet Web servers while maintaining a reasonable degree of queueing performance in case of a buffer overflow. Our simulation results have demonstrated the effectiveness of the proposed algorithm and proved the superiority over other algorithms. As a wish, the nature of interaction and speed is bound to change of transaction [5, 9, 10].

2 Our Model

The adoption of mobile technological innovation by the transaction world is seldem a neat, linear process. In our evolutionary model, the reinforcements can be either positive or negative, depending on whether the realized channel cost is greater or less than what the EC services need. Given the evolutionary approach method set A_i of EC agent i, where $A_i = \{a_{i,1}, a_{i,2}, a_{i,3}, \cdots, a_{i,Mi}\}$ respectively, there are alternative pure evolutionary approach to be performed by EC agent i, (i = 1, ..., M). EC agent i at each period uses an evolutionary approach method, and the state of the system in period t is denoted by $S_{t,i}$.

Note that here in this place $S_{t,i} = (S_{t,i}(a_{i,1}), S_{t,i}(a_{i,2}), S_{t,i}(a_{i,3}), ..., S_{t,i}(a_{i,Mi}))$ is the probability distribution of the evolutionary approach method set A_i in period t by EC agent i. If EC agent i plays evolutionary method $S_{t,i}$ in period t, then the resultant loading balance value is $S_{LV}(t, i, a_{t,i}, S_D)$. The EC agent's communication channel cost is denoted by $S_{MV}(t, i, a_{t,i}, S_D)$, and we set the loading balance value as $S_{BV}(t, i, a_{t,i}, S_D)$ $= S_{LV}(t, i, a_{t,i}, S_D) - S_{MV}(t, i, a_{t,i}, S_D)$. The S_D value is $\max(a_{i,k}, a_{i,t})$. Then, for i = 1,...,N and k =1, 2,...,Mi, the system state evolves in the following way:

$$S_{t+1,i}(a_{k,i}) = S_D * S_{BV}(t,i,a_{t,i},S_D) + (1 + |S_B(t,i,a_{t,i},S_D)|) * S_{t,i}(a_{k,i}) \quad (1)$$

Thus, it can be seen that if $S_{BV}(t, i, a_{t,i}, S_D)$ is positive, that means the EC agent is pleased with the outcome, and then the probability associated with the strategy will increase. In our proposed algorithm, EC transactions can be calculated in terms of link capacity, buffer size, queue length, etc. In addition, we can even update the switching function on the arrival of every transaction.

The key idea behind our proposed algorithm is to update the switching probability according to the loading strategy rather than the instantaneous or average loading weight, maintaining a single probability $S_{PV}(t, i, a_{t,i}, S_D)$ to transfer enqueued transactions.

I: Computing Switching Function

$$S_{SV}(t,i,e_{t,i},S_D) = (S_{BV} - (S_{TV} - S_{LV}(t,i,a_{t,i},S_D)))/S_{BV} \quad (2)$$

The system loading value in period t is denoted by $S_{LV}(t, i, e_{t,i}, S_D)$. We set a loading weight threshold, S_{TV}.

II: Computing Moving Probability

$$S_{SV}(t+1, i, a_{t+1,i}, S_D) = S_{PV}(t, i, a_{t,i}, S_D) * S_{BV}(t, i, a_{t,i}, S_D) \\ + S_{SV}(t, i, a_{t,i}, S_D) \tag{3}$$

This result can be derived from equations listed in Sect. 3. Thus, when the outcome satisfies the EC transaction services, the loading probability is increased. However, the switching probability is increased when the EC services are dissatisfied.

In the next section, we shall present our simulation results on our proposed algorithm and see how it compares with other algorithms in the same network environment. We will show the validity and features of our proposed EC services algorithm.

III: Our Loading Balance Method

1: Offspring generation.
2: EC system loading increase.
3: New parent selection among loading balance value.
4: Loading balance value updating.
5: Satisfied output the parents and loading balance value.

3 Our Loading Balance Method Performance

Certain media on Internet portray the transition to the mobile services. It prevents other transactions from accessing a shared data object before transaction is done. Simulation results show that our system outperforms such existing schedulers as branch and bound algorithm and the shifting bottleneck heuristic when an application requires an EC transaction model.

(1) Branch and bound algorithm: Branch and bound algorithm is enumerative search procedures based on construction of a tree of partial solutions. The tree contains entire set of feasible solutions in the leaves, while nodes inside the tree represent partial solution.
(2) Shifting bottleneck heuristic: The shifting bottleneck heuristic takes advantage of that scheduling problem with release time can be solved by bottleneck identification.
(3) Loading Balance Method: Our new scheduler is an evolutionary model to dynamically implement available transaction strategies by employing a loading balance value.

The offered value refers to the value given by the application when a transaction is submitted, and the final-obtained value indicates the net value after the transaction is successfully completed.

We examined real-time EC transactions under various conditions. According to the metrics of Commit times and throughput, the loading balance method has the best performance for distributed EC Web services using EC transaction models. In this experiment, we varied the arrival rate from 1 transactions/second to 5 trans/sec. Channel availability is number of bandwidth for EC transactions.

Table 1. Commit time simulation results of different method

Scheduler	Commit time (millisec)				
(Channel availability)	0.4	0.6	0.8	1	1.2
Branch and bound algorithm	195	175	130	100	90
Shifting bottleneck heuristic	215	200	170	135	105
Loading balance method	165	140	115	75	50

Table 2. Throughput simulation results of different method

Scheduler	Throughput (transaction/sec)				
(Channel availability)	0.4	0.6	0.8	1	1.2
Branch and bound algorithm	0.10	0.10	0.15	0.15	0.15
Shifting bottleneck heuristic	0.10	0.10	0.10	0.10	0.15
Loading balance method	0.20	0.25	0.30	0.30	0.35

Tables 1 and 2 show commit time and throughput results for EC services transactions. The performance orders are Loading balance method > Branch and bound algorithm> Shifting bottleneck heuristic, respectively.

The reason is that branch and bound algorithm and shifting bottleneck heuristic are both designed for a centralized case, and the impact of communication delays is not considered a scheduling factor. Such a phenomenon will frequently occur, as the traffic load gets higher. Branch and bound algorithm and shifting bottleneck heuristic perform poorly in commit time because they do not consider transaction relations. The performance of loading balance method is good at a high load because its scheduling policy in the under an overload situation.

Simulation results show that our system outperforms the others on throughput, and commit time. An EC transaction based on loading balance method, to each transaction resides in the ready queue with the highest will be executed. The appropriate setting for the communication delay of the real time transactions can meet their loading balance value on time under the simulation results.

The reasons for the superiority of loading balance method over the other algorithms are as follows. To begin with, the consideration of the loading characteristic in Web services gives a higher weight in the formula in the evolutionary model at the arrival of a transaction, since such a transaction requires an expensive cost for accessing data objects in the database.

However, the loading policy also depends on the reward ratio and loading balance value as well as the slack time of the system. In addition, the communication delays in loading balance method will result in a slightly higher weight for a remote transaction; hence, a local transaction will have a better chance to be executed completely under the adjustment of a transaction's reward ratio. Furthermore, loading balance method also takes care of the relations between transactions, taking into account the concept of slack time distribution.

4 Conclusion

Now, it is a portal to cyberspace an entry point to a worldwide network of information exchange and business transactions. We have presented a loading balance method to handle EC transactions on EC services systems for penetrate most areas of our daily life. Our loading balance method processes electronic commerce transactions to increase Web services performance only very limited support for processing Web content. Our loading balance method adjusts the transaction blocking probability according to the value of the switching function and its loading balance value.

Using loading balance method can enable the EC Web server to adapt to various network conditions and traffic characteristics intelligently and integration of data, information, knowledge, process and applications within business. Our results show that our system outperforms others on throughput and commit time, it beats such schedulers as branch and bound algorithm and the shifting bottleneck heuristic when an application requires an EC transaction model as enterprise resource planning from different product of implementing one link per supplier can be linked to a marketplaces.

Our loading balance method prevents the queue from turning into overflow and decreases the loss rate due to buffer overflow for reasons of cost and quality to adopt product as customer relationship management. Our loading balance method responses rapidly to the changes of the network load by adjusting the switching probability quickly within existing corporate information technology infrastructures solution. In this paper can be further developed into a set of networks that will help identify the best design alternative for high balance loading management based on the characteristics and parameters of given real time transactions on EC service applications as merge often require large-scale integration of existing information technology infrastructures. We shall focus on the development of new Web-base service management methods with QoS and differentiated service support for mobile services more openness, flexibility and dynamics.

References

1. Abbott, R. and Garcia-Molina, H. "Scheduling EC transactions." ACM SIGMOD Record 17(1):71-81, 1988.
2. B.Krishnam urthy and J.Rexford, Web protocols and practice: HTTP/1.1, networking protocols, caching, and traffic measurement, 1st ed., Addison Wesley, 2001.
3. D. Friedman, "On economic applications of evolutionary game theory," J. Evolutionary Economics, vol.8, no.1, pp.15–43, 1998.
4. El-Sayed, A.A., Hassanein, H.S., and El-Sharkawi, M.E. "Effect of shaping characteristics on the performance of transactions." Information and Software Technology 43(10): 579-590,2001.
5. E. Zitzler, K. Deb, and L. Thiele, "Comparison of multiobjective evolutionary algorithms: Empirical results," Evolutionary Computation, vol.8, no.2, pp.173–195, 2000.
6. Haritsa, J.R., Ramamritham, K., and Gupta, R. "The PROMPT real-time commit protocol." IEEE Trans. Parallel and Distributed Systems 11(2):160-181, 2000.
7. Huang, J. and Stankovic, J. "Real-Time Buffer Management." COINS TR 90-65. 1990.
8. H.Zh u and T.Y ang, "Cachuma: Class-based cache management for dynamic web content," Proc. IEEE INFOCOM 2001, pp.1215–1224, 2001.
9. J. Knowles and D.W. Corne, "Approximating the nondominated front using the Pareto archived evolution strategy," Evolutionary Computation, vol.8, no.2, pp.149–172, 2000.
10. J. W. Weibull, Evolutionary Game Theory, The MIT Press, 1995.
11. K. K. Leung, Y. Levy, "Global Mobility Management by Replicated Databases in Personal Communication Networks," IEEE Journal on selected areas in communications, Vol. 15, No. 8, pp1582-1596, 1997.

12. M. Arlitt and T. Jin, "Workload characterization of the 1998 world cup web site," IEEE Network, vol.14, no.3, pp.30–37, 2000.
13. M. Karam and F. Tobagi, "Rate and queue control random drop (RQRD): A buffer management scheme for Internet routers," Proc. Globecom'00, vol.1, no.1, pp.316–322, San Francisco, CA, Nov. 2000.
14. R. Pan, B. Prabhakar, and K. Psounis, "CHOKe: A stateless active queue management scheme for approximating fair bandwidth allocation," Proc. IEEE Infocom'00, vol.2, no.1, pp.942–951, March 2000.
15. U. Bodin, O. Schelen, and S. Pink, "Load-tolerant differentiation with active queue management," SIGCOMM Computer Communication Review, vol.30, no.3, pp.4–16, July 2000.
16. Whe Dar Lin, "EC Transactions Use Different Web-based Web systems," Lecture Notes in Computer Science, LNCS-2658, pp1059-1068, 2003.

A System of Patterns for Web Navigation

Mohammed Abul Khayes Akanda and Daniel M. German

Department of Computer Science, University of Victoria, Canada
maka@alumni.uvic.ca, dmgerman@uvic.ca

Abstract. In this paper we propose a system of design patterns for Web naviga-tion. We have collected patterns already published in the literature, selected ten of them, refined them and identified the relationships among them. The selected patterns are rewritten in the Gang of Four (GoF) notation. They are implemented and integrated together leading to a framework intended to be used as the central part in developing data intensive Web applications.

1 Introduction

Compared to software engineering –where there are several published books with de-sign patterns– hypermedia design patterns are in an early stage: they are scattered in the literature and they have barely been scrutinized. Paolini and Garzotto stated [13] "we have not seen many real 'booklets' of design patterns, ready to be used". The number of hypermedia design patterns keeps growing and it is becoming more difficult to keep track of them, to know whether there is a pattern that solves a determined problem, and, if there exists, to find it. In [9], we argued that it was necessary to:

- Unify the patterns. Some patterns provide insight that can enhance similar patterns. Some patterns provide different views of the same problem and they should be unified into a single super pattern including all the insights provided by the patterns individually.
- Patterns should be rewritten using a common pattern language and vocabulary. The hypermedia designers in general have not decided on a common vocabulary and this is reflected in the pattern descriptions.
- Patterns don't exist in isolation. There are many interdependencies between the patterns. A list of patterns doesn't reflect those relationships, and doesn't provide any guideline for their implementation. It also doesn't show how the patterns may evolve. Patterns should be organized into pattern systems. Buschmann et al. [4] de-fined a pattern system in the scope of software architecture. Their definition can be easily adapted to hypermedia application: a pattern system is a collection of pat-terns, together with guidelines for their implementation, combination and practical use in hypermedia development.

In this paper, we describe a system of patterns for Web navigation. Different authors are classifying the published patterns from different perspectives. But so far, there was no formalized system of patterns for hypermedia design patterns. Section 2 describes how we have created a system of patterns from the navigational hypermedia design patterns leading to develop a framework, implementing the patterns included in this

D. Lowe and M. Gaedke (Eds.): ICWE 2005, LNCS 3579, pp. 136–141, 2005.

system, intended to be used for the creation of data intensive Web applications. Section 3 describes the benefits of creating system of patterns and rewriting the patterns in Gamma notation.

2   A System of Patterns for Web Navigation

Our objective was to create a system of patterns for information navigation in hypermedia applications. According to Buschmann et al. [4] a system of patterns should satisfy the following requirements: it should (1) comprise a sufficient base of patterns, (2) describe all the patterns included in the system in a uniform notation, (3) expose the various relationships among the patterns, (4) organize its constituent patterns, (5) support the construction of hypermedia systems, (6) support its own evolution.

In particular, we wanted to concentrate in design patterns that would help address the following navigational problems: (1) making information easy to explore, (2) helping users to find the desired information quickly, (3) providing multiple navigation paths for different users, and (4) assisting users in knowing the current position in navigation.

We have found 96 hypermedia design patterns published in the literature and organized them in [3]. From these, we selected the following most frequently used navigational design patterns in web information systems or in data intensive web applications, based on behavioral relationships among the pattern which is described in Section 2.1: *Active Reference*[1, 8, 12, 14], *Guided Tour*[1], *Landmark*[15], *News*[1, 5, 11], *Set-Based Navigation*[1, 15], *Shopping Basket*[5], *Simple Search Interface*[1], *Selectable Search Space*[1]. In addition, we discovered two new patterns: *Visited Objects* [3], *Hierarchical Navigation* [3].

2.1   Relationships Among the Patterns

The patterns in this system were chosen based on behavioral relationships (i.e., how they interact with one another when they are used in an application together) such that when they were implemented and integrated together, would lead to a framework to be the central part of data intensive web application . Figure 1 depicts the relationships among the patterns. The diagram shows the flow of information from one pattern to another. For example, *Set based navigation* gets the search results to be explored from *Selectable search space* and *Simple search interface*. Set-Based Navigation plays a central part in this system, as many other patterns rely on it to display specific information to the user. This figure shows that *Simple search interface* is an extended version of *Selectable search space*, *Hierarchical navigation* is an extended version of the *Set based navigation*. We can get all the behaviors of *Selectable Search Space* using *Simple search interface*. The same is true for *Hierarchical navigation* and *Set based navigation*. In fact, still they all are strong enough to stand by themselves. *Shopping basket* is a special case of *Visited objects*. The set of all the elements of *Shopping basket* will be the subset of the set of all the elements of *Visited objects* when they both are instantiated in an application. In fact, it is not possible to get all the behaviors of *Shopping basket* using *Visited objects* only.

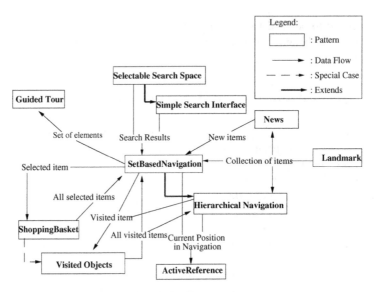

Fig. 1. Relationships between the patterns

2.2   Patterns in GoF Notation

The next step was to describe the patterns in a uniform notation and we decided to use the Gang-of-Four (GoF) one [6, 7]. One important aspect that we want to include in our descriptions is the diagrams that provide insight on how the pattern should be implemented. In the GoF notation, patterns are described using the UML notation. We felt that UML was not sufficient to describe navigational patterns, due to its inability to depict navigation. We decided to use UML-based Web engineering notation (UWE) [10]. Two diagrams of UWE have been particularly useful: *Navigation class* and *Presentation class*. The modeling element, *Navigation class* is used here to represent an information space to be explored and *Presentation class* is used to represent the actual pages or part of the pages created by different patterns to be shown in browser. Here we are including the description of the pattern *Hierarchical Navigation*. The rest of the patterns can be found in [3].

   Hierarchical Navigation

- **Name:** Hierarchical Navigation
- **Intent:** Organize the information by creating sets of related items recursively, create a hierarchical structure like tree of those sets and allow inter- and intra-set navigation.
- **Motivation:** Collections of objects are commonly displayed in a Web application. They need to be displayed in an easy-to-navigate way. The objects of collections can be explored like exploring the files in windows explorer or Konqueror.
- **Applicability:** This pattern will be applicable in exploring different collections of items in different Web Information Systems.
- **Structure:** Figure 2 shows the structure of the pattern.

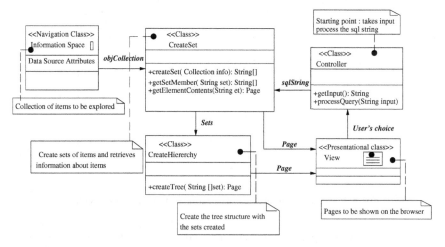

Fig. 2. The structure of Hierarchical Navigation

- **Participants:** The participants of this pattern are:
  1. *Information space:* It represents the collection of items to be explored like a collection of books, movies, CDs etc.
  2. *CreateSet class:* It creates the sets of related items. It may provide the detail information of an item of a particular set too.
  3. *CreateHierarchy class:* It creates a hierarchical structure using the sets created like the tree structure created using the files and/or directories in file explorer like Windows explorer or Konqueror.
  4. *Controller:* It processes the SQL string based on which sets will be created.
  5. *View:* It is the user interface to show the pages.
- **Collaborations:**
  1. *Information space:* This will provide the collection of items to be explored to CreateSet class.
  2. *CreateSet class:* It receives the collection of items from the Information space and provides the sets created to CreateHierarchy class. It also sends pages containing the element(s) of a set to View.
  3. *CreateHierarchy class:* It receives the sets from CreateSet class and provides pages containing the hierarchy of sets to View.
  4. *Controller:* It takes user input using the View and provides the SQL string to CreateSet class.
  5. *View:* It receives the pages from CreateSet class and CreateHierarchy class.
- **Known Uses:** Figure 3 shows the instance of the pattern in www.atPictures.com.
- **Related pattern:** This pattern is an extended version of Set based navigation.

2.3   Implementation

We have implemented all the patterns included in this system in the form of Java components (using the Tomcat Apache Web server) and we have developed a framework

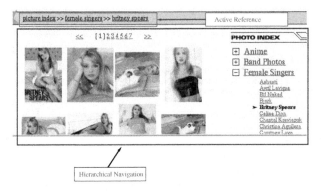

Fig. 3. Instance of Hierarchical navigation in www.atpictures.com

integrating all the developed components intended to be used to navigate an information space in Web.

A framework is a set of cooperating classes, some of which may be abstract, that make up of a reusable design for a specific class of software and usually incorporates several design patterns [16]. We have developed a navigational framework incorporating all the selected navigational design patterns. The individual components of the developed framework are independent. It is possible to use the components individually instead of the whole framework. It is also possible to replace one component by a different implementation as long as it maintains the same interface. This framework is extensible by incorporating more patterns as long as they maintain a behavioral relationship with the already incorporated patterns. The core concept of this framework of our implementation is that each pattern will be a component and we have described the implementation details in [2, 3].

3   Conclusions

A system of patterns shows how the patterns are connected together which will help in choosing a suitable pattern for a particular problem at hand. It provides guidelines for implementation, and facilitates in comparing the patterns, as all the patterns included in the system are written in a uniform notation. It shows practical uses of the patterns, and supports its own evolution. So, a system of patterns is arguably stronger than just a catalog of patterns.

One important contribution of this work is the structure diagram of each of the patterns, which represents the patterns graphically. None of the previous versions of these patterns contains a structure diagram of the patterns. We believe that the patterns described herein using this notation are more explanatory, easier to understand, and to use in practical applications.

The depicted relationships among the patterns shows how the patterns of this system are connected together or how they will interact with one another when they are being instantiated in application. This will help the users in choosing the required pattern(s) from the patterns included in this system for an e-commerce application or an Web Information Systems.

References

1. ACM-SIGWEB and University of Italian Switzerland. Hypermedia Design Pattern Repository. Available at http://www.designpattern.lu.unisi.ch/HypermediaHomePage.htm, January 2003.
2. M. A. K. Akanda and D. M. German. A Component Oriented Framework for the Implementation of Navigational Design Patterns. In *International Conference on Web Engineering (ICWE'03)*, pages 449–450, 2003.
3. Mohammed Abul Khayes Akanda. A system of patterns for web navigation. Master's thesis, University of Victoria, Canada, December 2003.
4. F. Buschmann, R. Meunier, H. Rohnert, P. Sommerlad, and M. Stal. *Pattern-Oriented Software Architecture- A System of Patterns*. John Wiley Sons Ltd., New York, 1996.
5. G. Rossi and D. Schwabe and F. Lyardet. Improving Web information Systems with Navigational Patterns. In *Proceedings of the 8th International World Wide Web Conference*, Available at www-di.inf.puc-rio.br/ schwabe/papers/www8.pdf, May 1999. W3C, Elsevier.
6. E. Gamma, R. Helm, R. Johnson, and J. Vlissides. *Design Patterns: Elements of Reusable Object-oriented Software*. Addison-Wesley, Reading, 1996.
7. Erich Gamma, Richard Helm, Ralph E. Johnson, and John M. Vlissides. Design Patterns: Abstraction and Reuse of Object-Oriented Design. In *ECOOP1993*, pages 406–431, 1993.
8. A. Garrido, G. Rossi, and D. Schwabe. Pattern Systems for Hypermedia. In *Proceedings of The 4th Pattern Languages of Programming Conference*, Available at http://st-www.cs.uiuc.edu/users/hanmer/PLoP-97/Workshops.html, 1997. University of Washington.
9. D. M. German and D. D. Cowan. Towards a unified catalog of hypermedia design patterns. In *Proceedings of the 33th Hawaii International Conference on System Sciences*, Available at http://www.turingmachine.org/ dmg/research/papers/dmg_hicss2000.pdf, Jan. 2000.
10. R. Hennicker and N. Koch. Systematic Design of Web Applications with UML. In *Unified Modeling Language: Systems Analysis, Design and Development Issues,2001, K. Siau and T. Halpin, Idea Group Publishing*, Available at http://www.pst.informatik.uni-muenchen.de/personen/kochn/publications.html, 2001.
11. F. Lyardet, G. Rossi, and D. Schwabe. Patterns for Dynamic Websites. In *Proceedings of The 4th Pattern Languages of Programming Conference*, Available at http://jerry.cs.uiuc.edu/ plop/plop98/final_submissions/P56.pdf, 1998.
12. F. Lyardet, G. Rossi, and D. Schwabe. Using Design Patterns in Educational Multimedia Applications. In *Proceedings of EDMedia'98*, Available at http://www.oohdm.telemidia.puc-rio.br/site_oohdm/oohdm.html, 1998.
13. P. Paolini and F. Garzotto. Design Patters for the WWW hypermedia: problems and proposals. In *Hypermedia Development: Design Patterns in Hypermedia*, 1999.
14. G. Rossi, D. Schwabe, and A. Garrido. Design Reuse in Hypermedia Applications Development. In *Proceedings of the Eighth ACM Conference on Hypertext*, Hypertext Design, pages 57–66, 1997.
15. G. Rossi, D. Schwabe, and F. Lyardet. Improving Web Information Systems with Navigational Patterns. In *Proceedings of the Eighth International World-Wide Web Conference*, Available at www-di.inf.puc-rio.br/ schwabe/papers/www8.pdf, 1999.
16. C. Szyperski. *Component Software*. Pearson Education Ltd., Great Britain, 1999.

A Design of Spatial XQuery
for Mobile and Location-Based Applications*

Soon-Young Park[1], Jae-Dong Lee[2], and Hae-Young Bae[1]

[1] Dept. of Computer Science and Information Engineering, Inha University
Yonghyun-dong, Nam-gu, Inchon, 402-751, Korea
sunny@dblab.inha.ac.kr, hybae@inha.ac.kr
[2] Dept. of Information and Computer Science, Dankook University
Hannam-ro, Yongsan-gu, Seoul, 140-714, Korea
letsdoit@dku.edu

Abstract. In this paper S-XML (Spatial-eXtensible Markup Language) is proposed for mobile and location-based applications. And in order to handle effectively the extension, a Spatial XQuery language and its processing modules has been designed. Because our work is based on a spatial DBMS, the Spatial XQuery statements are firstly translated into Spatial SQL statements. By working on an existing spatial DBMS, we can use its existing functions such as query optimization, spatial indexes, concurrency control mechanism, and recovery scheme. Translation of the Spatial XQuery into SQL has been explained using examples. Because the results from the spatial database system are in the form of tables, we again need to translate the results into S-XML statements. A working example of the proposed system as an Emergency Support System is also presented. Prospected application areas of the proposed system are almost all mobile and location-based systems such as m-commerce, ubiquitous systems in mobile environments.

1 Introduction

Recently the uses of mobile and location-based applications are popularized and extended. And requirements to geographic information systems also have been changed. Geography Markup Language (GML) [9] is the active standard for exchanging spatial data on the Internet and mobile devices, but it is limited only for text and graphic data of static geographic information. Location-based Services (LBS) can be provided as more attractive services when they utilize tracking information of moving objects. It would be very convenient if a car navigation system provides voice mode as well as the basic screen mode.

In this paper, S-XML (Spatial-eXtensible Markup Language) is proposed, which extends the GML by adding three schemas: voice schema, tracking schema, and POI (Point Of Interest). In order to handle the S-XML data effectively, a spatial XQuery language has been designed. In this research, the geographic data are stored in a spatial database management system and the spatial XQuery constructs submitted by users are translated into spatial SQL and evaluated by the SDBMS(Spatial Database Management System). The SDBMS supports the query optimization methods and concurrency control for processing multiple queries simultaneously.

* This research was supported by the MIC (Ministry of Information and Communication), Korea, under the ITRC (Information Technology Research Center) support program supervised by the IITA (Institute of Information Technology Assessment)

D. Lowe and M. Gaedke (Eds.): ICWE 2005, LNCS 3579, pp. 142–151, 2005.
© Springer-Verlag Berlin Heidelberg 2005

The spatial XQuery supports basic operations (e.g., =, <, and >), spatial operations (e.g., sp_disjoint, sp_intersects, and sp_contains), and operations for moving objects (e.g., mo_after, mo_before, mo_first, and mo_last). With these spatial operations and the operations for moving objects, the spatial XQuery can be effectively used on LBS (Location-Based Services) platforms. The spatial XQuery also supports the VOICE tag, using which the direction information can be provided by voice mode interface.

This paper is organized as follows. Section 2 summarizes the various approaches to handle XML queries. Section 3 presents the information model of S-XML and the syntax and semantics of spatial XQuery. Section 4 describes the overall processing of spatial XQuery. Spatial XQueries are first translated into equivalent spatial SQL statements and then evaluated by database management system with spatial operation. Section 5 provides a working scenario of using the spatial XQuery. In this scenario, the user first locates the nearest hospital from an accident and the driver of an ambulance from the hospital gets the direction to the accident site when the car approaches crossroads. Section 6 summarizes the contributions of the paper.

2   Related Work

Two research groups have contributed to the developments of XML query languages. First, the document research group has their experience in designing languages and tools for processing structured documents. Several query languages have been proposed for XML. For example, XQuery uses XPath in order to support operations on document path expressions. XQuery offers very powerful query capabilities. But XQuery does not provide much support for querying spatial elements. It simply treats spatial elements as numerical values [8]. Second, the database research group has their experience in designing query language and processors for data-oriented computations. XQuery also uses the basic structure of SQL language for relational databases [13].

In database approaches, XML documents are stored in preexisting database systems [1, 4, 9, 10] and the XML queries are translated into SQL or other database languages [6, 12]. The problems of updating XML data stored in tables [11] and indexing XML data [3, 7] have also been presented. Prototypes such as SilkRoute [5, 6] and XPERANTO [2] have proposed algorithms for efficiently encoding relational data as XML documents.

Consequently, database approaches make good use of the existing functions of database systems, which include query optimization, indexes, concurrency control, and recovery. On the other hand, native approaches are more customized for XML documents. Because huge amount of geographic information is already stored in spatial database systems, we take the database approach. By using the spatial XQuery language, the user can access not only the extended spatial information but also the ordinary text and graphic information in terms of XML forms.

3   S-XML and Spatial XQuery

In this section, the structure of S-XML is introduced at first and then the syntax and semantics of Spatial XQuery are proposed with some examples.

3.1 S-XML

S-XML is based on GML 3.0 and is designed to provide effective location based services to the user in mobile environments. S-XML consists of three main schemas, i.e., voice schema, tracking schema, and POI schema.

(a) Voice Schema

In mobile environments, voice information is often more useful than text or graphic information especially when the user is driving a car. To be effective, the grammar of the voice information is designed as simple as possible (see Fig. 1). The voice information can be either location information or turn information.

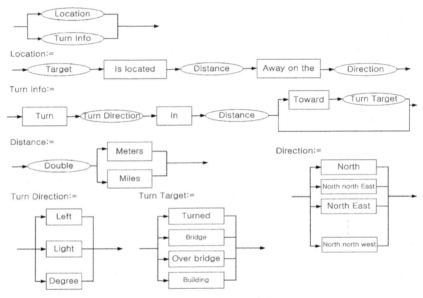

Fig. 1. Grammar of Voice Schema

(b) POI Schema

POI schema includes the location information of objects in specific area, the optimal path to destination, the type of moving objects (e.g., car, human, subway, etc.), information of the source and the destination, information of representative objects near the destination, and additional information about the destination (e.g., phone number and email address). Fig. 2 shows a part of POI schema, which includes a starting point, a target point and a route.

(c) Tracking Schema

Tracking schema specifies the changes of status of specific object as time changes. The information model includes the type of moving objects, information of specific points and the time when the point passed, and information of direction and velocity. Fig. 3 shows a part of Tracking Schema, which specifies the locus type. A locus consists of a series of points, time, location and direction.

```
<!-- access -->
<xs:complexType name="accessType">
    <xs:sequence>
        <xs:element ref="method"/>
        <xs:element name="ipoint" type="ipointType"/>
        <xs:element name="tpoint" type="tpointType"/>
        <xs:element name="route" type="routeType" minOccurs="0"/>
    </xs:sequence>
</xs:complexType>
<!-- access element(ipoint, tpoint, route) -->
<!-- ipoint -->
<xs:complexType name="ipointType">
    <xs:sequence>
        <xs:element ref="iclass"/>
        <xs:element ref="gml:location"/>
        <xs:element name="name" type="nameType" minOccurs="0"/>
    </xs:sequence>
</xs:complexType>
<!—tpoint -->
<xs:complexType name="tpointType">
    <xs:sequence>
        <xs:element ref="tclass"/>
        <xs:element ref="gml:location"/>
        <xs:element name="name" type="nameType" minOccurs="0"/>
    </xs:sequence>
</xs:complexType>
```

Fig. 2. Part of POI Schema that includes the specification of starting and target points

```
<!-- locus Type definition -->
<xs:complexType name="locusType">
<xs:sequence>
<xs:element name="point" type="sxml:pointType"/>
<xs:element name="dateTime" type="xs:dateTime"/>
<xs:element name="location" type="xs:string"/>
<xs:element name="dir" type="xs:unsignedShort"/>
</xs:sequence>
</xs:complexType>
```

Fig. 3. Part of Tracking Schema that includes the specification of locus

3.2 Spatial XQuery

Spatial XQuery follows basic FLWR (For Let Where Return) structure of XQuery with path expressions so that SQL users feel easy to use and the elements and attributes of S-XML can be effectively accessed. Spatial XQuery also supports the spatial data, spatial relational operators, and spatial functions that are recommended by OGC specifications [9]. In Spatial XQuery, spatial operators and spatial functions have 'sp' as a prefix in their names. Functions of moving objects have 'mo' as a prefix in their names. A list of operators and functions specified in Spatial XQuery are as follows.

(a) Basic Operator for Spatial Objects
   sp_Dimension (g Geometry): int, sp_GeometryType (g Geometry): string
   sp_AsText (g Geometry): string, sp_AsBinary (g Geometry): binary
   sp_IsEmpty (g Geometry): int, sp_IsSimple (g Geometry): int
   sp_Boundary (g Geometry): geometry, sp_Envelop (g Geometry): geometry

(b) Functions of Point Type

  sp_x (p Point): double, sp_y (p Point): double

(c) Functions of Curve Type

  sp_StartPoint(c Curve): point, sp_EndPoint(c Curve): point
  sp_IsClosed(c Curve,): int, sp_IsRing(c Curve): int, sp_Length(c Curve): double

(d) Functions of LineString Type

  sp_NumPoints(l LineString): int, sp_PointN(l LineString, n Int): point

(e) Functions of Surface Type

  sp_Centroid (s Surface): point, sp_PointOnSurface(s Surface): point, sp_Area(s Surface): double

(f) Functions of Polygon Type

  sp_ ExteriorRing(p polygon): linestring, sp_InteriorRingN(p polygon, n int): linestring
  sp_ NumInteriorRing(p polygon): int

(g) Functions of GeometryCollection Type

  sp_NumGeometries(g GeomCollection): int
  sp_GeometryN(g GeomCollection, n int): geometry

(h) Functions of MultiCurve Type

  sp_IsClosed(mc MultiCurve,): int, sp_Length(mc MultiCurve): double

(i) Topology Operators between two spatial objects

  sp_Equals(g1 Geometry, g2 Geometry): int, sp_Disjoint(g1 Geometry, g2 Geometry): int
  sp_Intersects(g1 Geometry, g2 Geometry): int, sp_Touches(g1 Geometry, g2 Geometry): int
  sp_Overlaps(g1 Geometry, g2 Geometry) int, sp_Crosses(g1 Geometry, g2 Geometry): int
  sp_Within(g1 Geometry, g2 Geometry)): int, sp_Contains(g1 Geometry, g2 Geometry): int

(j) Functions of Distance Relationship

  sp_Distance(g1 Geometry, g2 Geometry): double

(k) Functions of Spatial Operations

  sp_Intersection(g1 Geometry, g2 Geometry):geometry
  sp_Difference(g1 Geometry, g2 Geometry): geometry
  sp_Union(g1 Geometry, g2 Geometry): geometry
  sp_Symdifference(g1 Geometry, g2 Geometry): geometry
  sp_Buffer(g1 Geometry, d Double precision): geometry, sp_Convexhull(g Geometry): geometry

(l) Functions of Moving Objects

  mo_First(p Position, n Int): point, mo_Last(p Position, n Int): point
  mo_After(p Position, t Time): point, mo_Before(p Position, t Time): point
  mo_Snapshot(p Position, t Time): point, mo_Snapshot(p Position, g Geometry): time
  mo_Slice(p Position, pe Period(start, end)): Linestring
  mo_Slice(p Position, g Geometry): Linestring
  mo_Project(p Position): Linestring, mo_Project(pe Period(start, end, g Geometry): point

(m) Functions of Voice Service

  POIDirection(p Position): string, ShortestPathDirection(p Position, i Int): string

Details of XQuery syntax are not discussed in this paper. The meaning of Spatial XQuery will be clear from the following example.

Example 1. This query retrieves the names of cities that are located within 5 km from any river in rivers.xml.

```
for     $a in document("cities.xml") //city
        $b in document("rivers.xml") //river
where      sp_overlap($a/obj, sp_buffer($b/obj, 5000)) eq true
return     <Within5000CityName>$a/name</Within5000CityName>
```

4 Processing of Spatial XQuery

The query processor of Spatial XQuery consists of Parser, SQL Info Generator, Result Info Generator, and SQL Translator (see Fig. 4). The queries from the user interface are first parsed to generate parse trees, which are sent to SQL Info Generator and Result Info Generator. Spatial XQueries are finally translated into spatial SQL, based on the information generated by SQL Info Generator and Result Info Generator. SQL Info Generator analyzes the clauses FOR, LET, and WHERE from the Spatial XQuery statements and generates a mapping table for query translation. The RETURN clause of Spatial XQuery is analyzed by Result Info Generator and a linked list of tags and elements is generated.

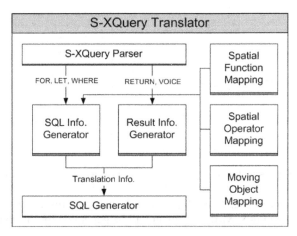

Fig. 4. Structure of the Query Processor of Spatial XQuery

Details of the procedure of translating Spatial XQuery are presented using an example. Consider the query in Example 1. By analyzing the FOR and WHERE clauses, we can generate the mapping table as in Table 1. In Table 1, tag names and variable names are translated into corresponding table names in spatial database. Operators in Spatial XQuery are also mapped into the corresponding ones in spatial database management system. Such mapping information is provided by *Spatial Operator Mapping* which is the Mapping Module of Spatial Operators. In this example, the spatial operator of Spatial XQuery *sp_overlap* in mapped into operator *overlap* in spatial database management system.

Table 1. Mapping from Spatial XQuery to Spatial SQL

	Spatial XQuery	Spatial SQL
From	Cities.xml//City Rivers.xml//River	City River
Select	$a/name	City.name
Where	sp_overlap($a/obj, Buffer($b/obj, 5000)) eq true	overlap(City.obj, Buffer(River.obj, 5000)) = true
Order by	NULL	NULL

Based on the mapping table in Table 1, spatial SQL query can be generated as follows.

Select City.name
From   City, River
Where overlap(City.obj, Buffer(River.obj, 5000)) = true;

The results from *SQL Info Generator* and *Result Info Generator* can be represented as a graph. The graph in Fig. 5 is generated for this example, which includes
nodes for start tag, table name, column name and end tag.

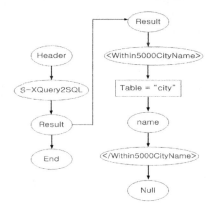

Fig. 5. Graphical Representation of results from *SQL Info Generator and Result Info Generator*

Using the results in Fig. 5 and the table returned as a result for the spatial SQL
statement, the following S-XML document will be generated for this example.

<Within5000CityName>
      <name> Han River </name>
</Within5000CityName>

5   Working Scenario

A scenario to apply Spatial XQuery in LBS environments is discussed in this section.
This is an example of Emergency Support System that includes POI Service and
Shortest Path Service. Suppose that a car accident takes place and there are some
injuries (see Fig. 6). The user of this system is looking for the nearest hospital and
wants an ambulance for injured people. Once the nearest hospital is identified by the
Emergency Support System, the hospital is requested to dispatch an ambulance to the
accident place. Then the driver of the ambulance asks the direction to the accident
place while he drives.

Fig. 7 is a Spatial XQuery that looks for the nearest hospital from the accident
place. The coordinates of the accident place are available from a GPS.

Fig. 8 is the spatial SQL query that is translated from the Spatial XQuery in Fig. 7.
The spatial operator *sp_distance* is translated into spatial database management op-
erator *distance* and for optimization the selection condition is included in the
WHERE clause.

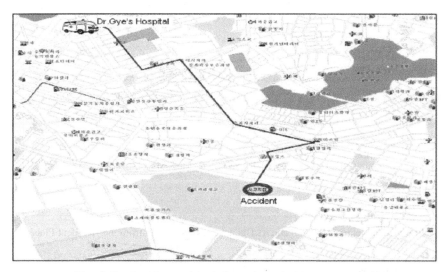

Fig. 6. Car Accident and Ambulance from the Nearest Hospital

```
for    $a in document("textshape.xml")//TextShape
let    $b := min(sp_distance($a/obj, point(4559734.910290 1348143.837131)))
where  contains($a/tex(), "%hospital%") and text_kind eq '50'
return <POI> {
            for $c in document("textshape.xml")//TextShape
            where contains($a/tex(), "%hospital%") and sp_distance($a/obj,
                            point(4559734.910290 1348143.837131)) <= $b and text_kind eq '50'
            return {
                        <Label> $c/text() </Label>
                        <Location> $c/obj </Location>
                        <Distance>
                            sp_distance($c/obj, point(4559734.910290 1348143.837131))
                        </Distance>
                        <voice>
                            <Direction>POIDirection(point(4559734.910290
                                        1348143.837131))</Direction>
                        </voice>
                    }
                }
        </POI>
```

Fig. 7. Spatial XQuery looking for the Nearest Hospital

```
select text, obj, distance(obj, point(4559734.910290 1348143.837131))
from  textshape
where text like '%hospital%' and distance(obj, point(4559734.910290 1348143.837131) ) <=
            (select min(distance( obj, point(4559734.910290 1348143.837131) )) from textshape where
            text like '%hospital%' ) and text_kind = '50';
```

Fig. 8. Spatial SQL that is translated from the Spatial XQuery in Fig. 7

From the result returned for the spatial SQL query in Fig. 8, an S-XML document
is generated as in Fig. 9. In Fig. 9, a hospital named "Dr. Gye's Hospital" is selected
and the distance and direction to it are included.

```
<POI>
  <Label>Dr. Gye's Hospital </Label>
  <Location>
    <gml:Point>
      <gml:coord>
        <gml:X>4559375.060000</gml:X><gml:Y>1348618.010000</gml:Y>
      </gml:coord>
    </gml:Point>
  </Location>
  <Distance>638.692749 </Distance>
  <vml>
    <Direction>east </Direction>
    <POIblock>
      Dr. Gye's Hospital is located 638.692749 meter away on the east
    </POIblock>
  </vml>
</POI>
```

Fig. 9. The Nearest Hospital and its Distance and Direction from the Accident Place

6   Conclusion

S-XML is proposed for mobile and location-based applications. In order to handle effectively the extension, we have designed a Spatial XQuery language and its processing modules. Because our work is based on a spatial database system, the Spatial XQuery statements are first translated into spatial SQL statements. By working on existing spatial database system, we can use the existing functions of database systems such as query optimization, spatial indexes, concurrency control, and crash recovery. Translation of the Spatial XQuery into spatial SQL has been explained using an example.

Application areas of the proposed system are almost all mobile and location-based systems such as LBS, ubiquitous systems, and distributed control and management systems. In order to be more powerful, it needs to be extended with various development tools. Naive users may have difficulties to program their queries using Spatial XQuery. Some user-friendly designed GUI tools could make the system more effective. Even current execution model allows multiple queries; we need to devise more sophisticated optimization strategies for multiple queries.

References

1. P. Bohannon, J. Freire, P. Roy, and J. Simeon, "From XML schema to relations: A cost-based approach to XML storage," Proceedings of IEEE International Conference on Data Engineering (ICDE), 2002.
2. M. Carey et al., "XPERANTO: Publishing Object-Relational Data as XML," Proceedings of Workshops on Web and Databases (WebDB), 2000.
3. B. Cooper et al., "A Fast Index for Semistructured Data," Proceedings of International Conference on Very Large Databases (VLDB), 2001.
4. A. Deutsch, M. Fernandez, and D. Suciu, "Storing semistructured data with STORED," Proceedings of the ACM SIGMOD International Conference on Management of Data (SIGMOD), 1999.
5. M. Fernandez et al., "Publishing Relational Data as XML: The SilkRoute Approach," IEEE Data Engineering Bulletin, 24(2), 2001.

6. M. Fernandex, Y. Kadiyska, A. Morishima, D. Suciu, and W. Tan, "SilkRoute: A frame-work for publishing relational data in XML," ACM Transactions on Database Systems, 2002.
7. D. Kha, M. Yoshikawa, and S. Uemura, "An XML Indexing Structure with Relative Region Coordinate," Proceedings of IEEE International Conference on Data Engineering (ICDE), 2001.
8. Z. Liu, E.-P. Lim, W.-K. Ng and D. H. Goh, On Querying Geospatial and Georeferenced Metadata Resources in G-Portal, Proceedings of Joint Conference on Digital Libraries (JCDL), 2003.
9. OGC, Geography Markup Language (GML) Implementation Specification 3.0, 2003.
10. S.-Y. Park, J.-D. Lee, and H.-Y. Bae, "Easily Accessible GML-based Geographic Informa-tion System for Multiple Data Server over the Web," Proceedings of International Confer-ence on Information System Technology and its Applications (ISTA), 2003.
11. I. Tatarinov, Z. Ives, A. Halevy, and D. Weld, "Updating XML," Proceedings of ACM SIGMOD International Conference on Management of Data (SIGMOD), 2001.
12. I. Tatarinov, S. Viglas, K. Beyer, J. Shanmugasundaram, E. Shekita, and C. Zhang, "Stor-ing and querying ordered XML using a relational database system," Proceedings of ACM SIGMOD International Conference on Management of Data (SIGMOD), 2002.
13. W3C, XQuery 1.0: An XML Query Language, 2002.

An Article Language Model for BBS Search

Jingfang Xu, Yangbo Zhu, and Xing Li

Department of Electronic Engineering, Tsinghua University
Beijing 100084, P.R. China
{xjf02,zhuyangbo99}@mails.tsinghua.edu.cn, xing@cernet.edu.cn

Abstract. Bulletin Board Systems (BBS), similar to blogs, newsgroups, online forums, etc., are online broadcasting spaces where people can exchange ideas and make announcements. As BBS are becoming valuable repositories of knowledge and information, effective BBS search engines are required to make the information universally accessible and useful. However, the techniques that have been proven successful for web search are not suitable for searching BBS articles due to the nature of BBS. In this paper, we propose a novel article language model (LM) to build an effective BBS search engine. We investigate the differences between BBS articles and web pages, then extend the traditional LM to author LM and category LM. The article LM is powerful in the sense that it can combine the three LMs into a single framework. Experimental results shows that our article LM substantially outperforms both INQUERY algorithm and the traditional LM.

1 Introduction

Bulletin Board System(BBS) are online broadcasting spaces where people can exchange ideas and make announcements. Unlike web site, where users only browse web pages, BBS are virtual places where, besides browsing, people carry on discussion with others. Some users post articles on BBS to ask questions, answer questions or share information with others, while others browse the articles in BBS for information they need. As BBS are valuable repositories of knowledge and information, there is a tremendous need for BBS search techniques.

BBS search can be simply defined as the search engine specific to BBS. Unfortunately, the techniques that have been proven successful for web search are not suitable to BBS search due to the nature of BBS. In this paper, BBS articles are defined as messages in BBS which contain documents, authors and categories. We investigate the differences between BBS articles and web pages to discover the nature of BBS which affects search performance. Comparing BBS articles and web pages, there are three primary differences. First, BBS articles consist of documents, authors who wrote it, and categories which them belong to. While web pages usually only contain documents; the authors and the categories of them are not available. Second, as users sometimes post articles to ask questions or answer questions, the articles are often shorter than web pages. Finally, there are no links between BBS articles while web pages are closely connected by hypertext links. Consequently, on the one hand many techniques

D. Lowe and M. Gaedke (Eds.): ICWE 2005, LNCS 3579, pp. 152–160, 2005.

applied in web search, e.g., link analysis and anchor text, are not suitable for BBS search; one the other hand, the authors and categories of BBS articles may be helpful for ranking retrieved articles. However, to our best knowledge, there is no effort devoted to building special models for BBS search.

In this paper, we explore the problem of building an effective BBS search with the article language model(LM). According to the nature of BBS, we apply the traditional document LM to the documents belong to an author or a category, and propose the author LM and the category LM. Combining the document, author and category LMs, the article LM is used to rank the retrieved articles according to the probability that the article LM produces the query. To improve the retrieval performance, we propose a smoothing method to address the problem that BBS articles are usually short, which affects the precision of sampling. Experimental results show that the article LM achieves significantly better performance than both INQUERY ranking algorithm and the traditional LM.

The rest of the paper is organized as follows. First we briefly review the related work in section 2. Then the traditional LM, the article LM, and a smoothing method for BBS search are described in section 3. Section 4 presents the experiments and results, which shows the effectiveness of the article LM empirically. Finally we conclude with future work in section 5.

2   Related Work

As BBS becomes more and more popular, considerable effort has been devoted to investigate the special phenomenon in BBS, such as its complex network model[1], its aliasing users[2], and its relationship of interests [3]. Many information retrieval(IR) techniques such as PageRank[4], HITS[5] and anchor text[6] are designed for web search, but they are not suitable for other applications. Therefore, many research have been done to improve IR performance in other context, e.g., web site[7], newsgroup[8], workplace[9], etc. In this paper we focus on improving the retrieval performance in BBS.

In the mean time, LMs, successfully used for speech recognition, have been applied to various IR systems, e.g., web search[10], resource selection[11], etc. Generally, IR systems can be classified by the underlying conceptual models, such as Boolean model, vector-space model, probabilistic model and LM. Ponte and Croft originally proposed LM for IR [10], then Song put emphasis on data smoothing techniques in LM[12]. Recently, many variations of traditional LM have been developed to improve IR performance, such as relevance-based language model[13], time-based language model[14] and title language model[15]. In this paper, we extend the traditional document LM to the author LM and the category LM according to the nature of BBS articles.

3   Language Model

3.1   Document Language Model

As described by Ponte and Croft[10], in document LM each document is viewed as a language sample and a query is treated as a generation process, sampled from the language model. Then the retrieved documents are ranked based on the probabilities of producing the query from the corresponding language models of them. Given the language model M_d of document d, the maximum likelihood estimate of the probability of term t produced by the corresponding LM is computed by Equation 1:

$$p_{(t|M_d)} = \frac{tf_{(t,d)}}{N_d} \tag{1}$$

where $tf_{t,d}$ is the raw term frequency of term t in document d, and N_d is the total number of tokens in document d. We treat a query as a sequence of terms. Then each term is viewed as an independent event, and the query is viewed as the joined event[12]. Consequently, the query probability is computed by multiplying the individual term probabilities, as shown in Equation 2:

$$p_{(Q|M_d)} = \prod_{t \in Q} p_{(t|M_d)} \tag{2}$$

where t is the term in the query sequence Q. Notice that, in this paper, first we use Boolean model to get the documents that contain the whole query, then apply LMs to rank them. So the zero probability problem does not exist in our research.

3.2   Author Language Model and Category Language Model

As mentioned above, each BBS article contains an author and a category, which can be used to improve the performance of BBS search. The traditional document LM infers a LM for each document and views the document as a sample of the model. Similarly, we infer an author LM for each author and a category LM for each category. That is to say, all the articles of an author are viewed as a huge document, a sample from the corresponding LM. Like probability in the document LM, we compute the probability of term t produced by the author LM M_a. We also get the category LM M_c, corresponding to all the articles belonging to a category, and compute the probability of producing the query term, as shown in Equantion 3, 4:

$$p_{(t|M_a)} = \frac{tf_{(t,a)}}{N_a} \tag{3}$$

$$p_{(t|M_c)} = \frac{tf_{(t,c)}}{N_c} \tag{4}$$

where $tf_{t,a}$ and N_a are the raw term frequency of term t and the total number of tokens in all articles written by author a, and $tf_{t,c}$ and N_c are the raw term frequency of term t and total number of tokens in all articles belong to category c.

3.3   Article Language Model

In order to improve the BBS search performance, we combine three LMs: document, author, and category LMs into the article LM. Each BBS article is viewed as a trigram (d, a, c), where d is the document text, a is the author and c is the category. Then the retrieved articles are ranked according to the probability $P_{(Q|article)}$ that the query is sampled form the article LM.

$$P_{(Q|article)} = P_{(Q|d,a,c)} = \prod_{t \in Q} P_{(t|d,a,c)} \tag{5}$$

Assuming that the three LMs are independent, $p_{(t|d,a,c)}$ is calculated as follows:

$$
\begin{aligned}
P_{(t|d,a,c)} &= \frac{P_{(d,a,c|t)}P_{(t)}}{P_{(d,a,c)}} \\
&= \frac{P_{(d|t)}P_{(a|t)}P_{(c|t)}P_{(t)}}{P_{(d,a,c)}} \\
&= \frac{\frac{P_{(t|d)}P_{(d)}}{P_{(t)}} \frac{P_{(t|a)}P_{(a)}}{P_{(t)}} \frac{P_{(t|c)}P_{(c)}}{P_{(t)}} P_{(t)}}{P_{(d)}P_{(a)}P_{(c)}} \\
&= \frac{P_{(t|d)}P_{(t|a)}P_{(t|c)}}{P_{(t)}^2}
\end{aligned}
\tag{6}
$$

where $p_{(t|d)}$ is the probability that the document LM produces the query term, $p_{(t|a)}$ is the probability of the author LM and $p_{(t|c)}$ is the probability of the category model. Therefore, $p_{(Q|article)}$ is the product of the probabilities in three LMs, as shown in Equation 7:

$$P_{(Q|article)} = \prod_{t \in Q} \frac{P_{(t|d)}P_{(t|a)}P_{(t|c)}}{P_{(t)}^2} = \prod_{t \in Q} \frac{P_{(t|M_d)}P_{(t|M_a)}P_{(t|M_c)}}{P_{(t)}^2} \tag{7}$$

where $p_{(t|M_d)}$, $p_{(t|M_a)}$ and $p_{(t|M_c)}$ are computed according to Equation 2, 3, 4 and $p_{(t)}$ can be computed according to Equation 8:

$$P_{(t)} = \frac{tf_{(t,corpus)}}{N_{corpus}} \tag{8}$$

where $tf(t, corpus)$ is the term frequency of term t and N_{corpus} is the total number of tokens in the corpus.

3.4   Data Smoothing

Some articles in BBS are too short, e.g., less than 15 words, as users post them only to ask or answer questions. The small length affects the precision of maximum likelihood estimate as the sparse sampling data can not reflect the underlying LM exactly. Moreover, the probability is biased towards short articles. To address this problem, we smooth the length by adding the average sample length of the LM to the original length. That is to say, in document LM N_d is replaced by $N_d + avegn_{N_d}$, where $avegn_{N_d}$ is the average length of all the documents. Similarly, some authors post few articles and some categories contain few articles, which lead to sparse sampling data in both the author LM and the category LM. We apply similar smoothing methods on the author LM M_a and the category LM M_c, as presented in Equation 9:

$$p_{(t|M_d)} = \frac{tf_{(t,d)}}{N_d + avegN_d}$$

$$p_{(t|M_a)} = \frac{tf_{(t,a)}}{N_a + avegN_a} \tag{9}$$

$$p_{(t|M_c)} = \frac{tf_{(t,c)}}{N_c + avegN_c}$$

4   Experimental Results

4.1   Data

To demonstrate the effectiveness of the article LM, we conducted experiments on a Chinese BBS site, *Tsinghua University BBS (SMTH)*[1], which is the most famous and most large BBS site in China. The BBS search engine that we build for SMTH is accessible on line[2]. As table 1 lists, in SMTH there are $1,954,689$ articles, totally 11 gigabytes information, belongs to $85,062$ authors and 424 categories. And the average lengthes of document, author and category are 150, $3,447$ and $691,517$.

Table 1. Statistics of SMTH BBS Data

Data Size	11G
#Articles	1,954,689
#Author	85,062
#Category	424
Average length of documents	150
Average length of author	3,447
Average length of category	691,517

4.2   Implementation

Three different ranking algorithms are used in our experiments. The article LM is compared with INQUERY ranking formula and the traditional document LM. INQUERY ranking formula, which uses Robertson's *tf* score and a standard *idf* score, is lists as follows:

$$p_{t,d} = 0.4 + 0.6 \times \frac{tf_{t,d}}{tf_{t,d} + 0.5 + 1.5\frac{N_d}{arvgN_d}} \times \frac{log(\frac{N+0.5}{df_t})}{log(N+1)} \tag{10}$$

where $p_{t,d}$ is that probability that document d is relevant to term t, N is number of documents in collection, and df_t is the document frequency in collection. In INQUERY system, documents are ranked by the probability $p_{t,d}$.

Traditional LM is described as the document LM above, and the retrieved documents are ranked based on the probability $p_{(t|M_d)}$. In the article LM, retrieved articles are ranked based on the probability $p_{(Q|article)}$.

---

[1] http://www.smth.org
[2] http://bbs.compass.edu.cn

4.3   Evaluation Metrics

The recall/precision and minimizing Kendall's τ distance [16] are chosen to measure the performance of various models. Recall measures how many relevant articles are retrieved, while precision measures how highly the retrieved articles are relevant to the query. In recall/precision metric, relevant articles are unordered, which is opposite to the fact that users review the result lists orderly. To evaluate the order of result lists, minimizing Kendall's τ distance is adopted to measure the similarity between the ground truth and the top-k lists produced by the models.

The minimizing Kendall's τ distance is defined as follows. Given two top k lists τ_1 and τ_2 with result domains $D_{\tau 1}$ and $D_{\tau 2}$, we define $P(\tau 1, \tau 2)$ to be the set of all unordered pairs of distinct elements in $D_{\tau 1} \cup D_{\tau 2}$. The minimizing Kendall's τ distance is calculated according to Equation 11:

$$K_{min}(\tau_1, \tau_2) = \frac{\sum_{\{i,j\} \in P_{(\tau_1, \tau_2)}} K^{min}_{\{i,j\}}(\tau_1, \tau_2)}{k \times (k-1)/2} \tag{11}$$

Let $r_{1,i}$ denote the rank of result i in list τ_1, and result i is ahead of result j in τ_1 if $r_{1,i} < r_{1,j}$. Then $K^{min}_{\{i,j\}}$ is calculated according to Equation 12:

$$K^{min}_{\{i,j\}} = sign\{(r_{1,i} - r_{1,j})(r_{2,i} - r_{2,j})\} \tag{12}$$

4.4   Results and Discussions

Several volunteers are required to pose 50 queries, which are the top frequent queries in the log of BBS search engine that we build, to three systems in our experiment. For each query, volunteers evaluate the relevance of the top 50 articles returned by each system. Then they list the top 20 relevant articles based on the relevance, which referred to as the ground truth.

Only considering the articles in the ground truth as relevant results, we calculate the eleven point recall/precison of the three systems, as shown in Table 2 and Figure 1. In table 2, column 2,3,4 compare the article LM to INQUERY, and column 5,6,7 compare the article LM to the traditional document LM. As we can see, the article LM outperforms INQUERY ranking algorithm at all levels of recall, and the article LM achieves better precision than the document LM expect at 0.9 level of recall. In addition, the eleven point average precision of three systems are 0.310, 0.356 and 0.449, and the article LM do 44.84% better than INQUERY and 26.12% better than the document LM.

The minimizing Kendall's τ distance is computed between the ground truth and the top 20 list of each system's search results. As Table 3 presents, the Kendall's τ distance of three systems and the ground truth are 0.461100, 0.446451 and 0.401906, among which the article LM has the shortest distance to the ground truth. It indicates that the order of the result list in article LM is most similar to the ground truth.

Experimental results shows that the article LM outperforms INQUERY ranking algorithm and the traditional LM. Not only the recall/precision of the article

Table 2. Comparing eleven point recall/precison of INQUERY, document LM and article LM

Recall	INQUERY	Article LM	%chg	Document LM	Article LM	%chg
			Precision			
0.0	-	-	-	-	-	-
0.1	0.576	0.740	+28%	0.610	0.740	+21%
0.2	0.473	0.707	+49%	0.555	0.707	+27%
0.3	0.463	0.666	+44%	0.525	0.666	+27%
0.4	0.442	0.613	+39%	0.484	0.613	+27%
0.5	0.376	0.552	+47%	0.419	0.552	+32%
0.6	0.318	0.507	+59%	0.348	0.507	+46%
0.7	0.233	0.394	+69%	0.282	0.394	+40%
0.8	0.180	0.240	+33%	0.218	0.280	+10%
0.9	0.040	0.063	+57%	0.111	0.063	-43%
1.0	0.003	0.003	0	0.003	0.003	0
Avg	0.310	0.449	+44.84%	0.356	0.449	+26.12%

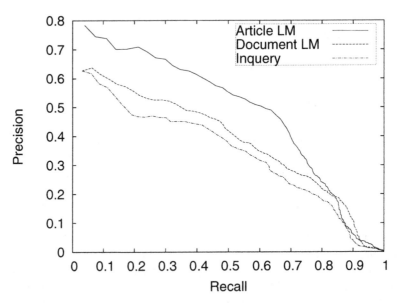

Fig. 1. Comparing eleven point recall/precison of INQUERY, document LM and article LM

LM is better than the others, but also the order of the relevant results in article LM is more close to the ground truth. The success is due to that the article LM makes use of the information from the author and the category. Each user or category has particular interests and different fields of knowledge. Obviously it will be helpful to improve IR performance that exploring differences between users or categories. Consequently, combing document, author and category LMs into the article LM would achieve significant improvement in BBS search.

Table 3. Minimizing Kendall's τ Distance Results

list τ_1	list τ_2	Kendall's τ distance
Ground Truth	INQUERY	0.461100
Ground Truth	Traditional Document LM	0.446451
Ground Truth	Article LM	0.401906

5 Conclusions and Future Work

In this paper, we propose a novel article LM for BBS search to improve the retrieval performance. According to the nature of BBS, we extend the traditional document LM to the author LM and the category LM. The article LM combines document, author, and category LMs into a single framework. Our experimental results show that the article LM outperforms significantly both INUQERY ranking algorithm and the traditional LM. It indicates that the information of the authors and the categories of the BBS articles are helpful to improve the retrieval performance in BBS search. The article LM can be easily applied in other similar systems such as blogs, newsgroups and forums.

For the future work we are planning to explore various smoothing method to improve retrieval performance. Moreover, we will explore to build an blogs search engine with our article LM. Making use of user informaion, personalized search in BBS or blogs is also planed to do.

References

1. Kou, Z., Zhang, C.: Reply networks on a bulletin board system. Physical Review E **67** (2003)
2. Novak, J., Raghavan, P., Tomkins, A.: Anti-aliasing on the web. Proceedings of the 13th international conference on World Wide Web (2004) 30–39
3. Kou, Z., , Bao, T., Zhang, C.: Discovery of relationships between intereswts from bulletin board system by dissimilarity reconstruction. Proceedings Lecture Notes in Artificial Intelligent **2843** (2003) 328–335
4. Brin, S., Page, L.: The anatomy of a large-scale hypertextual web search engine. Proceedings of the seventh international conference on World Wide Web 7 (1998) 107–117
5. Kraft, R., J.Zien: Authoritative sources in a hyperlinked environment. Proceedings of the ninth annual ACM-SIAM symposium on Discrete algorithms (1998) 668–677
6. Kraft, R., J.Zien: Mining anchor text for query refinement. Proceedings of the 13th international conference on World Wide Web (2004) 666–674
7. G.Xue, H.Zeng, Chen, Z., Ma, W., Lu, C.: Log mining to improve the performance of site search. Third International Conference on Web Information Systems Engineering (2002)
8. Xi, W., Lind, J., Brill, E.: Learning effective ranking functions for newsgroup search. Proceedings of the ACM SIGIR Conference on Research and Development in Information Retrieval (2004) 394–401
9. Fagin, R., Kumar, R., McCurley, K.: Searching the workplace web. Proceedings of the twelfth international conference on World Wide Web (2003) 366–375

10. Ponte, J., Croft, W.: A language modeling approach to information retrieval. Proceedings of the ACM SIGIR Conference on Research and Development in Information Retrieval (1998) 275–281
11. Si, L., Jin, R., Callan, J., Ogilvie, P.: A language modeling framework for resource selection and results merging. Proceedings of the eleventh international conference on Information and knowledge management (2002) 391–397
12. Song, F., Croft, W.: A general language model for information retrieval. Proceedings of the ACM SIGIR Conference on Research and Development in Information Retrieval (1999) 279–280
13. Lavrenko, V., Croft, W.: Relevance-based language models. Proceedings of the 24th annual international ACM SIGIR conference on Research and development in information retrieval (2001) 120–127
14. Li, X., Croft, W.: Time-based language models. Proceedings of the twelfth international conference on Information and knowledge management (2003) 469–475
15. R. Jin, A.G. Hauptmann, C.Z.: Title language model for information retrieval. Proceedings of the 24th annual international ACM SIGIR conference on Research and development in information retrieval (2002) 42–48
16. Fagin, R., Kumar, R., Sivakumar, D.: Comparing top k lists. Proceedings of the fourteenth annual ACM-SIAM symposium on Discrete algorithms (2003) 28–36

Conqueries:
An Agent That Supports Query Expansion

Jean-Yves Delort

Montpellier II University – LIRMM, 161 rue Ada, 34392 Montpellier, France
delort@lirmm.fr

Abstract. This article presents Conqueries, an agent that assists users during their searches on search engines. The system recommends terms and modifiers to users so that they can reformulate their queries. The system unobtrusively learns the user's current needs in order to propose personalized lists of keywords. The article presents the design and the architecture of Conqueries which has been implemented and describes the current version which has been used for almost a year.

1 Introduction

Different kinds of interactive systems may assist users seeking for information with a search engine. The main goal of these systems is to improve the user queries which are supposed to represent their information needs. Word re-weighting, search for similar pages, spelling correction and query expansion are among current query re-formulation techniques. Query-expansion consists in narrowing the scope of a search by adding new terms to a user's initial query.

Interactive query expansion tools are accessible from search engine interfaces[1]. However, insofar as they are on the server-side, they have a limited access to the user's interaction trails. Accordingly, they often neglect the users' behaviors. For example, they may rely on term co-occurrence in a corpus of documents, on a thesaurus or yet on a semantic net [1]. When they are tested on a wide-scale, recommendations provided by this approach (called global-analysis) are observed as being often ignored by users [2]. A likely reason is that the users' behaviors are not taken into account. Indeed, Web users' profiles, intentions and strategies may greatly differ.

Agents supporting searching on search engines using the users' behaviors have to cope with two main difficulties: 1) with a mean query size of 2.6 words [3], the representations of the users' needs are often imperfect and incomplete and, 2) users are often reluctant to send their feedbacks, because of privacy concerns or because it is time-consuming.

This article tackles with the issue of designing an agent which assists web searching through interactive query expansion. It presents Conqueries, an agent which helps users to reformulate their queries with recommended terms and modifiers. The query expansion algorithm is based on the content of the documents accessed by the user, a shift of focus detection algorithm and a heuristic to take into account the user's behavior with the suggestions themselves. The article reports feedbacks and design experience of Conqueries which has been used for almost a year.

---

[1] See for example Yahoo!, Excite, or Kartoo

D. Lowe and M. Gaedke (Eds.): ICWE 2005, LNCS 3579, pp. 161–166, 2005.

The paper is organized as follows. Section two outlines the general architecture of Conqueries. Section three explains the main features of the current algorithm query expansion of Conqueries. Section four describes how Conqueries can easily adapt to different search engine interfaces thanks to search engine templates. Finally, we survey other query expansion systems, discuss how they differ from Conqueries and conclude with the future improvements.

2 System Overview

We have developed a system called Conqueries that helps users to expand their queries during their searches on search engines. The system suggests personalized lists of keywords depending on the user's behavior. It is based on an unintrusive approach to learn the user's interests from their interaction trails.

Conqueries considers two kinds of user interactions:

1. An access to a *result list*, i.e. a page that contains links towards *result pages* retrieved by a search engine.
2. An access to a result page.

Subsection one presents an example of Web search with a search engine where the user is assisted by Conqueries to expand her queries[2]. Subsection two describes how Conqueries deals with the users' interactions. Subsection three addresses the issue of presenting a list of suggested terms to a user so that she can easily reformulate her previous query.

2.1 Example

Conqueries assists a user who is trying to expand her previous query because the results retrieved by the search engine did not satisfy her. The following scenario emphasizes the important steps in the search process and the time of Conqueries action. Let us denote by "SE" a search engine and by "Anna" a user looking for information about the major cities in Sweden[3]:

1. Anna formulates her initial query which is "Sweden cities" and she submits it to SE.
2. The result list page reports that 5,180,000 documents are relevant for the SE. Anna clicks on the first one in the list.
3. Anna looks at the content of the page which deals with tourism in Sweden. Her need is not satisfied and she gets back to the result list.
4. At that time, Conqueries recommends her the following terms, "cityguide", "Stockholm", "Malmö", "sightseeing" and "tours".
5. Anna chooses to insert "Stockholm" and "Malmö" (two of the major Swedish cities) in her query and she submits it to SE.
6. The result list reports now that about 140.000 are relevant. Among the top-ten results, Anna sees and clicks on a link to a document that looks really relevant to her.

---

[2] We will use the feminine pronoun (she, or) when referring to users of either gender
[3] This scenario was tested on Google.com, Feb. 9th 2005

7. Indeed, the document contains the list of the major cities in Sweden as well as their number of inhabitants. Anna's information need is satisfied.

This example shows how a query expansion system, like Conqueries, can support searching on a search engine. The next subsection reviews the different kinds of support query expansion systems should provide to the users.

2.2 Dealing with the User's Interactions

Conqueries is a Browser Helper Object (BHO) for Microsoft Internet Explorer. Accordingly, it can receive the browser's events triggered by the user's interactions.

When the user wants to access a page, Conqueries recognizes that the URL corresponds to a result list if it contains characteristic substrings like, the search engine domain name, the CGI name, an attribute, etc.

Conqueries finds out that a URL corresponds to a result page if the two following conditions hold:

1. the previously accessed page was a result list.
2. the URL is exactly contained in the enumeration of the previous result list. Indeed, the result list can contain other links (e.g. banners) which do not point towards result pages.

The second condition is checked as follow: First, two markers have two be looked for in the HTML content of the result list. Markers are strings saying precisely where the result enumeration starts and finishes. The URL is compared with all the URLs contained between the markers. If one matches, the URL corresponds to a result page.

If the user accesses a result list, Conqueries carries out the following actions:

1. the user query q is extracted (directly from the URL in the case of a GET or in the sent data in the case of a POST),
2. q is sent to the recommender system,
3. the new list of recommended terms is received from the recommender system,
4. the list is displayed in menu-words in Conqueries.

In the case of result page, Conqueries proceeds as follow:

1. it waits for the content of the result page to be completely displayed in the browser window,
2. the content of the page is sent to the recommender system.

2.3 Presenting Recommended Terms to the User

The interface of Conqueries is a toolbar in the browser window. Recommended terms are displayed in *menu-words*. The purpose of a menu-word is show the user the list of modifiers that can be used together with the word in the query. When a user clicks on an item in a menu-word, the content of the query field in the browser window is updated. An update consists either in appending a boolean modifier followed by the word to the query or in removing the chosen word from the query. Boolean modifiers can be "AND", "AND NOT", "NEAR", etc. They depend on the query language of the search engine. Figure 1 shows an example of a menu-word associated with the keyword "sweden" during a search on Google.

Fig. 1. A query-word

The query field is modified thanks to dynamically inserted Javascript into the content of the page when the page loads. Then, if the user clicks on a menu-item, a Javascript function is called.

The toolbar is made up with three areas [Fig. 2]:

1. "Settings": This single menu opens up a window where the user can tune the recommendation algorithm.
2. "History": This single menu contains the list of the user's previous queries. By clicking on a query, the user submits it again.
3. "Recommended terms": The fourth area displays the menu-words corresponding to the recommended terms.

Fig. 2. Conqueries toolbar

3 Query Expansion

In this section we briefly review the main features of the current algorithm used by Conqueries. Details of the algorithm can be found in [4]. The algorithm is based on the assumption that Web searchers often expand their queries with terms picked up in the content of previously accessed result pages [5]. Let us take an example to emphasize this idea. Let us suppose that a user needs information about health insurance in France and that her initial query is "insurance in France". Typically, existing search engines would retrieve millions of relevant pages. However, after browsing a few result pages, her next queries can contain refinement terms such as "health", "medical" or "security". We assume that often, these terms are picked up in the content of the accessed result pages.

The user confidence in the recommender system would probably decrease quickly if the system suggested irrelevant keywords. It can happen between the times when the user starts a new search and before she accesses a first result page. Then, the recommender system keeps recommending terms related to her previous interest because it is based on the last accessed result pages. We use a shift detection heuristic in order to avoid such a situation. When a shift occurs, Conqueries resets all the information about the user's needs it has saved so far.

Sometimes a term has been recommended several times in a row but the user has never used it. We consider that the user has no interest in it. Conqueries takes into account the previous recommendations in order not to recommend again terms that have been suggested more often than a given threshold.

4   Search Engine Templates

Conqueries can support searching on a great number of search engines provided that it knows useful information about the search engine:

1. the markers used to check if a URL belong to the result enumeration in a result list (let us denote them by, *startMarker* and *endMarker*)
2. the substrings used to check if a URL is a result list (*resultListCondition*).
3. the boolean modifiers and wildcards understood by the search engine (*modifier* in *modifierList*)
4. The form name (*formName*) and the name of the field where the query is entered (*formAttribute*).

These pieces of information are specific to each search engine.

Every time the user opens a browser instance, Conqueries connects to a server where it downloads the latest templates. If a search engine interface is changed then one only needs to update the template on the server-side so that every user of Conqueries can get the latest template.

5   Related Work and Conclusion

To our knowledge, [6] describes the closest system to Conqueries. It describes a meta-search system that recommends query expansion terms from the content of annotated relevant documents. However the system differs from Conqueries in the following reasons: First, the query expansion system requires the user explicit feedback. Second, it requires a specific architecture. Third, the user's shifts of focus and the behavior with respect to previous recommendations are not taken into account. [7] describes a link recommender system that automatically generates synthesized queries from terms contained in the previously accessed documents. The system is based on an algorithm that predicts whether a term is likely to occur in the last accessed relevant document or not. The approach is based on the idea that the last accessed document is the only relevant one. Unlike the query expansion algorithm used by Conqueries, this approach does not take into account the facts that user's needs can evolve during the search process and that the user may need to access several relevant pages before her information need is satisfied.

This article introduced Conqueries, an adaptive agent that assists users to reformulate their queries on search engines. Conqueries proposes a novel concept of interface for interactive query expansion. The interface has the ability to make the user reformulate her queries in only two clicks. Most users dislike systems that require explicit feedback that is why our query expansion algorithm is unintrusive. It has been improved thanks to the users' feedbacks which tend to emphasize the need of taking into account the shifts of focus and of filtering the unused recommendations.

The effectiveness of the algorithm implemented in Conqueries was studied in [5]. Future works will address the evaluation of the effectiveness of the interface we propose and the improvement of our current query expansion approach using a hybrid approach.

References

1. Stenmark, D.: Query expansion using an intranet-based semantic net. Proceedings of IRIS-26 (2003)
2. Anick, Peter: Using terminological feedback for web search refinement – a log-based study. Proceedings of the ACM Conference on Research and Development in Information Retrieval (2003) 88 – 95
3. Spink, A., Jansen, B. J., Wolfram, D., Saracevic, T.: From E-Sex to E-Commerce: Web Search Changes. IEEE Computer, Vol. 35 (3). (2002) 107 – 109
4. Delort, J.-Y.: Adaptive User Modeling for Query Expansion. Proceedings of the International Conference of Internet Technologies (2005)
5. Delort, J.-Y.: A User-Centered Approach for Evaluating Query Expansion Methods. (Under submission)
6. Smeaton, A. F., Crimmins, F.: Relevance feedback and query expansion for searching the web: A model for searching a digital library. Proceedings of The European Conference on Digital Librairies (1997)
7. Zhu, T., Greiner, R., Haubl, G.: Learning a Model of a Web User's Interests. Proceedings of the Ninth International Conference on User Modeling (2003)

Ubiquitous Information Retrieval
Using Multi-level Characteristics

Joonhee Kwon[1] and Sungrim Kim[2]

[1] Department of Computer Science, Kyonggi University,
San 94-6, Yiui-dong, Yeongtong-ku, Suwon-si, Kyonggi-do, Korea
kwonjh@kyonggi.ac.kr
[2] Department of Computer Science, Seoil College,
49-3, Myonmok-dong, Jungrang-Ku, Seoul, Korea
srkim@seoil.ac.kr

Abstract. Applications of ubiquitous computing are increasingly leveraging contextual information from several sources to provide users with behavior appropriate to their environment. The method of information retrieval is one of the most fundamental research issues in ubiquitous computing. Applications where user's contexts change continuously over time require prompt retrieval of relevant information. This paper proposes a new ubiquitous retrieval method that enables users to obtain relevant information efficiently using the multi level characteristics of the contexts. This paper describes the ubiquitous information retrieval process. Several experiments are performed and the results verify that proposed method has better retrieval performance.

1   Introduction

Weiser introduced the area of ubiquitous computing, and put forth a vision of people and environments augmented with computational resources that provide information and services whenever and wherever desired [1]. One of the most critical technologies in a variety of application services of ubiquitous computing is to supply adequate information or services depending on each context through context-awareness. The context is characterized by being continuously changed and defined as all information related to the entities such as users, space and objects [2, 3]. Ubiquitous computing applications need to be context-aware, adapting behavior based on information sensed from the physical and computational environment.

According to recent analysis on applications using context-aware ubiquitous computing, one of the most challenging research areas in the future is considered to be information retrieval methods in ubiquitous computing environment [4, 6]. The main consideration in information retrieval methods is how accurately it retrieves information required by the users and how rapidly it retrieves information even with the bulk of information to retrieve [4, 7]. Since existing ubiquitous computing retrieval methods get all detailed information for the target context in accordance with the continuous changes of contexts, the retrieval time takes longer. Moreover, since the retrieval results could lead to unwanted information for users, there is the problem in retrieving accurate information. Thus, new retrieval methods are required for rapid and accurate information retrieval.

We suggest a new ubiquitous retrieval method using multi level characteristics of contexts for rapid and accurate information retrieval. We adopt a multi level charac-

D. Lowe and M. Gaedke (Eds.): ICWE 2005, LNCS 3579, pp. 167–172, 2005.

teristic of contexts based on the observation that all information does not need to be retrieved at a time according to each context value. By using the multi level characteristics of contexts, we get more detailed information progressively as we get nearer to the context of interest. This enables more rapid and accurate information retrieval because of no access to the most detail information in the context values at a time.

Our discussion will proceed as follows. Section 2 will give an overview of related works. Section 3 will discuss the ubiquitous information retrieval process and section 4 will discuss the experimental results. Finally section 5 will conclude this paper.

2   Related Works

Most approaches to context-aware retrieval methods simply match user profiles to context values [6]. Because the mechanisms use only explicit information, there are limitations to retrieve useful information. Moreover, the method does not consider retrieving information rapidly.

An advanced approach to context-aware retrieval method in ubiquitous computing is proposed in [4]. It proposes a context-aware cache based on the context-aware diary. Based on the contents, the context-aware cache tries to capture the information the user is more likely to need in future contexts. It makes more immediate retrieval and reduces the cost of retrieving information by doing most of the work automatically. The context-aware diary stores past and future data that are explicitly informed. This approach, however, simply matches data from the context-aware diary to the current context, when the context-aware cache tries to capture future data.

The most recent approach to context-aware retrieval method is proposed in [8]. It uses a very similar approach to the approach we have taken. To retrieve information rapidly, this method locally stores the recommended information that the user is likely to need in the near future based on behavior patterns. To retrieve the information that would be required by the user, this method uses data mining methods. Moreover, using a multi-agent architecture, it allows continuous rapid and accurate information retrieval even with the change of user's contexts and solves the limitations of storage. However, this method retrieves the most detail information at a time causing unnecessary and slow information retrieval. Moreover, when the behavior pattern is not found, the method does not retrieve information rapidly and accurately.

The largest difference between our work and [8] is adoption of the multi level characteristics of context. It may reduce the amount of information requested for faster retrieval time and retrieve more accurate information for users.

3   Ubiquitous Information Retrieval Process

The proposed method for information retrieval is conceptually comprised of three main tasks, as shown in Figure 1. The first step is to extract the recommendation information rules related to the context values [8]. These are extracted using the association rule mining in the data mining [9] methods from the contexts database.

In the second step, the recommendation information in the near future is extracted using the current context value and recommendation information rules. In this paper, we call the window includes context values that have possibility of using in near future as "context window". When a behavior pattern [8] is found, the context values in

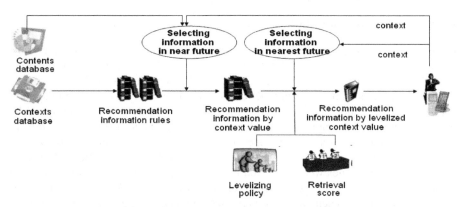

Fig. 1. Flow Diagram of the Proposed Method

context window is a behavior pattern, otherwise they are context values within a certain difference of value from the current context values.

In the final step, we extract the recommendation information to be appeared in the very near future using context value, levelizing policy and retrieval score. The recommendation information extracted in the second step can cause the storage capacity and transmitting rate to increase. To solve these problems, only the recommendation information that can be used in the very near future is stored and then this process is repeated.

The levelizing policy determines the level value of the current context value. In this paper, we assume that the levelizing policy is given. The level value means the level of detail of the information and determines properties of information to be retrieved. The information needed for a low level value is higher in priority and broader than it needed in a high level value. In this paper, we use the confidence in association rule mining as priority. For an example of the levelizing policy, the level value may be determined using the velocity in the location context. That is, faster (slower) velocity is considered as the request for simple (detailed) information on wider (narrower) area so that the level value is lower (higher).

For rapid and accurate information retrieval, we use the prefetching method. From the recommendation information by the second step, we extract recommendation information to be retrieved in the very near future using the current context value and level value. The size of context window in the very near future is determined by the level value and becomes larger in inverse proportion to the level value. We only extract information higher than priority allowed in current level value from the recommendation information of context values in the context window.

However, a replacement policy is needed by storage capacity limitation. Therefore, we propose the retrieval score. The retrieval score represents the priority of information determined by a level value of a context value when the context values are in the context window. The higher the retrieval score of information is, the higher the possibility to be accessed in the very near future is. We replace the information in the lower retrieval score with it in the higher retrieval score. It makes the high hit ratio in the client's storage. The retrieval score is zero in case the context values are not in the context window.

4 Experimental Evaluation

For experiments, we implemented both the proposed method called *System1* and the method in [8] called *System2*. All programs were written in Java. The server ran on a Pentium IV desktop computer. The client ran on a Pentium laptop computer.

In the experimental data, the number of context values was set to 100 and the number of recommendation rules was set to the number of context values multiplied by the row number of recommendation information. The number of rows of recommendation information was set to the number of rows of contents multiplied by 0.005.

The values of the contents were generated from number 1 to the number of the contents. The context values were generated from number 1 to the number of the context values. The action parts of recommendation rules were randomly generated from the values of contents for each condition parts, where condition parts are context values. The confidence of the rules is given randomly from 20 to 100. The number of levels in generated data is 4. For each level, the size of context window required in level value 1(2,3,4) is 10(7,4,1, respectively) and confidence allowed in level value 1(2,3,4) is 80(60,40,20, respectively). In addition, level values are higher whenever context values are changed in our experiment.

We evaluated the impact of the amount of contents for each level value. We ran an experiment 100 times for context values extracted at random for evaluation. In order to evaluate the impact of the row number of contents, we measured the average miss ratio in client for each context value to retrieve recommendation information. We set the maximum number of row allowed in client's storage to 100. For the comparison, we varied row numbers of contents by 10% from 10,000 to 31,384. The measurements of the evaluation for each level value are depicted in Figure 2.

As shown in Figure 2, for *System1*, the average miss ratio is near zero when the row number of contents decreases. However, average miss ratio for *System2* exceeds 50% in level value 1, 2 and 3. Only in level value 4, average miss ratio for *System1* and *System2* is almost the same. In level value 4, both *System1* and *System2* use the most detail information; therefore the results are almost the same. Several other observations are found on these results. First, the average miss ratio in *System1* consistently performs better than that in the *System2*. Second, as the level value is lower, the difference between the *System1* and *System2* is increased. As the level value is lower, the number of context values required in the near future is greater. The result shows the high miss ratios in *System2*.

5 Conclusion

Ubiquitous information retrieval is very promising but has not been sufficiently explored. This paper introduced a new ubiquitous retrieval method using multi level characteristics of contexts. The proposed method was explained with the system flow, the scenario, the algorithms and the experimental results.

There have been some studies in context-aware retrieval methods for ubiquitous computing. These methods however, all use the most detailed information. We suggest a new ubiquitous retrieval method using the multi level characteristics of contexts for rapid and accurate information retrieval. By the multi level characteristics of contexts, we get more detailed information progressively as we get nearer to the con-

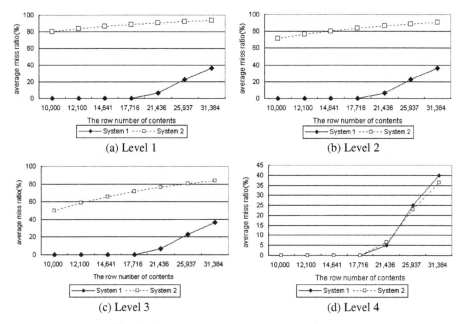

Fig. 2. The Impact of the Row Number of Contents

text of interest. This enables the rapid and accurate information retrieval, because of no access to the most detail information in all context value at a time.

The proposed method has several advantages. First, we presented a new ubiquitous information retrieval method using multi level characteristics of contexts. By using these multi level characteristics of contexts, information is retrieved rapidly and accurately. Second, we proposed a new prefetching and replacement method for levelized context-aware information. The proposed method could be used in ubiquitous applications to improve information retrieval.

Acknowledgements

This work was supported by grant No.R04-2004-000-10056-0 from the Basic Research Program of the Korea Research Foundation.

References

1. Mark Weiser: The computer for the 21st century. Scientific American, Vol. 265, No. 30, p.94-104, 1991
2. Anind K. Dey, Daniel Salber, Gregory D. Abowd: A Conceptual Framework and a Toolkit for Supporting the Rapid Prototyping of Context-Aware Applications. Anchor article of a special issue on Context-Aware Computing Human-Computer Interaction Journal, Vol. 16, No. 2-4, p.97-166, 2001
3. Paul Prekop, Mark Burnett: Activities, Context and Ubiquitous Computing. Special Issue on Ubiquitous Computing, Computer Communications, Autumn, 2002

4. P. J. Brown, G. J. F. Jones: Context-aware Retrieval: Exploring a New Environment for Information Retrieval and Information Filtering. Personal and Ubiquitous Computing, 2001, Volume 5, Issue 4, December, p.253 - 263, 2001
5. Jeffrey Hightower, Gaetano Borriello: Location Systems for Ubiquitous Computing. Computer, Vol. 34, No. 8, p 57-66, IEEE Computer Society Press, 2001
6. Getri Kappel, Birgit. Proll, Werner Retschitzegger, Wieland Schwinger: Customisation for Ubiquitous Web Applications - A Comparison of Approaches. International Journal of Web Engineering and Technology, Vol.1, No.1, p. 79-111, January, 2003
7. Bradley J. Rhodes, Pattie Maes: Just-in-time information retrieval agents. IBM Systems Journal, Vol. 39, No. 3&4, p.685-704, 2000
8. Joonhee Kwon, Sungrim Kim, Yongik Yoon: Just-In-Time Recommendation using Multi-Agents for Context-Awareness in Ubiquitous Computing Environment. Lecture Notes in Computer Science 2973, Mar, 2004
9. R. Agrawal, T. Imielinski, A. Swami: Mining association rules in large databases. In Proceedings of ACM SIGMOD Conference on Management of Data, Washington D.C., p.207-216, May 1993

First-Order Patterns for Information Integration

Mark A. Cameron and Kerry Taylor

CSIRO ICT Centre
GPO Box 664 Canberra, 2601, Australia
{Mark.Cameron,Kerry.Taylor}@csiro.au

Abstract. Advanced inter-enterprise applications operate in an environment that changes rapidly as autonomous services dynamically join and leave a community of interest at will. Well-designed integrated information views simplify inter-enterprise application development by hiding details of data distribution, extraction, filter and transformation from inter-enterprise applications, thereby shielding them from unwanted environment changes. Recently, the local-centric *local-as-view (LAV)* approach to integrated information view specification has attracted attention because of its maintainability advantage over the traditional *global-as-view (GAV)* approach. This paper introduces a first-order predicate calculus mapping language that admits LAV, GAV and *global-and-local-as-view (GLAV)* view mapping specifications over distributed database tables and service functions. Mapping patterns that apply to a wide range of integration problems are presented in the language. A case-study inter-enterprise application is used to illustrate the patterns in action.

1   Introduction

Despite a long and rich research history, data integration remains a key challenge in practice for modern business enterprises. Consumers are demanding that enterprises improve both the efficiency of internal processes and their internal knowledge of the dynamic and historical behaviour of their business. At the same time, rapidly changing business environments require rapid changes in business partner relationships and corporate structures. These two factors put enormous pressure on enterprise information sytems to keep up with the businesses they serve. Inevitably, data integration is required as information is extracted from legacy information systems and recombined and repurposed for new ones.

Lenzerini [1] formalizes an integration system $\mathcal{I}$ as consisting of $\langle \mathcal{G}, \mathcal{S}, \mathcal{M} \rangle$, where $\mathcal{G}$ is the global (integrated) schema, $\mathcal{S}$ are source schemas, and $\mathcal{M}$ is a set of assertions relating elements of the global schema with elements of the source schemas. $\mathcal{G}$, $\mathcal{S}$ and $\mathcal{M}$ are specified in some (though possibly different) suitable language. There are four flavours of mapping specification for $\mathcal{M}$: *global-as-view* (GAV), *local-as-view* (LAV), *global-and-local-as-view* (GLAV), and *peer-to-peer*, which we do not address further here.

In a GAV integration system, each mapping in $\mathcal{M}$ defines part of the global schema $\mathcal{G}$ in terms of queries over source schemas $\mathcal{S}$, in much the same way as

D. Lowe and M. Gaedke (Eds.): ICWE 2005, LNCS 3579, pp. 173–184, 2005.

one defines a view in SQL as a query over other relations or views. In a LAV setting, each mapping in $\mathcal{M}$ defines a source schema $\mathcal{S}$ in terms of queries over the global schema $\mathcal{G}$. The advantage of LAV mappings is that they treat sources independently: a mapping is phrased in terms of the relationship between a single source schema and the global view, without reference to other sources. GLAV mappings aim to exploit the value of a combined local and global approach. GLAV integration systems admit mappings $\mathcal{M}$ that are a mixture of GAV and LAV mappings, and may relate queries over multiple sources to queries over the global schema.

It is always possible to transform a LAV integration system into a GAV integration system [2], however the reverse is not always possible. The value of a GLAV approach is not well explored [3, 4], but there are two key reasons for preferring it. Despite the advantages of LAV for dynamic source integration, LAV alone does not permit the phrasing of mapping rules that take advantage of within-source joins, nor across-source joins through queries against the global schema.

Whatever style (GAV, LAV, GLAV) of integration mapping is applied, there are specific challenges that integration systems must meet. Data integration, according to [5], involves eight tasks, of which the sixth requires creating mappings between sources and the global schema. This step encapsulates the knowledge gained from all the previous steps, so it is important that the mapping language is sufficiently expressive to deal with the range of possible variation in the understanding developed in the previous steps. It is our goal to ensure that the mappings are both human-readable and directly computer-interpretable in order to actuate the data integration process at run-time (the final step).

In this paper we present such a mapping language, called **iMaPl**, based on the first-order predicate calculus (FOPC). It is a GLAV language, which means that it can express LAV and GAV mappings as degenerate cases. It is a declarative language, which means that it is amenable to interpretation and optimisation by computational means. We present mapping patterns that can be applied in many situations, to assist DBAs or domain experts to formulate the mappings they require for particular data integration projects. We have developed a comprehensive run-time environment for actuation of the mappings for data integration, but this is not presented here.

Outline. The paper is organised as follows. Next we describe a case-study application, Sydney's Information Highway. Then we introduce **iMaPl**. In section 4 we describe problems in information integration and the patterns expressed in **iMaPl** that apply to those problems, illustrated by reference to the case study. We then outline further work and conclude.

2   Case Study: Sydney's Information Highway

For an example in this paper we describe a case study of government information sharing associated with a major transport route in Sydney, Australia, known as the Sydney Information Highway (SIH) [6]. Local and state government agencies contribute information services to an inter-enterprise application that permits map-based search and display. Basic information services remain under the control and data management responsibility of the originating data custodians, being served to the Web from their own IT infrastructure. Users, including land developers, real estate investors, local government planning authorities and the general public have seamless access to information with a whole-of-government perspective. We introduce a conceptual model of the global schema for Sydney's Information Highway, together with sources and their schemas shown in figure 1.

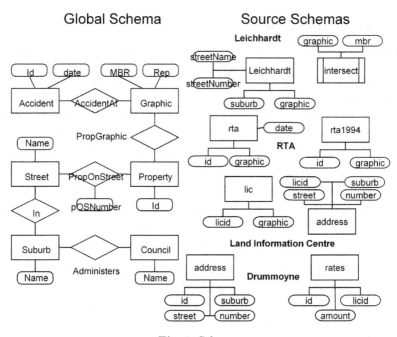

Fig. 1. Schemas

3 iMaPl Mapping Language

3.1 Preliminaries

For this paper, we will favour logic programming terminology and notation as defined in [7]. The **iMaPl** language consists of terms, atomic formulas, and compound formulas. A term is either a constant symbol (we use lowercase symbols, quoted symbols or numbers such as a, "a", 50), a variable symbol (strings starting with uppercase symbols X, or _ for an anonymous variable that is distinct from every other variable), or a compound term consisting of a function symbol and a sequence of terms such as $f(a, X)$. A predicate consists of a predicate symbol (lowercase or quoted symbols such as p or '$p@s$') and a sequence of terms (such as $p(X_1, ..., X_n)$). Constraints are binary operators $Op \in \{<, >, >=, =<\}$ applied to pairs of terms (such as $A < 23$). Compound formulas are formed in the usual way from predicates, constraints, logical connectives (conjunction $\wedge$, disjunction $\vee$, implication $\rightarrow$ or $\leftarrow$) and quantifiers $Quant \in \{\forall, \exists\}$. Quantified expressions are of the form $\forall(\bar{V}ar, P)$ and $\exists(\bar{V}ar, P)$ for formula P. By convention, we may omit universal quantifiers. Where notational detail is not important, we simplify term sequences such as $X_1, ..., X_n$ with $\bar{X}$ and indicate omission of detail with '...'.

Describing sources within the $\langle \mathcal{G}, \mathcal{S}, \mathcal{M} \rangle$ model requires a mapping language to connect a language for $\mathcal{S}$ to a language for $\mathcal{G}$. The @ operator ('p@s') identifies source predicates from $\mathcal{S}$ distinguishing them from global predicates in $\mathcal{G}$.

3.2   Language Definition

Our mapping language admits three forms of mapping statements: GAV, LAV and GLAV. $\mathcal{M}$ is comprised of assertions of these forms.

Each mapping statement is of the form $Quant(\bar{V}ar,(P \rightarrow Q))$. The logical connective implication ($\rightarrow$) partitions the statement into "if [P] then [Q] is a consequence". The implication ($Q \leftarrow P$) is a notational variation. This provides a convenient way to express what bindings are exchanged between expressions P and Q without having to write expressions using the logical connectives $\sim$, $\wedge$ or $\vee$.

The antecedent [P] and consequent [Q] are compound formulae comprised of predicates, quantifiers, constraints, conjuncts and disjuncts but never including negation or implication. All variables appearing in [Q] must also appear in [P] or else be existentially quantified. Free variables in a mapping statement are assumed to be universally quantified over the scope of the statement.

Using the @ operator to partition our $\mathcal{S}$ and $\mathcal{G}$ schemas, we can now establish syntactic patterns for GAV, LAV and GLAV mapping statements. One of the features of these patterns is that mapping expressions logically constrain models for $\mathcal{G}$ but they do not constrain models for $\mathcal{S}$. That is, mapping statements are unable to create new $\mathcal{S}$ entities–these must come from the sources themselves– and are unable to create inconsistencies in the sources. Therefore they are well suited to autonomous service-based systems. If necessary, integrity constraints can be used to ensure that agreed data quality standards are met.

GAV Mappings. GAV mappings are mapping implications ($P \rightarrow Q$) where the [P] expression is a compound formula and the [Q] expression consists of only one $\mathcal{G}$ schema predicate. This corresponds to conventional view definitions.

LAV Mappings. LAV mappings are mapping implications ($P \rightarrow Q$) where the [P] expression consists of one $\mathcal{S}$ predicate; the [Q] expression consists of conjuncts of $\mathcal{G}$ schema predicates. Quantifiers may be used within [P] and [Q].

Applying the LAV mapping scheme to the `leichhardt` schema at the Leichhardt source results in a mapping expression

$leichhardt(\_, \_, SuburbName, \_)@Leichhardt \rightarrow$
$suburb(SuburbName) \wedge suburbName(SuburbName, SuburbName)$

Which corresponds to the intention "if we obtain a value for `SuburbName` from `leichhardt@Leichhardt` then both `suburb(SuburbName)` and `suburbName(SuburbName, SuburbName)` hold in a model for $\mathcal{G}$".

GLAV Mappings. GLAV mappings are mapping implications (P $\rightarrow$ Q) where the [P] expression is unconstrained (i.e consists of zero or more $\mathcal{S}$ or $\mathcal{G}$ predicates conjuncts, disjuncts, quantifiers or constraint operators); the [Q] expression consists of conjuncts of $\mathcal{G}$ schema predicates and quantifiers.

4   Integration Patterns

The generic language definition patterns of Sect. 3 provide useful templates for GAV, LAV and GLAV mapping statements. These templates are common building blocks for the problem-centric patterns of schema mismatch, value mismatch and coverage constraints.

Mismatch between source and target schemas and values is a very common problem. Examples of schema mismatch include explicit vs implicit representation of concepts; tabular vs structured representations of entities; and composite vs atomic vs missing entity identifiers. The patterns of Sect. 4.1 are well suited to problems of schema mismatch. Value mismatches cover domain issues such as inconsistent units of measure (m/s vs ft/s), as well as formatting mismatches (capitalized vs lowercase vs camel case) and data entry errors. Section 4.2 documents patterns for addressing value mismatches between sources and the integrated schema. Often both value and schema mismatches occur simultaneously.

4.1   Patterns for Schema Mismatch

Problem: Making Implicit Information Explicit. Successfully incorporating legacy systems into an integrated federation often requires understanding the implicit assumptions developers made. In our example, both Drummoyne and Leichhardt record property information such as street name, number and suburb. Neither system explicitly understands that the suburbs and streets within their domain are administered by the respective council. The `council` entity and the `administers` relationship between Council and Suburb is implicit knowledge for both Leichhardt and Drummoyne.

Pattern: Integration Meta-data. While some data is not available directly from the participating source, we can use our knowledge of the environment to record the data directly within the integration schema. Within a mapping specification $\mathcal{M}$, one might use this GLAV pattern to augment an integrated $\mathcal{G}$ schema predicate with additional database instances that are missing from a source.

Example 1. Integration Meta-data

$council(leichhardt)\wedge$
$councilName(leichhardt, \text{``Leichhardt''})\leftarrow$

Problem: Structural $\mathcal{G}$ Schema Constraints. The token `leichhardt` used to identify Leichhardt as a member of `council` in ex. 1, is somewhat arbitrary, as the service representing Leichhardt cannot itself supply one. However, the relationship between `council` and `councilName` is a $\mathcal{G}$ schema constraint requiring that we use the same token (whatever it may be). Our example dependency is modest, but there are variations of this structural constraint problem that apply to more complex document structures [8, 9].

Pattern: Quantification.   Existential $\exists(\bar{Var}, Formula)$ and   universal $\forall(\bar{Var}, Formula)$ quantification enables mapping specifications to quantify what is known about individuals that meet criteria expressed in the statement scope. Existential quantification is useful where there are discrepancies in mapping attributes between $\mathcal{S}$ and $\mathcal{G}$ schemas i.e. where the $\mathcal{G}$ schema has more attributes than a source can contribute. More formally, if x is a variable and P is a well formed formula, then $\exists x(P)$ is an existential quantification of x over the scope P; "there exists [x] such that [P]"; and universal quantification "for each [x] such that [P]".

By using the same quantified variable within an expression scope covering structural constraints, it is possible to tie together $\mathcal{G}$ schema entities in a way that satisfies the structural constraints as well as provide values for known information.

Patterns in Action. In example 2, we rewrite the mapping statement of ex. 1 to replace occurrences of the token `leichhardt` with an existentially quantified variable C and simultaneously express a mapping implication to map tokens from our Leichhardt source onto the $\mathcal{G}$ schema entity `suburbName`.

Example 2. Quantification

$\exists(C, \ (council(C) \land$
$councilName(C, \text{``} Leichhardt\text{''}) \land$
$\forall(SuburbName, leichhardt(\_, \_, SuburbName, \_)@Leichhardt \rightarrow$
$\exists(Suburb, (suburb(Suburb) \land$
$suburbName(Suburb, SuburbName) \land$
$administers(C, Suburb))))))$

Informally, this mapping expression captures our desire that "there exists a C such that `council(C)` and `councilName(C,"Leichhardt")` and if we obtain a value for `SuburbName` from `leichhardt@Leichhardt` then there exists a Suburb such that `suburb(Suburb)` and `suburbName(Suburb, SuburbName)` and `administers(C,Suburb)`"

Problem: Transitive Closures. GLAV mappings open the possibility to write recursive mapping statements, for example to generate the transitive closure of a relation. Transitive closures may be needed when dealing with transitive relations obtained from multiple sources [10].

Pattern: Recursive Mappings. Recursive mapping expressions will generally have one or more base (non-recursive) cases, followed by a recursive case. In the example below, we use a recursive mapping pattern to obtain the `connected` relation through functional source operators `nextTo`.

Pattern in Action

Example 3. Recursive Mapping

$suburb($ "Glebe" $)\leftarrow$

$suburb(S) \wedge nextTo(S, P)@Leichhardt \rightarrow connected(S, P) \wedge suburb(P)$

$suburb(S) \wedge connected(S, P) \wedge nextTo(P, Q)@Leichhardt$
$\rightarrow connected(S, Q) \wedge suburb(Q)$

4.2 Patterns for Value Mismatch

Problem: Normalized Representation. Our example has shown how to obtain tokens representing suburb names from a source. Leichhardt council provides sentence case names while LIC provides uppercase names. Sometimes a $\mathcal{G}$ schema will require a single representation for tokens for a domain; suburb name in our example has two $\mathcal{S}$ representations, and with a $\mathcal{G}$ schema requirement for lowercase, neither $\mathcal{S}$ representation matches. The challenge for a mapping language is to enable encoding of transformations so that raw data from a source is processed into the normalized representation required by the integrated schema.

Pattern: Source Specific Normalization. The source specific normalization pattern encodes transformation knowledge directly into the $\mathcal{M}$ expression. The idea is that variables from data producers are connected directly to transformation operators, whose output is placed into the $\mathcal{G}$ schema. Source specific normalization follows the scheme: $[P(..., \bar{X})@S_i] \wedge [F(..., \bar{X}, ...\bar{Y})@S_j] \rightarrow [G(...\bar{Y})]$.

Patterns in Action. Example 4 shows this pattern applied to directly transforming Leichhardt source suburb names to lowercase expressed by a within-source join.

Example 4. Source Specific Normalization

$leichhardt(\_, \_, SuburbNameS, \_)@Leichhardt \wedge$
$to\_lowercase(SuburbNameS, SuburbName)@Leichhardt$
$\rightarrow$
$\exists(Suburb, (suburb(Suburb) \wedge$
$suburbName(Suburb, SuburbName)))))$

This pattern brings up a knowledge-engineering issue. Knowledge about how to manipulate and transform domain values (e.g transform the $\mathcal{S}$ specific domain SuburbNameS into the $\mathcal{G}$ schema SuburbName) has been tightly merged with knowledge about how to populate a schema from a source.

The following patterns encode an alternative strategy to formulating and writing mapping statements when a separation of knowledge about transforming data representations from populating domains is required.

Pattern: Domain Specific Normalization. In the domain specific normalization pattern, type domains are explicitly described in the $\mathcal{G}$ schema; and we set up domain-specific type transformation schemas, capturing our desire to transform data from one representation into another. These domain specific transformation schemas are global predicates that require implementations. These implementations will of course be delegated to the set of underlying operations offered by sources.

Our source mapping statements will then populate the appropriate $\mathcal{G}$ predicates by appealing to the domain specific transformation offered by the $\mathcal{G}$ schema. This pattern requires recursive mapping expressions. It is similar to techniques described in [10] for dealing with functional dependencies among $\mathcal{G}$ schema predicates; and [11] for dealing with sources with limited capabilities.

In our running example, we have a number of sources offering graphic entities. On closer inspection, one might discover that RTA offers point graphic entities of type OGISPoint, Leichhardt offers graphics of type mifmid, while LIC offers graphic entities of type OGISPolygon. Furthermore, the functionsRus service offers a suite of transformation operations: toMifMid, toOgisFeature, toSVG and toJPG, each of which is capable of transforming input data from a source type to a target type. The transform services form a directed graph (containing cycles) over the types.

The first part of the pattern requires setting up our domain for graphic entities; we use typeOf(V, T) to denote that values of V have type T. This domain functor provides a placeholder for two things: making statements (assertions) about data after it is retrieved from a source or transformed by a service; and acting as a constraint requiring that data be in a specified format. Example 5 shows how this pattern might apply to graphic data elements retrieved from Leichhardt. Similar statement patterns apply for the remaining resources.

Example 5. Populating Domain from Sources

$leichhardt(..., Graphic)@Leichhardt$
$\rightarrow$
$graphic(typeOf(Graphic, mifmid))$

The second part of the pattern requires setting up a typeTransform type transformation operator. This operator has two parts: an equality theory for the domain (a statement that says transformations between data in the same type is a no-op and a statement about the transitivity of type transformations); and statements about the services that implement the operator. Assume a functional dependency from input (first variable) to output. In example 6, the global operator will have implementations delegated to the appropriate service specific operations. Furthermore, notice the use of the domain functor `typeOf(V, T)` as a constraint (or precondition) on the type of information sent to the operation.

Example 6. Domain Rules & Type Transform Implementations

Domain Rules
$typeTransform(typeOf(X, Y), typeOf(X, Y))) \leftarrow$

$typeTransform(X, Y) \wedge typeTransform(Y, Z)$
$\rightarrow$
$typeTransform(X, Z))$

Mapping Rules
$toSVG(Graphic1, Graphic2)@functionsRus \wedge$
$(((Vector = shapeFile) \vee (Vector = mifmid))$
$\rightarrow$
$typeTransform(typeOf(Graphic1, Vector), typeOf(Graphic2, svg)))$
...

Queries over the $\mathcal{G}$ schema use `typeTransform(X,Y)` and `typeOf` to trigger the necessary type conversions. For example:

$$q(Y) \leftarrow graphic(X) \wedge typeTransform(X, typeOf(Y, svg)).$$

Problem: Object Reconciliation. For multiple data sources, shared error-free identifying fields are uncommon. We have shown two techniques, source specific normalization and domain normalization, which are suitable for cases where normalizing is a viable strategy.

Alternatively, value mismatch may be resolved by record linking techniques. There is a large literature focussed on record linkage techniques, software and methods [12–16].

Pattern: Object Reconciliation. In [17], steps for specifying a sequence of virtual services encapsulated in a composition for record linking are given. The virtual service has a $\mathcal{G}$ schema of `link(DataA, DataB, LinkedData)` relying on support predicates such as `standardize`, `index`, `compare` and `classify`. Intuitively, values from two sources are compared and a probabilistic match score is returned indicating the likelihood that values are the same. A pattern for mapping sources to any of the support predicates (F) follows: $[SF_m(..., \bar{X}, ..., \bar{Z})@S_a] \wedge [SF_n(\bar{Z}, ..., \bar{Y})@S_z] \rightarrow [F(step_{i-1}(\bar{X}), step_i(\bar{Y}))]$ The support predicates have function terms such as $step_i$ which work together to ensure that services are sequenced correctly.

4.3   Coverage Constraints

Problem: Logical Fragmentation. A coverage constraint is, informally, a statement about the range of values held for a relation in a particular source database. We should use coverage constraints in query planning to exclude sources from mapped queries when we know from the coverage constraint that those sources cannot contribute to the answers to our query. A coverage constraint is quite different to an integrity constraint, although these can also provide information to assist query planning [18].

Pattern: Coverage Constraint. Constraint expressions are formed from the standard constraint operators $Op \in \{<, >, >=, =<\}$ applied to terms. Our pattern for using coverage constraints requires that the constraints appear on the antecedent of the implication, all variables appearing in the constraint expression are universally quantified (the quantifier may be omitted by convention):
$\forall(\bar{X}, [P(..., \bar{X}, ...) \wedge Op(\bar{X})] \rightarrow [Q])$

In general, constraint reasoning (see [19] for example) is required to either eliminate mappings from source specific plans or tighten the source specific query bounds.

Patterns in Action. RTA data sources offer accident data based on date. Consider two RTA sources, one contributing data for 1994, and the other for subsequent years. This example demonstrates both coverage constraint and domain specific normalization.

Example 7. Coverage Constraint

$rta1994(..., Spatial)@rta1994 \wedge$
$ADate = 1994$
$\rightarrow$
$accident(ADate, ..., Spatial) \wedge graphic(typeOf(Spatial, ogisPoint))$

$rta(ADate, ..., Spatial)@rta \wedge$
$ADate > 1996$
$\rightarrow$
$accident(ADate, ..., Spatial) \wedge graphic(typeOf(Spatial, ogisFeature))$

Queries can constrain a predicate thus:

$q(T) \leftarrow accident(D, ..., S) \wedge typeTransform(S, typeOf(T, svg)) \wedge D > 2000.$

Constraint reasoning techniques are required to tighten the query bounds (and thus remove the redundant constraint $Date > 1996$ [19]) on the requests sent to sources. The coverage constraint pattern also applies to categorical domains as well as integer domains as we have shown in example 7.

5   Conclusion and Further Work

We have applied recent research on local-as-view query planning to the problem of dynamically building integration plans in response to user-defined requests. Our approach relies heavily on the run-time interpretation of expressive mapping rules that relate sources of data and functional data transformations to global concepts. In this paper we have defined a range of mapping patterns that are designed to address commonly-occurring integration problems. These patterns, expressed in the language of first order predicate calculus, may be interpreted by suitable planning engines, such as one we have under development. Because they are declarative, with a well-defined semantics, they may also be used as a benchmark for evaluating the capabilities of information integration systems.

Our approach subsumes well known GAV, LAV and GLAV mapping patterns for query planning, and extends to offer declarative local database coverage constraints, data type coercion, and recursive mappings. We have defined patterns that address specific information integration problems for schema and value mismatch and object reconciliation.

We are aware of some problems not adequately covered by these patterns, for example, negation, nested implication and mapping expressions that require second-order predicates. Some of these shortcomings in our mapping language arise from our goal for both human readability of the language and sound computational interpretation. We have preferred a syntactic description of the mapping language for ease of adoption by developers at the expense of admitting more expressive mappings that may be safely interpreted only if complex conditions about their construction are met. Ongoing work is extending our pattern set.

References

1. Lenzerini, M.: Data integration: A theoretical perspective. In: PODS, Madison, Wisconsin (2002) 233–246
2. Cali, A., De Giacomo, G., Lenzerini, M.: Models for information integration: turning local-as-view into global-as-view. In: Proceedings of International Workshop on Foundations of Models for Information Integration (10th Workshop in the series Foundations of Models and Languages for Data and Objects). (2001)
3. Lenzerini, M.: Data integration is harder than you thought. Keynote presentation, CoopIS 2001, Trento, Italy (2001)
4. Cali, A., Calvanese, D., De Giacomo, G., Lenzerini, M.: On the expressive power of data integration systems. In: Proc. of the 21st Int. Conf. on Conceptual Modeling (ER 2002). (2002)
5. Seligman, L., Rosenthal, A., Lehner, P., Smith, A.: Data Integration: Where Does the Time Go? Bulletin of the IEEE Computer Society Technical Committee on Data Engineering **25** (2002)
6. Cameron, M.A., Taylor, K.L., Abel, D.J.: The Internet Marketplace Template: An Architecture Template for Inter-enterprise Information Systems. In: Proccedings of the Sixth IFCIS International Conference on Cooperative Information Systems (CoopIS'2001). Volume 2172 of LNCS., Trento, Italy, Springer (2001) 329–343
7. Lloyd, J.W.: Foundations of Logic Programming. 2nd edn. Springer-Verlag (1987)

8. Levy, A.Y., Suciu, D.: Deciding containment for queries with complex objects. In: Proc. of the 16th ACM SIGMOD Symposium on Principles of Database Systems, Tucson, Arizona (1997) 20–31
9. Popa, L., Velegrakis, Y., Miller, R.J., Hernández, M.A., Fagin, R.: Translating web data. In: Proceedings of VLDB 2002, Hong Kong SAR, China (2002) 598–609
10. Duschka, O.M., Genesereth, M.R., Levy, A.Y.: Recursive query plans for data integration. Journal of Logic Programming **43** (2000) 49–73
11. Li, C., Chang, E.Y.: Query planning with limited source capabilities. In: ICDE. (2000) 401–412
12. Fellegi, L., Sunter, A.: A Theory for Record Linkage. Journal of the American Statistical Society **64** (1969) 1183–1210
13. Cohen, W.: Data integration using similarity joins and a word-based information representation language. ACM Transactions on Information Systems **18** (2000) 288–321
14. Elfeky, M., Verykios, V., Elmagarmid, A.: TAILOR: A Record Linkage Toolbox. In: Proc. of the 18th Int. Conf. on Data Engineering, IEEE (2002)
15. Christen, P., Churches, T., Hegland, M.: A parallel open source data linkage system. In: Proc. of the 8th Pacific-Asia Conference on Knowledge Discovery and Data Mining (PAKDD'04), Sydney (2004)
16. Nick Koudas, Amit Marathe, D.S.: Flexible string matching against large databases in practice. In: Proceedings of the 30th VLDB Conference, Toronto, Canada (2004)
17. Cameron, M.A., Taylor, K.L., Baxter, R.: Web Service Composition and Record Linking. In: Proceedings of the Workshop on Information Integration on the Web (IIWeb-2004), Toronto, Canada (2004)
18. Cali, A., Calvanese, D., De Giacomo, G., Lenzerini, M.: Accessing data integration systems through conceptual schemas. In: Proceedings of the 20th International Conference on Conceptual Modeling (ER'01), Yokohama, Japan (2001)
19. Guo, S., Sun, W., Weiss, M.A.: Solving satisfiability and implication problems in database systems. ACM Transactions on Database Systems (TODS) **21** (1996)

Web Application Development:
Java, .Net and Lamp at the Same Time*

Jaime Navón and Pablo Bustos

Computer Science Dept., P.Universidad Católica de Chile
Vicuña Mackenna 4860, Santiago, Chile
{jnavon,pbustos}@ing.puc.cl

Abstract. Web applications are usually built starting from incomplete design documents and proceeding directly to implementation for some specific software platform. The resulting application is usually difficult to change or extend. Although several methodologies have been proposed in the last few years, most of them use a concrete approach that leverages the features of a specific software platform or concrete Web elements. Model-driven development proposals, on the other hand, are difficult to adopt. This paper discusses a successful intermediate approach that allows the designer to work with abstract artifacts that can be readily mapped into any MVC-based (application) framework, independently of which software platform is used. This methodology is simple and easy to learn, even by those who are not platform experts. We present it in terms of a real-life running application for use by local governments in Chile.

1 Introduction

Over the last decade, society has become increasingly dependent on the Internet. In the wake of this phenomenon, software developers are finding themselves under pressure to build more and more complex applications in less and less time. Very often Web applications are built with little or no methodology behind them [1]. It is not unusual to find navigation diagrams mixed together with architectural designs, while important details are not documented at all. The resulting applications exhibit poor quality attributes and are hard to extend or adapt to the ever-changing requirements of the domain.

In the last five years there has been a significant effort in the research community to propose a sound and systematic methodology (method and artifacts). Most of these proposals fall into one of the following two categories:

- A concrete approach that leverages the features of a particular platform (i.e., Java, ASP.NET, etc.) or concrete Web elements (frames, anchors, etc.).
- A relatively abstract approach that is completely independent of the platform and even of the Web itself.

In our experience, neither approach is suitable. The first one is easy to sell: developers see an immediate solution to their concrete problems and it requires significant

---

* This research is supported in part by the Chilean National Fund for Science and Technology (Fondecyt Project 1020733)

D. Lowe and M. Gaedke (Eds.): ICWE 2005, LNCS 3579, pp. 185–190, 2005.

less effort to learn. In [2] the author defines an extension to UML, called Web Application Extension that models Web elements at a very concrete level. The resulting models are almost ready for implementation, but they remain tightly coupled to the software platform. In [3], the authors propose a methodology for developing all the components typical of Web applications but their methodology and architecture are closely linked to the Java 2 platform Enterprise Edition (J2EE) technology. Although J2EE defines a *de facto* standard for developing multi-tier interactive Web applications, it is not always easy to map these solutions to other popular Web platforms such as PHP (LAMP[1]) or ASP.NET.

As for the second approach, many designers are reluctant to adopt a platform-independent methodology. They find that it has little connection with the world they are dealing with, and feel it will take too long to arrive at a real solution once everything is modeled in the abstract world. This is the case, for example, with the artifacts of some proposals on operational specification of applications. Sequence diagrams, proposed in [4] and [5], cannot specify all possible paths an application would be required to handle. Activity diagrams as proposed in [6] improve the flows specification, but are deficient in components interaction specification. Moreover, most of these proposals share a troubling characteristic: they do not capture the fundamental characteristics of every Web application (i.e., http stateless, and therefore request-response roundtrips and session state). Their level of abstraction goes beyond middleware (i.e., J2EE, ASP.NET) to actually achieve Web independence, and their guides and artifacts can also be used to model a classic non-Web application. This independence, though it may at first seem to be desirable, in fact impedes the identification of essential Web components such as request filters (i.e., logged user session filters). Full platform independence as proposed by the Model Driven Architecture [7] movement is an interesting challenge, but only if the models are specific enough to feed the tools for automatic code generation. Otherwise, completely mapping an abstract model to the implementation platform will be a difficult task.

We have been developing an intermediate approach. It involves a UML-based methodology that is platform independent, but whose artifacts nevertheless can be mapped easily through appropriate restrictions to a specific platform. Furthermore, our approach is general enough to accommodate any Web application whose architecture fits the MVC pattern. In [8] we described the main features of our proposal, which included a first methodology. The key to our approach is a strong coupling with the Web in terms of how applications operate in this context independently of the implementation platforms. In a Web application, or more specifically in the Web tier, the only actor enabled to trigger an event is the user, and the application must always respond with a Web page. The application then operates in round-trip fashion, accepting user requests, processing them, and responding in HTML code. Making use of these restrictions, the level of abstraction of the models can be lowered to achieve an easier implementation, while still maintaining it high enough so the models can be used in any concrete Web platform.

We have tested our approach in two real-life projects. The methodology was easily learned and adopted and the application was built very quickly. Furthermore, though

---

[1] LAMP is the acronym user for a popular open source platform composed of Linux, Apache, MySql and PHP

using this methodology for the first time the users found the resulting design to be superior in terms of elegance and flexibility. The testing process also yielded important feedback about the methodology's weaknesses, in the light of which we have incorporated significant improvements. In the rest of the paper we present we present our approach trough a running example.

2 Example Application

Our running example is a simple real Web application that allows vehicle owners in Chile to pay vehicle license fees to their local governments over the Internet (CLIP, for Car License Internet Payment). Like most countries, Chile requires that every vehicle have a valid license, which must be renewed on an annual basis. The vehicle owner, known as a "contributor", pays an amount based on the vehicle's appraised and insured values to the local municipality. The contributor must also present a vehicle inspection certificate from an inspection station stating that the vehicle complies with road safety and environmental regulations. The basic requirements are:

- The contributor should be able to pay for her vehicle license over the Internet.
- The contributor should be able to choose between one-time payment, or two semi-annual payments.
- The contributor should be able to select one the insurance company of her choice
- The contributor should give proof of a valid car inspection (certificate number).
- If there are traffic violations associated with the vehicle, the system should allow the contributor to pay any outstanding fines together with the license fee.
- In the case of payments for the second semi-annual period, the system does not check for payment method, insurance, inspection certificates or traffic violations.

Once CLIP has collected all the necessary information for the license payment, it should notify the Payment-Module regarding the transaction to be performed (using Web services) in order to complete the process.

3 Abstract Specification of the Application

Most Web applications are built around the MVC architecture and therefore share a common architectural pattern. The advantages of this pattern have been demonstrated in practice. Some of the most popular implementation frameworks, such as Struts [9], are MVC-based. Consequently, our abstract specification is composed of, a model architecture, a view architecture and a controller architecture. We added a last specification that we call the components interaction specification.

The Model is a conceptual representation of the business domain. This component can be designed using any modern software methodology. As an example, we have successfully used the Unified Software Development Process. In spite of the Model's Web tier independence, specific interfaces for the two main clients, the View and the Controller, must be specified.

The responsibility of the View is to display the Web application's user interface. We have split the View model into two parts: the Interaction model and the Navigation model.

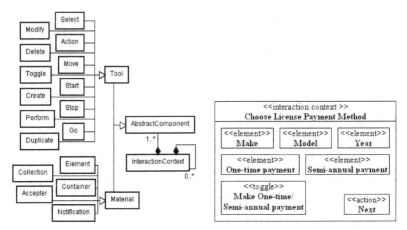

Fig. 1. The interaction context diagram metamodel (left) and one interaction context for the example application (right)

The interaction model of the View (Fig. 1) presents the graphic information of the Web pages displayed to the user. The model is made up of a set of interaction contexts each of which represents the system information and tools displayed to the user at a given moment. The interaction context diagrams are built using a UML extension based on Constantine Canonical Abstract Components ([8], [10]).

The navigation model (Fig. 2) captures the possible flows across the interaction contexts, and it is modeled with UML state charts. These diagrams can describe alternative and conditional flows [13] and the resulting diagrams are relatively small and easy to understand.

The Controller (Fig. 3) ensures coordination of the necessary components in order to process a user request, from reception to response. The Controller behavior is specified through activity UML diagrams. There are three different kinds of activities: model update, interaction context call and filtering.

The last item that must be dealt with in order to complete the description involves the specifics of how the Controller updates the Model and how the View prepares its materials to show the corresponding interaction context. To this end, each activity of the Controller model will map to a corresponding sequence diagram that shows either a Controller-Model interaction or a View-Model interaction.

4   Mapping to Specific Implementation Platforms

It is quite easy to get from here to the actual Java platform or ASP.NET design. We have developed detailed mappings for Java and ASP.NET. These two mappings are based on typical architectures for Java and .Net In a generic MVC Java architecture, a servlet receives the browser requests, filters them using the application filter classes, delegates their processing to the application controller classes, and finally, chooses a JSP to send the display of the interaction context. In the generic ASP.NET architecture, when a request for an ASPX is received, the asp elements are fed by the corresponding CodeBehind. The ASPX then renders the HTML to the browser. When a request from an ASPX form is received, its corresponding Code Behind processes it by querying and updating the application Model. CodeBehind then transfers control to the next ASPX. If the page is inherited from a filtered Web page, filtering is performed before any page processing.

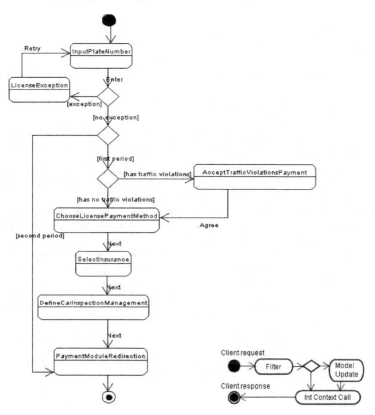

Fig. 2. Navigation Model for the example application (left). and a generic controller (right)

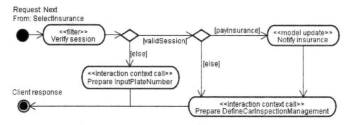

Fig. 3. A Controller Model with Filter for the example application

5 Conclusion

We have presented a methodology for creating Web applications that allows postponing platform specific details up to the very end of the project. Since the abstract artifacts relate closely to the concrete ones that appear in any MVC-based framework, the final mapping is direct and easy to perform. In our experience, our approach can be learned by Web developers and put to use almost immediately. Future tasks include process formalization and tool development for semiautomatic mapping of abstract to concrete artifacts.

References

1. A. Ginige and S. Murugesan, "Web Engineering: An Introduction". IEEE MultiMedia, vol. 8, N°3, 14-18 (2001).
2. J. Conallen, *Building Web Applications with UML.* The Addison-Wesley Object Technology Series. Addison Wesley, 1999.
3. J. Zhang and U. Buy, "A Framework for the Efficient Production of Web Applications", Proceedings of the Eighth IEEE International Symposium on Computers and Communication (ISCC'03) 1530-1346/03 (2003).
4. C. Kaewkasi and W. Rivepiboon, "WWM: A Practical Methodology for Web Application Modeling", Proceedings of the 26th Annual International Computer Software and Applications Conference (COMPSAC'02) 0730-3157/02 (2002).
5. L. Baresi, F. Garzotto, and P. Paolini, "Extending UML for Modeling Web Applications", Proceedings of the 34th Annual Hawaii International Conference on System Sciences (HICSS-34)-Volume 3, Page: 3055 (2001).
6. N. Koch and A. Kraus, "The Expressive Power of UML-based Web Engineering", Second International Workshop on Web-oriented Software Technology (IWWOST02) (2002).
7. OMG Model Driven Architecture (2004). http://www.omg.org/mda/
8. L. Ramirez and J. Navon, "Model Centric Web Development", Proceedings of the 7th Conference on Software Engineering and Applications, Marina del Rey, CA (M. Hamza editor) (2003).
9. T. Husted, *Struts in action: Building Web Applications with the Leading Java Framework*, Manning Publications Co, 2002.
10. L. Constantine, "Canonical Abstract Prototypes for Abstract Visual and Interaction Design", University of Technology, Sydney, Australia (2003).

A Security Acceleration Using XML Signcryption Scheme in Mobile Grid Web Services

Namje Park[1], Kiyoung Moon[1], Kyoil Chung[1], Dongho Won[2], and Yuliang Zheng[3]

[1] Information Security Research Division, ETRI,
161 Gajeong-dong, Yuseong-gu, Daejeon, 305-350, Korea
{namjepark,kymoon,kyoil}@etri.re.kr
[2] School of Information and Communication Engineering, Sungkyunkwan University,
300 Chunchun-dong, Jangan-gu, Suwon-si, Gyeonggi-do, 440-746, Korea
dhwon@dosan.skku.ac.kr
[3] The University of North Carolina at Charlotte,
9201 University City Boulevard, Charlotte, NC 28223-0001, USA
yzheng@uncc.edu

Abstract. Today's grid architecture encompasses a far greater breadth of applications than the traditional grid, which focused on distributed applications processing large amounts of data. Newer grid applications are more data-centric and more focused on distributed services. As these trends, mobile internet and the grid, are likely to find each other the resource constraints that wireless devices pose today affect the level of interoperability between them. The goal of this paper is to investigate how well the most limited wireless devices can make the use of grid security services. This paper describes a novel security approach on fast mobile grid services based on current mobile web services platform environment using XML signcryption mechanism.

1 Introduction

Besides mobile internet the traditional Internet computing is experiencing a conceptual shift from client-server model to grid and Peer-to-Peer (P2P) computing models. As these trends, mobile internet and the grid, are likely to find each other the resource constraints that wireless devices pose today affect the level of interoperability between them. As these key trends, mobile Internet and the grid, are likely to find each other the resource constraints that wireless devices pose today affect the level of interoperability between them [1].

Furthermore, open mobile grid service infrastructure will extend use of the grid technology or services up to business area using web services technology. Therefore differential resource access is a necessary operation for users to share their resources securely and willingly. Therefore, this paper describes a novel security approach on fast mobile grid services based on current mobile web services platform environment using XML signcryption mechanism.

2 The Performance Problem and XML Signcryption

XML-based messaging is at the heart of the current grid based on web services technology. XML's self-describing nature has significant advantages, but they come at the

D. Lowe and M. Gaedke (Eds.): ICWE 2005, LNCS 3579, pp. 191–196, 2005.

price of bandwidth and performance. XML-based messages are larger and require more processing than existing protocols such as RMI, RMI/IIOP or CORBA/IIOP: data is represented inefficiently, and binding requires more computation. For example, an RMI service can perform an order of magnitude faster than an equivalent web service-based grid. Use of HTTP as the transport for Web services messages is not a significant factor when compared to the binding of XML to programmatic objects [9].

Increased bandwidth usage affects both wired and wireless networks. Often the latter, e.g. mobile telephone network, have bandwidth restrictions allotted for communication by a network device. In addition, larger messages increase the possibility of retransmission since the smaller is the message, the less likely it will be corrupted in the air. Increased processing requirements affect network devices communicating using both types of networks (wired and wireless). A server may not be able to handle the throughput the 'network' demands of it. Mobile phone battery life may be reduced as a device uses more memory, performs more processing and spends more time transmitting information. As the scale of web services usage increases, these problems are likely to be exacerbated. Fast grid services attempts to solve these problems by defining binary-based messages that consume less bandwidth and are faster and require less memory to be processed. The price for this is loss of self-description. Fast grid service is not an attempt to replace XML-based messaging. It is designed to be an alternative that can be used when performance is an issue.

XML signcryption structure and schema has been proposed. Shown below is the XML signcryption XML document. The root element XML signcryption is the fundamental element of the XML documents. Within the root element are contained various other elements such as signed info and the signcryptionvalue, Rvalue and Svalue [6,7].

```
<?xml version="1.0" encoding="UTF-8" ?>
< XML_Signcryption >
  <SignedInfo>
    <CanonicalizationMethod Algorithm />
      <SignatureMethod Algorithm />
      <EncryptionMethod Algorithm />
      <Reference URI>
        <DigestMethod1 Algorithm />
        <DigestMethod2 Algorithm />
        <DigestValue />
      </Reference URI>
  </SignedInfo>
  <SigncryptionValue></SigncryptionValue>
  <Rvalue></RValue>
  <Svalue></Svalue>
</ XML_Signcryption>
```

Fig. 1. Proposed XML Signcryption Schema

The signedInfo element contains the information about the signcryption methodology used. It described about the implementation details about signcryption. Within the signed info element there are other elements such as CanonicalizationMethod Algorithm, SignatureMethod Algorithm, EncryptionMethod Algorithm and Reference URI.

The CanonicalizationMethod indicates the method that is used for canonicalization. The canonical method allows the use of different characters in the XML document. For example, if there are white spaces in the xml document, these are removed because of the XML canonicalization method used. The signatureMethod element indicates the signature element used in the signcryption process. EncryptionMethod is the encryption method that is used in the signcryption process. In our example, the algorithm used is DES. The element Reference indicates the link of the file that is being signcrypted. It contains the path of the file that is being signcrypted. The reference URI also contains the different Hashing algorithms that are being used in the signcryption process. In our implementation, we are using MD5 and SHA1.

As indicated in sections above, the result of signcryption are three values, namely c, r and s. these three values are required by the system to create the plain text from these messages. When signcryption is performed on a data, the output is a signcryption value. Signcryption requires different digest functions. The description of the hash functions and also the different parameters required for encryption. The encryption method that is used for signcryption is also shown in the XML document. This information is also shown in the Canonicalization method is used to embed a document in another document. Using Xpath filtering, an appropriate file is opened so that the file is opened using the application specified.

```
<element name="XML_Signcryption" type="SigncryptionType"/>
  <complexType name="SigncryptionType">
    <sequence>
      <element ref="SignedInfo"/>
        <element ref="SignatuereMethod"/>
        <element ref="EncrptionMethod" />
        <element ref="Reference" minOccurs="0"/>
    </sequence>
        <attribute name="Id" type="ID" use="optional"/>
        <attribute name="MimeType" type="MIME" use="optional"/>
        <attribute name="Mode" type="MODE" use="required"/>
        <attribute name="Type" type="TYPE" use="required"/>
        <attribute name="Encoding" type="CODING" use="optional"/>
  </complexType>
</element>
```

Fig. 2. Signcryption Schema

XML signcryption schema is shown above. The schema is required to validate the received XML message for its integrity. A part of the XML signcryption module is to create a technique where in badly formed XML documents need to be removed. Survey shows that a lot of attacks on XML servers are due to the fact that the XML documents created are not properly formed. The hardware-based solutions perform this additional task. The software-based module also needs to check the validity of the schema before the document is passed onto the next stages for verification.

The schema defines the various attributes and the elements that are required in a XML document. These attributes declare the feature of the XML document. The Id the element possesses and Multipurpose Internet Mail Extensions (MIME) so as to allow non-textual message to be passed can be incorporated into the XML document. The mode in which the signcryption has occurred, Type specifies a built-in data type.

The XML signcryption schema and is being used with Java Crypto Extensions and SAX parser to create a XML signcryption module. As the signcryption algorithm is faster compared to other signature algorithms, because of its reduced computation, the system is faster. This system introduces faster processing and also provides an additional feature of encryption along with the signature. Hence, the XML signcryption not only performs the integrity of the XML document, but also performs the confidentiality of the system. This additional facility is provided to the system with faster execution time.

The proposed XML signcryption test environment, as shown in figure 4, an XML document is parsed and schema is validated using SAX parser. After the XML document is validated, the information is passed to signcryption module. The signcryption components can verify/generate the signature for an XML document.

3   Middleware Framework for Secure Mobile Grid Service

A security framework using grid middleware for mobile grid services is as follows figure 3. Web services can be used to provide mobile security solutions by standardizing and integrating leading security solutions using XML messaging. XML messaging is referred to as the leading choice for a wireless communication protocol and there are security protocols for mobile applications based upon it. Among them are the follows. SAML (Security Assertions Markup Language) is a protocol to transport authentication and authorization information in an XML message. It could be used to provide single sign on web services. XML signatures define how to digitally sign part or all of an XML document to guarantee data integrity. The public key distributed with XML signatures can be wrapped in XKMS (XML Key Management Specification) formats.

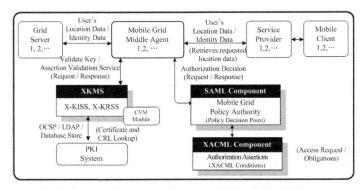

Fig. 3. Security Framework for Open Mobile Grid Middleware

XML encryption allows applications to encrypt part or all of an XML document using references to pre-agreed symmetric keys. The WS-Security, endorsed by IBM and Microsoft, is a complete solution to provide security to web services. It is based on XML signatures, XML encryption, and an authentication and authorization scheme similar to SAML. When a mobile device client requests access to a back-end application, it sends authentication information to the issuing authority. The issuing authority can then send a positive or negative authentication assertion depending upon the credentials presented by the mobile device client. While the user still has a session with the mobile applications, the issuing authority can use the earlier reference to send an authentication assertion stating that the user was, in fact, authenticated by a particular method at a specific time. As mentioned earlier, location-based authentication can be done at regular time intervals, which means that the issuing authority gives out location-based assertions periodically as long as the user credentials make for a positive authentication [4,5,8].

4   Test Configuration and Results

Components of the grid security are XML security library, service components API, application program. Although message service component is intended to support XML applications, it can also be used in other environments where the same management and deployment benefits are achievable. The figure for representing Testbed architecture of service component is as follows figure 4.

We will concentrate on the most limited category of wireless Java 2, Micro Edition (J2ME) devices that use Mobile Information Device Profile (MIDP). Applications that these devices understand are midlets. Typically maximum size of a midlet varies from 80-100kbs and user can download six to nine applications to his mobile phone. Midlet is a JAR-archive conforming to the midlet content specification [2]. The server is composed server service component of mobile grid platform package. And the message format is based on Specification of W3C (World Wide Web Consortium).

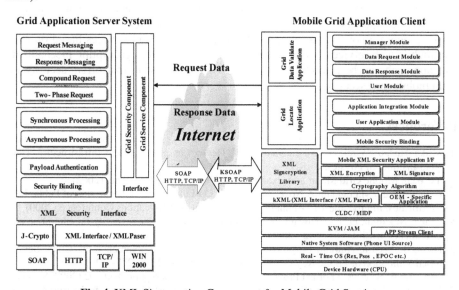

Fig. 4. XML Signcryption Component for Mobile Grid Services

Figure 5 shows the time taken for verification of the signature takes a longer time than the generation of the signcryption value itself. Figure 6 shows in the information in a graphical form. It can be noticed that as the number of iterations increase the amount of time taken per iteration decreases significantly. In the case of Unsigncryption the time taken per iteration is much more than the time taken for signcryption. The process provides both confidentiality and integrity at relatively lesser speed and lesser time as compared to other signature techniques.

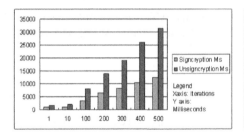
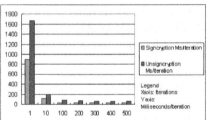

Fig. 5. Time taken plotted against number of iterations for Signcryption & Unsigncryption

Fig. 6. Average time/iteration mapped against the number iterations

5 Conclusion

Mobile grid services are so attractive that they can cover all walks of life. However, current grid is growing slower than expected. Many problems like accuracy, privacy, security, customer requirement have to be addressed. It should be understood that there is no single universal solution to grid. signcryption technique allows simultaneous processing of encryption-decryption and Signature. It has been proved that the use of signcryption decreases the processing time by 58%. signcryption is being programmed using the field theory. signcryption technique is very efficient as it uses only a single exponentiation for both encryption and signature.

We propose a novel security approach on fast mobile grid services based on current mobile web services platform environment using XML signcryption mechanism. Our approach can be a model for the future security system that offers security of open mobile grid security.

References

1. Miika Tuisku: Wireless Java-enabled MIDP Devices as peers in Grid Infrastructure. Helsinki Institute of Physics, CERN
2. Ye Wen: Mobile Grid Major area examination. University of California (2002)
3. E. Faldella and M.Prandini: A Novel Approach to On-Line Status Authentication of Public Key Certificates, in Proc. the 16th Annual Computer Security Applications Conference (2000)
4. Yuichi Nakamur, et. Al.: Toward the Integration of web services security on enterprise environments. IEEE SAINT '02 (2002)
5. Diana Berbecaru, Antonio Lioy: Towards Simplifying PKI Implementation, Client-Server based Validation of Public Key Certificates. IEEE ISSPIT (2002) 277-281
6. Joonsang Baek, et. Al.: Formal Proofs for the security of signcryption, PKC'02 (2002) 80 – 98
7. Y. Zheng: Digital signcryption or How to Achieve Cost(Signature & Encryption) << Cost(Signature) + Cost(Encryption), Advances in Cryptology – Crypto'97. Lecture Notes in Computer Science, Vol. 1294. Springer-Verlag (1997) 165-179
8. Wooyong Han, et. Al.: A Gateway and Framework for Telematics Systems Independent on Mobile Networks. ETRI Journal, Vol.27, No.1 (2005) 106-109
9. Jang Hyun Baek, et. Al.: An Efficient Two-Step Paging Strategy Using Base Station Paging Agents in Mobile Communication Networks. ETRI Journal, Vol.26, No.5 (2004) 493-496

Light-Weight Distributed Web Interfaces: Preparing the Web for Heterogeneous Environments

Chris Vandervelpen, Geert Vanderhulst, Kris Luyten, and Karin Coninx

Hasselt University, Expertise Centre for Digital Media
Agoralaan, gebouw D, B-3590 Diepenbeek, Belgium
{chris.vandervelpen,kris.luyten,karin.coninx}@uhasselt.be
geert.vanderhulst@student.uhasselt.be

Abstract. In this paper we show an approach that allows web interfaces to be dynamically distributed among several interconnected heterogeneous devices in an environment to support the tasks and activities the user performs. The approach uses a light-weight HTTP-based daemon as a distribution manager and RelaxNG schemas to describe the service user interfaces offered by native applications. From these service descriptions, the XHTML-based user interface is generated.

1 Introduction

With the emergence of web access and web-based applications on networked personal devices like PDAs and cellular phones, there is an opportunity to create *distributed interaction spaces*. Such an interaction space uses various resources that are available in the user's environment that can be accessed by the user. We distinguish between a *personal distributed interaction space* where one person interacts with the application and a *collaborative distributed interaction space* where different persons can use the (duplicated) distributed service user interface to interact with the application.

This paper presents an approach that serves two purposes. First, it allows *manual* and *automatic* distribution of web user interface parts among several heterogeneous devices in a transparent way. Secondly, it can be used to collaborate on a web application by sharing the user interfaces of particular application services among several users. The distribution and the duplication of particular web user interface parts are handled by a light-weight HTTP-based daemon. We call this daemon the *Interface Distribution Daemon (IDD)* in the rest of the paper.

2 Schema-Driven Web Interfaces

In contrast with distributed and migratable user interfaces as described in([2, 3, 5]), the approach we propose here does not require a new methodology or

D. Lowe and M. Gaedke (Eds.): ICWE 2005, LNCS 3579, pp. 197–202, 2005.

ontology [1] for designing a distributed web interface. However, it does rely on a suitable description to transform the functionality of a native application into a web interface. Traditionally, a web interface is rendered using a markup language that is created according to the vocabulary defined by a schema.

In our approach the schema language RelaxNG[1] is used to describe the services offered by the application, the structure of these services and the constraints between the different services (e.g. whether service A and B should always appear together). One of the advantages of RelaxNG over other schema languages is its simplicity and flexibility. Since RelaxNG also allows to define constraints for text values, it is possible to define a schema for an XML-file that only validates that specific file. This can be done by constraining each element, attribute and text value in the XML-file. This means an interface part for a service can be defined in XHTML, e.g. between `<div></div>` tags and converted to RelaxNG schema code. Moreover the original XML-instance can easily be regenerated from the schema.

We can create RelaxNG schema code for each service an application offers and give that service a name in the schema[2]. This allows the inclusion of service definitions of an application in a RelaxNG schema. This schema describes, for example, a web interface and constrains the `html`, `head`, `body`, `div`... elements. It can also constrain the included service definitions by referring to them inside RelaxNG patterns. Using RelaxNG we can put constraints on the occurrence of services (e.g. service S_1 and S_2 are optional but should always appear together). With this method we can create schemas that ensure the generated interface is suitable (valid) for the target device.

3   Distributed Web Session

Figure 1 shows a real distribution case in which parts of the user interface are distributed over a laptop and two PDAs. In our work, we identify three different types of possible web interface distributions: User-driven distribution, system-driven distribution and continuous distribution. These types are elaborated upon in the following subsections.

3.1   User-Driven Distribution

User-driven distribution relies on the initiative of the user: the end-user connects with the IDD and requests the web interface for her/his personal interaction space. In many cases this is preferred since the end-user has full control over the distribution of the web interface. Before the user can ask to distribute the interface of an application to selected clients, this application must be registered with the IDD. This is done by sending the schemas, representing the type of services offered, to the IDD. Figure 2(a) shows a sequence diagram describing

---

[1] RelaxNG specification: http://www.relaxng.org/spec-20011203.html

[2] RelaxNG supports so called "named patterns". A part of a RelaxNG schema can be given a name by which it can be referred in the rest of the schema

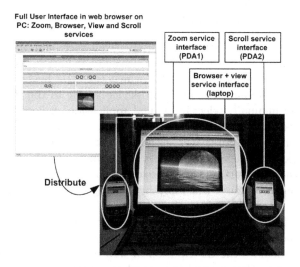

Fig. 1. Real distribution case

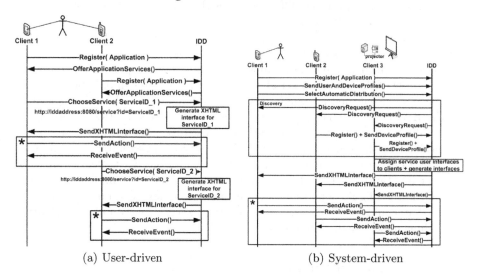

(a) User-driven   (b) System-driven

Fig. 2. Distribution System Sequence Diagrams

the interactions between the clients and the IDD. This figure shows how the user selects the application services she/he wants to use from which client device in the personal interaction space. The IDD then distributes the appropriate XHTML documents to the different clients. These XHTML documents are generated from the RelaxNG schemas available for that application (see section 2). The user can interact with the different devices, that together present a logical whole, while the IDD redirects the actions to the actual application. After some time, events from the application will be redirected to clients by the IDD (not shown in the figure).

3.2   System-Driven Distribution

While the user is in full control when user-driven user interface distribution is selected, this is not the case with system-driven distribution. Figure 2(b) shows how the user selects an application for which the IDD hosts the service user interfaces and how it sends the user and device profile to the IDD. Notice that the user does not manually select individual application services to present on the different devices in the personal interaction space. Instead, she/he lets the IDD decide where service user interfaces are migrated to. However, in this setting, the IDD does not know which client devices are available in the environment and neither what their properties are. Therefore, it broadcasts a discovery request. Subsequently, client devices will reply by sending their device profiles back to the IDD.

The device profiles sent by client devices are used to decide which clients a service interface will be migrated to in a distributed interactive session. To automatically calculate the distribution of web user interfaces, a cost function $C(v_1, ..., v_n)$ is used that recursively calculates the weight of the service user interface s_d. $v_1, ..., v_n$ are the different values that typify the weight of service s_d such as minimum screen size, minimum number of colors, minimum memory size, minimum network bandwidth, ... At this moment, only screen space has been used as input for the cost function, but this can be extended to incorporate more values. For each client device, the values specifying their properties are contained in the profile of the device. A set of service user interfaces can only be displayed by a client device if their accumulated weight does not exceed the weight specified by the device. The IDD calculates the distribution possibilities according to these values. Notice that the cost function is used together with the constraints as specified in the schema (section 2). Thus, for all possibilities indicated by the constraint paths in the schema, an optimal solution (w.r.t. the definition of the cost function) can be obtained by calculating the overall minimal weighted distribution configuration. In literature, more complex cost functions can be found that could be applied in this situation; several partitioning/paginating algorithms make use of a similar approach [4].

3.3   Continuous Distribution

When a user is engaged in a distributed interaction session, changes in her/his interaction space may trigger dynamic changes in the distribution of the user interface. Two main causes of environment changes can be distinguished in this context: client devices entering or client devices leaving the interaction space.

When a client leaves the interaction space its registration with the IDD will be canceled. This implies that the user interface of the service the client was interacting with must migrate to another substitute device without disturbing the execution of the application. Therefore, the IDD looks for a client in the environment that satisfies the requirements of the service user interface and migrates the generated XHTML document to the new client. When a new client enters the environment it announces its presence and sends its device profile to the IDD. If the new client device better fulfills the requirements for a user interface of a particular service already running in the interaction space, the IDD can decide to migrate the service interface to the new client (based on the cost function C).

4 Implementation Architecture

For a client to support user-driven distribution the only requirements are a network connection and an XHTML compliant browser that supports JavaScript and the XMLHttpRequest object[3]. This object can be used from within Java-Script code and enables the client to submit and receive XML data in the background without the need to reload the entire page. This is important because clients and applications communicate with each other by sending XML-based *action* and *event* messages. If the user performs an action, an action message is sent to the IDD. This action message is forwarded to the application that executes the action. The application on its turn can trigger an event and send an event message to the IDD with updated state information. The IDD now forwards this event message to all clients that registered as being interested in this particular event type. Notice that with this approach a user action performed on one device may trigger an event that is sent to multiple devices. The interface rendered on all of these client devices will be updated according to the new application state.

One of the main challenges we identified is that web browsers are focused on stateless client-server communication, while our communication model assumes bidirectional communication. This bidirectional communication is accomplished by sending a LISTEN[4] request to the IDD. However, the IDD does not answer this request immediately but waits until it receives an action or event message and forwards this message to the application or clients respectively by replying the appropriate LISTEN request(s) with the corresponding message attached.

To realize system-driven distribution the client devices in the environment need extra software to enable them to respond to the discovery messages from the IDD. The *Distribution Client (DC)* is responsible for this functionality. When it receives a discovery message, it responds by sending the device profile of the client to the IDD using an HTTP PUT-message. When the DC is started, it also announces itself to the IDD. When the IDD receives this announcement, it requests the device profile of the client device. This, again, is sent to the IDD through an HTTP PUT-message. A last responsibility of the DC is to listen for migration requests of the IDD. If the IDD wants the client to render an application service interface, it sends the interface's URL to the DC which redirects the client's browser to this URL. As a proof of concept we used Universal Plug and Play[5] (UPNP) for our discovery infrastructure.

---

[3] http://developer.apple.com/internet/webcontent/xmlhttpreq.html

[4] We added support for the LISTEN HTTP method to the IDD

[5] http://www.upnp.org

5   Conclusions and Future Work

The distribution of application user interfaces is an interesting concept in cases where a mobile user needs more functionality then her/his personal device offers (e.g. more screen space, more processing power, . . .). In this paper we presented a light-weight infrastructure to support this distribution process and we showed that distributing a user interface among heterogeneous devices is possible using existing technologies.

However, more research is necessary to support effective continuous distribution based on context information that is gathered from the environment, platform, available services and users.

On the following URL more information is available: `http://research.edm.luc.ac.be/cvandervelpen/research/icwe2005/`.

Acknowledgments

Part of the research at EDM is funded by EFRO (European Fund for Regional Development), the Flemish Government and the Flemish Interdisciplinary institute for Broadband technology (IBBT). The CoDAMoS[6] project (IWT 030320) is directly funded by the IWT (Flemish subsidy organization).

References

1. L. Balme, A. Demeure, N. Barralon, J. Coutaz, and G. Calvary. CAMELEON-RT: A Software Architecture Reference Model for Distributed, Migratable, and Plastic User Interfaces. volume 3295 of *LNCS*, pages 291–302, 2004.
2. R. Bandelloni and F. Paternò. Flexible Interface Migration. In *Proceedings of Intelligent User Interface 2004 (IUI 04)*, pages 148–155, 2004.
3. A. Larsson and E. Berglund. Programming ubiquitous software applications: requirments for distributed user interface. In *The Sixteenth International Conference on Software Engineering and Knowledge Engineering (SEKE4)*, 2004.
4. G. Menkhaus and S. Fischmeister. Dialog model clustering for user interface adaptation. In *Web Engineering, Proceedings of the International Conference on Web Engineering (ICWE 03)*, volume 2722 of *LNCS*, pages 194 – 203. Springer Verlag, 2003.
5. C. Vandervelpen and K. Coninx. Towards model-based design support for distributed user interfaces. In *Proceedings of the third Nordic Conference on Human-Computer Interaction*, pages 61–70. ACM Press, 2004.

---

[6] `http://www.cs.kuleuven.ac.be/cwis/research/distrinet/projects/CoDAMoS/`

Building Blocks for Identity Federations

Johannes Meinecke, Martin Nussbaumer, and Martin Gaedke

University of Karlsruhe, Institute of Telematics,
IT-Management and Web Engineering Research Group,
Engesserstr. 4, 76128 Karlsruhe, Germany
{meinecke,nussbaumer,gaedke}@tm.uni-karlsruhe.de

Abstract. Technologies like XML and Web Services have posed new requirements to authentication, authorization and identity management for the Web as
an application platform. Beyond merely providing access control for a single
isolated system, modern, flexible architectures support a business-spanning federation of applications and services by sharing digital identities. The diversity
of today's specifications and the many aspects to be considered, like e.g. privacy, system integrity and distribution in the Web, makes the construction of
these architectures a very time-consuming task. Thus, a uniform view on the
overall system is needed that abstracts from technological issues. This can be
achieved by extracting the core concepts from the emerging Federation technologies and specifications and formalize them to an extent that they can be
used as a foundation for configurable applications and services. In this paper,
we introduce a solution catalogue of reusable building blocks for Identity and
Access Management (IAM). We also present a configurable system that supports IAM solutions in Web-service-based applications.

1 Introduction

Among the many aspects to be considered during the engineering of Web-based applications and systems is the establishment of an adequate Identity and Access Management concept. Today we are faced with a large number of heterogeneous, partly
Web-based business applications from different companies that are all in need of
access control as well as the related management of identities. Moreover, many products implement their own access control mechanisms, leading to the challenge of
managing a company's overall security policy and raising unnecessary costs. Even
more difficulties have to be overcome when applications under the control of different
organizations are involved. These problems have been recognized [1] and resulted in
standardization efforts aimed at the construction of systems that are interoperable in
terms of security. The principal idea behind such solutions is to make use of Web
service technology to separate authentication and authorization mechanisms from the
applications themselves. Thus, federated architectures are realized by sharing identity
and access information. In this context, the Security Assertion Markup Language
(SAML) has been specified by OASIS as an XML-based notation for exchanging
security-relevant information [2]. Furthermore, the Liberty Alliance project is concerned with standardized mechanisms for discovering and offering identity-related
services and applications [3]. Similarly, WS-Federation defines access profiles that
describe, how and in which order the messages necessary for a federated authorization
process are exchanged between the involved browsers, clients and servers [4]. Be-

D. Lowe and M. Gaedke (Eds.): ICWE 2005, LNCS 3579, pp. 203–208, 2005.

cause of the high number of different aspects to be concerned, like security technologies, cryptographic algorithms, and communication protocols, solutions based on those standards entail a high degree of complexity, demanding for abstraction.

In this paper, we propose reusable building blocks based on a simple, extendable model, the Federated Identity Model. The building blocks provide solutions to common problems using concepts from security and federation specifications. They have also laid the foundation for the idFS system, an implementation of distributed Web access control that supports the building-block-based approach.

2   A UML-Based Federated Identity Model

The construction and operation of distributed, federated applications that apply the mentioned specifications and technologies demand for a dedicated and comprehensive support. Especially with large identity infrastructures, notations are required to model the structure of the architecture on an abstract level. As one step in this direction, we propose FIM, the Federated Identity Model. FIM is based on our experience and is not intentioned to cover all federation aspects in full. It should rather be seen as a framework that can be extended with additional elements, like for example pseudonym services, and will evolve over time. The model abstracts from the actual technologies in favor of a view centered on potential real-world scenarios. We chose UML to define a set of classes for the modeling elements. As FIM merely serves as the foundation for the focused building blocks, we omit the extensive UML diagram and give a brief description of the most important classes.

Resources are the parts of the system that provide the actual business functionality seen on an application/service level. In the context of federation, they represent the subjects to be shared between the federation partners. Unlike resources, **Security Token Services (STS)** are only auxiliary architecture components providing a safe and federation-enabled identity management infrastructure. Currently, the model comprises two types of STS, which issue the tokens necessary for accessing the resources. In the case of **Identity Providers (IP)**, the tokens concern identities (e.g. "The owner of this token, who signs messages with the cryptographic key A, has the identity B!"). In the case of **Resource Security Token Services**, they contain authorization statements (e.g. "The user with the identity B is allowed to access the Web site C to perform the set of operations D!").

Within the model, all resources and security token services (collectively denoted as **Federation Nodes**) own a certificate providing a private key for message security[1]. Every federation node can make statements in messages that nodes may choose to believe or not, depending on their trust relationships. This association is directed and simply means that one node knows another node by possessing its public key. Hence, it cryptographically trusts certain types of (signed) statements from the other node. The trust relationship plays a central role in FIM as it allows the realization of various trust models like e.g. described in [5].

On a higher level, federation nodes are grouped into **Security Realms**. All systems in one realm are under control of a certain owner, as for example the applications and

---

[1] For simplicity, we assume a PKI is used; other cryptographic options are also possible

services at a single company site. This implies that there exists a common role system or other form of access control strategy. If resource security token services are used, only one per realm is required. The establishment of trust between inner nodes is straightforward, as they are operated by the same party. However, two nodes do not necessarily need to trust each other just because they belong to the same realm.

Additional modeling classes represent abstract modules and user interfaces that can be seen as separate system parts, with the configuration specifying the concrete algorithms and mechanisms to be used (like e.g. **Authentication Mechanisms, Authorization Mechanisms, Delegation Mechanisms** or **Management Interfaces**).

3 Building Block Catalogue

The model presented in the previous section took a rather general approach, allowing for the description of a wide range of solutions. This also included very conventional systems, as for example a monolithic Web application with built-in authentication and authorization mechanisms, and an integrated account management interface for administrators. In the context of the mentioned identity management problems however, guidelines are required for building solutions in a high-quality and cost-effective way. Therefore, we present a catalogue of building blocks based on FIM. Similar to design patterns in Software Engineering [6], it contains a statement of a certain problem together with a description of how to solve this problem as well as a discussion of the solution. In the following, we describe a selection of four building blocks out of our catalogue.

Single Sign On (SSO): An organization runs several Web applications that require access control. Integrating IAM components into the applications would result in high management costs and inconveniences for the users who would have to remember all their credentials.

Corresponding to the approaches described in section 2, an IP and a resource STS is set up. The Web applications are all configured to send users requesting protected resources to the STS by performing an HTTP redirect. The STS redirects the user again, now to its configured IP that displays a sign-in form. In case valid credentials have been supplied, a security token is generated and passed on to the STS. The STS determines the permissions for the identity stated in the incoming token, generates a new token and redirects to the original application. When the user accesses one of the other federation-enabled applications within the same session, the IP will not have to show the sign-in form again, as it has already authenticated the user and the issued token is still available as session data. The separation of the authentication and authorization processes from the applications allows for reusing accounts and access policies. Any redundancy of identity information is avoided, which lowers the cost of management. A central STS enables the organization to define a uniform role system for all connected applications. Once the infrastructure exists, new applications can easily be integrated by just configuring them for the use of the STS.

Self-service Identity Management: The operation of large, Web-based systems with many different users causes high administration costs. A vast amount of effort is spent on identity-related tasks like creating user accounts for new employees or resetting passwords.

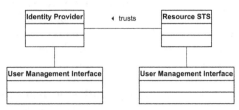

Fig. 1. Self-service Identity Management

To reduce management expenses, the tasks related to accounts and access policies are delegated to the users themselves as far as possible. Both IP and STS are equipped with management interfaces that are used by the account holders in a self-service manner (cf. Fig. 1). For the IP, this means, enabling users to make changes to their own accounts, like resetting passwords and changing contact details. Even the creation of accounts can occur without any dedicated staff involved, e.g. with online registration forms for anonymous users. In case of the STS, a self-service authorization mechanism can allow account holders to enter *activation codes* in order to put themselves in certain roles and, in a way, authorize themselves as foreseen by the business process. An obvious restriction to the self-service concept concerns the security aspect. Anonymously created accounts or role administration by users may not be suitable in high-security zones, but in other areas, close to 100% self-operating solutions can be achieved.

Distributed Web Service Access Control: An organization operates a service-oriented architecture (SOA) with a large number of Web services. These need to be partly available publicly, whereas some of their methods are only intended for a limited group of callers. The policy stating who is allowed to access which functionality changes frequently. If this policy was wired into the services statically, the resulting maintenance would raise unnecessary costs.

The organization may already have set up an IP and an STS for their Web applications. Similarly to the Single Sign On building block, the Web services are configured to trust a central STS, which itself trusts a central IP. Any accessing program has to first call the SOAP interfaces of the IP and the STS to receive the necessary security tokens. For the duration of the token validity, applications can then attach these to all of their SOAP requests. Hence, a standardized way of accessing the organization's Web services is provided. When implementing this relatively complex approach to secure Web services, the impact on performance has to be considered carefully. In the worst case, the number of Web service calls is tripled, with each call requiring time-intensive cryptographic operations. However, the solution brings with itself a lot of advantages regarding flexibility. The same infrastructure that is already applied to handle application access control is reused. Thus, it is possible to treat individual programs and their owners with the same technical concept.

Identity Federation of Enterprises: Separate enterprises want to cooperate by the interconnecting of users, applications and systems. This includes problems for the arrangements of transcendental access to distributed processing and data sharing.

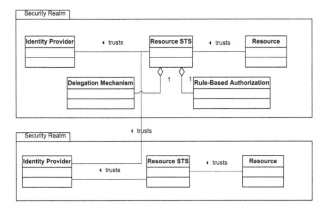

Fig. 2. Identity Federation of Enterprises

As a solution, the security infrastructures of the partners are linked up by connecting their security realms, for example as depicted in Fig. 2. Trust relationships are established between the STS of the realm where resources need to be accessed and the identity providers of the realms where the accessing users have their accounts. When a user accesses a resource, the responsible STS dynamically allocates the proper identity provider based on the rules of a delegation mechanisms. When the security token returns back from the IP to the STS, it is quite possible that the stated foreign identity is unknown in this realm. Therefore, an authorization mechanism should be applied that issues permissions depending on rules. Although the identification process is delegated to an external system, the partners are still in full control of their access policies. External users do not receive permissions unless this has been explicitly stated at the STS. Users of a federation partner do not need an extra account for the external sites and only sign in once at their enterprise. The full potential of this solution relies on the fact that the work of the users transcends organizational borders, as business processes demand.

4 System Support by idFS

As a technological infrastructure for supporting Web-service-based architectures in correspondence to the Federated Identity Model (FIM), we developed the Identity Federation System (idFS). It consists of configurable components that offer the necessary SOAP and Web application interfaces for identity providers, security token services and protected Web resources. As the underlying technological platform, the .NET Framework was used, which already offers some support for WS-Security. The FIM building blocks can be realized by configuring solutions for the use of different security token formats, protocols and security token services. In the current version, these underlying federation concepts are implemented with the standards WS-Federation and SAML. This allows e.g. to establish Single Sign On (SSO) in compliance with the WS-Federation specification, with SAML being used as the security token format. The screenshot in Fig. 3 shows the application of idFS in a real world scenario at the University of Karlsruhe campus, demonstrating the combined use of two federation concepts: SSO and self-service identity management. idFS can be downloaded at http://mwrg.tm.uni-karlsruhe.de/downloadcenter/.

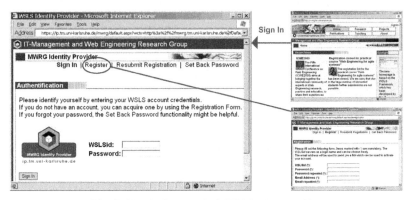

Fig. 3. Sign-in form at the idFS identity provider

5   Conclusion and Future Work

In this paper, we looked at various concepts of federated identity management. Founded on the model FIM, we presented a catalogue of building blocks that can be applied to support scenarios which take full advantage of the federation idea. Early experiences with the implemented supporting system idFS led already to very promising results: the maintenance effort of student accounts was practically eliminated, existing heterogeneous account systems of the university could be integrated, and the participation of legacy applications and services in the research group's partner network was achieved almost without complications. We are now working on a shift towards a more agile approach to configuration, which focuses the whole life cycle of all interacting federation nodes.

References

1. Witty, R.J. and Wagner, R.: The Growing Need for Identity and Access Management. 2003: Stamford, CT
2. Maler, E., Mishra, P., and Philpott, R.: Assertions and Protocol for the OASIS Security Assertion Markup Language (SAML) V1.1 – OASIS Standard (2003): http://www.oasis-open.org/specs/ (18.10.2004)
3. Liberty Alliance Specifications – Web site (2004), Liberty Alliance Group: http://www.projectliberty.org/resources/specifications.php (18.10.2004)
4. Bajaj, S., et al.: Web Services Federation Language (WS-Federation) – IBM (2003): http://www-106.ibm.com/developerworks/webservices/library/ws-fed/ (14.10.2004)
5. Linn, J., et al.: Trust Models Guidelines – OASIS Working Draft (2004): http://www.oasis-open.org/committees/tc_home.php?wg_abbrev=security (19.01.2005)
6. Gamma, E., et al.: Design patterns: elements of reusable object-oriented software. Addison-Wesley professional computing series. 1995, Reading.: Addison-Wesley. xv, 395

Level of Detail Concepts
in Data-Intensive Web Applications

Sara Comai

Politecnico di Milano, Dipartimento di Elettronica e Informazione
P.zza L. da Vinci, 32, 20133 Milano, Italy
sara.comai@polimi.it

Abstract. Current *data-intensive* Web applications, such as on-line trading, e-commerce, corporate portals and so on, are becoming more and more complex, both in terms of density of information and in terms of navigational paths. At this aim different techniques have been proposed in literature for optimizing the information to be shown to the user. In this paper we present a technique for tuning the amount of data presented to the user, directly inspired to the concept of *Levels of Details (LoD)*, commonly used in computer graphics. Like in computer graphics the idea is to simplify the original model, without loosing the main characteristics of the objects to be shown. The approach is based on the application of LoD operators to the compositional and navigational structure of a Web application, expressed through an hypertextual model.

1 Introduction

Today *data-intensive* Web applications, allowing access and maintenance of large amounts of structured data, typically stored in a database management system, represent a broad class of applications [4]. They include, for example, on-line trading and e-commerce applications, institutional Web sites of private and public organizations, corporate portals and so on. Thanks to the availability of CASE tools supporting the design and, possibly, their automatic generation, such applications are becoming more and more complex. The complexity entails both the density of the information presented to the user (like in portals, sites presenting news or products) and long navigational paths to reach the desired information content.

To deal with this increasing trend, the need for new techniques for optimizing the information to be shown to the user has been recognized. In literature, different approaches have been proposed, such as the adaptive hypermedia systems [1] [3], aiming at the adaptation of the content and of the navigational paths of the application according to the user interests. In this paper we present a different technique inspired to the concept of Levels of Details, which can be seen as complementary to adaptivity.

The concept of *Levels of Details (LoD)* was first introduced in computer graphics by Clark [2], for defining simpler versions of the geometry for objects that have lesser visual importance, such as those who would be far away from the viewer. Complex geometries can be simplified by removing graphical primitives in order to produce simpler models, which retain the important visual characteristics of the original object. This technique, applied to complex objects or to complex portions of the scene to be rendered, allows to obtain a whole series of simplifications with dif-

D. Lowe and M. Gaedke (Eds.): ICWE 2005, LNCS 3579, pp. 209–220, 2005.

ferent *amount of detail*, and to choose the simplified version according to the size, distance or importance of the object components.

We believe that this kind of technique can be successfully transposed also in the Web design context, especially to data-intensive Web applications.

The idea is to exploit a dividi-et-impera technique, where different *hierarchical abstraction levels are applied to the representation of an hypertext*. While Web designers apply these techniques to master the complexity of the design of a Web application, here the same technique is offered to the final users, to master the complexity, in terms of *amount of data*, of the information provided by the site, so that the site be more readable, the loading of the pages becomes faster, the needed information can be easily found, and so on.

This kind of approach presents several benefits:

- The performances, in terms of amount of data to be transmitted to the client, can be improved, when low levels of details are required.
- The user can scale the information of the visited site according to her needs: typically, first users need more information (and appealing sites with lots of graphics); frequent users claim a fast access to the data.
- The usability of the site can be better supported, as stated also in [6].

Essential aspects of the LoD concept have been employed in the techniques for adaptivity [1] [3], where the content and the links of the pages are adapted according to the interests of the user. However, the proposed approach presents some differences compared to adaptivity. First of all, adaptivity is typically applied server-side: the application takes the decision of the content/link to present to the user, according to her past behavior or to her explicit declaration of interests. Therefore, a user model is built at this aim. Instead, the approach proposed in this paper does not rely on a user model (which could however be integrated), but provides a mean to the final user for tuning the amount of data rendered by the application. It can be seen as a client-side approach, which can be used also by non-registered users or by users refusing cookies. In any case, it does not exclude the application of adaptive techniques, which could be combined with it.

An approach similar to the one presented in this paper has been studied in [6], where a stratification is defined on the application data and access to the data is provided according to such stratification. However, as we will see, such an approach presents some limits when applied to complex Web applications. With respect to this work, in this paper the application of the Level of Details concept is defined on a conceptual hypertext model, suited for complex applications.

The paper is structured as follows: Section 2 presents an overview of the issues related to the LoD approach, which are then formalized in Section 3. Section 4 compares our approach with related work, and finally Section 5 draws the conclusions and presents future work.

2   The LoD Approach Applied to Web Applications Concepts

In computer graphics the LoD technique allows the representation of graphical objects with a level of detail bound to the *distance/importance* of the object from the observer. Distant objects can be simplified; when they are in front of the viewer their

LoD is increased. In the same way it is possible to apply LoD techniques to Web pages, with a level of detail bound to the *amount of information* that the user would like to receive. Unlike in computer graphics, in case of Web applications, the user can tune the "distance/importance", which is the metric used to choose the desired LoD.

The amount of information can be simplified using alternative LoD operators, such as *filtering*, for cropping from the Web page the less important data, *summarization*, for substituting less important data with meta-data describing it; or, in a complementary way, important information can be highlighted with *zooming* operators (analogous operators have been define in adaptive hypermedia systems [1] [3]). In the sequel, we will refer to the filtering operator, but the results easily extend also to the other operators.

The LoD concept can be applied orthogonally to the three traditional design levels composing a Web application: the *data* of the application, the *hypertext* that represent the navigational interfaces used to publish the application data, and the *presentational aspects* of the hypertext. For example, among the data of a particular object (e.g., the data concerning a book) some pieces of information are considered fundamental, while others could be filtered when the user navigates with a low LoD. In the same way, inside a given page some objects (which can include also advertisements[1]) are more important than others and different LoDs could be defined. At the presentational level, LoD operators can be applied to the rendering of the graphical objects.

In order to consider all the main aspects of complex Web applications, we have conducted our analysis on a Web specification language, namely WebML [4]; however, the presented examples and results can be mapped also to other notations. A brief summary of the WebML concepts is presented to understand our solution. The LoD approach will be illustrated on a relatively simple Web application (the site about WebML), but containing a quite rich compositional and navigational structure.

2.1 A Brief Overview of the Web Concepts Through WebML

WebML consists of a *data model,* describing application data, of a *hypertext model*, expressing the Web interface used to publish this data, and of a *presentation model*.

The data model. The WebML data model is the standard Entity-Relationship (E-R) model. As an example, Fig. 1 shows the E-R schema describing part of the database of the webml site [11]. Every entity has a unique identifier attribute, named ID, which is not depicted to avoid clutter. It contains the news, the papers about WebML organized into different categories, and the persons working on the project and authors of the papers. Moreover, it stores the data of a book, organized in parts, chapters and sample pages; exercises and additional materials are associated to chapters.

The hypertext model. Upon the same data model it is possible to define different hypertexts (e.g., for different types of users or for different publishing devices), called site views. A *site view* is a graph of *pages*, allowing users from the corresponding group to perform their specific activities. Pages consist of connected *units*, representing at a conceptual level atomic pieces of homogeneous information. They publish

---

[1] The LoD technique presented in this paper to application data, can be applied also to commercial objects to be included in the site

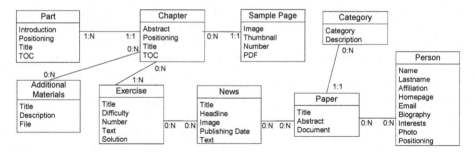

Fig. 1. Sample data model for the official WebML Web site

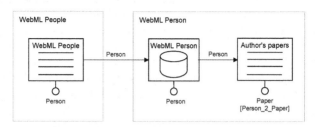

Fig. 2. Sample hypertext model for webml.org

content retrieved from the entities of the underlying data model. In particular, they show a subset of the attributes of a given entity. Units within a Web site are often related to each other through *links* carrying data from a unit to another, to allow the computation of the hypertext. To determine the data that are displayed by a unit, a *selector* is specified, which tests complex logical conditions over the unit's entity.

The hypertext fragment in Fig. 2 shows two pages: the WebML People page presents a list of persons (through an *index unit* called "WebML people" and defined over the Person entity); when the user selects a person from the index, the link exiting the unit is followed, carrying the identifier of the selected person. The WebML person page shows the details of the selected person (through a *data unit* called "WebML Person" defined over the Person entity). Notice that only the Person corresponding to the identifier received from the incoming link is shown. The person page lists also the papers written by the person (through the index unit called "Papers of Selected Author", defined over the Paper entity, and extended with a selector for retrieving only the papers of the selected person).

The language includes several other units and modularization constructs for organizing complex applications into hierarchies. For further details about the language the reader may refer to [4].

The **presentation model** addresses the definition of the presentation rules specifying the page layout, the position of the units and of the links in the page, and the position of the attributes specified inside a unit.

In the next subsections we present some simple examples specified in WebML to provide an overview of the possible issues concerned with LoDs. Then, in the section 3 we formalize our approach by describing how LoDs are built.

2.2 Different Hypertexts on the Same Data

The core model in the design of a Web application is represented by the *hypertext model, which is based on the data model and drives the presentation design.* We therefore face our analysis focusing on this model, which includes also the data to be shown. Indeed, as we will see, different hypertext fragments defined on the same data may require different LoD specifications with respect to such data.

Consider, for example, the hypertext fragment, shown in Fig. 3, representing the person and the paper pages in the webml Web site. Both are defined on the person and paper entities and their relationship. In the former page, the most important data appearing at the top of the page relate to the person, in the latter, the most important data concern the paper. They can be defined as the lowest level of detail to be shown in the page (LoD_1). In both cases, to the less important information (in LoD_2) a simplifying LoD operator could be applied. For example, if the parts in LoD_2 are summarized, they are replaced with meta-data indicating to the user which kind of data are not shown at the lowest level LoD_1. Notice, that even if the portion of data model on which the two hypertexts are based is the same, different stratifications of the data are implied from these two pages, as shown in the bottom part of Fig. 3. The LoD-based approach must be therefore applied *top-down*, starting from the hypertext and examining at a second level the underlying data, so that all the possible combinations of data can be considered.

2.3 Different Access Paths to the Same Hypertext Fragment

The application of the LoD technique to an hypertext must also consider all the possible access paths to a given page. Indeed, in complex Web applications the same page can be reached through different navigational paths, to facilitate access to users.

For example, consider the hypertext in Fig. 4: it shows an exercise (Exercise data unit), extracted from a particular chapter (whose details are retrieved by the Chapter data unit) of the book. Also the list of the exercises of the same chapter is shown (Exercises of the chapter index unit).

This page can be accessed in two ways: either with the link towards the Exercise data unit (access A) or with the link towards the Chapter data unit (access B). In the former case, the user, after selecting *a particular exercise* in another page, is led to this page to see the details about that exercise. The exercise data are therefore important (in LOD_1), while the list of all the other exercises of the chapter, to which the selected exercise belongs could be displayed at a second level (in LOD_2). In the latter case, the user, after selecting a *particular chapter* in another page, is led to this page to see one (or more) exercise(s) related to that chapter. In this case, the list of the exercises available for the selected chapter must be shown to user, so that she can select the desired exercise. If a default exercise is shown to the user for the selected chapter, also the Exercise unit plays an important role in this page: in such case all the units belong to the same initial LoD.

Different LoDs could be therefore defined according to the access path followed by the user. This simple example, shows that the same hypertext, used with different access paths, may imply different stratifications of the hypertext.

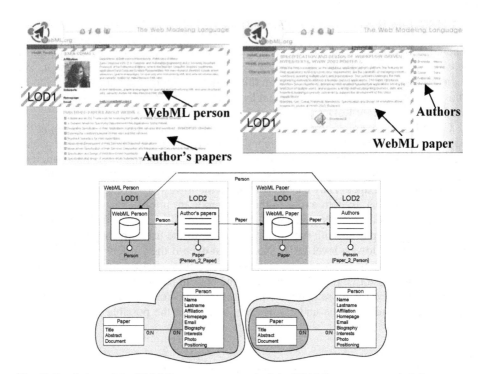

Fig. 3. Rendering of the WebML person page and of the WebML paper page; their hypertextual representation and the inferred stratification on the data model

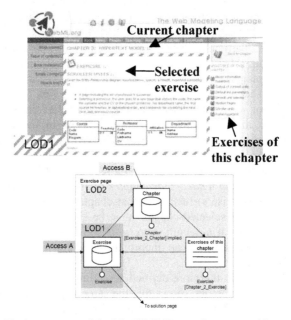

Fig. 4. The hypertext model of the WebML exercise page and its rendering

3   LoD Definition

In order to apply the LoD technique it is necessary to assign priorities to the elements of a page, and render them according to such priorities. However, some rules are needed to maintain the consistency with the complete Web application and to preserve the meaning conveyed by the designer for its pages. An important *hypothesis* at the basis of our technique is that any LoD operation must preserve the topology of the Web application and the general layout of the page, in order to preserve also its usability.

In an hypertext, LoDs can be applied at three main concepts: the content of a page, the content of a single information unit, and the links. We will focus on the former, since it represents the core element of a Web application.

3.1   Content of a Page and Rules for Defining the LoDs

A page shows the content of different units, typically having a certain degree of cohesion. In WebML the specification of the content of a page can be seen as a *graph of units, connected by links*.

In particular, in WebML we can identify:

- *Context-free units*, which do not depend on other units (they have no incoming links).
- *Externally dependent units*, requiring mandatory input (through a link) from a unit in a different page.
- *Internally dependent units*, requiring input only from units inside the same page.

For example, consider the WebML Chapter page (see Fig. 5): it describes the content of a chapter (Chapter data unit), and provides some sample pages (Sample pages index), a link to the part containing such chapter (Part data unit), and indexes of related exercises and additional materials. Other chapters can be browsed through scrolling commands (Chapter browsing scroller unit).

According to the above classification, the Chapter browsing scroller unit is a context free unit since it has no incoming links, the Chapter data unit is an externally dependent unit since it has an external incoming link, and the other units are internally dependent unit, since their incoming links depart from internal units.

Taking into account the composition of a page, we can define a set of rules for assigning correct LoDs to the units.

Let us call *K-unit*, the key unit with the highest priority to be always shown in the page[2]. In the Chapter page in Fig. 5 the key unit is the Chapter data unit, showing the details about the chapter. Notice that the K-unit may be any kind of unit (a data, an index, and so on), and may be positioned in any node in the graph.

A unit is (statically) *computable* if all the units providing input to it can be computed. For example, the index unit Exercises needs in input the current chapter to compute the list of exercises of the chapter: it can be computed once the Chapter unit has been computed. Notice that context-free units are always computable. Externally

---

[2]   In this paper we limit our analysis to exactly one key unit per page, which is consistent with most of the current data-intensive Web sites

dependent units are computable when their link coming from the external page is navigated and, if other inputs are needed from internal units, also such the internal units can be computed.

This property can be checked statically on the graph of units, for each possible access modality to the page. The assignment of the LoDs to the page must take into account the computability of the units, to guarantee that the units belonging to a given LoD be actually computable.

A K_1-cluster is composed by a set of units (and their connecting links) containing in particular a sequence $u_1, ..,u_n$ where u_1 is a) an externally dependent unit, if the page is accessed through it, or b) a context-free unit otherwise, and u_n is a K-unit (u_1 may coincide with u_n).

A K_1-cluster is *computable* if the K-unit contained in it is computable.

For each access modality to the page a computable K_1-cluster has to be defined.

Starting from a computable K_i-cluster it is possible to extend it to a computable K_{i+1} cluster (for each $1 <= i <$ max level), by adding a set of units that are computable starting from the units in the K_i-cluster.

To each K_i-cluster a LoD is assigned, which can be defined on the hypertext by assigning *priorities* to the units. The units having a priority less or equal to a given value i belong to the same LoD. Notice that there are as many priorities for each unit as the number of different distinct access modalities.

The LoDs generated from the above definitions allow to easily implement a mechanism to provide *feedback to the user* about the amount of filtered information, calculated as the difference of the LoD at the maximum level and the LoD of the current level.

Consider, for example, the Chapter page in Fig. 5, whose K-unit is represented by the Chapter data unit: two access modalities are possible, either through a link pointing to the whole page, or through the link towards the Chapter data unit. In the former case the K_1-cluster must contain at least the Chapter browsing unit (which is the only context-free unit contained in this page) and the Chapter data unit (which is the K-unit). In the latter, the Chapter data unit represents both the externally dependent unit and the K-unit, so it can be the only unit in K_1-cluster. According to the definition the K_1-cluster may contain also other units, if they are statically computable. For example, in both access modalities the set {Chapter browsing scroller unit, Chapter data unit, Part data unit} is a valid K_1-cluster, since it is possible to statically compute all such units. The next clusters may then extend the K_1-cluster with the other units, to which different priorities may be applied. For example, K_2-cluster= K_1-cluster U {Sample Pages index} and K_3-cluster= K_2-cluster U {Additional Materials index, Exercises index} is a valid set of clusters (see Fig. 6). Notice that, as shown in this example, it is always possible to define a K_1-cluster including all the access modalities: in this case, a unique priority for each unit can be defined.

As another example, consider the Exercise page in Fig. 4: through access A the described LoDs are determined by K_1-cluster={Exercise data unit} and K_2-cluster= K_1-cluster U {Chapter data unit, Exercises of this chapter index}; for access B the K_1-cluster contains all the units. Notice that for access A the K_1-cluster could also include all the units, or valid LoDs could be produced also with K_1-cluster={Exercise data unit}, K_2-cluster= K_1-cluster U {Chapter data unit}, and K_3-cluster= K_2-cluster U {Exercises of this chapter index}.

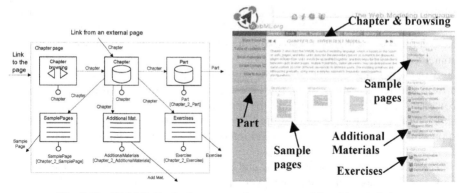

Fig. 5. The WebML Book chapter page hypertext model and its rendering.

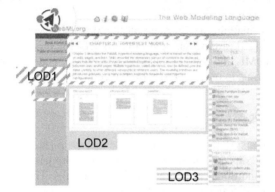

Fig. 6. Example of a possible LoD definition for the WebML Book chapter page

3.2 Links and Content of a Unit

The LoD operators may also be applied to links activating operations or leading to other pages[3], or to the content of each unit: e.g., among a set of links exiting the page it is possible to filter the less important, or among a set of attributes displayed by a unit, some priorities could be defined. In this latter case, the approach is similar to the data stratification proposed in [6], and does not require particular rules in the priority assignments. However, also at this level the same kind unit in different pages or two different kinds of units defined on the same entity may require different criteria for selecting the attributes to which the LoD operators are applied. Therefore, for each unit/page priorities can be assigned to the attributes and links.

3.3 Implementation

The proof of concepts of the proposed approach has been implemented using tclhttpd [9], a Web server built entirely in Tcl [8]. Tclhttpd provides a Tcl+HTML template

---

[3] Notice that intra-page links connecting two units are treated by the rules defined in Section 3.1, since a cluster contains a set of units and the links connecting them

facility that allows to mix Tcl commands with HTML. We have built a Tcl package linkable from tclhttpd implementing the WebML units. The Tcl+HTML template we have defined is composed of two parts: the first part computes the content of the units contained in the page; unit computation is performed through a call to a Tcl procedure implementing the unit. WebML units are instantiated with a designer-defined priority created according to the rules presented in Section 3.1. In the second part, the content of the unit is inserted into the markup describing the page. For storing the application data we have used Sqlite [7], an embeddable relational database library, supporting SQL92 and providing a Tcl interface. The WebML units interact with the database through such interface.

The rules for specifying the LoDs and their computation have been proven on the most complex pages of several real Web applications specified with WebML such as our department Web site (http://www.elet.polimi.it), a complex application including a set of B2B portals (http://www.metalc.it), and other business sites (http://www.acer-euro.it, http://www.webratio.com).

Currently we are mapping these rules on the WebML specification supported by the WebRatio tool [12], a development environment for the visual specification of applications in WebML and the automatic generation of code for the J2EE and Microsoft .NET platforms, in order to test it on the complete applications.

4 Related Work

Adaptive hypermedia systems (surveyed and described in [1], [3]) and adaptive Web approaches [5] also consider the removal of objects from pages, e.g. by introducing conditional links, conditional fragments, and hidden links. Therefore also adaptivity applies to navigational structures, and page content, and also in the adaptive context operators like filtering/summarization/zooming are used. However, adaptivity is based on the user's interests and *knowledge*, given by the information already visited by the user. When we filter some information our aim is not that of removing useless information for the user (all the data of the page are always available and can be seen by setting the maximum LoD), but to assign different priorities to the different pieces of information, so that the user can select to explore the site with the desired LoD and increase or decrease it according to her interests. Our approach is *orthogonal* to adaptive systems: it can be applied also to the results of an adapted page, to assign different priorities to the information that could be interesting for the user. On the other hand, the information to which the LoD operators apply could be determined with an adaptive approach: this would allow to apply sophisticated heuristics in the assignment of the priorities to the units, attributes and links shown in a page. Another important difference is that we do not assume a priori knowlegde about the interests of the user and therefore our approach can be applied to any kind of Web application. Moreover, with our approach it is the user (at client-side) that selects the amount of information to be displayed according to her needs, and the decision about the amount of detail is not taken by the system.

To our knowledge, the only work providing a stratification of the information of a Web Information System with the aim of assigning different priorities is that presented in [6]. In this work the authors apply a stratification to the information space, described by a model called Progressive Access Model (PAM), possibly connected to functional, hypermedia and user models. The proposed approach is *bottom-up*, since the stratification is defined on the *data model* and then the other models use such stratification. We also face the problem of managing different LoDs to provide a progressive access to the information, but our approach is *top-down*: the stratification is applied to the *hypertext* and then, for each object contained in the hypertext, a stratification can be defined on the displayed attributes or links. This allows us to consider *complex Web applications*, typically providing different point of views of the same underlying data and different access facilities to the same data.

5 Conclusions and Future Work

In this paper we have presented an approach for applying different LoDs to the concepts of a Web application, focussing in particular on the content of a page. We have shown through some examples, that complex Web applications built on several inter-related data and providing different access paths to such data, require the assignment of different LoDs, and a top-down approach starting from the hypertextual layer. We have provided a set of basic rules that must be satisfied to produce significant priority rules for guaranteeing the computation of the page.

Such an approach can be extended to be effectively applied also in adaptive Web applications, by extending users profiles with the information about the priorities associated with the Web concepts.

Moreover, also accessibility [10] could take advantage from this approach, since different LoDs can be assigned to the information of a Web application taking into account their importance for the different classes of users. For example, someone who cannot use the mouse needs shortcuts, which can be filtered to all the other classes of users; images can be filtered to blind users; and so on.

As future work we plan to automatize the phase for assigning the priorities to the content of the Web pages, by defining heuristics for the identification of the key units and for inferencing the priorities of the other units contained in a page. Moreover, we plan to study more sophisticated clustering algorithms involving multiple stratifications, and, finally, we would like to investigate the possibility to remove the assumption of preserving the site topology, by applying merging/splitting operators at the page level.

Acknowledgements

I wish to thank Alberto Allara for helpful discussions and contributions to the implementation of the proposed approach.

References

1. Peter Brusilovsky Methods and Techniques of Adaptive Hypermedia. *User Modeling and User Adapted Interaction*, 1996, V. 6, N. 2-3, 87-129
2. Clark, J. H. Hierarchical geometric models for visible surface algorithms. *Communications of the ACM*, 1976, 19:547-554
3. Paul De Bra, Peter Brusilovsky, Geert-Jan Houben. Adaptive Hypermedia: From Systems to Framework.. *ACM Computing Surveys*, Vol. 31(4), 12, 1999, ACM Press

4. S. Ceri, P. Fraternali, A. Bongio, M. Brambilla, S. Comai, M. Matera: *Designing Data-Intensive Web Applications*, Morgan-Kaufmann, December 2002.
5. Mike Perkowitz, Oren Etzioni. Towards adaptive Web sites: Conceptual framework and Case Study. *Artificial Intelligence*, 118 (2000), 245-275
6. M. Villanova-Oliver, J. Gensel, H. Martin. A Progressive Access Approach fro Web-Based Information Systems. *Journal of Web Engineering*, Vol. 2, (1&2) (2003) 027-057
7. Sqlite. http://www.sqlite.org/
8. Tcl. http://www.tcl.tk/
9. Tclhttpd - Tcl Web server. http://www.tcl.tk/software/tclhttpd/
10. W3C. Web Content Accessibility Guidelines 2.0, Working Draft 30 July 2004. http://www.w3.org/TR/2004/WD-WCAG20-20040730/
11. WebML Site. http://www.webml.org
12. WebRatio. http://www.webratio.com

Separation of Navigation Routing Code in J2EE Web Applications

Minmin Han and Christine Hofmeister

Computer Science and Engineering Dept, Lehigh University
19 Memorial Dr. W., Bethlehem, PA 18015, USA
mih9@lehigh.edu, Hofmeister@cse.lehigh.edu

Abstract. The navigation routing code of a web application is the part of the code involved in routing a request from a web page through the appropriate components on the server, typically ending with the display of a response page. Common maintenance activities are to change the sequence of pages or the processing for a page, and for these activities the navigation routing code must be located, understood, and possibly modified. But in J2EE applications this code is spread among a number of components, making maintenance costly. We describe an approach for separating this navigation routing code, using either Aspect Oriented Programming (AOP) or conventional OO techniques. We demonstrate how this improves maintainability by converting three exemplar applications from Sun and Oracle, with a 4- to 11-fold reduction in the number of files containing navigation routing code and in the lines of code in these files.

1   Introduction

A navigation map, which describes the possible sequences of web pages displayed to a user, is typically part of the documentation of a web application. But to get from one page to another, a request from one page is usually routed through a series of components on the server, ending with the display of the response page. We define the *navigation path* of a request to be the sequence of components that handle this request. Then we define an application's *navigation routing* to be the union of all possible navigation paths for requests in that application. Navigation routing must be understood and potentially modified when the navigation map changes, when external links embedded in pages change, when the content of a page changes, or when processing required for a request changes.

Since changes of these types are common in web applications, the developer should be able to efficiently understand and modify the navigation routing. However, existing web application platforms such as J2EE make this difficult. One problem is the complexity of the navigation routing code: it is usually scattered through many components, interspersed with processing code, and uses a wide variety of techniques for routing a request. A second problem is that the platform invokes the server components implicitly, using information in a deployment descriptor file (web.xml in J2EE). This requires the developer to have a thorough understanding of the platform's navigation routing rules in order to follow the navigation routing.

In this paper we address the first problem, the complexity of the navigation routing code, by presenting an approach that

- separates the navigation routing from the rest of the application, and
- uses a small set of implementation conventions to reduce the variability in navigation routing code.

D. Lowe and M. Gaedke (Eds.): ICWE 2005, LNCS 3579, pp. 221–231, 2005.
© Springer-Verlag Berlin Heidelberg 2005

Even in well-designed J2EE applications, navigation routing code is located in several types of components: JSPs (Java Server Pages), filter classes, servlet classes, and a deployment descriptor file (web.xml) [18].

The starting point of a navigation path is a request originating from a link or form in a JSP page. The "target URI" of the request determines where the request is routed. In the simplest case the target URI is another JSP page that is displayed by J2EE server. Otherwise the web server looks up the target URI in web.xml in order to determine which filter or servlet will next receive the request.

Upon receipt of a request, a filter or servlet often does some processing for the request, perhaps using the target URI in order to distinguish requests from different JSPs. For example, when the Front Controller design pattern is used [1], a single component receives all requests from the client then passes them to the appropriate component. To pass the request along to another component or display the response page, a component invokes one of several platform methods (chain, forward, sendRedirect), passing along a target URI. Each time the request is passed to another component, web.xml uses the target URI to determine which component should receive the request. Of course, the target URI does not have to be a hardcoded string that is passed immutably through the components. It could come from any expression that evaluates to a string, and could be changed by any component along the navigation route.

All of these variations are possible while still following the recommended design guidelines. But these guidelines are not obligatory, and in addition to having navigation routing code located in any number of JSPs, filters, servlets, and web.xml, it could be located in any number of other classes on the server side. The guidelines do nothing to prevent navigation routing code from being interspersed with code for processing the request, and they do not limit the large variety of ways the target URI can be set.

Our approach for addressing the complexity of navigation routing code separates it from the processing code, locates it in a small number of modules, and does not force a particular structure on the application. For example, some existing approaches put navigation routing in a separate table but require the use of a Front Controller servlet provided by a library. With our approach, requests can be routed through any number of components in any order with any desired target URI.

Separating out the navigation routing code already applies some implementation conventions, which helps reduce the variability of this code, but it still leaves too much variability in how a component can modify a target URI as it processes a request. After looking at existing applications for different ways that a component determines the outgoing target URI for a given incoming target URI, and considering other ways that might be used, we see that these are covered by three categories.

The first is *static routing*, where there is only one possible outgoing URI for a given incoming URI. This could be hardcoded in the component or looked up from a table. It could even be computed by the component, although this is unlikely since in static routing the outgoing URI is determined at development time, not runtime.

The second is *conditional routing*. In this case the set of possible outgoing URIs is determined at development time, but the choice among them is made at runtime. When processing a request the component can use a number of different ways to make the choice, such as using data located in the request, using a session variable, looking up data in a table or database, using the current date and time, etc. Both static and conditional routing are supported by many current table-driven frameworks.

The third type of navigation routing is *cached routing*. As in conditional routing the set of possible outgoing URIs is known at development time and the choice is made at runtime, but in this case the choice is not made by the component. Instead the choice was made by another component when processing a prior request or possibly earlier in the processing of this request. Thus the outgoing URI is retrieved from a variable in which it was cached earlier. Note that cached routing could be treated as a case of conditional routing where the selection of outgoing URI is made by retrieving it from a variable. However, because this case occurs frequently, creating a third category allows us to preserve the particular semantics of this type of routing.

In our experience these three categories cover all of the variants on navigation routing that occur within web applications. The case where a user enters an arbitrary URI is not relevant because we are interested only in the navigation routing within an application, where the routing choices should be known at development time and only the selection is made at runtime. Having defined these three categories, we can create standard implementation conventions for each, thus greatly reducing the variability in navigation routing code.

In the next section we describe our approach, comparing it to current table-driven frameworks. Section 3 presents our evaluation of the approach. Section 4 describes related work, and Section 5 concludes the paper.

2   Separation of Navigation Routing Code

2.1   Our Approach

Our approach to separating navigation routing code has two variants. Our first version uses aspect-oriented programming (AOP), which supports the modularization of concerns that would otherwise be spread across many modules. This is done by creating aspect modules that contain *advice*, the code for that concern, and *pointcuts* that identify where the advice should be inserted in the application. Because we are working with J2EE web applications, we use AspectJ [5], an AOP language for Java applications.

We create three aspect modules, one each for the navigation routing code in web pages, filter classes and servlet classes. For JSP pages, we place all navigation routing code (the URIs) in a PageNavigation aspect. Since AspectJ cannot define pointcuts in JSP script language, we create a dummy function insertURI() and call this function to get the URI for each form or link in a web page. Then a PageNavigation aspect module intercepts all calls to insertURI() and computes the URI for all requests generated from JSP pages. It accepts two parameters, page name and form name, and returns a string containing the URI.

To create a ServletNavigation aspect, first any processing needed for a request is encapsulated in a method, so that each incoming request has a single processing method (or perhaps none at all). These methods have two parameters, for the request and response objects, and return either nothing or a string containing the processing result.

The doPost/doGet methods that normally process a request are left empty, and instead the navigation routing code is placed in a ServletNavigation aspect module. This module may contain several pairs of pointcuts and around advice, one pair for each servlet. The pointcut says that the corresponding advice should be executed instead of the servlet's doPost or doGet method. Inside the advice, the incoming URI is used to invoke the appropriate processing method. For static routing the outgoing URI is hardcoded then the request is passed along. For conditional routing the result of the processing method is used to determine the outgoing URI, and for cached routing the outgoing URI is retrieved from a session variable.

Fig.1 shows the pointcut and around advice for a servlet named Dispatcher. For incoming requests with URI "/transferAck.do", the "makeTransfer" method is called to process the request. Then the request is forwarded with URI "/transferAck.screen" if makeTransfer returns "success". Thus this is an example that uses conditional routing.

```
aspect ServletNavigation {
    pointcut DispatcherNav(HttpServletRequest req, HttpServletResponse res):
        execution(* Dispatcher. do* (HttpServletRequest, HttpServletResponse))
            && args(req,res);
    void around (Dispatcher dp, HttpServletRequest req, HttpServletResponse res) :
            DispatcherNav(req,res) && target(dp)  {
    String targetURI=req.getServletPath(); //Get target URI.
    if (targetURI.compareTo("/transferAck.do") == 0)  {
        String returnValue = dp.makeTransfer(req,res);
        try  {
            if (returnValue.compareTo("success") == 0) {
            // forward to transferAck web page
            req.getRequestDispatcher("/transferAck.screen").forward(req,res);
            } ...
```

Fig. 1. ServletNavigation Aspect Module

Filters are treated almost exactly the same as servlets are, except that the pointcut specifies doChain, which is the normal processing method for filters, and the pointcuts and advice go into the FilterNavigation aspect.

Besides the three aspect modules, there is some navigation routing information in web.xml. Since the J2EE platform forwards the requests according to the deployment description in web.xml, we cannot modify it to look someplace else. Thus we leave web.xml as it is.

The number of the aspect modules can be altered since aspect modules could be combined or split without affecting the functionality. But according to our experience with small- and medium-sized applications, it works well to use the three aspect modules we describe above.

However, this approach has some shortcomings. A developer need not be an expert in AOP because our implementation conventions describe exactly how to write the aspects. But without some understanding of AOP, he or she may have difficulty understanding how advice is woven into the application at the locations specified in the pointcuts. Another problem is the complexity of compilation and deployment of the aspect modules, especially for JSP web pages. Because AspectJ does not understand the JSP scripting language, JSPs must be converted into Java files before weaving in the aspects.

But it turns out that AOP is not essential to our approach. The reason for this is that the weaving we require is simple: we ask the weaver to replace a dummy method with the advice given in the aspect rather than asking it to weave advice into various places in the body of a method. Thus our approach can also be implemented using only standard OO techniques.

For the OO variant of our approach, we use regular classes instead of aspect modules. For the navigation routing code in JSPs, we use a PageNavigationManager class. It provides a function that is called whenever the navigation routing information is needed. This function takes the web page name and form/link name as parameters and returns the URI.

The servlet classes need to be structured in almost the same way as for the AOP variant: divide processing into functions for different URIs, but in this case remove the doGet/doPost methods.

For the navigation routing code in the servlet, we use a class ServletFramework instead of the servlet aspect module. In this class, both doGet and doPost call a `proceed` function. The `proceed` function looks much like the servlet advice: identify the incoming request's URI, call corresponding functions in original servlet class, set session variables if necessary and forward the request.

All servlet classes inherit from this ServletFramework class. Since we do not define doPost/doGet in the servlet classes, every time a request reaches a servlet class, the `proceed` function in ServletFramework is invoked by its doGet/doPost. Function `proceed` uses introspection to find out which servlet class was invoked, then invokes the appropriate method.

As before, filters are treated in a similar way to servlets.

Fig. 2 shows part of the proceed function in the ServletFramework class corresponding to Fig.1. First it checks if the instance is the Dispatcher class; then identifies the incoming request's URI; invokes the method "makeTransfer" in the Dispatcher, and forwards the request with URI "/trasferAck.screen" if the return value is "success".

```
private void proceed(HttpServletRequest request, HttpServletResponse response {
    Class theServletClass = getClass();
    String incomingURI = request.getServletPath();
    ...
    if (theServletClass.getName().compareTo("com.sun.ebank.web.Dispatcher")==0) {
        if (incomingURI.compareTo("/transferAck.do")==0) {
            theMethod = theServletClass.getMethod("makeTransfer", paramTypeList);
            returnValue = theMethod.invoke(this, paramList);
            if (((String)returnValue).compareTo("success")==0)
                forwardingURI = "/transferAck.screen";
    ...}}
    request.getRequestDispatcher("/"+forwardingURI).forward(request, response);
    ...
```

Fig. 2. Proceed Function in ServletFramework Class

2.2 Comparison with Current Table-Driven Frameworks

We also studied the existing frameworks (Struts[14] and others) for developing web applications to find out how the current techniques handle navigation routing. Most frameworks are similar with regard to navigation routing, so we will only discuss Struts in this section. The discussion of other web application frameworks is in section 5.

J2EE web applications using the Struts use the ActionServlet servlet class of the Struts library as a Front Controller. For all requests received by the ActionServlet class, part of the navigation routing is defined in a separate XML file, which includes incoming requests' URI, the Action class that will process the request, the possible return values, and the corresponding forwarding URI. Thus this table-driven framework supports both static and conditional routing.

```
<action-mappings>
    <action path="/transferAck"
            type="com.sun.ebank.web.transferFundsAction" ...>
            <forward name="success" path="/transferAck.screen" />
    </action>   ...
```

Fig. 3. Struts-config.xml

Fig. 3 shows part of the struts-config.xml for the same Dispatcher servlet shown in Fig.1 and Fig. 2. The incoming request with URI "/transferAck" will invoke the Action class "transferFundsAction", which works as the makeTransfer function in our approach. Then the transferFundsAction class forwards the request to the URI ("path" in Fig. 3) associated with "success".

We compare our approach and Struts in Table 1 according to seven criteria. There are two main concerns for a developer choosing an approach for supporting navigation routing: coverage and effort. For coverage, we see if the approach covers all three navigation routing categories described in Section 1, which types of components it covers, and what kind of constraints it applies to the application structure. For effort, we see how easy it is to understand, compile and deploy, debug, and implement the approach.

A checkmark in the table means the approach satisfies this criterion well. Most of the table content is self-explanatory so we do not repeat the details here. Our AOP and OO variants separate the navigation routing code in the same basic way, but each has some shortcomings. The AOP variant is more difficult to compile and deploy. The OO variant requires the servlet and filter classes to inherit from our navigation routing class framework.

Struts does not separate the whole navigation routing but only those parts used by the front controller. Strut uses XML tables to store navigation routing information. It cannot support cached routing because its table structure does not allow that. We can also use tables for our approach, rather than hardcoding the same information in the source code. Then we provide developers the navigation routing classes as a library. Since our tables cover navigation routing code for all component types, the table must have different sections for different component types. They must also support cached routing.

The most obvious advantage of a table-driven approach is that to change navigation routing inside a table is easier than to change the source code in an aspect module or class. No recompilation and redeployment is necessary for modifications in a table.

Table 1. Struts vs Our Approach

		Struts	Our Approach	
			AOP Variant	OO Variant
Coverage	Navigation Routing Categories	Static and conditional routing.	√ Static, conditional, and cached routing.	
	Component Types	Only the front controller servlet.	√ JSPs, servlet classes, and filter classes.	
	Application Structure	Must use front controller pattern.	√ No pattern is enforced. Also it can be applied on top of Struts.	
Effort	Understandability	√ OK if the developer is familiar with Struts.	√ Ok if the developer understands AOP and weaving.	√ OK.
	Compilation and Deployment	√ Relatively easy.	Difficult. JSP files need to be converted to Java, and aspects need to be woven into other modules.	√ Relatively easy.
	Debugging	The library code is not open source, so it cannot be traced at runtime.	Aspect modules make the control flow hard to follow and debug.	√ Relatively easy.
	Implementation Support	√ Library code is provided.	√ Aspect module framework is provided.	√ Navigation routing class framework is provided.

Putting the navigation routing in a table may make it easier for non-specialists to understand and modify the navigation routing, since they do not need to understand a programming language like Java. However, when the table contents get complicated, it may be easier for a developer to understand code rather than a table. Supporting all component types and all three navigation routing categories significantly complicates the table structure.

3 Evaluation

To evaluate our solution for improving the maintainability of web applications by separating navigation routing code, we describe our experiences refactoring existing applications.

We[1] have applied our solution to a number of existing applications. Some are small sample applications provided with the J2EE server 1.4, but the three we discuss here are more comprehensive: Duke's Bank [16], PetStore [17] and Virtual Shopping Mall [10]. The first two of these exemplar applications are provided by Sun, and the third is provided by Oracle.

---

[1] Here "we" stands for one author and another graduate student who was not involved in the research but converted the applications after receiving an explanation of the approach. The numbers we give for effort (time) are the average time spent among us

Table 2. Metrics for the original applications

	Dukes Bank	Mall	Pet Store
Total LOC	7133	19248	34048
# web pages	10	35	16
# filters	0	0	2
# servlets	1	7	2
# modules with nav. routing	12	44	21
LOC modules with nav. routing	1015	6154	9059

Table 2 shows some metrics for the original applications and Table 3 shows how these changed after our AOP solution, OO solution, or the Struts technique was applied. Duke's Bank 1 uses the AOP solution, Duke's Bank 2 uses the OO solution, Duke's Bank 3 uses the Struts technique, and Mall and Petstore use the AOP solution.

Duke's Bank is a comparatively small on-line banking application. We spent three hours applying the AOP variant of our solution on this web application (Duke's Bank 1 in Table 3): one hour moving code from the JSPs to the Page Navigation aspect module and one hour moving code from the servlet to the Servlet Navigation aspect module, including separating out three functions for three types of request processing. The remaining hour was needed to compile, test, and deploy the aspect modules and modified java files.

When we used the OO variant of our approach (Duke's Bank 2), the time we spent was very similar: one hour moving code from JSPs to the Page Navigation class and one hour moving code from servlets to the ServletFramework class and separating out three functions. We spent less time compiling, testing, and deploying than with the aspect modules.

We also used Struts on Duke's Bank (Duke's Bank 3 in Table 3). We spent less time with Struts since not all navigation routing code is separated. JSPs remain untouched because Struts cannot separate the navigation routing code in JSP pages. Less than one hour was spent moving code from the original servlet to three new action classes. It is very much like separating out functions in our approach. One hour was spent compiling, testing, and deploying. The longer time here was because it is not easy to debug when Struts is used. The library source code is not available, so when there are errors the debugger cannot trace the servlet code.

Virtual Shopping Mall is a medium-sized on-line retail store application. Since we found that six of the web pages simply forward the request to other web pages, we treated them as servlets. This application uses the Struts framework, so part of the navigation routing code is already separated. We applied our approach on top of the Struts framework to separate the leftover navigation routing code (mostly in web pages), which took three hours. An additional two hours was spent compiling, testing, and deploying.

PetStore is another medium-sized on-line store application. Petstore uses WAF (a framework very similar to Struts for navigation routing). But there is still navigation routing code in filter classes and web pages. We spent one and a half hours converting the JSPs and creating the Page Navigation aspect module. One hour was spent modifying the servlet classes and creating the Servlet Navigation aspect module, and another hour was spent doing the same to the filters. The remaining two hours were needed for compiling, testing and deploying.

Table 3. Metrics after applying AOP solution

	Duke's Bank 1 (AOP)	Duke's Bank 2 (OO)	Duke's Bank 3 (Struts)	Mall (AOP)	Pet Store (AOP)
# modules with nav. rout.	3	3	12	4	4
LOC modules with nav. rout.	200	324	929	637	339
# methods	3	3	3	27	11
LOC methods	120	120	154	3175	2016
Modification Time (in hours)	3	2.5	1.5	5	5.5

As evidence that our solution improves maintainability, we first look at the number of files that contain navigation routing code before and after applying our solution. For example, in PetStore originally there were twenty-one files containing navigation routing code: 16 web pages, 2 filters, 2 servlets and web.xml. After applying our solution there are only the three aspect files and web.xml. Since the developer can focus on a smaller number of files, any maintenance involving navigation routing is easier to perform. Duke's Bank and Virtual Shopping Mall have similar improvements: from 12 to 3 and from 44 to 4 files containing navigation routing code. In Table 2, Mall has one additional file containing navigation routing because it uses a Struts configuration file.

If we look the size of these files before and after applying our AOP solution, we find a 5- to 25-fold reduction in the LOC. The main reason for the large decrease is that originally many files contain a small portion of navigation routing code along with other code. After conversion the files with navigation routing code contain only navigation routing code (except web.xml, which still contains other deployment information). This clearly reduces the amount of time a developer spends in locating and understanding navigation routing code.

Reviewing the modification time for the applications, we find that a developer needs about three hours to apply our solution for an existing small web application and five to six hours for an existing medium-size web application. For a 4- to 11-fold reduction in the number of files containing navigation routing code and 5- to 25-fold reduction in the lines of code in these files, the cost is not high. For the AOP variant, since the aspect modules are woven into the other source code before executing, performance is not affected.

4 Related Work

It is clear that researchers believe navigation is an important part of web applications. Rossi [12] identifies a number of common navigation patterns used in web applications. Reina [11] states that it is necessary to separate the navigation concerns into aspect modules but does not present a specific solution.

We studied other web application frameworks besides Struts. Web application frameworks like WAF[15], Tapestry[7], Expresso[2], Maverick[8] are close to Struts when considering only the navigation routing. A table is used to define part of the navigation routing and a front controller is used. However, Tapestry provides more separation of navigation routing code at the JSP side since it separates the client side HTML and the server side code in the JSPs.

Another web application framework, Barracuda [1], uses a more complicated event model, which is closer to the event model in swing applications. The events are hierarchically organized. The request from the web pages is first received by a servlet class that converts them to events. Then the listener classes process the events and may send more events. Finally, a response request indicates the corresponding web page to be sent back to the client. In Barracuda, the navigation routing can include more than one server component as in our approach while the Struts cannot. However, Barracuda does not separate the navigation routing code and navigation routing is harder to understand because of the hierarchical event model.

To the best of our knowledge, there is no other similar approach for separating navigation routing code. AspectJ has been applied to many different kinds of applications to separate other kinds of concerns, such as [6], [13]. Most of the results are considered a success and better than a pure Java implementation.

Kienzle [6] concludes that AOP can be good for code factorization but only for experienced programmers. Also since concurrency and failures are simulated by objects (not part of the object semantics), they are very difficult to aspectize. Our results are that navigation routing is not simulated by objects and is not difficult to aspectize. We do expect developers to have some knowledge of AOP.

Murphy et.al. [9] present a study on applying AOP to separate concerns for two common scenarios: separating concerns tangled within a method and between classes. They conclude that a concern may be easier to separate if it is encapsulated in methods and classes or if its code is in contiguous chunks. We use a similar idea: for doPost/doGet/doChain, we first gather the processing for each intermediate target URL and put it into a separate method, such as "makeTransfer". After that we put the remaining navigation routing code into aspect modules.

5   Conclusion

Our approach can be applied to both new application design and for refactoring existing applications. To show its benefit, we evaluated it by refactoring three commercial applications with a variety of navigation routing patterns: some with a Front Controller and some without, some with multiple filters and servlets, some with JSPs only, some with servlets only, and some using an XML table for part of the navigation routing. While it took 3-6 hours to refactor these small- to medium-sized applications, the number of files containing navigation routing code and the lines of code in these files was greatly reduced (a 4- to 11-fold reduction in number of files and a 5 -to 25-fold reduction in lines of code in these files).

We found a large improvement in maintainability as a result of separating the navigation routing code into a handful of modules. Clearly most of this was the result of gathering together the navigation routing code, making it easier to locate and understand. But our solution also forces a more standard way of encoding navigation routing, which facilitates maintenance.

However, separation of concerns alone is not sufficient for solving the maintainability problem. Because server components are implicitly invoked by the J2EE framework, the navigation routing is difficult to follow even after locating the code. A model that explicitly describes the navigation routing can help the developer during maintenance. Our solution to this problem, described in [4], is a formal navigation routing model and a set of tools to analyze the model, generate implementation code, and extract a model from the code. An implementation-level solution such as the one described in this paper enables this model to be automatically extracted from the code. We have also proposed the Navigation Routing Diagram as a visualization of this model. In addition, we can use the navigation routing model as an indication of the complexity of an application's navigation routing.

References

1. Barracuda Presentation Framework. http://barracudamvc.org/Barracuda/index.html
2. Expresso Web Services. http://www.jcorporate.com/
3. Gamma, E., Helm, R., Johnson, R. and Vlissides, J. Design Patterns. Addison-Wesley Professional. 1995.
4. Han, M. and Hofmeister, C. Modeling Navigation Routing in J2EE Web Applications. Lehigh University Technical Report, 2004.
5. Kiczales, G., Hilsdale, E., Hugunin, J., Kersten, M., Pal J., and Griswold, W.G. An Overview of AspectJ. J. In *Proceedings of the European Conference on Object-Oriented Programming (ECOOP '01)* (Budapest, Hungary, June 18-22, 2001) Springer-Verlag LNCS 2072, 2001, 327-353.
6. Kienzle, J. and Guerraoui, R. AOP: Does It Make Sense? The Case of Concurrency and Failures. In *Proceedings of the European Conference on Object-Oriented Programming (ECOOP '02)* (Malaga, Spain, June 10-14, 2002) Springer-Verlag LNCS 2374, 2002, 37-61.
7. Lewis Ship, H. M. Tapestry in Action. Manning Publications. 2004.
8. Maverick. http://mav.sourceforge.net/
9. Murphy, G.C., Lai, A., Walker, R.J., and Robillard, M.P. Separating Features in Source Code: An Exploratory Study. In *Proceedings of the 23rd International Conference on Software Engineering (ICSE '01)* (Toronto, Canada, May 12-19, 2001) ACM Press, New York, NY, 2001, 275-284.
10. Oracle J2EE sample code. Virtual Shopping Mall. http://www.oracle.com/technology/sample_code/tech/java/j2ee/vsm13/index.html
11. Reina, A.M. and Torres, J. Analysing the Navigational Aspect. *In Proceedings of Second Aspect-Oriented Software Development Workshop (AOSD '02)* (Germany, February 2002).
12. Rossi, G., Schwabe, D. and Lyardet, F. Improving Web Information Systems with Navigational Patterns. In *Proceedings of the 8th International Conference on WWW* (Toronto, Canada, 1999) Elsevier North-Hooland, Inc., New York, NY, 1999, 1667-1678.
13. Soares, S., Laureano, E. and Borba, P. Implementing distribution and persistence aspects with AspectJ. In *Proceedings of 17th Annual ACM conference on Object-oriented programming, systems, languages, and applications (OOPSLA '02)* (Seattle, Washington, November 4-8, 2002) ACM Press, New York, NY, 2002, 174-190.
14. Struts. http://struts.apache.org/
15. Sun Java Blueprints: Guidelines, Patterns, and Code for End-to-end Applications. http://java.sun.com/reference/blueprints/index.html
16. Sun Java Center. The Duke's Bank Application. http://java.sun.com/j2ee/1.4/docs/tutorial/doc/Ebank.html
17. Sun Java Center. Java Petstore 1.1.2. http://java.sun.com/developer/releases/petstore/petstore1_1_2.html
18. Sun Java Center. Java Servlet Technology. http://java.sun.com/products/servlet/

Video-Based Sign Language Content Annotation
by Incorporation of MPEG-7 Standard

Rashad Aouf and Steve Hansen

[1] University of Western Sydney, School of Computing and Information Technology,
Sydney, Australia
{r.aouf,s.hansen}@uws.edu.au

Abstract. The advanced progress in multimedia technology increases the demand on delivering effective content in term of quality with the ability to describe content. From the W3C initiative into the web accessibility (WAI), there is a dedicated effort to make data accessible by every person even by people with disabilities. Accordingly, this paper balances the portion between the minimum bandwidth and the optimum required data to display customized video-based sign language. It also describes a systematic approach derived from the MPEG-7 multimedia content description standard to annotate sign language information. A new approach is proposed by this paper. It makes use of an "intermediary" signage object rather than immediate transmission of sign language video clips. Based on the signage object, this research analyses the components in order to enhance the display quality for video-based sign language with less data consumption by determining the accurate display parameters.

1 Introduction

Delivering multimedia data on a Web client is currently a significant area of research due to the bandwidth bottleneck [15] in particular with streaming video. The current compression technology (e.g. MPEG) proved its efficiency in minimizing the data rate that is relevant to ADSL and ISDN [15] [7] internet connection which are still expensive. However this technology is still not enough to deliver multimedia data with good quality for 56 kbps modem connection which is commonly being used to access internet. Meanwhile accessibility is still a current issue in the web environment in term of disability. The WAI [5] specified set of scenarios to access telecommunication systems by disabled people such as video captioning for deaf [4]. From the web accessibility issue and the enhancement in generic Web blended multimedia data presentation this research is looking in a systematic approach to provide effective sign language transmission with the minimum bandwidth needed.

Making use of the intermediary object, rather than immediate transmission of sign language video clips, provides access to sign language related information and allow enhancement in content (e.g. include graphics or animation) and minimize data (e.g. adjust display parameters – frame rates, resolution, and colors). This work make use of the MPEG-7 Multimedia Description Scheme [14] (MDS) to manage signage information.

This paper is organized as follows. Section 2 introduces sign language status in the web. Section 3 outlines the proposed signage information system. Section 4 explains in detail the system architecture. Section 5 presents a summary and conclusion, and declaration of future work.

D. Lowe and M. Gaedke (Eds.): ICWE 2005, LNCS 3579, pp. 232–236, 2005.

2 Sign Language

Sign language [2] is the natural approach of communication for deaf and hearing impaired people and providing sign language information within the Web will assist these people to access telecommunication systems.

Nowadays studies that focus in digitally handling sign language in the web environment is extremely limited (ViSiCast [6], DePaul University Project [16] [17], Dublin City University Project [18], and Gallaudet University[19]) and need more contribution from researchers around the continents while the statistics show a trend for these people to use web services.

Sign language has wealth of information to be clearly shown in video-based sign language [1] without jerky object movements and low-temporal resolution [10]. The next sections of this paper show how it is possible to adjust display quality parameters (frame rates, resolution, and colors) in order to minimize data while respecting the acceptable appearance of sign language attributes within a video-based sign language.

3 Proposed System

Currently, it is aimed to integrate sign language information system into the Web environment making use of XML-based technology [3] [8] (i.e. MPEG-7 standard). The goal of this research is to produce a signage information system that will balance the portion between the minimum bandwidth and the optimum required data to be displayed in video-based sign language transmission.

As outlined above, an intermediary object is defined to store multimedia data extracted from the original message (i.e. video-based sign language). This object is wrapped with additional information related to sign language such as users' preferences (e.g. display parameters, sign language components, etc), speech acts (e.g. interrogation, exclamation, etc) and emotional state (e.g. happiness, sadness, etc).

The role of the system is to improve in the presentation of the original message in term of display quality with minimum data rate transmission by associating of other web objects such as graphics (i.e. style) that supports the content of the description.

4 System Architecture

The system is built on client/server environment. This paper focuses on the server side in term of describing data modularity. The server contains 4 modules: MPEG-7 Framework, AV Storage System, User Information Storage System, and Intermediate Signage Object Generation.

4.1 MPEG-7 Framework

This research examines the extension of MPEG-7 Multimedia Description Scheme (MDS) [14] tools to include sign language attributes. However, MPEG-7 is considered as a library of description tools whereas creation and application of the descriptors are outside its scope. Therefore, the application specific domain [12] has to extract and extend MPEG-7 data model and select an appropriate subset of MPEG-7

Framework. According to the MPEG-7 Requirements Document [13] MPEG-7 framework consists of Descriptors Ds (low level features such as colors, texture, etc), Description Schemes DSs (high level features such as audio visual segment, etc), and the Description Definition language DDL [9] (i.e. XML-Schema Document) to extend or define new DSs and Ds to describe sign language AV content.

MPEG-7 Framework is addressed by two associated areas: AV Storage System and Users' Information Storage System. More details are given in the following sections.

4.2 AV Storage System

This system is to store video based sign language content and their description documents. It consists of two main parts: the AV content and their associated MPEG-7 description documents.

The MPEG-7 description documents provide information about the AV content making use of MPEG-7 description schemes and descriptors related to the AV content structure.

However, the description process produced a document that describes the content in generic form except with the "TextAnnotation" DS [11], free text is used to annotate low level sign language information. High level sign language attributes require extending normalized DSs through the DDL schema (section 4.4).

4.3 User Information Storage System

The user information storage system is an essential module while making a decision about the display quality of the AV content. This model consists of two parts: User's Information and MPEG-7 Preferences.

The user's information is a set of data collected from the user and then transformed into MPEG-7 descriptions (i.e. User Interaction Tools). This information is used in order to customize the display quality and minimize data consumption.

A DDL document has been generated to extend existed DSs in order to define the description structure, relationship among description schemes or descriptors and to constraint the values. Section 4.4 shows two samples of MPEG-7 XML Schemas.

4.4 Intermediate Signage Object Generation

The intermediary signage object is the generic object, defined above, wrapped with additional attributes that are extracted to enhance the original signed message. Attributes that are related to sign language are defined in the DDL XML-based schema. Existed DSs are selected to be used with the DDL for extension in order to include high level interpretation of audiovisual sign language.

From the signer's face, high level sign language attributes can be extracted to define other related attributes such as style and speech action. The intermediary object that contains these attributes will be associated with other web objects (e.g. animation) in order to enhance in the appearance of the signed message. The other attributes will be treated to ensure clear appearance of sign language parameters in the video clips in complicated conditions such as busy background, clothes color not contrast with skin color or even other objects that hide parts of the signer.

The following fragment of MPEG-7 Schema Definition (DDL) shows how to extend the MovingRegion DS that defined as PersonType in the code above to include additional elements related to sign language such as the "EmotionalState" and the "SpeechActs" elements and attributes related to sign language video clips.

```
<complexType name="MovingRegionType" final="#all">
 <complexContent><extension base="mpeg7:VisualDType">
   <element name="EmotionalState">
    <simpleType><restriction base="mpeg7:ModelStateType">
                <pattern value="Happy|Sad|Angry"/>
                </restriction></simpleType></element>
   <element name="SpeechActs">
    <simpleType><restriction base="mpeg7:TextType">
                <pattern value="Interrogation| Exclamation| Af-
                firmative"/>
                </restriction></simpleType></element>
 </extension></complexContent></complexType>
```

Code 1. Extends MovingRegion DS to include SignerFace

The following fragment of MPEG-7 Schema Definition (DDL) shows how to extend another DS called "MediaProfiles" that belongs to the MPEG-7 Content Management Tools [14] to include additional elements related to sign language display quality such as the "Resolution", "FrameRate", and "Color".

```
<complexType name="MediaInformationType" final="#all">
 <complexContent>
   <extension base="mpeg7:MediaProfilesType">
    <element name="Resolution">
     <simpleType><restriction base="mpeg7:VectorType">
                 <length value="2" /></restriction>
     </simpleType></element><element name="FrameRate">
     <simpleType><restriction base="mpeg7:unsigned6">
                 <pattern value="5|10|15|25"/>
                 </restriction></simpleType></element>
    <element name="Color"><simpleType>
      <restriction base="mpeg7:ColorSpaceType">
       <pattern value="RGB|GrayScale|BlackAndWhite" />
      </restriction></simpleType></element>
 </extension></complexContent></complexType>
```

Code 2. Extends the MediaProfiles DS within MediaInformaiton

Finally, the user's preferences are also taken into account in order to determine the final MPEG-7 content description document. User's preferences are sent to the multimedia servers to be combined with the original signage object and "actively" recommend customized signage content with minimum data rate transmission.

5   Summary and Conclusion

This paper gives an overview of a project being investigated into methodologies to integrate signage information into the web. Accordingly, sign language attributes are initiated according to their importance while addressing a signed message throughout computer mediated communication. In addition, user's preferences are considered in order to deliver customized signage content in term of display quality editing, with minimum data transmission rates in conjunction with other web objects that can be interact with content and style. MPEG-7 standard provides an appropriate markup environment to annotate various related content depicted by the intermediary signage object. To extensively broaden the accessibility issue in the web, this project looks forward for deeper examination of signage image and video content such as automatic facial expressions extraction and analysis rather than embed them manually.

References

1. Agrafiotis, D. and Canagarajah, N., Perceptually Optimized Aign Language Video Coding based on Eye Tracking Analysis. Electronics letters, 2003. **39**.
2. Aouf, R. and Hansen, S. Integration of Signage Information into the Web Environment. in Proceedings of the 9th International Conference on Computer Helping People with Special Needs, ICCHP. 2004. Paris, France: Springer-Verlag GmbH.
3. Aouf, R., Hansen, S., and Salter, G. Incorporation of Signage Information with Multimedia Data Processing by Making Use of XML Technology. in Proceedings of the International Conference on Computers in Education, ICCE. 2004. Melbourn, Australia.
4. Brewer, J., Scenarios of People with Disabilities Using the Web. 2000.
5. Brewer, J., WebAccessibility Initiative WAI. 2003.
6. Elliott, R., Glauert, J., Kennaway, J., and Marshall, I. The Development of Language Processing Support for the ViSiCAST Project. in Proceedings of the Fourth International ACM Conference on Assistive Technologies. 2000. Virginia, USA.
7. Foulds, R., A., Biomechanical and Perceptual Constraints on the Bandwidth Requirements of Sign Language. IEEE, 2004. **12**: p. 65-72.
8. Han, W., Buttler, D., and Pu, C., Wrapping Web data into XML. SIGMOD, 2001. **30**.
9. Hunter, J., An Overview of the MPEG-7 Descripiton Definition Language (DDL), in IEEE Transactions on Circuits and Systems for Video Technology. 2001. p. 765-772.
10. Manoranjan, M., D., Practical Low-Cost Visual Communication Using Binary Images for Deaf Sign Language. IEEE, 2000. **8**: p. 81-88.
11. Martinez, J., M., Overview of the MPEG-7 Standard V5.0. 2001, ISO/IEC JTC1/SC29/WG11 N4031 Coding of Moving Pictures and Audio: Singapore. p. 1-88.
12. Pereira, F., MPEG-7 Application Document. 1998, ISO/IEC JTC1/SC29/WG11 MPEG98/N2462 Coding of Moving Pictures and Audio: Atlantic City. p. 1-25.
13. Pereira, F., MPEG-7 Requirements Document V.15. 2001, ISO/IEC JTC1/SC29/WG11 N4317 Coding of Moving Pictures and Audio: Sydney. p. 1-30.
14. Salembier, P. and Smith, J., R., MPEG-7 Multimedia Description Schemes, in IEEE Transactions on Circuits and Systems for Video Technology. 2001. p. 748-759.
15. Sandini, G. and Nielsen, J., Image-based Personal Communication Using an Innvative Space-Variant CMOS Sensor. 1997.
16. University, D., The DePaul University American Sign Language Project. 2002, School of Computer Science, Telecommunication and Information Systems: Chicago.
17. University, D., The DePaul University American Sign Language Project Overview. 2002, School of Computer Science, Telecommunication and Information Systems: Chicago.
18. University, D.C., Research Studentships in the School of Computer. 2003, School of Computing.
19. University, G., Gallaudet University: E-Learning Online Graduate Degrees. 2004.

E-Legislative Services: Issues and Architecture

Elena Sánchez-Nielsen[1] and Francisco Chávez-Gutiérrez[2]

[1] Departamento de E.I.O. y Computación. Universidad de La Laguna, 38271 La Laguna, Spain
enielsen@ull.es
[2] Parlamento de Canarias. C/ Teobaldo Power, 7, 38002 S/C de Tenerife, Spain
fchavez@parcan.es

Abstract. Current legislative institutions demand information and services exchange between similar entities. However, legislative applications are composed of autonomous, heterogeneous and distributed components. In this paper, we describe a Web Services based model for legislative distributed institutions that use heterogeneous and autonomous information systems. Our approach is focused on four essential challenges: (1) maintaining the independence and equality among all the participating, (2) no modification of the information systems of each one of the legislative participating, (3) an efficient security mechanism in order to provide a successful system performance and (4) an open and scalar approach that allows incorporating new legislative institutions in a dynamic way.

1 Introduction

The use of procedures that allows legislative institutions to collaborate between them is a political priority of CALRE (conference of European regional parliament's presidents). At the same time, different initiatives directed towards the use of information and communication technologies (ICT) are promoted from European Commission [1].

The purpose of this paper is to describe our Web Services approach for exchange of information and cooperation between Spanish legislative assemblies. Information online about documentation, procedure on the laws, legislative initiatives, consultation of the librarian funds, as well as, statistic data on the legislative activities are illustrative examples of the need of cooperative services between the legislative institutions. One of the main features of our approach is based on extending this approach to other organizations within Europe and internationally. That is, the proposed solution allows anytime new incorporations without requiring infrastructure modification of the present institutions.

The remainder of this paper is organized as follows. In Section 2, we address the different issues and requirements. In Section 3 is provided a brief overview of Web Services technology. Section 4 illustrates the architecture and describes the different layers of functionality. Finally, some concluding remarks are given in Section 5.

2 Requirements Analysis

In order to provide a plausible solution, several requirements must be addressed:

- *Autonomy*: the approach for sharing data from distributed and heterogeneous information systems must be based on a decentralized schema, due to no legislative institution can play a superior role on another.

D. Lowe and M. Gaedke (Eds.): ICWE 2005, LNCS 3579, pp. 237–242, 2005.

- *Flexibility*: the resulting system must be an open solution. That is, non-specific architecture or programming language should be required.
- *Security*: the security model in order to be resistant to unwanted breakdowns and malicious attacks must be characterized by the following features: (1) each institution must be able to add or delete their users or revoke and grant permissions if it is needed, (2) it is the responsibility of every institution to contain an accessible medium for other institutions in order to check an user and sensible operations, (3) every institution must log every sensible access or operation to be performed, (4) it is assumed that every legislative institution includes a firewall defending the internal networks and systems (intranet) and (5) no special security considerations are required for several operations or information requests, i.e., public documents, announcements, bibliographic information, etc. Therefore, an anonymous or public access level with no restrictions in use is also involved.
- *Scalability*: new legislative incorporations must be supported without requiring infrastructure modification of the present and future institutions.

3 Web Services Technology

The Web Services paradigm [2, 3, 4] offers and consumes software as services. Interactions among Web Services involve three types of participants [4]: service provider, service requestor (also known as service consumers) and service registry. This way, service providers are the owners that offer services. They define descriptions of their services and publish them in the service registry. Service requestors use a find operation to locate services of interest. The registry returns the description of each relevant service. The requestor uses this description to invoke the corresponding Web Service. Three standardization initiatives XML-based technology have been submitted to W3C consortium to support interactions among Web Services: WSDL [5], UDDI [6] and SOAP [7]. Figure 1 illustrates Web Services functionalities.

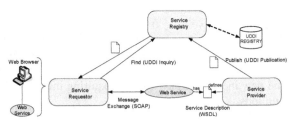

Fig. 1. Web Service reference model

4 Architecture

In the design of the architecture, several issues have been taken into account:

- At the present, all the Spanish legislative assemblies have all the information that they decide to share in some internal database. However, the assemblies provide a myriad of heterogeneous databases. Although the variety of databases is wide, the development of applications that allow the consultation of these databases is feasible. Therefore, the development of a Web Service that allows the consulting of the required information of some database is feasible at the same time.

– It is each assembly's task, to impose restrictions on the access to certain information.

– Each assembly can publish new services or modifying the current services in an autonomous way. It is advisable for each assembly to have available a Web Service Registry (UDDI), where all the modifications carried out in each assembly's UDDI would be replied autonomously to the rest of the assemblies. This condition is not essential, due to a single Web Service Registry could be implemented in a single assembly, however it would imply that any modification in a Web Service of an assembly would need the permission from the assembly that manages the Web Service Registry.

– A new institution can be incorporated anytime for consulting information provided by the other institutions, for offering new services to the other institutions or both situations.

The global architecture of our approach is illustrated in Figure 2. Three layers of functionality are involved: (i) Process Manager Layer, (ii) Web Services Layer and (iii) Security Processors Layer. The development of three modular Web Services in order to provide consultations to: legislative data (L), legislative activities (LA) and library resources (B) are initially proposed for sharing data. The following sections describe each layer of functionality of the proposed architecture.

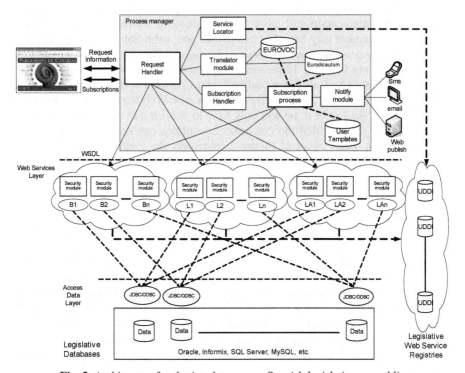

Fig. 2. Architecture for sharing data among Spanish legislative assemblies

4.1 Process Manager Layer

The *process manager* layer is used to process all the incoming requests from the users of the system. Two types of requests are supported by the system: request information and request subscriptions. This process will allow each user to be able to carry out consultations about certain information in a simultaneous way in all the assemblies that have enabled the appropriate Web Service. The *process manager* will be located in each legislative institution and will be implemented in function of the available resources. All requests are received and processed by the *request handler* module. To cover all aspects of location, discovery and invocation of available Web Services, a *service locator* module is used by the *request handler* module. The *service locator* discovers the available Web Services through the examination of the Web Service Registry (UDDI). The *request handler* module can improve the consultation of the system's information using the *translator* module. This module is based on the use of the multilingual thesaurus Eurovoc [8] and Eurodicautom [9].

Besides requests of information, the system allows the user to be informed when something of his interest is published in some assembly. The *user templates* module stores all the relative information about the subscriptions of the registered users.

4.2 Web Service Layer

For each service that is required to be implemented (initially three services proposed, focused on consultations to: legislative data - L, legislative activities – LA and library resources - B), an application will be deployed to implement the corresponding Web Service and this application will allow the consulting to the relative information of that service in a remote way for other assemblies and institutions. Since the architecture is completely decentralized, it allows each assembly to decide to implement their Web Services or not to do so. In the same way, each autonomous assembly can only deploy a Web Service of all those outlined, or to perform it in a progressive way. When a *provider* assembly chooses to *publish* his new Web Service so that the other assemblies can make use of it, he will only have to *publish* it in a Web *Service Registry* (UDDI) with the idea that the *consumer* assemblies can know its existence and consultation form. Each cloud of Figure 2 represents the logical group of all Web Services that have been published about one type of Web Service (B, L or LA).

4.3 Security Layer

The development of security component is based on: (1) flexibility, (2) modularity and (3) ubiquity. The ubiquity approach leads to user accessing to the system like an all-system. With this purpose, the security model is composed of three modules. Figure 3, shows graphically the security module for a user service request. The continue line represents a client call and the dash line represents a response, B_1, B_2 to B_n corresponds to the one kind of Web Services proposed. The user program only involves the *request module* through the use of his *id session*. The *id* session allows obtaining the session that is a data structure which includes name, login, source assembly, IP connection address, *id* requested service, parameters and other data, in order to identify and localize the user. The security restrictions provide two general possible scenarios: (i) a requested public service, e.g., request of public information, where non-user identification is required and (ii) a requested private service.

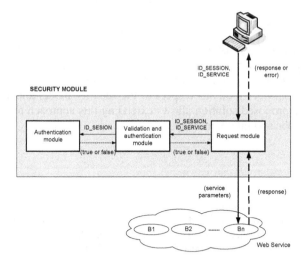

Fig. 3. The security module for a user service request

The security politic is based on an active components model that we call *sentinels* approach. Each Web Service, or Web Services organization, are associated with one or more sentinels. When a service request is received by the *request* module, the user credentials to access (*id* session, *id* requested service) are checked for each associated *sentinel* to the requested service. When the user *id* session does not belong to the assembly that provides the requested service, a session transport protocol is settled up, requesting to the appropriate assembly the information. In this context, the authentication and security requirements must be checked at legislative assembly layer using an asymmetric cryptography approach. The request operation is aborted if anyone of the sentinels refuses the request service. An error message is returned to the user program, showing the rejection reason and the mechanism to use for solving the problem, if it proceeds. In other case, when all the sentinels are consenting to, the operation is executed and the results are returned to the user program. Different *sentinel* models can be implemented. The simplest *sentinel* model is based on user authentication. That is, it is checked that the supplied *id* session maps a true session. Other security schemas are based on the use of access control list (ACL).

The use of the proposed security model presents the following advantages: (1) the different responsibilities are clearly distinguished, which leads to a reduction of the development process and modifications of the system, (2) a transparency approach of Web Services modules respect to the security model. That is, it is not required knowledge by the Web Services modules about the *sentinel's* implementation approach and vice versa, and (3) the transport session provides a monolithic appearance due to the user is authenticated for all the legislative assemblies once the user has been authenticated in an only assembly.

5 Conclusions

In this paper, architecture for data exchange among heterogeneous and distributed legislative assemblies based on a Web Services paradigm has been presented. The development of our approach is based on the use of three major concepts: (1) a decentralized schema for the cooperation problem between the legislative assemblies, (2) Web Services technology as wrappers that enable access to and interoperability amongst legislative assemblies and (3) flexible and modular security model, which is supported by a *sentinel* approach that provides a transparency approach of the development of Web Services modules respect to the security model and vice versa. The flexibility of the proposed solution allows extending this approach to other organizations within Europe and internationally.

References

1. Europe 2005 Action Plan. 2002.
   http://europa.eu.int/information_society/eeurope/2005/index_en.htm
2. Olivera Marjanovic.: Web Services Business Context- The Normative Perspective. Interantional Jornal of Web Services Research, 1(2), 16-36, April-June 2004.
3. FEA Working Group. E-Gov Enterprise Architecture Guidance (Common Referent Model), July 2002.
4. S. Vinoski. 2002. Web Services Interactions Models, Part 1: Current Practice. *In IEEE Internet Computing,* Vol 6, N° 3, pp. 89-91.
5. W3C: World Wide Web Consortium. 2003. *Web Services Description Language (WSDL).* http://www.w3.org/TR/wsdl
6. OASIS UDDI. 2003. *Universal Description, Discovery, and Integration.* http://www.uddi.org/
7. W3C: World Wide Web Consortium. 2003. *Simple Object Access Protocol. (SOAP).* http://www.w3.org/TR/soap/
8. The Office for Official Publications of the European Communities. *Eurovoc Thesaurus.* http://europa.eu.int/celex/eurovoc/
9. The Office for Official Publications of the European Communities. 1973 *Eurodicautom* http://europa.eu.int/eurodicautom

An Application Framework for Collaborative Learning

Aiman Turani[1], Rafael A. Calvo[1], and Peter Goodyear[2]

[1] Web Engineering Group, School of Electrical and Information Engineering,
The University of Sydney, Australia
{aimant,rafa}@ee.usyd.edu.au
http://www.weg.ee.usyd.edu.au
[2] CoCo, Faculty of Education, The University of Sydney, Australia
p.goodyear@edfac.usyd.edu.au

Abstract. We present the design of a new web application framework for collaborative learning. The framework guides users (i.e. teachers) in implementing online activities based on well-known pedagogical techniques, and simplifies the development of collaboration tools needed to carry out those techniques. There are common tasks across various techniques and our framework organizes them in a layer of abstraction. The framework model has four abstraction layers: Pedagogical Models, Pedagogical Techniques, Collaboration Tasks Patterns, and CSCL Tools. By using this framework, developers will place the control of designing and implementing new functionalities in the teacher's hand rather than in the software designer's.

1 Introduction

Learning usually happens when students are active and collaborate in solving a problem in a social environment [1]. In fact, recent pedagogical research shows that learning [2] is not simply knowledge assimilated with the help of a more knowledgeable person or mediated by a computer system, but also jointly constructed through solving problems with peers by a process of building shared understanding [3]. Collaboration software can be used to support this process, but generic collaboration software is not always appropriate or sufficient to build a meaningful learning experience. Collaborative learning software, as the one described here, brings into the software design the good practices of the established educational design methodology.

Figure 1 shows a model for a collaborative learning process. This process is described as an interactive flow. First the process starts with course objectives specified by the instructor or department. Then the educational context [4] is used to help teachers select a pedagogical technique. Boyley, defines a pedagogical technique as a manner of accomplishing teaching objectives according to how the technique prescribes student interaction with other students and resources [5].

In order to improve the quality and reduce the cost of online teaching, researchers are studying how to increase the reuse of learning content and instructional design. Today, a lot of the research by learning technologists emphasizes 'learning objects' (a way of packaging content modules) reuse. Regrettably, this work might reinforce the idea of learning as information 'transfer' (from the teacher or content to the student) which is a cause of low learner motivation, low engagement, and isolation [6]. Meanwhile, there has been a recent paradigm shift among university teachers, in which activities and collaboration take priority over content delivery. This shift has

D. Lowe and M. Gaedke (Eds.): ICWE 2005, LNCS 3579, pp. 243–251, 2005.

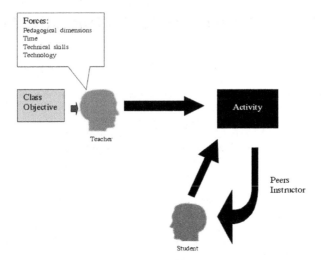

Fig. 1. Collaboration learning process

significant implications for online teaching, where software systems must be built to support these new pedagogical designs. Companies and universities have addressed this new paradigm with a variety of approaches, but in most cases these institutions lack software systems that embody these teaching strategies and support teachers in the design of courses with a strong collaborative component. Where these systems exist, they tend to focus on managing content rather than collaboration.

Engineers design software with abstractions and patterns as part of their standard software engineering practice. The essence of this practice is constructing representations that can communicate the commonalities in a number of problem/solution scenarios. Meanwhile, educational researchers have found that there are commonalities between many of the learning tasks and have defined and designed several 'Pedagogical Techniques' currently used by many teachers [7, 8]. We use these in the process of producing the abstractions we describe later.

Currently, there are several approaches for building software that supports those pedagogical techniques in an online environment. The first, a bottom-up approach, is the most commonly used and involves providing generic collaboration tools such as e-mail, bulletin boards, text chat, or computer conferencing [8] that the teacher then 'bundles' and sequences to create a pedagogical technique. For most pedagogical techniques, those individual tools are not enough [9]. For example, a teacher, who wants his students to participate in a brainstorming technique, might restrict his selection to a bulletin board and a text chat but he will probably need more than that. He might, for example, need an idea chart to hold the posted ideas, a timing tool to keep up the time, a voting tool to select the best idea, etc. Therefore, more than one tool might be required to carry out the brainstorming session. The *technical* solution is to provide more tools, other than those four, for teachers to select from, and enable them to sequence those tools according to the technique structure. If the tools were available, we could build new techniques, but would also put more pressure on the teacher to learn what are the best tools and how to configure them to carry out the activities. Finally this approach would also introduce more difficulties to students.

A second approach would be to provide teachers with specific bundles of tools for each pedagogical technique. This would be hard to implement due to three main reasons: first, the large number of possible pedagogical techniques [9], second, the same pedagogical technique might be performed with different scenarios since no single pedagogical technique structure is agreed upon among all teachers, third, teachers should be able to design new pedagogical techniques.

Our web engineering approach uses the domain specific knowledge from educational designers who have noticed that there are common components embedded in most pedagogical techniques, such as forming groups, provisioning topic information, monitoring, text-based discussion, etc. These components are at a different level from the tools used in the first approach. In this approach we also use the concept of application frameworks [10] that benefits the development of reusable, flexible, and customizable components in designing CSCL applications [11]. However, application frameworks consist not only of software components but also of design patterns. The component represents code reuse while a pattern represents design reuse [12]. Pedagogical techniques can provide the design reuse. In other words, a structure of a certain pedagogical technique, for example a debate in a political science class, could be reused in other learning domains. There is a big potential benefit from applying this new paradigm but the problem lies in the identification and dimensioning of components due to the large variety of abstraction methods used by pedagogical researchers and software engineers. Our approach to this problem is the four layered framework model introduced in this paper. This framework design will provide the basis of an implementation that helps teachers choose a pedagogical technique, and if necessary design the most appropriate tool for that technique. Section 2 describes each of the abstraction levels and Section 3 concludes the discussion.

2   Four Layers of Abstraction

A key design requirement in our application framework is that the teacher should be able to manage, customize and reuse ideas in the whole instructional design process. First, teachers would select which pedagogical model to use according to certain environmental forces. Second, a list of suggested pedagogical techniques associated with the selected model would be presented. Teachers would select the pedagogical technique according to what kind of problem students were asked to solve (learning objectives) and its context. Third, based on design reuse, the system would automatically present a suggested list of tasks to be preformed by the teacher and learners. At this point, a teachers' participation in the design process would terminate. Fourth, the system would map each task to a certain collaboration tool and then assemble all mapped tools to a single tool. Figure 2 shows how the four functional layers are related. This is followed by a detailed description of each layer.

2.1   The First Layer (Collaborative Pedagogical Models)

This is the most general layer as it describes the different collaboration pedagogical models. Morten [8] pioneered work in defining a framework for pedagogical CMC models. His contribution was to divide the existing models into four groups according to four communication paradigms used in computer-mediated communication. The

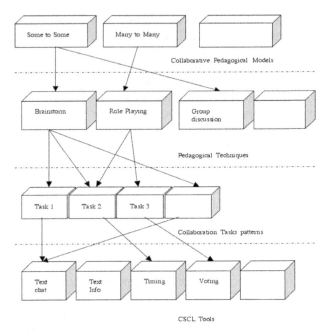

Fig. 2. The four layers of abstraction

first model is classified as *one-alone*, which can be preformed by retrieving information from online resources without communication with the teacher or other students. The second model is classified as *one-to-one*, which can be conducted via e-mail applications. The third model is classified as *one-to-many*, which typically is conducted via bulletin boards. Finally, *many-to-many* techniques, which can be organized within computer conferencing systems or bulletin board systems. As discussed before, defining the models around fixed communication tools makes them hard to adapt or used in other contexts. Pedagogical models should be divided according to their learning objectives, context and forces, not upon tools. Forces could be divided into three types: class size, time and technology. The class size is an important factor in choosing which model to follow. For example, a *one-to-one* model is difficult to implement in a class with 100 students. The second type of force is time. Time plays a major role in design considerations, and often it is the most important factor for a teacher designing a learning activity. A teacher needs to know how much time might be required in designing and facilitating the activity, and how much time students would be required to spend on it. The third type of force is technological which has two aspects, 'tools' particularly which CSCL tools are available and 'technical difficulty' that indicates how much time the teacher would need to learn the tool.

2.2   The Second Layer (Pedagogical Techniques)

Instructional design researchers have documented many different pedagogical techniques. We will build on work by Morten [8] who listed some of the pedagogical techniques used in adult education. Some differences are worth noting: his *one-alone* model was not used because our focus is on collaboration. Second, we have subdivided the *many-to-many* model into: *some-to-many* and *some-to-some* model. The *some-to-many* model is used to categorize some techniques that imply a small group acting in front of a larger group. The *some-to-some* model is used to categorize small groups interacts within. Figure 3 shows how pedagogical techniques are categorized.

In order to help teachers select the appropriate pedagogical technique, each technique is represented by a pattern. A pattern describes a problem repeatedly in the environment, and then describes the solution [13]. The solution is an essential part of a pattern since it provides the basic knowledge to identify and form the pattern's list of tasks. Table 1 shows a Group Discussion technique pattern.

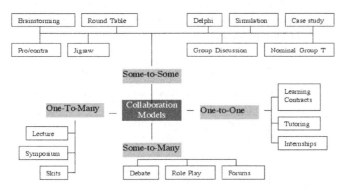

Fig. 3. Pedagogical techniques categorization

Table 1. Group discussion technique pattern

Pedagogical Technique	Group Discussion
Problem	How to establish and encourage group knowledge sharing among students
Example	Discussing how to improve writing and speaking skills for a foreign student
Context	Small groups with different skills and backgrounds interact to develop more knowledge among them
Solution	▪ Teacher specifies the discussion topic, related material and the time ▪ Student will start a Free discussion according to their experience and may build upon others' knowledge ▪ Teacher will guide the discussion when needed
Actors	▪ Teacher ▪ Learner ▪ System

2.3 The Third Layer (Collaboration Tasks Patterns CTP)

Pedagogical techniques are composed of a set of tasks that need to be performed by teachers and students. Therefore pedagogical techniques are considered to be task-oriented. Most of the pedagogical techniques (brainstorming, debate, group discussion, role-play, etc) have many tasks commonalities between them, such as a session creation task, a group forming task, a guiding task, a text interaction task, etc. Tasks are mainly subdivided between three roles: Teacher, Learner, and System. Some of these tasks are mandatory and some are optional. Teacher tasks can be subdivided into four main components: management tasks, information provision tasks, guiding tasks and assessments tasks. Learner tasks can also be subdivided into four components: group level tasks, individual level tasks, management tasks (for some roles) and additional tasks.

A primary list of tasks is identified after careful analysis of 10 well known pedagogical techniques (Brainstorming, Group Nomination, Group discussion, Round Table discussion, Debate, Role playing, Jigsaw, Pro/Contra, Lecture, One to One Tutoring), which cover all activity models (one-to-one, one-to-many, some-to-some, many-to many) [8]. There are currently 39 common tasks that could form any of those pedagogical techniques. The list of common tasks for the teacher is shown in Table 2 followed by the list of common tasks for students in Table 3.

Table 2. List of common tasks for teacher

Managements Tasks	1	Creating a collaboration session based on pedagogical technique
	2	Group formation
	3	Controlling the session (Activating, Terminating)
	4	Controlling the floor during session process
	5	Setting and controlling the timing
Guiding Tasks	6	Monitoring groups through the process
	7	Tracking participants interactions levels
	8	System Automatic Tracking and Supporting
	9	Providing Guidance
	10	Asking and Answering questions
Provision Tasks	11	Defining the objective of the session (title)
	12	Providing subject related info
	13	Providing sub-subject related info to a specific Role/Group
	14	Providing the session rules and instructions
	15	Preparing presentation text slides
	16	Preparing presentation Flash animations slides
	17	Video presentation
	18	White board drawing
Assessments	19	Results Evaluation
	20	Viewing session details

These tasks will enable the teacher to play a major role in the development of the collaboration tools in three ways: First, the teacher can select one of the supported pedagogical techniques to form a list. Each pedagogical technique will have it's own default tasks list based on a detailed study on that technique. Second, for flexibility, the teacher can: agree with the defaults tasks, delete some of those tasks and/or add new tasks. This will help the teacher to reshape the technique without losing the original pedagogical structure embedded inside. Third, a tasks list can provide a suitable mean for teacher and developer to generate a new pedagogical technique by simply dragging tasks from the list. This will make the designing of a new pedagogical technique's tool simple enough to place the control of the design in the teacher's hand rather than the software designer's hand.

Table 3. List of common tasks for learner

Group level Tasks	21	Group Joining
	22	Small group discussion (Free/Round)
	23	Large group discussion (Controlled by Facilitator/System)
	24	Debating (Controlled by Facilitator/Script)
	25	Role Playing (Controlled by Facilitator/Script)
	26	Ideas posting
	27	Application sharing
Individual Tasks	28	Private writing
	29	Asking/answering/needing teacher's help
	30	Summarizing the result (resolution/conclusion)
	31	*one-to-one* interaction
	32	Individual assigned reading
Management Tasks	33	Controlling the floor
	34	Controlling the timing
Additional Tasks	35	Participating in ideas voting to select the best idea
	36	Participating in yes/no questionnaires
	37	Participating in multiple choice questionnaires
	38	Participating with emoticons
	39	Joining multiple groups

Table 4 shows a default list of tasks needed to conduct Group Discussion technique. There are some tasks mandatory to all techniques such as 1,2,10 while the rest of the 13 tasks are driven from the solution part in Table 2

Table 4. Group discussion technique list of tasks

Teacher tasks:	Task No.
✓ Creating a Group Discussion session	1
✓ Group formation	2
✓ Defining the Group Discussion session title	10
✓ Providing subject related information	11
✓ Controlling the session (Activating, Terminating)	3
✓ Controlling the floor	4
✓ Setting and controlling timing	5
✓ Monitoring groups through the process	6
✓ Providing Guidance	8
✓ Results evaluation	19
Learner tasks:	
✓ Group joining	21
✓ Small group discussion (Free)	22

The Task list associated with any technique can lead to a description of the system architecture. To bridge the gab between teachers and software engineering, first each task is represented by a pattern object. For example, task 1 (Creating a collaboration session) is directly related to the *Session Creation* object. Second, we apply the UML (Unified Modeling Language)[14]. This holds the basic information to drive both the Use Case diagram and the Class diagram.

2.4   The Fourth Layer (CSCL Tools)

In the last layer, the system will map each task in the list to one of the CSCL tools along with any configurations. The final result, what learners see, is the bundle of CSCL tools, tasks and configurations that the designer has included in his pedagogical technique. For example, task number 10 (Defining The Title) will be mapped to a static info box tool and the same will be done to all selected tasks. CSCL tools consist mainly of traditional tools, such as chat, audio, video, whiteboard, forum, but with some additional attributes. First, some tools (Text Chat, Audio,) should have different levels of control. Second, the communication direction should be specified. Third, the text chat should have two additional attributes: Numbering and Authentication. Besides that, some additional tools are needed for some pedagogical techniques, such as Info text box, Voting tool, Timing tool and Gestures tool. Info text can be divided into two parts: static and dynamic. The static component is needed to hold information written by the teacher during the activity design time, such as Title, Problem Related info, etc, while the dynamic component is needed to hold temporary information, such as guiding info, is broadcast during the runtime, such as guiding info. A teacher can show/hide some of these tools embedded in the main tool to synchronize the activities sequence during the run time. Figure 4 shows a screen shot of the prototype for a brainstorming tool.

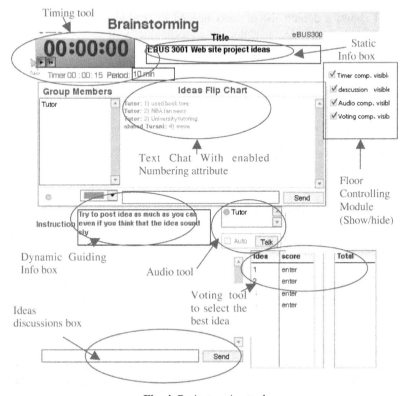

Fig. 4. Brainstorming tool

3 Conclusion

We have described the functional design of a framework to support teachers in selecting a suitable pedagogical technique and to support the construction of new ones. The theoretical framework has been successfully applied on ten well-known pedagogical techniques. The use of the application framework will also enable teachers to develop new pedagogical technique tools with minimum effort. A list of tasks that the teacher and learners should take before, during and after the collaboration session will drive the construction of the desired tool. For customization, it is possible for the teacher to change some of these tasks according to his needs. This approach will prevent losing the pedagogic structure embodied in the original learning activity while providing different kinds of tools for different techniques. We have only reported here the functional requirements and design of the framework. A prototype system is being built using the dotLRN Learning Management System and Macromedia's Collaboration Server. The two systems interact exchanging XML messages according to the IMS Learning Design specification.

References

1. Laurillard, D., *Rethinking University Teaching*. 2nd ed. 2002: Routledge Falmer.
2. Scardamalia, M. and C. Bereiter, *Computer Support for Knowledge-Building Communities*. The Journal of the Learning Sciences, 1994. **3**(3): p. 265-283.
3. Wasson, B. and S. Ludvigsen, *Designing for Knowledge Building*, in *ITU Report*. 2003, University of Oslo Press: Oslo, Norway.
4. Goodyear, P. *Patterns, pattern languages and educational design*. in *ASCILITE*. 2004. Perth, Australia: Australasian Society for Computers in Learning in Tertiary Education.
5. Boyle, P.G., *Planning Better Programs*. 1981, New York: McGraw-Hill Book Company.
6. Stacey, P., *People to People, not just people to content*. 2003, Vancouver.
7. Dimitriadis, Y.A., et al., *Component-Based Software Engineering and CSCL in the Field of e-Learning*. UPGRADE, 2003. **IV**(5): p. 21-27.
8. Paulsen, M.F., *The Online Report on Pedagogical Techniques for Computer-Mediated Communication*. 1995, nki.
9. Baumgartne, P. and I. Bergner, *Categorization of Virtual Learning Activities*. 2004: Hagen.
10. Fayad, M., D. Schmidt, and R. Johnson, *Building Application Frameworks Object-oriented foundations of framework design*. 1999: Wiley.
11. Asensio, J.I., et al., *Collaborative Learning Patterns: Assisting the Development of Component-Based CSCL Applications*. 12th Euromicro Conference on Parallel, Distributed and Network-based, 2004: p. 218-224.
12. Goodyear, P., et al. *Towards a Pattern Language for Networked Learning*. in *Networked Learning*. 2004.
13. Leo, D.H., J.I.A. Perez, and Y.A. Dimitriadis, *IMS Learning Design Support for the Formalization of Collaborative Learning Patterns*. 2004: Spain.
14. Fowler, M., *UML Distilled*. Second ed. 2000: Addison Wesley Longman.

An Investigation of Cloning in Web Applications

Damith C. Rajapakse and Stan Jarzabek

Department of Computer Science, School of Computing
National University of Singapore
{damithch,stan}@comp.nus.edu.sg

Abstract. Cloning (ad hoc reuse by duplication of design or code) speeds up development, but also hinders future maintenance. Cloning also hints at reuse opportunities that, if exploited systematically, might have positive impact on development and maintenance productivity. Unstable requirements and tight schedules pose unique challenges for Web Application engineering that encourage cloning. We conducted a systematic study of cloning in 17 Web Applications of different sizes, developed using a range of Web technologies, and serving diverse purposes. We found cloning rates 17-63% in both newly developed and already maintained Web Applications. Contribution of this paper is two-fold: (1) our results confirm potential benefits of reuse-based methods in addressing the key challenges of Web engineering, and (2) a framework of metrics and presentation views that we defined and applied in our study may be useful in other similar studies.

1 Introduction

Today, web sites are changing from mere collections of static hypertext documents to full blown software applications, commonly called Web applications (WA). In contrast to static web sites, WAs are bigger, more complex, more business critical, and more close to traditional software applications, requiring bigger initial investments and longer payback periods. WAs also have dramatically short development life-cycles, and fuzzy initial requirements resulting in frequent latent changes. All these add to the challenge of engineering and maintaining WAs.

Cloning has been recognized as a pervasive problem in maintenance of traditional software applications. It has been the focus of research for at least a decade. Cloning increases the tendency for update anomalies (inconsistencies in updating). Cloning also increases the effort required in program comprehension. Both these negatively affect maintenance. Reasons for cloning are manifold; most of them are related to programmer's intent to reuse the implementation of some abstraction [1]. It is a commonplace practice and cloning levels as high as 68% [8] have been reported in traditional software. With the recent proliferation of WAs, cloning in web domain is becoming an issue worthy of attention. As one benefit of cloning is the reduction of initial development time, shorter time-to-market requirement of WAs makes them ideal breeding grounds for clones. Also, the lack of suitable reuse and delegation mechanisms in HTML makes WAs a good candidates for clone proliferation [5]. On the positive side, the same similarity patterns that make cloning possible also signify valuable reuse opportunities. By exploiting such reuse opportunities systematically, we may cut development effort and ease future maintenance of WAs. Technologies for realizing this potential exist (server side scripting, template engines, meta-level techniques), but it is not known how well they fare in current state of the practice. As per our knowledge, no systematic study of cloning in the web domain has been done so far. In research on cloning in Web domain [3],[4],[5],[6],[11],[12], we did not find a published work giving concrete evidence of the extent of cloning in Web domain. Particularly, it is not known how the cloning problem in Web domain compares to that in the traditional software domain.

The above observations encouraged us to conduct a study of cloning in the WA domain, as described in this paper. The contribution of the paper is two-fold. (1) We conducted a comprehensive study of cloning in many types of WAs. We used WAs of different sizes, developed using a range of technologies, to cater for different application domains, by teams of different structures, using different development/business models, in different development environments. From our study, we were able to confirm potential benefits of reuse-based methods in addressing the key challenges of Web engineering. (2) We defined similarity metrics and clone analysis presentation views to be used in evaluating the extent of cloning in WAs. We adopted a general-purpose clone detector CCFinder [9] for analysis of the many types of sources that form WAs. We used, and validated, our clone evaluation framework in the study and we believe it will provide useful guidelines for future similar studies done by others, not only in Web domain, but in other domains as well.

Our study indicates that the extent of cloning in WAs is indeed substantial, exceeding cloning rates that we find in traditional applications. This shows the importance of investigating engineering techniques capable of defining generic solutions to avoid counter-productive cloning. Current technologies make a step in the right direction, but our analysis shows that there is room for improvement.

The remainder of this paper is organized as follows. In Section 2 we describe the experiment method, giving details of tools, metrics and graphs used. The results of the study are presented in Section 3, followed by related work is given in Section 4. Conclusions end the paper.

2   Experiment Method

In this experiment, we analyzed 17 WAs covering the following.

- **Languages/technologies** - Java, JSP, ASP, ASP.net, C#, PHP, Python, Perl, Web services, proprietary template mechanisms
- **Application domains** - collaboration portals, e-commerce applications, web based DB administration tools, conference management, corporate intranets, bulletin boards, etc.
- **System sizes** - 33 ~1719 files
- **License types** – free, commercial, internal use,
- **Development models** – open source, closed source
- **Life cycle stage** – pre/first/post release, dead
- **Usage types** – off-the-shelf, one-time-use, custom-built, model applications
- **Team structures** – single author, centralized teams, distributed teams
- **Organizations** – software development companies including Microsoft, Sun Microsystems, and Apache Software Foundation, free lance software developers, in-house development teams of non-software companies

In our choice of WAs, we have tried to represent the diversity of WA domain in an unbiased manner. Due to practical limitations, the number of WAs we could include in the study was limited to 17. Although it was possible to increase the sample size by including many readily available open source WAs, we refrained from doing that, in order to keep a balance between open source WAs and (less readily available) closed source WAs. The scope of analysis was clones in *any* text file that is likely to be maintained by hand, including files not normally considered 'source code'. More than 11000 files were analyzed in total.

We used CCFinder [9] as our clone detector. CCFinder can detect exact clones and parameterized clones. Our experiment needed to detect clones in files written in many languages, not necessarily languages supported by CCFinder. Therefore, we instructed CCFinder to assume all input files as 'plain text'. In this mode, only exact clones were detected. We also instructed CCFinder to ignore trivially short clones (i.e. clones shorter than 20 tokens) and clones occurring within the same file, in order to keep the volume of reported clones within manageable limits. We developed a Java program called 'Clone Analyzer' to control the clone detection process and to analyze the clones detected by CCFinder. Fig. 1 shows the steps of clone analysis process. Next, we describe the metrics and visualizations used in the experiment.

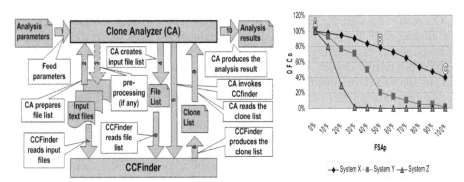

Fig. 1. Clone analysis workflow   **Fig. 2.** Sample FSCurves

Total Cloned Tokens (TCT): We defined TCT of a system as the sum of clone related tokens, i.e., tokens that form a part of any of the clones in that system. *TCTp* is *TCT* expressed as a percentage of total number of tokens in the system. When *TCTp* is high, *update anomaly risk* (the risk of inadvertently creating an update anomaly while modifying the system) is also high. If the *TCTp* is greater than 50%, system has more clones than non-clones; every update to the system has a higher chance of involving a clone than not; and hence runs a high risk of creating an update anomaly. We can call such systems *high update anomaly risks*.

File Similarity (FSA): While *TCTp* is a good indication of the overall cloning level of a system, it can be further complemented by a measure of file similarity. For example, consider two systems X and Y of similar size, both having the same *TCTp*. In X, clones are scattered across the system in such a way that no two files are substantially similar. But In Y, clones are well concentrated into a certain set of files. From a clone treatment perspective, system Y is more interesting than X because the clones in Y are more easily treatable than that of X. To identify the similarity of a file f to other files, we calculated the metric $FSA(f)$. We defined $FSA(f)$ as follows (This is analogous to $RSA(f)$ defined in [13]).

$$FSA(f) = \frac{1}{Tn(f)} \sum_{c \in CF(f)} Tn(c)$$

Here, $Tn(f)$ is the number of tokens in file f, $CF(f)$ is a set of code fragments which are included in file f and have a clone relation with some code fragments in other files, and c is an element of $CF(f)$. In this summation, overlapped code portions are counted only once. $FSA(f)$ is a direct measure of the similarity (resulting from cloning) of file f to other files in the system. For example, $FSA=0.6$ for a given file f means 60% of f has been cloned from other files of the system. For convenience, we defined the metric $FSAp$ as FSA given as a percentage (i.e., $FSAp(f) = FSA(f) * 100\%$)

Qualifying File Count (QFC): We define Qualifying File Count for $FSAp$ value v, $QFC(v)$, as the number of files for which $FSAp$ is not less than v. For example, $QFC(30\%)$ gives the number of files in the system having a $FSAp$ value not less than 30%. $QFCp$ is QFC expressed as a percentage of the total number of files in the system. For example, $QFCp(60\%) = 43\%$ means, in 43% of files in the system, 60% or more have been cloned.

File Similarity Curve (FSCurve): To observe the overall file similarity characteristics across an entire system, we used File Similarity Curve (FSCurve). An FSCurve is created by plotting $QFCp$ against $FSAp$. In the example FSCurve shown in Fig. 2, we have marked points A, B and C to illustrate how to interpret FSCurves. Point A indicates the invariant property that in 100% of files at least 0% has been cloned. At the other extreme, point C indicates that 40% of the files in System X have been completely (100%) cloned. Similarly, point B denotes that for System X, $QFC(50\%) \approx 80\%$. i.e. in about 80% of the files in System X, at least 50% of the contents have come from other files. From FSCurves we can also get an idea about relative file similarity characteristics of different systems. For example, from the three FSCurves in Fig. 2, we can clearly see that file similarity in system Y is generally less than that of X but more than that of Z. i.e. Higher the position of the curve, higher the file similarity.

3 Experiment Results

3.1 Overall Cloning Level

The initial phase of our investigation was focused on the overall cloning level in WAs. Given in Fig. 3 is the *TCTp* of each WA we studied. Only one WA has a *TCTp* below 20%. The average *TCTp* is 41% (with a standard deviation of 15%). Five WAs are high update anomaly risks (*TCTp*>50%) while three more are close behind.

From these data alone, the level of cloning in WAs seems substantial. Still, these data do not include clones with parametric variations (parameterized clones) and non-parametric variations (gapped clones). As a result, the actual cloning level in WAs could be even higher than the levels indicated by these data. We tested this hypothesis by comparing cloning level reported by CCFinder and a web-specific clone detector described in [3]. This clone detector (for convenience, we refer to it as *WSFinder*) detects the similarity among web-specific files. We did not use it as our main clone detector because it currently supports HTML and JSP files only. WSFinder reports three different values of file similarity based on 1. HTML tags, 2. Text included inside HTML tags, and 3. Scripts included in the file (only applicable to JSP pages). For a small set of HTML and JSP pages, we applied both CCFinder and WSFinder to compare results. To make the comparison least biased towards the hypothesis, we compared the minimum of the three values reported by WSFinder against CCFinder results. As shown in Fig. 4, CCFinder almost always reported a cloning level less than or equal to that reported by WSFinder. This supports our hypothesis that actual cloning level in WAs could be even higher than what is reported in this paper.

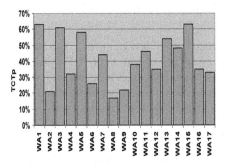

Fig. 3. Cloning level in each WA

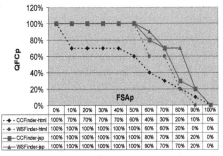

Fig. 4. CCFinder Vs WSFinder

A high level of cloning does not necessarily mean a high reuse potential. The clones detected could be too small, too dispersed, or false positives. Since our minimum clone length was 20 tokens, these results could include clones as short as 20 tokens. (We did not use a higher minimum clone length, in the hope of capturing some of the parameterized clones or gapped clones; a parameterized/gapped clone contains a number of smaller exact clones). This could prompt one to argue that clones detected are trivially short ones, not worthy of elimination. To address this concern, we used the breakdown of the clones by length, in each system (as shown in Fig. 5). Clone size increases from 20 to 100+ as we go from top to bottom of each bar. Increasingly larger clones are shown in increasingly darker colors. As an average LOC is accounted by 6-8 tokens, a 100 token clone is roughly 15 LOC long. Therefore, this graph shows that most clones we detected are longer than 15 LOC.

To address the issue of clones dispersed across the system too thinly, we generated FSCurves for each system. To save space, we show all the FSCurves together in Fig. 6, with the average, the minimum, and the maximum curves marked with dashed lines. According to the average curve, close to 50% of the files have at least 50% of their content cloned. Fig. 7 represents two cross sections of Fig. 6, namely, at *FSAp*=50% and *FSAp*=90%. We use this graph to give a bit more detailed view of the clone concentration in each WA. It shows the percentage of files in each system that we can consider 'cloned' ($FSAp \geq 50\%$) and 'highly cloned' ($FSAp \geq 90\%$). In eleven of the WAs, we find more than 10% of the files have been highly cloned. In five, we find more than 20% of the files have been highly cloned. Aggregating all the WAs, the percentages of cloned and highly cloned files are 48% and 17% respectively. These data suggest that there is good clone concentration in files.

With regards to the issue of false positives, it is not practical to manually weed out the false positives in a study of this scale. However, since we detected only exact clones, we believe the false positives are at a minimum.

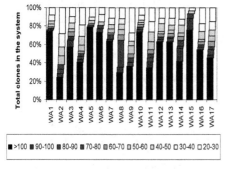

Fig. 5. Distribution of clone size   **Fig. 6.** FSCurves for all WAs

3.2   Cloning Level in WAs Vs Cloning Level in Traditional Applications

Since cloning in Traditional Applications (TAs) has been widely accepted as a problem, we wanted to compare cloning levels of WAs to that of TAs. We started by separating the files in WAs into two categories:

- WA-specific files – files that use WA-specific technologies, e.g., style sheets, HTML files, ASP/JSP/PHP files
- General files – files equally likely to occur in WAs and TAs. e.g., program files written in Java/C/C#, build scripts

We found 13 of the WAs had both type of files, while some smaller WAs had only Web-specific files. For WAs with both type of files, we calculated $TCTp\_W$ ($TCTp$ for WA-specific files) and $TCTp\_G$ ($TCTp$ for general files) as given in Fig. 8. The last two columns show that overall $TCTp\_W$ was 43% and overall $TCTp\_G$ was 35%. The $TCTp$ comparison of individual WAs shows that in 6 WAs $TCTp\_W$ is significantly higher ($TCTp\_W > TCTp\_G$ by more than 10%), in 3 WAs levels are similar ($|TCTp\_W\text{-}TCTp\_G| \leq 10\%$), and only in 4 WAs $TCTp\_G$ was significantly higher ($TCTp\_G > TCTp\_W$ by more than 10%). These figures suggest that WA-specific files have more cloning than general files. But we can reasonably assume that cloning in full fledged TAs is not worse than cloning in these general files. This infers that cloning in WAs is worse than cloning in TAs.

3.3   Factors Affecting the Cloning Level

Our investigation also included collecting quantitative data on different factors that might affect cloning in WAs. We started by investigating whether system size has any effect on the cloning level. However, a comparison of average cloning level in small, medium, and large WAs (Table 1) showed that cloning level does not significantly depend on the system size.

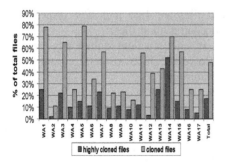

Fig. 7. Percentage of cloned files

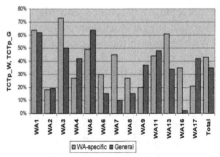

Fig. 8. WA-specific files Vs General files

Table 1. Average cloning for WAs of different size

Size (in # of files)	Avg $TCTp$	Std. Deviation
Small (size < 100)	40%	21%
Medium (100 ≤ size < 1000)	42%	14%
Large (size ≥ 1000)	40%	16%
All	41%	15%

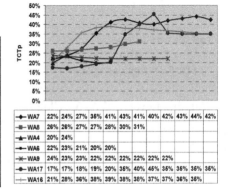

WA7	22%	24%	27%	35%	41%	43%	41%	40%	42%	43%	44%	42%
WA8	26%	26%	27%	27%	28%	30%	31%					
WA4	20%	24%										
WA6	22%	23%	21%	20%	20%							
WA9	24%	23%	23%	22%	22%	22%	22%	22%	22%			
WA17	17%	17%	18%	19%	20%	35%	40%	45%	35%	35%	35%	35%
WA16	21%	28%	36%	38%	39%	38%	38%	37%	37%	36%	35%	

Fig. 9. Movement of cloning level over time

Continuing, we also investigated the progression of cloning level over time. For this, we used seven of the WAs for which at least four past releases were readily available. All seven suitable WAs were open source, and of medium or large size. In the Fig. 9, we show the moving average (calculated by averaging three neighboring values) of *TCTp* over past versions, up to the current version. According to this graph, all WAs show an initial upward trend in the cloning level. Some WAs have managed to bring down the *TCTp* during the latter stages, even though current levels still remain higher than the initial levels. This indicates that the cloning level is likely to get worse over time. WA9, and to a smaller extent WA6, are the only exceptions, but this may be due to non-availability of the versions corresponding to the initial stage.
kkk

3.4 Identifying the Source of Clones

Finally, we attempted to obtain some quantitative data that could be useful for devising a solution to the cloning problem. We were interested to find which of the following file categories contributed most clones

i. **Static files (STA)** – files that needs to be delivered 'as is' to the browser. Includes markup files, style sheets and client side scripts (e.g., HTML, CSS, XSL, JavaScripts).
ii. **Server pages (SPG)** – files containing embedded server side scripting. These generate dynamic content at runtime (e.g., JSP, PHP, ASP, ASP.NET).
iii. **Templates (TPL)** – files related to additional templating mechanisms used.
iv. **Program files (PRG)** – files containing code written in a full fledged programming language (e.g., Java, Perl, C#, Python)
v. **Administrative files (ADM)** – build scripts, database scripts, configuration files
vi. **Other files (OTH)** – files that do not belong to other five types.

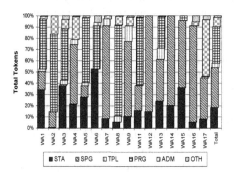 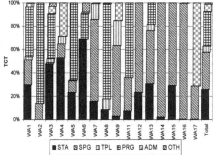

Fig. 10. Contribution of different file types to system size

Fig. 11. Contribution of different file types to cloning

Fig. 10 gives the contribution of each file type towards system size while Fig. 11 gives the contribution of each file type towards cloning. The rightmost column of each graph shows the overall situation (aggregation all the WAs). The salient feature of these graphs is that there is no single file type that clearly dominates the composition of the system, or the composition of the clones. At least three types (STA, SPG, and PRG) shows dominant influence, while the influences of TPL and ADM are smaller, but not negligible. This shows that a successful solution to the cloning problem has to be applicable equally to the entire range of file types. Moreover, the high influence of WA-specific types (STA, SPG and to a lesser extent, TPL) suggests that a solution rooted in TAs might not be successful in solving the cloning problem in WAs.

4 Related Work

Clones have been defined in slightly different ways by different researches. These differences are usually related to different detection strategies used and the different domains focused on by each researcher. Accordingly, there are clone definitions specific to web domain; [5] defines HTML clones as pages that include the same set of tags while [4] defines clones as pages that have the same, or a very similar structure. In [3], web page clones are classified into three types based on similarity in page structure, content, and scripts. Since our study considers all text files for clone detection, not just HTML pages or script files, we use a simpler definition of clones, i.e., clones are similar text fragments.

Existing research in clone detection (CD) is based on two major approaches [7]: (1) Using structural information about the code. E.g., metrics, AST, control/data flow, slices, structure of the code/expressions, PDG, etc. (2) Using string-based matches. Our main detection tool CCFinder [9] falls into the 2nd category. It was developed at Osaka University, Japan. Since then, it has been used [10] and evaluated [2] by independent researchers. The string based approach of CCFinder is well suited for studies like ours involving text written in many languages including natural languages. Clone detection (CD) have many applications, like detecting plagiarism, program comprehension, reengineering, quality evaluation etc. and is an area extensively studied in the context of traditional software domain. Syntax errors and routine use of multiple programming languages make clone detection in the web domain harder [12]. There are CD tools/techniques specific to web being proposed [4],[5],[6],[12]. Technique in [5] detects clones in static pages only, but in [4] it was extended to include ASP pages. A (semi) automatic process aimed at identifying static web pages that can be transformed into dynamic ones, using clustering to recognize a common structure of web pages, is described in [11]. Technique in [3] identifies HTML and JSP pages that are more similar to each other than a specified threshold.

Gemini [13] is a maintenance support environment that augments CCFinder. Gemini provides the user with functions to analyze the code clones detected by CCFinder. It primarily provides two visualizations: scatter plot and metrics graph. The scatter plot graphically shows the locations of code clones among source codes. The metrics graph shows different metric values for clones. We regularly use Gemini in our research and have found it to be a very useful tool. However, there were three main limitations of Gemini that led us to write our own Clone Analyzer. First, when using Gemini, it is difficult to grasp the total cloning activity in the system [10]. Size of the clone metric graph in particular grows out of control when a large number of files are involved. Second, Gemini does not provide an API to access the analysis data. When using Gemini, it is not possible to analyze the clones beyond the visual data provided by the tool itself. And third, due to its visual nature, Gemini is more resource intensive compared to CCFinder; the number of clones it could handle is limited. Our Clone Analyzer overcomes these issues and was very useful in cutting down the time required to analyze the large amount of clone data generated in this study.

5 Conclusions and Future Work

We conducted a study of cloning in 17 Web Applications of different sizes, developed using a range of Web technologies, and serving diverse purposes. We found cloning rates 17-63% in both newly developed and already maintained Web Applications. To emphasize the reuse potential signified by these clones, we showed that most of the clones are substantially long, well concentrated and unlikely to be false positives. With the aid of a Web-specific clone detector, we substantiated our hypothesis that actual cloning level could be even higher than the levels reported here. We also showed that cloning equally affect small, medium or large WAs, and cloning gets worse over time. More importantly, we showed that cloning in WAs could be even worse than that of traditional applications. Firstly, our findings provide the concrete evidence of cloning in WAs we set out to produce at the start of this study. In doing so, it confirms the potential benefits of reuse-based methods in addressing the key challenges of Web engineering. Secondly, our study defines and validates a framework of tools, metrics, and presentation views that may be useful in other similar studies.

One explanation of substantial cloning we found is extensive similarity within WA modules, across modules and across WAs. The existence of those similarities, exceeding the rates of similarity we are likely to find in traditional software, underlines the importance of investigating techniques to improve the effectiveness of reuse mechanisms in Web Engineering. The study itself revealed an important consideration when devising such mechanisms. That is, it shows that a number of files categories – some of which use Web-specific technologies – contribute towards cloning in WAs. This suggests that any successful solution need to be uniformly applicable to all text sources, not just code written in a particular language.

In our future work, we hope to complement this quantitative analysis with more qualitative analysis. We hope such work will result in further insights into the nature of problem of cloning in WAs. We also plan to address design-level similarities, so-called structural clones. Structural clones usually represent larger parts of programs than the 'simple' clones detected by current clone detectors like CCFinder; therefore their treatment could be even more beneficial.

All the WAs included in this study are one-off products. Going further, a promising area we hope to work on is cloning in WA product lines. In the absence of effective reuse mechanisms, whole WAs could be cloned to create members of the product line, resulting in much worse levels of cloning than reported here. Server side scripting, current technology of choice for adding run time variability to WAs, may fall well short of the construction time variability a product line situation demands. We plan to explore this area to find synergies between run time and construction time technologies in solving the cloning problem of WA domain in general, and WA product lines in particular.

Acknowledgements

Authors thank following persons for their contributions during the study: Andrea De Lucia and Giuseppe Scanniello (Università di Salerno, Italy), Katsuro Inoue, Shinji Kusumoto, and Higo Yoshiki (Osaka Uni. Japan), Toshihiro Kamiya (PRESTO, Japan), Sidath Dissanayake (SriLogic Pvt Ltd, Sri Lanka), Ulf Patterson (SES Systems Pte Ltd., Singapore), Yeo Ann Kian, Lai Zit Seng, and Chan Chee Heng (National University of Singapore).

References

1. Baxter, I., Yahin, A., Moura, L., and Anna, M. S., "Clone detection using abstract syntax trees," *Proc. Intl. Conference on Software Maintenance* (ICSM '98), pp. 368-377.
2. Burd, E., and Bailey, J., "Evaluating Clone Detection Tools for Use during Preventative Maintenance," *Second IEEE Intl. Workshop on Source Code Analysis and Manipulation (SCAM'02)* pp. 36-43.

3. De Lucia, A., Scanniello, G., and Tortora, G., "Identifying Clones in Dynamic Web Sites Using Similarity Thresholds," Proc. Intl. Conf. on Enterprise Information Systems (ICEIS'04), pp.391-396.

4. Di Lucca, G.A., Di Penta, M., Fasolino, A.R., "An approach to identify duplicated web pages," *Proc. 26th Annual Intl. Computer Software and Applications Conference* (COMPSAC 2002), pp. 481 – 486.

5. Di Lucca, G. A., Di Penta, M., Fasilio, A. R., and Granato, P., "Clone analysis in the web era: An approach to identify cloned web pages," *Seventh IEEE Workshop on Empirical Studies of Software Maintenance* (WESS 2001), pp. 107–113.

6. Lanubile, F., Mallardo, T., "Finding function clones in Web applications," Proc. Seventh European Conference on Software Maintenance and Reengineering, (CSMR' 2003). pp.379 – 386.

7. Marcus, A., and Maletic, J. I., "Identification of High-Level Concept Clones in Source Code," Proc. Automated Software Engineering, 2001, pp. 107-114.

8. Jarzabek, S. and Shubiao, L., "Eliminating Redundancies with a "Composition with Adaptation" Meta-programming Technique," Proc. European Software Engineering Conference and ACM SIGSOFT Symposium on the Foundations of Software Engineering (ESEC-FSE'03), pp. 237-246.

9. Kamiya, T., Kusumoto, S, and Inoue, K., "CCFinder: A multi-linguistic token-based code clone detection system for large scale source code," IEEE Trans. Software Engineering, vol. 28 no. 7, July 2002, pp. 654 – 670.

10. Kapser, C., and Godfrey, M. W., "Toward a taxonomy of clones in source code: A case study," *In Evolution of Large Scale Industrial Software Architectures*, 2003.

11. Ricca, F., Tonella, P., "Using clustering to support the migration from static to dynamic web pages," *Proc. 11th IEEE International Workshop on Program Comprehension,* (IWPC' 2003), pp. 207 – 216.

12. Synytskyy, N. Cordy, J. R., Dean, T., "Resolution of static clones in dynamic Web pages," *Proc. Fifth IEEE Intl. Workshop on Web Site Evolution,* (IWSE'2003), pp. 49 – 56.

13. Ueda, Y., Kamiya, T., Kusumoto, S., and Inoue, K., "Gemini: Maintenance Support Environment Based on Code Clone Analysis," *Proc. Eighth IEEE Symposium on Software Metrics*, pp. 67-76, 2002.

Intelligent Web Information Service Model
for Minimizing Information Gap Among People
in E-Government

Gye Hang Hong[1], Jang Hee Lee[2], Tae Hyun Kim[3],
Sang Chan Park[3], Hyung Min Rho[4], and Dong Sik Jang[1]

[1] Industrial System and Information Engineering, Korea University, Seoul, Republic of Korea
{kistduck,jang}@korea.ac.kr
[2] Industrial Management, Korea University of Technology and Education,
Chunan, Republic of Korea
janghlee@kut.ac.kr
[3] Industrial Engineering, Korea Advanced Institute of Science and Technology,
Daejeon Republic of Korea
{imiss,sangchanpark}@kaist.ac.kr
[4] CADCAM center, Korea Institute of Science and Technology, Seoul, Republic of Korea
hmrho@kist.re.kr

Abstract. We suggested a web information service model for minimizing information gap among people. A difference of information access environment, ability to understand and information pursuit desire, etc among people makes people to use different kinds of information on their decision-making. We designed an intelligent web information service model, consisting of a web usage analysis and a personalized web service module.

1 Introduction

E-government is defined as an application of IT to government service [1]. An access to information service, one of the common e-government services provides various kinds of public information to the users having various demands for supporting their decision-making. Because education level, information pursuit desire, different network connection environment, and so on are different according to the users, the web service of government which does not consider these differences may not satisfy some users of them. For reducing these differences, many researches are developed in the fields of both web design and personalization.

Marchionini G. and M. Levi [2] suggested a design method where many kinds of information are contained in minimum pages and the same information is presented as the various different types, which all users can understand easily.

A personalization is that information about the specific user is used to develop an electronic profile based on different types of user-specific information. So, users can have benefit for reducing searching time of information [3].

We have formulated the following conjectures by examining the research results and the e-government environment.

Firstly, we verify that the information gap among advantaged people and disadvantaged people has an effect on difference of profit/loss in their economic behaviors.

D. Lowe and M. Gaedke (Eds.): ICWE 2005, LNCS 3579, pp. 263–266, 2005.

Secondly, we show that causes of the information gap occur from the level of understanding information among people. So, we identify the web pages, which advantaged people refer for their decision-making and the web pages, which disadvantaged people do. We analyze differences of the two kinds of web pages from the viewpoint of the dimension complexity and the decision variables.

2   Current Web Information Service System of MAF in Korea

A current public institution's web service system in MAF was made to deliver beneficial agriculture information to farmers. Web contents in the web service system of MAF are mainly statistic analysis of product transaction in market. Although the current system serves many kinds of web pages to satisfy various demands of users, the many kinds of web pages caused increase of searching time and some kinds of web pages could not be understood by some people because of summarizing data by many dimensions.

3   Intelligent Web Information Service (*IWIS*) Model

3.1   Web Usage Analysis Module(*WUAM*)

WUAM is defined as the module for identifying information gap between advantaged people and disadvantaged people, then discovering knowledge, key web pages and those dimensions and decision variables, for reducing the information gap.The *WUAM* discovers the knowledge by the following steps.

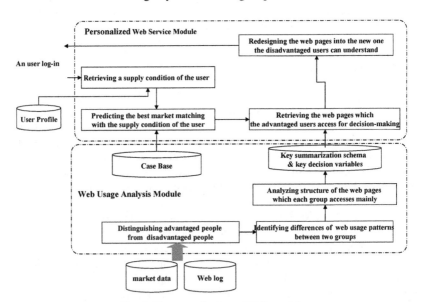

Fig. 1. Framework of our IWIS model

Firstly, we distinguish advantaged people from disadvantaged people in terms of three factors: Total Profit or loss (TP), Probability For Profit (*PFP*), and Probability

For Loss (*PFL*). By evaluating the factors simultaneously, we can distinguish advantaged people from the others. For evaluating the factors simultaneously, we segment people into several groups having a similar features with SOM(Self-Organizing-Map), one of the clustering methods [4].

Secondly, we identify differences of web usage patterns between advantaged group and disadvantaged group. The differences are the kinds of web page accessed for decision-making and the level of understanding information. The following sub-steps identify the difference of web pages accessed between two groups.

1) We calculate access count of user to web page by analyzing web-log data. The access count is transformed into one of the five levels: High(*H*), Low(*L*), Average(*A*), Above Average(*AA*), and Below Average(*BA*).
2) We identify the important web pages which can distinguish two groups. We use the C4.5 which is one of classification methods [5]. Table 1 shows the result of classification. Disadvantaged people think price and quality data a day as important information, while advantaged people think quantity and it's trend data a week as important information.

Table 1. Summary of the schema and decision variables characterizing each group

	No. web pages	Degree of reference	Dimension and decision variable
Advantaged people	A01	<=AA	Dimension: time(daily), item, market Decision variables: price and quality
	A15	> A	Dimension: time(week), market, supplier, item Decision variables: quantities and its trend
disadvantaged people	A01	> AA	Dimension: daily, item, market Decision variables: price and quality

3.2 Personalized Web Service Module(*PWSM*)

PWSM is defined as the module for predicting the best decision-making under current supply condition of the user accessed in the system, then redesigning the web pages regarded to the best decision-making.

Firstly, we retrieve a supply condition of the accessed user from the user' profile database and market database.

Secondly, we predict the best market matching the supply condition of the user. We use a hybrid approach of Memory And Neural Network based learning (MANN) [6] for the prediction.

Thirdly, we retrieve the web pages which advantaged people mainly access for decision-making.

Lastly, we redesign the retrieved web pages into new one the disadvantaged people can understand easily.

Fig. 2 shows one of the redesigned web pages which the disadvantaged people can understand easily. Fig 2 (a) is web information, advantaged people access mainly, summarized according to four dimensions of item, supplier, market, and time. Because the web information consists of many web pages of combination of four dimensions, disadvantaged people consider many web pages for decision-making.

Therefore, we predict the good alternatives under condition of disadvantaged people, present the good alternatives by two dimension of time and item. Fig 2(b) shows

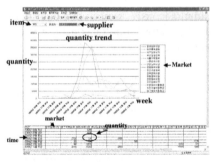 

(a) One of the web pages that advantaged people access for decision-making

(b) The web page which is redesigned to understand disadvantaged people

Fig. 2. Redesigning an web-page (Some Korean words were translated into English)

the redesigned web page summarized according to only item and time by fixing the optimal supplier and the optimal market. As a result, disadvantaged people consider a little of web pages and they can make the better decision.

4 Conclusion

Due to the differences of information access environment, the ability to understand information and the information pursuit desire, people use different kinds of information. To provide the losers with the same profit as a minimization of the information gap, we collected web-log data of users and profit data of the users. We divided people into the advantaged people and the disadvantaged people. We identified differences of web usage, web pages accessed mainly for decision-making and a level of understanding the web pages, between the two groups. Then, we identified important factors for decision-making by analyzing the dimension and decision variables included in the web pages used by the advantaged users. The factors and the level of understanding information of each group are used for a personalization service. If a user logged in the system, the system retrieved profiles of the user and the factors and predicted potential alternatives. Then the system designed information of the potential alternatives to a type of web pages which the user can understand easily.

References

1. Marchionini G., Sanan H., and L. Brabdt: Digital Government, Communications of the ACM, vol. 46, No.1 (2003) 25-27
2. Marchionini G., M. Levi: Digital Government Information Services: The Bureau of Labor Statistics Case, Interactions, Vol. 10 (2003) 18-27
3. Hinnant C. C. and J.A.O'Looney: Examining pre-adoption interest in on-line innovations: An exploratory study of e-service personalization in public sector, IEEE Transactions on engineering management, vol.50,No.4 (2003) 436-447.
4. T.Kohonen: Self-oranized formation of topologically correct feature maps, Biolog. Cybern., vol.43 (1982) 59-69.
5. Quinlan,J.R.: C4.5: Programs for machine learning, San Mateo, CA: MaGrw-Hill (1993).
6. C.K. Shin, U.T Yun, H.K. Kim and S.C. Park: A Hybrid Approach of Neural Network and Memory-Based Learning to Data Mining. Int J IEEE Trans. on Neural Networks. Vol.11, No.3 (2000).

Intelligent Website Evolution of Public Sector Based on Data Mining Tools

Jang Hee Lee[1] and Gye Hang Hong[2]

[1] School of Industrial Management, Korea University of Technology and Education,
307 Gajeon-ri, Byeong cheon-myun, Cheonan City,
Choongnam Province 330-708, South Korea
janghlee@kut.ac.kr
[2] Industrial System and Information Engineering, Korea University
kistduck@nate.com

Abstract. As one of means for the electronic government embodiment, the website construction and its complement of public sector such as government agency and public institution has been importantly considered. The public sector's website is operated for public benefit and consequently needs to be continuously redesigned for the users with lower performance in the satisfaction level and effect of using it based on the served information by evaluating whether the performance is different between the users with the various different backgrounds, areas and etc. In this study we present an intelligent evolution model of public sector's website based on data mining tools in order to improve the whole users' satisfaction and the effects of using it, especially the users with lower performances by continuously redesigning and complementing the current key web pages.

1 Introduction

As one of means for the electronic government embodiment, the website construction of public sectors such as government agencies and public institutions/enterprises have been actively propelled. Electronic government construction aims at providing citizen with service quickly and accurately, effectiveness of government work, innovation by redesigning work process, and raising national competitiveness by improving productivity [1].

Public sector's website ultimately differs with the private sector's website in its seeking the public benefit and equability. It provides beneficial public information to various kinds of users with different types of backgrounds, education levels, various needs and etc. (e.g., citizens, researchers, public servants in a government agency, other government agency and etc.). Since the users of public sector's website are varied and vast, it is difficult to improve the satisfaction of all users on it and the effects of using it based on the served information.

This study presents an intelligent website evolution model of public sector that can evolve its website and consequently satisfy the users of it and give them an improvement of profits after using it. It consists of 4 steps: current website evaluation based on user satisfaction survey, segmentation of the users into groups based on the survey, finding crucial website evaluation factors (i.e., discriminating factors) and key

D. Lowe and M. Gaedke (Eds.): ICWE 2005, LNCS 3579, pp. 267–272, 2005.

web pages through pairwise comparison between two groups and finally redesigning the pages in terms of the discriminating factors to suit the targeted group. These steps are continuing and therefore the website evolves.

2 Public Sector's Website Evaluation

Website means the information system of Internet based on web to interactively exchange information and knowledge. The website of public sector provides useful public information to support decision-makings of various people as well as constructs the direct conversation channel between government and people and promotes quick collection of public opinion and citizen's participation for public decision-makings.

The research on the website evaluation of public sector has been recently attempted. The technical aspects of Internet such as the connection speed, error rate, number of URL, convenience of use and user's satisfaction in administration service side were proposed as the major criteria of public sector's website evaluation [2]. The research group of cyberspace policy in the university of Arizona proposed 2 evaluation criteria, transparency and accessibility, which focused on the openness of administration [3]. Alesander and Tate proposed 5 evaluation criteria, the information authority, information accuracy, information objectivity, information currency and information coverage of web page [4]. The web support group in New Zealand proposed the evaluation criteria such as scope of content, layout, accessibility, update frequency, extent of feedback, interactivity, site performance, etc [5].

3 Intelligent Website Evolution Model of Public Sector

We propose a new intelligent evolution model for public sector's website. As stated before, it consists of 4 steps: current website evaluation based on user satisfaction survey, segmentation of the users into groups based on the survey, finding discriminating factors and key web pages through pairwise comparison between two groups and finally redesigning the pages in terms of the discriminating factors to suit the targeted group.

3.1 Current Website Evaluation Based on User Satisfaction Survey

As the first step of intelligent evolution model of public sector's website, we evaluate the level of user's satisfaction about the current website service and the outcomes such as the level of user's reuse intentions, trust on the website and user's profit obtained by using the website information for user's economic behavior according to our new evaluation model of it.

In this study, for the rational design of public sector's website evolution model, we make a new its website evaluation model to use the major criteria for the website evaluation of federal government of the U.S and NCSI (National Customer Satisfaction Index) model for measuring customer satisfaction in Korea. The model describes the cause and effect relationship in the user satisfaction on public sector's website and outcomes such as reuse, trust, and profit/loss (refer to Fig. 1).

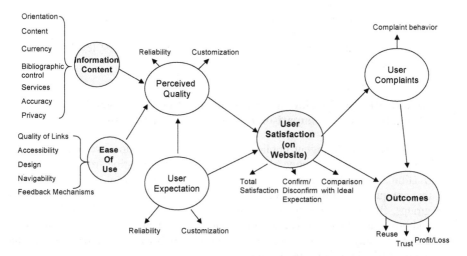

Fig. 1. Evaluation model of public sector's website in our study

In our model, 'Information Content' and 'Ease of Use' are major criteria for the website evaluation of federal government of the U.S [6]. 'Information content' criteria evaluate the substantive aspects of the website and have 7 sub-criteria, orientation to website, content, currency, bibliographic control, services, accuracy, and privacy. 'Ease of use' criteria evaluate physical movement through the website and have 5 sub-criteria, quality of links, feedback mechanisms, accessibility, design and navigability. The 'Perceived Quality' after using the public sector's website affects 'User Satisfaction' and accordingly 'Outcomes' such as reuse, trust on it and user's profit/loss.

Based on our model, we conduct the user satisfaction survey on the public sector's website. The survey asks all the registered users of website to rate 59 questions addressing criteria such as 'Information Content', 'Ease of Use', the level of user's satisfaction, reuse intentions, trust on the website and the level of user's profit to obtain after using the website information for user's economic behavior, user's demographic information and so on.

For most questions, a seven-point scale is used with the ratings of very dissatisfied/strongly disagree (1.0), dissatisfied/disagree (2.0), somewhat dissatisfied/weakly disagree (3.0), fair/moderate (4.0), somewhat satisfied/weakly agree (5.0), satisfied/agree (6.0), very satisfied/ strongly agree (7.0). A "don't know (0)" option is also provided.

3.2   Segmentation of the Users into Groups Based on the Survey

As the second step of intelligent public sector's website evolution model, we analyze the survey data and segment all the surveyed users into the group with similar patterns in their levels of satisfaction, reuse intentions, trust on the website and profit to obtain after using the website information for their economic behaviors.

To segment all the surveyed users, we use SOM (Self-Organizing Map), a special type of neural network using an unsupervised learning scheme, as a clustering tool

[7]. After SOM using, we can obtain several user groups with similar patterns in the satisfaction, reuse intentions, trust and profits and select an user group among them for the pairwise comparison in the third step, which has the highest level of satisfaction, reuse intentions, trust and profit.

3.3 Identification of Discriminating Factors and Key Web Pages Through Pairwise Comparison Between Two User Groups

As the third step of intelligent public sector's website evolution, we firstly identify the discriminating factors among all factors (e.g., the 'Orientation'-related factors of 'Information Content' criteria, the 'Accessibility'-related factors of 'Ease-of-Use', etc.) that are questioned in the survey, which can discriminate between the two paired user groups, the user group with the highest level of satisfaction, reuse intentions, trust and profit and the other user group among the segmented user groups. The other user group certainly has lower levels than the user group with the highest ones in the satisfaction, reuse intentions, trust and profit.

Pairwise comparion presents constituents such as discriminating factors in the survey and key web pages in web usage patterns in which the other user group with the lower levels is relatively lacking through comparison with the user group with the highest ones. If we obtain ten segmented user groups after SOM using, we conduct 9 pairwise comparisons.

In pairwise comparison, we conduct the analysis of survey data using C4.5 [8], a decision tree learning tool, in order to extract the discriminating factors in the user satisfaction survey. We choose the nodes appeared in the decision tree generated by C4.5 discriminating factors, which can classify the surveyed users into the user with the highest levels of satisfaction, reuse intentions, trust and profit and the other user with lower ones.

In addition to finding discriminating factors, we identify the difference of website usage patterns between the two paired groups by analyzing their web-log data and consequently find the key web pages to be redesigned in the public's sector website for the other users' improvement in the level of satisfaction, reuse intentions, trust and profit (refer to Fig. 2).

For the identification of key web pages, we firstly make the summarization table of user, user's total access frequency and connection time of web page during an analyzing time period and the user group to which the user belongs by analyzing user's web-log data. The table describes the access frequency and connection time of all users belonging to the two paired user groups for all possible web pages of current website.

We secondly identify key web pages that can distinguish the users (group) with the highest levels from the other users (groups) on the basis of website usage patterns by using C 4.5. Like the same way in the identification of discriminating factors, we choose the nodes appeared in the decision tree generated by C4.5 key web pages. The generated nodes are the connection time or access frequency of key web pages (e.g., the connection time of web page 38, the access frequency of web page 36) among all possible web pages of current website.

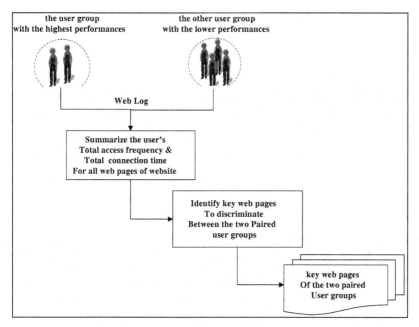

Fig. 2. Key web pages identification steps

3.4 Redesigning Current Key Web Pages in Terms of the Discriminating Factors

After finding the key web pages for all paired user groups, we differently redesign current those web pages (e.g., web page 38 and 36) in terms of the identified discriminating factors (e.g., content-related factors, design-related factors) for the improvement in the level of satisfaction, reuse intentions, trust and profit of the user group with lower levels.

Since the discriminating factors can discriminate between the user group with the highest levels and the other user group with lower ones in the satisfaction, reuse intentions, trust and profit, they influence the level of user's satisfaction, reuse intentions, trust and profit. If we provide the users with lower levels with the redesigned key web pages on the basis of discriminating factors, their level of satisfaction, reuse intentions, trust and profit can be improved.

For the intelligent evolution of public sector's website, we propose that the above described 4 steps are regularly and continuously executed. Through the website evolution, all the users with different backgrounds, education and experience levels, etc. are continuously satisfied with the website, trust and reuse it and can obtain more profits by easy and correct using the website information for their economic behaviors.

4 Conclusion

Incorporating intelligence into website is increasingly important, especially in public sector, as the cross-section of user communities is various, vast and increasingly growing. Our study presents an intelligent evolution model of public sector's website based on data mining tools, which can continuously provide all the users with the lower levels of satisfaction, trust, reuse and benefits with the beneficial information service to improve their levels by continuously and suitably redesigning key web pages in the website.

Our evolution model can decide what to change next in the website for the performance improvement of users through the analysis of user satisfaction survey data using data mining tools. We will progress further work about the application of our model to other areas and the supplement of our evaluation model for public sector's website in Usability engineering, requirements engineering, prototyping, and information design.

References

1. Lee J. A. and Jung J. W.: Strategy for Implementing High Level e-Government based on Customer Relationship Management. Korean National Computerization Agency. (2004)
2. Korean National Computerization Agency.: Guide of construction, operation and information resource management of public institution's website. Korean National Computerization Agency. (1999)
3. Research group of cyberspace policy of the university of Arizona.: http://w3.arizona.edu
4. Alesander and Tate.: http://www.widener.edu/wolfgram-memorial-library/inform.htm
5. Web support group of New Zealand.: http://www.theweb.co.nz/govtweb/0115.html
6. Kristin R. E., John C. B., Charles R. M., Steven K. W.: Accessing U.S. Federal Government Websites. Government Information Quarterly. Vol. 14. (1997) 173-189
7. Kohonen, T.: Self-Organization & Associative Memory. 3rd ed. Springer-Verlag, Berlin (1989)
8. Quinlan, J. R.: C4.5: Programs for Machine Learning. Morgan Kaufmann Publishers. San Mateo California (1993)

An Experiment on the Matching and Reuse of XML Schemas

Jianguo Lu[1], Shengrui Wang[2], and Ju Wang[1]

[1] School of Computer Science, University of Windsor
jlu@cs.uwindsor.ca, ju_wang@yahoo.com
[2] Department of Computer Science, University of Sherbrooke
Shengrui.wang@usherbrooke.ca

Abstract. XML Schema is becoming an indispensable component in developing web applications. With its widespread adoption and its web accessibility, XML Schema reuse is becoming imperative. To support XML Schema reuse, the first step is to develop mechanism to search for relevant XML Schemas over the web. This paper describes a XML Schema matching system that compares two XML Schemas. Our matching system can find accurate matches and scales to large XML Schemas with hundreds of elements. In this system, XML Schemas are modelled as labeled, unordered and rooted trees, and a new tree matching algorithm is developed. Compared with the tree edit-distance algorithm and other schema matching systems, it is faster and more suitable for XML Schema matching.

1 Introduction

XML Schema has become an indispensable component in web application development. Schemas are used to represent all kinds of data structure in programming, and are often mapped to classes. To some extent, we can think XML Schemas are similar to data types or classes in traditional programming language. What makes XML Schema different from traditional software components is that it is widely available on the web, encoded in XML and programming language independent, and adopted by all the major software vendors. All these features make XML Schema reuse not only imperative, but also have the potential to succeed beyond traditional software component reuse. We can envision that almost any data structure that you can think of will be available on the web. Programmers need a search tool to find the relevant schema instead of developing the schema from scratch.

Schema matching has its root in software component search and software agent search. Both have a long history. [17] provides a good survey in component search, and [22] is the seminal paper on software agent matching, which also inspired numerous works on web service searching. Schema matching is also widely studied in the area of database area [6] [14], with the aim to integrate relational and semi-structured data. [18] surveys the works in this area.

This paper describes a schema matching system that generates element mappings between two schemas. One design rationale of the system is that it should work effectively and efficiently – generating good results in acceptable time, such that it is capable of matching real life schemas with several hundreds of elements. We model an

D. Lowe and M. Gaedke (Eds.): ICWE 2005, LNCS 3579, pp. 273–284, 2005.
© Springer-Verlag Berlin Heidelberg 2005

XML Schema as an unordered, labeled and rooted tree. In general, an XML schema corresponds to a directed graph in which recursive definitions are represented by loops and reference definitions are represented by cross edges. The graph representation is not adopted in our work for two reasons. First, intuitively the directed graph representation of an XML Schema still encompasses a hierarchical structure similar to a tree, with a few "loop" exceptions. Secondly and more importantly, approximate graph matching [3] is too computationally costly as we have investigated in [11]. Our recent algorithm in graph matching employed strong heuristics to reduce search space, but still can only deal with graphs with dozens of node [11]. Obviously, graph matching algorithms would be difficult to match XML Schemas with hundreds of nodes.

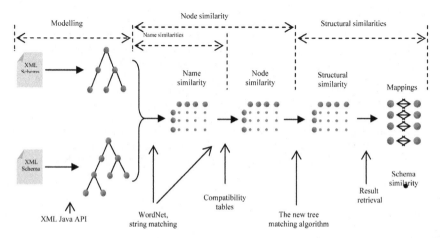

Fig. 1. Matching process

Our new tree matching algorithm identifies the structural relations by extracting approximate common substructures in two trees. Our observation on the properties of XML Schemas shows that similar schemas are made up of similar elements and these elements are connected similarly, that is, similar schemas (or similar portions of schemas) have similar ancestor-descendent and sibling relations. Based on this, the algorithm uses heuristics to reduce the searching space dramatically, and achieves a trade-off between matching optimality and time complexity.

Figure 1 depicts the structure of the matching system. We compute three types of similarities for every node pairs, i.e., *name similarity*, *node similarity* and *structural similarity*. Name similarity is related to calculating the relationship between two names. It is the main entity used for computing similarity between two nodes, other entities include data types and cardinalities information. The structural similarity shows the relation between two sub-trees rooted at these two nodes.

The system is tested extensively using about 600 XML Schemas in total. We evaluated both matching accuracy and computational efficiency of our system. Comparisons were made with the traditional edit distance tree matching algorithm [24] and a popular XML Schema matching system COMA [6]. The results show that our new tree matching algorithm outperforms these two methods, and can be used to match larger schemas that contain hundreds of elements.

2   Modelling XML Schemas as Trees

An XML Schema is modeled as a *labeled unordered rooted tree*. Each element or attribute of the schema is translated into a *node*. Attributes and elements that reside inside an element are translated as children of the element node. The names of elements and attributes, along with some optional information such as data types and cardinalities, are the labels of the nodes.

The modelled tree does not include every detail of an XML Schema. Excluded information falls into two categories. One is related to elements or attributes such as default value and value range. The other is relevant to structure, such as element order indicators. Although by XML Schema standard the order of the elements matters, it is ignored in our tree model based on the assumption that the order does not make differences as big as changing the labels.

Modelling XML Schema is a tedious task due to the complexity of XML Schema. During the modelling, we need to take care of the following constructs in XML Schema, to insure that a schema is modelled as a tree.

Reference Definition

Reference definition is a mechanism to simplify schema through the sharing of common segments. To transform this structure into a tree, we duplicate the shared segment under the node that refers to it. By doing this, we increased the number of nodes.

There are two types of references in XML Schema specification: data type reference and name reference. Data type reference is created by the clause '*type=dataTypeName*' (where '*dataTypeName*' is not a built-in data type), and the referred segment is a *<complexType>* or *<simpleType>*; while name reference is created by '*ref=elementName*', and referred segment must be a *<element>*. All the referred types or elements must be *top level* such that they are nested in *<schema>* only. Therefore, our solution is that: build two lists called '*referred*' and '*referring*', list 'referred' contained all the top level elements and types (both complex and simple), and list 'referring' contain the elements having 'type' or 'ref' reference; then after scanning the schema file, for every element in 'referring', we physically duplicate the segment which they refer. Solving those segments which are from outside of the schema file follows the same method as *importing* and *inclusion*.

Recursive Definition

Recursive definition happens when a leaf element refers to one of its ancestors. This definition also breaks the tree structure, and it has to be solved differently from the way of solving reference definition, otherwise it falls into infinite loop.

Matching recursively defined node is equivalent to matching the inner node being referred. So we utilize a detecting procedure, which scans the path from a node up to the root of the tree to find out whether this node refers to its ancestor or not. Once a node which has recursive definition is found, we cut the connection and mark the node with recursive property to distinguish it from its referred ancestor.

Namespace

Namespace is a way to avoid name ambiguity, such as two same data type names in one schema file, by assigning them to different vocabularies. This is accomplished by adding unique *URI*s and giving them aliases. The aliases serve as prefixes, such as 'xsd:' in the example, to associate the terms with certain vocabularies – namespaces. In our implementation, namespace affects reference definitions in three ways: built-in data type, user-defined data type, and element reference. To support this feature, our program tracks every prefix and its corresponding URI, takes them and the term right after the prefix as one unit, then put this unit into the reference solving.

Importing and Including
Importing and *including* are mechanisms of reusing elements and attributes defined in other schema files. Including limits the sharing within the same namespace, and importing can cross different namespaces. When being imported, the imported schema file's information is provided in the <import> tag, including the file name, location and the imported namespace. Our program also parses and models this schema, then together with its namespace, brings its top level elements and types into the 'referred' list. If any of them are referred by the components in the original schema file, they will be handled by the reference solving process. For including, the included file's information is kept in <include> tag, and the same method is applied to solve including with the difference of namespace. The namespace for including is as the same as the original schema file.

Extension
Extension allows new elements and attributes being added. For this situation, we first need to solve the type reference, so we treat the base clause as the same as type reference. After getting the base type being duplicated, we process the newly added components, converting them to nodes and join them as siblings to the duplicated ones.

Grouping
Grouping is similar to complex type definition, providing a way of reusing predefined components. The most often used grouping is attribute grouping, which is specified by *<attributeGroup>* tag. We use the same way as type reference to solve this situation, i.e., add the *<attributeGroup>* definition and reference element to the 'referred' list, then duplicate the referred group.

3 Node Similarity

Since a label of a node consists of name, datatype, and cardinality information, the node similarity is computed based on these entities. Among them the name similarity is the most complex one.

3.1 Name Similarity

Name similarity is a score that reflects the relation between the meanings of two names, such as tag name or attribute name, which usually comprised of multiple words or acronyms. The steps of computing name similarity include tokenization, computing the semantic similarities of words by WordNet, determining the relations of tokens by a string matching algorithm if they can not be solved by WordNet, and calculating the similarity between two token lists.

Tokenization

Quite often a tag name consists of a few words. It is necessary to split up the name into tokens before computing the semantic similarity with another one. This operation is called *tokenization*. A *token* could be a word, or an abbreviation. Although there are no strict rules of combining tokens together, conventionally, we have some clues to separate them from each other such as case switching, hyphen, under line, and number. For instance: 'clientName' is tokenized into 'client' and name, and 'ship2Addr' to 'ship', '2', and 'Addr'.

Computing Semantic Similarity Using WordNet

Once a name is tokenized into a list of words, we use WordNet [25] to compute the similarity between the words. WordNet builds connections between four types of POS (Part of Speech), i.e., noun, verb, adjective, and adverb. The smallest unit in WordNet is *synset*, which represents a specific meaning of a word. It includes the word, its explanation, and the synonyms of this meaning. A specific meaning of one word under one type of POS is called a *sense*. Each sense of a word is in a different synset. For one word, one type of POS, if there are more than one sense, WordNet organizes them in the order from the most frequently used to the least frequently used.

Based on WordNet and its API, we use synonym and hypernym relations to capture the semantic similarities of tokens. Given a pair of words, once a path that connects the two words is found, we determine their similarity according to two factors: the length of the path and the order of the sense involved in this path.

Searching the connection between two words in WordNet is an expensive operation due to the huge searching space. We impose two restrictions in order to reduce the computational cost. The first one is that only synonym and hypernym relations are considered, since exhausting all the relations is too costly. This restriction is also adopted in some related works [1]. Another restriction is to limit the length of the searching path. If a path has not been connected within a length limit, we stop further searching and report no path found.

In our implementation, we use the following formula to calculate the semantic similarity: $wordSim(s,t) = senseWeight(s) * senseWeight(t) / pathLength$

Where s and t denote the source and target words being compared. *senseWeight* denotes a weight calculated according to the order of this sense and the count of total senses.

We performed a comparison with seven other approaches on the set of word pairs in [12]. In terms of correlation, ours exceeds four approaches and falls behind three of them. Considering that the method we use is simpler and scalable, our similarity measure is acceptable.

Similarity Between Words Outside Vocabulary

Words outside English vocabulary are often used in schemas definition, such as abbreviations ("qty") and acronyms ('purchase order' as PO). In this case WordNet is no longer applicable, and we use edit-distance string matching algorithm. By doing this, the measurement reflects the relations between the patterns of the two strings, rather than the meaning of the words.

Similarity Between Token Lists

After breaking names into token lists, we determine the similarity between two names by computing the similarity of those two token lists, which is reduced to the bipartite graph matching problem [13]. It can be described as follows: the node set of a graph G can be partitioned into two subsets of disjoint nodes X and Y such that every edge connects a node in X with a node in Y, and each edge has a non-negative weight. The task is to find a subset of node-disjoint edges that has the maximum total weight.

3.2 Similarity of Built-In Data Type

In XML Schema there are 44 built-in data types, including nineteen primitive ones and twenty-five derived ones. To reduce the number of combinations, we create seven data type categories, i.e., *binary*, *boolean*, *dataTime*, *float*, *idRef*, *integer*, and *string* that cover the 44 data types. The compatibility table is built for the seven categories. After this, when comparing two data types, first we check which category these types belong to, then extract the similarity measure from the category compatibility table.

3.3 Similarity of Cardinalities

XML Schema allows the specification of minimum and maximum occurrences, i.e., cardinality, for elements. The range of cardinality is from 0 to unbounded. It is impossible and unnecessary to compare all the cardinalities in this range. As a result, we apply a threshold. When cardinalities are equal to or bigger than it, we treat the cardinality as this threshold.

4   Approximate Tree Matching

Tree matching is an extensively studied problem. The classical tree edit distance matching algorithm [28] is not an adequate solution for 1) it is not fast enough as is shown in our experiment explained in section 5; 2) it must preserve the tree ancestor structure during the match, hence may miss better matches.

Take the two schemas in Figure 2 for example. In those two schemas, there are two substructures that are very similar. One is about car information, the other one is driver information. Intuitively we would like to match those substructures. However, with the traditional tree edit distance algorithms, that kind of matching is not easy to achieve because shifting two sub-trees (e.g., exchange the position of driver information with car information in Schema 1) requires many edit operations. Based on this observation, we generalized the concept of common substructures between two trees to approximate common substructures (ACS), and developed an efficient tree matching algorithm for extracting a disjoint set of the largest ACSs [25]. This disjoint set of ACSs represents the most likely matches between substructures in the two schemas. In addition, the algorithm provides structural similarity estimate for each pair of substructures including, of course, the overall similarity between the two schemas. Using our algorithm to match the above car-driver schemas, both driver and car nodes and their components can be matched, even though car is an ancestor of driver in schema one, and it is the other way around in schema two.

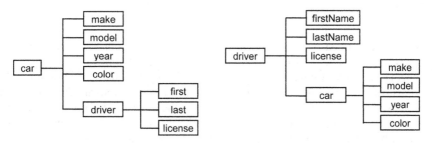

Schema 1, from car rental company   Schema 2, from insurance company

Fig. 2. Example schemas from two businesses

5 Experiment

Our system is compared with the traditional edit distance tree matching algorithm for labeled unordered trees [19] that is implemented by us, and the popular schema matching system COMA [6].

5.1 Data

The experiments are performed upon the XML Schemas we collected from various sources. The first group comprises five purchase order schemas which are used in the evaluation of COMA [6]. We choose the same test data to compare with COMA. The second group includes 86 large schemas from www.xml.org. These are large schemas that are proposed by companies and organizations to describe the concepts and standards for particular areas. We use these large schemas to evaluate system efficiency. The third group consists of 95 schemas that are collected from HITIS [10]. These schemas are designed to be the standards of interfaces between hospitality related information systems, such as hotel searching, room reservation, etc. Group four consists of 419 schemas extracted from WSDL files that describe the schemas of the parameters of web service operations. These schemas are small in general. Group three and four are used to test the accuracy of our matching system. Since most of them are relatively small, they are easy to read and judge manually.

5.2 Accuracy

Comparison with Edit-Distance Algorithm

Figure 3 compares the precision and recall between our algorithm (method 1) and edit distance algorithm (method 2). The test cases are from data group 1, which consists of 5 purchase orders that are also used in COMA.

The figure shows that our algorithm outperforms the edit distance tree matching algorithm consistently. Both algorithms adopt node removal operation and use iterative improvement heuristic to search the approximate result. The major difference between these two algorithms is that we deal with two nodes (one for each tree) each time, recursively match two trees from leaves to roots, and the node removal operation is limited to the child level of current nodes only. The edit distance tree matching algorithm always takes two trees, tries to remove some nodes in the range of entire trees each time, compares and keeps the state with smallest distance. Reviewing these five purchase order schemas supports our schema properties observation again – similar concepts described by XML are made up of similar elements, and these elements are constructed in similar ways. Simply speaking, good mappings between two similar schemas could be found by a few node removal operations. Our algorithm takes advantage of this condition and limits the range of node removal. Therefore it removes fewer nodes, but achieves better result. On the other hand, for the edit distance tree matching algorithm, when the input size is large, the wide range of node removal increases the searching space and decreases the chance of getting good mappings.

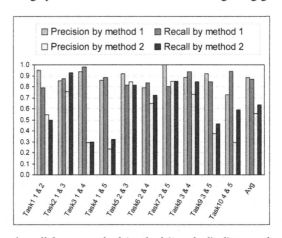

Fig. 3. Precision and recall for our method (method 1) and edit-distance algorithm (method 2)

Comparison with COMA

COMA maintains a library of different matchers (matching methods) and can flexibly combine them to work out the result. It introduced a manual reuse strategy which can improve the results but needs human assistance. Besides precision and recall, COMA adopts the overall measurement that combines precision and recall.

We focus on two matcher combinations in COMA, i.e., 'All' – the best no-reuse combination, and 'All+SchemaM' – the best reuse involved combination. Together with the result of our matching system, the precision, recall and overall measure are compared in Table 1.

Table 1. COMA and our algorithm

	COMA (All)	COMA (All+ SchemaM)	Ours
Precision	0.95	0.93	0.88
Recall	0.78	0.89	0.87
Overall	0.73	0.82	0.75

From this table, we can conclude that in terms of overall accuracy, our matching system outperforms COMA 'All' combination, and falls behind 'All+SchemaM' combination on matching the given five purchase order schemas. Considering the 'All+Schema' needs human assistance, our matching system works well.

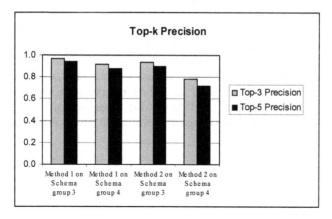

Fig. 4. Top-3 and top-5 precision

Top-k Precision

We use Top-k precision method to assess the schema relations reported by our algorithm and tree edit distance algorithm. *Top-k precision* is defined as $p_{Top-k} = |ReportCorrect_k| / k$, where $ReportCorrect_k$ is the set of correct results in the top-k return ones. The experiment for assessing the schema relations is performed on data group three and four, and is designed as follows: in each group, we randomly pick a schema; compare it with every schema in this group using both algorithms; then we sort the returned schemas. Next, we take the union of top-k schemas from the two lists, subsequently, based on the union set, we manually determine which schema(s) should not be ranked in top-k, and finally compute the top-k precision for each algorithm. In order to get better overall measurement, we compute top-3 and top-5 precisions, repeat above process, and take averages. Figure 4 summarizes the evaluation results which are based on 10 random schemas in group 3 and 20 schemas in group 4.

The result shows that 1) using either algorithm in a schema group, top-3 precision is better than top-5 precision; 2) both algorithms get better precision on schema group 3; and 3) our algorithm gets better overall results than the edit distance algorithm.

The reason of better top-3 and top-5 precisions for group 3 is that all the schemas in this group are collected from one domain. Most files have similar piece of information, a few of them are even identical.

5.3 Performance

The performance is assessed using group two that consists of 86 large schemas. This experiment is performed on a computer with single Intel Pentium 4 3.0GHz CPU and 1G memory. The operating system is Red Hat Linux release 9. We match every two schemas in this group are matched, so there are 3655 matching tasks in total. Due to the high computation cost of method 2, we bypass this method for schemas that exceed 150 nodes. Therefore, the count of matching tasks that the two algorithms participate is different.

Figure 5 shows the execution times of the three methods. We divide the input size, represented by the multiplication of node count of the two trees, into several intervals, then count the number of matching tasks, and calculate the average execution times for each interval. As we can see, for method 2, there are only six matching tasks when input size is from 16k to 20k, and there is no task when input size is over 20k.

It illustrates the increasing trend for all of the three execution times while the input size gets large. Besides, we can conclude that the preparing part is a heavy job, and the new tree matching algorithm is faster than the edit distance tree matching algorithm.

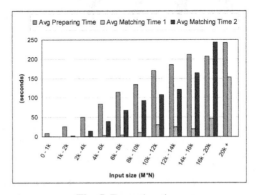

Fig. 5. Execution time

There are some tasks in preparing part, including modelling, computing node similarity, and preparing related data structures for later matching. Clearly, the majority cost is spent on computing node similarity, and more specifically, on computing semantic similarities. Computing semantic similarities is a very expensive task: given two words, the program exhausts their relations stored in WordNet, and tries to find the highest ranked connection. Even through we restrict the relation to synonymy and hypernym only, the searching space is still huge. However, we could adopt some alternatives to reduce the dependence of WordNet, such as reuse pre-calculated result and build user-specified similarity tables.

Our tree matching algorithm is faster than the edit distance tree matching algorithm. Due to the same reason describe in previous section, our tree matching algorithm limits node removal operation, therefore it reduces the searching space.

In conclusion, compared with the edit distance tree matching algorithm, our algorithm generates better results in shorter time for most of the matching tasks, especially when input size is large. Therefore it is more applicable in real life schema matching problems.

5.4 Implementation of the Matching System

This system is developed in Java. SAX XML parser is used to analyse XML schema, and WordNet API JWNL is used to access WordNet's dictionaries. The experiments generate huge amount of result data, therefore, we employ Oracle database to manage the data.

6 Conclusion and Future Work

This paper presents our first step in creating an XML Schema searching system to support schema reuse. There are already hundreds of thousands of XML Schemas on the web, which need to be collected, classified, indexed, and searched upon. We are developing an XML Schema repository, and providing various search mechanisms ranging from simple keyword search to the sophisticated tree matchings as described in this paper.

To achieve this goal, one salient feature of our system is our exhaustive approach to each step in the matching process, coping with the engineering details in real application scenario, with the ultimate goal for practical application. For example, we considered the details of modelling a XML Schema to a tree, and the practical issues in using WordNet to compute the name similarity. Most existing schema matching systems are prototypes that omitted those engineering details.

The experiment results also show that our new tree matching algorithm can match large trees with hundreds of nodes effectively and efficiently. In a matching task, most executing time is spent on computing node similarities, especially the connection time with WordNet. We are improving this by precalculating and caching the word relationships.

We are also applying schema matching system in web service searching, since the major components in web services are XML Schemas which defines the parameters in the operations of a web service.

References

1. S. Banerjee, T. Pedersen. Extended Gloss Overlaps as a Measure of Semantic Relatedness. *IJCAI*, 2003.
2. H. Bunke. On a relation between graph edit distance and maximum common subgraph. *Pattern Recognition Lett.* 1997 18(8), 689-694.
3. H. Bunke, Recent Developments in Graph Matching, *Proc. 15th Int. Conf. on Pattern Recognition*, Barcelona, 2000, Vol 2, 117 – 124.
4. P. V. Biron, A. Malhotra (ed.), W3C, April 2000, 'XML Schema Part 2: Datatypes', http://www.w3.org/TR/xmlschema-2/
5. A. Budanitsky, G. Hirst. Semantic distance in WordNet: An experimental, application-oriented evaluation of five measures. In *Proceedings of the NAACL 2001 Workshop on WordNet and Other Lexical Resources*, Pittsburgh, June 2001.
6. H. Do, E. Rahm. COMA A system for flexible combination of schema matching approaches. *VLDB* 2002
7. H. Do., S. Melnik, E. Rahm, Comparison of Schema Matching Evaluations, *Proc. GI-Workshop "Web and Databases"*, Erfurt, Oct. 2002.
8. A. Doan, P. Domingos, A. Halevy. Reconciling schemas of disparate data sources: A machine-learning approach. In *proc. SIGMOD Conference*, 2001
9. Gupta, N. Nishimura. Finding largest subtrees and smallest supertrees. *Algorithmica*, 21:183-210, 1998
10. HITIS - Hospitality Industry Technology Integration Standard, http://www.hitis.org.
11. A. Hlaoui and S. Wang, "A Node-Mapping-Based Algorithm for Graph Matching", submitted (and revised) to J. Discrete Algorithms 2004.
12. M. Jarmasz, S. Szpakowicz. Roget's Thesaurus and Semantic Similarity. *RANLP* 2003
13. H. W. KUHN. The Hungarian method for the assignment problem. *Naval Research Logistics Quarterly 2* (1955), 83–97.

14. M. L. Lee, L. H. Yang, W. Hsu, X. Yang. XClust: clustering XML schemas for effective integration. In *Proceedings of the eleventh international conference on Information and knowledge management*, Pages: 292 - 299, 2002
15. J. Madhavan, P. A. Bernstein, E. Rahm. Generic schema matching with Cupid. *VLDB*, 2001.
16. S. Melnik, H. Garcia-Molina, E. Rahm. Similarity flooding: a versatile graph matching algorithm and its application to schema matching. *ICDE* 2002.
17. A Mili, R Mili, RT Mittermeir, A survey of software reuse libraries, Annals of Software Engineering, 1998.
18. E. Rahm, P. A. Bernstein. A survey of approaches to automatic schema matching. *VLDB J.*, 10(4):334-350, 2001.
19. D. Shasha, J. Wang, K. Zhang, F. Y. Shih. Exact and approximate algorithms for unordered tree matching. *IEEE Transactions on Systems, Man, and Cybernetics*. Vol 24, NO.4, April 1994.
20. D. Shasha, J. T. L. Wang, R. Giugno, Algorithmics and Applications of Tree and Graph Searching, In *Proc. PODS'02*, June 3-5 2002.
21. H. Su, S. Padmanabhan, M. Lo. Identification of syntactically similar DTD Elements for schema matching. *WAIM*, 2001.
22. K. Sycara, M. Klusch, S. Widoff, J. Lu, Dynamic Service Matchmaking among Agents in Open Information Environments, Journal of ACM SIGMOD Record, 28(1):47-53, 1999.
23. H. S. Thompson, D. Beech, M. Maloney, N. Mendelsohn (ed.), W3C, April 2000, 'XML Schema Part 1: Structures', http://www.w3.org/TR/xmlschema-1/.
24. J. Wang, B. A. Shapiro, D. Shasha, K. Zhang, K. M. Currey. An algorithm for finding the largest approximately common substructures of two trees. *IEEE Trans. PAMI* 20, 1998, 889-895.
25. Shengrui Wang, Jianguo Lu, Ju Wang, Approximate Common Structures in XML Schema Matching. Submitted.
26. WordNet – a lexical database for English. http://www.cogsci.princeton.edu/~wn/
27. K. Zhang, D. Shasha. Simple fast algorithms for the editing distance between trees and related problems. *SIAM Journal of Computing*, 18(6):1245-1263, Dec. 1989.
28. K. Zhang, D. Shasha, J. T. L. Wang, Approximate Tree Matching in the Presence of Variable Length Don't Cares, *Journal of Algorithms*, 16(1):33-66.

Aggregation in Ontologies: Practical Implementations in OWL

Csaba Veres

Dept. of Computer and Information Science (IDI)
Norwegian University of Science and Technology (NTNU)
N-7491 Trondheim-NTNU
Csaba.Veres@idi.ntnu.no

Abstract. Data modeling for Web Applications needs to be guided not only by the specific requirements of a particular application, but also by the goal of maximizing interoperability between systems. This necessitates the adoption of widely accepted design methods and a set of rich, theoretically motivated principles for organizing data in ontologies. This paper presents one set of such principles. It is based on the observation that current ontologies emphasize the abstraction mechanism of generalization but ignore the various forms of aggregation. We explore possible techniques for modeling aggregation with OWL, investigate the semantics of aggregation, and consider the merits of aggregation over generalization for modeling knowledge in particular situations.

1 Introduction

Aggregation is variously defined as[1]

- The act of aggregating, or the state of being aggregated; collection into a mass or sum; a collection of particulars; an aggregate. (Webster's Revised Unabridged Dictionary)
- several things grouped together or considered as a whole (WordNet 2.0)
- <programming> A composition technique for building a new object from one or more existing objects that support some or all of the new object's required interfaces. (The Free On-line Dictionary of Computing)

These definitions show that some form of *aggregation* is useful when thinking about conceptual entities that are somehow constituted from smaller, self contained entities.

In data modeling, *aggregation* and *generalization* are two major forms of *abstraction* that can help organize data [11]. Similarly, object oriented analysis and design as implemented in the Unified Modeling Language (UML)[2] includes these abstraction mechanisms. However in spite of its widespread use, *aggregation* appears to be a troublesome concept. In data modeling, the term is used in several distinct senses. While [10] considers an attribute which includes a numeric quantity and the unit of measure (e.g. "12 cases") a form of *aggregation*,

---

[1] All definitions from http://www.dict.org
[2] http://www.uml.org

D. Lowe and M. Gaedke (Eds.): ICWE 2005, LNCS 3579, pp. 285–295, 2005.

[9] defines an *aggregate object* as a "named collection of other objects and their connections" which is useful for describing the model, but is not itself implemented. In UML the semantics of *aggregation* has not been made clear. Martin Fowler laments that "... the difficult thing is considering what the difference is between aggregation and association" [3]. Aggregation is sometimes treated as *part-of*, as in "a wheel is part of a car". Indeed this *part-whole aggregation* seems to be the sense that is often illustrated in connection with UML *aggregation*. However, the *part-of* relation is only one of many possible aggregation mechanisms, and is itself problematical partly because of its diverse semantics [2]. Since the representation of part-whole hierarchies is of primary importance in medical informatics, its use in ontologies has been widely investigated [8], and will not be further considered here.

The literature on *semantic data modeling* also considers the role of various sorts of aggregates and composites in data modeling. A primary aim of semantic data modeling is to model objects and the relationships between them directly [1], for the purpose of constructing databases whose organisation mirrors naturally occurring structures, under the assumption that this will make it easier to represent the primitives of a problem domain than if they first had to be translated into some sort of artificial specification constructs [4]. In defining the Semantic Data Model (SDM), [4] specifies a number of possible groupings:

1. grouping class - based on shared attribute (e.g. SHIP_TYPES contains groups of similar types of SHIP)
2. enumerated grouping class - useful when we wish to group similar types, but there is no clear attribute to define the type. This is a class whose members are other classes. (e.g. TYPES_OF_HAZARDOUS_SHIPS)
3. user-controllable grouping class - simple *aggregates* of arbitrary elements in a class. This is a class whose members are themselves members of a different class. Once again the member elements are of the same type (e.g. CONVOY)

Along similar lines [6] introduces *composition* and *collection* as methods for aggregation in the Format Model. The currently relevant constructor is *collection* which " ... allows one to specify the formation of the sets of objects, all of a given type" [6] (p. 522). For example a CONVOY is a set of SHIPS and STAFF is a collection of STAFF-MEMBER, which is in turn a *classification* (a sort of generalization) of FACULTY-MEMBER and SUPPORT-EMPLOYEE.

Given the somewhat conflicting views of aggregates, there is sometimes a confusion in modeling about whether or not aggregation or generalization is a more useful way to model a particular relationship. For example [13] considers the "EAGLE/SPECIES problem" [14] in which it seems that an entity (EAGLE) has to be represented as both an individual (instance of SPECIES) and a class (set of all EAGLES), in order to accommodate the necessary domain facts. But [13] argues that replacing some of the generalizations with an aggregation helps solve the problem. Briefly, the main problem with the model was that EAGLE was modeled as a subclass of SPECIES. But considering the Linnaean taxonomy suggests that the relationship should be modeled as a form of aggregation in which the class SPECIES (more correctly, FAMILY ACCIPITRIDAE) is not a supertype, but an aggregate of the classes EAGLE, HAWK, etc. Replacing the *generalization* with *aggregation* is part of the solution to the problem.

Turning now to a novel but we think natural source of information about semantics, the linguist Anna Wierzbicka claims that concepts involving collections are even more common than the ones we have considered thus far [15]. In fact, many of the concepts that might be commonly modeled as types are better describes as collections. For example, "a gun is a subtype of weapon", or "knife is a subtype of cutlery" are erroneous modeling decisions because the categories WEAPON and CUTLERY are not taxonomic. That is, the categories do not consist of entities of a single type. Instead, they aggregate entities of different types into one supercategory, with the aggregation based on one of several possible criteria. These aggregation classes relate to particular human needs, which tend not to be about the typology of things, but about their utility and origin. Thus WEAPON is a concept that aggregates other concepts like GUN or KNIFE or sometimes even FEATHER-PILLOW on the basis of their possible functions. Clearly, classifying FEATHER-PILLOW a as a subtype of WEAPON would be odd. [12] presents theoretical arguments for the usefulness of the various class types in constructing ontologies, which avoids odd classifications such as the preceding example. The different categories of such aggregates are, briefly:

- **purely functional** (e.g. WEAPON). Artifacts are often made to fulfill specific roles, so it is easy to think of a GUN as a *kind of weapon*. But really it is an artifact that can be used as a WEAPON. These categories are fuzzy and to some extent open, such that almost anything *could* be a weapon but nothing definitely is. Is a KNIFE a kind of WEAPON? Is it a WEAPON as much as a GUN is? Is a ROCK a kind of WEAPON? Is a FEATHER PILLOW a kind of WEAPON?
- **functional + origin** (Why is it there? "What for?" and "Where from?"). As an example, the term VEGETABLE means, roughly: "a thing of any kind that people cause to grow out of the ground for people to cook for food" [15], (p. 323). Similarly, MEDICINES have a function to cure disease, but must also be manufactured by people. This class classifies heterogeneous entities by their function, origin, and sometimes mode of use. But they are not collocations because the entities are not 'used together'.

    The terms for these concepts have an interesting syntax in English: they appear to be count nouns but their interpretation is not that of typical count nouns. If I say "I had two vegetables for dinner", I am likely to mean two different sorts of vegetable (e.g. carrot and broccoli) rather than two pieces of the same vegetable (e.g. two carrots). Compare this to "I have two birds in my cage", which could easily refer to two parrots.
- **collocations**. These have to be used/placed together in some sense.

    - **functional** (e.g. FURNITURE, TABLEWARE, NIGHTWEAR). These are defined by function but in addition, they have to be collected in a place (and/or time). That they differ from purely functional categories is demonstrated by the observation that a table that never made it out of the manufacturer's warehouse is not FURNITURE, but a home made explosive device kept in the basement can still be considered a WEAPON.

- **reason** (why is it together?) (e.g. GARBAGE, CONTENTS, DISHES (as in "dirty dishes" after a meal)). These are collections that require a unity of place, but without reference to function. LEFTOVERS form a collection because they came from the same place/source: they have the same immediate origin. The CONTENTS of a bag have all been placed together by someone, for some reason.

While there appear to be some similarities between these linguistically hypothesized categories and those proposed for semantic data models, there are three important points of difference. First, the linguistic categories specify a set of conditions under which natural collections exist, which potentially limits the possible sorts of, for example, enumerated- and user controllable groupings in [4]. Secondly, Wierzbicka's non taxonomic supercategories are composed of heterogeneous types, whereas the semantic data model collections are of like types. For example the functional category WEAPON consists of many diverse types including HANDGUN, INTERCONTINENTAL-BALLISTIC-MISSILE and, sometimes, FEATHER-PILLOW, whereas a CONVOY consists entirely in SHIPS. But possibly the most important feature of these categories is that they correlate with grammatical properties such as singular/plural, presence of determiners and numerals, and so on. That is, it should be possible to determine if a category descriptor belongs to one of these categories based on grammatical cues alone. This is not only of considerable theoretical interest, but also enhances the process of automatic ontology generation. In summary these linguistically motivated categories are nontaxonomic supercategories that complement taxonomic supercategories and previously identified categories that are aggregations of like types, and can be automatically discovered on the basis of their grammatical status.

The theoretical basis for the usefulness of these categories for constructing ontologies appears in [12]. In the present paper, we explore different ways of capturing their semantics in OWL. The suggestions are in the spirit of the Semantic Web Best Practices and Deployment Working Group[3] in providing engineering guidelines for OWL developers, rather than a rigorous formal semantics. However, we will see that the subtle semantics inherent in these categories will require a novel way to represent meaning.

2   Implementation

There are two immediately obvious approaches to implement these collections in OWL, both involving their own drawbacks. Both approaches involve using *enumerated* classes, where the class is defined simply by enumerating its members, and implemented with *rdf:parseType="Collection"*. In what follows, we investigate the relative merits of each proposal. We will also see that a novel technique is required for expressing all four distinct semantic relationships with the same formal representational device.

---

[3] http://www.w3.org/2001/sw/BestPractices/

2.1   Sets of Sets (SOS Solution)

One possibility is that the different sorts of heterogeneous collections be treated as set of sets. Thus, for example, VEGETABLE is considered as a set that acts as a container for a collection other sets. The members of the set are other sets like CARROT, TOMATO, and so on. Consider the difference between the subclass view of VEGETABLE as (1) a set which has subsets CARROT and TOMATO versus (2) VEGETABLE as a set which has as elements the sets CARROT and TOMATO:

1. $S_{vegetable} == \{carrot_1, carrot_2, tomato_1, tomato_2\}$
   - (a) $S_{carrot} == \{carrot_1, carrot_2\}$
   - (b) $S_{tomato} == \{tomato_1, tomato_2\}$
2. $S_{vegetable} == \{S_{carrot}, S_{tomato}\}$

The subset relationship in 1. expresses the semantics of the subtype interpretation of *is-a*. $Carrot_1$ is an element of the set *carrot* and it is also a member of the set *vegetable*. It is a subtype because it can be picked out with other "like" elements of *vegetable* to form a subset. But once again it is literally true that a carrot (e.g. $carrot_1$) is a *vegetable* because it is also an element of *vegetable*. Conversely, any defining property that is true of the members of *vegetable* must also be true of the members of *carrot*.

But the suggested representation in 2. is quite different. Here, the elements of the set *vegetable* are other sets. The set *vegetable* is an abstract entity that has other sets as members, not the elements of those sets. All we can say about $carrot_1$ is that it is an element of *carrot*, and not that it is an element of *vegetable*. Since an instance of the set *carrot* is not also an instance of the set *vegetable*, it follows that "two carrots" are not "two vegetables", as the linguistic intuition requires.

This solution implements the set of sets idea by defining the class *vegetable* as consisting of an enumerated collection of the sets comprising the class, as shown below.

```
<owl:Class rdf:ID="Vegetable">
 <owl:oneOf rdf:parseType="Collection">
  <owl:Thing rdf:about="#Carrot"/>
  <owl:Thing rdf:about="#Tomato"/>
 </owl:oneOf>
</owl:Class>
```

This solution retains important components of the meaning. For example 'two vegetables' can be interpreted as referring to two elements of the set *vegetable*, which in this example are the sets *carrot* and *tomato*. So if I had 'two vegetables' for dinner then I would have had two 'types' of *vegetable* as required. There are two drawbacks of this solution. The first is that it can only be implemented in OWL-Full because it requires classes to be treated as individuals. In this case inference becomes undecidable [5], so that automatic classification and consistency checking becomes impossible. Second, properties cannot be inherited from the collection class to its members, which are individuals. In OWL, property restrictions are only inherited by subclasses. We will explore this problem in more depth after we consider the second possible implementation.

2.2   Union of Sets (UOS Solution)

The following solution has the advantage that it is compatible with OWL-DL. Once again we use a collection class, but this time it is defined as the union of the component sets:

```
<owl:Class rdf:ID="Vegetable">
  <owl:unionOf rdf:parseType="Collection">
    <owl:Class rdf:about="#Carrot"/>
    <owl:Class rdf:about="#Tomato"/>
  </owl:unionOf>
</owl:Class>
```

This class axiom states that the class extension of *Vegetable* exactly corresponds to the union of the class extensions of *Carrot* and *Tomato*. This results in a set that is identical to definition 1., but it specifically disables the inheritance of properties that is made available through the *rdfs:subClassOf* property. The definition also loses the desirable property of the previous solution that the types of vegetable can be treated as pseudo-substances. In the present definition "two vegetables" could refer to two individual carrots. In this sense the definition captures the semantics of collections less faithfully than the first proposal.

2.3   Unique Features

We have previously noted that one potential problem is that neither of the proposed solutions will result in the contained classes inheriting properties from the container classes. For example, it might be useful to have all VEGETABLES have a property *hasVitamin*. Then CARROT might have vitamin A and C, TOMATO C and D, and so on. If CARROT and TOMATO were (standardly) defined as subclasses of VEGETABLE and *hasVitamin* had VEGETABLE as its domain, then all subclasses of VEGETABLE would inherit the property. If the range were further restricted in each subclass to the union of the appropriate (member of the disjoint classes of) VITAMIN, this would serve as a constraint in assigning the vitamin contents of each instance of CARROT, for example. But this is not possible if the subclass relationship is not explicitly defined. To overcome this limitation we introduce a unique solution by introducing some further concepts in the ontology. We will demonstrate this with the SOS approach, since many of the steps are identical for UOS.

The first point is that, since CARROT and so on are no longer modeled as subclasses of VEGETABLE, we need to decide if they are subclasses of something else. One reference source that can help identify the superclasses (*hypernyms*) of

Sense 2
carrot, cultivated carrot, Daucus carota sativa
   => **plant, flora, plant life** – (a living organism lacking the power of locomotion)
   => **entity** – (that which is perceived or known or inferred to have its own distinct existence (living or nonliving))
Sense 3
carrot – (orange root; important source of carotene)
   => **root vegetable** – (any of various fleshy edible underground roots or tubers)
      => **food** – (any solid substance (as opposed to liquid) that is used as a source of nourishment; "food and drink")
         => **entity** – (that which is perceived or known or inferred to have its own distinct existence (living or nonliving))

Fig. 1. Relevant WordNet senses for carrot, showing a selection of their hypernyms

words in everyday English is WordNet[4] which classifies nouns according to the *is-a-kind-of* relation [7]. There is some evidence that WordNet classifications are useful in constructing ontologies (e.g. [13]). Figure 1 shows selected *hypernyms* for *carrot*.

The first point of note is that there are two distinct relevant senses of *carrot*, only one of them being the vegetable sense we are discussing. The second sense classifies *carrot* as a type of *plant* (among other things). Since we are suggesting that VEGETABLE is not a taxonomic concept we take only the hyponymy in sense 2 into consideration. Thus CARROT is modeled as a subclass of PLANT. In order to represent that VEGETABLE is an aggregate concept, we create a separate hierarchy of concepts to represent the four possible kinds of non taxonomic aggregations that the linguistic descriptor *is-a* can indicate. Figure 2. is a screen shot of the Protege ontology editor displaying these classes[5].

Interestingly *aggregation (group, grouping)* appears in WordNet as one of the unique beginners in the noun hierarchy. It is of considerable theoretical interest that WordNet independently assigns such priority to this concept, strengthening arguments both for the utility of WordNet in structuring domain ontologies, and for the present use of aggregation in modeling real world domains.

But now we have a way to tackle the problem of property inheritance. In figure 2 we show a property *hasVitamin* whose domain is defined as VEGETABLE. We can then create an instance of VEGETABLE, say *carrot1*, which gives the desired result of instantiating the *hasVitamin* property. In OWL it is possible to define individuals with multiple types, so we add the type definition for CARROT to *carrot1* so that the individual can instantiate the properties of CARROTS as well. The net effect is that *carrot1* now has all properties from PLANT and VEGETABLE.

---

[4] http://wordnet.princeton.edu
[5] Notice that VEGETABLE is a subclass of FUNCTION_ORIGIN. This is not strictly speaking correct. A cleaner approach might be to use the metaclass facility. However, this is not possible with OWL-DL

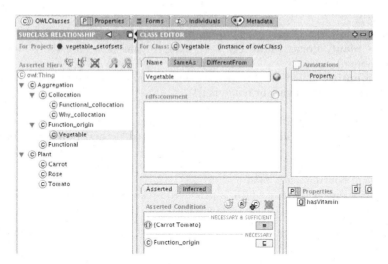

Fig. 2. Protege showing definition of collection classes

Unfortunately this solution as implemented with SOS introduces a severe problem. In the definition of VEGETABLE we stipulate that its only instances are the classes CARROT and TOMATO ("asserted conditions" in figure 2). But this will prevent the creation of an ordinary instance VEGETABLE:*carrot1*, unless it was inferred that *carrot1* was the same as either one of the defined members CARROT or TOMATO.

Let us now turn to the UOS solution. It is obvious that the only difference is that we define VEGETABLE as:

$$Vegetable \equiv Broccoli \sqcup Carrot \sqcup Lettuce \sqcup Spinach \sqcup Tomato$$

One immediate negative outcome is that some of the desirable semantics is lost: now, "two carrots" are also "two vegetables". But the opposite result that instances of VEGETABLE are also instances of CARROT is exactly what is required for solving the property inheritance problem as suggested above. The solution will therefore work in UOS. An individual *carrot1* can be defined with multiple types CARROT and VEGETABLE. Alternatively two differently named individual instances of the two classes can be equated with *owl:sameAs* as shown below.

```
<Vegetable rdf:ID="carrot">
 <owl:sameAs>
  <Carrot rdf:ID="carrot1">
   <owl:sameAs rdf:resource="#carrot"/>
  </Carrot>
 </owl:sameAs>
</Vegetable>
```

Either method will allow inheritance of properties from both classes. The other consequence of the change in definition is that the taxonomy is OWL - DL, allowing us to take advantage of available description logic reasoners. Classifying the taxonomy with Racer then reveals the result shown in figure 3. The inferred hierarchy is identical to an ontology that might have been built with more "traditional" approaches in which the subclass relationships were asserted. Retaining the originally asserted hierarchy as the foundational ontology maintains the benefit of explicit semantics while computing subsumption relations is beneficial for downward compatibility with ontologies in which the subclass relations are asserted.

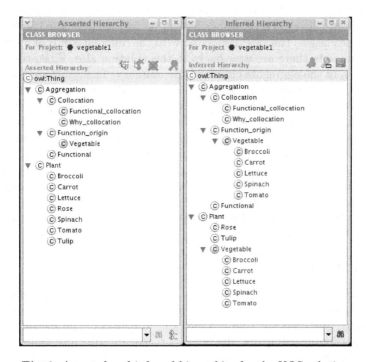

Fig. 3. Asserted and inferred hierarchies for the UOS solution

TO summarize thus far, it seems that SOS will not work, but UOS will work with one possible exception. But an important novel feature of the solutions is that the semantics of the categories is explicitly represented because the nature of the aggregation can be "read off" the ontology. In this example the reason for the category can be defined in that it represents a collection of entities that serve the same purpose or function (to provide a certain kind of nutrition) and have the same origin (growing in the ground). The specific function and origin are therefore facts that can be represented in the ontology. Perhaps the usefulness of this is less obvious for VEGETABLE than a concept like WEAPON. Here, division into subclasses would appear odd if the subclasses of WEAPON included GUN, KNIFE, ICE-PICK, FEATHER PILLOW, and DECK CHAIR. Collecting them in an aggregation whose intent was defined would clear up the mystery.

As a result of creating a separate hierarchy for aggregations, a third possible implementation solution presents itself. Called this the Instance Solution (IS), it involves modeling VEGETABLE as an instance of FUNCTION_ORIGIN, rather than as a subclass. The motivation for this solution is that it overcomes a possibly awkward feature of the previous solutions, that the subclass structure of, say, vegetable, is defined through the collection feature of OWL. If a new kind of vegetable were to be added, VEGETABLE would be redefined. It is necessary under this proposal to create two more properties *hasMember* (domain: AGGREGATION, range: PLANT in the current example) and its inverse *memberOf* to describe the relationship between the various subclasses of PLANT and the instances of the AGGREGATION classes. These properties can be used to infer the instances (and therefore the classes) that are associated with the different kinds of aggregation.

Unfortunately there are drawbacks to this solution also. First, there is now no definition of the aggregate classes in the ontology. That is, there is no reason why TULIP, GUN, or anything else could not be made a *memberOf* VEGETABLE. Second, direct inheritance of properties from VEGETABLE is not possible because VEGETABLE is now an instance. One possible workaround for this is to define datatype properties for the aggregate classes that can be used to describe the purpose of their instances. In our implementation we have three such properties (*function*, *origin*, and *purpose*) which can be used in various combinations to describe each instance of the subclasses of AGGREGATION. For example VEG-ETABLE has *function:eating, origin: grown_in_ground*. This can be used by an application to infer additional properties for an instance of CARROT through its *memberOf:vegetable* property.

3   Conclusion

We have suggested that aggregation is a useful alternative to generalization for some concepts. We investigated three approaches to modeling aggregation in OWL-DL. Each has their advantages and drawbacks. The second approach, UOS, seems most useful, but the last approach, IS, also has some merit. We have also noted that none of the approaches can fully capture the intended semantics, and suggested some possible ways in which a more complete semantics can be captured in more expressive logics. However, the research agenda involves an evaluation of the usefulness of these slightly imperfect implementations in developing workable ontologies in a tractable logic like OWL-DL.

Acknowledgements

This work was partly sponsored by the Norwegian Research Council through the WISEMOD project, number 160126V30 in the IKT-2010 program.

References

1. Abiteboul, S. and Hull, R. IFO: A Formal Semantic Database Model. ACM Transactions on Database Systems, Vol. 12, No. 4, December 1987, Pages 525-565. (1987).

2. Artale, A., Franconi, E., Guarino, N., and Pazzi, L. Part-whole relations in object-centered systems: An overview. Data & Knowledge Engineering, 20(3):347-383. (1996).

3. Fowler, M. and Scott, K. UML Distilled: Applying the Standard Object Modeling Language. The Addison-Wesley Object Technology Series (1997).

4. Hammer, M. and McLeod, D. Database Description with SDM: A Semantic Database Model. ACM transactions on Database Systems, Vol. 6, No. 3, September 1981, Pages 351-386. (1981).

5. Horrocks, I., Patel-Schneider, P. and F. van Harmelen. From SHIQ and RDF to OWL: The making of a web ontology language". Journal of Web Semantics, 1(1):7–26, (2003).

6. Hull, R. and Yap, C. K. The Format Model: A Theory of Database Organization. Journal of the Association for Computing Machinery, Vol 31, No 3, pp. 518-537. (1984).

7. Miller, G. Nouns in WordNet. In C. Fellbaum (Ed.) WordNet: An Electronic Lexical Database. MIT Press, Cambridge, MA. (1998).

8. Rector, A. Medical Informatics. In F. Baader, D. Calvanese, D. McGuinness, D. Nardi, P. Patel-Schneider (Eds.) The Description Logic Handbook: Theory, Implementation and Applications. Cambridge University Press (2003).

9. Ross, R. G. Entity Modeling: Techniques and Application. Database Research Group, Boston, Massachusetts, (1987).

10. Simsion, G. C. Data Modeling Essentials: Analysis, Design, and Innovation, 2nd edition. Coriolis, Scottsdale, Arizona, (2001).

11. Smith, J. M. and Smith, D. C. P. Database Abstrctions: Aggregation and Generalisation. ACM Transactions on Database Systems, Vol. 2, No. 2, (1977).

12. Verec, C., Ontology and Taxonomy: why "is-a" still isn't just "is-a". In Proceedings of The 2005 International Conference on e-Business, Enterprise Information Systems, e-Government, and Outsourcing, EEE'05 Las Vegas, Nevada, (2005).

13. Veres, C. Refining our intuitions with WordNet: a tool for building principled ontologies. In Proceedings of ISoneWORLD, Las Vegas, Nevada, (2004).

14. Welty, C., and Ferrucci, D. What's in an Instance? RPI Computer Science Technical Report. 1994.

15. Wierzbicka, A. Apples are not a 'kind of fruit': the semantics of human categorization. American Ethnologist, 313–328 (1984).

Recursive Application of Structural Templates to Efficiently Compress Parsed XML

Akira Kinno[1], Hideki Yukitomo[2], Takehiro Nakayama[1], and Atsushi Takeshita[1]

[1] Multimedia Labs. NTT DoCoMo, Inc.,
3-5 Hikari-no-oka, Yokosuka, Kanagawa, Japan
{kinno,nakayama,takeshita}@mml.yrp.nttdocomo.co.jp
[2] Panasonic Mobile Communications Co., Ltd.
600 Saedo-cho, Tsuzuki-ku, Yokohama, Japan
Yukitomo.Hideki@jp.panasonic.com

Abstract. This paper proposes an efficient compression method for parsed XML. Our method involves structure-based compression (SBC). In contrast to SBC, our method recursively inputs compressed parsed XML by parsing template instances as a node. Simulation results show that our method can reduce the memory requirements for real XML contents by almost 18%, and retains its compression efficiency even if the application domain changes, while that of SBC varies depending on the structural templates provided. One application of our method is to accelerate the response to native XML database queries.

1 Introduction

XML is increasingly used as a data format for adapted contents delivery which involves the integration of material from several source XML documents according to the user's preference and device capability.

For storing XML documents, which are targeted for adaptation, native XML databases(NXDBs) are suitable. Because they efficiently support XML-specific capabilities not included in most relational databases(RDBs) currently available. However, NXDB still has considerable points compared to RDBs. One point is at the access level. Large volumes of XML data stored in textural form are hard to access, because parsing is an expensive process. To improve the speed of accessing XML data, caching parsed XML in-memorycan be a promising approach. However, parsed XML has huge memory requirements [4].

In this paper, we propose an efficient method for compressing parsed XML. It uses structure-based compression (SBC) in which the structural information of parsed XML is replaced by structural templates given in advance [5]. Further, it replaces the structures in compressed XML, which also include template instances, with structural templates. This enables higher compression efficiency through the use of small templates, which can be more easily created, than is offered by SBC with the same structural templates. Simulations verify the efficiency of our method, and prove that it well handles even actual XML in terms of the compression ratio.

Eqauations and terms in this paper are refered to Appendix.

D. Lowe and M. Gaedke (Eds.): ICWE 2005, LNCS 3579, pp. 296–301, 2005.
© Springer-Verlag Berlin Heidelberg 2005

2   Structure-Based Compression

With structure-based compression(SBC), parsed XML can be compressed while still supporting the ability of prompt traverse. The basic idea of SBC is to substitute the pure structure with structural templates given in advance [5].SBC is defined as below.

Method 1 *Structure-based compression replaces subgraph $G' \subseteq G$ with template instance $T' \subseteq T_i$, when $G' = g \subseteq G^*$ and joint type of edge, which joins $\forall v \in G'$ and $w \in (G \cap \overline{G'})$, equals J^* of isomorphism $\phi(v) = \nu^* \in g$.*

It is obvious that compression efficiency increases with the number of nodes in the templates and the frequency with which the templates are used. The level of efficiency is, however, somewhat suspect since it strongly depends on the XML data and chosen templates. To make SBC generally practical, we have to identify the set with the best (or quasi-best)structural templates that minimize the total data size of the templates set and compressed XML . In other words, we have to find large and frequent sub-trees in the forest, and this is, in general, a time consuming process [6]. Moreover, SBC has to minimize the data size of the template set. Because SBC must have a template set to extract compressed XML, the best structural templates must offer the minimum data size of template set.

3   Recursive SBC

3.1   The Basic Idea

Our method avoids the difficulties associated with identifying the best templates; it achieves higher compression efficiency with the use of small template sets, i.e. few structural templates, that have few nodes, than is true with SBC. In general, small template sets are easier to create and their data size can be made reduced. However, in SBC, their compression efficiency is small. Our method is defined below.

Method 2 *In Method 1, our method contracts graph G' into node $v_{G'} \notin G$. That is, our method generates contracted graph G/G'. Moreover, our method recursively inputs G/G' as G.*

A unique characteristic of our method is that it replaces subgraphs, which also include template instances, with structural templates. In other words, our method replaces subgraphs with combined structural templates. That is, while the data size of template sets is small, the compression efficiency of our method with the small template sets is the same with that of SBC with the large template sets, which consist of templates combined with each template in the small template sets.

Since our recursive matching approach contributes that the number of times that structural templates are applied exceeds that with SBC. Since templates are replaced more frequently, our method has higher compression efficiency than SBC assuming the use of the same template set.

3.2 Comparison of Memory Consumption

To evaluate the efficiency of our method, we compared the memory consumption of parsed XML treated by our method to those required by non-compressed parsed XML and SBC-treated XML. Memory consumption follows the definition by [5]. The memory consumption of non-compressed parsed XML U(x) and that of parsed XML treated by SBC C(x) are given by equations (1)(2)(3).

We acknowledge that our method incurs some recursion overhead because it generates a new node to contract subgraphs for each template application. Thus, our method may be, overall, worse than SBC if the overhead exceeds the gains made in compression efficiency. We define the memory consumption of parsed XML treated by our method $C^*(x)$ that is given by equations (4)(5).

4 Simulation

4.1 Conditions

We conducted a simulation to examine the space efficiency of our method. In this section we compare memory consumption $C(x), C^*(x)$ for each site. We implemented our method and SBC using Apache Xalan's DTM. We used a simple algorithm to find every place at which the structural template matched the XML documents. For each XML document, every structural template was tested as to whether it matched the subtree rooted by each node in the depth first manner from leaf node side. After that, our method recursively processed the compressed XML. To solve recursion overhead problem of our method, we applied a simple recursion terminating algorithm; our method compares the current results, i.e., compression ratio, of recursion with the previous results, and if the current results are worse than the previous results, recurison is terminated and the previous results are output.

Table 1. Sample data information

Site	# of documents	Ave. file size [KB]	Ave. # of nodes	contents
A	933	27.4	1143.7	rumors, tips about misc. topics
B	629	17.0	698.2	technology-related news article

As the input XML documents, we collected HTML documents from two web sites (Table 1). By complementing the illegal notation in HTML documents, we translated them to valid XML documents. Some elements or tags of the documents were complemented in advance to yield validated XML. Note that, we treated a single HTML file as a single document in this simulation. We carefully chose 6 structural templates to compare our method with SBC (Figure 1). The rule of making our templates is that when we combine our templates by using recursive SBC, we get templates used in [5].

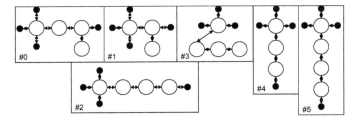

Fig. 1. Structural templates used in simulation. Filled and hollow circles represent open-joint information and nodes, respectively. The relationships are represented by arrows. Note that, we took care of components of templates' open-joint information for Apache Xalan to permit parsing of the compressed XML

4.2   Simulation Results and Discussion

The simulation results show that our method is better than SBC(Figure 2). In terms of average compression ratio, moreover, its compression efficiency remains high even if the application domain changes, while that of SBC falls depending which structural templates were given in advance. Considering the use of our method in NXDB, the latter result supports our contention that our method is better than SBC. In general, the structures of XML data in NXDB are defined by various schema to better utilize the NXDB characteristic, which is that NXDB can treat native XML data. In this case, our method performs more efficiently than SBC. Moreover we discuss the relationship between NXDB performance and compression ratio. Assuming that the time taken to put XML data into memory is much shorter than that taken for XML processing, the average processing speed without any compression method S is given by equation (6). On the other hand, the average processing speed with compression method S' is given by equation (7). Thus, the progress rate of processing speed by compression R is given by equation (8). If cache hit ratio h and parsing cost r are high, equation (8) shows that R can be made very high by increasing compression rate C_r. This assumption is reasonable when querying NXDB for two reasons. The first reason is that parsing is an expensive process and unsuitable when ran-

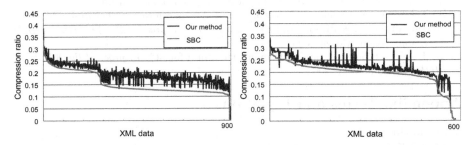

Fig. 2. Compression ratios of compressed pared XML created by our method and SBC for the documents of sites A (a) and B (b).The average compression ratios are written in parentheses

domly accessing individual elements of a data structure (i.e., querying process). The other is that caching XML documents is effective, because we can assume the locality of data querying from NXDB is high.

Other approachs to improve the speed of XML process, [3], [2] and [1] are also text based approaches, but aim at query-enabling XML compression. However, they do not well support content adaptation because content adaptation requires the partial addition, deletion, and alternation of XML documents. To support these features, the whole XML document should be kept in parsed form, and the compression of parsed XML should be considered.

5   Conclusion

This paper proposed an efficient method for compressing parsed XML. It replaces the structures in compressed XML, which also includes template instances, with structural templates. This enables higher compression efficiency through the use of small templates than is possible with structure-based compression (SBC) [5] with the same structural templates. Simulations showed that our compression ratios were better than those of SBC in the two actual sites examined. Moreover, they showed that our method keeps its compression efficiency even if the application domain changes, unlike SBC since the latter must use the structural templates given in advance.

Our future work includes evaluating the impact of our method on the time needed for querying. This paper used only simulations to examine the compression efficiency and why the compression of parsed XML can accelerate query speeds. We will elucidate how much our method can decrease the time needed for querying.

References

1. J. Cheng and W. Ng, "XQzip: Querying Compress XML Using Structural Indexing".In proc. of Extending Database Technology, 2004.
2. J.K. Min, M.J. Park, and C.W. Chung, "XPRESS: A Queriable Comression for XML Data". In proc. of ACM Symp. on the Management of Data, 2003.
3. P.M. Tolani and J.R. Haritsa,"XGRIND:A Query-friendly XML Compressor". In proc.of Int. Conf. of Data Engineering, 2002.
4. XSLT Processor Xalan, http://xml.apache.org/xalan-j/index.html.
5. H. Yukitomo, A. Kinno, T. Nakayama and A. Takeshita, "Structure-based compression of parsed XML for Content Adaptation". In proc. of the 49th IPSJ SigDD workshop, Tokyo, March 2005.
6. M. J. Zaki, "Efficiently mining frequent trees in a forest". In proc. of the 8th ACM SIGKDD, Edmonton, 2002.

Appendix: Terms and Equations

Terms in this paper:
Parsed XML is a graph $G_s = (V_s, E_s)$. Each node $v_s \in V_s$ has node type, name, and value. Each edge $e_s \in E_s$ has *relationships*.

Relationship is a set of edge types between nodes, i.e., parent, first child, and previous and next sibling.

Pure structure is a graph $G = (V, E)$, where $E = (\epsilon, J)$, where $\epsilon \subseteq [V]^2$, and J is a set of *relationships*. In contrast to *parsed XML*, it is unconcerned with node type, name and value.

Open-joint information is a set of references between a node included in a *structural template* and an outside node. Let open-joint information $Ex = (\nu^*, J^*)$, where $\nu^* \subseteq V^*$ and J^* is the relationship between $\forall v \in \nu^*$ and $w \in (V \cap \overline{V^*})$.

Structural template is a data structure to represent a fragment of the *pure structure*. Let a structural template $\mathrm{T} = (T_{id}^*, G^*, Ex)$, where T_{id}^* is a set of template identifiers, and G^* is a set of fragments of the pure structure G.

Template instance is a data structure to represent a part of parsed XML in compressed XML. It consists of an instance identifier T_{id}, a reference to the *structural template* T_{id}^*, node information V_t, and outer joint information E_t. Let a template instance $T_i = (T_{id}, T_{id}^*, V_t, E_t)$.

Equations[1] in this paper:

$$U(x) = 4 \cdot 4N_x + 4 \cdot 2N_x + D(x), \tag{1}$$

$$C(x) = 4(\sum A(t_i, x)(J(t_i) + 2) + 4M_x) + 4 \cdot 2N_x + D(x), \tag{2}$$

$$M_x = N_x - \sum A(t_i, x) \cdot N_{t_i}, \tag{3}$$

$$C^*(x) = 4(\sum A^*(t_i, x)(J(t_i) + 2) + 4M_x^*) + 4 \cdot 2N_x + D(x), \tag{4}$$

$$M_x^* = N_x - \sum A^*(t_i, x) \cdot N_{t_i} + \sum A^*(t_i, x), \tag{5}$$

$$S = ((1 - r)W)h + (r \cdot W + (1 - r)W)(1 - h), \tag{6}$$

$$S' = (r \cdot W + (1 - r)W)(1 + C_r)h$$
$$+ (r \cdot W + (1 - r)W)(1 - (1 + C_r)h), \tag{7}$$

$$R = \frac{S - S'}{S} = \frac{h \cdot r}{1 - r \cdot h} \cdot C_r \tag{8}$$

---

[1] Explanatory note: $U(x)$:memory consumption of non-compressed content, $C(x)$:that of content treated by SBC, $C^*(x)$:that of content treated by our method, N_x:# of nodes in content x, $D(x)$:the sum of string data, M_x: # of nodes for which no template was applied, t_i:i-th structural template, $A(t, x)$:# of times structural template t occurs in content x, $J(t)$ is the size of joint information for structural template t, M_x^*:# of nodes to which no template was applied even our method applying, A^*:# of times structural template occurs in content, S:average processing speed without any compression method, S':that with compression method, R:progress rate of that by compression, W:the whole XML processing speed, r:the time cost ratio of the parsing process among all processes, h:the cache hit ratio, and C_r:the compression ratio

Matching Semantic Web Services
Using Different Ontologies

Le Duy Ngan and Angela Goh

School of Computer Engineering, Nanyang Technological University, Singapore
{ledu0001,ASESGOH}@ntu.edu.sg
http://www.ntu.edu.sg

Abstract. The rapid development of semantic web services has led to a demand for a discovery mechanism. To perform discovery, researchers have developed Matchmakers to match web service requesters and providers. Current Matchmakers do not support the matching of semantic web services that use different ontologies. Thus, even if the web service providers meet the requirement of web service requesters, such a match may be missed. This paper introduces a framework which supports matching web services using different ontologies. The Matchmaker algorithm, which incorporates a means of distinguishing different ontologies, is presented.

1 Introduction

Semantic web service is a technology which is based on semantic web and web service technologies. It has become a core technology in e-business due to its strengths in discovery, composition, invocation, monitoring and so on. Discovery is the most important task in the web because web services are useless if they cannot be found. To perform discovery, researchers have developed Matchmakers [1, 2, 3, 4] to match web service requesters with web service providers.

Current Matchmakers are adequate when the web service requester and provider use the same ontology. Unfortunately, they do not support the situation where a web service requester and provider use different ontologies. In the real world, a web service provider can provide an exact service to the requester even though both services use different ontologies. The web service requester and provider operate independently; therefore, they usually define their own ontologies to describe their services.

Hence, a Matchmaker that supports web services using different ontologies is extremely important and provides the motivation behind this work. In the proposed framework, we assume that the building and maintaining of the ontologies are outside the scope of our work. The rest of the paper is as follows. Section 2 describes the matchmaker algorithm. Related work in matching web services is presented in section 3, followed by the conclusion and future work.

2 Matching Algorithm

2.1 Semantic Web Service

A semantic web service defined in languages such as DAML-S and OWL-S [5] includes four basic classes, namely Service, ServiceProfile, ServiceModel, and ServiceGrounding (figure 1). For matching, only ServiceProfile is used because it con-

D. Lowe and M. Gaedke (Eds.): ICWE 2005, LNCS 3579, pp. 302–307, 2005.

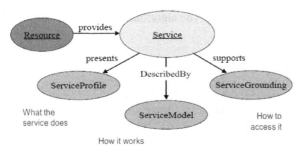

Fig. 1. Top level of the service ontology [5]

tains the description about the service to be discovered. The ServiceProfile [6] describes three basic types of information, namely, contact information, functional description of the service, and additional properties.

The contact information contains textDescription [6] which provides a brief description of the service. It describes what the service offers, or what service is requested. The functional description of the service is the most important declaration used for matching. It specifies the parameters of the inputs, outputs, preconditions, and effects of the service. The Profile also declares an operation of the web service.

2.2 Matchmaker Description

Before matching can take place, the web service providers must advertise their information to the Matchmaker and the advertised information will be stored in the Matchmaker. When a requester with a certain requirement wants to find a service, the Matchmaker will attempt to match the profiles of the requester with the advertised information of providers in its database. As the result of the matching, the Matchmaker will output a list of sufficiently similar [2] providers to the requested service. It is necessary to define the term "sufficiently similar". We define four degrees of similarity, namely, exact match, plug-in match, relaxed match, and fail match [2, 4]. Two web services are called sufficiently similar when the result of matching is Exact match, Plug-in match, or Subsumes match.

Exact match is the most accurate match. It happens when the two descriptions are semantically equivalent. In this case, two web services point to the same concept. Plug-in match is less accurate than exact match. This is when the advertisement service is more general than the requested service. Subsumes match is the least accurate. It is the inverse of Plug-in match and happens when the requested service is more general than the advertisement service. Fail match happens because of three reasons. Firstly, when there is no subsumption relation between advertisement and request. Secondly, when the requested service and advertisement service use different ontologies and two web services have different descriptions. Finally, it happens when the distance of two concepts in different ontologies exceeds a specific threshold (section 2.3).

2.3 Matchmaker Algorithm

The proposed matchmaker divides the matching into four stages [4] that include input matching, output matching, operation matching, and user-defined matching. Each stage is independent of the other. The algorithm uses [2] as a starting point, which can be described as follows:

```
match(request) {
   resultMatch = empty_list;
   forall adv in advertisementsDB do{
      if match(request, adv) then
      resultMatch.add(adv,degreeMatch)}
   return sort_Result(resultMatch);
}
```

The requested service is matched against all the advertisements stored in the database of the matchmaker. If the advertisement service is sufficiently similar to the requested service, we add the advertised information and its degree of match to the *resultMatch*. After the requested service is matched with all advertisements, *sort_Result* function will return a sorted list with a number of advertisements which fits the requester, based on the degree of matching. The matching process is elaborated as follows:

```
match(request, adv) {
   degreeUser = user-definedMatching;
   if (degreeUser = Fail)return Fail;
   else( if (inputMatch(req,adv) != Fail)
            degreeInput = inputMatch(req,adv);
         else return Fail;
         if (outputMatch(req,adv) !=Fail);
            degreeOutput= outputMatch(req,adv);
         else return Fail;
         if (operationMatch(req,adv) !=Fail)
            degreeOperation= operationMatch(req,adv);
         else return Fail;
   return
   round_avg(degreeInput,degreeOutput,degreeOperation)
}
```

Users can refine the result by specifying the similarity degree of each stage. In addition, the user-defined stage can be used to narrow the result of matching by declaring some constraints or rules. For example, a requester wishing to buy a computer describes a web service with price as input and configuration of the computer as output. They may also declare more constraints relating to the computer. For instance, the computer must be manufactured by a particular company. These constraints or rules will be matched against the advertisement and the result of user-defined matching is "match" or "not match". If the advertisement does not match the constraints, the matching will fail. Otherwise, the final matching will be computed based on the average degree of input, output, operation matching.

Input matching first checks if two web services use the same ontology. If they do, we will match each input of the advertised service with an input of the request services. If they use different ontologies, we will check if the two services have the same description. If the descriptions are different, the two web services cannot be matched. In other words, matching fails. Otherwise, input matching computes the distance between two concepts. The algorithm for input matching is as follows:

```
inputMatch(request, adv){
  degreeMax = 0;
  for all inputAdv in adv do{
    for all inputReq in request do{
      if( checkOntology(inputAdv, inputReq)){
        degree = computDegree(inputAdv, inputReq);
        if degree>degreeMax then degreeMax=degree;}
      else{ if{checkDescription(inputAdv, inputReq){
            d = computeDistance(inputAdv, inputReq)
            if (d>threshold) return fail;
            else{ if d>degreeMax then degreeMax = d;}
          else return fail}
  return degreeMatch
}
```

The threshold referred to in the algorithm is a value which depends on a specific application and domain. The input match will return the degree of the input. Both output and operation processing are carried out in the same manner as input. But in output matching, all output from the requested service will be matched with each output in the advertised service. In operation matching, service category of the requested and service category the advertised service are matched. The results of these two matching are the degree of output matching and operation matching respectively.

After matching two services, the semantic distance of the match will be the sum of all four stages. This will be stored in the database. After matching with all advertisements from the database, the matched list will be sorted by the degree of similarity of advertisement web service and returned to the requester.

The semantic distance within the same ontology is computed based on the relationship between two concepts in the ontology. We assume that A and B are two concepts of an ontology. The function to compute the distance between A and B is as follows:

```
computDegree (A, B){
  if (A=B) return exact;
  if (A subsumes B) return subsumes;
  if (B subsumes A) return plug-in;
  otherwise return fail;
}
```

2.4 Compute Distance and Description

To check if two web services have the same description we use clustering technology. Clustering is a process that divides a set of items into groups of similar items [7]. Each group is a cluster and consists of items that are similar to each other. If two textDescription (section 2.1) belong to the same group, we say that they refer to the same function. Otherwise, two web services cannot be matched.

To compute the distance between two concepts from different ontologies, we use [8] to define rules to compute the semantic distance between labels, properties, super-concepts or sub-concepts of two concepts. The final distance of two concepts A and B is the summation of the three components with weight w_i.

$$similarity(A,B) = \sum_{i=1}^{n} w_i similarity_i(A,B) .$$

w_i is application and domain specific. n is number of rules. When requested and advertisement web service use different ontologies, similarity (A, B) will be used to compute the similarity matching of input, output, and operation matching.

3 Related Work

Since web services use different languages to describe the services and hence, are semantically incompatible, the LARKS (Language for Advertisement and Request for Knowledge Sharing) project [3, 4] defined a common language called ADCL (Agent Capability Description Language). LARKS includes five different filters for matching. However, ADCL is not a standard of W3C (www.w3c.org) and is difficult to write. Furthermore, LARKS does not support other commonly used languages such as DAML-S and OWL-S.

The Matchmaker from the collaboration between Toshiba and Carnegie Mellon University [10] is based on LARKS and the algorithm from [2] to overcome the drawbacks of LARKS. Similar to LARKS, it allows users to decide which filters they would like to use to narrow the result of matching. However, it has two drawbacks; first, it does not support operation matching which is very important in matching operations; second, the Text Filter which is useful to minimize missed matches is inefficient.

Li and Horrocks [1] have developed a framework for matchmaking based on DAML-S. It tries to match the profiles of requested service and advertised service respectively directly, instead of dividing the matching into several stages. Service profile is part of any web service description language and includes information such as input, output, precondition, effective, user information etc. Therefore, without dividing the matching into several stages, it will be difficult to automate reasoning techniques to compute semantic matching and the matching will be time-consuming.

The Matchmaker from TU-Berlin [4] is a good example of a matching algorithm. It is divided into four stages. By dividing the matching algorithm, the Matchmaker not only avoids the drawback from [1] but also helps users to choose the degree of matching from each stage. However, the matchmaker is quite simple and one of the drawbacks is that it is very difficult for users to utilize user-defined matching. With user-defined matching, the user must define their rules without user-friendly graphical user-interfaces.

All of the above matchmakers assume that the requested service and advertised services use the same ontology and support one semantic description language. The proposed Matchmaker supports matching of web services using different ontologies and different description languages.

4 Conclusions and Future Work

In this paper we have introduced an algorithm and engine which supports matching of web services using different ontologies. The proposed algorithm is based on [2, 4]. The algorithm in [2] is extended to support matching of web services using different ontologies. It also supports the matching of web services which use different web service description languages such as OWL-S, DAML-S, and RDFS by using different reasoners. Each reasoner will be responsible for a different web services description language. However, to determine if two web services have the same description by using clustering technology has limitations when the number of services is not large enough. The approach in computing the distance of two concepts from different ontologies is also too simplistic. Alternative solutions to these issues are being looked into, as well as implementation of the framework.

References

1. L. Li and I. Horrocks: A software framework for matching based on semantic web technology. 12th International World Wide Web Conference (WWW 2003), pp. 331-339, Budapest, Hungary, 2003.
2. M. Paolucci, T. Kawamura, T. R. Payne, K. Sycara: Semantic Matching of Web services Capabilities. 1st International Semantic Web Conference (ISWC 2002), pp. 333-347, Sardinia, Italy, 2002.
3. K. Sycara, S. Widoff, M. Klusch, J. Lu: LARKS: Dynamic Matchmaking Among Heterogeneous Software Agents in Cyberspace. Autonomous Agents and Multi- Agent Systems, Vol.5, pp.173-203, 2002.
4. M.C.Jaeger, S. Tang and C. Liebetruth: The TUB OWL-S Matcher. Available at http://ivs.tu-berlin.de/Projekte/owlsmatcher/index.html
5. W3C: OWL-S 1.0 Release. Available at: http://www.daml.org/services/owl-s/1.0/
6. OWL Profile: http://www.daml.org/services/owl-s/1.0/Profile.owl
7. P. Berkhin, Survey of Clustering Data Mining Techniques: Technical Report. Accure Software. Available at: http://citesseer.nj.nec.com/berkhin02servey.html
8. M. Ehrig, Y. Sure: Ontology Mapping – An Integrated Approach. 1st European Semantic Web Symposium, Heraklion, Greece, 2004.

Improving Semantic Consistency of Web Sites by Quantifying User Intent

Carsten Stolz[1], Maximilian Viermetz[2], Michal Skubacz[3], and Ralph Neuneier[4]

[1] University of Eichstätt-Ingolstadt, Germany
carsten.stolz@ku-eichstaett.de
[2] Heinrich-Heine-Universität Düsseldorf, Germany
maximilian@viermetz.net
[3] Siemens AG, Corporate Technology, Germany
michal.skubacz@siemens.com
[4] Siemens Corporate Research Princeton, USA
ralph.neuneier@siemens.com

Abstract. The design and organization of a website reflects the authors intent. Since user perception and understanding of websites may differ from the authors, we propose a means to identify and quantify this difference in perception. In our approach we extract perceived semantic focus by analyzing user behavior in conjunction with keyword similarity.

By combining usage and content data we identify user groups with regard to the subject of the pages they visited. Our real world data shows that these user groups are nicely distinguishable by their content focus. By introducing a distance measure of keyword coincidence between web pages and user groups, we can identify pages of similar perceived interest. A discrepancy between perceived distance and link distance in the web graph indicates an inconsistency in the web site's design. Determining usage similarity allows the web site author to optimize the content to the users needs.

1 Introduction

Web Mining provides many approaches to analyze usage, user navigation behavior, as well as content and structure of web sites. They are used for a variety of purposes ranging from reporting through personalization and marketing intelligence. In most cases the results obtained, such as user groups or clickstreams, are difficult to interpret. Moreover practical application of them is even more difficult. We would like to present a way to analyze web data giving clear recommendations for web site authors on how to improve the web site by adapting it to user's interest. For this purpose we have to first identify and evaluate the interest. Since we analyze corporate web sites that mainly provide information, but no e-commerce, there is no transactional data available. Transactions usually provide insight into the user's interest: what the user is buying, that is what he or she is interested in. But facing purely information driven web sites, other approaches must be developed in order to reveal user interest. Our goal is to automatically generate recommendations for information driven web sites enabling authors to incorporate user's perception of the site in the process of optimizing it.

D. Lowe and M. Gaedke (Eds.): ICWE 2005, LNCS 3579, pp. 308–317, 2005.

We achieve the goal by combining and analyzing web site structure, content as well as usage data. For the purpose we collect the content and structure data using an automatic crawler. The usage data we gather with the help of a web tracking system integrated into a large corporate web site. The content and structure data are collected by a crawler.

Contribution: Combining usage and content data and applying clustering techniques, we create user interest vectors. We analyze the relationships between web pages based on the common user interest, defined by the previously created user interest vectors. Finally we compare the structure of the web site with the user perceived semantic structure. The comparison of both structure analyses helps us to generate recommendations for web site enhancements.

Related Work: A similar approach is described by Zhu et al in [15]. The Authors analyze user paths to find semantic relations between web pages with the aim to improve search by constructing a conceptual link hierarchy. Mobasher et al. [8] combine user and content data in a similar way in order to create content profiles. These profiles are used in a framework for web site personalization. Mobasher and Dai analyze user behavior in context of the Semantic Web in [5], using the advantages of ontologies and taxonomies. User Interest is also the focus of Oberle et al. in [9]. They enhance web usage data with formal semantics from existing ontologies. The main goal of this work is to resolve cryptic URLs by semantic information provided by a Semantic Web. In our approach we do not use explicit semantic information, because Semantic Web extensions are not available for the web sites we analyze. How semantic information from a Semantic Web can be provided and applied is covered by Berendt et al in [1]. Like Cooley describes in [4], we also combine Web Content, Structure and Usage. Cooley uses their combination for a better data preprocessing and product page classification. We have instead chosen to use standard multivariate analysis for identification of user and content cluster. In [12] we have outlined a technique for smoothing the keyword space in order to reduce dimensionality and improve clustering results.

A comparison of perceived user's interest and author's intentions manifested in the web site content and structure can be regarded as a web metric. A systematic survey of web related metrics can be found at Dhyani et al. [6] and Calero et al.[3]. Usability and information accessibility aspects of our approach can be regarded in the context of Vanderdonckt et al.[14] presenting a guideline-based automatic HTML check on usability of web sites.

Overview: Our approach is described in sections 2 through 4. In the sections 2.1 and 2.2 we describe different datasets, their preprocessing and the combination of user and content data. The identification process of user interest groups is described in 3.1 and 3.2. By comparing Web Site Structure with the user perceived semantic structure of a web site, we identify discrepancies of the web site in section 4. The application and evaluation of our approach is presented in section 5 by analyzing real world data of a corporate web site.

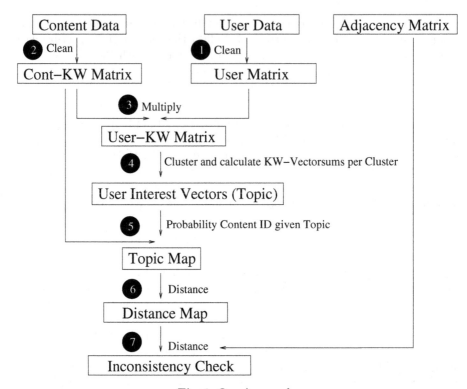

Fig. 1. Our Approach

2   Data Preparation

For our approach we analyze usage as well as content data. We consider usage data to be user actions on a web site which are collected by a tracking mechanism. We extract content data from web pages with the help of a crawler. Figure 1 depicts the major steps of our algorithm. The data preparation steps 1 and 2 are described in 2.1. Section 2.2 describes step 3, where usage and content data are combined. Further the combined data is used for the identification of the user interest groups in 3.1. To identify topics we calculate the key word vector sums of each cluster in 3.2. Step 5, in which probabilities of a web page belonging to one topic is calculated, is explained in 3.2. Afterwards in 4.1 the distances between the web page are calculated, in order to compare them in the last step 4.2 with the distances in the link graph. As a result we can identify inconsistencies between web pages organized by the web designer and web pages grouped by users with the same interest.

2.1   User Data Extraction and Cleaning

A tracking mechanism on the analyzed web sites collects each click, session information as well as additional user details. In an ETL (Extraction-Transform-Load) process user sessions are created. The problem of session identification occurring with logfiles is overcome by the tracking mechanism, which allows easy construction of sessions. The resulting session information was afterwards manually cleaned by the following steps:

Exclude Crawler: We identify foreign potential crawler activity thus ignoring bots and crawlers searching the web site since we are solely interested in user interaction.

Exclude Navigational Pages: Furthermore we identify special navigation and support pages which do not contribute to the semantics of a user session. *Home, Sitemap, Search* are unique pages occurring often in a clickstream, giving hints about navigational behavior but providing no information about the content focus of a user session. Using i sessions and j web pages (identified by Content IDs) we can now create the user session matrix $U_{i,j}$.

Content Data Extraction and Cleaning: The visited pages of a web site are crawled and their content extracted.

Exclude Single Occurring Keywords: Keywords that occur only on one web page can not contribute to web page similarity and can therefore be excluded. This helps to reduce dimensionality.

Stopwords and Stemming: To further reduce noise in the data set additional processing is necessary, in particular applying a stopword list which removes given names, months, fill words and other non-essential text elements. Afterwards we reduce words to their stems with Porter's stemming [10] method.

Ignore Navigation Bars: Due to the fact that the web pages are supplied by a special content management system (CMS), the crawler can send a modified request to the CMS to deliver the web page without navigation. This allows us to concentrate on the content of a web page and not on the structural and navigational elements. With help of the CMS we achieve a focused content selection which others approaches like [11] concentrate on in detail. From these distilled pages we collect textual information, HTML markup and meta information.

HTML-Tags, Metainformation: In [12] we have evaluated meta-information and found that they are not consistently maintained throughout web sites. Also, HTML markup cannot be relied upon to reflect the semantic structure of web pages. In general HTML tends to carry design information, but does not emphasize importance of information within a page.

Number of Keywords per Web Page: From the web page text we have extracted all words. In order to increase effectivity, one usually only considers the most common occurring key words. In general the resulting key word vector for each web page is proportional to text length. In our experiments in section 5 we decided to use all words of a web page since by limiting their number one loses infrequent but important words. Since we analyze single corporate web sites, which concentrate on one area of interest, it is reasonable to have a detailed content description to distinguish between only slightly different topics.

Navigational Pages: In order to have compatible data sets, we exclude navigation pages, which we also eliminated from the above explained user data $U_{i,j}$. From this cleaned database with j web pages (Content IDs) and k unique keywords we create the content matrix $C_{j,k}$.

2.2   Combine User and Content Information

One objective of this approach is to identify what users are interested in. In order to achieve this, it is not sufficient to know which pages a user has visited, but the content of all pages in a user session. Therefore we combine user data $U_{i,j}$ with content data $C_{j,k}$, by multiplying both matrices obtaining a user-keyword-matrix $CF_{i,k} = U_{i,j} \times C_{j,k}$. This matrix shows the content of a user session, represented by keywords.

3   Reveal User Interest

3.1   Identify User Interest Groups

In order to find user session groups with similar interest, we cluster sessions by keywords.

Number of Clusters: In order to estimate the n number of groups, we perform a principal component analysis on the scaled matrix $CF_{i,j}$ and inspect the data visually.

Select Start Partition for Clustering: In order to create reliable cluster partitions with k-Means, we have to define an initial partitioning of the data. We do so by clustering $CF_{i,k}$ hierarchically. We have evaluated the results of hierarchical clustering using Single-, Complete- and Average-Linkage methods. For all data sets the Complete-Linkage method has shown the best experimental results. We extract n groups defined by the hierarchical clustering and calculate the within group distance $dist(partition_n)$. The data point with the minimum distance within $partition_n$ is chosen as one of n starting points of the initial partitioning for the k-Means algorithm.

Identifying User Interest Groups by k-Means Clustering: The previously determined partitioning initializes a standard k-Means clustering assigning each user session to a cluster. We identify user groups with regard to the subject of the pages they visited, clustering users with the same interest.

To find out in which topics the users in each group are interested in, we regard the keyword vectors in each cluster.

3.2   Identifying Interest of User Groups

We create an interest vector for each user group by summing up the keyword vectors of all user sessions within one cluster. The result is a user interest matrix $UI_{k,n}$ for all n clusters. Afterwards we subtract the mean value over all cluster of each keyword from the keyword value in each cluster.

Figure 2 shows two topic vectors. The keywords are spaced along the horizontal axis, while the vertical axis represents the relative importance (or unimportance) of individual keywords to this user interest vector. One sees, that the user perceived topics are nicely separable.

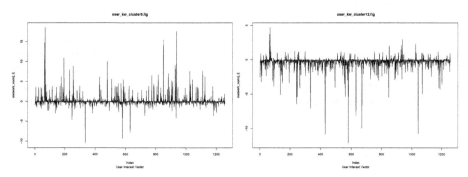

Fig. 2. User Interest Vectors

4   Comparison Between User Perceived Semantic Distance and Web Site Link Distance

4.1   Measure Distance of Keyword Coincidence

Having the keyword based topic vectors for each user group $UI_{k,n}$ available, we combine them with the content matrix $C_{j,k} \times UI_{k,n}$ from 2.1. The resulting matrix $CI_{j,n}$ explains how strong each content ID (web page) is related to each User Interest Group $UI_{k,n}$. The degree of similarity between content perceived by the user can now be seen as the distances between content IDs based on the $CI_{j,n}$ matrix. The shorter the distance, the greater the similarity of content IDs in the eyes of the users.

4.2   Identify Inconsistencies

Adjacency Matrix: We compare the above calculated distance matrix CI_{dist} with the distances in an adjacency matrix of the web graph of the regarded web site. For this adjacency matrix we use the shortest click distance between two web pages. This distance matrix is calculated by the Dijkstra Algorithm, which calculates shortest paths in a graph.

Discrepancies: Comparing both distance matrices, discrepancy between perceived distance and link distance in the web graph indicates an inconsistency in the web sites design. If two pages have the similar distance regarding user perception as well as link distance, then users and web authors have the same understanding of the content of the two pages and their relation to each other. If the distances are different, then either users do not use the pages in the same context or they need more clicks than their content focus would permit. In the eyes of the user, the two pages belong together but are not linked, or the other way around.

5   Case Study

We applied the above presented approach to two corporate web sites. Each deals with different topics and is different concerning size, subject and number of user accesses. With this case study we evaluate our approach employing it on both web sites. We begin with the data preparation of content and usage data and the reduction of dimensionality during this process. See figure 1 for details of the whole process.

5.1   Data Collection and Preparation

In all projects dealing with real world data the inspection and preparation of data is essential for reasonable results.

User Data: Raw usage data consists of 13302 user accesses in 5439 sessions.

Table 1. Data Cleaning Steps for User Data

Cleaning Step	Data Sets	Dimensions (SessionID x Keyword)
Raw Data	13398	5349 x 283
Exclude Crawler	13228	5343 x 280
Adapt to Content Data	13012	5291 x 267

Content Data: 278 web pages are crawled first. Table 2 explains the cleaning steps and the thereby following dimensionality reductions.

We have evaluated the possibility to reduce the keyword vector space even more by excluding keywords occurring only on two or three pages.

5.2   Identification of User Interest Groups

In step 3 in figure 1 we combine user and content data by multiplying both matrices obtaining a user-keyword-matrix $CF_{i,k} = U_{i,j} * C_{j,k}$ with $i = 4568$ *user sessions*, $j = 247$ *content IDs* and $k = 1258$ *keywords*. We perform a

Table 2. Data Cleaning Steps for Content Data

Cleaning Step	Data Sets	Dimensions (ContentID x Keyword)
Raw Data	2001	278 x 501
ContentIDs wrong language	1940	270 x 471
Exclude Home, Sitemap, Search	1904	264 x 468
Exclude Crawler	1879	261 x 466
Delete Single Keywords	1650	261 x 237
Delete Company Name	1435	261 x 236

principal component analysis on the matrix $CF_{i,k}$ to determine the n number of clusters. This number varies from 9 to 30 cluster depending on the size of the matrix and the subjects the web site is dealing with. The Kaiser criteria can help to determine the number of principal components necessary to explain half of the total sample variance, like in figure 3. We choose different number of clusters varying around this criteria and could not see major changes in the resulting cluster numbers. Standard k-Means clustering provided the grouping of $CF_{i,k}$ into n cluster.

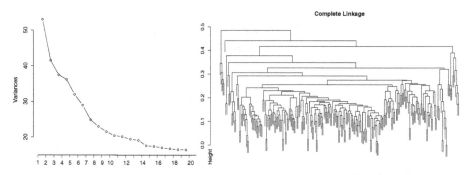

Fig. 3. Principal Component Analysis and Hierarchichal Clustering

We calculate the keyword vector sums per each cluster, building the total keyword vector for each cluster. The result is a user group interest matrix $UI_{k,n}$ Part of an user interest vector is given here: *treasur — solu — finan — servi — detai.*

We proceed as described above in 4.1 with the calculating the user perceived interest. The crawler has gathered all links, which we use for building the adjacency matrix.

We now want to provide a deeper insight into the application of the results. We have calculated the distance matrix $dist(CI_{j,n})$ as described in 4.1.

5.3 Identify Inconsistencies

We scale both distance matrices, the user $dist(CI_{j,n})$ and adjacency matrix $Dist_{Link}$ to variance 1 and mean 0 in order to make them comparable. Then we calculate their difference $Dist_{UserInterest} - Dist_{Link}$. We get a matrix with as many columns and rows as there are web pages, comparing all web page (content IDs) with each other. We are interested in the differences between user perception and author intention, which are identifyable as peak values when subtracting the user matrix from the adjacency matrix, clearly visible in Fig. 4. The set of peaks, identifying pairs of web pages, now forms the candidates put forward for manual scrutiny by the web site author, who can update the web site structure if he or she deems it necessary.

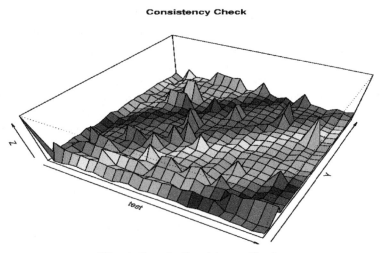

Fig. 4. Sample Consistency Check

6   Conclusion

We have presented a way to show weaknesses in the current structure of a web site in terms of how user perceive the content of that site. We have evaluated our approach on two different web sites, different in subject, size and organization. The recommendation provided by this approach has still to be evaluated manually, but since we face huge web sites, it helps to focus on problems the users have. Solving them promises a positive effect on web site acceptance. The ultimate goal will be measurable by a continued positive response over time.

This work is part of the idea to make information driven web pages evaluable. Our current research will extend this approach with the goal to create metrics, that should give clues about the degree of success of a user session. A metric of this kind would make the success of the whole web site more tangible. For evaluation of a successful user session we will use the referrer information of users coming from search engines. The referrer provides us with these search strings. Compared with the user interest vector a session can be made more evaluable.

References

1. B. Berendt, A. Hotho, G. Stumme; Towards Semantic Web Mining, The Semantic Web - ISWC 2002, 2002, p. 264
2. S. Chakrabarti; Mining the Web - Discovering Knowledge from Hypertext Data. Morgan Kaufmann, 2002
3. C. Calero, J. Ruiz, M. Piattini; A Web Metrics Survey Using WQM Web Engineering, 4th Int. Conf. ICWE 2004, Proc. p.147-160
4. R. Cooley; The Use of Web Structure and Content to Identify Subjectively Interesting Web Usage Patterns ACM Transaction on Internet Technology, 2003, Vol.3 Nr.2 p. 93–116
5. H. Dai, B. Mobasher; Using ontologies to discover domain-level web usage profiles,PKDD 2001
6. D. Dhyani, NG. Keong, S.S. Bhowmick; A Survey of Web Metrics, ACM Computing Surveys, 2002, vol. 34, nr. 4, p. 469-503
7. X. He, H. Zha, C. Ding, and H. Simon; Web document clustering using hyperlink structures Computational Statistics and Data Analysis, 41:19-45, 2002
8. B. Mobasher, H. Dai, T. Luo, Y. Sun, and J. Zhu; Integrating Web Usage and Content Mining for More Effective Personalization. Proc. of the Int'l Conf. on E-Commerce and Web Technologies (ECWeb2000)(2000)
9. D. Oberle, B. Berendt, A. Hotho, J. Gonzalez; Conceptual User Tracking, Proc. of the Atlantic Web Intelligence Conference,2002, p. 155 - 164
10. M. F. Porter; An algorithm for suffix stripping. Program, 14:130–137, (1980)
11. R. Song and H. Liu and J. Wen and W. Ma; Learning important models for web page blocks based on layout and content analysis SIGKDD Explor. Newsl. vol.6, nr. 2, 2004, p.14–23
12. C. Stolz, V. Gedov, K. Yu, R. Neuneier, M. Skubacz; Measuring Semantic Relations of Web Sites by Clustering of Local Context, ICWE2004, München (2004) In Proc. Int. Conf. on Web Engineering 2004, Springer, p. 182–186
13. A.Sun and E.-P. Lim; Web Unit Mining: Finding and Classifying Subgraphs of Web Pages. In Proceedings 12th Int. Conf. on Information and Knowledge Management, p. 108–115. ACM Press, 2003.
14. J. Vadnerdonckt, A. Beirekdar, M. Noirhomme-Fraiture; Automated Evaluation of Web Usability and Accessibility by Guideline Review, In Proc. Int. Conf. Web Engineering 2004, Springer, p. 17-30
15. J. Zhu, J. Hong, J.G.Hughes; PageCluster: Mining Conceptual Link Hierarchies from Web Log Files for Adaptive Web Site Navigation, ACM Journal Transaction on Internet Technology,2004, Vol.4,Nr.2, p. 185-208

A Framework to Support QoS-Aware Usage
of Web Services*

Eunjoo Lee[1], Woosung Jung[1], Wookjin Lee[1], Youngjoo Park[1],
Byungjeong Lee[2,**], Heechern Kim[3], and Chisu Wu[1]

[1] School of Computer Science and Engineering, Seoul National University, Seoul, Korea
{ejlee,wsjung,duri96,ppang,wuchisu}@selab.snu.ac.kr
[2] School of Computer Science, University of Seoul, Korea
bjlee@venus.uos.ac.kr
[3] Dept. of Computer Science, Korea National Open University, Seoul, Korea
hckim@knou.ac.kr

Abstract. Web services offer an easier, effective, efficient way to support a service paradigm. However, there is lack of adequate QoS support in using web services. In this paper, we propose a framework to support QoS aspects of web services. Three new elements are added to the original web service framework: QoS Server, QoS UDDI Broker and QoS Agent. In this framework, a requester is able to query more flexibly by using history QoS data of each web service with few load.

1 Introduction

A Web service is a software interface that describes a collection of operations that can be accessed through standardized XML messaging over the network [1] [2]. Due to the rapid growth of web service applications and the abundance of service providers, the requester must choose the "right" service provider. In such a scenario, the quality of service (QoS) serves as a benchmark to differentiate service providers [3]. However, most of today's web service implementations fail to guarantee good quality of service to their users. In fact, UDDI is currently a registry database that allows requesters to look for Web services based on their functionality and not on QoS information [4]. The lack of adequate QoS support prevents the adoption of performance sensitive web services [5].

Recently, several studies have been carried out on framework supporting web services with QoS [3], [5], [6], [7]. They all commonly dealt with QoS support framework for web services. Yet, there is lack of consideration about end users' condition. And most of the studies require some operations in requester's side, which bring about a load on end user. Typically, QoS enabled web services are associated with a service level agreement that providers present. However, there is no mechanism to quantify the trustworthiness of providers [3]. Therefore, QoS aware framework needs to be independent of provider.

In this paper, we suggest a framework to support QoS-aware usage of web services using an agent, a broker and a QoS Server. In this framework, the extensive history

* This work was supported by grant No. R01-2002-000-00135-0 from the Basic Research Program of the Korea Science & Engineering Foundation
** Corresponding author

D. Lowe and M. Gaedke (Eds.): ICWE 2005, LNCS 3579, pp. 318–327, 2005.

data of each web service can be utilized for more flexible query. History data of a web service include area, response time, access date and time, etc. A QoS Agent regularly collects that data and is consequently processed into QoS information of each web service. Each requester has diverse condition according to the requester's usage pattern. That is, a requester uses a web service only during peak hours and the requester ignores performance aspects of the web service during off-hours. Those are expressed as requester-specific conditions in a requester's query. History data is utilized to find the most suitable web service that meets the specific conditions.

The remaining parts of this paper are organized as follows. Section 2 presents the related works and the inherent problems. Section 3 presents our proposed framework. Section 4 describes a scenario illustrating an operation in a web service where our framework is applied. Section 5 presents comparisons between our framework and other frameworks. Finally, Sect. 6 describes contribution and limitation of our study.

2 Related Works

Several studies on a web service framework with QoS support have been carried out thus far. Tian et al. presented an approach that allows not only QoS integration in Web services, but also the selection of appropriate services based on QoS requirements [7]. They classified QoS parameters as 'Web service layer QoS support' and 'the network layer QoS support'. Processing time, availability and various other requirements were included in the former. Bandwidth, packet loss and several other data points were included in the latter. A Web service Broker (WSB) was used in the proposed architecture, which fetches information of offers that requester could be interested in. WSB tests the web services that meet functional requirements and it returns the most appropriate services to requester. That is, WSB helps the requester to find appropriate offers according to 'Web service layer QoS support'. The requester and server have a requester side QoS proxy and server side QoS proxy, respectively. The proxies handle 'the network layer QoS support' at runtime. Two implementations of WSB exist; one uses a local object within the application and the other uses a remote web service. In [7], there is lack of feedback mechanism that can reflect requester's state. Also, there is no way of using history data related to QoS properties.

Singhera et al. extend web services framework installed with a Monitor [6]. In this framework, non-functional characteristics of a web service are determined at run-time and requesters are offered services that best meet their non-functional requirements as well as functional requirements. Monitor consists of a Registration Module, Service Monitoring Module, Uplink Module, Rules Engine and History Analyzer. These modules collect the non-functional characteristics, perform the necessary tests and select the best web service.

In [3], architecture with verity and which uses a reputation system was introduced. The reputation system is intended to aggregate and disseminate feedback on the past behaviors of the participants [8]. This system encourages trustworthiness and help requester choose the most appropriate system for service request. A requester and a service broker contain different profiles of the reputation vector. The service broker calculates the global verity, while the requester calculates the local verity. To determine the verity value used in quality driven selection, the user employs a weighted sum mechanism. However, most requesters are reluctant to store database and a cal-

culator in their server. Moreover, they are particularly sensitive about leakage of their
server logs to the outside. Another drawback is that it is difficult to manage certain
elements such as a calculator in requester. Yu and Lin proposed two resource allocation algorithms (Homogeneous Resource Allocation algorithm; HQ and Non-
homogeneous Resource Allocation algorithm; RQ) [5]. The purpose of the algorithms
is to achieve a high average system utility and avoid making frequent resource reconfigurations. The resource allocation in a server can be effectively adjusted so that
requesters can avoid experiencing unstable performance.

3   Proposed Framework

A general web service framework is composed of three parts: Provider, Requester
and discovery mechanism like UDDI. Requester and Provider can communicate via
message using XML, SOAP, WSDL technology. Yet, there are only few mechanisms
that can reflect Requester's QoS requirements.

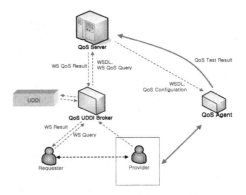

Fig. 1. QoS-Aware Framework

A QoS UDDI Broker obtains suitable set of web services, which is determined by
some information in a query sent by a Requester. Figure 2 shows an example of a
query in XML. The information includes not only data about general UDDI search
for functionally suitable web services, but each weight value for QoS properties and
condition information about time, period and area. A wide spectrum of metrics that
reflect the QoS of web services have been introduced by the research community
with often varying interpretation [3][9]. We consider 'reputation', 'response time',
'availability', 'reliability' as QoS properties in our example, and those QoS properties
can be measured with the existing QoS metrics. QoS properties can be added to or
removed from those according to a policy. QoS Server has history data for each web
service that have been registered in the QoS Server. Each registered web service has
wsid, its unique identifier.

At first, functionally suitable web services are returned to UDDI QoS Broker from
UDDI. If some web services don't have *wsid*, the web services are newly registered
in the QoS Server. Next, A QoS Server calculates metric value of each QoS properties based on its history data using search conditions, such as time, period and area.
Finally, each weight value is applied to get the last resulting list sorted by decreasing

order according to user's preference. In addition to the list, evaluated data (grade) of each web service in the list are shown. And more, the history data is illustrated as a form of graph, which helps a user know the usage pattern of the web service and select more appropriate one. The whole selecting process is described in Fig. 3.

```
<?xml version="1.0" encoding="UTF-8" ?>
<QoS_Query>
<Category id="1" />
<Keywords>
        <Keyword>medical</Keyword>
        <Keyword>record</Keyword>
</Keywords>
<Weight>
        <Availability>30</Availability>
        <Reliability>40</Reliability>
        <Reputation>10</Reputation>
        <ResponseTime>20</ResponseTime>
</Weight>
<Period>
        <FromDate>2004-02-01</FromDate>
        <ToDate>2005-01-31</ToDate>
</Period>
 <Area id="3" />
</QoS_Query>
```

Fig. 2. An example of a query

1. $S=\{s_1, s_2, ..., s_n\}$ // S is a set of functionally suitable web services, $s_1, s_2, ..., s_n$.
2. Extract condition and weights for QoS properties from query.
          $cond=\{time, area, period\}$
          $W=<w_1, w_2, ..., w_m>$ // W is a set of weights for each QoS properties.
3. Determine grades of each web services based on the condition using the history data. A group of web services that have no history data is listed separately.
          $G_i=\{g_1, ..., g_m\}$ // G_i is s_i's grade for each QoS properties
4. Calculate ranks of the web service with this following formula.

$$f(s_i) = \sum_{k=1}^{m} w_k \bullet g_k \qquad (f(s_i) \text{ is an evaluation function for each web service } s_i)$$

5. Get the network delay time between a requester and each provider of candidate web services using some technique such as '*ping*'.
6. Return the list of resulting web services with network delay time in decreasing order.

Fig. 3. Process for selecting QoS suitable web services

Compared to distributed components operated on intranet environments, web services are expected to be used based on not only intranet, but also internet. Therefore we decompose 'response time' into local response time in a provider's side and network delay time between an agent and a provider. And then, we take local response time as 'response time', for network delay may be serious factor in internet environment. Local response time can be obtained with actual response time and network delay time. In our framework, several agents test at diverse area because network status tends to be varied according to some condition, for example, area. If a web service is tested by only one agent, the result may be distorted for the condition reason.

A QoS Agent regularly tests web services registered in a QoS Server according to the configuration forwarded by a QoS Server, and it stores the test result in QoS

Server as history data of each web services. Figure 4 shows a main part of an example of QoS configuration delivered from a QoS Server to a QoS Agent. QoS configuration mainly includes testing condition (time interval, timeout). When a QoS Server is established initially, a manager registers a list of web services as one of initial setting to collect history data for the first search. When a QoS Agent tests a web service, it uses test data automatically generated from a WSDL of the web service, particularly the type information of parameters in the WSDL. When errors occur in testing due to test data, it should be fixed manually with a log message about the error.

UDDI tracks on changes on web services [10]. When a web service is changed, QoS Agent updates test modules if necessary. When a web service is not available any more, *wsid* of the web service is unregistered in the QoS Server.

```xml
<?xml version="1.0" encoding="euc-kr" ?>
<AgentCommands>
  <!-- From QoS Server To QoS Agent  -->
  <Configuration>
      <!-- Agent Overall Configuration  -->
      <Interval unit="min">10</Interval>
      <Timeout unit="sec">30</Timeout>
   </Configuration>
  <Command>
      <Configuration>
      <!-- Configuration For Target  -->
      <Interval unit="min">10</Interval>
      <Timeout unit="sec">30</Timeout>
      </Configuration>
      <Target type="URI">http://violet.snu.ac.kr/wsdl/TestWebService.wsdl</Target>
      <Operations>
         <!--Operations to be tested  -->
         <Operation id="/definitions/portType/operation[@name='getCharCount']">
          <!-- test configuration  -->
          <Configuration>
             <!-- Configuration For Operation  -->
             <Interval unit="min">10</Interval>
             <Timeout unit="sec">30</Timeout>
          </Configuration>
         <TestMsg>
          <!-- Test SOAP Message  -->
          <soap:Envelope xmlns:soap="http://schemas.xmlsoap.org/soap/envelope/" xmlns:m="some-uri">
             <soap:Body>
                <m:getCharCountRequest>
                    <arg0>0321146182</arg0>
                </m:getCharCountRequest>
             </soap:Body>
          </soap:Envelope>
         </TestMsg>
         <ResultMsg>
          .............
```

Fig. 4. An example of QoS configuration

4 Scenario Under the Proposed Framework

This section presents a scenario of a requester using the web services that meets both its functional and non-functional requirements by applying our framework. We also show a simple example of a conditional QoS query at the end of this section. We assume that the various web services are defined in WSDL and registered in UDDI registries.

1. The QoS Server let a QoS Agent regularly test web services and collect some data such as testing date, time, area and response time, etc., which are processed into QoS information by QoS Server. QoS information of web services becomes piled up in the database. The QoS information of each web service is graded by QoS Server's grading scheme.
2. A requester sends a query to the QoS UDDI Broker. Functional requirement, QoS requirement and requester-specific condition can be included in that query. QoS requirements are a set of pairs, <QoS information, weight value>, for example, {<reliability, 35%>, <availability, 45%>, <response time, 20%>} (Fig. 5(a)). A requester can select QoS properties such as reliability, availability. If any property is not selected, all properties are considered to have same weight value.
3. A QoS UDDI Broker extracts functional parts and sends them to UDDI. UDDI finds the web services that is compatible with functional part in that query and returns the list of the web services to the QoS UDDI Broker.

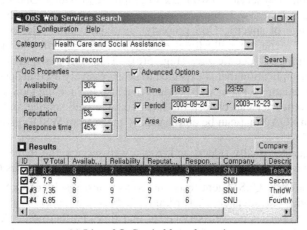

(a) List of QoS suitable web services

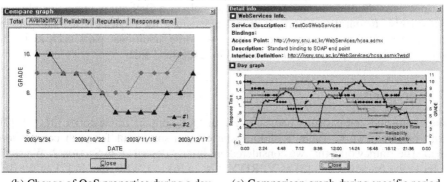

(b) Change of QoS properties during a day   (c) Comparison graph during specific period

Fig. 5. A sample screenshot of search result

4. To the functionally suitable web services listed in the previous step 3, following process are applied to show a list of QoS suitable web services. Figure 5(a) shows the result of this search process. The functional and QoS requirements in Fig.5(a) is transformed into query as a form shown in Fig. 2.

   (a) Basic search process

   QoS Server lists resulting web services with total ranking order. Total ranking can be calculated with each weight value and predefined QoS grade.

   (b) Advanced search process

   If requester-specific condition exists in that query, the condition is applied for advanced search process. For example, if the condition is "{<area, Seoul>, <time, P.M. 8:00-P.M.11:00>}", advanced search process are executed onto web services' history data that have been recorded by a QoS Agent that had tested the web services in Seoul, from eight to eleven o'clock P.M. Total ranking is determined based on the history data in accord with the specific condition.

   Change graphs for QoS properties are displayed, which can help requester select a more suitable web service. Two types of graph are provided. One shows comparison among selected web services during specified period (Fig. 5(b)). Fig. 5(b) shows change of specific QoS property 'availability' for selected web services '#1' and '#2'. The other illustrates change of QoS properties for a specific web services during a specific day (Fig. 5(c)). This one day graph is helpful to building an application that is expected to be excessively used in specific time.

5. A requester obtains a list of web services that also include the QoS data concerned with it. A requester can choose the most suitable web service and it can be accessed with SOAP that can be automatically made from WSDL given by the provider.

6. After a requester finally selects and uses a web service, the requester can give a QoS Agent a rate of the QoS UDDI Broker for reputation properties (optional).

In this framework, QoS Agent tests and collects test results of QoS properties of each web service, in advance. Accordingly, it becomes unnecessary to check the value of QoS properties of web services at real time. Furthermore, the history data collected by QoS Agent are saved and managed by QoS Server, which can be used at various parts. In other words, requesters can deliver a QoS query more flexibly and extensively. In our framework, it is not mandatory for requesters to take part in checking reputation ranking. And at the same time, additional parts such as Local verity calculator in [3] need not be located in requesters' side.

5 Comparison

We conducted comparisons between several QoS support frameworks [3], [6], [7] with our framework. Table 1 outlines the comparison result for each comparison item. The frameworks that we considered are briefly described in Section 2. We shall refer to the framework in [3] as VERITY, that in [6] as EWSF, that in [7] as WSBF, and our framework as QAF, for convenience. Data related to QoS properties are logged in history data and they can be useful in web service selection. Usually a requester selects a web service in practice by using the results of QoS test, which includes not only the current data but also past data, for the right selection. Storage capacity has to be enough to store the massive history data. In that respect, QAF shall have the demerit of storage demand. That is, there is a tradeoff between the history data and storage demand.

In QAF, a requester is able to query more flexibly compared with others. For example, with QAF, it would be possible to execute operations as described in the previous section by using the history data. It is expected to be helpful in real usage of web service, because a requester may want to know a specific condition where web services are used. In VERITY and our QAF, requesters' feedback is supported explicitly. But VERITY allows the requesters to maintain database and a calculator in their server, and at the same time, allows their logs to be used outside. This is a burden to the requesters, which in turn poses as a usage barrier in the real market. To the contrary, QAF does not force requesters to provide feedbacks, and moreover, only the QoS Agent performs all miscellaneous operations.

The item, Requester's view, is a measure of what the web service takes into consideration as a requester. Local verity in VERITY can reflect requester's position but it has a tradeoff relationship with 'Requester's load'. In our QAF, QoS Agent executes the test of finally selected web services under requester's condition such that the condition of the requester is partly reflected on the test results.

For dynamic QoS aspect, proxies in a requester and a server handle the network layer QoS support concerning the network performance in WSBF. EWSF supports run-time non-functional QoS parameters by relying on a monitor. Similarly to EWSF, QAF makes use of history data but provides more flexible and extensive usage of the data. QAF and VERITY support users' feedback, however QAF does not put a burden on the requester with mandatory provisions of feedbacks nor require for additional elements to be installed in the requester's side as in the case of VERITY. WSBF takes into consideration dynamic aspects that are not presented to QAF. And yet WSBF doesn't utilize helpful history QoS data and feedback mechanism. Also, its local WSB is operated in the requester side.

QAF focuses on the flexibility of the usage of QoS support web service from a requester's perspective. In addition, it activates QoS Agent performing concerned executions, which lessens the load of a requester.

Table 1. Comparison with other frameworks

	VERITY	EWSF	WSBF	QAF
History data	not use	use	not use	use
Requester's view	concern	ignore	partly concern	concern
Flexibility of query	low	low	low	high
Feedback	support (mandatory)	ignore	ignore	support (voluntary)
Storage demand	medium	high	medium	high
Requester's load	heavy	light	medium	light
Dynamic QoS	ignore	partly support	support	ignore

6 Conclusion

We have proposed a QoS aware framework that can support the QoS aspects of web services. QoS Server, QoS UDDI Broker and QoS Agent have been newly added to the original web service framework, where a requester could initially find web services to meet only functional requirements. QoS appropriate web services are selected based on QoS history data that are regularly collected by QoS Agents. In our framework, history data are utilized for more flexible and extensive usage and additional parts are not necessarily located on the requesters' side. Furthermore, the requester's view is considered and load of requester is reduced. The main contribution of our framework can be summarized as follows:

- Requesters can query more flexibly, fitting to their specific condition. Also, the resulting web services is visually shown as graph with their history data in many ways, which helps user select suitable one.
- History data can be utilized for obtaining more information and estimating the future usage of web services through data mining process.
- In our framework, selecting scheme is not dependent on provider; testing data are generated using type information in WSDL of web services, and test results are managed by a QoS Server. Therefore, requesters can get more unbiased QoS information of concerned web service.
- A requester can get tailored results using the rich set of history data and flexible query with no additional processing. Most web services did not consider a specific user's environment and preference in QoS support. Even if considering, special data such as a user's profile [3] is needed. However, we let several agents test regularly in diverse area, and we decompose response time into an agent's network delay and local response time in a provider's side. And more, requesters can actively reflect their condition and preference using extensive query.

Our framework has several limitations:

- We restrict our work to a single web service, not concerning web service composition.
- We assume the testing is conducted on mutual agreement between agents and each provider. Only authorized agent can access a provider, which requires considering security aspect.
- Dynamic QoS support is not considered. History data cannot fully satisfy the performance requirement in dynamic situation.

In the future work, we will focus on implementing three elements, QoS Server, QoS UDDI Broker, and QoS Agent. Furthermore, we'll extend our framework to achieve a more adaptive usage of web services supported by the network layer.

References

1. IBM Web services, http://www-136.ibm.com/developerworks/webservices/
2. W3C, "Web Servicesk Description Requirements." W3C Working Draft, October 2002.
3. 3. Kalepu, S., Krishnaswamy, S. and Loke, S. W., Verity: A QoS Metric for Selecting Web services and Providers, the Fourth International Conference on Web Information Systems Engineering Workshops (WISEW'03), pp.131 – 139, 2003.
4. UDDI, "UDDI Technical White Paper." uddi.org, September 2000.
5. Yu, T. and Lin, K., The Design of QoS Broker Algorithms for QoS-Capable Web services, IEEE Conference on e-Technology, e-Commerce and e-Service(EEE'04), 2004.

6. Singhera, Z. U., Extended Web services Framework to Meet Non-Functional Requirements, International Symposium on Applications and the Internet Workshops (SAINTW'04), 2004.
7. Tian, M., Gramm, A., Naumowicz, T., Ritter, H., and Schiller, J., A Concept for QoS Integration in Web services, the Fourth International Conference on Web Information Systems Engineering Workshops(WISEW'03), 2003.
8. Resnick, P., Zeckhauser, R., Friedman, E., and Kuwabara, K., Reputation Systems, Communications of the ACM Volume 43, Issue 12, December 2000.
9. Zeng, L., Benatallah, B., Ngu, A. H. H., Dumas, M, Kalagnanam, J., and Chang, H., QoS-Aware Middleware for Web Services Composition, IEEE Transactions on Software Engineering, Vol. 30, No. 5, May 2004.
10. http://uddi.org/pubs/uddi-v3.0.2-20041019.htm#_Toc85908401

Integrating Web Applications and Web Services

Nicholas L. Carroll and Rafael A. Calvo

Web Engineering Group
School of Electrical and Information Engineering
University of Sydney, NSW 2006
Australia
{ncarroll,rafa}@ee.usyd.edu.au

Abstract. Database systems are an essential component in multi-tiered web applications. These applications increasingly interact with others using web services. In this paper, we describe and compare two architectures for integrating web services into web applications, and perform performance benchmarks using the Google web service. For one of the architectures we contribute a SOAP interface to the PostgreSQL Relational Database Management System, implemented as a user-defined function that allows developers to make service calls from within the database. We show that SQL can be used to easily query data provided by web services, and therefore as a way of accessing and using web services in a database-driven web application.

1 Introduction

Database-driven web applications store, access, process and serve information using a database and application server. Recently, these applications have been able to access data stored in other systems using web services. An understanding of how different service oriented architectures affect system performance and development effort is important to support the right design decisions in web development. Integration of web services into a web application usually occurs within the application's business logic. However, in recent releases of databases such as Oracle and DB2, it is now possible to request web services directly from the database system. Due to these new possibilities we should reassess the best architectures for integrating web services. This paper contributes to this reassessment by comparing two architectures.

We will use a reference scenario that defines a need for integrating web services into a web application: integrating a student information portal with a search engine web service, and using contextual information to improve the accuracy of search results [1]. In practical terms this can be achieved by integrating the search engine with the business logic of an application. For example, a student searching for third year electives from her University's course catalogue, might simply enter a general search for "third year courses" into the search engine. The results of the search would list third year courses provided by all faculties at the University.

D. Lowe and M. Gaedke (Eds.): ICWE 2005, LNCS 3579, pp. 328–333, 2005.

Depending on the number of results returned, narrowing the results down to third year courses may prove to be time consuming. If the search engine is integrated into the application as a web service as described in Section 2, it could implicitly use such facts as the student's prior course history to improve the accuracy of the search results. The integration could provide a more complete query without the student needing to describe the context, thereby limiting the search results to courses that the student qualifies for enrolment. This type of integration is not commonly used despite its potential benefit [2]. Two key issues need to be addressed to improve the uptake: 1) the performance of such systems cannot be degraded, and 2) developers must find it easy to integrate these data sources into their applications. We address the first in Section 3 and the latter in Section 4, and Section 5 concludes.

2   Integrating Web Service Requesters

The two architectures described here are both distributed, multi-tier architectures consisting of: a presentation component, business logic, database, and a web services requester that binds to a web service provider. The differing factor between the two architectures is the positioning of the web services requester component for integration with the web application. This difference is conveyed in Fig. 1, where Architecture 1, the most commonly used, integrates web services into the business logic component [3], and Architecture 2 integrates web services into the database component. The last architecture is not very popular but recent releases of Oracle and DB2 are now capable of using SOAP [4], as the XML messaging specification for communications between a web service requester and web service provider.

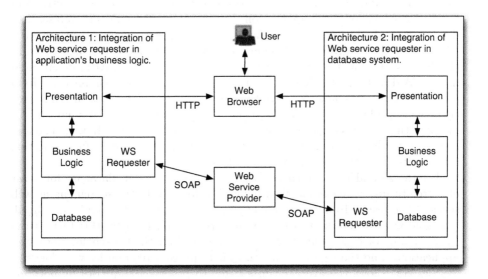

Fig. 1. Two architectures for web services integration

Both architectures were implemented using the same technologies wherever possible. We used Java to implement two simple applications using each architecture. Both web applications provide the functionality described in our reference scenario. For Architecture 1, we integrated the Google web service requester directly into the business logic component, which was as trivial as calling specific methods supplied by the Google Web API. In Architecture 2, we integrated a "SOAP client into the database through user-defined functions" [5]. Most database systems support user-defined functions, which means this approach for integrating a SOAP client into a database system can be generally applied. The SOAP client functioned as the web service requester component within the database system. We used PostgreSQL in both cases.

3   Performance Analysis

The performance analysis that we conducted was limited to the time taken to access and combine information from multiple data sources. In our scenario, we use the provided student ID to query the local database system for information about the student, which can then be used in conjunction with an external data source, to produce more accurate search results. Analysing the accuracy of the search results is beyond the scope of this paper. For this scenario, we assume that associating context with a search engine query improves the accuracy of search results based on efforts in [1].

3.1   Experiment One: Benchmarking with Google

Our first objective was to compare the performance of accessing a web service from within a database system, to accessing the same web service directly from the business logic of a web application. An advantage of requesting web services directly from the business logic is the convenience of accessing web service APIs provided by the programming language used to implement the business logic. In the first test (business logic integration) we used Google's Web API implemented in Java. A drawback of this architecture is that if the information returned from a web service call is connected with the data stored in the database in some way, then there would be an inefficiency caused by the overhead of communications between the database and web service via the business logic. It was therefore necessary to determine if there was in fact a performance gain for requesting web services directly from within the database.

For the second test, we chose to query the PostgreSQL database for a list of search terms, which would then be used to forward to the search engine web service. The results from the search engine web service would then be displayed. The goal was to determine which architecture could perform this task in the least amount of time. This task was performed ten times each for both web applications, and the times for all ten runs to process 100 queries were logged.

Fig. 2(a) shows the average times taken to process 100 queries by both architectures. The graph indicates that requesting a web service from within the

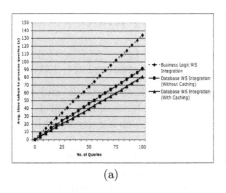 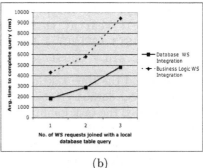

(a)   (b)

Fig. 2. a) Average time taken to execute web service requests. b) Average time taken to join data from different data sources

database is more efficient than consuming web services directly from the business logic component of a web application. The business logic web service integration architecture achieved on average 0.75 queries/sec, while the database web service architecture achieved on average 1.23 queries/sec when PostgreSQL was allowed to use its internal default caching mechanism, and 1.10 queries/sec when it was disabled.

3.2   Experiment Two: Adding Context to Google's Queries

Our second objective for our performance analysis was to compare the efficiency of both architectures in joining information from multiple data sources. To evaluate this, we created a table in the database that matches a student ID to the URL of the faculty that they are enrolled in. The goal was to query the database table for the URL of the faculty that the student is enrolled in. Then use the retrieved URL to filter the results from the search engine to limit the results for the student's search query to a faculty web site. This task was designed to simulate our reference scenario of associating context to a search query.

For the database web service, the task can be summarised as one SQL SE-LECT statement as shown below. In fact, joining additional web services together to query from was as trivial as listing the user-defined functions to the respective web service requesters after the FROM keyword in the SQL SELECT statement. Implementing this task was not as straight-forward in the business logic web services architecture, especially when joining information from more than one data source. Our implementation required loops to iterate through the search engine results to find web pages that match the faculty URL. It was observed that joining information from multiple data sources from within the database required considerably less code to implement than doing the equivalent in the business logic. The benefits of which are reduced complexity and improved maintainability of the source code.

```
SELECT summary, url, snippet, title, directorytitle
   FROM google_search('third year courses') gs
   WHERE EXISTS (SELECT 1 FROM faculty_urls fac
   WHERE fac.sid = 200517790 AND gs.url LIKE fac.url || '%' )
```

We measured the time taken to complete the task of accessing and joining data from a local database table with a web service for a single search query. We then repeated the task joining a second, and third web service in addition to the existing data sources. These tasks were completed ten times each, and the average times for each task are shown in Fig. 2(b). The results show that the database web services architecture performed the tasks up to 50 percent quicker than when the web services requester was integrated directly into the business logic. Also the performance of the database web services architecture did not degrade as much as the business logic web services architecture when additional web services were joined to the query.

4   Scenario-Based Evaluation

It is difficult to define "optimum architectures" since comparisons cannot be abstracted from the circumstances the systems are used in [6]. In fact, according to the Architecture Tradeoff Analysis Method (ATAM) described by Bass et al [6], the architectures must be evaluated based on a set of quality goals. These quality goals can only be based on specific scenarios and on the perceptions that different stakeholders have of them. This method is out of the scope of this paper but we will address three of the ATAM quality goals: usability, performance and scalability.

Performance and scalability are important since the system would perform a large number of interactions with the web services provider. A drawback of the common architecture for integrating web services directly into the business logic is that, if data returned from a web service is connected with the data stored in the database in some way, then there will be an inefficiency caused by the overhead of communications between the database and web service via the business logic component. The database web service architecture does away with this overhead, leaving the database to obtain data from web services directly.

An important limitation of the database web service architecture is that it can only be used to query data-provisioning web services. Data-provisioning web services are services that use SOAP RPC, as oppose to the SOAP Document style. The SOAP Document style is used for "complex web services that deal with the composition of other web services to formulate workflows for business processes" [7]. Business composition web services rely on meta-data for their composition with other web services. A more suitable query language for business composition web services is XQuery, which is "XML based and can process meta-data" [8]. XQuery is suited more towards architectures that integrate web services into the business logic component of a web application.

Most database systems provide support for user-defined functions where developers can add their own implementations to the function catalog of a database system. The advantage of this approach is that the integration of web services is not dependent on extending SQL to support web services. Secondly, access to web services is totally transparent to the application developer, as the invocation of a web service is only a call to an SQL compliant database function.

5   Conclusion

We studied two architectures for integrating web services into database driven web applications. The first architecture presented, integrated a web service requester directly into the business logic component. The second architecture, with the web service requester in the database, consolidates access to multiple data sources through a single data access point. These architectures allow web developers to implement systems that can produce queries to external data sources with contextual information provided by the business logic and internal data sources, as was demonstrated through the use of a reference scenario. We have shown that the database integration is more efficient (Section 3) due to a better coupling of the query and contextual information. This architecture therefore provides an alternative for web developers looking at integrating web services into their database-driven web applications. The main disadvantage (Section 4) is the lack of support, but this is changing due to new products.

References

1. Leake, D.B., Scherle, R.: Towards context-based search engine selection. In: IUI '01: Proceedings of the 6th international conference on Intelligent user interfaces, Santa Fe, New Mexico, United States, ACM Press (2001) 109–112
2. Barros, F.A., Goncaolves, P.F., Santos, T.L.: Providing context to web searches: The use of ontologies to enhance search engine's accuracy. Journal of the Brazilian Computer Society 5 (1998)
3. Geetanjali, A., Kishore, S.: XML Web Services – Professional Projects. Premier Press (2002)
4. Malaika, S., Nelin, C.J., Qu, R., Reinwald, B., Wolfson, D.C.: Db2 and web services. IBM Systems Journal 41 (2002) 666–685
5. Carroll, N., Calvo, R.: Querying data from distributed heterogeneous database systems through web services. In: The Tenth Australian World Wide Web Conference (AUSWEB'04). (2004)
6. Bass, L., Clements, P., Kazman, R.: Software Architecture in Practice, 2/E. Addison Wesley Professional (2003)
7. Curbera, F., Khalef, R., Mukhi, N., Tai, S., Weerawarana, S.: The next step in web services. Communications of the ACM 46 (2003) 29 – 34
8. Hoschek, W.: A unified peer-to-peer database framework for scalable service and resource discovery. In: Lecture Notes in Computer Science - Proceedings of the Third International Workshop on Grid Computing. (2002) 126–144

The Semantic Web Services Tetrahedron: Achieving Integration with Semantic Web Services[*]

Juan Miguel Gómez[1], Mariano Rico[2],
Francisco García-Sánchez[3], and César J. Acuña[4]

[1] DERI Ireland, National University of Ireland, Galway, Ireland
juan.gomez@deri.org
[2] Universidad Autónoma de Madrid
Mariano.rico@uam.es
[3] Universidad de Murcia
frgarcia@um.es
[4] Kybele Research Group, Universidad Rey Juan Carlos
cesar.acuna@urjc.es

Abstract. Web Engineering is going through several major changes. New promising application fields related to the Web such as the Semantic Web and Web Services, and its combination, Semantic Web Services, are transforming the Web from a mere repository of information into a new vehicle for business transactions and information exchange. However, the lack of integration among different Web Applications such as Web Portals and web services is hindering the potential leverage of the Web. In this paper, we present a novel approach for integration in Web engineering based on Semantic Web Services. Our approach enables the combination in a Tetrahedron of a fully-fledged architecture consisting of three layers. An application integration layer, a second layer based on goal-oriented and intelligent user-interaction and finally, a common middleware platform for Semantic Web Services. We describe the implementation of our architecture and its benefits by achieving full integration all over Web applications.

1 Introduction

The Web is changing from a mere repository of information to a new vehicle for business transactions and information exchange. Large organizations are increasingly relying on Web Services technologies for large-scale software development and sharing or exposing of services within an organization. Web Services are loosely coupled software components published, located and invoked across the web. The growing number of Web Services available on the Web raises a new and challenging problem, the integration among heterogeneous applications.

---

[*] This work is founded by the Ministry of Science and Technology of Spain under the project DAWIS (TIC2002-04050-C02-01) and Arcadia (TIC2002-1948); by the European Commission under the projects DIP, Knowledge Web, Ontoweb, SEKT, and SWWS; by Science Foundation Ireland under the DERI-Lion project; and by the Austrian government under the CoOperate programme. We also thanks FUNDESOCO for it support through the project FDS-2004-001-01

D. Lowe and M. Gaedke (Eds.): ICWE 2005, LNCS 3579, pp. 334–339, 2005.
© Springer-Verlag Berlin Heidelberg 2005

The Semantic Web is about adding machine-understandable and machine-processable metadata to Web resources through its key-enabling technology: ontologies. Ontologies are a formal, explicit and shared specification of a conceptualization. The breakthrough of adding semantics to Web Services leads to the Semantic Web Services paradigm. Several Semantic Web Services initiatives such as OWL-S [7], which offers semantic markup based on OWL [2] or the newly established WSMO [9] have recently gained momentum.

However, the problem of integration remains since, to our knowledge, nobody has attempted to define architecture and implementation to integrate several Semantic Web Services from a rich user-interaction perspective i.e. by enabling specifying user request with natural language and presenting the results properly. In this paper, we present a novel approach to address those challenges and solve the integration problem regarding to searching, finding, interacting and integrating Semantic Web Services. Our contribution is an overall solution based on a Tetrahedron composing a fully-fledged architecture consisting of three layers. The presentation layer deals with intelligent user human-interaction through the Jacinta [8] and GODO [3] applications. The intermediate layer is based on WSMX [6] a common middleware platform for Semantic Web Services and finally, an integration layer composed of Web Services and Web Portal wrapper applications.

The remainder of the paper is organized as follows. Section 2 describes the common middleware platform for Semantic Web services. In Section 3 and Section 4, Jacinta and GODO, the components of the presentation layer are introduced. Section 5 presents the integration layer regarding Web Portals and finally, the whole architecture is depicted in Section 6. Conclusions and Related Work are discussed in Section 7.

2   WSMX: Middleware for Semantic Web Services

WSMX is the reference implementation for WSMO, aiming to provide both a test bed for WSMO and to demonstrate the viability of using Semantic Web Services as a means to achieve dynamic inter-operation of Semantic Web Services.

The current architecture of WSMX provides dynamic discovery, mediation, selection and invocation and a simple but complete implementation of these components. In short, its functionality could be summarized as performing discovery, mediation selection and invocation of several Web Services on receiving a user goal specified in WSML [1], the underlying formal language of WSMO. The user goal is matched with the description of a Web Service, then the Web Service is invoked and the result is returned. Presently the WSMX architecture relies on a set of loosely-coupled main components. The core component is the WSMX manager, an event-based driven coordinator managing the other components. The Matchmaker component attempts to match the user goal to a Capability of a Web Service and the Mediator component bridges the gap between different ontologies in the matchmaking process. The Message Parser and Compiler components deal with the understanding and interpretation of WSML messages. Various repositories store descriptions and ontologies of Web Services. Transforming message formats is a task for the Message Adapters and finally, the Invoker component performs the required SOAP request (invocation) to the chosen Web Service.

3 Jacinta: User-Interaction for Semantic Web Services

In principle, the Semantic Web could be viewed as a "web for agents, not for humans", but this is only the case of the B2B aspect. The B2C aspect has to deal with a human user. As a first step in this direction, we proposed the creation of a simple, specialized type of agent, to which we will refer as Jacinta, who mediates between traditional Web Services and end users. This mediator agent is invoked by human users who interact with it using a traditional web browser, so that the mediator (Jacinta) invokes traditional Web Services on behalf of the user and show the results in the most appropriated way. Jacinta can be seen as a Semantic Agent (SA) specialized in interaction with human users. The main objective of Jacinta is not the creation of Semantic Web Services (SWS) or SA but the development of techniques for interacting with the end user. Once SA-SWS will become a reality, as it is case of WSMX (see section 2), Jacinta can be used as a module for Human-Agent interaction. Firstly, dealing with the physical features of the interaction user device such as PDA, mobile phones or other small devices. Secondly, delegating a more sophisticated aesthetic to specialized enterprises so that human user can choose the most appropriated or fashionable.

4 GODO: Goal-Oriented Discovery for Semantic Web Services

As mentioned in Section 2, WSMX [6] enables automatic discovery, selection, mediation, invocation and interoperation of the Semantic Web Services. It accepts *goals* in a specified format as input and returns the Web Services invocation results. GODO [3] can be seen as a software agent that aims at helping users to send their goals to WSMX. It can either accept a text in natural language or define a set of rules to determine the user wishes. Once GODO has inferred what the user wants, it creates the goals WSMX have to execute in order to achieve it.

GODO is composed of six main components. The most important is the *Control Manager*. It supervises the whole process and acts as an intermediary among the other components. The *Language Analyzer* is in charge of understanding the text in natural language with the users' whishes. Another important component is the *Rules Loader*, which loads the rules generated by the rules-based system. It helps users to express exactly what they want. The *Goal Loader* looks for goals either in the WSMO goal repository or in an internal repository with goals templates. These goals will be compared with the users' whishes by the *Goal Matcher*. The goals accepted are then composed by the *Control Manager*. Finally, the *Goal Sender* sends individually the goals to WSMX.

5 WP2WS: Using Web Portals as Web Services

There is still, a huge amount of information and functionality available in the Web in the form of traditional Web Portals. Nowadays lot of research and industrial efforts are focused in web services integration, but they mostly ignore the information and services offered by those traditional Web Portals. That is, only a few Web Portals offer their information and functionality in the form of Web Services (i.e. amazon.com). Achieving full web integration requires taking into account those Web Portals.

WP2WS (Web Portals to Web Services) is a tool which allows the semi-automatic generation of web extraction modules or wrappers. On the one hand, WP2WS generates the modules to automatically extract the Web Portals information and the modules to access the Web Portal services. On the other hand, it generates the WSDL Web Services description to allow the web wrapper to be invoked as a Web Service.

WP2WS follows an ontology-based approach. It uses domain-specific ontologies in conjunction with some heuristics to locate constants present in the Web Portal and constructs objects with them. WP2WS is a semi-automatic tool because while the tool is running, it requests the user for feedback to accurately construct the proper object to data extraction or to functionality access. The user also decides which of the detected data and functionality is going to be available as Web Services. Depending on the selected data and functionalities, WP2WS generates the modules in charge to process the Web Portal in order to use the offered functionality or data.

6   The Tetrahedron Approach: Achieving Integration with Semantic Web Services

The main objective of this work is to integrate and articulate in a fully-fledged architecture the described applications in order to solve the problem of integration of Web Services over the Internet. Our architecture uses WSMX as its middleware technology. It partitions into three well defined layers: presentation, intermediate and integration layer. In Figure 1 the layer model of the integrated architecture is shown.

The first layer in the figure is the presentation layer constituted by GODO and Jacinta. As middleware and facilitator for the integration we find WSMX in the second layer. Finally, WP2WS is sited in the bottom layer, as it has to provide access to the data and functionality provided by the portals and a number of Web Services distributed over the Internet.

For the sake of clarity, we will detail how the user interacts with the architecture and how it solves the user problems regarding integration. The process takes place as follows:

1. Users access GODO. Their have two possibilities for the input. They can either write a sentence in natural language or indicate what they exactly want through a set of rules.
2. It is the GODO task to analyze that input and to determine the goals it has to send to WSMX in order to achieve the user wishes.
3. WSMX receives the goals, process it, and infers the Web Services it has to invoke.
4. Some of the Web Services invoked will be the ones proportioned by WP2WS. They enable us to access to the information contained in several portals distributed on the Internet and also to their functionality.
5. WSMX receives the responses from the Web Services and send them directly to Jacinta.
6. Finally, Jacinta determines the better way this information can be shown to the users, formats it and presents it to the user.

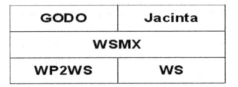

Fig. 1. Our fully-fledged layered architecture

The use of the Tetrahedron metaphor is justified by the interdependence of those applications in terms of the common middleware platform (the common vortex) on top of the three other applications.

7 Conclusions and Related Work

As the use of Web Services grows, the problem for searching, interacting and integrating relevant services will get more acute. In this paper, we proposed a layered architecture based on a Tetrahedron and an effective implementation to integrate Semantic Web Services. While this paper focuses mainly on Semantic Web Services concerns about integration, there is a whole plethora of integration problems in many other domains. The forthcomings of our approach are mainly two: namely the ease of user interaction and application integration. Ease of user interaction, since he can specify in natural language what he is expected to achieve and without worrying about heterogeneity problems and the input and results for interaction are handled in an intelligent and user-friendly manner. Application integration is achieved by means of mediation and interaction with loosely-coupled distributed software components.

There are several other approaches to the ones presented in this paper. In [5], the author points out how the ontology languages of the Semantic Web can lead to more powerful agent-based approaches for using services offered on the Web. The importance of the use of ontologies in agent-to-agent communication has also been highlighted. In [4], the authors outline their experiences of building semantically rich Web Services based on the integration of OWL-S [7] based Web Services and an agent communication language (it is done to separate the domain-specific and the domain-independent aspect of communication).

References

1. Bruijn, J.,Foxvog, D.,Fensel, D.: WSML-Core, Working Draft, 2004..
2. Dean, M. Schreiber, G.editors. *OWL Web Ontology Language Reference*. 2004. W3C Recommendation 10 February 2004.
3. Gómez, J.M, Rico, M., García-Sánchez, F., Martínez-Béjar, R., Bussler, C. (2004) GODO: Goal-driven orchestration for Semantic Web Services. Proceedings of the Workshop on Web Services Modeling Ontology Implementations (WIW 2004). Frankfurt, Alemania, September 29-30, 2004.
4. Gibbins, N., Harris, S., Shadbolt, N. (2003). Agent-based Semantic Web Services. In Proc. of the 12th Int. World Wide Web Conference, May 2003.
5. Hendler, J. (2001). Agents and the Semantic Web. IEEE Intelligent Systems, 16(2): 30-37, March/April 2001.

6. Oren, E., Zaremba, M., Moran M.: Overview and Scope of WSMX. WSMX Working Draft, 2004. Available from http://www.wsmo.org/2004/d13/d13.0/v0.1/20040611/.
7. OWL-S: Semantic Markup for Web Services. http://www.daml.org/owls
8. Rico, M., Castells, P. Jacinta: a mediator agent for human-agent interaction in semantic web services. In Proc. The Semantic Web - International Semantic Web Conference (ISWC) 2004. Selected Posters., Hiroshima, Japan, November 2004.
9. Roman, D. Lausen, H., Keller, U.: Web Service Modeling Ontology Standard. WSMO Working Draft v02, 2004. Available from http://www.wsmo.org/2004/d2/v02/20040306/

Secure Web Forms with Client-Side Signatures

Mikko Honkala and Petri Vuorimaa

Telecommunications Software and Multimedia Laboratory,
Helsinki University of Technology,
P.O. Box 5400 FIN-02015 HUT Finland
{Mikko.Honkala,Petri.Vuorimaa}@tml.hut.fi

Abstract. The World Wide Web is evolving from a platform for information access into a platform for interactive services. The interaction of the services is provided by forms. Some of these services, such as banking and e-commerce, require secure, non-repudiable transactions. This paper presents a novel scheme for extending the current Web forms language, XForms, with secure client-side digital signatures, using the XML Signatures language. The requirements for the scheme are derived from representative use cases. A key requirement, also for legal validity of the signature, is the reconstruction of the signed form, when validating the signature. All the resources, referenced by the form, including client-side default stylesheets, have to be included within the signature. Finally, this paper presents, as a proof of concept, an implementation of the scheme and a related use case. Both are included in an open-source XML browser, X-Smiles.

1 Introduction

Commerce and communication tasks, such as ordering items from a shop or using e-mail are becoming popular in the World Wide Web (WWW), and therefore WWW is transforming from a platform for information access into a platform for interactive services [1]. Unfortunately, some of the technologies used today are outdated and, infact, were not originally designed for the complex use case scenarios of today's applications, for instance, secure transactions.

The Wold Wide Web Consortium (W3C) has recently developed a successor to HyperText Markup Language (HTML) forms, called XForms [2]. It removes need for scripts from the forms and separates the form's model from the presentation. It can use any XML grammar to describe the content of the form.

Digital signatures are a primary way of creating legally binding transactions in information networks, such as WWW. Unfortunately, digital signatures are hard to apply to HTML [3]. Using eXtensible Markup Language (XML) helps, since a conforming XML processor is not allowed to accept non-well-formed XML. Also, W3C and Internet Engineering Task Force (IETF) have specified a standard way of signing XML data, i.e., XML Signature.

XML Signatures is a language, which provides the necessary framework for encoding, serializing, and transmitting signatures in XML format. The main focus is signing XML, but it can also function as the signature description language

D. Lowe and M. Gaedke (Eds.): ICWE 2005, LNCS 3579, pp. 340–351, 2005.

for any ASCII or binary data. In that case, the additional data is included in the signature as a reference. [4].

Why are client-side signatures needed? In order to be legally binding, the signature must be created in a secure way using the private key of the signer. Usually, this can be done in a tamper-proof smart card or a similar device. Because of this requirement, it is not possible to create the signature at the server side along with the other application logic.

Why to integrate signatures into XForms? Signature is usually attached in data produced by the user, not by the author, and XForms is a technology for collecting user input. Signature must be serialized and transmitted to the receiver. XForms submission is a good way of submitting digital signatures encoded in XML.

How to make signatures over forms legally binding? Signatures can be made legally binding in many countries, if the signing process fulfills some requirements. A basic requirement, apart from the technical requirements for the signature, is that the signer must see everything that she is signing. Also, it must be possible to reconstruct the document that the signer has signed later.

1.1 What You See Is What You Sign

An important, but often overlooked, property of a signing application is the capability to express the signature over everything that was represented to the user. This principle is usually called "What you see is what you sign" (WYSIWYS). To accomplish this, it is normally necessary to secure as exactly as practical the information that was presented to that user [3]. This can be done by literally signing what was presented, such as the screen images shown to a user. However, this may result in data, which is difficult for subsequent software to manipulate. Instead, one can sign the data along with whatever filters, style sheets, client profile or other information that affects its presentation. [4]

1.2 Related Work

Previous work in the field includes, e.g., Extensible Forms Description Language (XFDL) [3]. In XFDL, all information related to the form is included in a single XML file, including form definition, styling information, form data, and even binary attachments, and the signature is created over this single file. This approach does not fit well to signing Web pages consisting of decoupled resources, such as stylesheets and images, which is the target for this paper.

There is also research on specific algorithms on determining whether unsigned areas are visually overlapping with signed areas [5]. This is required, if signatures over a partial form are allowed. Unfortunately, this approach requires certain type of layout, and thus it cannot easily be extended to languages with different layout models, such as SVG (absolute layout) and XHTML (flow and absolute layout), or different modalities, such as Voice XML (speech modality).

2   Research Problem

The research problem of this paper is *how to create legally binding secure services in the WWW*. Secure transmission technologies, such as Secure Sockets Layer (SSL), are already widely used, but they do not support the notion of a client-side signature. Thus, the main focus is to enable the services on the WWW to allow digital signatures over the user's input. This is achieved by allowing XForms forms to be signed by the user. A subproblem is to ensure that the user has a clear understanding what she is signing (WYSIWYS). Another important subproblem is to ensure the full reconstruction of the signed form, when validating the signature.

2.1   Use Cases

We have identified three basic use cases that should be supported by the scheme:

USE CASE 1, Single form: In the most basic use case, the user downloads a form, which is to be signed. She fills the form and initiates the signing process. Within the signing process there is the possibility to select the key, which is used in the signing. When the form is signed, she submits the form. The form can, for instance, be an email that she fills and signs before sending.

USE CASE 2, Form approving: When the first user has signed the form, the form is sent to her supervisor, who adds some data, and then signs it with her own key. The supervisor's signature should also cover the already signed portion of the form, since she approves also the data signed by the first user.

USE CASE 3, Multiparty form: Third use case, a joint insurance claim filing, is depicted in Fig. 1. Multiple parties are filing a single insurance claim. It should be possible to add new parties and attachments, but each of the parties signature must not allow changes in the core information of the claim form.

In all use cases 1-3, it must be possible to verify the resulting signature's integrity at any future time, and any change to the signed form, including all referenced items (e.g., stylesheets, images, etc.), must invalidate the signature.

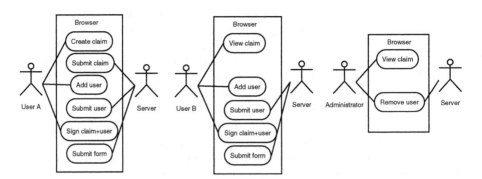

Fig. 1. Use case 3: Multiparty form

2.2   Requirements

From the basic use cases, the following requirements for the XML Signature and XForms integration were gathered:

Signature security. *Technical requirements for secure signatures.*
 Client-side. The signature must be generated client-side so that the user can check the signature validity before submitting. Also, support for signing with secure smart card must be supported.
 Common algorithms. The signature must be generated using common, trusted, algorithms for maximum security.
 Signed form reconstruction. It must be possible to reconstruct the signed form in case of dispute.
Signature coverage. *Which parts of the form need to be signed (WYSIWYS).*
 User input. The data user inputted through the form.
 UI. The UI document, which describes the layout of the form.
 All referenced data. Stylesheets, images, objects, applets, scripts, schemas, external instances, etc.
 The user agent info. Information about the user agent.
Complex signature support. *Support for complex signing scenarios.*
 Partial signature. Support signing only part of the form.
 Multiple signatures. Support multiple signatures within one form.
Form language integration.
 Ease of authoring. Provide as easy syntax as possible for authors.
 Ease of implementation. Use of off-the-shelf libraries should be possible.
 Modality and host language independence. The design should be independent of modality and host language.

An XForms form is independent of its presentation, which fulfills the **Modality and host language independence** requirement. As a language, XForms requires a host language in order to realize the presentation. It must be kept in mind, that the layout strategy (e.g., SVG, XHTML) or even the modality (e.g., Voice XML) is not fixed when using XForms. That is why the goals of this paper differ, e.g., from [5], which expects a box layout, and based on that is able to have fine-grained author control over the signature.

3   Design

We considered two different approaches to the XForms XML Signature integration, keeping in mind the requirements above. First option was the addition of new submission filter, which would create the signature at submission time. The second option, which was chosen, was to create a new XForms compatible action for the signature processing. This is more flexible than the submission filter, and it fits better to the XForms processing model, thus fulfilling the **Form language integration** requirement. The only drawback is that the author must explicitly have a placeholder in the XForms instance data, where to store the signature.

Since XForms can represent dependencies between fields in the form, it is hard to implement the **Partial signature** requirement at the client side, while fulfilling the WYSIWYS paradigm. Because of this, in our scheme, the whole form is always signed with the related resources, and no signatures over a partial form are allowed. Thus, the **Partial signature** requirement must be fulfilled at the server-side. Fortunately, XForms provides functionality to make this task easier, and we demonstrate this with an implemented use case in Sect. 5.1.

3.1   Process Description

The overall process in the scheme can can be divided into three steps: 1) Retrieving and filling the form, 2) attaching the digital signature into the form, and submitting the signed form into the server, and 3) validating the submitted form data and the signature. This is depicted in Fig. 2.

There are four main actors involved in the process: a) *the user* fills and signs the form, b) *the browser* displays the form, and creates the signature, c) *the smart card* signs the hash of the signed form, and d) *the server* validates the submitted form data and the signature. If a lesser security level is appropriate, the hash can be signed using the browser instead of the smart card.

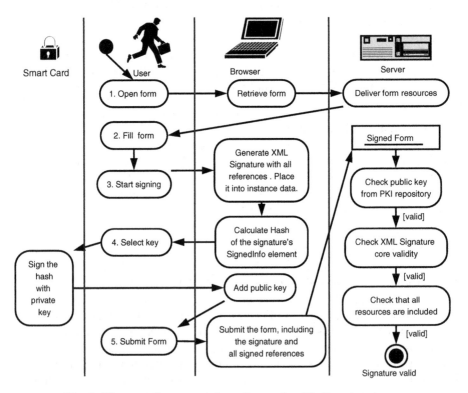

Fig. 2. The overall process of creating and validating signatures

3.2 Signature Creation with XForms Extension "sign"

XForms language was extended with a namespace *"http://www.xsmiles.org/2002 /signature"* and a single element *sign* in that namespace. The element integrates to XForms processing model in two ways: first, it is an XML Events action, similar to *xforms:send* [2]. Second, it uses the XForms single node binding to specify where to store the signature.

Attribute: to an XPath expression specifying the node, under which the signed content is placed. All previous children of that node are destroyed. The result of the evaluation must be a document or a element node. If the node is the document node, then the content is placed as the document element.

Operation is as follows:
The signature operation consists of the following steps, each of which must follow XML Signatures' *core generation* rules [4]. See Fig. 2 for overall description of the process.

1. Disable any user stylesheets. These stylesheets might prevent some parts of the form from displaying.
2. If the document is not a top-level document (e.g., is inside a frameset or embedded in another document), abort signature creation. This ensures that the user has clear view of the complete content he will be signing.
3. Evaluate the XPath expression in @*to* attribute, using the XForms' default context node (first model, first instance, document element) as the context node and context nodeset, and the sign element as the namespace context element, and XForms functions in scope. The node *"target"* is the first node in the resulting nodeset. If the result is not a nodeset, or the first node is not an element or document node, the processing stops.
4. Remove all child nodes of *"target"* node.
5. Create a signature with the following references:
   – Always create an enveloping signature.
   – Create an <dsig:Object id="x"> and <dsig:Reference URI="#x"> elements for each live instance data, and copy to contents of the live instance inside the object element. The id 'x' must be replaced by an arbitrary unique id.
   – Create <dsig:Object id="y"> and <dsig:Reference URI="#y"> elements for all user agent and user stylesheets, which have been used for displaying the form, and copy the stylesheets as the text content of the root node of the object. The id 'y' must be replaced by an arbitrary unique id.
6. Create detached references to all URLs referenced by the host document:
   – The host document
   – All referenced URLs separately: images, objects, applets, stylesheets, scripts, XForms external instances, xinclude, xlink, XSLT, etc.
7. Create a valid signature over all the references with the users private key.
8. Create a valid dsig:KeyInfo element containing the signers public key.
9. Place the dsig:Signature element as the only child of the *"target"* node.

Example of the usage of the signature action is below. The XForms trigger element contains the sign element, which creates an enveloping signature to an empty instance with id "signature", when the DOMActivate event is caught, for instance, when the user activates the trigger.

```
<trigger>
  <label>Sign message</label>
  <sign:sign to="instance('signature')/.." ev:event="DOMActivate"/>
</trigger>
```

Note that all resources that are used to render the document must be included in the signature. This includes images, objects, applets, stylesheets, scripts, XForms external instances, xinclude, xlink, XSLT, etc. The resources that are fetched using an get operation with an URL, are added as detached references.

The user agent has its own default CSS stylesheets. The signature must contain all stylesheets that have been applied when the page has been displayed. Since the default stylesheets cannot be identified with an URL, they must be included as inline objects within the signature.

3.3   Event: "signature-done"

In order to notify the form after the signature has finished, a notification DOM event *signature-done* was added. It's target is the sign action element. It bubbles, is cancellable, and does not have any context information. The signature-done event does not have any default action. It allows the creation of XML Events listeners for a certain sign action element.

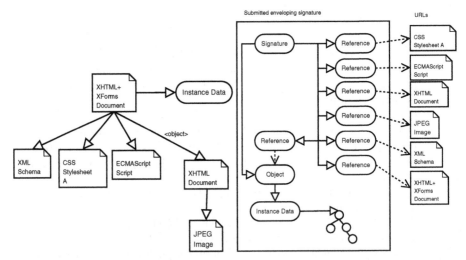

Fig. 3. Left: A Document with references. Right: The signature over the document

3.4   Signature Validation

The validation of the signature has the following steps (cf. Fig. 2 for a general description of the process):

1. Find the Signature element from the submitted instance data.
2. Read the public key from the KeyInfo element and check from a Key repository that it corresponds the users identity. If it does not, abort the validation process.
3. Validate the Signature element according to the XML Signatures' core validation rules [4]. If the validation fails, abort the validation process.
4. Do application-specific validation of all resources. For detached references, this is simple: just check that the URL is correct (the hash and the signature has been checked in the previous step already). For enveloped resources, application-specific logic must be included in the validation. For instance, XForms calculations, defined in the form, should be run in the server-side, in order to check the correctness of the submitted instance data. If any check fails, abort the validation process.
5. The Signature is accepted if none of the above checks fails.

4   Implementation

The first author has implemented the current complete implementation with the processing described in this paper. It is based on an earlier experimental implementation, which was done in co-operation with Heng Guo [6].

4.1   X-Smiles XML Browser

The signature processor was integrated with the XForms processor in the X-Smiles browser [7]. X-Smiles is a modular XML browser, which allows registering different components for different XML namespaces, thus allowing easy creation of XML "plugins", which are called Markup Language Functional Components (MLFC) [8]. The sign element and it's namespace were created as a new MLFC. Note that the signature MLFC is purely a processing component, i.e., it does not have an associated UI rendering component.

4.2   Implementation Cost when Integrating
to the XForms Processor

A requirement for building modular software is to decouple components and use well-defined interfaces for inter-component communication. In the integration of XML Signature and XForms processors, we used the DOM interfaces as much as possible. The signature element is part of the UI DOM tree, so it can naturally access the tree with the XML and XForms DOM access. A DOM 3 XPath component for XPath evaluation, extended with XForms functions, is used by the @to attribute. We have decided that the XForms context node inheritance rules do not apply to the sign element, since it is not in the XForms namespace.

The XML signature is created using the *Apache XML Security 1.1 for Java* library[1]. This library is a complete XML Signature implementation. It is also responsible for creation of the external references in the signature.

The user agent must provide an interface to access the list of resources, which were loaded for the form being signed. Some of these resources can be referenced via an universal URL (such as the images), while others are local to the processor. Both must be provided through this interface.

5   Results

5.1   Use Case: Joint Insurance Claim

We implemented a joint insurance claim application, which implements the use case *Multiparty form*, using the proposed scheme. The application consists of one XHTML+XForms page and a server-side process (servlet).

In the application, it is the responsibility of the servlet to filter the instance data so that, at each step, the correct parts of the insurance data are transmitted to the client. For instance, since the signatures are not related to each other (remember that it must be possible to add new signers or remove them without affecting the validity of the other signatures), the servlet filters out the other user's data and signatures for the "add user" view. Similarly, in the verify view, only the related users' data is included. Finally, in the "view claim" view, nothing is filtered out, resulting in the complete view of the claim (cf. Fig. 4). The filtering is implemented using simple XPath statements in the servlet.

The use case and it's source code are included in the X-Smiles distribution. The application was created as a Java servlet. The main logic of the servlet was to store the signatures and the form data and to filter the data according to the current view of the user. The servlet's Java files have 1300 lines, half of which are general utility functions, which can be reused in similar applications.

5.2   Memory Requirements

The XML Security library was stripped down in order to facilitate the integration to the X-Smiles browser distribution. The XML encryption features were removed from the library. The final storage size of the library is 331 KB. The storage size of classes in X-Smiles, related to the implementation, is 25 KB. The total storage size is then 356 KB, which is small enough to be added to the binary distribution of X-Smiles, which is about 8 000 KB of size.

5.3   Applicability to HTML Forms

The presented scheme works for XForms forms. XForms language has certain attributes, which make applying digital signatures easier. The main attributes

---

[1] XML Security for Java and C++, Software, Apache Foundation. http://xml.apache.org/security/

Fig. 4. Viewing the claim and attaching new signers

are the lack of scripting and a pure XML format. Also, the state of the form is reflected exclusively in the instance data, and not in the presentation DOM.

The scheme could be extended to cover XHTML or even HTML forms as well. XHTML forms without scripting is the easiest case; the outgoing message (e.g., the URL encoded form submission), needs to be signed as a enveloped binary reference. The XHTML document can be signed as an detached reference, either as XML or binary.

Scripting makes the case a bit more complex, since the state of the form is captured in the presentation DOM. The signature in that case, should include the serialized DOM at the moment the signature was created. XHTML serialization is rather straight-forward, but HTML serialization is more complex, foremost because browsers tend to accept and fix ill-formed HTML content, making machine-validation of the serialized HTML difficult, even impossible.

5.4   Complex Signatures

Use case 1, *Single form*, presented in Sect. 2.1, can directly be solved using our proposed extension. We have demonstrated use case 3, *Multiparty form* using a combination of our extension and a server side process, where the server side process has to filter the data sent to the client according to the current view. Use case 2, *Form approving* can be solved in a similar fashion, where the server side process serves the same data in slightly modified form for different signing parties. For instance, the first party is allowed to input the data in the form, and sign it, while for the supervisor, the data and the signature of the first users just shown, and he is only allowed to create a signature on top of it. Validating the signatures in case of a dispute is still straightforward.

5.5   Security Analysis

WWW has an open model, where any compatible user agent can connect and use internet services. This adds extra requirements for the security model of the scheme. First assumption is that the user trusts the user agent, which she is using. That means, that the user agent itself cannot be hostile, and for instance, show the user different content to what it signs. Second assumption is that a key distribution scheme, such as PKI, is used. This way, the server can be sure about the identity of the signer. The signature itself should be done on a smart card or similar device, which does not allow exporting the private key. The scheme presented here detects if a third party inserts content into the form. The signature over this kind of form does not validate, since the server detects a faulty hash for the detached reference.

CSS layout model allows re-flowing the content based on the browser windows width. Also, it allows the use of layers (i.e., absolute and relative blocks), thus potentially hiding content of the form for some browser window widths. Therefore, the author of the form should check the form with all screen widths. Best option is not to use layers in the layout at all. Additional security could be provided by adding a screen dump of the form as an enveloped reference.

6   Conclusion

This paper describes a successful research and implementation of secure Web based services. A extension was added to the XForms language, allowing authors to add digital signing features to XForms applications, without the use of scripting or other client-side languages. The extension was implemented in the X-Smiles XML browser, and a demonstration application was created. The application is included in the online demos of the browser distribution.

After analyzing three use cases and the XForms language, four groups of requirements for the signature integration were gathered: *Signature security*, *Signature coverage*, *Complex signature support*, and *Form language integration*. These requirements lead to design of one declarative action called *sign* and one DOM event called *signature-done*. The action creates a enveloping signature that covers all information related to the form, thus fulfilling the *WYSIWYS* paradigm.

The integration is therefore quite simple at the XML language level. This is good, since it provides ease of authoring. The integration was implemented in a real user agent, X-Smiles, in order to asses the implementation cost of the integration. The results from the integration is that only few hidden properties of the XForms processor need to be exposed, i.e., the integration can be done at the DOM level. The user agent must provide an interface to determine the different resources, which are related to a document that is presented to the user. These resources include images, stylesheets, etc. Some of these resources are never available in the DOM (e.g., the user agent default stylesheet), and therefore they should all be exposed using the same interface.

7   Future Work

The scheme presented in this paper always creates enveloping signatures, and it uses the default signature and canonicalization algorithms defined in the XML Signature specification. While this solves most of the use cases, sometimes it is needed to have better control over the type of signature (e.g., enveloped instead of enveloping) and the signature algorithms. This is left as a future work item.

In the implementation, the user agent information is not included in the signature, which can be a problem when disputes are being solved. A possible future work item would be to include some information about the user agent, which was used to create the signature. One possibility would be to include the Composite Capabilities / Preferences Profile (CC/PP) description of the client as one of the signed objects. CC/PP is not currently very widely adopted, and therefore a simpler scheme could be needed.

Some processing markup languages allow dereferencing external URLs and placing the content of the URL inline within the host document. Examples are XInclude and XHTML 2.0 @src attribute. It is an open question whether to process these languages and place the additional content within the host document or add the referenced URLs as external references in the signature.

Currently, the implementation does not check whether the document, which is to be signed, is a top-level window or not.

Acknowledgment

This research was funded by the TEKES GO-MM project to whose partners and researchers the authors would like to express their gratitude. We would also like to thank Mr. Pablo Cesar for many valuable comments about this paper.

References

1. Hostetter, M., Kranz, D., Seed, C., C. Terman, S.W.: Curl, a gentle slope language for the web. World Wide Web Journal (1997)
2. Dubinko, M., et al. (eds.): XForms 1.0. W3C Recommendation (2003)
3. Blair, B., Boyer, J.: XFDL: creating electronic commerce transaction records using xml. In: WWW '99: Proceeding of the eighth international conference on World Wide Web, Elsevier North-Holland, Inc. (1999) 1611–1622
4. Bartel, M., et.al.: XML-Signature syntax and processing. W3C Recommendation (2002)
5. Boyer, J.M.: Bulletproof business process automation: securing XML forms with document subset signatures. In: Proceedings of the 2003 ACM workshop on XML security, ACM Press (2003) 104–111
6. Guo, H.: Implementation of secure web forms by using XML Signature and XForms. Master's thesis, Helsinki University of Technology (2003)
7. Vuorimaa, P., Ropponen, T., von Knorring, N., Honkala, M.: A java based XML browser for consumer devices. In: 17th ACM Symposium on Applied Computing, Madrid, Spain (2002)
8. Pihkala, K., Honkala, M., Vuorimaa, P.: A browser framework for hybrid XML documents. In: Internet and Multimedia Systems and Applications, IMSA 2002, IMSA (2002)

Robust and Simple Authentication Protocol for Secure Communication on the Web

Eun-Jun Yoon[1], Woo-Hun Kim[2], and Kee-Young Yoo[1,*]

[1] Department of Computer Engineering, Kyungpook National University,
Daegu 702-701, Republic of Korea
`ejyoon@infosec.knu.ac.kr, yook@knu.ac.kr`
[2] Department of Information Security, Kyungpook National University,
Daegu 702-701, Republic of Korea
`whkim@infosec.knu.ac.kr`

Abstract. User authentication is an important part of security, along with confidentiality and integrity, for systems that allow remote access over untrustworthy networks, such as the Internet Web environment. In 2005, Chien-Wang-Yang (CWY) pointed out that Chien-Jan's ROSI protocol required state synchronization between the client and the server, and then its state-synchronization property was vulnerable to the Denial of Service (DoS) attack. Furthermore, they proposed an improved protocol that conquered the weaknesses and extended its key agreement functions, and improved the server's performance. Nevertheless, CWY's improved ROSI protocol does not provide perfect forward secrecy and is vulnerable to a Denning-Sacco attack. Accordingly, the current paper demonstrates that CWY's protocol does not provide perfect forward secrecy and is susceptible to a Denning-Sacco attack. We then present an enhanced protocol to isolate such problems.

Keyword: Cryptography, Security, Authentication, Smart card, Key establishment, Forward Secrecy, Denning-Sacco attack

1 Introduction

Perhaps the environment in which authentication is the most crucial is the Internet Web environment. Therefore, user authentication is an important part of security, along with confidentiality and integrity, for systems that allow remote access over untrustworthy networks, such as the Internet Web environment. Every day, there are vast numbers of authentication processes taking place. From logging in to a corporate system or database, reading your e-mail, making a purchase online, or performing a financial transaction, each of these common tasks require an authentication phase. As such, a remote password authentication scheme authenticates the legitimacy of users over an insecure channel, where the password is often regarded as a secret shared between the remote system and the user. Based on knowledge of the password, the user can create and send a

---

* Corresponding author. Tel.: +82-53-950-5553; Fax: +82-53-957-4846

D. Lowe and M. Gaedke (Eds.): ICWE 2005, LNCS 3579, pp. 352–362, 2005.

valid login message to a remote system in order to gain access. Meanwhile, the remote system also uses the shared password to check the validity of the login message and authenticates the user. However, a password-based protocol is vulnerable to a password guessing attack, replay attack, stolen-verifier problem, denial of service (DoS) attack or a forgery attack [1][2]. These attacks affect the integrity of the SAS protocol [3], the revised SAS-1 [4], the revised SAS-2 [4] or the OSPA protocol [5].

ISO 10202 standards have been established for the security of financial transaction systems using integrated circuit cards (IC cards or smart cards). A smart card originates from an IC memory card used which has been in the industry for about 10 years [6][7]. The main characteristics of a smart card are its small size and low-power consumption. Generally speaking, a smart card contains a microprocessor which can quickly manipulate logical and mathematical operations, RAM which is used as a data or instruction buffer, and ROM which stores the user's secret key and the necessary public parameters and algorithmic descriptions of the executing programs. The merits of a smart card for password authentication are its high simplicity and its efficiency regarding of the log-in and authentication processes.

Based upon low-cost smart cards that support only simple hashing operations, ROSI [8] is a highly efficient password-based authentication protocol. Its simplicity, resistance to existing known attacks and high performance make it much more attractive than its counterparts. In 2005, Chien-Wang-Yang [9], however, pointed out that the ROSI protocol requires state synchronization between the client and the server, and then its state-synchronization property makes it vulnerable to a Denial of Service (DoS) attack. In addition, they proposed an improved protocol that overcomes its weaknesses, extends its key agreement functions, and improves the server's overall performance.

Nevertheless, CWY's improved ROSI protocol does not provide perfect forward secrecy [10] and is vulnerable to a Denning-Sacco attack [11]. Accordingly, the current paper demonstrates that CWY's protocol does not provide perfect forward secrecy and susceptible to a Denning-Sacco attack, where an attacker can easily obtain legal client's secret value. We then present an enhanced protocol to isolate such problems.

The remainder of the paper is organized as follows: Section 2 defines the security properties. Section 3 briefly reviews CWY's improved ROSI protocol, then Section 4 demonstrates the security weaknesses of CWY's protocol. The proposed ROSI protocol is presented in Section 5, while Section 6 discusses the security and efficiency of the proposed protocol. The conclusion is given in Section 7.

2   Security Properties

The following security properties of the authentication protocols should be considered [1].

(1) **Guessing attack:** A guessing attack involves an adversary (randomly or systematically) trying long-term private keys (e.g. user password or server secret key), one at a time, in the hope of finding the correct private key. Ensuring long-term private keys chosen from a sufficiently large space can reduce exhaustive searches. Most users, however, select passwords from a small subset of the full password space. Such weak passwords with low entropy are easily guessed by using the so-called dictionary attack.

(2) **Replay attack:** A replay attack is an offensive action in which an adversary impersonates or deceives another legitimate participant through the reuse of information obtained in a protocol.

(3) **Stolen-verifier attack:** In most applications, the server stores verifiers of users' passwords (e.g. hashed passwords) instead of the clear text of passwords. The stolen-verifier attack means that an adversary who steals the password-verifier from the server can use it *directly* to masquerade as a legitimate user in a user authentication execution.

In addition, the following security properties of session key agreement protocols should be considered since they are often desirable in some environments [1].

(1) **Denning-Sacco attack:** The Dennig-Sacco attack is where an attacker compromises an old session key and tries to find a long-term private key (e.g. user password or server private key) or other session keys.

(2) **Implicit key authentication:** Implicit key authentication is the property obtained when identifying a party based on a shared session key, which assures that no other entity than the specifically identified entity can gain access to the session key.

(3) **Explicit key authentication:** Explicit key authentication is the property obtained when both implicit key authentication and key confirmation hold.

(4) **Mutual authentication:** Mutual authentication means that both the client and server are authenticated to each other within the same protocol.

(5) **Perfect forward secrecy:** Perfect forward secrecy means that if a long-term private key (e.g. user password or server private key) is compromised, this does not compromise any earlier session keys.

3   Review of CWY's ROSI Protocol

This section briefly reviews CWY's ROSI protocol. Some of the notations used in this paper are defined as follows:

- ID: public user identity of client.
- PW: secret and possibly weak user password.
- x: server's strong secret key.
- N_c, N_s: random nonce chosen by the client and server, respectively.
- p, q: large prime numbers p and q such that $q|p - 1$.

- g: generator with order q in the Galois Field $GF(p)$, in which the Diffie-Hellman problem is considered hard.
- c, s: session-independent random exponents $\in [1, q-1]$ chosen by the client and server, respectively.
- K: shared fresh session key computed by the client and server.
- $h(\cdot)$: secure one-way hash function.
- $||$: concatenation operation.
- $\oplus$: bit-wise XOR operation.

CWY's ROSI protocol consists of two phases; the registration phase, and the authentication and key establishment phase.

3.1 Registration Phase

(1) The user submits his ID and PW to the server through a secure channel.
(2) The server issues the user a smart card that stores $R = h(x||ID) \oplus PW$ and $h(\cdot)$.

3.2 Authentication and Key Establishment Phase

The user who has obtained the server-issued smart card can perform the following steps to log on to the server and establish a fresh session key with the server. CWY's authentication and key establishment phase is illustrated in Figure 1.

(1) Client→Server: ID, c_1, c_2
    The user inserts his smart card into the terminal and inputs his ID and PW. The card then extracts $h(x||ID)$ by computing $R \oplus PW$, chooses a random nonce N_c and computes $c_1 = h(x||ID) \oplus N_c$ and $c_2 = h(ID||N_c)$. The card sends (ID, c_1, c_2) to the server.
(2) Server→Client: c_3, c_4
    Based on the received ID, the server computes $h(x||ID)$, extracts the nonce N_c by computing $c_1 \oplus h(x||ID)$ and verifies the data by checking whether $h(ID||N_c)$ equals c_2. If the verification fails, then the server stops the authentication; otherwise, it chooses a random nonce N_s and computes the session key $K = h(h(x||ID)||N_c||N_s)$, $c_3 = h(N_c) \oplus N_s$ and $c_4 = h(K||N_c||N_s)$. The server finally sends (c_3, c_4) to the client.
(3) Client→Server: c_5
    Upon receiving (c_3, c_4), the client first derives $N_s = c_3 \oplus h(N_c)$, computes the session key $K = h(h(x||ID)||N_c||N_s)$ and then verifies whether $h(K||N_c||N_s)$ equals the received c_4. If the verification fails, it stops the authentication; otherwise, it sends back $c_5 = h(N_s||N_c||K)$ to the server.
(4) Upon receiving the data c_5, the server verifies whether c_5 equals $h(N_s||N_c||K)$. If the verification fails, it refuses the request; otherwise, mutual authentication is completed and the fresh session key K is confirmed.

Shared information: Hash function $h(\cdot)$.
Information held by Client: Identity ID. Password PW. Smart card.
Information held by Server: Secret key x.

Client		**Server**
Input ID, PW		
Extract $h(x\|\|ID) = R \oplus PW$		
Choose N_c		
Compute $c_1 = h(x\|\|ID) \oplus N_c$		
Compute $c_2 = h(ID\|\|N_c)$	$\xrightarrow{ID, c_1, c_2}$	Compute $h(x\|\|ID)$
		Extract $N_c = c_1 \oplus h(x\|\|ID)$
		Compute $h(ID\|\|N_c)$
		Verify $h(ID\|\|N_c) \overset{?}{=} c_2$
		Choose N_s
		Compute $K = h(h(x\|\|ID)\|\|N_c\|\|N_s)$
		Compute $c_3 = h(N_c) \oplus N_s$
Extract $N_s = c_3 \oplus h(N_c)$	$\xleftarrow{c_3, c_4}$	Compute $c_4 = h(K\|\|N_c\|\|N_s)$
Compute $K = h(h(x\|\|ID)\|\|N_c\|\|N_s)$		
Verify $h(K\|\|N_c\|\|N_s) \overset{?}{=} c_4$		
Compute $c_5 = h(N_s\|\|N_c\|\|K)$	$\xrightarrow{c_5}$	Verify $h(N_s\|\|N_c\|\|K) \overset{?}{=} c_5$

Fresh session key $K = h(h(x\|\|ID)\|\|N_c\|\|N_s)$

Fig. 1. CWY's authentication and key establishment phase

4   Cryptanalysis of CWY's ROSI Protocol

This section shows that CWY's improved ROSI protocol does not provide perfect forward secrecy and is vulnerable to a Denning-Sacco attack.

4.1   Perfect Forward Secrecy Problem

Perfect forward secrecy is a very important security requirement in evaluating a strong protocol. A protocol with perfect forward secrecy assures that even if one entity's long-term key is compromised, it will never reveal any session keys used before. For example, the well-known Diffie-Hellman key agreement scheme [3] can provide perfect forward secrecy. CWY's ROSI protocol, however, does not provide it because once the secret key x of the server is disclosed, all previous fresh session keys K will also be opened and hence previous communication messages will be learned.

In the CWY's ROSI protocol, suppose an attacker E obtains the secret key x from the compromised server and intercepts transmitted values (ID, c_1, c_2, c_3), then E can compute $h(x\|\|ID)$ and extract the client's random nonce N_c by computing $c_1 \oplus h(x\|\|ID)$. Using the extracted N_c, E can also extract server's random nonce N_s by computing $c_3 \oplus h(N_c)$. Finally, E can compute the session key $K = h(h(x\|\|ID)\|\|N_c\|\|N_s)$ by using $h(x\|\|ID)$, N_c and N_s. Obviously, CWY's ROSI protocol does not provide perfect forward secrecy.

4.2   Denning-Sacco Attack

This attack arises from the fact that the compromise of a random nonce or fresh session key enables the protocol to be compromised. Such attacks have long been known. Please refer the Denning-Sacco attack in [1]. If N_c becomes known to an attacker E, then E can use this knowledge to impersonate the client to the server in this instance of the protocol. This is a typical and uncontroversial assumption for an authentication protocol; however, we show below that if such a random nonce N_c is ever disclosed, even long after the protocol is executed, then a serious attack is possible.

In the CWY's ROSI protocol, suppose E has intercepted messages c_1 of the protocol and learned the random nonce N_c in c_1 by some means. Then, knowledge of N_c will enable $h(x||ID)$ to be discovered from c_1 by computing $c_1 \oplus N_c$ (since N_c included in c_1 is known to E). Compromise of the user's secret value $h(x||ID)$ will enable the attacker to impersonate the client freely. For example, E chooses a random nonce N_e and computes $c_1^* = h(x||ID) \oplus N_e$ and $c_2^* = h(ID||N_e)$, by using the compromised user's secret value $h(x||ID)$. If E sends these modified values (ID, c_1^*, c_2^*) to the server, then the server will authenticate E by performing the authentication and key establishment phase. Therefore, CWY's ROSI protocol is obviously insecure against a Denning-Sacco attack.

5   Proposed ROSI Protocol

This section proposes an improved ROSI protocol by providing perfect forward secrecy in order to overcome the above mentioned problems with CWY's protocol. The improved protocol also consists of two phases; the registration phase, and the authentication and key establishment phase.

5.1   Registration Phase

(1) The user submits his ID and PW to the server through a secure channel.
(2) The server issues the user a smart card that stores $R = h(x||ID) \oplus PW$, $h(\cdot)$, p and g.

5.2   Authentication and Key Establishment Phase

The user who has obtained the server-issued smart card can perform the following steps to log on to the server and establish fresh session keys with the server. The proposed authentication and key establishment phase is illustrated in Figure 2.

(1) Client→Server: ID, c_1, c_2
    The user inserts his smart card into the terminal and inputs his ID and PW. The card then extracts $h(x||ID)$ by computing $R \oplus PW$, chooses a random exponent $c \in Z_p^*$ and computes $c_1 = g^c \pmod{p}$ and $c_2 = h(h(x||ID)||g^c)$. The card sends (ID, c_1, c_2) to the server.

Shared information: Generator g of Z_p^* of prime order q. Hash function $h(\cdot)$.
Information held by Client: Identity ID. Password PW. Smart card.
Information held by Server: Secret key x.

Client		**Server**
Input ID, PW		
Extract $h(x\|ID) = R \oplus PW$		
Choose $c \in Z_p^*$		
Compute $c_1 = g^c (\bmod p)$		
Compute $c_2 = h(h(x\|ID)\|g^c)$	$\xrightarrow{\;ID, c_1, c_2\;}$	Compute $h(x\|ID)$
		Verify $h(h(x\|ID)\|c_1) \overset{?}{=} c_2$
		Choose $s \in Z_p^*$
		Compute $K = g^{cs}(\bmod p)$
Compute $K = (c_3)^c = g^{cs}(\bmod p)$	$\xleftarrow{\;c_3, c_4\;}$	Compute $c_3 = g^s(\bmod p)$
		Compute $c_4 = h(K\|c_1)$
Verify $h(K\|g^c) \overset{?}{=} c_4$		
Compute $c_5 = h(K\|c_3)$	$\xrightarrow{\;c_5\;}$	Verify $h(K\|g^s) \overset{?}{=} c_5$
	Fresh session key $K = g^{cs}(\bmod p)$	

Fig. 2. Proposed authentication and key establishment phase

---

(2) Server→Client: c_3, c_4

Based on the received ID, the server computes $h(x\|ID)$ and verifies the data by checking whether $h(h(x\|ID)\|c_1)$ equals c_2. If the verification fails, then the server stops the authentication; otherwise, it chooses a random exponent $s \in Z_p^*$ and computes the session key $K = g^{cs}(\bmod p)$, $c_3 = g^s(\bmod p)$ and $c_4 = h(K\|c_1)$. The server finally sends (c_3, c_4) to the client.

(3) Client→Server: c_5

Upon receiving (c_3, c_4), the client first computes the session key $K = (c_3)^c = g^{cs}(\bmod p)$ and then verifies whether $h(K\|g^c)$ equals the received c_4. If the verification fails, it stops the authentication; otherwise, it sends back $c_5 = h(K\|c_3)$ to the server.

(4) Upon receiving the data c_5, the server verifies whether c_5 equals $h(K\|g^s)$. If the verification fails, it refuses the request; otherwise, mutual authentication is completed and the fresh session key K is confirmed.

6   Security Analysis and a Comparison of Performance

This section discusses the security and efficiency of the proposed ROSI protocol.

6.1   Security Analysis

This subsection analyzes the security of the proposed ROSI protocol. At first, we define the security terms needed for the analysis of the proposed ROSI protocol.

Definition 1. *A weak secret (password) is a value of low entropy $W(k)$, which can be guessed in polynomial time.*

Definition 2. *A strong secret key is a value of high entropy $H(k)$, which cannot be guessed in polynomial time.*

Definition 3. *A secure one-way hash function $y = h(x)$ is one where given x it is easy to compute y and where given y it is hard to compute x.*

Definition 4. *The discrete logarithm problem (DLP) is explained by the following: Given a prime p, a generator g of Z_p^*, and an element $\beta \in Z_p^*$, find the integer α, $0 \le \alpha \le p - 2$, such that $g^\alpha \equiv \beta (\bmod p)$.*

Definition 5. *The Diffie-Hellman problem (DHP) is explained by the following: Given a prime p, a generator g of Z_p^*, and elements $g^c (\bmod p)$ and $g^s (\bmod p)$, find $g^{cs} (\bmod p)$.*

Here, six security properties: Guessing attack, replay attack, stolen-verifier attack, Denning-Sacco attack, mutual authentication, and perfect forward secrecy, would be considered for the proposed ROSI protocol. Under the above definitions, the following theorems are used to analyze the six security properties in the proposed protocol.

Theorem 1. *The proposed ROSI protocol can resist the server's secret key guessing attack.*

Proof. An attacker E can intercept a login request message (ID, c_1, c_2) sent by the client in Step (1) over a public network. Due to Definition 3, however, that a secure one-way hash function is computationally difficult to invert, he cannot derive the client's secret value $h(x||ID)$ from c_2. Suppose that an attacker obtains the client's secret value $h(x||ID)$. Due to Definitions 2 and 3, however, it is also extremely hard for any attacker to derive the server's strong secret key x from $h(x||ID)$.

Theorem 2. *The proposed ROSI protocol can resist the replay and an impersonation attack.*

Proof. An attacker E can intercept (ID, c_1, c_2) and use it to impersonate the client when sending the next login message. For a random challenge, however, the g^c and g^s separately generated by the client and server are different every time. Since the client and server always verify the integrity of the fresh session key K by checking c_4 and c_5, the replayed messages can be detected by the client and server, respectively. Furthermore, obtaining random exponents c and s from g^c and g^s is computationally infeasible, as it is a discrete logarithm problem of Definition 4. Therefore, E cannot compute K without knowing c and s. In addition, it is also computationally infeasible to obtain the fresh session key $K = g^{cs}$ from g^c and g^s, as it is the Diffie-Hellman problem of Definition 5. As a result, E cannot impersonate the client or the server.

Theorem 3. *The proposed ROSI protocol can resist the stolen-verifier attack.*

Proof. Servers are always the target of attacks. An attacker may try to steal or modify the verification table stored in the server. If the verification table is stolen by an attacker, the attacker may masquerade as a legitimate user. If the verification table is modified, a legitimate user cannot successfully login to the system. This results in a denial-of-service attack. The proposed protocol is a nonce-based authentication protocol, but it does not require a verification table in the server. Obviously, the proposed protocol can prevent the stolen-verifier attack.

Theorem 4. *The proposed ROSI protocol can resist the Denning-Sacco attack.*

Proof. Although an attacker E obtains g^c, g^s and fresh session key g^{cs}, E cannot obtains the client's secret value $h(x||ID)$ from $c_2 = h(h(x||ID)||g^c)$ because x is a strong secret key by Definition 1 and $h(\cdot)$ is a secure one-way hash function by Definition 3. Obviously, the proposed protocol can prevent the Denning-Sacco attack.

Theorem 5. *The proposed ROSI protocol provides mutual authentication.*

Proof. Mutual authentication means that both the client and server are authenticated to each other within the same protocol, while explicit key authentication is the property obtained when both implicit key authentication and key confirmation hold. As such, the improved protocol uses the Diffie-Hellman key exchange algorithm to provide mutual authentication, then the key is explicitly authenticated by a mutual confirmation fresh session key K.

Theorem 6. *The proposed ROSI protocol provides perfect forward secrecy.*

Proof. Even if both client's password PW and server's secret key x are compromised simultaneously, an attacker E can derive only the fresh session key at this time. Previous fresh session keys cannot be opened because the fresh session key is constructed under the Diffie-Hellman key agreement scheme. That is, it is computationally infeasible to obtain the fresh session key $K = g^{cs}$ from g^c and g^s by Definition 5. So the proposed ROSI protocol provides perfect forward secrecy.

The security properties of CWY's ROSI protocol, and the proposed ROSI protocol are summarized in Table 1.

6.2   Performance Comparison

The computational costs of CWY's ROSI protocol and the proposed ROSI protocol in the authentication and key establishment phase are summarized in Table 2. The computational costs of the registration phase are the same. In the authentication and key establishment phase, CWY's protocol requires a total of

Table 1. Comparisons of security properties

	CWY's protocol	Proposed protocol
Guessing attack	Secure	Secure
Replay attack	Secure	Secure
Impersonation attack	Secure	Secure
Stolen-verifier attack	Secure	Secure
Denial of Service attack	Secure	Secure
Denning-Sacco attack	Insecure	Secure
Mutual authentication	Provided	Provided
Perfect forward secrecy	No provided	Provided

Table 2. Comparisons of computational costs

	CWY's protocol		Proposed protocol	
	Client	Server	Client	Server
Exponent operation	0	0	2	2
Hash operation	4	6	3	4
XOR operation	3	3	1	0

ten hashing operations and six exclusive-or operations, but the proposed protocol requires a total of two exponent operations, seven hashing operations and one exclusive-or operations. Two exponent operations are needed to prevent a Denning-Sacco attack and to provide perfect forward secrecy.

When considering hashing and exclusive-or operations, in CWY's protocol, one hashing and one exclusive-or operation for the server are required for a user to register and get his smart card. In the authentication and key establishment phase, four hashing and three exclusive-or operations for the client and six hashing and three exclusive-or operations for the server are required. In the proposed protocol, however, one hashing and one exclusive-or operations in the server are required for a user to register and get his smart card. In the authentication and key establishment phase, three hashing and one exclusive-or operations in the client and four hashing operations in the server are required. Obviously, the proposed protocol is more efficient than CWY's protocol.

7   Conclusions

The current paper demonstrated that CWY's improved ROSI protocol does not provide perfect forward secrecy and is susceptible to a Denning-Sacco attack. We then presented an enhancement to the protocol in order to isolate such problems. The proposed ROSI protocol can resist various attacks including guessing, replay, stolen-verifier, and Denning-Sacco. In addition mutual authentication and perfect forward secrecy are provided. The computational costs also are significantly less than those of the CWY's protocol. As a result, in contrast to CWY's protocol and the existing SAS-like authentication protocols [3–5, 8], the proposed ROSI protocol can efficiently and securely perform key agreement for secure communication on the Internet Web environment.

Acknowledgements

This research was supported by the MIC (Ministry of Information and Communication), Korea, under the ITRC (Information Technology Research Center) support program supervised by the IITA (Institute of Information Technology Assessment).

References

1. Menezes, A.J., Oorschot, P.C., Vanstone, S.A.: Handbook of Applied Cryptograph. CRC Press. New York (1997)
2. Lin, C.L., Hwang, T.: A Password Authentication Scheme with Secure Password Updation. Computers & Security. Vol. 22. No. 1. (2003) 68-72
3. Sandirigama, M., Shimizu, A., Noda, M.T.: Simple and Secure Password Authentication Protocol (SAS). IEICE Transactions on Communications. Vol. E83-B. No. 6. (2000) 1363-1365
4. Kamioka, T., Shimizum, A.: The Examination of the Security of SAS One-time Password Authentication. IEICE Technical Report. OFS2001-48. No. 435. (2001) 53-58
5. Lin, C.L., Sun, H.M., Hwang, T.: Attacks and Solutions on Strong-password Authentication. IEICE Transactions on Communications. Vol. E84-B. No. 9. (2001) 2622-2627
6. Peyret, P., Lisimaque, G., Chua, T.Y.: Smart Cards Provide Very High Security and Flexibility in Subscribers Management. IEEE Transactions on Consumer Electronics. Vol. 36. No. 3. (1990) 744-752
7. Sternglass, D.: The Future Is in the PC Cards. IEEE Spectrum. Vol. 29. No. 6. (1992) 46-50
8. Chien, H.Y., Jan, J.K.: Robust and Simple Authentication Protocol. The Computer Journal. Vol. 46. No. 2. (2003) 193-201
9. Chien, H.Y., Wang, R.C., Yang, C.C.: Note on Robust and Simple Authentication Protocol. The Computer Journal. Vol. 48. No. 1. (2005) 27-29
10. Steiner, M., Tsudik, G., Waidner, M.: Refinement and Extension of Encrypted Key Exchange. ACM Operating Systems Review. Vol. 29. No. 3. (1995) 22-30
11. Denning, D., Sacco, G.: Timestamps in Key Distribution Systems. Communications of the ACM. Vol. 24. (1981) 533-536

Offline Expansion of XACML Policies Based on P3P Metadata

Claudio Ardagna, Ernesto Damiani, Sabrina De Capitani di Vimercati,
Cristiano Fugazza, and Pierangela Samarati

Dipartimento di Tecnologie dell'Informazione
Università degli Studi di Milano
v. Bramante 65, 26013 Crema, Italy
{ardagna,damiani,decapita,fugazza,samarati}@dti.unimi.it

Abstract. In the last few years XML-based access control languages like XACML have been increasingly used for specifying complex policies regulating access to network resources. Today, growing interest in semantic-Web style metadata for describing resources and users is stimulating research on how to express access control policies based on advanced descriptions rather than on single attributes.
In this paper, we discuss how standard XACML policies can handle ontology-based resource and subject descriptions based on the standard P3P base data schema. We show that XACML conditions can be transparently expanded according to ontology-based models representing semantics. Our expansion technique greatly reduces the need for online reasoning and decreases the system administrator's effort for producing consistent rules when users' descriptions comprise multiple credentials with redundant attributes.

1 Introduction

Semantic-Web style ontologies are aimed at providing a common framework that allows data to be shared and reused by applications across enterprise and community boundaries. While interest for ontology-based data representation is now growing in many application fields, access control techniques still do not take full advantage of semantic Web metadata. Recent proposals for specifying and exchanging access control policies adopt XML-based languages such as the *eXtensible Access Control Markup Language* (XACML) [4]. Although very expressive and flexible, XACML is severely limited by the comparatively low expressive power of formalisms used to describe resources and users requesting them.

In this paper we present a practical and efficient approach for increasing XACML expressive power by incorporating into XACML policies ontology-based resource and subject descriptions based on the standard P3P base data schema [8]. In particular, we describe how XACML conditions can be expanded taking into account ontology-based models representing user profiles and resources semantics. Our expansion technique greatly reduces the need for on-line

D. Lowe and M. Gaedke (Eds.): ICWE 2005, LNCS 3579, pp. 363–374, 2005.

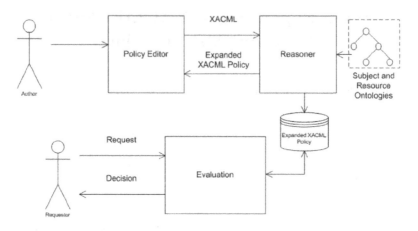

Fig. 1. Scenario

reasoning, relieving the (potentially heavy) computational burden of supporting resource and users' semantics in policy definition and evaluation. As far as
user descriptions are concerned, we rely on P3P-based credentials [8], which are
increasingly used to represent subject-related personal information in privacy
policies. In our approach, the standard P3P base data schema for credential definition is converted into semantic-Web style metadata that can be easily checked
in the framework of policy evaluation[1]. Figure 1 illustrates the scenario we consider. The XACML policies are created via the *Policy editor* component. The
Reasoner takes such XACML policies together with the subject and resource ontologies as input and computes the expanded XACML policies including semantically equivalent additional conditions. These conditions, specified in disjunction
with the original ones, allow for increasing the original policy's expressive power.
Our semantically expanded XACML policies can be straightforwardly used as a
replacement of the original ones or, more interestingly, can be evaluated side by
side with them, flagging cases of inconsistency in the policies' semantics.

Therefore, our solution allows the definition of rules based on generic assertions defined over concepts in the ontologies that control metadata content. The
result is a semantic-aware policy language exploiting the high expressive power
of ontology-based models. The remainder of this paper is organized as follows.
Section 2 describes our semantic-Web style representation of the standard P3P
base data schema. Section 3 shows a simple example of XACML policy expansion, deriving possible alternatives obtained by straightforward reasoning over
context information. Section 4 illustrates how the reasoning process derives the
actual credential users should provide to be granted access to a given resource
by taking into account an explicit representation of resources. Finally, Section 5
shows how a complex condition is modeled and how the ontology is used to
deduce some semantically equivalent alternatives.

---

[1] More specifically, the ontology used in this paper relies on the revised P3P base data
schema introduced in our previous work [3, 6]

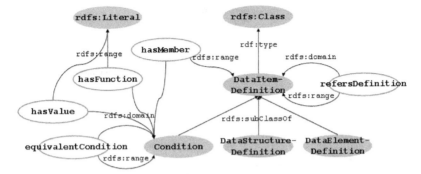

Fig. 2. The language layer defining the building blocks of our RDFS-based representation of the standard P3P base data schema

2   Representing Heterogeneous Credential Information

We start from a simple RDFS representation of the standard P3P base data schema. Fig. 2 shows the first level of RDF Schema definitions [10] (the *language layer*) for our semantic-Web style representation of the standard P3P base data schema [8]. Here, classes have a grey background color while properties have borders and no background color. Root class `DataItemDefinition` is sub-classed by `DataStructureDefinition` and `DataElementDefinition` to model P3P *data structures* and *data elements*, respectively, and by a class `Condition` used to model policy conditions by means of the associated properties `hasFunction`, `hasMember`, and `hasValue`. More precisely, these properties represent the evaluation function, the variables, and the literal values used in the condition, respectively. `Conditions` can feature alternatives by means of property `equivalentCondition`. We denote the inclusion between `DataItems` with property `refersDefinition` whose domain and range (in RDFS terms `rdfs:domain` and `rdfs:range`) coincide with the `DataItemDefinition` class. This property, together with the `rdfs:subClassOf` property, will be used throughout the paper to query the knowledge base for alternatives to data items.

Below the language layer, the *ontology layer* (see Fig. 3) comprises data elements and structures represented as classes and linked with each other by means of the `refersDefinition` property. This layer models the semi-lattice structure of the P3P base data schema [6]. At the bottom of the model, the *instance layer* contains the actual negotiable user credential expressed as instances of the classes defined by the ontology layer. Credentials are connected by the `refersInstance` property, modeling the tree structure linking literal values to nodes representing credential instances as a whole. For the sake of simplicity, rather than bending the built-in inference rules associated with ontology languages like OWL [7], we rely on plain RDFS and define from scratch a rule set representing the reasoning patterns required by our application. In the following, the examples make use only of the implications in the ontology layer, hence the instance layer is not further described.

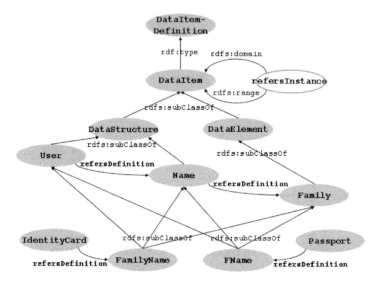

Fig. 3. The ontology layer integrating the standard P3P base data schema with credential definitions

3   Referencing Credential Information in Policies

We are now ready to describe some worked out examples of ontology-based policy expansion. In the first example, we show how using an ontology to link independent credentials to the P3P base data schema allows for easily specifying alternatives. Fig. 4 shows an XACML condition that references data items of the extended context provided by the ontology via the `urn:...:BaseDataSchema:User:Name:Family` URN, matching it with the literal "Rossi". From the URN we can note that the referenced data items:

– belong to the underlying P3P base data schema and can correspond to different alternatives (one for each possible credential);
– have type `Family`, which is part of the `Name` context associated with the `User` requiring a resource or service.

From this URN, the following RDQL [11] query can be derived.

```
SELECT ?DataElement
WHERE
(<http://.../BaseDataSchema#Family><http://.../BaseDataSchema#refersDefinition>?DataElement)
(?DataElement rdfs:type <http://.../BaseDataSchema#SubjectAttribute>)
```

The query extracts the referenced data items from the P3P base data schema (note that class `SubjectAttribute` allows for distinguishing subject credentials from resources types). Let us now examine in more details the (hopefully rather self-explanatory) RDQL syntax. First of all, in the selection clause we collect all ontology nodes referenced by the `Family` node. Since `Family` is a leaf and `refersDefinition` is a reflexive property (i.e., `?Credential`

```
<Rule RuleId="urn:...:ruleid:1" Effect="Permit">
  <Description/>
  <Target/>
  <Condition>
    <Apply FunctionId="urn:oasis:...:function:string-equal">
      <AttributeValue DataType="http://www.w3.org/2001/XMLSchema#string">
        Rossi
      </AttributeValue>
      <SubjectAttributeDesignator AttributeId="| urn:...:BaseDataSchema:User:Name:Family |"
        DataType="http://www.w3.org/2001/XMLSchema#string"/>
    </Apply>
  </Condition>
</Rule>
```

Fig. 4. A simple XACML condition referencing the extended context

`refersDefinition ?Credential` holds for any candidate credential), the only result is:

`<http://.../BaseDataSchema#Family>`

Then, we query the information base for data items semantically equivalent to `BaseDataSchema#Family`. Note that the other elements specified in the URN (i.e., `User` and `Name`) act as constraints. We then derive the following RDQL query:

```
SELECT ?DataElement
WHERE
(?DataElement rdfs:subClassOf <http://.../BaseDataSchema#User>)
(?DataElement rdfs:subClassOf <http://.../BaseDataSchema#Name>)
(?DataElement rdfs:subClassOf <http://.../BaseDataSchema#Family>)
(?DataElement rdfs:type <http://.../BaseDataSchema#SubjectAttribute>)
```

The RDFS reasoning engine returns two results:

`<http://.../Passport#FName>`
`<http://.../IdentityCard# FamilyName>`

The entities are then mapped to the URNs `urn:...:Passport:FName`, and `urn:...:IdentityCard:FamilyName`, respectively, and the original condition is expanded as illustrated in Fig. 5.

Note that, as long as the two parties agree on the extended context, our expansion procedure does not affect the asymptotic complexity of evaluation, since the expanded condition can still be evaluated by applying XACML standard functions to literal values. Our policy expansion process has therefore the advantage of hiding the complexity of the structure of the user description metadata.

4   Referencing Proprietary Representations of Resources

P3P base data schema is normally used for describing user-related personal information. However, the scope of our technique can be easily enlarged to encompass resource descriptions. The availability of a common data schema allows

```
<Condition>
  <Apply FunctionId="urn:oasis:...:function:or">
    <Apply FunctionId="urn:oasis:...:function:string-equal">
      <AttributeValue DataType="http://www.w3.org/2001/XMLSchema#string">
        Rossi
      </AttributeValue>
      <SubjectAttributeDesignator AttributeId="urn:...:BaseDataSchema:User:Name:Family"
        DataType="http://www.w3.org/2001/XMLSchema#string"/>
    </Apply>
    <Apply FunctionId="urn:oasis:...:function:string-equal">
      <AttributeValue DataType="http://www.w3.org/2001/XMLSchema#string">
        Rossi
      </AttributeValue>
      <SubjectAttributeDesignator AttributeId="urn:...:IdentityCard:FamilyName"
        DataType="http://www.w3.org/2001/XMLSchema#string"/>
    </Apply>
    <Apply FunctionId="urn:oasis:...:function:string-equal">
      <AttributeValue DataType="http://www.w3.org/2001/XMLSchema#string">
        Rossi
      </AttributeValue>
      <SubjectAttributeDesignator AttributeId="urn:...:Passport:FName"
        DataType="http://www.w3.org/2001/XMLSchema#string"/>
    </Apply>
  </Apply>
</Condition>
```

Fig. 5. The XACML condition of Fig. 4 after the expansion

```
<Condition>
  <Apply FunctionId="urn:...:functions:semantic-match">
    <ResourceAttributeDesignator AttributeId="urn:...:Document:Creator"
      DataType="urn:...:datatypes:structured-type"/>
    <SubjectAttributeDesignator AttributeId="urn:...:BaseDataSchema:User"
      DataType="urn:...:datatypes:structured-type"/>
  </Apply>
</Condition>
```

Fig. 6. XACML condition referencing an arbitrary categorization of resources

for rooting an arbitrary representation model for describing resources metadata: actual credentials can then be associated with this information. Following the standard XACML approach, our second example introduces a custom matching function, called semantic-match, that will be applied to structured data items, indicated by the custom data type structured-type. As an example, consider the XACML condition in Fig. 6. This condition is evaluated to true when the Document:Creator data structure describing a resource matches the User data structure from the base data schema. The task of finding the right credential against which to match the resource's Creator can then be left to the reasoning engine.

In this example, our semantic-match function works as follows:

- First, it retrieves data items identifying a document's creator (for the sake of conciseness, we assume that authors are uniquely defined by their first name, last name, and e-mail). Here, class ResourceAttribute allows for distinguishing resource types from subject credentials:

```
SELECT ?DataElement
WHERE
(<http://.../Documents#Creator><http://.../BaseDataSchema#refersDefinition>?DataElement)
(?DataElement rdfs:type <http://.../BaseDataSchema#ResourceAttribute>)
```

According to our assumption, this query returns three values:

```
<http://.../Document#FirstName>
<http://.../Document#FamilyName>
<http://.../Document#EmailAddress>
```

- Since resources descriptions are not credentials, their definitions need not be shared. Thus, for each of the data items retrieved, the corresponding super-classes in the base data schema are identified[2]. For instance, the following RDQL query selects data items in the base data schema that are equivalent to data element FirstName.

```
SELECT ?DataElement
WHERE
(<http://.../Documents#FirstName> rdfs:subClassOf ?DataElement)
(?DataElement rdfs:type <http://.../BaseDataSchema#SubjectAttribute>)
```

The result of this query is

```
<http://.../BaseDataSchema#Given>
```

- At this point, all data items can be retrieved as in Section 3, taking into account the User constraint in the SubjectAttributeDesignator:

```
SELECT ?DataElement
WHERE
(?DataElement rdfs:subClassOf <http://.../BaseDataSchema#User>)
(?DataElement rdfs:subClassOf <http://.../BaseDataSchema#Given>)
(?DataElement rdfs:type <http://.../BaseDataSchema#SubjectAttribute>)
```

This query returns two values:

```
<http://.../Passport#GName>
<http://.../IdentityCard#FirstName>
```

After translating all the alternatives into URNs, the condition is expanded according to the translation's results. Once again, we remark that the expanded policy is fully compliant with the XACML standard schema defined in [4]. For the sake of conciseness, the (rather verbose) result of the expansion is shown in Appendix A.

---

[2] Note that these super-classes are themselves leaves induced in the P3P base data schema by the refersDescription property

```
<Condition>
  <Apply FunctionId="urn:oasis:...:function:string-match">
    <AttributeValue DataType="http://www.w3.org/2001/XMLSchema#string">
    Milano
    </AttributeValue>
    <SubjectAttributeDesignator AttributeId="| urn:...:IdentityCard:CityOfBirth |"
    DataType="http://www.w3.org/2001/XMLSchema#string"/>
  </Apply>
</Condition>
```

Fig. 7. A condition on the city of birth of the requestor

5   Expressing Advanced Semantics-Aware Conditions

In this Section, our expansion technique is extended to take into account not only the metadata context being referenced by a policy, but also how data items are combined or evaluated in conditions. As we will see, complex translations schemes can be defined, leading to equivalent conditions in terms of the attributes being compared, the function being applied, and also the right-end value of the comparison. In other words, our example will take into account not only the context composed of attributes associated with subjects and resources, but also the operational semantics of the policy language describing the rules. Here, metadata represents not only the data items being exchanged, but also the conditions applied to them.

The conditions shown in Figure 7 states that the city of birth of the requestor should be equal to `Milano`.

In triple format this condition can be expressed as follows:

```
COND-001 rdf:type dom:Condition
COND-001 dom:hasFunction 'urn:oasis:...:function:string-match'
COND-001 dom:hasValue 'Milano'
COND-001 dom:hasMember IdentityCard:PlaceOfBirth
```

Our expansion technique derives an equivalence between these triples and the ones below:

```
COND-002 rdf:type dom:Condition
COND-002 dom:hasFunction 'urn:oasis:...:function:string-regexp-match'
COND-002 dom:hasValue '/11(\w)F205(\w)'
COND-002 dom:hasMember CodiceFiscale
```

In other words, we can generate the following assertion:

```
COND-001 dom:equivalentCondition COND-002
```

Note that condition `COND-002` has left and right terms different from those of `COND-001` and also uses a different evaluation function. However these two conditions are equivalent because the Italian tax code, called *codice fiscale*, is a 16 digits alphanumeric code uniquely defined by the first name, last name, gender, date, and city of birth. The city code F205 appearing in positions 12 to 15, indicates Milano as the city of birth and therefore the original condition

```
<Condition>
  <Apply FunctionId="urn:oasis:names:tc:xacml:1.0:function:or">
    <Apply FunctionId="urn:oasis:...:function:string-match">
      <AttributeValue DataType="http://www.w3.org/2001/XMLSchema#string">
        Milano
      </AttributeValue>
      <SubjectAttributeDesignator AttributeId="urn:...:IdentityCard:PlaceOfBirth"
        DataType="http://www.w3.org/2001/XMLSchema#string"/>
    </Apply>
    <Apply FunctionId="urn:oasis:...:function:string-regexp-match">
      <AttributeValue DataType="http://www.w3.org/2001/XMLSchema#string">
        /11(\w)F205(\w)
      </AttributeValue>
      <SubjectAttributeDesignator AttributeId="urn:...:CodiceFiscale"
        DataType="http://www.w3.org/2001/XMLSchema#string"/>
    </Apply>
  </Apply>
</Condition>
```

Fig. 8. The condition of Fig. 7 after the expansion

can also be expressed in XACML by matching the *codice fiscale* against the regular expression '/11(\w)F205(\w)'. The expanded condition is represented in Fig. 8.

Computationally, the equivalence between the two conditions can be checked by direct mapping with tabled values, such as the city codes appearing in the CodiceFiscale, or else provided by means of numeric or string conversion functions.

6 Extending XACML to Support Complex Conditions

The previous examples have shown how we can expand XACML conditions expressing a predicate (e.g., equality) between an attribute and a literal or between two attributes by means of an ontology based on the standard P3P data schema. One step further toward increasing the policy language expressive power beyond plain XACML would require dealing with more complex logic conditions, including variables and quantifiers. For instance, the complex condition *"User X can see document Y if there exists at least another document Z with the same creation date"* cannot be expressed in plain XACML. Also, evaluating this kind of conditions is known to be a difficult computational problem [2]. For this, we need to define a different XML-syntax, based on a BNF grammar like the one shown below:

```
Q varList booleanExprPred.
booleanExprPred ← pred, booleanExprPred.
                ← pred; booleanExpression.
                ← pred.
                ← ¬ pred.
pred ← predName(varList).
varList ← varName, varList.
        ← varName.
Q ← ∃, ∀.
```

Note that with this approach the evaluation mechanism of the new policy language will need to perform ontology-based reasoning as an integral part of the policy evaluation mechanism rather than using it to explicitly expand policies. The evaluation of complex conditions requires a component (currently being developed [1]) traslating XML-based logic conditions into RDQL queries to be submitted to an ontology-based reasoner during the evaluation phase. Online reasoning about conditions, of course, will require careful design in order to keep the computational burden of policy evaluation under control; also, it may lead to unexpected results, as the effects on policy evaluation of the semantic information stored in the ontology are not available for inspection. For this reason it might be necessary to publish, for transparency, also the inference rules used for the evaluation. We plan to deal with this subject as future work.

7   Conclusions

We have illustrated how XACML policies can be expanded on the base of ontology-based resource and subject descriptions encoding the P3P base data schema. Our approach can be used with any P3P data schema to derive, given a specified policy, a policy that includes semantically equivalent additional conditions on users and resource description metadata. The advantage of our solution is twofold. First, it permits to automatically extend available access control policies taking into account resources whose metadata express similarity with other resources already mentioned in the policies. Second, it allows to check consistency of existing policies with respect to different resources and users having a similar semantic status.

Acknowledgments

This work was supported in part by the European Union within the PRIME Project in the FP6/IST Programme under contract IST-2002-507591 and by the Italian MIUR within the KIWI and MAPS projects.

References

1. C.A. Ardagna, E. Damiani, S. De Capitani di Vimercati, M. Cremonini, and P. Samarati – *Towards Identity Management for E-Services* – In Proc. of the TED Conference on e-Government Electronic democracy: The challenge ahead, Bozen, Italy, March 2005.
2. P. A. Bonatti, P. Samarati – *A Uniform Framework for Regulating Service Access and Information Release on the Web* – Journal of Computer Security 10(3): 241-272 (2002)
3. E. Damiani, S. De Capitani di Vimercati, C. Fugazza, and P. Samarati – *Extending Policy Languages to the Semantic Web* - In Proc. of ICWE 2004, Munich, 2004, Lecture Notes in Computer Science 3140.

4. *eXtensible Access Control Markup Language* (XACML) – Organization for the Advancement of Structured Information Standards – http://www.oasis-open.org/committees/tc_home.php?wg_abbrev=xacml

5. Jeff Z. Pan, Ian Horrocks – *Metamodeling Architecture of Web Ontology Languages* – In Proc. of the Semantic Web Working Symposium 2001

6. P. Ceravolo, E. Damiani, S. De Capitani di Vimercati, C. Fugazza, and P. Samarati – *Advanced Metadata for Privacy-Aware Representation of Credentials* – In Proc. of the ICDE Workshop on Privacy Data Management (PDM 05)

7. *OWL Web Ontology Language – Overview* – W3C Recommendation, December 2003 – http://www.w3.org/TR/owl-features/

8. *Platform for Privacy Preferences* (P3P) – W3C Recommendation, 16 April 2002 – http://www.w3.org/TR/P3P/

9. *Privacy and Identity Management for Europe* (PRIME) – European RTD Integrated Project – http://www.prime-project.eu.org/

10. *RDF Vocabulary Description Language* (RDFS) – W3C Recommendation, 10 February 2004 – http://www.w3.org/TR/rdf-schema/

11. *RDQL – A Query Language for RDF* – W3C Member Submission, 9 January 2004 – http://www.w3.org/Submission/2004/SUBM-RDQL-20040109/

A   Expansion of the Condition in Fig. 6

```
<Condition>
  <Apply FunctionId="urn:oasis:names:tc:xacml:1.0:function:and">
    <Apply FunctionId="urn:oasis:names:tc:xacml:1.0:function:or">
      <Apply FunctionId="urn:oasis:names:tc:xacml:1.0:function:string-equal">
        <ResourceAttributeDesignator AttributeId=" urn:...:Document:Creator:FirstName "
          DataType="http://www.w3.org/2001/XMLSchema#string"/>
        <SubjectAttributeDesignator AttributeId=" urn:...:User:Name:Given "
          DataType="http://www.w3.org/2001/XMLSchema#string"/>
      </Apply Apply FunctionId="urn:oasis:names:tc:xacml:1.0:function:string-equal">
        <ResourceAttributeDesignator AttributeId=" urn:...:Document:Creator:FirstName "
          DataType="http://www.w3.org/2001/XMLSchema#string"/>
        <SubjectAttributeDesignator AttributeId=" urn:...:IdentityCard:GivenName "
          DataType="http://www.w3.org/2001/XMLSchema#string"/>
      </Apply>
      <Apply FunctionId="urn:oasis:names:tc:xacml:1.0:function:string-equal">
        <ResourceAttributeDesignator AttributeId=" urn:...:Document:Creator:FirstName "
          DataType="http://www.w3.org/2001/XMLSchema#string"/>
        <SubjectAttributeDesignator AttributeId=" urn:...:Passport:GName "
          DataType="http://www.w3.org/2001/XMLSchema#string"/>
      </Apply>
    </Apply>
    <Apply FunctionId="urn:oasis:names:tc:xacml:1.0:function:or">
      <Apply FunctionId="urn:oasis:names:tc:xacml:1.0:function:string-equal">
        <ResourceAttributeDesignator AttributeId=" urn:...:Document:Creator:FamilyName "
          DataType="http://www.w3.org/2001/XMLSchema#string"/>
        <SubjectAttributeDesignator AttributeId=" urn:...:User:Name:Family "
          DataType="http://www.w3.org/2001/XMLSchema#string"/>
      </Apply>
      <Apply FunctionId="urn:oasis:names:tc:xacml:1.0:function:string-equal">
        <ResourceAttributeDesignator AttributeId=" urn:...:Document:Creator:FamilyName "
          DataType="http://www.w3.org/2001/XMLSchema#string"/>
        <SubjectAttributeDesignator AttributeId=" urn:...:IdentityCard:FamilyName "
```

```
    DataType="http://www.w3.org/2001/XMLSchema#string"/>
  </Apply>
  <Apply FunctionId="urn:oasis:names:tc:xacml:1.0:function:string-equal">
    <ResourceAttributeDesignator AttributeId=" urn:...:Document:Creator:FamilyName "
    DataType="http://www.w3.org/2001/XMLSchema#string"/>
    <SubjectAttributeDesignator AttributeId=" urn:...:Passport:FName "
    DataType="http://www.w3.org/2001/XMLSchema#string"/>
  </Apply>
  </Apply>
  <Apply FunctionId="urn:oasis:names:tc:xacml:1.0:function:date-equal">
    <ResourceAttributeDesignator AttributeId=" urn:...:Document:Creator:EmailAddress "
    DataType="http://www.w3.org/2001/XMLSchema#string"/>
    <SubjectAttributeDesignator AttributeId=" urn:...:User:Online:Email "
    DataType="http://www.w3.org/2001/XMLSchema#string"/>
  </Apply>
  </Apply>
</Condition>
```

B RDQL Basics

RDQL queries have the following general form:

```
SELECT ?a
FROM <http://input-model.rdf>
WHERE (?a, <http://some-predicate>, ?b)
AND ?b < 5
```

Question marks indicate variables, each variable in the SELECT clause determines a column in the output. The FROM clause allows for selecting a specific file as the input model; this functionality is not used in the paper.

The WHERE clause simply defines triples that must be found in the knowledge base for a result to be selected: in the example, elements eligible for the ?a placeholder must have property some-predicate linking to some element ?b.

Finally, the AND clause allows for evaluating literal values according to a set of standard functions: in the example, the element ?b linked to a candidate result ?a must evaluate as < 5. Also this functionality is not used in the paper.

Automatic Optimization of Web Recommendations Using Feedback and Ontology Graphs

Nick Golovin and Erhard Rahm

University of Leipzig, Augustusplatz 10-11, 04109, Leipzig, Germany
{golovin,rahm}@informatik.uni-leipzig.de
dbs.uni-leipzig.de

Abstract. Web recommendation systems have become a popular means to improve the usability of web sites. This paper describes the architecture of a rule-based recommendation system and presents its evaluation on two real-life applications. The architecture combines recommendations from different algorithms in a recommendation database and applies feedback-based machine learning to optimize the selection of the presented recommendations. The recommendations database also stores ontology graphs, which are used to semantically enrich the recommendations. We describe the general architecture of the system and the test setting, illustrate the application of several optimization approaches and present comparative results.

1 Introduction

Many modern websites use web recommendations to increase usability, customer satisfaction and commercial profit. A number of algorithms were developed, which generate recommendations by applying different statistical or data mining approaches to some available to them information, for example on characteristics of the current page, product, web user, buying history etc.[5, 9] However, so far no single algorithm uses the benefits of all the available knowledge sources and no single algorithm shows clear superiority over all others. Therefore, the need for hybrid approaches which combine the benefits of multiple algorithms has been recognized [5].

In this paper, we present a new approach, capable of combining many recommender algorithms (or shortly *recommenders*). Our approach utilizes a central recommendation database for storing the recommendations, coming from different recommender algorithms and applies machine learning techniques to continuously optimize the stored recommendations. Optimization of the recommendations is based on how "useful" they are to users and to the website, i.e. how willingly the users click them or how much profit they bring. The incentive for our optimization approach was the observation, that the popularity and perceived relevance of individual recommendations are not always well predicted by the recommenders.

The information about the website and the users is represented in the recommendation database in form of ontology graphs. This allows us to semantically enrich the recommendations and bring in the knowledge from additional sources. It is also practicable for the adaptation of the system to the different types of websites.

The preliminary version of the architecture was sketched in [7]. In the current paper, we describe the architecture of the prototype implementations of the system and present evaluation results.

D. Lowe and M. Gaedke (Eds.): ICWE 2005, LNCS 3579, pp. 375–386, 2005.

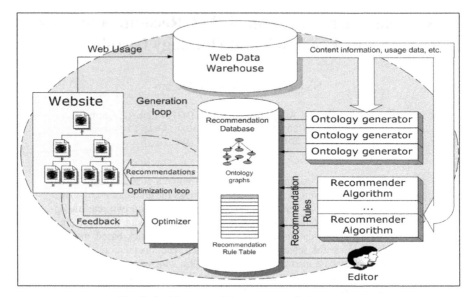

Fig. 1. Architecture of the recommendation system

We have implemented the prototype of our system on two websites: a website of the Database Group, University of Leipzig http://dbs.uni-leipzig.de and internet software shop http://www.softunity.com. To denote the origin of the examples and notions in the paper, we mark them either with EDU (educational) for the Database Group website or with EC (e-commerce) for www.softunity.com.

In the next section we explain the architecture of the system and its main components. Section 3 describes the selection of recommendations using ontology graphs and recommendation rules. In Section 4 we explain the recommenders and generation of the recommendations. The optimization techniques are presented in Section 5. Section 6 contains the evaluations of the real-life experimental data. In Section 7 we provide an overview of the related work. Section 8 summarizes the paper.

2 Architecture Overview

The architecture of our recommendation system is shown in Fig. 1. The *website* interacts with the web user, presents recommendations and gathers the feedback. The *web data warehouse* stores information about the content of the website (e.g., products and product catalog, HTML pages, etc.), users, and the usage logs generated by the web server or the application server. It serves as an information source for the recommender algorithms and ontology generators and allows OLAP evaluations of the usage data and the efficiency of recommendations. The *recommendation database* stores the semantic information in form of three directed acyclic ontology graphs (for the website content, web users and time) and the recommendations in form of recommendation rules, which are described in the next section. The set of *ontology generators* is responsible for generating the ontology graphs. The set of *recommender algorithms* generates recommendations using data from the web data warehouse.

Ontology graphs and recommendation rules can also be created and edited by a *human editor*. The *optimizer* refines the recommendation database based on the feedback obtained from the website using machine learning.

In our recommendation system we distinguish the generation loop and the optimization loop. The generation loop is executed at regular intervals of time. It involves generating/updating the ontology and the recommendation rules utilizing the information on the content and recent usage information from the web data warehouse. The optimization loop is continuously executed, and selects and presents the recommendations from the recommendation database. Furthermore, feedback is gathered, i.e. user reactions to presented recommendations. The optimizer uses this information to refine the recommendations in the database and to influence the selection of future recommendations.

3   Recommendation Selection Using Ontology Graphs

Fig. 2 shows the selection of recommendations using ontology graphs. To request recommendations to present, the website specifies the current *website context* and the desired number of recommendations. The website context is a set of parameters, which characterize the currently viewed website content, current web user and present point in time. An example of a website context is given below:

WebsiteContext{ ProductID="ECD00345"; UserCountry="DE";
UserOperatingSystem="Windows"; Date ="21.03.2005";...} (EC).

Obviously, the choice of suitable parameters in the website context depends on the specific website, especially with respect to the current content.

The recommendation system maps the provided website context into a *semantic context*, which consists of nodes of the three ontology graphs {ContentNodes, UserNodes, TimeNodes}. Using a selection policy, recommendations associated with the relevant nodes of the ontology graphs are selected and finally presented. This two-step selection process aims at supporting application-oriented recommendation strategies and high flexibility. Assigning recommendations to semantic concepts is expected to be more stable than directly using low-level website contexts whose values may change frequently (e.g. due to website restructuring).

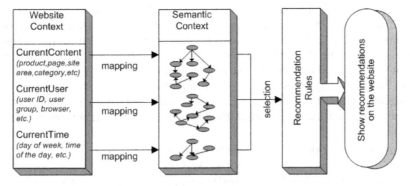

Fig. 2. Selecting recommendations using semantic context

Fig. 3 shows an example of an ontology graph for website content. Ontology graphs for web users and time are built in a similar way. We use directed edges to point from more specific concepts to more general concepts, from subcomponents to aggregated components, etc. Recommendations can be assigned to any node in such a graph. Highlighted with thick lines in Fig. 3 is an example of how the semantics stored in the ontology graph can be used to search for additional recommendations for Product4. We are able to retrieve the recommendations directly for Product4 as well the recommendations that are bound to some common property that Product4 possesses (in our case Hardcover) and the recommendations to some product catalog topics that Product4 is a part of (History, Books).

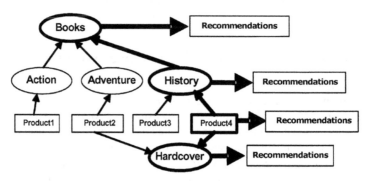

Fig. 3. A sample ontology graph for content dimension (EC)

The mapping between website and semantic contexts is specified by mapping clauses, which are statements written in a simple predicate language. The predicate language supports logical operators (AND, OR, NOT), comparison operators ($<$, $>$, $=,<>,>=,<=$) and operator LIKE, which does string matching with wildcard, similar to the SQL-operator with the same name. Some of the nodes in the ontology graphs immediately correspond to a certain set of parameters and can be mapped using mapping clauses. Others represent abstract notions and can be reached only by traversing the ontology graph and have no associated mapping clauses.

The ontology graphs are automatically generated by ontology generators and can be edited manually by the editors of the website. Each of the three ontology graphs is mapped separately. In our EC application, the ontology graphs are created by ontology generators using the product catalog, common properties of products and the business logic of the website. Application EDU uses the manually specified website content hierarchy and user groups determined by data mining (J48 decision tree algorithm). Most mapping clauses are automatically determined by the ontology generators together with the creation of the ontology and simply use an equality operator. Manually specified mapping clauses may be more complex. Examples of mapping clauses are:

ProductID="ECD00345"   -> ContentNode=1342 (EC)
UserCountry="DE"   -> UserNode=3 (EC)
UserDomain LIKE '%.edu' OR UserDomain LIKE '%uni-%' -> UserNode =2 (EDU)

The recommendations associated to nodes in the ontology graphs are represented by rules stored in the recommendation database. Recommendation rules have the form:

$$RuleContext\{Content, User, Time\} \rightarrow RecommendedContent, Weight$$

RuleContext refers to nodes in one or several of the three ontology graphs. These values can also be set to NULL, denoting that the rule does not depend on the corresponding dimension. RecommendedContent is the pointer to the content being recommended, e.g. recommended product or URL. The Weight is used as a criterion for the selection of the recommendation rules for presentations.

We have implemented several policies for selecting nodes of the ontology graphs and thus to select the associated recommendations. These policies include: "direct match", "direct + parents" and "combined". The "direct match" policy selects the recommendations using only the nodes matched using mapping clauses. The policy "direct + parents" uses these nodes as well as all their parents in the ontology graphs. In the "combined" policy the "direct match" policy is applied first. If this policy is unable to return the requested number of recommendations, the policy "direct + parents" is applied.

After the current semantic context is ascertained by selecting the nodes in the ontology graphs, we use the following general SQL query to select the recommendations from the rule table of the recommendation database:

```
SELECT TOP N RecomNode From Rules  WHERE
       (ContentNode in (CurrentContentNode1, CurrentContentNode2,...) OR
       ContentNode is NULL)  AND
       (UserNode in (CurrenUserNode1, CurrentUserNode2,...) OR
       UserNode is NULL)  AND
       (TimeNode in (CurrentTimeNode1, CurrentTimeNode2,...) OR
       TimeNode is NULL)
ORDER BY Weight DESC
```

We order the recommendations by weight and return the requested number of recommendations with the highest weight.

4 Creating Recommendation Rules

The recommendation rules are generated by the recommender algorithms and stored in the recommendation database. A recommender algorithm may also supply an initial weight for every generated recommendation rule from the interval [0 .. 1]. In the prototype implementation, we determine product recommendations with the following recommenders:

1. Content similarity. This recommender determines for each product (EC) or HTML page (EDU) (content node) the M most similar products using TF/IDF text similarity score.
2. Sequence patterns. Products (EC) or HTML Pages(EDU)most often succeeding other products/pages in the same user session are recommended to them.
3. Item-to-Item collaborative filtering.(EC) Products, which most often appear together in one user's basket, are recommended for each other.

4. Search Engine recommender (EDU). This recommender is applicable to the users coming from a search engine. It extracts search keywords from the HTTP Referrer field and uses the website's internal search engine to generate recommendations for each keyword. The recommender was first described and implemented in [17].

If the recommender algorithms generate a rule, which already exists in the recommendation rule table with different weight, the weight in the recommendation rule table takes preference over the weight supplied by the recommenders. We have explored two approaches to setting the initial weights of newly generated recommendation rules. In the first approach, we simply set all initial weights to zero (ZeroStart). The second approach uses normalized recommender-specific weights or relative priorities for the respective contexts. When several recommenders generate the same recommendation we use the maximum of their weights. The initial weights are expected to be relevant primarily for new recommendations since the weights for presented recommendations are continuously adapted.

5   Feedback-Based Optimization

The goal of our optimization is to adjust the weights of the recommendation rules in such a way, that the more useful recommendations are shown more often, than less useful. In our applications, we determine utility through the *acceptance rate* of the recommendations, which is:

$$AcceptanceRate = Nclicked / Npresented,$$

where *Nclicked* is number of times the recommendation was clicked and *Npres* is number of times the recommendation was presented.

However, our optimization algorithm is also able to work with utility determined otherwise, for example as sales turnover or profit brought by the recommendation.

Every time a web user requests a web page with recommendations, several recommendation rules from the recommendation database are selected and shown. We call such an event a *presentation*. The web user then may take some action in respect to the presented recommendations. For example, the user may click a recommendation, buy the recommended product, or ignore the recommendation. Each of these actions has a real value associated with it, called *feedback*.

The optimizer evaluates all presentations and adjusts the weights of the participating recommendation rules according to the obtained feedback. New recommendation rules can be added to the recommendation database at any time. Both online and offline optimization are possible.

There are two key aspects, which have to be addressed in our optimization algorithm. First, the utility of the individual recommendations may change over time, due to the "drift of interests" of the web users. The optimization algorithm must promptly react to the significant changes in user interests without overreacting to short-term fluctuations. Also, we are facing the "exploration vs. exploitation" dilemma. On one side, we would like to present the recommendations, which are the most "useful" according to our current knowledge, i.e. be "greedy". On the other side, we would like to learn, how good are the other recommendations, for which our current knowledge is insufficient [16, 8]. In the next subsections, we discuss these aspects in more detail.

5.1 "Drift of Interest"

We can handle the "drift of interest" in several ways:

- consider older feedback and newer feedback to be equally important (no aging). In this case, the weight of the recommendation rule is equal to the acceptance rate of the recommendation and the "drift of interest" is not taken into account.
- store the last n feedback values for each recommendation rule and generate the weights of the recommendation rules from them. This approach, however, requires additional memory in case of online optimization.
- use *aging by division* (also called *exponential smoothing*). Here, with every presentation the original weight of the recommendation rule is decreased by a fraction of its value:

$$Q(r) = (1-1/T)*Q(r) + Feedback(r) / T.$$

In this formula, $Q(r)$ is the weight of the recommendation rule r, T is the aging parameter (T>1). Feedback is the numerical value which describes a user's response to the presentation of the given recommendation. Multiplying the weight by (1-1/T) implements the aging, since this way the latest presentations have the most impact on the resulting weight value while the contribution of past presentations decreases exponentially with each next presentation. The exact value of parameter T should be determined experimentally, depending on how dynamic the user interests for a website are.

5.2 Exploration Versus Exploitation

We have investigated two techniques of balancing between exploration and exploitation. In the *reward-only* technique, the tradeoff between exploration and exploitation is set statically through the parameter ε. With probability (1- ε) the technique selects the best recommendations according to their weights. With probability ε it selects random recommendations for presentation to give them a chance to be explored. This technique is also called ε-greedy in the literature [16]. The benefit of this technique is a very simple and understandable control over exploitation vs. exploration. The drawback is that it explores all recommendations with equal probability, not taking into account how promising they might be. The values of Feedback(r) for this technique are as follows:

    1   if the recommendation r was clicked
    0   if the recommendation r was not clicked

In the *reward-penalty* technique the balancing between exploration and exploitation is done dynamically using negative feedback. When some recommendation r in a presentation is clicked, r receives positive feedback, all other recommendations receive negative feedback. When no recommendation is clicked, after a predefined timeout all participating recommendations receive negative feedback. To prevent the weights from sliding into the extreme values, the feedback values should be chosen in such a way, that for any given context an approximate equilibrium is maintained throughout the process:

$$\Sigma(positive\ feedback) \approx -\Sigma(negative\ feedback)$$

For example:

      1   if the recommendation r was clicked

     -p if the recommendation r was not clicked

where p is the probability, that a recommendation is clicked, averaged over all recommendation presentations on the web site. For both our applications. (EDU) and (EC), the value of $p \approx 0.01$.

With the reward-penalty technique we do not have to always sacrifice a fixed share of presentations for exploration. However, the drawback of this technique is the need for careful selection of the feedback values, because otherwise the learning process degenerates. It is also possible to combine the reward-penalty technique with the ε-random selection of the recommendations for exploration.

6   Prototype and Evaluation

In this section we describe the implementations of our prototype and evaluate the obtained results. In subsection 6.1 we present technical details of the implementation and effects of the recommendations on the buying behavior of the users. In subsection 6.2 we compare different optimization algorithms and recommendation rule selection policies.

6.1   Prototype Implementations, Click Rates and Economic Efficiency

A prototype of the system was implemented and applied at two websites. The first one is the website of the Database Group, University of Leipzig (http://dbs.uni-leipzig.de, approximately 2000 page views per day). It shows two (N=2) recommendations on all html-pages of the site. The second application is a small commercial online software store (http://www.softunity.com, approximately 5000 page views per day). Here, our approach is used to automatically select and present five (N=5) recommendations on product detail pages. Both websites have around 2500 content pages. The recommendation database contains about 60000 rules for (EDU) and 35000 rules for (EC).

The prototype uses a MySQL database server for the recommendation database and Microsoft SQL Server for the web data warehouse. All recommenders and the optimizer, as well as the websites themselves, are implemented using the PHP scripting language.

Fig. 4 shows the that the number of clicks per recommendation rule is distributed according to a Zipfian-like law (in the figure, only the recommendations with at least 100 presentations are considered.). The data shows that a relatively small percentage of the recommendation rules brings the majority of clicks. This supports our optimization heuristic, since it shows that we may achieve overall improvement of the acceptance rate by presenting the most successful recommendations more often.

In general, 2.07 % web users of www.softunity.com are becoming customers (this metric is usually regarded as CCR – Customer Conversion Rate). For web users who clicked a recommendation this value is 8.55 %, i.e. more than four times higher.

The analysis of the customer and purchase data has also shown, that 3.04 % of all purchased products were bought immediately after clicking the recommendation, and 3.43 % of all purchased products were recommended in the same session.

Fig. 5 shows the effects of our optimization algorithm in terms of buying behavior, in contrast to the non-optimized selection of the recommendations. The non-optimized algorithm uses the initial weights supplied by the recommenders to select the recommendations, and does no feedback-based optimization. The figure shows that the optimized approach results in a noticeable increase of the number of additions to shopping carts.

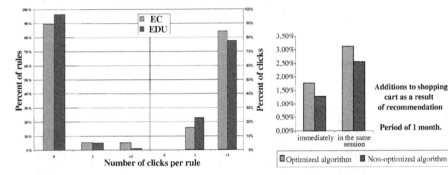

Fig. 4. A small number of recommendations brings the majority of clicks (EC, EDU)

Fig. 5. Additions to basket as a result of recommendation (EC)

6.2 Optimization Algorithms and Recommendation Selection Policies

To evaluate the effectiveness of the different optimization algorithms, we have compared the performance of the reward-only and reward-penalty optimization algorithms with the selection of recommendations based on the initial weight supplied by recommender. For an evaluation period of several months the selection algorithm was chosen with equal probability from one of the following:

- reward-only, $\varepsilon=0.2$, no aging
- reward-only, $\varepsilon=0.05$, no aging
- reward-penalty, aging by division with T=200
- reward-penalty, aging by division with T=500
- without optimization

Fig. 6 shows that the optimized algorithms achieve higher acceptance rates than the algorithms without optimization. The algorithm, which uses penalty as well as reward, was able to achieve somewhat higher acceptance rates than the algorithm which uses only reward and with some probability selects random recommendation rules for exploration. Too quick aging (in our case T=200) can adversely affect the optimization. The relatively small improvement of the reward-penalty algorithm can be attributed to the fact, that in our applications the successful and unsuccessful recommendations can be distinctly separated even by the simpler algorithms. The algorithm which used zero as initial weights for the recommendation rules was tested on the EDU website. Its acceptance rate was only 4% lower than that of the algorithm which used recommender-specific initial weights.

Fig. 7 shows the session acceptance rates (number of sessions where at least one recommendation was accepted divided through total number of sessions) for different recommendation selection policies introduced in Section 3. Five policies were tested. The random policy was used for comparison. In addition to the policies described in section 3, we have tested policies "only parents" and "only siblings" which were used to simulate the scenarios when no directly matching recommendations can be found. The policy "only parents" ignores the direct matching recommendations and takes only recommendations from the higher hierarchy levels. The policy "only siblings" searches for recommendations among the hierarchy siblings (nodes having a common parent with the current node), also ignoring the direct matches. According to the test results, the "direct match" policy performs better then the policy "direct+parents". However, the "direct+parent" policy is able to find recommendations even in cases, when no directly matching recommendations are available.

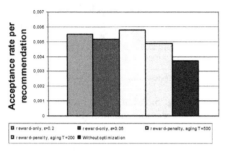

Fig. 6. Acceptance rate of different optimization algorithms(EC)

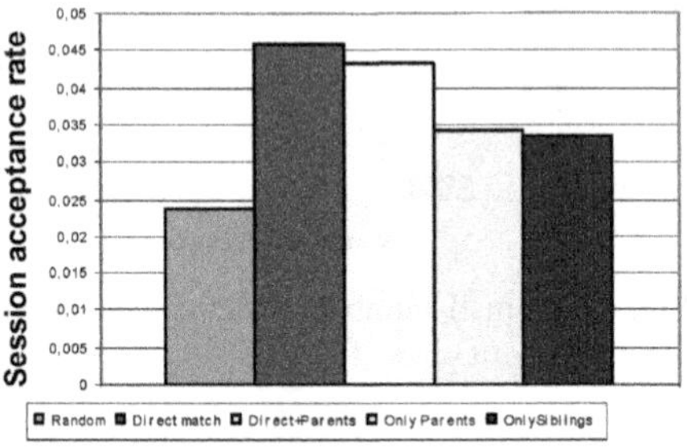

Fig. 7. Session Acceptance rate of the rule selection policies(EDU)

6.3 User Groups

Fig. 8 shows the comparison of the acceptance rates for different user groups. The user groups were built using a decision tree algorithm J48 over the usage data of several months from the EDU website. The DBS website is structured in several areas of interest, most important of which are Study and Research: For the decision tree algorithm, the area of interest (Research/Study) visited by a web user, has served as a classification attribute; other attributes were country, browser and operating system of the web user. However, after the tree was pruned, only the attribute country appeared to be of importance in addition to the area of interest. The resulting tree was transformed into ontology graph nodes with mapping clauses. Fig. 8 indicates that the acceptance rates differ substantially for the user groups and that for the considered website research-oriented users accept presented recommendations almost twice as much than study-oriented users.

Fig. 9 shows how good our user groups are in predicting the user interests. Here, differently colored bars show the acceptance for recommendations pointing to content of different interest areas. The user group Research appears to be quite effective, since its users have only clicked the recommendations leading to the research area of the website. Users of group Study preferred study-related recommendations but the corresponding acceptance rate is not much higher than for users not belonging to any of the two specific user groups.

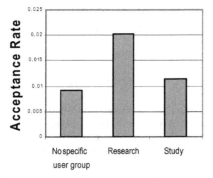
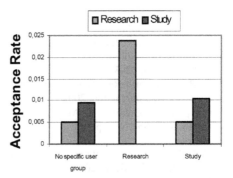

Fig. 8. Acceptance rates of different user groups (EDU)

Fig. 9. Acceptance rates of user group based recommendation rules (EDU)

7 Related Work

A survey of hybrid recommender systems including a list of strengths and weaknesses of different recommender algorithms and a classification of the hybridization methods can be found in the [5].

The work in [17] also employs data warehouse to store usage information and implicit user feedback. However, in [17] the feedback is used to learn how to switch different recommender algorithms, which work independently, whereas in our approach the feedback influences the weights of individual recommendations ("switched" approach vs. "weighted" approach according to the classification in [5]). [17] describes several strategies, according to which the best recommender can be chosen.

Combining the collaborative filtering with content-based algorithms is addressed in [6], [13] and [3]. Their approaches strive to combine both algorithms in one algorithm in an algorithm-specific way. Our approach, in contrast, views these algorithms as independent, but dynamically combines their results in a way, optimized for the given website.

8 Summary

We described the architecture, implementation and use of a novel recommendation system. It uses multiple techniques to generate recommendations, stores them in a semantically enabled recommendation database and then refines them using online optimization. Our results for two sample websites showed that feedback-based optimization can significantly increase the acceptance rate of the recommendations. Even the simple optimization techniques could substantially improve acceptance of recommendations compared to the non-optimized algorithm. We have also shown that web recommendations and our optimization approach have considerable impact on the buying behavior of the customers of an e-commerce web site.

References

1. S. Acharyya, J. Ghosh: Context-Sensitive Modeling of Web-Surfing Behavior using Concept Trees. Proc. WebKDD, 2003

2. M. Balabanovic: An Adaptive Web Page Recommendation Service. CACM, 1997
3. J.Basilico, T.Hofmann.: Unifying collaborative and content-based filtering. Proc. 21th ICML Conference. Banff, Canada, 2004
4. S. Baron, M. Spiliopoulou: Monitoring the Evolution of Web Usage Patterns. Proc. ECML/PKDD, 2003
5. R. Burke: Hybrid Recommender Systems: Survey and Experiments. User Modeling and User-Adapted Interaction, 2002
6. Claypool, M., Gokhale, A., Miranda, T.: Combining Content-Based and Collaborative Filters in an Online Newspaper. In: Proc. ACM SIGIR Workshop on Recommender Systems, 1999
7. N. Golovin, E. Rahm: Reinforcement Learning Architecture for Web Recommendations. Proc. ITCC2004, IEEE, 2004
8. S. ten Hagen, M. van Someren and V. Hollink: Exploration/exploitation in adaptive recommender systems. Proc. European Symposium on Intelligent Technologies, Hybrid Systems and their Implementation in Smart Adaptive Systems, Oulu, Finland. 2003
9. A. Jameson, J. Konstan, J. Riedl: AI Techniques for Personalized Recommendation. Tutorial presented at AAAI, 2002
10. G. Linden, B. Smith, and J. York: Amazon.com Recommendations: Item-to-Item Collaborative Filtering. IEEE Internet Computing. Jan. 2003
11. B. Mobasher, X. Jin, Y. Zhou. Semantically Enhanced Collaborative Filtering on the Web. Proc. European Web Mining Forum, LNAI, Springer 2004
12. M. Nakagawa, B. Mobasher: A Hybrid Web Personalization Model Based on Site Connectivity. Proc. 5th WEBKDD workshop, Washington, DC, USA, Aug. 2003
13. P. Paulson, A. Tzanavari: Combining Collaborative and Content-Based Filtering Using Conceptual Graphs. Lecture Notes in Computer Science 2873 Springer 2003
14. E. Reategui, J. Campbell, R. Torres, R. Using Item Descriptors in Recommender Systems, AAAI Workshop on Semantic Web Personalization, San Jose, USA, 2004
15. B. Sarwar, G. Karypis, J. Konstan, J. Riedl: Analysis of Recommendation Algorithms for E-Commerce. Proc. ACM E-Commerce, 2000
16. R.S. Sutton, A.G. Barto: Reinforcement Learning: An Introduction. MIT Press,1998.
17. A. Thor, E. Rahm: AWESOME - A Data Warehouse-based System for Adaptive Website Recommendations. Proc. 30th Intl. Conf. on Very Large Databases (VLDB), Toronto, Aug. 2004

Recommender Systems Using Support Vector Machines

Sung-Hwan Min and Ingoo Han

Graduate School of Management, Korea Advanced Institute of Science and Technology,
207-43 Cheongrangri-dong, Dongdaemun-gu, Seoul 130-722, Korea
`shmin@kgsm.kaist.ac.kr`

Abstract. Due to the explosion of e-commerce, recommender systems are rapidly becoming a core tool to accelerate cross-selling and strengthen customer loyalty. There are two prevalent approaches for building recommender systems – content-based recommending and collaborative filtering (CF). This study focuses on improving the performance of recommender systems by using data mining techniques. This paper proposes an SVM based recommender system. Furthermore this paper presents the methods for improving the performance of the SVM based recommender system in two aspects: feature subset selection and parameter optimization. GA is used to optimize both the feature subset and parameters of SVM simultaneously for the recommendation problem. The results of the evaluation experiment show the proposed model's improvement in making recommendations.

1 Introduction

Recommender systems are the information filtering process to supply personalized information by predicting user's preferences to specific items. In a world where the number of choices can be overwhelming, recommender systems help users find and evaluate items of interest [11]. Due to the explosion of e-commerce, recommender systems are rapidly becoming a core tool to accelerate cross-selling and strengthen customer loyalty. To date, a variety of techniques for building recommender systems have been developed. These techniques can be classified into two main categories: content-based filtering and collaborative filtering (CF). CF is the most successful recommendation technique, which has been used in a number of different applications such as recommending movies, articles, products, Web pages [1, 10]. CF is built on the assumption that a good way to predict the preference of the active consumer for a target product is to find other consumers who have similar preferences, and then use those similar consumer's preferences for that product to make a prediction [6].

Support Vector Machines have attracted most interest in the last few years which is developed by [16]. SVM implements the principle of Structural Risk Minimization by constructing an optimal separating hyperplane in the hidden feature space, using quadratic programming to find a unique solution. Compared with most other learning techniques, SVM has shown remarkable results in pattern recognition [13], text categorization [9], speaker identification [12] and financial time series prediction [2, 4, 8]. But only a small number of studies used SVM in recommendation problem. Furthermore there has been few research which uses optimized SVM model in recommendation problems. In general, the performance of SVM model is sensitive not only to some parameters but also to feature subset. Therefore it is very critical to optimize SVM model for more accurate performance.

D. Lowe and M. Gaedke (Eds.): ICWE 2005, LNCS 3579, pp. 387–393, 2005.

This study proposes an SVM based recommender system. Furthermore this study presents the methods for improving the performance of the SVM based recommender system in two aspects: feature subset selection and parameter optimization. GA is used to optimize both the feature subset and parameters of the SVM simultaneously for more accurate recommendations.

2   Background

2.1   Genetic Algorithm

Genetic Algorithm (GA) is an artificial intelligence procedure based on the theory of natural selection and evolution. GA uses the idea of survival of the fittest by progressively accepting better solutions to the problems. It is inspired by and named after biological processes of inheritance, mutation, natural selection, and the genetic crossover that occurs when parents mate to produce offspring [5]. GA differs from conventional non-linear optimization techniques in that it searches by maintaining a population (or data base) of solutions from which better solutions are created rather than making incremental changes to a single solution to the problem. GA simultaneously possesses a large amount of candidate solutions to a problem, called population. The key feature of a GA is the manipulation of a population whose individuals are characterized by possessing a chromosome.

Two important issues in GA are the genetic coding used to define the problem and the evaluation function, called the fitness function. Each individual solution in GA is represented by a string called the chromosome. Initial solution population could be generated randomly, which evolve to the next generation by genetic operators such as selection, crossover and mutation. The solutions coded by strings are evaluated by the fitness function. Selection operator allows strings with higher fitness to appear with higher probability in the next generation [7]. Crossover is performed between two selected individuals, called parents, by exchanging parts of their strings, starting from a randomly chosen crossover point. This operator tends to enable to the evolutionary process to move toward promising regions of the search space. Mutation is used to search further space of problem and to avoid local convergence of the GA [15].

2.2   Support Vector Machine(SVM)

Support Vector Machine (SVM) is a novel learning machine introduced by [16]. The SVM has emerged in recent years as powerful techniques both for regression and classification. The SVM learns a separating hyperplane to maximize the margin and to produce good generalization ability. Recently the SVM has been successfully applied in many areas and has shown remarkable results.

The SVM is based on the Structural Risk Minimization principle for which error-bound analysis has been theoretically motivated. The SVM performs pattern recognition for two-class problems by determining the separating hyperplane with maximum distance to the closest points of the training set. These points are called support vectors. In its simplest linear form, an SVM is a hyperplane that separates a set of positive examples from a set of negative examples with maximum margin. Suppose N observations has a pair $(\mathbf{x}_1, y_1), (\mathbf{x}_2, y_2), (\mathbf{x}_3, y_3), \ldots, (\mathbf{x}_n, y_n)$: a vector

$x_i \in R_n, y_i \in \{-1, 1\}$. The task of the SVM is to learn mapping the pair, $x_i \rightarrow y_i \in \{-1, 1\}$. The formula for the output of a linear SVM is $u = \vec{w} \cdot \vec{x} - b$ where $\vec{w}$ is the normal vector to the hyperplane, and $\vec{x}$ is the input vector. In the linear case, the margin is defined by the distance of the hyperplane to the nearest of the positive and negative examples. Maximizing the margin can be expressed as an optimization problem: minimize $\frac{1}{2} \| \vec{w} \|^2$ subject to $y_i(\vec{w} \cdot \vec{x} - b) \geq 1, \forall i$ where x_i is the ith training example and y_i is the correct output of the SVM for the ith training example.

The algorithms for solving linearly separable cases can be extended so that they can solve linearly non-separable cases as well by either introducing soft margin hyperplanes, or by mapping the original data vectors to a higher dimensional space where the new features contain interaction terms of the original features, and the data points in the new space become linearly separable [3]. In the non linear problem, we first map the data to some other Euclidean space H, using mapping, $\Phi : \mathbf{R}^d \mapsto \mathrm{H}$. Then instead of the form of dot products, "kernel function" K is used such that $K(\mathbf{x}_i, \mathbf{y}_i) = \Phi(\mathbf{x}_i) \bullet \Phi(\mathbf{x}_j)$.

3 Hybrid GA-SVM Model

This study presents the methods for improving the performance of an SVM based recommender system in two aspects: feature subset selection and parameter optimization. GA is used to optimize both the feature subset and parameters of SVM simultaneously for recommendation model.

3.1 Optimizing Feature Subset

Feature subset selection is essentially an optimization problem, which involves searching the space of possible features to find one that is optimum or near-optimal with respect to certain performance measures such as accuracy. In a classification problem, the selection of features is important for many reasons: good generalization performance, running time requirements and constraints imposed by the problem itself.

In the literature there are known two general approaches to solve the feature selection problem: The filter approach and the wrapper approach [14]. The distinction made depending on whether feature subset selection is done independently of the learning algorithm used to construct the classifier (i.e., filter) or not (i.e., wrapper). In the filter approach, feature selection is performed before applying the classifier to the selected feature subset. The filter approach is computationally more efficient than a wrapper approach. Wrapper approach train the classifier system with a given feature subset as an input and estimate the classification error using a validation set. Although this is a slower procedure, the features selected are usually more optimal for the classifier employed.

In a classification problem, feature subset selection plays an important role in the performance of prediction. Furthermore its importance increases when the number of features is large. This study seeks to improve SVM based recommender system. We propose the GA as the method of feature subset selection in the SVM system. This study uses the wrapper approach to select optimal feature subset of the SVM model using GA.

3.2 Optimizing the Parameters of SVM

One of the big problems in SVM is the selection of the value of parameters that will allow good performance. Selecting appropriate values for parameters of SVM plays an important role in the performance of SVM. But, it is not known beforehand which values are the best for one problem. Optimizing the parameters of SVM is crucial for the best prediction performance.

This study proposes GA as the method of optimizing parameters of SVM. In this study, the radial basis function (RBF) is used as the kernel function for SVM based recommender system. There are two parameters while using RBF kernels: C and δ^2. These two parameters play an important role in the performance of SVMs [2]. In this study, C and δ^2 are encoded as binary strings, and optimized by GA.

3.3 Simultaneous Optimization of SVM Using GA

In general, the choice of the feature subset has an influence on the appropriate kernel parameters and vice versa. Therefore feature subset and parameters of SVM need to be optimized simultaneously for the best prediction performance. The proposed model optimizes both feature subset and parameters of SVM simultaneously. The overall procedure of the proposed model starts with the randomly selected chromosomes which represent feature subset and parameters of SVM. Each new chromosome is evaluated by sending it to the SVM model. The SVM model uses the feature subset and parameters in order to obtain the performance measure (e.g. hit ratio). This performance measure is used as the fitness function and is evolved by GA.

The chromosomes for the feature subset are encoded as binary strings standing for some subset of the original feature set list. Each bit of the chromosome represents whether the corresponding feature is selected or not. 1 in each bit means the corresponding feature is selected, whereas 0 means it is not selected. The chromosomes for parameters of SVM are encoded as a 16-bit string which consists of 8 bits standing for C and 8 bits standing for δ^2. Fig. 1 shows examples of encoding for GA.

Each of the selected feature subsets and parameters is evaluated using SVM. This process is iterated until the best feature subset and values of parameters are found.

The data set is divided into a training set and a validation portion. The training set (T) consists of both T_1 and T_2.

GA evolves a number of populations. Each population consists of sets of features of a given size and the values of parameters. The fitness of an individual of the population is based on the performance of SVM. SVM is trained on T_1 using only the features of the individual and the values of parameters of the individual. The fitness is the prediction accuracy of the SVM model over T_2. At each generation new individuals are created and inserted into the population by selecting fit parents which are mutated and recombined.

The fitness function is represented mathematically as follows:

$$Fitness = \frac{\sum_{i=1}^{n} H_i}{n}$$

(1)

where H_i is 1 if actual output equal to the predicted value of the SVM model, otherwise H_i is zero.

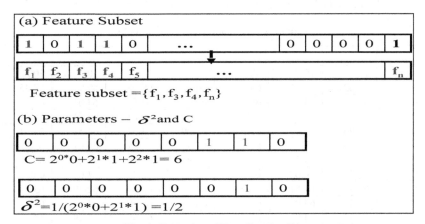

Fig. 1. Examples of Encoding for GA

4 Experimental Evaluation

We conducted experiments to evaluate the proposed model. For experiments we used the EachMovie database, provided by Comaq Systems Research Center (http://www.research.compaq.com/SRC/eachmovie). The dataset contains explicit rating data provided by each user for various movies. The EachMovie dataset has rating information on 1,628 movies by 72,916 users during an 18 month period from 1996. The ratings in the EachMovie are discretized into six levels, as 0, 0.2, 0.4, 0.6, 0.8 and 1. In the following, we defined a move "interesting" to an individual customer if his/her preference rating for this movie is greater than 0.5.

We used hit ratio as our choice of evaluation metric to report prediction experiments. First we selected 1000 users with more than 100 rated items. We divided the data set into a training set and a test portion.

We use the term, "GA-SVM" model as the proposed model which is simultaneous optimization of SVM using GA. To compare the performance of the proposed GA-SVM model we used the traditional CF algorithm as the benchmark model. The traditional CF recommendation employs the Pearson nearest neighbor algorithm.

Table 1 shows the classification accuracies of various parameters in SVM. The experimental results show that the prediction performance of SVM is sensitive to various parameters. Table 2 describes the average prediction accuracy of each model. In

SVM, we used the best result on the validation set out of results of Table 1. In Table 2, the proposed GA-SVM model shows better performance than SVM and TCF model.

The McNemar tests are used to examine whether the proposed model significantly outperforms the other models. This test is a nonparametric test for two related samples using the chi-square distribution. The McNemar test assesses the significance of the difference between two dependent samples when the variable of interest is a dichotomy. It is useful for detecting changes in responses due to experimental intervention in "before-and-after" designs.

Table 3 shows the results of McNemar test. As shown in Table 3, GA-SVM outperforms SVM and TCF with the 5% statistical significant level.

Table 1. Classification accuracy of SVM

C	δ^2						
	1	10	30	50	80	100	200
1	65.02	64.51	63.51	60.47	60.98	59.97	58.45
10	64.51	63	65.03	65.52	64.51	64.01	64.51
30	58.96	63	62	65.02	64.01	64.51	64.01
50	57.95	62.49	62.5	61.99	64.51	64.51	64.51
70	58.96	63.5	64.01	61.99	64.01	64.01	63.5
90	58.45	64.51	63	61.99	62.49	64.01	63
100	58.96	66.03	63	62.49	62.49	64.01	63
150	60.47	64.51	62.49	63.5	62.49	62.49	63
200	58.45	65.02	63	63.5	61.99	63	63.5
250	57.44	64.01	63	63	61.99	62.49	63

Table 2. Average prediction accuracy

Model		Hit Raio(%)
Proposed Model	GASVM	67.85
	SVM	66.03
Traditional Model	TCF	65.58

Table 3. p values of McNemar test

Model		p-value	
		SVM	TCF
Proposed Model	GASVM	0.032[a]	0.017**
	SVM	.	0.363
Traditional Model (TCF)			

[a] Significant at the 5% level

5 Conclusion

Due to the explosion of e-commerce, recommender systems are rapidly becoming a core tool to accelerate cross-selling and strengthen customer loyalty. This study focused on improving the performance of recommender system by using data mining techniques. This paper proposed an SVM based recommender system. Furthermore this study presented the methods for improving the performance of an SVM based recommender system in two aspects: feature subset selection and parameter optimization. GA was used to optimize both the feature subset and parameters of the SVM simultaneously.

We conducted an experiment to evaluate the proposed model on the EachMovie data set and compared them with the traditional CF algorithm. The results show the proposed model's improvement in making recommendations.

In our future work, we intend to optimize kernel function, parameters and feature subset simultaneously. We would also like to expand this model to apply to the instance selection problems.

References

1. Breese, J.S., Heckerman, D., Kadie, C. (1998). Empirical Analysis of Predictive Algorighms for Collaborative Filtering. Proceedings of the 14th Conference on Uncertainty in Artificial Intelligence (UAI-98), pp. 43-52.
2. Cao, L., Tay, F.E.H., (2001), Financial Forecasting Using Support Vector Machines, Neural Computing & Applications 10. pp. 184-192.
3. Cortes, C., and Vapnik, V., Support vector networks. Machine Learning, 20, 273-297, 1995.
4. Fan, A., Palaniswami, M., (2000). Selecting Bankruptcy Predictors Using A support Vector Machine Approach, Proceeding of the International Joint Conf. on Neural Network 6. 354-359.
5. Goldberg, D. E., Genetic Algorithms in Search, Optimization and Machine Learning (Addison-Wesley, New York 1989)
6. Herlocker, J.L., Konstan, J.A. and Riedl, J., (2000). Explaining collaborative filtering recommendations. Proceedings on the ACM 2000 Conference on Computer Supported Cooperative Work, (pp. 241–250). Philadelphia.
7. Holland, J. H., Adaptation in natural and artificial systems (The University of Michigan Press, Ann Arbor, 1975)
8. Huang, Zan., Che, Hsinchun., Hsu, Chia-Jung., Chen, Wun-Hwa., Soushan Wu, (2004). Credit rating analysis with support vector machines and neural networks: a Market comparative study, Decision Support Systems 37. 543-558.
9. Joachims, T. (1997). Text Categorization with Support Vector Machines, Technical report, LS VIII Number 23, University of Dormund
10. Sarwar,B.M., Konstan,J.A., Borchers,A., Herlocker,J.L., Miller,B.N., Ried1,J. (1998). Using filtering agents to improve prediction quality in the grouplens research collaborative filtering system. Proceedings of CSCW'98. Seattle, WA.
11. Schafer, J.B., Konstan, J.A. and Riedl, J. (2001). Electronic Commerce Recommender Applications. Data Mining and Knowledge Discovery 5(1/2), pp. 115-153.
12. Schmidt, M. S. (1996). Identifying Speaker with Support Vector Networks, In Interface '96 Proceedings, Sydney.
13. Sclkopf, B., Burges, C., Vapnik, V., (1995). Extracting support data for a given task. In U.M Fayyad and R. Uthurusamy, editors, Proceedings, First International Conference on Knowledge Discovery & Data Mining. AAAI Press, Menlo Park, CA.
14. Sun, Z., Bebis, G., Miller, R., Object Detection using Feature Subset Selection, Pattern Recognition 27 (2004) 2165-2176
15. Tang, K. S., Man, K. F., Kwong, S., He, Q., Genetic Algorithms and Their Applications, IEEE Signal Processing Magazine 13 (1996) 22-37.
16. Vapnik, VN., (1995). The Nature of Statistical Learning Theory (New York, Springer-Verlag.
17. http://www.research.compaq.com/SRC/eachmovie

Multi-channel Publication of Interactive Media Content for Web Information Systems

Nico Oorts[1], Filip Hendrickx[2], Tom Beckers[3], and Rik Van De Walle[3]

[1] VRT, A. Reyerslaan 52, Brussels, Belgium
nico.oorts@vrt.be
[2] IMEC, Kapeldreef 75, Leuven, Belgium
filip.hendrickx@imec.be
[3] Ghent University-IBBT, Sint-Pietersnieuwstraat 41, Ghent, Belgium
tom.beckers@xmt.be, rik.vandewalle@ugent.be

Abstract. The increasing number of devices for multimedia consumption poses a significant challenge on the device independence of Web Information Systems. Moreover, media content itself becomes increasingly complex, requiring not only an adaptive layout model, but also support for interactivity and synchronisation of resources.

In this paper, we use the XiMPF document model integrated with descriptive languages for layout, synchronisation and interaction. This integration preserves the uniformity which XiMPF handles singular resources and composed multimedia items with. Moreover, it improves the reusability and automatic adaptation of multimedia content. We focus on the introduction of interactivity in this model and present a publication engine which processes XiMPF items and their descriptions, and generates different versions of the content for different platforms.

1   Introduction

The emergence of powerful networked devices such as mobile phones, personal digital assistants and set-top boxes brings about a dramatic diversification of the means of multimedia consumption. Web Information Systems need to be able to select and adapt content in order to target diverse types of client devices.

Our approach allows fine grained adaptation of multimedia content to the capabilities of target devices and user preferences while maintaining maximum publisher control options. It aims to facilitate the reuse of multimedia resources and presentational information across heterogeneous consumption platforms. This is accomplished by a rigorous separation of concerns (content, structure, positioning, styling, synchronisation, behavior/interactivity) in the hierarchically structured XiMPF document model.

2   The XiMPF Document Model

In order to give the publisher maximal control of the output specification and to maximize reuse possibilities, we have continued development of the XiMPF

D. Lowe and M. Gaedke (Eds.): ICWE 2005, LNCS 3579, pp. 394–399, 2005.

document model (see [3, 6, 7] for a detailed introduction and examples). Fashioned after the MPEG-21 Digital Item Declaration (DID) model [5], it defines a semantically richer set of elements to structure and annotate the presentation content.

The XiMPF document model defines a document as a tree aggregating composing items. The nodes of the tree consist of (sets of) description fragments and content resources. The document model makes abstraction of item content: atomic multimedia resources are allowed as alternatives for composite presentation fragments, for example a picture and caption combination can be substituted for a video.

For the aggregation of textual and multimedia content, descriptions of structure, layout, synchronisation and behavior are used. We currently use available W3C technologies (XHTML, CSS, SMIL) supplemented with custom developed description languages where needed (e.g. interactivity). By not limiting the descriptive languages to be used, a flexible and future-proof framework guarantees the ability to cope with new target platforms.

Composite presentation fragments and atomic multimedia resources are treated in a similar fashion. Both can be automatically transformed or adapted to the target platform by the publication engine. The publisher can:

- leave the selection between alternatives to the publication engine - based on the client capabilities and preferences, or
- point to the version he deems fit for a certain presentation.

3   Use Case Description

To demonstrate the validity of the XiMPF model and the feasibility of a web information system in a multimedia, multichannel context, we operated within a specific use case scenario: the development of a new publication infrastructure for the present VRTNieuws.net website [2]. At the moment, the leading Belgian public broadcast company VRT (Vlaamse Radio en Televisie) produces news content for television, radio and internet. The internet publication engine produces only two fundamentally different versions: a full multimedia and a text-only version, both targeted towards a PC browser.

The new engine separates the editing of content from the adaptation and presentation for different platforms. Several versions of the news content (including text content as well as multimedia resources) are automatically derived from the same source material but the publisher retains control over the layout of the document presented to the customer.

In this use case, we generate output adapted to the following platforms:

- a television set with a set-top box and a large, high quality screen;
- a PC system with adequate system resources and a medium sized screen;
- a personal hand-held device (PDA) with wireless network connection.

4   Introducing Interactivity

Adding interactive behavior to media publications usually requires some form of programming. This often results in implementation code being spread across the entire publication. Such entanglement complicates adaptation of the document to support different platforms. It also interferes with reuse of the non interactive parts of the media publication, as these parts cannot be easily separated from the interaction code. In this section, we elaborate on a method to integrate interactive components in the XiMPF model in a way that leaves the separation of concerns intact.

An example is a user controlled slideshow developed for the news site use case. Visually, the slideshow consists of an image and a back and forward button. When the user clicks one of the buttons, the image changes. In a web environment, this requires adding some code to the buttons via the onclick attribute. This code is usually a call to a function in a separate script element or external file. The external code contains a reference to the image element that must change when the user clicks a button. During an initialisation phase, the images are preloaded and stored in an array. The back and forward functions can access this array and show the correct image.

While this is a simple example of interactivity, it already shows that the implementation of the behavior is tightly coupled with the rest of the document. There are links between the buttons, the images, the initialization phase and the rest of the code. Even though a Javascript and a VBScript implementation are conceptually identical, replacing one with the other will not be trivial, as several pieces of code throughout the whole document must be changed. This complicates reuse of the rest of the application (structure, layout and synchronisation).

Publishing this interactive presentation on a fundamentally different platform, like a television with Java based set-top box, will be cumbersome, as manual editing of the whole presentation is inevitable.

Our approach is based on a strict separation of the – possibly platform specific – implementation of the interactive behavior from the rest of the document. This ensures reusability of the rest of the media application. Three pieces of information are required to enable this separation (see figure 1).

1. An *API* defines the generic interface of the interactive behavior. For the slideshow, it defines the parameters for the initialisation phase (a list of images and a reference to the container for the images) and the supported features (back, forward) together with their parameters if present.
2. An *interaction description* in the XiMPF document links the parameters and features from the API with specific XiMPF items. These links are independent from the actual implementation of the interactive behavior.
3. An *implementation* of the API for a certain platform. When targeting a web browser, this implementation will for example define an `onclick` attribute for the back and forward buttons and an `onload` attribute for the `body` element. The attribute values will contain a Javascript function call implementing the desired behavior. The referred functions are also defined in the implementation.

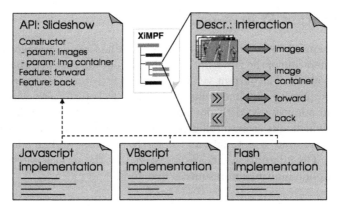

Fig. 1. Interactivity is added to media content via an API defining the behavior, an interaction description in the XiMPF document linking parameters and features with specific XiMPF items and an implementation

To illustrate this method, we will describe the necessary steps to add a feature to an interactive document. This feature will allow a user to push a button to move a slideshow one image forward. To add the 'forward' feature to the slideshow example, one needs to list the feature with its parameters (name and type) (in this case none) in the API. In the XiMPF interaction description, this feature is bound to a GUI item (in this case an image defined in the structure definition that will serve as a button through the inclusion of an onClick method). If needed, items or values are added as parameters to this feature binding in the XiMPF interaction description. The implementation file defines the construction of the code fragments that need to be added to the output document. This construction includes XSLT processing to replace parameters with their actual values. Parameters are replaced with the facet (selected in the implementation, e.g. item ID or item source path) of the parameter item (as declared in the interaction description). The publication engine constructs the code fragments and weaves them into the output publication.

This method of describing the interactive behavior of the slideshow application enables reuse of the XiMPF document, including the interaction description, for different platforms. For example, if we want to use Java or Flash instead of Javascript when publishing the slideshow, we only need to add the corresponding Java or Flash implementation alongside the Javascript implementation. As long as the new implementation adheres to the slideshow API, a publication of the interactive application in the correct format is possible without changes to the XiMPF document.

While the slideshow is a simple example, describing more complex interactive behavior is equally straightforward. Once the API is defined, it can be used in XiMPF documents without any dependency on the actual implementation (complexity).

5   Publication Framework

Our publication infrastructure, based on the Apache Cocoon framework [1], performs the generation of the news site described in our use case and the adaptation of atomic resources. The current version of our architecture (see figure 2) consists of an XML processing pipeline including a XiMPF Transformer, responsible for resolving and adapting XiMPF documents to a specific presentation version, a core engine, which acts as an intelligent broker, a resource and metadata (device characteristics, resource metadata and so forth) database and an adaptation service registry. The adaptation services registered by the service registry are used to process atomic multimedia resources like audio and video.

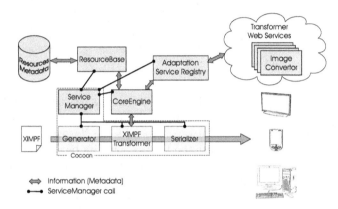

Fig. 2. The publication framework based on Cocoon

6   Related Work

A lot of the standard multimedia document models like SMIL and RIML [8], lack appropriate modeling primitives to enable reuse of multimedia content in different presentations and contexts. For example, SMIL's layout mechanism only allows fixed positioning of media items with regard to each other, and thus forces the author to create separate layouts for devices with highly differing screen sizes. XHTML and CSS take the approach of separating structure and layout but still lack adequate support for true single authoring. Different style sheets are needed to accommodate various platforms. To enable content creation and reuse for complex content applications, a more rigorous separation of presentational aspects is required, together with a high level document model like MPEG-21 DID. However, the practicability of MPEG-21 DID is vague and the model needs extensions for description types and structure which are introduced by the XiMPF model. Model-driven methodologies, like Hera [4] distinguish three design steps: conceptual, navigational and presentation design. Hera's navigation model offers flexible support for form-based interactivity in data-intensive applications. This is complementary to the XiMPF interactivity model, which is more geared towards dynamic content. Note also that Hera does not support synchronisation.

7 Conclusions

Device independent content management is an important challenge for Web Information Systems. This is especially true for dynamic multimedia content. In this context, we have indicated the strengths of the XiMPF document model, namely reuse of both media resources and presentational information at a fine level of granularity, and support for automatic adaptation of both singular and composed media content. The introduction of interactivity in a reusable and implementation independent manner demonstrates the extensibility of XiMPF. We built an extensible publication framework able to adapt media resources and descriptions, and generate specific output documents for different client terminals. We applied it to the news site of the leading Belgian broadcaster VRT, generating adapted news publications including interactive JavaScript, VBScript and Flash components for 3 different platforms.

Acknowledgements

This work is the result of a joint collaboration between VRT, IMEC, Vrije Universiteit Brussel and Universiteit Gent, funded by the Flemish government. The authors want to thank their colleague Peter Soetens for his valuable input regarding the publication framework.

References

1. The apache cocoon project. Available at http://cocoon.apache.org.
2. Vrtnieuws.net. Available at http://www.vrtnieuws.net.
3. T. Beckers, N. Oorts, F. Hendrickx, and R. Van de Walle. Multichannel publication of interactive media documents in a news environment. To be published in Proceedings of the Twelfth International World Wide Web Conference, 2005.
4. G.-J. Houben, F. Frasnicar, P. Barna, and R. Vdovjak. Modeling user input and hypermedia dynamics in Hera. In *Proceedings of the 4th International Conference on Web Engineering*, pages 60–73, Munich, Germany, July 2004. Springer Verlag.
5. ISO/IEC. *MPEG-21 – Part 2: Digital Item Declaration – ISO/IEC FDIS 21000-2*.
6. S. Van Assche, F. Hendrickx, and L. Nachtergaele. Multichannel publication using MPEG-21 DIDL and extensions. In *Proceedings of the Twelfth International World Wide Web Conference*. W3C, 2003. Poster.
7. S. Van Assche, F. Hendrickx, N. Oorts, and L. Nachtergaele. Multi-channel publishing of interactive multimedia presentations. *Computers & Graphics*, 2004(5):193–206.
8. T. Ziegert, M. Lauff, and L. Heuser. Device independent web applications - the author once - display everywhere approach. In *Proceedings of the 4th International Conference on Web Engineering*, pages 244–255, Munich, Germany, July 2004. Springer Verlag.

Classification of RSS-Formatted Documents Using Full Text Similarity Measures

Katarzyna Wegrzyn-Wolska[1] and Piotr S. Szczepaniak[2,3]

[1] Ecole Supérieure d'Ingenieurs en Informatique et Génie de Télécommunication
77-200 Avon-Fontainebleau, France
[2] Institute of Computer Science, Technical University of Lodz,
ul. Wolczanska 215, 93-005 Lodz, Poland
[3] Systems Research Institute, Polish Academy of Sciences
ul. Newelska 6, 01-447 Warsaw, Poland

Abstract. The Web is enormous, unlimited and dynamically changed source of useful and varied kinds of information. The news is one of the most rapidly changing kinds of information. The departure for this paper is presentation of RSS, an useful data format used frequently by publishers of news; some statistics related to news syndication illustrate the actual situation. Then, two recently developed methods for examination of similarity of textual documents are briefly presented. Since RSS-supplied records always contain the same type of information (headlines, links, article summaries, etc.), application of methods of presented type makes their diverse applications like automatic news classification and filtering easier.

1 Introduction

This paper describes some general problems of publishing, retrieving and filtering news information on the Web. The first section introduces the principle of the news publication on the Web. The second section explains the main problems of exploration and filtering of the news data from the presentation Web pages. The following sections present the problems of the contents syndication on the Web and present some statistical results of the experiments carried out. Then the RSS feed data formats is introduced. The following sections show potential and features of this format. The last sections present methods for classification of documents using full text similarity measures. The conclusion summarizes the problems presented.

2 News Published on the Web

There are a lot of web sites which publish news. The news sites publish different kinds of information in different presentation forms [3, 6]. News is a very dynamic kind of information, constantly updated. The news sites have to be verified very often so as not to miss any of the news information. In Table 1 the updating frequency for some Web news sites is presented.Some parameters are significant

D. Lowe and M. Gaedke (Eds.): ICWE 2005, LNCS 3579, pp. 400–405, 2005.

Table 1. Example of updating news frequency (provided by the sites administrators)

Service news	URL	Update
Google	http://news.google.com	about 20 min
Voila actuality	http://actu.voila.fr	every day
TF1 news	http://new.tf1.fr/news	instantaneously
News now	http://ww.newsnow.co.uk	about 5 min
CategoryNet	http://www.categorynet.com	every day
CNN	http://www.cnn.com	instantaneously
Company news groups	http://www.companynewsgroup.com	about 40 per day

for automatic treatment; frequency of data updating, the size of the transferred data and extraction and filtering facilities on news sites. We have done some statistical tests to evaluate the updating frequency [13] of news.

The results shown (Fig.1a) the different behavior of interrogated sites: the news updated very regular or irregular when information is updated when present. Some news sites present periodic activity: ex. the news site of the French television channel TF1 is updated only during working hours. The results confirm that the content of the news sites change very often. This is one of the most important reasons for careful optimization the data flux format. The traffic generated on the net by news is high and it is interesting to optimize it. We have done some comparative tests (Fig. 1b) of the transferred data size for the news presented in HTML and in XML (RSS).

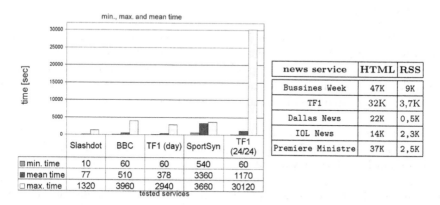

Fig. 1. a) Values of updating frequency; b) comparative size of HTML and RSS

3 News Data Formats: HTML and RSS

There are two the most frequently used data format for news publishing; the HTML non-structured data format and the dedicated format, named RSS-feed. These formats have different aspects for publication and presentation and for retrieving and exploring the data by other tools such as catalogues, search-engines and meta-search tools.

3.1 HTML Presentation

There are a lot of news Web sites that present the news using only the standard HTML page form. This page contains a lot of diverse data, not only lists of selected news items, but also much additional information. This additional information is completely useless for the retrieving tools (Search Engine, Meta-Search Engine, etc.) [11, 12]. The searching news' agent needs to extract only the significant data. Additional and non-essential data increases the complexity of analysis. The HTML pages, which include the informational and presentational data, are not optimal for data extraction and information content updating. The HTML pages are also not optimal for data transfer because of their size.

Data Extraction Problems. The format of the HTML news pages are not standardized. Their form does not lend itself to information extraction. There are two kinds of extraction problems. Firstly, finding all of the news description with their links included in the news page and then identifying only the pertinent ones. The most important difficulties of information extraction are: complex linking, difficulties in recognizing and following links to framed pages and then extraction of the information in this frame, difficulties in identifying links in image maps and in the script code sources like a JavaScript, etc. There is also some information, which is not static, for example, thematic publicity selected automatically and frequently changed. The retrieving tool has to distinguish which piece of data is the news information and select only the significant links.

3.2 RSS Feed

RSS (RDF Site Summary) is an XML-based special format that enables web developers to describe and syndicate web site content. The original RSS, was designed as a format for building portals of headlines to mainstream news sites. But RSS is not designed just for news and news-like sites, it became one of the basic weblog-oriented products and other web-based publishing software.

RSS Advantages. RSS provides a static and well-structured format for all the textual documents. The RSS file contains only the informational data formatted in a standardized format without any presentation parts. This well structured document is easy to parse. It is possible to analyze, monitor and to extract the data automatically. When we aim at off-line filtering or classification of news or other documents the RSS format seems to be a good proposition for simple extracting textual records which needs to be evaluated on their relevance. In the evaluation, human-similar comparison of textual documents (words, sentences, abstracts, full documents, etc.) is a key problem.

4 Similarity of Textual Records

So far, the methods used for text comparison have been based mainly on the classical identity relation, according to which two given texts are either identical or not. Diverse similarity or distance measures for sequence of characters have been developed. Examples of simple indices are Hamming and Levenstein distances. However, conventional methods are of limited usefulness and reliability, in particular for languages having reach inflexion (e.g.Slavonic languages). Here, two more sophisticated methods that make use of different independent ways of looking for similarity - similarity in terms of fuzzy sets theory [7, 9, 10] and sequence kernels [2, 4, 5], are proposed as possible solution. Although they exhibit certain similarities in their behavior, in many aspects the methods differ in an essential way. Here, only the first method is briefly presented; for the second one we refer to the given literature.

Fuzzy Measure. To enable a computer compare textual documents, the fuzzy similarity measure proposed in [7] (cf. also [9, 10]) can be used. Because in the considered case we deal with relatively frequently changing sources of textual information, the less time-consuming version of the method [8] analogous to the n-gram method described in [1] is recommended.

Let W be the set of all words from a considered dictionary (universe of discourse).

Definition 1. *The similarity measure takes the form*

$$\forall w_1, w_2 \in W : \quad \mu_{RW}(w_1, w_2) = \frac{1}{N-k+1} \sum_{j=1}^{N(w_1)-k+1} h(k,j) \qquad (1)$$

where: $h(i,j) = 1$, if a sub-sequence containing i letters of word w_1 and beginning from its j-th position in w_1, appears at least once in word w_2; otherwise: $h(i,j) = 0$;
$h(i,j) = 0$ also if $i > N(s_2)$ or $i > N(s_1)$;
$N = max\{N(w_1), N(w_2)\}$ - the maximum of $N(w_1), N(w_2)$- the number of letters in words w_1, w_2, respectively;
k denotes length of the considered string.

The function μ_{RW} can obviously be interpreted as fuzzy relation in terms of the fuzzy sets theory. This fuzzy relation is reflexive: $\mu_{RW}(w, w) = 1$ for any word w; but in general it is not symmetrical. This inconvenience can be easily avoided by the use of minimum operation. Note that the human intuition is considered because the bigger is the difference in length of two words, the more different they are, and the more common letters are contained in two words, the more similar they are.

However, the value of the membership function contains no information on the sense or semantics of the arguments. In a natural way, the sentence comparison bases on word similarity measure and any two textual records which are sets of words (sentences or not) can be compared using formula (2).

Definition 2. *The fuzzy relation on S - the set of all sentences, is of the form* $RS = \{(\langle s_1, s_2 \rangle, \mu_{RW}(s_1, s_2)) : s_1, s_2 \in S\}$, *with the membership function* μ_{RS} : $S \times S \to [0, 1]$

$$\mu_{RS}(s_1, s_2) = \frac{1}{N} \sum_{i=1}^{N(s_1)} \max_{j \in \{1, \ldots, N(s_2)\}} \mu_{RW}(w_i, w_j), \tag{2}$$

where: w_i- the word number i in the s_1 sentence, w_j- the word number j in the s_2 sentence,$\mu_{RW}(w_i, w_j)$ - the value of the μ_{RW} function for the pair (w_i, w_j),
$N(s_1), N(s_2)$ - the number of words in sentences s_1, s_2,
$N = max\{N(s_1), N(s_2)\}$ - the number of words in the longer of the two sentences under comparison.

In the summary, we state that both methods, i.e. fuzzy concept based, and sequence kernels, used to find the similarity of words can be also applied to establish similarity of sentences or even whole documents. In the first method, some similarity function on the sentences or documents must be defined, cf.(2). In the second one, instead of letters, the alphabet should contain words or sentences. Both methods are non-sensitive to mistakes or other misshapen language constructions but standard preprocessing is recommended. Unfortunately, they do not use semantic information existing in the natural language. To increase the rate of comparison correctness a dictionary of synonyms should support the method applied.

5   Summary

At the beginning, RSS feed files were used only for the news sites. Now, with thousands of RSS-enabled sites, this format has become more popular, perhaps the most widely seen kind of XML. RSS-feed is easy to use and well optimized to retrieve the news from the source sites. That is why it is useful to publish the news in two formats; firstly HTML dedicated to visual presentation and secondly XML-based format which is more useful for retrieving-tools. The RSS format seems to be a good proposition for simple extracting textual records which play the same role in different documents and therefore needs to be evaluated on their mutual similarity or similarity to certain pattern. For human-similar automatic evaluation of document relevance more sophisticated methods for text comparison than simple classical identity relation must be applied. Comparison of longer textual documents (words, sentences, abstracts, full documents, etc.) becomes a key problem. Examples of two methods based on quantitative measures were presented. Because of their character, they should be integrated with other approaches and applied off-line, eg. as an intelligent agent module.

References

1. H. Bandemer and S. Gottwald. Fuzzy sets, fuzzy logic, fuzzy methods with applications. *John Wiley and Sons*, 1995.
2. N. Canccedda, E. Gaussier, C. Goutte, and J. M. Renders. Word-sequence kernels. *Journal of Machine Learning Research*, 3:pp. 1059–1082, 2003.

3. L. Kangchan, M. Jaehong, and P. Kishik. A design and implementation of xml-based mediation framework(xmf)for integration of internet information resources*. In *Proceedings of the 35th Hawaii International Conference on System Sciences*, New York, 2002. Association for Computing Machinery.
4. H. Lodhi, N. Cristianini, J Shave-Taylor, and C. Watkins. Text classification using string kernel. *Advances in Neural Information Processing System, MIT Press*, 13, 2001.
5. H. Lodhi, C. Sanders, J. Shave-Taylor, N. Cristianini, and C. Watkins. Text classification using string kernels. *Journal of Machine Learning Research*, 2:419–444, 2002.
6. E.T. Mueller. Machine-understandable news for e-commerce andweb applications. In CSREA Press, editor, *Proceedings of the 2001 International Conference on Artificial Intelligence*, pages 1113–1119, New York, 2001. Association for Computing Machinery.
7. A. Niewiadomski. Appliance of fuzzy relations for text documents comparing. In *Proceedings of the 5th Conference on Neural Networks and Soft Computing*, pages 347–352, Zakopane, Poland, 2000.
8. A. Niewiadomski, P. Kryger, and P.S. Szczepaniak. Fuzzy comparison of strings in faq answering. In *BIS 2004. Proceedings of 7th International Conference on Business Information Systems*, pages 355–362, Poznan, Poland, 2004. W.Abramowicz (Ed.), Wydawnictwo Akademii Ekonomicznej.
9. P.S. Szczepaniak and A. Niewiadomski. Clustering of documents on the basis of text fuzzy similarity. In Abramowicz W. (Ed.), editor, *Knowledge-based information retrieval and filtering from the Web*, pages 219–230. Kluwer Academic Publ, London, Boston, New York, Dordrecht, 2003.
10. P.S Szczepaniak and A. Niewiadomski. Internet search based on text intuitionistic fuzzy similarity. In P.S. Szczepaniak, J. Segovia, J. Kacprzyk, and L. Zadeh, editors, *Physica-Verlag, A., Intelligent Exploration of the Web*. Springer ï+$\frac{1}{2}$Verlag Company,, Heidelberg, New York, 2003.
11. K. Wegrzyn-Wolska. *Etude et realisation d'un meta-indexeur pour la recherche sur le Web de documents produits par l'administration francaise*. PhD thesis, Ecoles Superieures de Mines de Paris, DEC 2001.
12. K. Wegrzyn-Wolska. Fim-metaindexer a meta-search engine purpose-bilt for the french civil service and the statistical classification and evaluation of the interrogated search engines. In *The Second International Workshop on Web-based Support Systems, In IEEE WIC ACM WI/AT'04*, pages 163–170, 2004.
13. K. Wegrzyn-Wolska. Le document numerique: une etoile filante dans l'espace documentaire. *Colloque EBSI-ENSSIB; Montreal 2004*, 2004.

Modelling Adaptivity with Aspects[*]

Hubert Baumeister[1], Alexander Knapp[1], Nora Koch[1,2], and Gefei Zhang[1]

[1] Ludwig-Maximilians-Universität München
{baumeist,knapp,kochn,zhangg}@pst.ifi.lmu.de
[2] F.A.S.T. GmbH, Germany
koch@fast.de

Abstract. Modelling adaptive Web applications is a difficult and complex task. Usually, the development of general system functionality and context adaptation is intertwined. However, adaptivity is a cross-cutting concern of an adaptive Web application, and thus is naturally viewed as an aspect. Using aspect-oriented modelling techniques from the very beginning in the design of adaptive Web applications we achieve a systematic separation of general system functionality and context adaptation. We show the benefits of this approach by making navigation adaptive.

1 Introduction

Adaptive Web applications are an alternative to the traditional "one-size-fits-all" approach in the development of Web systems. An adaptive Web application provides more appropriate pages to the user by being aware of user or context properties. Modelling adaptive Web applications is a difficult task because general system functionality aspects and adaptation aspects are tightly interwoven. We propose to view adaptivity as a cross-cutting concern and thus to use aspect-oriented modelling techniques to the modelling of adaptive Web applications. The advantages of using aspects when modelling adaptation is the removal of redundant modelling information, the increase in maintainability of models, and the better modularity of designs by grouping interrelated facets [9]. In particular, aspects make explicit where and how adaptivity interacts with the functional features of the Web application. Building less redundant models has the additional advantage of bug reduction in an implementation based on these models.

We demonstrate how aspect-oriented modelling techniques for adaptivity can be used to specify common types of adaptive navigation. In particular, we present aspects for adaptive link hiding, adaptive link annotation and adaptive link generation [5]. This demonstration is done in the context of the UML-based Web Engineering (UWE [13]) method and the SmexWeb (Student Modelled Exercising on the Web [1]) framework for adaptive Web-based systems which has been developed at the University of Munich[1].

The remainder of this paper is structured as follows: We first provide an overview of UWE and of adaptivity in Web applications. Next, we present our approach to modelling adaptivity with aspects. As a running example, we use a SmexWeb instance that

---

[*] This research has been partially sponsored by the EC 5th Framework project AGILE (IST-2001-32747) and Deutsche Forschungsgemeinschaft (DFG) within the project MAEWA (WI 841/7-1)

[1] http://smexweb.pst.informatik.uni-muenchen.de

D. Lowe and M. Gaedke (Eds.): ICWE 2005, LNCS 3579, pp. 406–416, 2005.

implements a lesson on the topic of EBNF (Extended Backus-Naur Form). We conclude with a discussion of related work and some remarks on future research.

2   UML-Based Web Engineering

Separate modelling of Web application concerns is a main feature of UML-based Web Engineering (UWE) as well as of other Web engineering methods. Thus, different models are built for each point of view: the content, the navigation structure, the business processes, and the presentation. The distinguishing feature of UWE is its UML compliance [15] since UWE is defined in the form of a UML profile and an extension of the UML metamodel (for more details, see [12, 13]).

In UWE, the content of Web applications is modelled in a conceptual model where the classes of the objects that will be used in the Web application are represented by instances of «conceptual class» which is a subclass of the UML Class. Relationships between contents are modelled by UML associations between conceptual classes.

The navigation model is based on the conceptual model and represents the navigation paths of the Web application being modelled. A «navigation class» represents a navigable node in the Web application and is associated to a conceptual class containing the information of the node. Navigation paths are represented by associations: An association between two navigation nodes represents a direct link between them. Additional navigation nodes are access primitives used to reach multiple navigation nodes («index» and «guided tour») or a selection of items («query»). Alternative navigation paths are modelled by «menu»s.

A navigation model can be enriched by the results of the process modelling which deals with the business process logic of a Web application and takes place in the process model. The presentation model is used to sketch the layout of the Web pages associated to the navigation nodes.

Figure 1 shows a simplified navigation model of our SmexWeb example [1]: an EBNF lesson, in which a grammar for constructing mountains is developed. After an introductory session, the user can select among three alternatives: "recognising mountains" or "building mountains", or to solve directly. First the user interactively solves the exercise with the support of the system. Subsequently, the user can apply his EBNF knowledge to solve a similar exercise without support.

3   Adaptivity

Adaptive Web applications allow for personalisation and contextualisation of Web systems. An adaptive Web application provides more appropriate pages to the user by being aware of user or context properties. User properties are characteristics such as tasks, knowledge, background, preferences or user's interests. Context properties are those related to the environment and not to the users themselves comprising both, user location (place and time) and user platform (hardware, software, network bandwidth). These properties are kept in a user model or context model, which is continuously updated based on the observation the system makes of the user behaviour or the environment, or on modifications of the user or context profile explicitly performed by the user.

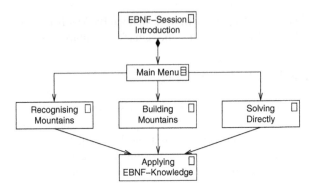

Fig. 1. SmexWeb: Navigation model for the EBNF lesson

We distinguish three levels of adaptation [12]: content adaptation, link or navigation adaptation and presentation adaptation. Others, like Brusilovsky [5], distinguish only between content and link level adaptation, where content adaptation refers as well to changes in the layout as to differences in the contents. Adaptive content comprises text adaptation and multimedia adaptation, whereas well known techniques for text adaptation are inserting/removing/altering of fragments, stretchtext and dimming fragments. Techniques to implement adaptive presentation are modality (selection, e.g., between written text or audio), multi-language (text translation into another language) and layout variations (e.g., resizing of images and ordering of text fragments or multimedia elements). Adaptive navigation support is achieved by adaptive link ordering, adaptive link hiding/removing/disabling, adaptive link annotation and adaptive link generation. The direct guidance and map adaptation techniques proposed by Brusilovsky [4, 5] can be implemented by the adaptation link techniques mentioned above: ordering, annotation, hiding and generation; thus we limit the description to those techniques:

- *adaptive link ordering* is the technique of sorting a group of links belonging to a particular navigation node. The criteria used for sorting are given by the current values of the user model: e.g., the closer to the top of the list, the more relevant the link is. Sorted links are only applicable to non-contextual links and are useful in information retrieval applications, but they can disorient the user as the link list may change each time the user enters the page.
- *adaptive link annotation* consists of the augmentation of the links with textual comments or graphical icons, which provide the user with additional information about the current state of the nodes behind the annotated links. Link annotation is a helpful and frequently used technique, also used for user-independent annotation.
- *adaptive link hiding* can be easily implemented by removing, disabling or hiding of links. All three techniques reduce the cognitive-overload of the user with the advantage of more stable nodes when links are added incrementally.
- *adaptive link generation* is a runtime feature for adding new anchors for links to a node based on the current status of the user model. The typical implementation are user model dependent shortcuts.

In our SmexWeb example we use the techniques of adaptive link annotation, adaptive link ordering and adaptive link hiding for link adaptation. Depending on the acquired knowledge, the user skills and the estimated cognitive abilities of the user – contained in the current user model (see below) – the system offers different links, sorted in a different way and differently annotated with emoticons.

The current user model for the EBNF course comprises three sub-models: domain, navigation and individual model. Values of the domain model represent the learner's knowledge about the topic of the course. The most important attribute of the navigation model captures the learner's navigation behaviour. The individual model represents learning preferences, for instance with brief or extended explanations, more abstract or more pragmatic descriptions. The initial values of all sub-models are assigned on basis of the answers to the initial questionnaire the user has to go through before starting the lesson. From there on, values of the user model will change dynamically according to the user's behaviour while navigating or solving an exercise. For further details about the user modelling techniques implemented in SmexWeb see [1, 12].

4   Modelling Adaptivity with Aspects

Adaptivity often cross-cuts the main functionalities of a Web application, e.g., counting the visits to a link and presenting the link differently depending on the number of visits are orthogonal to the navigation structure. It is not desirable to model such cross-cutting features in the principal model for each affected model element separately, since this would lead to redundancy and make the models error-prone. Instead, the techniques of aspect-oriented modelling [9] should be used.

Aspect-oriented modelling is a maturing modelling paradigm which aims at *quantification* and *obliviousness* by introducing a new construct: *aspect*. By quantification model elements of a cross-cutting feature are selected and comprised in an aspect and thus redundancy can be reduced; obliviousness means that the principal model does not need to be aware of the existence of the aspects and provides thus a better separation of concerns.

An aspect consists of a *pointcut* part and an *advice* part. It is a (graphical) statement saying that additionally to the features specified in the principal model, each model element selected by the pointcut also has the features specified by the advice. In other words, a complete description including both general system functionality and additional, cross-cutting features of the quantified model elements is given by the composition of the principal model and the aspect. The process of composition is called *weaving*. Building on a simple extension of the UML by aspects, we illustrate the use of aspect-oriented modelling for modelling adaptivity in our running example SmexWeb.

4.1   Aspects in the Unified Modeling Language

The UML [15] does not show genuine support for aspect-oriented modelling. In fact, several proposals have been made for integrating aspect orientation with the object-oriented paradigm followed by the UML, ranging from representing the programming language features of AspectJ in the UML [16] to integrating aspects in UML 2.0 as components [3], for an overview see, e.g., [9].

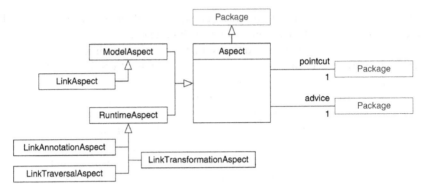

Fig. 2. Extension of UML metamodel

We restrict ourselves to a rather lightweight extension of the UML that merely composes the main ingredients of aspect-oriented modelling into a subclass (stereotype «aspect») of the UML metaclass Package: pointcut and advice; see Fig. 2. The pointcut package comprises (references to) all model elements on whose occurrence the advice package is to be applied. Both packages may contain constraints that either detail the application condition or the effect of an aspect. The semantics of applying an advice on a pointcut depends on whether an aspect is to be woven statically («model aspect») at the model level or dynamically («runtime aspect») at runtime. The different kinds of aspects we use for modelling navigation adaptation are discussed in the subsequent sections.

4.2   Extension of the UWE Metamodel

In order to capture adaptive link ordering, link annotation, and link hiding, we extend the UWE metamodel for designing navigation structures of Web applications by a NavigationAnnotation metaclass, see Fig. 3. In navigation structure models, navigation annotations thus can be attached to any navigation link. The details of how to represent the annotation, ordering or hiding in a specific Web application can thus be deferred to the choice of the designer.

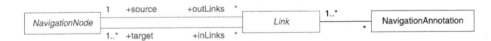

Fig. 3. Extended UWE metamodel (fragment)

4.3   Model Aspects

Adaptive navigation behaviour of Web applications has to rely on parameterisable features of the underlying navigation model. Thus, the integration of adaptability into

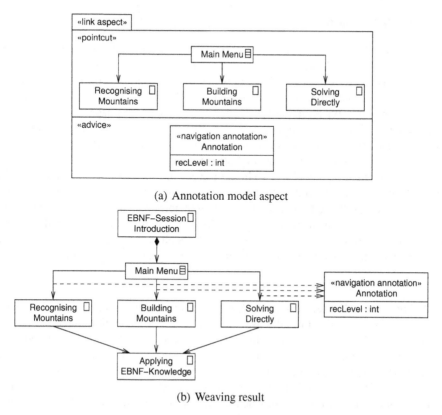

(a) Annotation model aspect

(b) Weaving result

Fig. 4. Adding annotations to the SmexWeb navigation structure

UWE navigation structures is most simply achieved by adding annotations to navigation links: these annotations reflect the adaptations to the user model incurred by observed user behaviour [12]. Such an extension, in particular, has to take place on the navigation model level. On the one hand, each navigation link that shall be subject to adaptation has to be marked; on the other, the marking may not be desired to be uniform, but to be restricted to a certain part of the navigation model.

In Fig. 4(a), we show how the partial introduction of annotations can be achieved by using a model aspect for the SmexWeb navigation structure (cf. Fig. 1). This aspect separates the annotation feature from the navigational behaviour and documents the adaptability possibilities in a dedicated place. Each model aspect is woven statically with the principal model at design time. The pointcut of the ≪link aspect≫ describes those parts of the navigation structure model which are to be made amenable to adaptation. The advice part of the aspect specifies that the class Annotation, which is an instance of NavigationAnnotation, has to be added to all the links (hence the name ≪link aspect≫) present in the pointcut. The attribute recLevel of the annotation represents the recommendation level of a link. The result of the weaving is shown in Fig. 4(b).

4.4   Runtime Aspects

The difference between a run time aspect and a model time aspect is that the effect of weaving the aspect with the navigation model is based on information only available at runtime. This includes information about which link is being traversed and the state of the user model. In addition, a run time aspect may change the runtime environment.

There are three types of run time aspects, link annotation aspects, link traversal aspects, and link transformation aspects (cf. Fig. 2). A ≪link annotation aspect≫ is used for adaptation of the link's annotation attributes depending, for example, on the experience of the user. A ≪link traversal aspect≫ allows us to model the adaptation of the user and navigation model when a link is traversed, e.g., to count how often a certain link is followed and, in combination with a ≪link annotation aspect≫, to increase the link's priority, if followed often. With a ≪link transformation aspect≫ new navigation links which were not available in the original navigation model can be introduced and existing links removed. For example it can be modelled that a direct navigation link is added when the system discovers that the user navigates to a navigation node quite often.

Link Annotation/Traversal Aspect. Both, link annotation and link traversal aspects, have a similar structure. In both cases the pointcut is a navigation diagram and the advice is an OCL constraint. The difference is the type of OCL constraint and how weaving is performed. With a link annotation aspect the constraint is an invariant, and, for all links which are instances of the links in the navigation diagram of the pointcut, the constraint is required to hold. In contrast, with a link traversal aspect, the constraint is a postcondition constraint, and, whenever a link instance of one of the links of the pointcut is being traversed, the postcondition has to hold after the traversal of the link.

In the advice of a ≪link annotation aspect≫ we refer to the current session by using thisSession, assuming that thisSession is an instance of class Session which has at least an association to a class User representing the current user of this session (cf. Fig. 5). In addition, we assume that the variable link refers to an instance of a link in the navigation diagram defined in the pointcut. This makes it possible for the constraint to navigate to the current user and the links in the navigation diagram.

The semantics of a ≪link annotation aspect≫ is that at runtime, for all links that are instances of links in the navigation diagram defined in the pointcut of that aspect, the instance diagram has to satisfy the constraint of the advice. Note that we are modelling the behaviour of aspects but not how this behaviour is implemented. Thus the implementation of the aspect has to ensure that the constraint is satisfied.

In the example, cf. Fig. 6, the constraint of the advice ensures that the attribute recLevel of the annotation associated with a navigation link from the navigation dia-

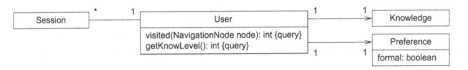

Fig. 5. Relationship between sessions and users

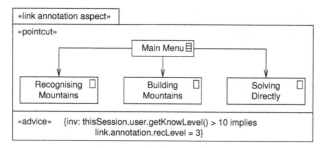

Fig. 6. Example of the use of a ≪link annotation aspect≫

gram is set to 3 when the current user has a knowledge level greater than 10. When a link from the navigation diagram is displayed, the value of recLevel can be used, for example, to display a smiley for a high recommendation level, or a frowny for a low recommendation level.

In the case of a ≪link traversal aspect≫, an advice is an OCL postcondition constraint in the context of an instance of the navigation diagram given by the pointcut of the aspect. As in an advice for a ≪link annotation aspect≫, the constraint may refer to the current session by thisSession. The result of weaving a ≪link traversal aspect≫ into the navigation model is that when a link corresponding to the navigation diagram of the pointcut is traversed, the constraint of the advice is true w.r.t. the states of the system before and after the traversal of the link. Similar to the ≪link annotation aspect≫, the postcondition has to be ensured by the implementor of the aspect after the link has been traversed. Using an aspect-oriented language, the postcondition can be implemented by an `after` advice where the pointcut is the method in the runtime environment that traverses the link. In the example, cf. Fig. 7, the constraint of the advice ensures that the traversal of links in the navigation diagram by the current user is counted.

Link Transformation Aspect. Adaptive link generation and removal can also be modelled using aspects in a modularised way. In the SmexWeb example (cf. 1), a shortcut from Main Menu to Apply EBNF-Knowledge should be added to the navigation model after the user has solved the mountain grammar exercise directly. The pointcut of a ≪link transformation aspect≫ has the form of a navigation model, consisting of the navigation nodes, between whom extra links are to be added or removed and which can use OCL constraints specifying when the advice should be applied. The advice is another navigation model, consisting of the classes contained in the pointcut and the

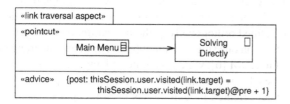

Fig. 7. Example of the use of a ≪link traversal aspect≫

new navigation structure between them. Figure 8 shows an aspect where a link from Main Menu to Apply EBNF-Knowledge should be introduced when the user has visited node Solving Directly at least once.

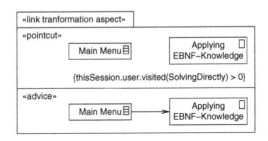

Fig. 8. Example of a ≪link transformation aspect≫

5   Related Work

Most of the currently existing methodologies tackle the modelling of adaptive Web applications by defining a rule or a filter for each point in the application where adaptation applies. As far as we know, only some of them view adaptivity as a cross-cutting feature and none of them uses aspects for modelling adaptivity.

The Hera methodology [10] provides an RMM-based notation for the representation of slices and links, which are the basic model elements of the application model. An application model is used to represent the navigation structure and presentation aspects of the Web application. Adaptation is on the one hand modelled explicitly, e.g., specifying the possible choices with links and alternative sub-slices. On the other hand, Hera constructs a rule-based adaptation model, but does not offer a visual representation of these rules. Rules are allowed to be composed recursively; Hera, however, assumes a confluent and terminating rule set.

The OO-H approach [11] proposes the use of personalisation rules to adaptivity. These rules are associated to the navigation links of the navigation model. This means that if a navigation node requires adaptation, this will be performed at runtime by execution of these rules. When a node is reachable by several links, for each link the corresponding filter has to be defined. This introduces additional redundancy, which opens the door for bugs, like forgetting a required filter for adaptation on a link.

In WSDM [7], an adaptation specification language is defined that allows designers to specify at the level of the navigation model which adaptations of the navigation structure can be performed at runtime. Although a visual representation of the rules is missing, rules are defined orthogonally to the navigation functionality as designers are allowed to define rules on one single element (node, link) and on group of elements. Another approach is OOHDM [6], which separates adaptation from navigation by adding a wrapper class for each navigation node which requires adaptation.

The use of aspect-oriented modelling has been recognised as a general means to improve the modularity of software models [9]. Our pragmatic approach to the aspect-oriented design of adaptive Web applications takes up some aspect techniques, but is rather geared towards the application of aspect-oriented modelling. In particular, Stein et al. [17] propose a more elaborate graphical notation for selecting model elements. It supports the application of wildcards for pattern matching model element names. This notation can be used to extend our approach in specifying pointcuts. Furthermore, Straw et al. [18] have given directives such as `add`, `remove`, and `override` for composing class diagrams. The directives can be used to describe how to weave two class diagrams together and thus the weaving process in our approach may be described by their composition directives. Theme/UML [8] uses templates to model aspects. Its main focus is a generic extension of the behaviour of classes where classes and their operations are bound to the formal parameters of the templates. In our approach aspects are used to describe additional concerns of links and associations.

6   Conclusions and Future Work

We have demonstrated the use of aspects for modelling adaptive Web applications in the UWE method by separating the navigation model from the adaptation model. A link aspect introduces navigation annotations to particular links for link reordering, annotating, or hiding due to user behaviour. This link aspect is applied at model time and thus captures cross-cutting model information in a dedicated place. During runtime, link annotation and link traversal aspects record information of the user behaviour and accordingly adapt the annotations or the user model for further use in the presentation layer. Additionally, the navigation structure becomes adaptable by link transformation aspects, that allow the designer to have fine-grained control on when links are added or removed.

We expect that contents adaptation and presentation adaptation can also be described by aspect-oriented modelling techniques, and we plan to investigate this topic in more detail. In particular, the effect of adding and modifying annotations on the navigation level to the presentation can again be described by aspects. We have restricted ourselves to a rather lightweight approach to integrating aspects into the UML and UWE in that we used the built-in extension facilities provided by the UML to define UML profiles. A more elaborate pointcut and advice description language is certainly desirable and subject to future research. For tool support, we plan to integrate adaptivity aspects in the open-source Web application modelling tool ArgoUWE.

References

1. Florian Albrecht, Nora Koch, and Thomas Tiller. SmexWeb: An Adaptive Web-based Hypermedia Teaching System. *J. Interactive Learning Research*, 11(3–4):367–388, 2000.
2. Thomas Baar, Alfred Strohmeier, Ana Moreira, and Stephen J. Mellor, editors. *Proc. 7th Int. Conf. Unified Modeling Language (UML'04)*, volume 3273 of *Lect. Notes Comp. Sci.* Springer, Berlin, 2004.
3. Eduardo Barra, Gonzalo Génova, and Juan Llorens. An Approach to Aspect Modelling with UML 2.0. In *Proc. 5th Wsh. Aspect-Oriented Modeling (AOM'04)*, Lisboa, 2004.
4. Peter Brusilovsky. Methods and Techniques of Adaptive Hypermedia. *User Model. User-Adapt. Interact.*, 6(2–3):87–129, 1996.

5. Peter Brusilovsky. Adaptive Hypermedia. *User Model. User-Adapt. Interact.*, 11:87–110, 2001.
6. Juan Cappi, Gustavo Rossi, Andres Fortier, and Daniel Schwabe. Seamless Personalization of E-commerce Applications. In Hiroshi Arisawa, Yahiko Kambayashi, Vijay Kumar, Heinrich C. Mayr, and Ingrid Hunt, editors, *Proc. Wsh. Conceptual Modeling in E-Commerce (eCOMO'01)*, volume 2465 of *Lect. Notes Comp. Sci.*, pages 457–470. Springer, Berlin, 2003.
7. Sven Casteleyn, Olga De Troyer, and Saar Brockmans. Design Time Support for Adaptive Behavior in Web Sites. In *Proc. 18th ACM Symp. Applied Computing*, pages 1222–1228. ACM Press, 2003.
8. Siobhán Clarke. Extending Standard UML with Model Composition Semantics. *Sci. Comp. Prog.*, 44(1):71–100, 2002.
9. Robert E. Filman, Tzilla Elrad, Siobhán Clarke, and Mehmet Aksit, editors. *Aspect-Oriented Software Development*. Addison-Wesley, 2004.
10. Flavius Frasincar, Geert-Jan Houben, and Richard Vdovjak. Specification Framework for Engineering Adaptive Web Applications. In *Proc. 11th Int. Conf. World Wide Web (WWW'02), Web Engineering Track*, Honolulu, 2002.
11. Irene Garrigós, Jaime Gómez, and Cristina Cachero. Modelling Dynamic Personalization in Web Applications. In Lovelle et al. [14], pages 472–475.
12. Nora Koch. *Software Engineering for Adaptive Hypermedia Systems: Reference Model, Modeling Techniques and Development Process*. PhD thesis, Ludwig-Maximilians-Universität München, 2001.
13. Nora Koch and Andreas Kraus. Towards a Common Metamodel for the Development of Web Applications. In Lovelle et al. [14], pages 497–506.
14. Juan Manuel Cueva Lovelle, Bernardo Martín González Rodríguez, Luis Joyanes Aguilar, José Emilio Labra Gayo, and María del Puerto Paule Ruíz, editors. *Proc. 3rd Int. Conf. Web Engineering (ICWE'03)*, volume 2722 of *Lect. Notes Comp. Sci.* Springer, Berlin, 2003.
15. Object Management Group. Unified Modeling Language Specification, Version 2.0 (Superstructure). Revised final adopted draft, OMG, 2004.
    `http://www.omg.org/cgi-bin/doc?ptc/2004-10-02`.
16. Dominik Stein, Stefan Hanenberg, and Rainer Unland. An UML-based Aspect-Oriented Design Notation For AspectJ. In *Proc. 1st Int. Conf. Aspect-Oriented Software Development*, pages 106–112. ACM, 2002.
17. Dominik Stein, Stefan Hanenberg, and Rainer Unland. Query Models. In Baar et al. [2], pages 98–112.
18. Greg Straw, Geri Georg, Eunjee Song, Sudipto Ghosh, Robert France, and James M. Bieman. Model Composition Directives. In Baar et al. [2], pages 84–97.

An Approach to User-Behavior-Aware Web Applications

Stefano Ceri[1], Florian Daniel[1], Vera Demaldé[2], and Federico M. Facca[1]

[1] Dipartimento di Elettronica e Informazione, Politecnico di Milano
P.zza Leonardo da Vinci 32, I-20133 Milano, Italy
{ceri,daniel,facca}@elet.polimi.it
[2] Istituto di Tecnologie della Comunicazione, Università della Svizzera Italiana
Via Lambertenghi 10 A, CH-6904 Lugano, Switzerland
demaldev@lu.unisi.ch

Abstract. The *Adaptive Web* is a new research area addressing the personalization of the Web experience for each user. In this paper we propose a new high-level model for the specification of Web applications that take into account the manner users interact with the application for supplying appropriate contents or gathering profile data. We therefore consider entire *processes* (rather than single *properties*) as smallest information units, allowing for automatic restructuring of application components. For this purpose, a high-level *Event-Condition-Action* (ECA) paradigm is proposed, which enables capturing arbitrary (and timed) clicking behaviors. Also, a possible architecture as well as a first prototype implementation are discussed.

1 Introduction

As the Web is a steadily growing environment and users, rather than navigating relatively simple (static) Web sites with structures that evolve only very slowly in time, nowadays users are more and more faced with complex Web applications, dynamically generated contents and highly variable site structures. Continuously, they are confronted with huge amounts of non pertaining contents or changed interaction paths. As a consequence, users may feel uncomfortable when navigating the Web.

Several techniques have been introduced that aim at augmenting the efficiency of navigation and content delivery. Content *personalization* allows for more efficiently tailoring contents to their recipients by taking into account predefined roles or proper user *profiles*. The relevance of information to be presented is derived from both user profile data and explicitly stated preferences.

Context-aware or *adaptive* Web applications [1, 2] go one step further and aim at personalizing delivered contents or layout and presentation properties not only with respect to the identity of users, but also by taking into account the context of the interaction involving users and applications. Besides proper user profiles, the term *context* usually refers to *environmental* (e.g temperature, position) or *technological* (e.g. device, communication channel) factors.

D. Lowe and M. Gaedke (Eds.): ICWE 2005, LNCS 3579, pp. 417–428, 2005.

Along a somewhat orthogonal dimension, *workflow-driven* Web applications address the problem of showing the right information at the right time by explicitly modeling the hidden (business) process structure underlying determined usage scenarios, especially within business-oriented domains. Whereas several commercial workflow management systems [3] exist that allow specifying processes by means of proper visual modeling tools and also support Web-based user interfaces, Brambilla et al. [4] propose a hybrid solution that weaves the necessary process logic into high-level, conceptual WebML site models [5].

Eventually, usability studies and Web log analysis efforts [6] try to examine the usability and thus ergonomics problem by means of an ex-post approach with the aim of deriving structural weaknesses, checking assumptions made about expected user navigations and mine unforeseen navigation behaviors for already deployed Web applications. Final goal of these approaches is the incremental enhancement of the application under investigation in order to meet the newly identified requirements.

We believe that a new approach and an open paradigm that combines adaptive and process-centric perspectives can open new ways for both (coase-grained) application adaptation and (online) usability analysis. In this paper we propose a model and a methodology to easily design *behavior-aware* Web applications that allow performing actions in response to the user's fulfillment of predefined navigation patterns. Our proposal is based on the conceptual framework provided by WebML, but we also propose a new formalism, WBM (*Web Behavior Model*), a simple and intuitive model for describing navigation goals. The two models are combined to form a high-level *Event-Condition-Action* paradigm providing the necessary expressive power for capturing the way users interact with applications. Despite the adoption of WebML for hypertext design, the proposed solution is of general validity and can thus be applied to arbitrary Web applications.

The paper is organized as follows: Section 2 introduces WebML and WBM as conceptual background; in Section 3 we define the ECA paradigm by combining WebML and WBM. In Section 4 we discuss a possible SW architecture, Section 5 illustrates an applicative example, and Section 6 outlines experiences gained so far. In Section 7 we discuss related research work and, finally, in Section 8 we address future research efforts.

2   Background Models

2.1   WebML: An Overview

WebML (Web Modeling Language) is a conceptual model and development methodology for Web application design [5], accompanied with a CASE tool [5, 7] and an automatic code generation mechanism. WebML offers a set of visual primitives for defining conceptual schemas that represent the organization of contents into hypertext interfaces. Visual primitives are also provided with an XML-based textual representation, which allows specifying additional properties, not conveniently expressible in the visual notation. For specifying the data structure, upon which hypertexts are defined, WebML adopts the well known Entity-Relationship model (ER).

WebML allows designers to describe hypertextual views over the application data, called *site views*. Site views describe browsable interfaces, which can be restricted to particular classes of users. Multiple site views can be defined for the same application. Site views are organized into hypertext modules, called *areas*. Areas and site views contain *pages* that are composed of containers of elementary pieces of content, called *content units*. Content units are linked to entities of the underlying data schema, holding the actual content to be displayed, and restricted by means of proper selector conditions. There are several predefined units (such as *data, index, multidata* or *entry* units) that express different ways of publishing or gathering data within hypertext interfaces; also, proprietary units can be defined. Arbitrary business actions can be modeled by means of so-called *operation units* and performed through navigating a relative input link. WebML incorporates some predefined operations for creating, modifying and deleting data instances and relationships among entities, and allows developers to extend this set with own operations.

Finally, pages or units can be connected by means of directed arcs, the *links*. The aim of links is twofold: permitting users to navigate contents (possibly displaying a new page, if the destination unit is placed in a different page), and passing parameters from a source unit to a destination unit for providing possible selector variables with respective values. For further details on WebML, the reader is referred to [5].

Recently, WebML has been extended to support the design of context-aware or adaptive Web applications [1]. Adaptive pages are continuously refreshed and, according to possible changes within the model of the application's context, content or layout adaptations as well as automatic navigation actions can be performed before rendering the HTML response. WebML operation chains are associated to adaptive pages and express proper actions to be carried out.

2.2 WBM: An Overview

The *Web Behavior Model* (WBM) is a timed state-transition automata for representing classes of user behaviors on the Web. Graphically, WBM models are expressed by labeled graphs, allowing for an easily comprehensible syntax; cf. Figure 1.

A *state* represents the user's inspection of a specific portion of Web hypertext (i.e., a page or a collection of pages), which is loaded on his browser, or the user's activation of a specific Web operation, such as "buy" on an e-commerce site, or "download" of a given file. A *transition* represents the navigation from one state to another. State labels are mandatory and correspond to names of pages or page collections or operations; transition labels are optional and express constraints enabling or disabling transitions, in terms of both used hypertext links and time. Each WBM specification, called *script*, has at least an initial state, indicated by an incoming unlabeled arc, and at least one accepting state, highlighted by dou-

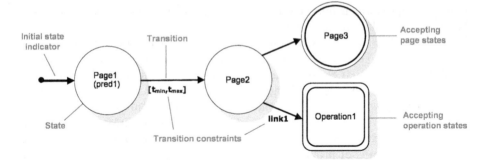

Fig. 1. Example of WBM script with state, link, time constraints and multiple exiting transitions from one state. Basic WBM primitives are named: page states are expressed by circles, operation states by rectangles

ble border lines; Figure 1 provides an overview of WBM primitives. Transitions can be constrained by state, link, and time constraints as follows.

- **State constraints.** Entering a state may be subject to the evaluation of a state constraint, expressing a predicate over properties of the pages being accessed or operation being fired. Such predicate may refer to contents displayed within pages or to operation parameters. The state is accessed iff the predicate evaluation yields to true.
- **Link constraints.** Each transition may be labeled with the name of a link entering the page or enabling the operation. The state is accessed iff the specified link is navigated.
- **Time constraints.** Each transition from a source to a target state may be labeled with a pair $[t_{min}, t_{max}]$ expressing a time interval within which the transition can occur. Either t_{min} or t_{max} may be missing, indicating open interval boundaries. If a transition does not fire within t_{max} time units, it can no longer occur; on the other hand, navigation actions that occur before t_{min} are lost. The use of suitable time constraints may thus cause the invalidation of running scripts.

One important aspect of WBM models is, that not all navigation alternatives must be covered. As the aim of WBM is to capture a concise set of user interactions, describing particular navigation goals and respective "milestones", only a subset of all possible navigation alternatives is relevant. E-commerce Web sites, for example, make heavy use of so-called *access-pages* that only serve the purpose of providing users with browsable categories for retrieving the actual products offered. Furthermore, Web sites usually provide several different access paths toward their core contents. Therefore, by concentrating only on those interactions that really express navigation goals, WBM allows both abstracting from unnecessary details and defining small and easily comprehensible specifications. Only performing specified target interactions – in the modeled order – may thus cause WBM state changes.

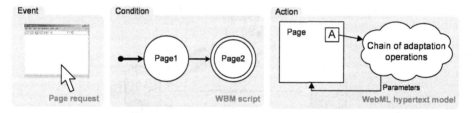

Fig. 2. High-level ECA rule components

Figure 1 shows an example WBM script. Entering the state denoted by *Page1* is constrained by *pred1*, which must evaluate to true. The transition from the first state to the second state must occur within t_{min} and t_{max} time units from the moment the script has been initiated, otherwise the script fails. The script in Figure 1 also presents two exiting transitions from state *Page2*. States labeled *Operation1* and *Page3* are "competing", as a browsing activity in *Page2* may lead to either *Operation1* or *Page3*. We constrain WBM scripts to have only one active state at time, only transitions may cause changes to it. Therefore, either a user browses from *Page2* to *Page3* (the transition *Page2* to *Page3* is triggered) and the script reaches the accepting state denoted by *Page3*, or the transition to accepting state *Operation1* occurs if *Operation1* is performed by using *link1*.

Despite the use of WebML for specifying example hypertext structures, WBM as adopted in this paper can be used to describe navigation behaviors on top of arbitrarily developed hypertexts. For further details on WBM and its propositional logic, the reader is referred to [8].

3   ECA Rule Model

To build the ECA rules that finally make Web applications aware of predefined user behaviors, we now combine WBM scripts and WebML adaptation mechanisms. Commonly, the ECA paradigm describes a general syntax (**on** *event* **if** *condition* **do** *action*) where the event part specifies *when* the rule should be triggered, the condition part assesses whether given *constraints* are satisfied, and the action part states the *actions* to be automatically performed if the condition holds.

In our view, the event consists in a *page* or *operation request*, the condition is a set of requirements on the user navigations (expressed as a *WBM script*), and the action part specifies some adaptivity actions to be forced in the Web application and expressed as WebML *operation chain*. Events are generated only for explicitly labeled pages (A-label) denoting the *scope* of the rule, and proper rule priorities resolve possible conflicts among concurrently activated rules. Figure 2 graphically represents such ECA rules.

Consider for instance the rule of Figure 2. The rule reacts to a user's visit to *Page1* followed by a visit to *Page2*. Thus, the expressed condition only holds when the script gets to the accepting state *Page2*. Once the accepting state is

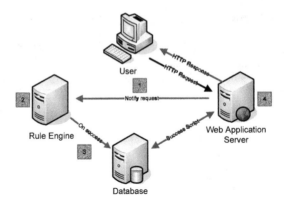

Fig. 3. A schema representing the architecture of the ReActive Web System

reached, the actions (expressed as cloud in Figure 2) are executed and, after a re-computation of page parameters, possible adaptations may be performed.

4   The ReActive Web System Architecture

Our so-called ReActive Web framework requires an extension of standard Web architectures: a new server, called *Rule Engine*, is introduced as illustrated in Figure 3. It collects and evaluates HTTP requests in order to track the user's navigational behavior, and hosts a repository of WBM scripts, which can be executed on behalf of individual users.

The behavior of the Rule Engine is described by the following steps (cf. Figure 3).

1. URL requests as generated by user clicks are notified to the Rule Engine.
2. A request can cause either the instantiation of a new script, or a state change of a given running script, or nothing.
3. When a WBM script reaches an accepting state for a certain user, the Rule Engine changes a record in the shared database, storing the information about the completed script and the user's session. Also, variables used by the WBM script are stored in the database.
4. Finally, if the request refers to a page contained within the rule's scope, the application interprets the modified data record as request for activating the adaptation chain associated to that page. Accordingly, it executes the operation chain, possibly generating a modified hypertext.

While the above steps represent the core of the Rule Engine's behavior, several variants are possible regarding the interaction between the three servers. For example, the Rule Engine server can act as stand-alone system for usability analysis or validation of given Web applications. The use of a distributed architecture offers some significant advantages:

- Since script handling is assigned to a dedicated server, which is neither the database nor the Web server, the overall application's performance is not affected by the time required for rule processing[1].
- The Rule Engine is not bound to the technology used to develop the Web application, and a single Rule Engine can handle rules for more than a single Web application.
- The Web application remains operational, even in case of Rule Engine slowdowns or crashes.
- The Rule Engine can be recovered independently from the rest of the Web application.

Synchronous as well as *asynchronous* rule execution models can be achieved with the presented architecture. In the synchronous case, if a rule is successfully triggered, the action part of the rule is executed immediately at the first page request. To avoid possible performance slowdowns (due to time spent for script evaluation), the asynchronous configuration defers rule evaluation to the next (automatic) page refresh. This allows for parallel tasks and short response times. The strong decoupling of application server and Rule Engine allows for independent resource management and parallel and scalable configurations[2].

5   Case Study: An E-Learning Web Application

In this section we introduce a case study to explore some aspects of the potential of our approach. In particular, we chose the e-learning domain due to the large possibility of personalization and adaptation possibilities it offers. A sketch of the e-learning Web application model – without the adaptation layer – is depicted in Figure 4. When a user logs in to the application, he is forwarded to the *Home* page, where *User Data* and *Suggested Courses* – only if there is any suggestion for the current user in the database – are displayed. From the *Home* page the user can ask for the *Courses* page. When requesting that page, if there is no *ExpertiseLevel* (a value corresponding to the user's current level of knowledge) available for the current user, he is redirected to the *Test* page. In this case, a multiple choice test for the lowest level of knowledge is proposed to the user. When he submits the filled test to the Web application, his new *ExpertiseLevel* is computed and he is redirected to the *Courses* page, where suitable concepts for its level are presented. From here, the user can browse new contents (*Course* page) or navigate to the *Test* page and perform a new test to verify if his level is increased after having studied new contents.

In the following we introduce two examples that add an adaptation layer to the presented Web application.

---

[1] This result requires, in addition, to instrument the Rule Engine as asynchronous process, as will be discussed later

[2] Further details on the implementation of the Rule Engine can be found at `http://dblambs.elet.polimi.it`

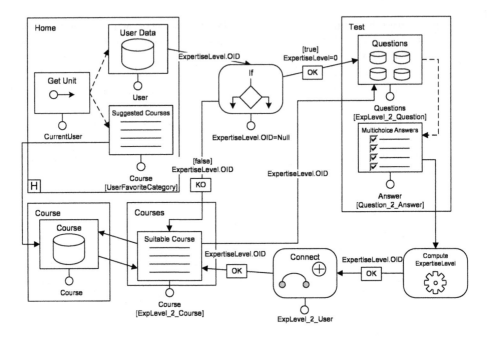

Fig. 4. The WebML model of the proposed educational Web site

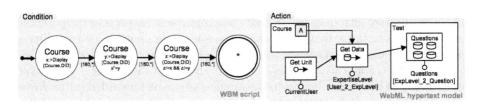

Fig. 5. An ECA adaptive rule to trigger evaluation of a student's knowledge level

Example 1. Evolving the Level of User Expertise. Figure 5 models an ECA rule to redirect the user to the *Test* page for the next experience level after having visited 3 courses; i.e., 3 different instances of *Course* pages, spending at least 3 minutes over each page. The WebML operation chain for adaptation is actually performed when the user asks again for a *Course* page. The * in the final state of the WBM script specifies the acceptance of any arbitrary page. The WebML model in figure serves the purpose of providing the user with new questions and answers allowing him to assess progress.

Example 2. User Profiling. Suppose we want to personalize the application according to the user's preferences traceable from his navigational choices (cf. Figure 6). We detect that a user is interested in a certain category of courses when he navigates at least three different *Course* pages presenting three courses belonging to the same category. In response to this behavior, the WebML chain

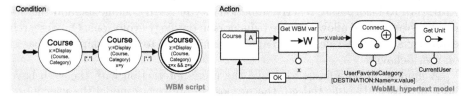

Fig. 6. An ECA adaptive rule to profile users according to their navigational behavior

stores the preference reported by the user – captured by the `Get WBM Variable Unit` – in the database. Now, courses belonging to the same category are presented to the user by means of the *Suggested Courses* unit in the *Home* page.

6   Experiments

A first prototype of the presented architecture has been developed and tested by implementing the reactive Web application of the previous case study (see Section 5). So far, we have fully implemented only link and time constraints provided by WBM, while only few of the mechanisms required by WBM state constraints have been realized. At this step, we are using a Web service for the interaction between Web application and Rule Engine. First feedback from experiments are quite positive: experiments proved that the whole mechanism is feasible and that the use of the asynchronous execution model effectively avoids Rule Engine response times to impact on user navigation. Besides positive initial considerations, experiments revealed a problem of performance in the architecture. We observed an excessive lag between the start of a notification of a page request and the final computation of the new state by the Rule Engine (around 2.5 seconds to manage 100 user requests). Further studies proved that the bottleneck of the system was not the Rule Engine (a stand-alone version of the Rule Engine can process the same 100 requests in less than 60 milliseconds). The actual bottleneck was found to be the time needed to generate the SOAP request by the client. We will fix this problem in the upcoming prototype and test the impact on performance caused by the introduction of complex state constraints[3].

7   Related Works

The ECA rule paradigm was first implemented in active database systems in the early nineties [9, 10] to improve the robustness and maintainability of database applications. Recently, they have been also exploited in other contexts such as

---

[3] Experiments were realized using an AMD AthlonXP 1800+, 512MB of RAM and with Tomcat as web server. WBM scripts used were more complex than the ones described in this paper

XML [11], to incorporate reactive functionality in XML documents, and the Semantic Web [12], to allow reactive behaviors in ontology evolutions. Our research explicitly adds ECA-rules to web application systems to allow adaptation based on user behavior.

A number of paradigms to model the user's interaction with the Web have been proposed [13, 14]. Indeed, the proposed approaches model the user interaction from the Web application's point of view: they have been designed to describe the navigational model of Web applications and not to model the user interacting with the application. Nevertheless, they can be adapted to model the user behavior disregarding the navigational design of the Web application. The main advantage of these models is their strong formal definition, as they are based on well known formal models like Petri Nets [13] or UML StateCharts [14].

WBM, on the other hand, is a general purpose model to describe at high level the user's interaction with Web applications, focusing only on navigational alternatives able to capture navigation goals. Besides that, WBM has an easy visual paradigm that allows designers to specify arbitrary user's behavior models.

A variety of design models have been proposed for Adaptive Hypermedia [15–17]. While most of these methods differ in approach, all methods aim to provide mechanisms for describing Adaptive Hypermedia (see [18, 19] for a survey). Most of them do not use a full ECA paradigm and rather deal with a CA paradigm [17]. Others [15] are not conscious to use an ECA paradigm and hence do not refer directly to it or do not propose a formal model, based on such a well-known paradigm. Some of them focus only on the adaptation, disregarding an effective description of the user's behavior that should trigger the adaptation [20]. A comprehensive overview of commercially available solutions is presented in [21]. The author points out that commercial user modeling solutions are very behavior-oriented: observed user actions or action patterns often lead directly to adaptations without an explicit representation of the user characteristics.

AHAM [15], in literature, is often referred to as the reference model for Adaptive Hypertext. It is based on Dexter [22], an early model for hypertext, and uses maps of concepts. The model presents many valid ideas (e.g. the 3-layer model capturing all the adaptive semantics) but suffers for the use of an old-fashioned model such as Dexter and is more suited for e-learning domain. The model introduced in [20] extends WSDM [23], a Web design method, with an Adaptation Specification Language that allows specifying the adaptive behavior. In particular, the extension allows specifying deep adaptation in the Web application model, but lacks expressive power as regards the specification of the user's behavior that triggers the adaptation. No discussion on an architecture implementation of the proposed design method is provided. In [17] the authors propose a Software Engineering oriented model based on UML and OCL to describe in a visual and a formal way an adaptive hypertext application. The adaptation model is based on a Condition-Action paradigm that allows expressing conditions on the user's behavior. The proposed visual notation lacks of immediacy and suffers the use of a visual paradigm born outside the Web area. Likewise, [2] proposes an interesting framework for context-aware adaptivity based on ECA rules, but it fails in proposing a real design model. It is not even clear if the original idea has been really used in experimental applications and with which results.

Compared to the cited researches, our model allows for an easy specification of user-behavior-driven, adaptive Web applications, and we heavily exploit expressive power derived by ECA rules. Furthermore, we supported our ideas by implementing and testing the proposed architecture underlying the model, allowing for automatic code generation from the Web application design model.

8 Conclusion and Future Work

In this paper we proposed a general purpose model for building behavior-aware Web applications. Our proposal is based upon WebML and WBM, and combines these two models into a visual ECA paradigm that opens the road to the implementation of high-level CASE tools for designing advanced Web sites. In this context, we are currently investigating the use of well-known modeling primitives, such as UML statecharts, for expressing WBM and its notation, as they are already supported by proper CASE tools.

Within our future work, we will develop proper policies for dealing with priorities and conflicts. Currently, we adopt the simple policy of always choosing the rule at highest priority, but this can be improved. Furthermore, we did not consider the problem of rule termination yet, which might arise when rules trigger each other. Also, dynamic activation and deactivation of rules and of rule groups will be considered.

A first prototype of the reactive Web environment has been implemented. It demonstrates the applicability and power of the approach, as it supports rules of arbitrary complexity and therefore can build arbitrary reactive applications. The implementation of a second generation prototype is ongoing, with optimized rule management and offering full graphic user interfaces to designers.

References

1. Ceri, S., Daniel, F., Matera, M.: Extending webml for modeling multi-channel context-aware web applications. In: Proceedings of Fourth International Conference on Web Information Systems Engineering Workshops (WISEW'03), Rome, Italy, December 12 -13, 2003, IEEE Press (2003) 225–233
2. Finkelstein, A.C., Savigni, A., Kappel, G., Retschitzegger, W., Kimmerstorfer, E., Schwinger, W., Hofer, T., Pröll, B., Feichtner, C.: Ubiquitous web application development - a framework for understanding. In: Proceedings of the 6th World Multiconference on Systemics, Cybernetics and Informatics (SCI). (2002) 431–438
3. IBM: MQ-Series Workflow.
   http://www-306.ibm.com/software/integration/wmqwf/.
4. Brambilla, M., Ceri, S., Comai, S., Fraternali, P., Manolescu, I.: Specification and design of workflow-driven hypertexts. Journal of Web Engineering (JWE) 1 (2003) 163–182

5. Ceri, S., Fraternali, P., Bongio, A., Brambilla, M., Comai, S., Matera, M.: Designing Data-Intensive Web Applications. Morgan Kauffmann (2002)
6. Facca, F.M., Lanzi, P.L.: Recent developments in web usage mining research. In: Data Warehousing and Knowledge Discovery, 5th International Conference, DaWaK 2003, Prague, Czech Republic, September 3-5,2003. Volume 2737 of Lecture Notes in Computer Science., Springer (2003) 140–150
7. WebModels srl: WebRatio. http://www.webratio.com.
8. Armani, J., Ceri, S., Demaldè, V.: Modeling of user's behaviors in web applications: a model and a case study. Technical report, Institute of Communication Technologies, Università della Svizzera italiana (2004)
9. Widom, J.: The starburst active database rule system. IEEE Trans. Knowl. Data Eng. 8 (1996) 583–595
10. Ceri, S., Fraternali, P., Paraboschi, S., Tanca, L.: Active rule management in Chimera. In: Active Database Systems: Triggers and Rules for Advanced Database Processing. Morgan Kaufmann, San Francisco, California (1996)
11. Bonifati, A., Ceri, S., Paraboschi, S.: Active rules for xml: A new paradigm for e-services. The VLDB Journal 10 (2001) 39–47
12. Papamarkos, G., Poulovassilis, A., Wood, P.T.: Event-condition-action rule languages for the semantic web. In: Proceedings of SWDB'03, Berlin, Germany, September 7-8, 2003. (2003) 309–327
13. Stotts, P.D., Furuta, R.: Petri-net-based hypertext: Document structure with browsing semantics. ACM Transactions on Information Systems 7 (1989) 3–29
14. Turine, M.A.S., de Oliveira, M.C.F., Masiero, P.C.: A navigation-oriented hypertext model based on statecharts. In: HYPERTEXT '97: Proceedings of the eighth ACM conference on Hypertext, New York, NY, USA, ACM Press (1997) 102–111
15. Bra, P.D., Houben, G.J., Wu, H.: Aham: a dexter-based reference model for adaptive hypermedia. In: Proceedings of the tenth ACM Conference on Hypertext and hypermedia : returning to our diverse roots. (1999) 147–156
16. Casteleyn, S., Troyer, O.D., Brockmans, S.: Design time support for adaptive behavior in web sites. In: Proceedings of the 2003 ACM symposium on Applied computing. (2003) 1222–1228
17. Koch, N., Wirsing, M.: The munich reference model for adaptive hypermedia applications. In: Proceedings of the Second International Conference on Adaptive Hypermedia and Adaptive Web-Based Systems, Springer-Verlag (2002) 213–222
18. Brusilovsky, P.: Adaptive hypermedia. User Modeling and User-Adapted Interaction 11 (2001) 87–110
19. Cannataro, M., Pugliese, A.: A survey of architectures for adaptive hypermedia. In Levene, M., Poulovassilis, A., eds.: Web Dynamics. Springer-Verlag, Berlin (2004) 357–386
20. Casteleyn, S., Troyer, O.D., Brockmans, S.: Design time support for adaptive behavior in web sites. In: Proceedings of the 2003 ACM symposium on Applied computing. (2003) 1222–1228
21. Kobsa, A.: Generic user modeling systems. User Model. User-Adapt. Interact. 11 (2001) 49–63
22. Halasz, F., Schwartz, M.: The Dexter hypertext reference model. Communications of the ACM 37 (1994) 30–39
23. Troyer, O.D. In: Audience-driven Web Design. Idea Group (2001) 442–462

A Component-Based Reflective Middleware Approach to Context-Aware Adaptive Systems

Zhang Kuo, Wu Yanni, Zheng Zhenkun, Wang Xiaoge, and Chen Yu

Department of Computer Science and Technology
Tsinghua University, Beijing 100084, China
{zhangkuo99,wuyanni98,zhengzhenkun98}@mails.tsinghua.edu.cn
{wangxg,yuchen}@mail.tsinghua.edu.cn
http://os.riit.tsinghua.edu.cn

Abstract. In ubiquitous computing environment, a middleware abstracting a unified service for various types of applications operating over a static environment is not valid; in particular, ubiquitous applications does not benefit from dynamic reconfiguration and adaptive computing. In this paper, we introduce our reflective middleware platform PURPLE[1], which is designed and implemented to fit the varying requirement of ubiquitous computing: such as adaptability, configurability, context awareness.

1 Introduction

Ubiquitous(or Pervasive) computing focuses on integrating computers with the physical environments, to make computing and communication essentially transparent. Devices that operate in these environments are usually embedded and use low-power wireless communication means; topologies of the networks are dynamic due to arbitrary node mobility, and usually contain no dedicated network connectivity devices. So ubiquitous applications should address the characteristics: such as context awareness and dynamic configurations.

We argue that these two characteristics specify the need for system support, while not application-specific, for both development and runtime services in ubiquitous environments. In this respect, middleware-oriented approaches can be very effective if they can reduce the effort required to develop ubiquitous software and provide appropriate runtime services for applications with the two characteristics above. However, most current middleware solutions are not adequate to support context-awareness and dynamic reconfigurations for real-time. Moreover, most currently available middleware for ubiquitous computing, are based on existed component-platforms, which are modular but static; it means that middleware developers need to pay additional attention to code reuse and leveraging existing systems, as well as adding features to make the system more flexible.

Research on reflective middleware has a history of ten years. Earlier projects mostly concentrated on what a real reflective middleware should be like and how to

---

[1] Supported by the National High-Tech Research and Development Plan of China (No.2003AA1Z2090), National Natural Science Foundation of China (No. 60203024), and Tsinghua University Research Found (No. JC2003021)

D. Lowe and M. Gaedke (Eds.): ICWE 2005, LNCS 3579, pp. 429–434, 2005.

build it, such as Open ORB [1], OpenCorba, mChaRM; Recent projects usually have more explicit application background including reflective middleware for pervasive/ubiquitous computing and mobile computing. Some significant projects are LegORB [3], Chisel, CARISMA, ReMMoC [5]. The applications of reflective middleware cover almost every hot research area in recent years, such as component based OS [4] P2P, and Grid computing and programmable networking [2], etc. The results of the research in reflection are also being incorporated in industrial-strength middleware, such as JBoss 4.0.

In this paper, we present a reflective middleware, which is based on EFL component platform, to facilitate the applications development in ubiquitous computing. It has the features of context-aware, dynamic-configurable and policy-driven to fit the requirement of constantly changed context. Unlike most adaptive middleware, it supports dynamic reconfiguration at both middleware and application layers by the help of reflection. We also innovatively present a multilevel Meta data, which reflects information and capabilities of the system from different perspectives with different resolution. An abstraction of components' interactions and dynamic reconfigurations is expressed in a high-level declarative language written in XML which is customizable and extendable.

2   Reflections in EFL Component Platform

EFL is a lightweight, efficient and reflective component platform running on Linux developed by our group. It is written in C for best performance and minimum memory footprint. Its specification adopts the design of Microsoft's DCOM, such as binary level interoperability standard, transparent local/remote invocations. And the platform deploys a standard runtime substrate that manages the running context of an EFL component. Many new features are brought into this component model. Our middleware is built upon on EFL component platform, so we focus on the implementation of reflection on the substrate of the system. During the study of the design and implementation of reflective middleware, various possibilities of constructing meta-level are investigated. Finally, an innovative multi-levels reflection model is proposed.

This model provides fine-grained metadata from different levels of a program. It can reflect information and capabilities of the system from different sources with different resolving power. In this novel multi-level reflection model, the metadata is distributed on three levels: the Interface-level, the Component-level and the Middleware-level. They are used to reflect the base level information in different perspectives and granularities. The first two levels are directly supported by EFL. The fundamental concepts of an EFL component are interfaces; Interface-level Meta data contains the definition of interfaces, functions and parameters. It provides the finest grain of self-description information of the system, and it is obtained by using the IMetaInterface interface of EFL component. With the help of this, middleware can dynamically load components and invoke the method without generating accessing code. Component-level Meta data is used to describe an EFL component's requirement of context for running (such as hardware and OS requirement). The Meta data in this level also contains the info of the reliance of dependency that one component lies on others. Component-level Meta data can be accessed by ICompMetaInterface

interface of EFL component. The Middleware-level Meta data describes a graph of runtime components on middleware platform, and provide the dynamic reconfiguration strategy.

3 Middleware System Overview

3.1 Architecture

The architecture of PURPLE is shown in Figure 1. Firstly, we will present an overview of PURPLE in this section.

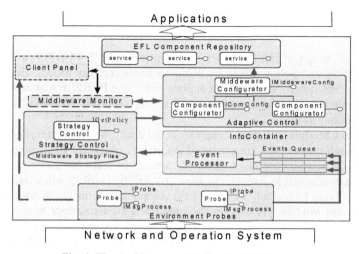

Fig. 1. The Architecture of Reflective Middleware

The PURPLE programming model is based upon the concept of described abstract services, such as WSDL. The underlying concrete implementations are supplied by groups of service components in *EFL Component Repository Module*. The tools for maintaining the repository is provided, so that developers can enrich the repository to meet applications' requirement. The components in this repository are classified as base-level components.

The support to the dynamic adaptation of the base-level components is offered by *Adaptive Control Module*. This module functions as the controller of Components' Runtime view; in other words, it is the graph of runtime components, the most important part of Middleware-level Meta data. Dynamic reconfiguration strategy is another part of Middleware-level Meta data. This information is maintained by *Strategy Control* Module. The strategies are recorded in strategy files and describe the actions should be taken when context value matches. The context specifications are presented in section 3.3, developers can customized their own strategy files according to the Schema we provide. *InfoContainer* Module is in charge of environment information analyzing and events maintenance and dispatching. Environment information includes various changes in network status, machine resources and connectivity status. Details are demonstrated in section 3.2. *Environment Probes* Module makes a real time collection of platform environment information, such as CPU usage, Battery info, Network info, etc. It provides the context-aware ability and raises a series of events to Event processor. Probes can be reconfigured and deployed into Probes container dynamically. So it is easily extendable in future.

Client Panel and *Middleware Monitor* are drawn in broken line in figure 1, that's because these two modules are optional in our platform. Client Panel can provide the visualization and runtime configuration of the middleware structure. It collects system info through Middleware Monitor, and represents the running context info by subscribing message from Environment Probes. Middleware Monitor interacts with Adaptive Control Module, and becomes a channel between Client Panel and other Middleware Modules.

3.2 Context-Awareness

The detailed design of InfoContainer is shown in Figure 2. PURPLE achieves context-awareness and policy-driven by using an Event Trigger Model. Event Trigger Model supports subscription from all entities within the PURPLE platform, including system components (such as component for strategy control), base-level components and applications as well.

The Event Module in Figure 2 represents the entity which is interested in special contexts. Each module is a composite of Receivers, which are EFL components implementing IClientSink interface. Selected methods in IClientSink interfaces are registered to a customizable Event Container, and will be invoked when interested contexts meet. Event Container is also an EFL component; it maintains the connections from all Event Module and triggers the subscribed events at right time. Each Event Container subscribes several interested context info to Event Processor. When context information comes to InfoContainer, Events Queue module unmarshals the message and filters the useless information, and then useful context information is classified, cashed and dispatched to Event Processor immediately. Event Processor takes care of the activity of each Event Container and injects the subscribed context info into specified Event Containers.

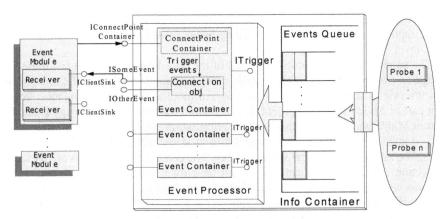

Fig. 2. The structure of InfoContainer

There are two problems exist. Firstly, large amount of events can be triggered simultaneously when context changes obviously. The property of priority for each Event Module is added; this priority is registered to its Event Container and maintained by Event Processor, so that concurrent events can be triggered orderly according to their priority. Secondly, the Events Containers can be customized by developers to subscribe variety of context information, but it can't be deployed dynamically without compiling; further more, composition of primitive context to form a hierarchical context is needed in system adaptation. We achieve these by introducing Strategy Control Module. Strategy files are maintained by this module; these files are written in XML format, providing the direction of system adaptation when context changed (detail of this is discussed in section 3.3), and these files can be deployed into Strategy Control Module on the fly, too.

The context specifications in strategy files are presented in next section.

3.3 Context Specification for Policy-Driven

Using the strategy file, the context-awareness of the adaptive system can be expressed by associating context expressions along with the application-level behavior. The elements of strategy file are presented in the following part. *Context Items* are expressions that return Boolean values which indicate different situations in specific context. For example, a context item C1 can refer to a 0%~50% CPU usage expression as C1= ($0 <= CPU\_Usage <= 0.5$), the value of C1 is either true or false; and C2 may represent the equipment used in a Cellular Network Context (C2 = (Network-Context = = GPRS). *Context Operators* are operators to specify the relationships among multiple Context Items. *Context Expressions* are expressions to represent the relations among context items using context operators. (Such as C1 & C2 specifies a specific context).

The operators can be used to specify the relations between Context Items or Expressions. In this sense, we can define a complex expression recursively by using simpler expression. For example: (C1->C2) in t represents that C2 becomes true within the time t until C1 being true; ((C1|C2) & (~C3)) in t means that C3 is not true while C1 or C2 is true for the last time period t. What associate with context expressions is *Strategy Information*; it is explicitly related to application-level behavior. The strategy info describe the actions should be taken when the value of Context Expression becomes true; and the actions can be concluded into dynamic reconfigurations to middleware platform. For instance, usually we use different components in charge of different wireless access solutions, such as 3G/B3G, IEEE 802.1x; when context exchanges from one to another, the components should be dynamically replaced immediately.

4   Conclusions and Future Work

This paper presents PURPLE, an adaptive, context-aware and component-based middleware for ubiquitous computing. The use of EFL component platform offers the technique in multi-level reflection, which provides the advantages of flexibility in implementing and extension. Specifically, we discussed the context-awareness mechanism for system-level reconfiguration using strategy control and the working process in adaptation and system consistency control. Based on our testing result, we conclude that the overhead by introducing reflection is small enough to be negligible. Finally, the work does not address a number of key issues within ubiquitous computing domain, such as the support for mobility, agent-based programming paradigm. Meanwhile, we would strengthen the collaboration with the development of ubiquitous computing applications to better understand the need and requirement of middleware support.

References

1. G S Blair, G Coulson, P Robin, M Papathomas. "An Architecture for Next Generation Middleware", In: Proceedings of IFIP International Conference on Distributed Systems Platforms and Open Distributed Processing (Middleware'98). Springer-Verlag, (1998). 191–206
2. Coulson, G., Blair, G.S., Gomes, A.T. et al, "A Reflective Middleware-based Approach to Programmable Networking", Proceedings of 2nd Intl. Workshop on Reflective and Adaptive Middleware (located with ACM/IFIP/USENIX Middleware 2003), Rio de Janeiro, Brazil, June, (2003)
3. Manuel Roman, M Dennis Mickunas, Fabio Kon, R H Campbell. "LegORB and Ubiquitous CORBA", IFIP/ACM Middleware'2000 Workshop on Reflective Middleware. IBM Palisades Executive Conference Center, NY, (2000)
4. Fabio Kon, Manuel Román, Ping Liu et al. "Monitoring, Security, and Dynamic Configuration with the dynamicTAO Reflective ORB", The IFIP/ACM International Conference on Distributed Systems Platforms and Open Distributed Processing. New York, New York, USA, 2000
5. Paul Grace, Gordon S Blair, Sam Samuel. "ReMMoC: A Reflective Middleware to Support Mobile Client Interoperability", Proceedings of International Symposium on Distributed Objects and Applications, volume 2888 of LNCS. Berlin & Heidelberg, Germany: Springer-Verlag Berlin Heidelberg, (2003). 1170-1187

Adaptation of Web Pages for Hand-Held Devices

Venkatakrishnan Balasubramanian Appiah and San Murugesan

School of Multimedia and Information Technology, Southern Cross University
Coffs Harbour, NSW 2457, Australia
{vbalasub,smurugesan}@scu.edu.au

Abstract. Web browsing using hand-held devices is becoming more common. But the relatively small display area of hand-held devices, compared to desktop computers, requires that Web pages designed for desktops are adapted to suit hand-held devices for convenient browsing. Web page adaptation techniques for hand-held devices takes into account device's screen size, limited bandwidth and input capabilities. Although several techniques have been proposed to adapt Web pages for smaller screen, each of them is better suited for specific scenarios and requirements. Hence a better understanding of the features and limitations of these techniques are required for successful development of Web pages for mobile devices. This paper presents a concise overview and comparative evaluation of the state-of-the-art of the techniques for adapting Web pages for hand-held devices.

1 Introduction

Nowadays, hand-held computing and communication devices such as PDAs, pocket PCs and mobile phones have come into wider use. As they become ubiquitous and are widely used there is increasing demand for providing Web-browsing-like services on these devices as in desktop PCs. However, accessing Web pages using hand-held devices has limitations because of the device's small screen size. Therefore, it becomes necessary that the presentation of the Web pages be tailored to hand-held device's screen size. Hence the need for suitable adaptation techniques to present Web pages on hand-held devices. But the diversity of existing devices makes no one particular adaptation technique suitable for all the devices or requirements, and most of the adaptive techniques have been developed for specific scenarios or requirements. Hence a comparative evaluation of Web page adaptation techniques is useful for the development of mobile Web applications. Such an evaluation will help Web developers to choose a more appropriate technique for a given requirement and to get a better understanding of relative strengths and weaknesses of the techniques. However, no such evaluation or an overview of various techniques has been made available in literature. This paper addresses this need and presents an overview and comparison of several adaptation techniques for presenting existing Web pages on hand-held devices.

The paper is organized as follows. A brief overview on Web pages on mobile devices is presented in Section 2. Several techniques for manipulating Web pages developed for desktops for presentation on mobile devices are discussed in Section 3. Section 4 provides a comparative evaluation of these techniques, and concluding remarks are presented in Section 5.

D. Lowe and M. Gaedke (Eds.): ICWE 2005, LNCS 3579, pp. 435–440, 2005.

2 Web Pages on Mobile Devices

There is a growing demand for viewing Web pages on mobile devices, but the display area of these devices is much smaller than that of desktop computers. For example, the display area of typical PDA is 6 x 8 cms while that of notebook/desktop computer is 28 x 21 cms [1]. Following gives a brief description about reauthoring and presentation methods used to adapt Web pages for hand-held devices.

2.1 Reauthoring Web Pages

Web pages designed for desktops need to be tailored for presentation on hand-held devices. This could be done by manual reauthoring or by automatic reauthoring [2]. In manual reauthoring, Web authors prepare manually multiple versions of a Web page targeted to resource profiles of each type of hand-held device. Although this approach could produce well-tailored, high-quality pages for a given device, it severely limits the number of Web pages that can be presented through hand-held devices, as the author has to manually recreate all the existing Web pages for each type of device. Moreover, updating and maintaining hand-held version of (dynamic) Web pages is cumbersome and costly. In automatic reauthoring, a transcoding [3] module transparently converts individual Web pages, making them accessible by hand-held devices. Automatic reauthoring techniques convert the original Web pages in to XML tree-like structure using Document Object Model (DOM) APIs and   Extensible Style Sheet Language Transformation (XSLT) to generate Wireless Markup Language (WML) and HTML content for display on mobile devices [3].

2.2 Web Page Content

While the wireless Web access could provide users with anytime, anywhere access to the same information they would get on in their desktops, it also facilitate provision of new and value-added services which might be based on user's location, preference and device capabilities that are specific to mobile use.

Web page content developed for desktops can be presented in three ways (Figure 1):

- Web page content (*Verbatim*) – without tailoring – can be adapted to be viewable by hand-held devices.
- Web page content is generically tailored and adapted to be viewable by hand-held devices.
- Context-aware Web content. Many users of mobile services prefer to access only those information that is relevant to their current situation or use. To cater to this need mobile wireless service must provide adaptation capabilities to handle dynamically changing environments. Based on the context, such as user's location, information of interest and device capabilities, the system could adapt the Web *content* before presenting to the hand-held devices.

It is especially difficult to browse a document by scrolling in small screen area and the user needs more time and keystrokes to get their target data/hyperlinks. Hence, it is highly desirable or even necessary to manipulate and minimize the content of a

Web page for presentation in hand-held devices. Segmentation and regrouping [4], table of contents [12], summarization and hybrid schemes [2] are some of the generic approaches proposed for this purpose. The next section describes different techniques for presenting Web pages on hand-held devices.

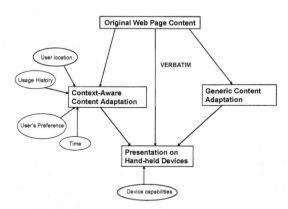

Fig. 1. Presentation of Web page on hand-held devices

3   Web Page Presentation

Web page presentation should enable the users to easily navigate the presented content and also be appealing, intuitive, informative and useful. For presentation of Web pages on hand-held devices different techniques have been proposed. They include: page block, zonezoom, fisheye, thumbnail, director and structure-aware directory. A brief description of them follows.

Page Block: In this approach, a Web page's structure is analyzed and the Web page is split (using page-analysis algorithm) into smaller, logically related units that can fit onto a hand-held device's screen. The Web page is then be adapted to form a two-level hierarchy with thumbnail representation at the top level, providing a global view, and an index to a set of sub pages at the bottom level providing detailed information [5].

ZoneZoom: ZoneZoom [6] is a navigational technique that lets users traverse large information space on mobile phones. It segments a given view of an information space into nine sub-segments and each segment is mapped to a key on the number keypad of the mobile phones [6]. The user can then initiate an animated zoom into one of these sub-segments by pressing the number key that corresponds to that segment [7].

Fisheye: The fisheye presents an overview of the entire large screen. Normally HTML control is used to display a Web page in hand-held devices [9]. In PDAs and mobile phones, this view takes up most of the screen, but the gutter around the edges displays small icons. The icons in the gutter will indicate whether there is an image, table, or text below, above, or to the side of the current position on the page [8].

Thumbnail: Thumbnails, also called "graphical summaries," are useful in conveying information quickly [10]. Users familiar with a Web page on the screen can often recognize it in thumbnail form. The user is free to zoom into any part of the thumbnail without having to scroll to get there. When resized, the thumbnail shows the page as desktop browser would, with wrapping and layout identical to that of a typical desktop browser.

Directory: Directory type presentation can be described as Mobile Link (m-link) infrastructure for utilizing existing Web content and services on hand-held devices [12]. As not all Web information is appropriately "linked", the Mobile links uses a middleware proxy – navigation engine – to incorporate data-detectors to extract bits of useful information such as names, phone numbers and addresses and link them appropriately. It makes Web navigation on small devices faster and less disorienting, which led culling the links from the content.

Structure-Aware Directory: Structure-aware presentation is similar to directory presentation but it focuses on structure-aware transcoding heuristics, which preserve the original Web page's underlying layout as much as possible [2]. Most of the complex Web sites generally uses multiple repeated layout patterns [2]. The transcoding module groups the different repeated pattern and creates a separate link for each layout, which maintains the relative importance of Web page components. A detailed comparative evaluation of these presentation techniques is presented below.

4   Comparative Evaluation

A set of experiments [5] showed that page block approach is better suited for pages with multiple topics, but it falters for single-topic pages such as pure news content pages. Although page block technique splits the Web page for easy navigation, both thumbnail and page block techniques present an overall content of a Web page which happens to be larger size for mobile phone display area. Familiar Web sites that have multiple topics and user's spatial memory [11] make page block and thumbnail suitable presentation techniques for these Web sites. ZoneZoom is a presentation technique specifically designed for browsing a map. Geographical Web sites which deal with maps of local-area are well suited for this kind of presentation; it also provides an easy navigation for users, using D-pad (numbers from 1 to 9 in a keypad), for any kind of small screen devices. Fisheye view presents an exact replica of original Web sites designed for desktops with minor modifications by omitting flash, Java scripts, and other embedded objects which are not suitable or compatible for hand-held devices. This presentation technique allows hand-held device users to get to see the exact Web page as they might see it in desktops. By doing so, fisheye presentation presents all the available information in the Web page to the users. But navigation of entire Web pages using hand-held devices takes lot of scrolling and keystrokes. Directory type presentation, which provides links for Web information in directory-like structure, is considered to be most primitive and is easily navigable for hand-held devices. Informative Web sites that give less importance to images and other multimedia objects can use this type of presentation. Structure-aware directory can be considered as an enhanced directory type presentation which maintains the relevant importance of Web page components and is more appealing than directory-like structure. A comparison of these techniques is presented in Table 1.

Table 1. Comparison of Web Page Presentation Methods

Presentation Type	Examples of Compatible Web Pages	Compatible Devices	Merits	Demerits
Page Block	www.cnn.com www.msn.com www.bbc.com	PDAs, Palmtop	• Easy navigation • Appealing • Intuitive	• Not much informative. • Not suitable for unfamiliar Web sites
ZoneZoom	www.whereis.com.au, www.nationalgeographic.com	All Hand-held devices	• Easy navigation • Appealing • Intuitive • Informative	• Applicable only for Geographical Web sites
Fisheye	All types of Web sites	All Hand-held devices	• Informative	• Requires a lot of scrolling. • Not intuitive.
Thumbnail	www.cnn.com, www.msn.com, www.bbc.com	PDAs, Palmtop	• Easy navigation • Appealing • Intuitive • Informative	• Unfamiliar Web sites are less informative
Directory	Corporate Web sites like: www.ibm.com, www.cisco.com	All Hand-held devices	• Very easy navigation • Intuitive • Specifically Informative	• Not appealing
Structure-Aware Directory	All types of Web sites	All Hand-held devices	• Very easy navigation • Intuitive • Informative	

5 Conclusion

In this paper, we presented a brief overview of how Web page content could be presented in hand-held devices in three different ways. We also briefly described and compared different presentation techniques. Our comparison shows that no particular technique is suitable for all types of Web sites satisfying most of the user requirements. We need better presentation techniques that satisfy most of the user requirements for all types of Web sites. It is hoped that this work can serve as useful information resource for Web developers and researchers in developing better presentation technique.

References

1. Karkkainen, L., Laarni, J.: Designing for Small Display Screens, Proceedings of the Second Nordic Conference on Human Computer Interaction. Arhus, Denmark (2002) 227–230
2. Hwang, Y., Kim, J., Seo, E.: Structure-Aware Web Transcoding for Mobile Devices, IEEE Internet Computing, Sep./Oct. (2003) 14-21
3. Hwang, Y., Jung, C., Jihong Kim, Chung S.: WebAlchemist: A Web Transcoding System for Mobile Web Access in Handheld Devices. Proceedings of the Mobile Computing Data Management. Denver, Colorado, August 2001
4. Rahman, F. R., Alam, H., Hartono, R.: Understanding the Flow of Content in Summarizing HTML Documents. Proceedings of Document Layout Interpretation and its Application Workshop (DLIA01). Seattle, USA (2001)

5. Chen, Y., Xie, X., Ma, W., Zhang, H.: Adapting Web Pages for Small-Screen Devices. IEEE Internet Computing, Jan./Feb. (2005) 50- 56
6. Daniel, C.R., Cutrell, E., Sarin, R., Horvitz, E.: ZoneZoom: Map Navigation for   Smartphones with Recursive View Segmentation. Proceedings of the Working Conference on Advanced Visual Interfaces. Gallipoli, Italy (2004) 231 - 234
7. Hinckley, K., Jacob, R., Ware, C.: Input/Output Devices and Interaction Techniques. In CRC Computer Science and Engineering Handbook, A. B. Tucker, ed. CRC Press LLC: Boca Raton, FL. to appear
8. Fulk, M.: Improving Web Browsing on Handheld Devices. CHI '01 extended abstracts on Human factors in computing systems. Atlanta, Georgia (2001) 395 - 396
9. C. Gutwin, C. Fedak.: Interaction with Big Interfaces on Small Screens: a Comparison of Fisheye, Zoom, and Panning Techniques. Proceedings of Graphics Interface 2004. London, Ontario (2004) 145 – 152
10. Jacob, O.W., Forlizzi, J., Scott, E. H., Brad, A. M.: WebThumb: Interaction Techniques for Small-Screen Browsers, Proceedings of the 15th annual ACM symposium on User interface software and technology. Paris, France (2002) 205 – 208
11. Robertson, G., Czerwinski, M., Robbins, K., Thiel, D.C., van Dantzich, M.: Data Mountain: Using spatial memory for document management. Proceedings of the 11th annual ACM symposium on User interface software and technology. San Francisco, USA (1998) 153 – 162
12. Schilit, B. N., Trevor, J., Hilbert, D. M., Tzu, K. K.: m-Links: An infrastructure for very Small Internet Devices. Proceedings of the 7th annual international conference on Mobile computing and networking. Rome, Italy (2001) 122 – 131

A Model-Based Approach for Integrating Third Party Systems with Web Applications

Nathalie Moreno and Antonio Vallecillo

Dpto. de Lenguajes y Ciencias de la Computación
Universidad de Málaga, Spain
{vergara,av}@lcc.uma.es

Abstract. New Web applications are rapidly moving from stand-alone systems to distributed applications that need to interoperate with third party systems, such as external Web services or legacy applications. In most cases, this integration is not properly addressed by current Web Engineering proposals, that either achieve it only at one single level (user interface, process, code or data), or assume the existence of a central conceptual model, something which is not always true in a service-oriented scenario. This paper presents a model-based framework that provides concepts and mechanisms for facilitating the high-level integration of Web applications with third party systems, allowing the manipulation of the external entities of such systems as native elements of our models.

1 Introduction

We are currently witnessing an evolution of Web applications, which are rapidly moving from stand-alone systems to distributed applications that need to interoperate with third party systems, such as external portlets, Web services or legacy applications.

In most cases, this integration is not properly addressed by existing Web Engineering proposals (such as WebML [1], OOHDM [2], UWE [3], OO-H [4], W2000 [5] or WSDM [6]). They provide excellent methodologies and tools for the design and development of Web applications. However, they have also shown some limitations when external and legacy systems need to be integrated into the applications they build. For instance, they either achieve this integration only at one single level (user interface, process, code, or data – see e.g., [7]) or assume the existence of a central model (usually called the conceptual or structural model), around which the rest of their models are built. However, the existence of such a central model is not always true, as it happens, for instance, in service-oriented scenarios where each party can have its own data schema. Finally, most of these Web proposals do not supply mechanisms for making explicit their provided and required interfaces, their processes, choreographies, data models, and business logic. Such a sort of "componentization" of Web application development is required in order to properly exchange information and services with other systems.

D. Lowe and M. Gaedke (Eds.): ICWE 2005, LNCS 3579, pp. 441–452, 2005.

Integration problems also depend on the kind of external systems being considered. Web services have become the Internet standard for exchanging functionality between loosely coupled clients and servers. Portlets [8] allow the exchange of presentation, on top of basic functionality, for Web portals construction. Finally, legacy software have been defined as "software that works". Although usually poorly documented, difficult to maintain, and complex to adapt and integrate with other systems, this kind of applications cannot be ignored because they support core business functions, embed business rules not documented anywhere else, and preserve the strategy and finances of most large organizations.

A proper integration approach requires an structured an efficient way to assist software architects and developers achieve it not only at implementation level, but also during all phases of the development process.

This paper presents a model-based framework that provides the concepts and mechanisms required for facilitating the high-level integration of Web applications with third party systems, allowing the manipulation of the external entities of such systems as native elements of our models. It is based on the MDA principles [9, 10], that aim at providing portability, interoperability and reusability through architectural separation of concerns. MDA prescribes certain kinds of models to be used (i.e, CIM, PIM and PSM), how those models may be prepared, and the relationships between the different kinds of models.

The basis for prescribing these models is the concept of viewpoint, where a viewpoint on a system is a technique for abstraction using a selected set of concepts and structuring rules, in order to focus on particular concerns within that system. In this regard, our framework identifies a set of models related to the development of a Web application, each one addressing a key concern.

The rest of the paper is structured as follows. Section 2 briefly introduces the framework, identifies its main layers and models, and defines guidelines for using the viewpoints prescribed by the framework for structuring Web applications development. Section 3 details how to use the framework for facilitating integration of Web applications with third party systems, using a classical example to illustrate the approach. Finally, Section 4 draws some conclusions and outlines some future research work.

2   A Framework for Building Web Applications Within the MDA Context

Our framework tries to help organize complex systems by separating the different concerns that matter for model-driven Web application development. As depicted in Figure 1, it is organized in three main independent layers, each one corresponding to a *viewpoint*. Consequently, a Web application in our approach distinguishes three main PIMs, one for each layer (User interface, Business logic, and Data). These PIMs comprise a set of models defined in terms of the entities that are relevant to the corresponding concerns, and the relationships between the models.

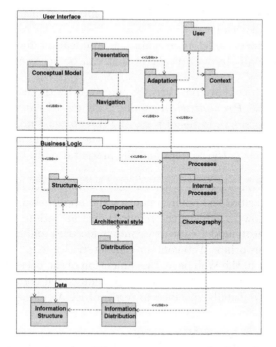

Fig. 1. Models representing the different concerns involved in the development of a Web application

2.1 The Data Viewpoint

The **Data structure** level describes the organization of the persistent information managed by the application (that could be finally stored in, e.g., a relational database). Information is represented in terms of the data elements that constitute its information base and the semantic relationships between them. This level is organized in two models:

- The *Information Structure* model deals with the information that has to be made persistent before it gets stored in a database.
- The *Information Distribution* model describes the distribution and replication of the data being modeled, since information can be fragmented in *Nodes* or replicated in different *Locations*.

2.2 The User Interface Viewpoint

The **User interface** level is responsible for accepting persistent, processed or structured data from the *Process* and *Data* viewpoints, in order to interact with the end user and deliver the application contents in a suitable format. Originally, Web applications were specifically conceived to deal mainly with navigation and presentation concerns, but currently they also need to address other relevant issues:

- The *Conceptual* model encapsulates the information handled by the rest of the models at this level.
- The *Navigation* model represents the application navigational requirements in terms of *Access Structures* that can be accessed via *Navigational Links*.
- Navigational objects are not directly perceived by the user, rather they are accessed via the *Presentation* model. This model captures the presentational requirements in terms of a set of *Presentation Units*.
- The *User* model describes and manages the user characteristics with the purpose of adapting the content and the presentation to the users' needs and preferences.
- The *Context* model deals with *Device, Network, Location* and *Time* aspects, and describes the environment of the application. These are needed to determine how to achieve the required customization.
- The *Adaptation* model captures context features and user preferences to obtain the appropriate Web content characteristics (e.g., the number of embedded objects in the Web page, the dimension of the base-Web page without components, or the total dimension of the embedded components). Adaptation policies are usually specified in terms of ECA rules.

2.3 The Business Logic Viewpoint

The **Business Logic** level encapsulates the application's business logic, i.e., how the information is processed, and how the application interacts with other computerized systems.

- The *Structure* model describes the major classes or component types representing services in the system (*BusinessProcessInformation*), their attributes (*Attributes*), the signature of their operations (*Signature*), and the relationships between them (*Association*). The design of the *Structure* model is driven by the needs of the processes that implement the business logic of the system, taking into account the tasks that users can perform.
- The *Internal Processes* model specifies the precise behavior of every *BusinessProcessInformation* or component as well as the set of activities that are executed in order to achieve a business objective. For a complete description of a business process, apart from the *Structure* model, we need information related to the *Activities* carried out by the *BusinessProcessInformation*, expressing their behaviour and the *Flows* that pass around objects or data.
- The *Choreography* model defines the valid sequences of messages and interactions that the different objects of the system may exchange [11]. The choreography may be individually oriented, specifying the contract a component exhibits to other components (*PartialChoreography*) or, it may be globally oriented, specifying the flow of messages within a global composition (*GlobalChoreography*).
- The *Distribution* model describes how its basic entities, the *Nodes*, are connected by means of point to point connections or *Links*. While the *Information Distribution* model of the *Data* viewpoint specifies the distribution of

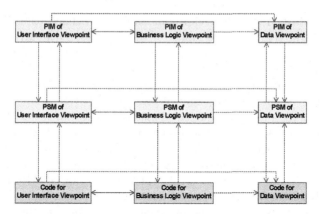

Fig. 2. PIMs required in the development of a Web applications, and their transformation to code (adapted from [13])

the data, this model describes the distribution of the processes that achieve the business logic of the system.

- The **Architectural Style** model defines the fundamental organization of a system in terms of its components, their relationships, and the principles guiding its design and evolution [12], i.e., how functionality is encapsulated into business components and services.

2.4 How the Framework Is Used

The development of a typical Web application with data, business process and hypertext requirements involves the definition of at least three PIMs, each one corresponding to a *viewpoint* (see top of Figure 2). Looking at the different viewpoints, we realized that they can be naturally integrated using the MDA architecture and its facilities for relating them.

The process begins by determining the scope of the system, by means of identifying the framework metamodels that need to be instantiated. For data-intensive Web applications, the *Data viewpoint* modeling is the cornerstone for all the other viewpoints. In consequence, our starting point is an *Information Structure* model of the application, which is represented in our proposal by a UML class diagram marked with the stereotypes defined in Table 1. The *Information Structure* model is then refined to represent how information is distributed in ≪Nodes≫, with attribute Location specifying their location. As shown in Table 1, external data sources will be referenced in the *Information Structure* model as ≪ExternalInformationUnit≫ UML classes, related to ≪InformationUnit≫ UML classes by means of ≪ExternalRelationship≫ associations.

Please notice that the fact that stereotypes of UML 2.0 Profiles may have associated attributes is very useful [14]. They add information to the stereotypes when marking the models – allowing us, for instance, to include information about the Location of a ≪Node≫, the kind and characteristics of an external association marked with ≪ExternalRelationship≫, etc.

Once the PIM of the *Data* viewpoint has been defined, the behavioral details are given in the *Structure* model of the *Business Logic* layer. This model captures the Web application functionality. It can be modeled in many different ways, including, e.g., preconditions, postconditions or invariants, or using any other notation that allows the semi-automatic generation of implementations (e.g., an Action Semantic Language). When external systems are used, they will be included in the model as ≪ExternalBusinessProcessInformation≫ UML classes. Their relationships with our ≪BusinessProcessInformation≫ UML classes will be represented by ≪ExternalAssociation≫ UML associations. Again, the use of attributes in stereotypes will allow us to represent (at a later stage) the kind of external services and the way to invoke them, e.g., using SOAP in case of Web services, JSR-168 or WSRP in case of portlets, etc.

Integration at this level is the most interesting but also the most difficult, because it may require interoperability between processes that may not have common a behavioral model (e.g., action semantics or granularity).

At this point, the system functionality can be refined into two additional models: the *Internal Process* model and the *Choreography* specification. Both of them are UML activity diagrams marked with the stereotypes defined in Table 1. Notice that the ≪ExternalActivity≫ and ≪ExternalFlow≫ marks allow to handle external business process and workflows as elements of our models.

The issues related to the architectural style (i.e., how processes are encapsulated into ≪Components≫) and process distribution (e.g., how and where components are deployed) complete the description of the *Business Logic* layer in marked UML component diagrams. Finally, the PIM of the *Business Logic viewpoint* is obtained by merging the previous models into a single one that contains all the information. In this regard, not only class, activity or component diagrams can be marked, but also UML deployment diagrams. The stereotypes ≪StaticNode≫, ≪ComputingNode≫, ≪MobileNode≫ and ≪ExternalNode≫ have been defined to represent system artifacts as nodes, which are connected through communication paths (≪Link≫ and ≪ExternalLink≫) to create network systems. Nodes can be either hardware devices (≪Device≫), places (≪Place≫), actors (≪Actor≫) or software execution environments (≪ComputingNode≫).

Finally, the description of how the information is displayed to the user starts with the definition of the *Conceptual* model of the *User Interface* viewpoint. Two main stereotypes distinguish between internal information objects that require to be manipulated at presentation level (≪UserKnowledgeUnit≫), and information objects that are created by external entities and that need to be displayed by our application (≪ExternalUserKnowledgeUnit≫) – as it happens, for instance, with portlets. Then, the *Conceptual* model is enriched with *Access Structures*, that determine how to reach the information objects using ≪Indexes≫, ≪Menus≫ or ≪GuidedTours≫. Finally, in order to obtain the PIM of the *User Interface* viewpoint, we need to provide for each ≪UserKnowledgeUnit≫ UML class and for each *Access Structure*, a graphical representation using the stereotypes defined in Table 1.

Table 1. Framework Models Entities

Level	Model	Concepts
Data	Information Structure	InformationUnit, ExternalInformationUnit, Attribute, Relationship, ExternalRelationship, AccessOperation, Parameter, Constraint, Transaction
	Information Location	Node, ExternalNode, Link, ExternalLink, Location
User Interface	Conceptual	UserKnowledgeUnit, ExternalUserKnowledgeUnit, Attribute, Association, Generalization, Specialization, Aggregation, Perspective, Dependency Relationship
	Navigation	NavigationUnit, NavigationLink, ExternalNavigationUnit, ExternalNavigationLink, LandmarkNavigationUnit, ContextNavigation, Event, Access Structure (Indexes, Menus, Guided Tour), OptionMenu, IndexOption
	Presentation	PresentationUnit, SinglePresentationUnit (Text, Image, Input element, Text area, Selection element, etc.), GroupPresentationUnit (Section, Page, Form,ExternalPage, etc.), Tabbed
	Context	Context, Device, Network, Location, Time
	User	History, Session, User, Role, UserFeature, Preference, Previous Knowledge
	Adaptation	Event, Rule, Condition, Action, Entity
Business Logic	Structure	BusinessProcessInformation, Attributes, Signature, Association, ExternalBusinessProcessInformation, ExternalAssociation
	Internal Processes	Activity, ExternalActivity, ActivityType, StartActivity, EndActivity, Flow, ExternalFlow, ControlStructure, ConditionalStructure
	Choreography	PartialChoreography, GlobalChoreography, Activity, Transition, AtomicActivity, ComplexActivity, ExecutionMode, Exception, ControlStructure, ConditionalStructure, Connection
	Architecture	Component, Module, Layer, Sub-module, Client, Server, Master, Slave, Pipe, Filter, Broker, Peer, Event bus, Sources, Channel, Bus, Listener, Model, View, Controller, Adapter, Interpreter
	Distribution	Node, StaticNode (Device, Place, Actor), ComputingNode, MobileNode, System, ExternalNode, Network, Link, ExternalLink

Depending on whether adaptation is required or not, a *User* model, a *Context* model and the adaptation rules of the *Adaptation* model need to be specified. These three models are merged to complete the *User Interface* PIM specification.

Once the three PIMs are appropriately marked, we just have to follow the MDA transformation process from PIMs to PSMs, applying a set of mapping rules (one for each mark and for each marked element). The result of the application of such mapping rules are a set of class diagrams marked according to the target technologies (e.g. Java, JSP, Oracle, etc.). Finally, the PSMs are translated to code applying a transformation process again (see Figure 2). As mentioned in [13], special care should be taken with the bridges between the three PIMs and their corresponding PSMs, for which transformations are also required.

3   Proof of Concept: The Travel Agency System

In order to illustrate our proposal, this section describes how to design a Travel Agency Web application that interacts with both customers through a Web interface, and with external service providers using Web services. The Travel Agency sells vacation packages to its customers. The packages include flights, hotel rooms, car rentals, and combinations of these. External service providers include transportation companies (airlines, hotels and car rentals) and financial organizations (credit companies and banks).

To book a vacation package, the customer will provide details about his preferred dates, destinations, and accommodation options to the Travel Agency System (TAS). Based on this information, the TAS will request its service providers for offers that fulfill the user's requirements, and then will present the list of offers to the customer. At this point, the customer may either select one of the offered packages, reject them all and quit, or refine his requirements and start the process again. If the customer selects one of the packages, the TAS will book the individual services to the corresponding transportation companies, and charge the customer. Based on these requirements, there is no need for persistent storage or for adaptation in this case. Thus, only two PIMs are required: the *User Interface* PIM and the *Business Logic* PIM.

The PIM of the *User Interface* viewpoint is developed starting from its *Conceptual* model. For service-oriented scenarios, it has to be defined from scratch taking into account the information that needs to be presented to the user during a session. Therefore, our *Conceptual* model will consist of seven ≪UserInformationUnits≫ UML classes, namely TravelAgency, HolidayPackage, Booking, Customer, Flight, Room and Car (see Fig. 3). Please note how the three latter classes have been added to the model to store temporarily returned values of invoked external services, and to handle the transactions. Besides, these entities will act as bridges between the Travel Agency Interface and the external Web services interfaces (marked as ≪ExternalUserInformationUnits≫ in the *Conceptual* model).

Then, the *Navigation* model is built as a refinement of the *Conceptual* model. The *Navigation* model specifies the navigational structures of the Travel Agency, i.e., how users navigate through the available information using *Indexes* (≪Index≫ HolidayPackageIndex), *Menus* (≪Menu≫ HolidayPackageMenu, ≪Menu≫ BookingMenu, ≪Menu≫ CustomerMenu) or *Guided Tours* (≪GuidedTour≫ BookingGuidedTour). With this purpose, each ≪UserInformationUnit≫ in the *Conceptual* model has been mapped to one or more ≪NavigationUnits≫ in the *Navigation* model, in the same way as *Associations* of the *Conceptual* model have been mapped to ≪NavigationLinks≫.

To reference the external points of navigation outside the scope of the application, ≪ExternalUserInformationUnit≫ UML classes (Airline, CarHire or Hotel) have been marked as ≪ExternalNavigationUnit≫ in the *Navigation* model. Likewise, the relationships between internal and external ≪NavigationUnits≫ have been marked as ≪ExternalNavigationLinks≫ in this model. We have added constraints to ≪NavigationLinks≫ describing which events will trigger the navigation through the link (e.g., when a process finishes, after clicking a ≪MenuOption≫, etc.)

The *Presentation* model further refers to groups of pages organized around ≪PresentationUnits≫ as: (*i*) ≪SinglePresentationUnits≫, with their attributes

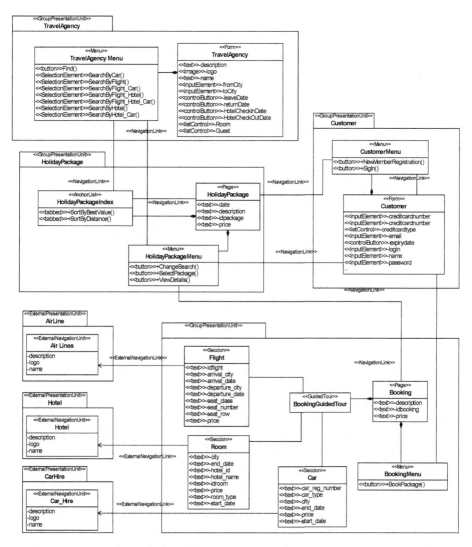

Fig. 3. The PIM for the User Interface viewpoint

marked as ≪text≫, ≪image≫, ≪button≫, etc.; and (ii) ≪GroupPresentationUnits≫ that comprise UML classes and packages stereotyped ≪page≫, ≪section≫ or ≪form≫. Basically, we have used in our example ≪section≫ to display service responses and ≪page≫ to display the main portal pages. We have also marked as ≪forms≫ those UML classes that invoke external services.

Since adaptation is not required in this case, the final PIM of the *User Interface* viewpoint (shown in Figure 3) is obtained by merging these three models.

The PIM for the *Business Logic* layer can be developed in parallel starting from the *Structure* model. As shown in Figure 4, it involves component types representing internal system services (≪BusinessProcessInformation≫), their

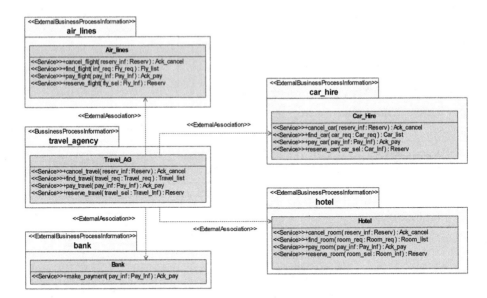

Fig. 4. Business Logic Structure Model

attributes (≪Attributes≫), the signature of their operations (≪Services≫), and the relationships between them (≪Associations≫). External system interfaces have been modeled as ≪ExternalBusinessProcessInformation≫ and their relationships with other ≪BusinessProcessInformation≫ processes as ≪ExternalAssociations≫.

Please notice that we can easily model these external services by making use of their actual specifications (i.e., interfaces, choreography, behavior) if we know them. Alternatively, we can always model their abstract (i.e., required) specifications, and then use adaptors at the PSM level when the actual services are decided [15].

The next step consists of providing a specific description of how internal processes (marked as ≪Services≫) find_travel, reserve_travel, pay_travel and cancel_travel work. This is described in the *Internal Process* model (not shown here). Then, the interactions between internal and external processes are detailed in the *Choreography* model (see Figure 5). Notice that both the *Internal Process* and the *Choreography* models are UML activity diagrams marked with the stereotypes defined in Table 1.

Finally, the *Component* and *Distribution* models (in this order) will reveal how the internal processes are grouped according to the software architecture style, and encapsulated for distribution in the final platform.

In addition to the *User Interface* and the *Business Logic* PIMs, the bridges between them (represented by dependency relationships in our framework) need to be specified. OCL restrictions and dependency relationships between elements from different models are used for that. For example, *events* in *Navigation* model establish when *activities* in the *Internal Process* model can start or finish.

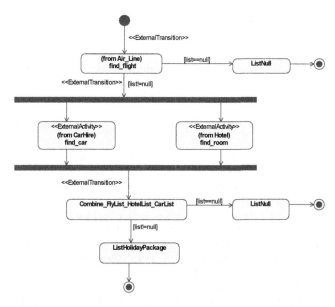

Fig. 5. An excerpt of the choreography for find_travel

Once the PIMs of our application are described, we need to generate their respective PSMs. Using a set of model transformations (as detailed in [13]), we can obtain a Java PSM for the *Business Logic* PIM and a Web presentation (e.g. a WAE PSM) for the *User Interface* PIM, for example. Then, another set of transformations is required (from PSMs to code) to produce the final code and Web pages of the application – but these transformations are already well-known and documented (see, e.g., [16]).

4   Concluding Remarks

Web applications are no longer isolated system, they need to interoperate with other external systems. Model-driven Web engineering proposals should take this fact into account, being able to incorporate these external applications into their models. In this paper we have presented a model-based framework that allows the high-level integration of Web applications with third party systems, enabling the manipulation of the external entities of such systems as other elements of our models.

Once the framework has been defined, there are some issues that need to be addressed. First, the specification of the bridges between the different PIMs have to be improved so precise correspondences between their elements can be established. Second, we plan to make use of QVT languages for defining the model transformations, so they can be easily re-used and integrated into an MDA tool. Finally, we plan to work on the interoperability issues that arise when (not necessarily compatible) external applications need to be smoothly integrated.

Acknowledgements

The authors would like to thank anonymous referees for their helpful comments and remarks. This work has been supported by Spanish Research Project TIC2002- 04309-C02-02.

References

1. Ceri, S., Fraternali, P., Bongio, A.: Web modelling language (WebML): a modelling language for designing web sites. Proc. of WWW9 (2000) Amsterdam, Netherlands.
2. Rossi, G., Schwabe, D., Guimaraes, R.: Designing personalized web applications. Proc. of WWW10 (2001) 275–284 Hong Kong, China.
3. Koch, N., Kraus., A.: Towards a common metamodel for the development of Web applications. Proc. of ICWE'03 **LNCS 2722** (2003) 495–506 Berlin.
4. Garrigós, I., Gómez, J., Cachero., C.: Modelling Dynamic Personalization in Web Applications. Proc. of ICWE'03 **LNCS 2722** (2003) 472–475 Oviedo, Spain.
5. Baresi, L., Garzotto, F., Paolini, P.: Extending UML for Modelling Web Applications. Proc. of HICSS-34 (2001)
6. Troyer, O.D., Leune, C.: WSDM: A User-Centered Design Method for Web Sites. Proc. of WWW07 (1998) 85–94
7. Brambilla, M., Ceri, S., Comai, S., Fraternali, P., Manolescu, I.: Model-driven specification of web services composition and integration with data-intensive web applications. IEEE Data Eng. Bull. **25** (2002) 53–59
8. Bellas, F., Fernández, D., Muiño, A.: A flexible framework for engineering "my" portals. Proc. of WWW13 (2004) 234–243
9. Miller, J., Mukerji, J.: MDA Guide. Object Management Group. (2003) OMG document ab/2003-06-01.
10. OMG: Model Driven Architecture. A Technical Perspective. Object Management Group. (2001) OMG document ab/2001-01-01.
11. OMG: A UML Profile for Enterprise Distributed Object Computing. Object Management Group. (2002) OMG document PTC/2002-02-05.
12. IEEE: Recommened Practice for Architectural Description of Software-Intensive Systems. IEEE Std. 1471-2000. (2000)
13. Kleppe, A., Warmer, J., Bast, W.: MDA Explained. The Model Driven Architecture: Practice and Promise. Addison-Wesley (2003)
14. Fuentes, L., Vallecillo, A.: An introduction to UML profiles. UPGRADE, The European Journal for the Informatics Professional **5** (2004) 5–13
15. Moreno, N., Vallecillo, A.: What to we do with re-use in MDA? Second European Workshop on Model Driven Architecture (EWMDA-2) (2004) Canterbury, Kent.
16. Bézivin, J., Hammoudi, S., Lopes, D., Jouault, F.: Applying MDA approach for Web service platform. In: Proc. of EDOC 2004, Monterey, California, IEEE CS Press (2004) 58–70

A Model-Driven Approach for Designing Distributed Web Information Systems

Richard Vdovjak* and Geert-Jan Houben

Eindhoven University of Technology,
POBox 513, 5600MB, Eindhoven,
The Netherlands
{r.vdovjak,g.j.houben}@tue.nl

Abstract. There is an apparent need for specifying the integration of multiple knowledge sources during the design of Web Information Systems (WIS) where the actual data is often retrieved from several content providers. Despite that, there exists very little work on integration within the context of WIS engineering and the related design methodologies in particular. We argue that this new context brings several additional requirements which must be dealt with in order to be able to successfully deploy distributed WIS. In this paper we elaborate a model that covers the integration phase of the WIS design trajectory. We centered our approach around the emerging data standard on the Semantic Web – RDF. The proposed integration model is able to reconcile many semantic heterogeneities that frequently occur among disparate RDF sources. We also address the issues of distributed RDF query processing and optimization, and test the performance of our framework.

1 Introduction

The need for handling multiple sources of knowledge and information is very apparent in the context of engineering Web Information Systems (WIS). The actual data presented in a typical WIS is often retrieved from several (possibly heterogeneous) set of sources. While the integration problem was carefully studied in isolation in the database field, there exists very little work on integration in the context of Web engineering applications and of the design methodologies that support them in particular. We argue that this new context brings several additional requirements that must be dealt with in order to be able to successfully design a distributed WIS. The separation-of-concerns principle together with the model-based approach has proven to be an efficient remedy to the complexity of the WIS design. In this paper we elaborate a model that covers the integration and data retrieval phase of the WIS design trajectory. We centered our approach around the emerging data standard on the Semantic Web, the Resource Description Framework (RDF) [1]. RDF is the modeling foundation of the Semantic Web. Despite its inherently distributed nature, most of the current RDF processing engines store the RDF data locally as a single knowledge

---

* Richard Vdovjak is also affiliated with Philips Research Eindhoven, The Netherlands

D. Lowe and M. Gaedke (Eds.): ICWE 2005, LNCS 3579, pp. 453–464, 2005.

repository, i.e. RDF models from remote sources are replicated and merged into a single model. Distribution is retained only virtually through the use of namespaces to distinguish between different models. We argue that many interesting applications on the Semantic Web would benefit from, or even require an RDF infrastructure that supports real distribution of information sources that can be accessed from a single point. In this paper we focuss on the RDF integration problem taking into account the context of WIS.

The rest of the paper is structured as follows. In section 2 we introduce the Hera WIS design framework and derive some WIS specific requirements for the integration phase. Section 3 summarizes the semantics of RDF(S) and formally defines some important terms used in our integration suite. Section 4 describes the Integration Model formalism which is able to deal with many semantic heterogeneities that frequently occur among sources on the Semantic Web. Section 5 addresses the issues of distributed query processing and optimization, and describes the performance of our system. Section 6 presents concluding remarks.

2   Modeling WIS in Hera

A primary focus of the Hera project is to support Web-based information system (WIS) design and implementation. A WIS generates a hypermedia presentation for the data that is retrieved from the data storage in response to a user query. This entire process of retrieving data and presenting it in hypermedia format needs to be specified during the design of the WIS. The typical structure of the WIS design in the Hera perspective consists of three layers: the semantic layer focusing on the application's semantics and the integration aspects, the application layer designing a navigational view over the data, and the presentation layer dealing with a concrete rendering platform such as HTML, WML or SMIL.

In this paper we focus mainly on the semantic layer of the Hera methodology. After the process of integration, the conceptual model instances are generated as response to a user query. Figure 1 presents an overview of the semantic layer with its central component – the mediator.

2.1   Related Work

As opposed to Hera, most of the web engineering approaches (e.g. UWE [2], WebML [3] or XWMF [4]) do not explicitly consider integration. A notable exception is the OntoWebber [5] system which we detail below.

OntoWebber is a system for building and managing data-intensive websites. Similarly to Hera, it adopts a model-driven ontology-based approach for declarative website management and data integration. It advocates the use of ontologies as the basis for constructing different models necessary for WIS design. OntoWebber supports the integration of heterogeneous data sources based on RDF as common format for modeling semistructured data. In the first step OntoWebber focuses on syntax reconciliation converting all source data into RDF. This RDF data (both the schema and the instances) is replicated and stored locally. From

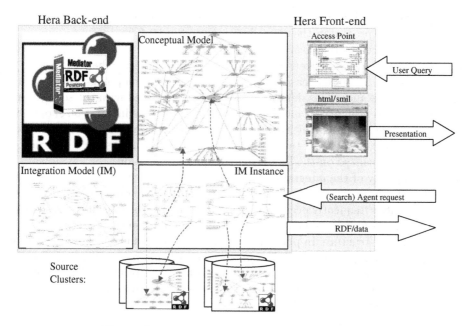

Fig. 1. An overview of the semantic layer of Hera

this point of view, OntoWebber acts as a data warehouse and does not guarantee the freshness of its data, as opposed to the Hera integration framework which implements the on-demand retrieval paradigm, assuring that the retrieved data is always up-to-date. After the replication phase, the local copies of the source data are articulated by the designer in terms of a reference ontology which captures the domain of interest.

2.2   Hera Requirements for RDF(S) Data Integration in the Context of WIS

By analyzing the specifics of WIS, we form the following set of requirements for our integration framework. The existing approaches to data integration, e.g. [6] often do not meet some of these important prerequisites which renders them less suitable for designing WIS. Below we summarize the list of requirements for the Hera integration framework.

- The use of (open) WWW standards.
  While in the past the main consumer of the information provided by WIS was usually a human, currently there are more and more (Web) applications that need to process this information as well. Moreover, WIS themselves often consist of a complex composition of collaborating (Web) components, such as the components in the Hera software suite. This requires the use of Web standards throughout the entire process. To promote the re-use of integration specifications by other parties on the Semantic Web, it is useful

that both the information to be integrated, and the integration specification itself are expressed in the same description standard.

– Ontology level, model-based approach.
  Since WIS are data-intensive applications with large numbers of instances per concept, it is not feasible to specify integration mappings for every individual instance. This data-intensive nature combined with the separation-of-concerns principle adopted by Hera implies that the integration should be expressible in an explicit model which reasons in terms of source ontologies rather than in terms of the actual data instances. The instance integration has to be realized on-the-fly during the query evaluation.

– Expressivity of the integration formalism.
  The integration formalism must be able to cover a wide range of semantic heterogeneities frequently occurring on the Semantic Web. This includes schema heterogeneities where the source ontologies can differ in their concepts, properties, and structure. In particular, RDFS models often contain sequences of connected properties – so-called ontology or schema paths. These paths can differ considerably among the sources and the conceptual model. To reconcile these discrepancies is an essential prerequisite to successful evaluation of join queries across multiple sources.

– Freshness of data.
  Hera has the ambition to support the engineering of WIS which often use as content providers other autonomous Web sources. Both the structure and the data of these sources may change without notification. While the structural changes are assumed to be less frequent, the actual data can change frequently. In this context the freshness of the gathered data is an important aspect and should be guaranteed.

3   RDF(S) and Ontologies

An RDF triple model is similar to a directed labeled graph [1]. The nodes in the graph are used to represent resources or literals. Literals (strings) denote content that is not processed further by the RDF processor[1]. The nodes that represent resources can be further classified as nodes representing URI references or blank nodes. All non-blank nodes are (explicitly) labeled with resource identifiers (URIs) or string values. The edges in the graph represent properties and are also labeled by URIs. The set of all labels occurring in the graph is called the vocabulary of the graph. In order to associate formal semantics to an RDF graph, all labels in its vocabulary must have an interpretation. An interpretation specifies for every URI reference what it stands for as well as whether it is a property, resource, or a literal value. In case of a property it also describes what value that property can take for things in the domain of discourse. To be able to reason about sources at schema level we must extend the initial vocabulary

---

[1] In this work we consider only plain literals but our approach can be easily extended to typed literals as well

with the standardized set of URI references defined in the RDF vocabulary and
RDF Schema vocabulary [7].

Definition 1 *An RDFS interpretation of a vocabulary V is defined as 7-tuple:*

$$(IR, IP, IC, LV, IS, IEXT, ICEXT)$$

*where IR is a set of resources, IP is a set of properties, IC is a set of classes,
LV is a set of literal values, IS is a mapping $V \to IR$ defining the interpretation
(meaning) of URI references and literals, and IEXT is a mapping $IP \to 2^{IR \times IR}$
defining the extent of properties[2]. ICEXT defines an extent of every class. Moreover, every RDFS interpretation has to satisfy several semantic conditions, e.g.
the transitivity and reflexivity of rdfs:subClassOf and rdfs:subPropertyOf.
We refer to [7] for the complete condition list.*

3.1 RDFS Ontologies

Both, the WIS that we need to populate with data and the sources are represented by their ontological descriptions. The ontology captures their domain of
discourse. When we refer to ontology, we mainly mean the hierarchy of concepts
together with their properties. The actual data that populates these concepts
is referred to as ontology instances. Note that due to the intensional nature of
RDF(S) semantics the antisymmetry property is not guaranteed to hold and
therefore we cannot say that there is a partial order on the set of classes and
properties. In the ontology definition below we use the pre-order relation – a
binary relation that satisfies the reflexivity and transitivity, but not necessarily
the antisymmetry.

Definition 2 *An RDFS ontology O as a 4-tuple $(G, I, \preccurlyeq_{IC}, \preccurlyeq_{IP})$, where*

- *G is an RDF graph.*
- *I is an RDFS interpretation of the vocabulary of G and I holds that $IR = IP \cup IC$, i.e. there are no 'instance' resources.*
- *$\preccurlyeq_{IC}$ is a pre-order relation on the set IC defined by
  $IEXT(I(rdfs:subClassOf))$*
- *$\preccurlyeq_{IP}$ is a pre-order relation on the set IP defined by
  $IEXT(I(rdfs:subPropertyOf))$*

If an RDF graph (and its interpretation) adheres to a given ontology O, i.e.
uses the properties and classes defined in O, it is considered to be an instantiation
of O.

Definition 3 *Let G be an RDF graph and I its RDFS interpretation. The pair
(G, I) is an instantiation of the ontology O $(G', I', \preccurlyeq_{IC}, \preccurlyeq_{IP})$ if the following
holds: $\{c \mid (x, c) \in IEXT(I(rdf:type))\} \subset I'.IC$, and $I.IP \subset I'.IP$, and the
types from the extent of every non-system property in G follow the types defined
in O by the $I'(rdfs:domain)$, and $I'(rdfs:range)$ for that particular property.*

---

[2] When an interpretation I is applied to a single URI reference, it represents a straightforward application of the IS function of I

Definition 4 *A single path in ontology O $(G, I, \preccurlyeq_{IC}, \preccurlyeq_{IP})$ is defined as triple (C, P, T) where $C \in I.IC$, $P \in I.IP$, $T \in I.IC \cup \{I(rdfs{:}Literal)\}$ and $(P, C) \in IEXT(I(rdfs{:}domain))$ and $(P, T) \in IEXT(I(rdfs{:}ramnge))$.*

Informally, a single ontology path is a property together with its domain and range classes. By using the following definition we can combine single ontology paths into an arbitrarily long path expression.

Definition 5 *Let $p_1, \ldots p_n$ be a sequence of single paths. They together constitute a composed ontology path expression if for any neighboring single paths $p_i(C_i, P_i, T_i)$ and $p_{i+1}(C_{i+1}, P_{i+1}, T_{i+1})$ the following holds:*

$$T_i \neq I(rdfs{:}Literal) \land$$
$$((P_i, C_{i+1}) \in IEXT(I(rdfs{:}range)) \lor$$
$$(P_{i+1}, T_i) \in IEXT(I(rdfs{:}domain)) \lor$$
$$(T_i, C_{i+1}) \in IEXT(I(rdfs{:}subClassOf)) \lor$$
$$(C_{i+1}, T_i) \in IEXT(I(rdfs{:}subClassOf)))$$

4   Integration Model

The official RDF semantics [7] makes a strong assumption about URI references: they are assumed to be globally coherent, so that a single URI reference can be considered to have the same meaning wherever it occurs. However, in the heterogenous world of the WWW we often have to relax this assumption if we want to integrate data from different sources. In Fig. 2 we depict an example of two sources with different vocabularies and interpretations. Both however describe the same domain and the integration model is a way to specify how they relate to the conceptual model. The solid lines indicate mappings established during the integration phase, and the dashed lines denote results during the query answering process[3]. The integration model defines a set of articulations which create semantic mappings between the sources and the CM.

4.1   Articulations

The simplest form of articulation is that combining two single path expressions. Informally, this articulation establishes a schema level link between two properties (one from a source and one from the CM). During the query resolution, the instances of the source property are translated into instances of the property from the CM.

Definition 6 *Let O_S be an RDFS ontology describing the source S and O_{CM} the (traget) RDFS ontology describing the WIS which we need to populate with instances. A simple articulation As is defined as a pair (Q, R), where $Q(C, P, T)$ and $R(C, P, T)$ are single ontology paths in O_{CM} and O_S, respectively. At instance level, the As is a function which transforms the source instances into CM*

---

[3] The property extent mappings $IEXT$ are omitted for the sake of readability

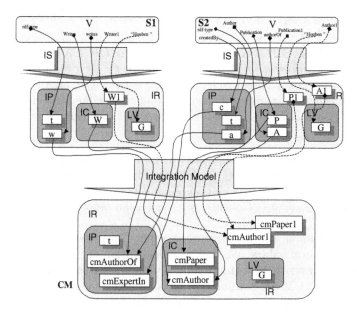

Fig. 2. Sources with different vocabularies and interpretations linked to the CM

instances. Let $Inst_S$ be the instantiation of the source ontology O_S. The instantiation of the O_{CM} is augmented such that the following holds:
$\forall(x,y) \in Inst_S.I.IEXT(R.P) \; \exists(x',y') \in Inst_{CM}.I.IEXT(Q.P) \wedge (x',Q.C) \in Inst_{CM}.I.IEXT(I(rdf{:}type)) \wedge ((y',Q.T) \in Inst_{CM}.I.IEXT(I(rdf{:}type)) \vee Q.T = I(rdfs{:}Literal))$.

Although a simple articulation allows for different vocabularies, when also the structure of the two ontologies differs we need a more sophisticated integration tool. A *path articulation* defined below allows for the mapping of ontology path expressions of different length. The idea is to link the beginning and the end of the two paths and to apply simple articulations where they exist. In case there exist some parts of the path in the CM which are not covered by the source path expression, e.g. due to structural heterogeneity, we generate blank node instances in the CM to keep the path connected.

Definition 7 *Let O_S be an RDFS ontology describing the source S and O_{CM} the (traget) RDFS ontology describing the WIS which we need to populate with instances. A path articulation Ap is defined as a pair (p, q) where p, and q are ontology path expressions in O_{CM} and O_S, respectively.*
Let (C_{1x}, P_{1x}, T_{1x}) and (C_{-x}, P_{-x}, T_{-x}) denote respectively the first and the last single path of the composed path expression x. The semantics of Ap is defined as the augmentation of the instantiation of the O_{CM} in the following way. For every instance of the path q we assume an instance of the path p consisting of blank nodes between the defined properties of p such that the path is connected. We generate instances to replace (some of) the blank nodes such that the fol-

lowing holds: $\forall x \in Inst_S.I.ICEXT(C_1q)\ \exists x' \in Inst_{CM}.I.ICEXT(C_1p)$ *i.e. we generate class instances for the beginning of the path p. We do the same also for its end:* $\forall x \in Inst_S.I.ICEXT(T_1q)\ \exists x' \in Inst_{CM}.I.ICEXT(T_1p)$. *Unless the end is a literal property, i.e.* $T_{-S} = I(rdfs{:}Literal)$, *then the literal values are copied:* $\forall(x,y) \in Inst_S.I.IEXT(P_{-q})\ \exists(x',y') \in Inst_{CM}.I.IEXT(P_{-p}) : y = y'$. *Further, we generate appropriate instances and replace the blank nodes for every single path in p that has a simple articulation that associates it to a single path from q.*

To cover also the cases when a (literal) value in the conceptual model is obtained from several paths, possibly distributed among different sources, we introduce a multiple source articulation. A multiple source articulation is defined as a tuple $(p_T, q_{S_1}, \ldots q_{S_n}, Concat)$, where p_T is an ontology path expression in O_{CM}, $q_{S_1}, \ldots q_{S_n}$ are ontology path expressions in source otologies, and $Concat$ is a function defining the concatenation result. Note that this articulation applies only for literal values. We omit the description of its semantics as it is a straightforward extension of the path articulation. For the converse where several values in the CM are obtained by splitting one value from a source we have a multiple CM articulation: $(p_{CM_1}, \ldots p_{CM_n}, q_S, Split)$.

4.2 RDF(S) Representation of the Integration Model

As we stated in the requirements, it is useful that the integration framework can be expressed in the same data format as the actual data that are integrated. It both facilitates the semantic interoperability and allows for reasoning about the integration phase at a higher level of abstraction. We translated the concepts of our theoretical integration framework into an RDF schema called Integration Model Ontology (IMO). This ontology describes in the RDF syntax the notion of path expressions, articulations, etc. The integration model instances (IMI) are created by the designer (or generated by a mapping tool) for a concrete integration problem. Due to lack of space we do not present in detail the verbose RDF serialization here, interested reader is referred to the Hera website[4]. The IMO together with IMI are used by the mediator during the query processing.

5   Distributed RDF Query Processing

The mediator component is responsible for finding the answer to the user query by consulting the available sources based on the integration model instances. The mediator takes as input the user query formulated in SeRQL [8].

```
SELECT A, P
FROM  {A} expertIn  {TA};  authorOf  {P},
      {P} concerns  {TP};  frontPage {F},
      {F} mentions  {A}
WHERE TA=TP
```

---

[4] http://wwwis.win.tue.nl:8080/~ hera

To illustrate the query processing in our mediator, consider the above SeRQL query example[5]. In this example we assume a total distribution, i.e. all properties reside on different sources and the mediator performs all partial joins.

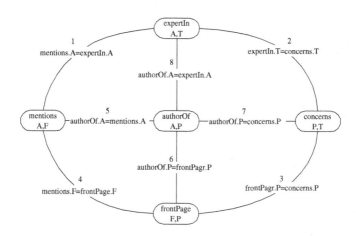

Fig. 3. Join graph

The query in our example is processed as follows.

- We first normalize the SeRQL query in the sense that all variables that are explicitly declared equal in the *Where* clause are given identical names (variables TP and TA are both renamed to T).
- From the normalized query we create a join graph (see Fig. 3) in which every property in the *From* clause stands for a relation with two attributes defined by the variable names. In the join graph we represent these relations as nodes and connect every two nodes that share an attribute[6]. Every edge in the join graph is interpreted as a join condition between the two connected relations.
- Next, we assign a random order to the edges of the join graph (the order is depicted by numbers above the edges) and recursively fold the join graph by combing the two nodes that are connected by the edge with the smallest number. The folding sequence for our join graph is depicted in Fig. 4. Dashed lines indicate the edges which are removed in that particular folding step[7]. The folding sequence essentially represents a query plan: a folding step is equivalent to a join operator and every edge which is removed in that particular step represents one conjunct in the join condition. To minimize the execution costs, this initial query plan is subsequently optimized by reordering the joins.

---

[5] *"Retrieve all authors and their papers, where the author is an expert in the topic that concerns the paper and he is also mentioned on the front-page of the paper"*
[6] If the nodes share more attributes, we create one edge for each such attribute
[7] For the sake of clarity, the node names were abbreviated to their starting letters

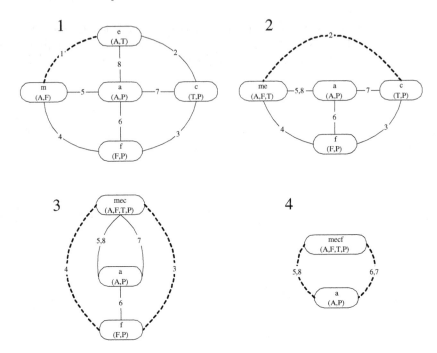

Fig. 4. Join graph folding

- To consult the sources, the mediator locates for every property in the join graph an articulation. From this articulation, it determines the source that provides an answer to it together with an appropriately translated path expression. This path expression is transformed into a SeRQL query and executed on that particular source. The sources are consulted in a multi-threaded fashion in order to achieve a high degree of parallelization. The mediator subsequently collects the partial results and performs the necessary join operations according to the query plan determined by the optimizer.

5.1   Query Optimization and Performance Evaluation

To test our integration framework we synthesized an RDFS schema of approximately 50MB and instantiated it with 500MB of RDF instances. Note that a schema/instance ratio of 10% is quite large; in normal circumstances, the size of the schema seldom reaches even 1% of the size of the instances. This represented for us a worst case scenario since the mediator has to join partial path results, the bigger schema the more potential paths to join. The data set was distributed among several computers connected by the Internet, and the underlying sources were using the Sesame RDF storage system[8].

Note that the sources, unlike the mediator, contain instance indices and are therefore very efficient for joining the path queries. Creating an instance index at

---

[8] http://www.openrdf.org/

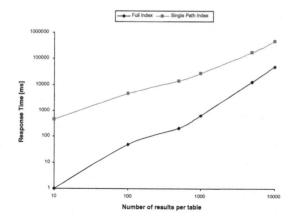

Fig. 5. The improvement with the use of path indexing

the mediator would require to gather all the data from the sources and thus turning our virtual repository into a datawarehouse with all its disadvantages like the freshness problem, the maintenance problem, data ownership issues etc. Instead, we adopted a schema based approach. Since the mediator has the schemas of the underlying sources, in order to minimize its workload a sophisticated ontology path indexing takes place. The main idea is to push down to the sources the longest possible paths they can answer, reducing the number of joins at the mediator. The performance improvement gained by schema indexing is depicted in Fig. 5.

While the path indexing is clearly beneficial, especially for larger results sets the joining at the mediator still represents a bottleneck. In order to minimize the joining time, which in turn due to different cardinalities and join selectivities largely depends on the order in which the joins are performed, we implemented a join ordering heuristic as a combination of iterative improvement and simulated annealing [9]. As depicted in Fig. 6, this improved the performance of the system even further, especially after the initial calibration phase.

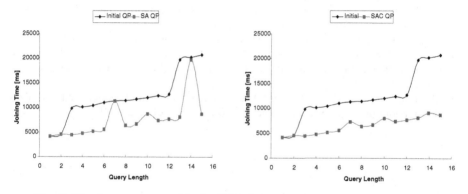

Fig. 6. The improvement with the IISA, left: uncalibrated, right: calibrated

6 Conclusions

As the nature of WIS changes under the influence of the Semantic Web (SW) initiative, the need to capture the semantics of the application data increases. In the typical WIS, the data is often gathered from several sources and it is crucial to understand their semantic annotations. We derived a set of integration requirements in the context of WIS. To address them, we presented our integration framework that helps to overcome semantic heterogeneities of RDFS meta-data from different sources. We also evaluated the performance of our system and proposed several optimization techniques to improve the the query evaluation. As future work we intend to extend the expressive power of our integration model towards higher level ontology languages such as OWL, and to investigate other possibilities to improve the performance of our implementation. One of the promising directions to minimize both the mediator's workload and the data transfer from the sources is to establish a network of collaborating mediators that would perform some query processing tasks, e.g. joins, on request.

References

1. Ora Lassila and Ralph R. Swick. Resource description framework (rdf) model and syntax specification. W3C Recommendation 22 February 1999.
2. Nora Koch, Andreas Kraus, and Rolf Hennicker. The authoring process of the uml-based web engineering approach. In *First International Workshop on Web-Oriented Software Technology*, 2001.
3. Stefano Ceri, Piero Fraternali, and Maristella Matera. Conceptual modeling of data-intensive web applications. *IEEE Internet Computing*, 6(4):20–30, 2002.
4. Reinhold Klapsing and Gustaf Neumann. Applying the resource description framework to web engineering. In *Electronic Commerce and Web Technologies, First International Conference, EC-Web 2000*, volume 1875 of *Lecture Notes in Computer Science*, pages 229–238. Springer, 2000.
5. Yuhui Jin, Stefan Decker, and Gio Wiederhold. Ontowebber: A novel approach for managing data on the web. In *Proceedings of the 18th International Conference on Data Engineering (ICDE'02)*, pages 488–489, 2002.
6. Jeffrey D. Ulman. Information integration using logical views. In *Proceedings of the 6th Int. Conference on Database Theory, ICDT'97*, volume 1186 of *Lecture Notes in Computer Science*, pages 19–40. Springer, 1997.
7. Patrick Hayes. Rdf semantics. W3C Recommendation 10 February 2004, 2004.
8. Jeen Broekstra and Arjohn Kampman. Query language definition, (on-to-knowledge eu-ist-1999-10132 deliverable 9). Technical report, Aidministrator Nederland b.v., 2001.
9. M. Steinbrunn, G. Moerkotte, and A. Kemper. Heuristic and randomized optimization for join ordering problem. *The VLDB Journal*, 6:191–208, 1997.

MDA Transformations Applied
to Web Application Development*

Santiago Meliá[1], Andreas Kraus[2], and Nora Koch[2,3]

[1] Universidad de Alicante, Spain
santi@dlsi.ua.es
[2] Ludwig-Maximilians-Universität München, Germany
{kochn,krausa}@pst.ifi.lmu.de
[3] F.A.S.T GmbH, Germany

Abstract. Current Web generation techniques are mainly hard-coded for prede-fined architectures of Web applications. Consequently, there is a gap between Web design models and the final implementation. We solve this problem, fol-lowing with our approach the Model-Driven Architecture (MDA) principles of automatic generation of software systems based on model transformations. In this context, we present a transformation process and propose a visual and tex-tual specification for the transformations using the forthcoming OMG standard Query /Views/ Transformations (QVT). Our proposal is illustrated by transfor-mations involving elements of the UML-based Web Engineering (UWE) meta-model and the WebSA metamodel, showing this way how both approaches are integrated.

1 Introduction

Models, modelling approaches and model transformations that follow the key princi-ples defined by the Model-Driven Architecture (MDA) are gaining consensus within many organizations involved in the development of complex software. They are at-tracted by the final MDA goal that is the automatic generation of a complete software system from a model with as less human interaction in the generation process as pos-sible. Such vision has enormous consequences for the development and maintenance of the increasing amount of Web software that is being produced. However, the cur-rent Web generation techniques are totally or partially hard-coded for predefined architectures of Web applications. We propose a generation process using an MDA approach in which the model transformations are driven by different architecture models.

In order to define the transformations between different models, there are several initiatives related to the MDA approach, among others the Request for Proposals for a Query/Views/Transformations (QVT) [11] language. From the received proposals, QVT-P [12] is, in our opinion, the most interesting one as it is a well defined lan-guage and it comprises a graphical as well as a textual notation.

In this article we present the WebSA approach [7] based on architectural-centric transformations from design to implementation models. This approach proposes (1) a

---

* This research has been partially sponsored by the EC 5th FP AGILE (IST-2001-32747) the German BMBF project GLOWA-Danube, and the Spanish METASING (TIN2004-00779)

D. Lowe and M. Gaedke (Eds.): ICWE 2005, LNCS 3579, pp. 465–471, 2005.

development process based on MDA, (2) a set of architectural models and (3) a set of transformations that permit the automatic integration of these architectural models with the functional models of a Web application using the QVT-P notation. The functional models, like navigation are those proposed by any Web design method such as WebML [2], OO-H [3] or UWE [5].

Sections 2 and 3 give an overview of the WebSA development process and the UWE design method, respectively. Section 4 presents the specification of the transformations and finally in section 5 some future steps of the use of WebSA for the development of Web applications are outlined.

2   The WebSA Approach: An Overview

WebSA is a proposal whose main objective is to cover all phases of Web application development focusing on software architecture. It contributes to fill the gap currently existing between traditional Web design models and the final implementation. In order to achieve this, WebSA defines a set of architectural models to specify the architectural viewpoint which complements current Web engineering methodologies [3, 5]. Furthermore, WebSA also establishes an instance of the MDA development process [4], which allows for the integration of the different viewpoints of a Web application by means of transformations between models.

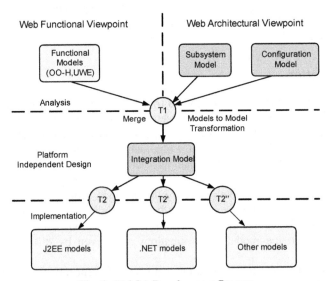

Fig. 1. WebSA Development Process

The WebSA development process is based on the MDA development process in which the artifacts that result from each phase must be models, which represent the different abstraction levels in the system specification. In the analysis phase the Web application specification is vertically divided into two viewpoints, as shown in the diagram flow of Fig. 1. On the one side, the functional-perspective is given by the Web functional models provided by Web methods (see [2, 3, 5]). On the other side, the Subsystem Model (SM) and the Configuration Model (CM) define the software architecture of the Web Application. The SM and CM architectural models use two different architectural styles to specify a Web application: a subsystem (or layer style) and a component style.

The PIM-to-PIM transformation (T1 in Fig. 1) which goes from analysis models to platform independent design models. It integrates the information about functionality and architecture (see sect. 4.1) in a single Integration Model (IM). This transformation type will be called T1. Also, the Integration Model, is the basis on which several PIM-to-PSM transformations, one for each target platform (see e.g. T2, T2' and T2'' in Fig. 1), can be defined. The output of these transformations is the specification of the Web application for a given platform (see sect. 4.2). This transformation type will be named T2 in the rest of the article.

3 A Web Functional Design Method: The UWE Approach

The distinguishing feature of the UML-based Web Engineering (UWE) approach in relation to other Web design methods is its UML compliance. The metamodel of UWE [6] is defined as a conservative extension of the UML metamodel which has a mapping to a UML profile [5]. Similarly to other Web design methods, UWE separates the concerns of a Web application supporting the modelling of different points of view: content, navigation structure, business processes and presentation.

The content of a Web application is modelled in UWE by a conceptual model that is represented as a UML class diagram. The navigation model is based on all conceptual classes that are relevant for the navigation structure and represents the navigation paths of the Web application. The model elements used to build nodes and links are primarily «navigation class» and «navigation link». In addition, access primitives (a special kind of nodes), such as «index» or «guided tour» are used to reach multiple instances of Web nodes.

Navigation models are enriched by «process class»es and «process link»s showing how the workflows are integrated in the navigation structure. These process classes and process links are part of the process model, which deals with the business logic of a Web application. The behavioural aspects of the business logic are modelled by a process flow model represented as a UML activity diagram. In UWE, the presentation model is used to sketch the layout of the Web pages associated to the navigation nodes.

In contrast to many other methods, UWE defines a systematic method, which supports semi-automatic generation of the models described above. Although, until now, UWE has not referred to these automatic generation steps explicitly as a transformation-based "model-driven development" feature, those steps correspond to a model driven development approach. UWE allows e.g. for the generation of the navigation model based on the set of conceptual classes marked as relevant for navigation. Further, indexes and menus are included automatically in the navigation model with additional model transformations that apply on the navigation model. A basic presentation model can be defined by transformations based on the navigation model.

In our case, the WebSA and UWE metamodels play an important role in the WebSA development process, because they contain the information necessary to specify the model transformations T1 and T2.

4   The WebSA Transformation Process

The WebSA transformation policy is defined by a set of transformations in which the first class citizens are the classes of the architectural view. The WebSA development process consists of two types of transformations: T1 and T2 (Fig. 1). T1 merges the elements of the architectural models of WebSA with those of the functional models, and translates them into the Integration Model. T2 maps the platform specific implementation models (e.g. J2EE or .NET) from the Integration Model. Both transformations are complex, i.e. they are built of a set of smaller transformations, which are executed in a deterministic way.

In MDA [9] there are different alternatives to get the information to transform one model into another (e.g. using a profile, using metamodels, patterns and markings, etc). For WebSA we have selected a metamodel mapping approach to specify the transformations. In order to obtain the integration we extend the MDA model transformation pattern of Bézivin [1] for UWE and WebSA models. The metamodels based on the MOF language are the source of the transformation rules that establish the transformation into target metamodel elements. For more details about the metamodels refer to [6] and [8].

The transformation rules are defined in the QVT language [11] which is an MDA standard also based on MOF 2.0. We selected the QVT-P [12] proposal, which comprises a rich graphical and textual notation. Both notations can be used to declaratively define transformations without specifying how a transformation is actually executed. Simple queries can be expressed by a (graphical or textual) pattern matching language that allows matching instances, sets of instances and associations with specific properties. For more complex queries the (additional) use of OCL 2.0 expressions is recommended. QVT-P transformations can be composed and extended by inheritance or overriding which is needed for scalability and reusability. In contrast with other transformation proposals (like graphs, XSLT, etc.), QVT-P has a smaller learning curve because the transformations themselves are models based on standards as MOF and OCL.

Next, we present an example of a T1 transformation using the graphical notation of QVT-P and also an example of a T2 transformation in the textual notation of QVT-P.

4.1   Transformation T1: Merging Web Functionality and Architectural Models

Due to the complexity of the T1 transformation, it is helpful to build a map of transformations that indicates the flow of execution and avoids redundancies in the specification. In the transformation map each transformation is related to the rest by means of three different relationships: (1) Composition – A transformation can be composed by one or more transformations (2) Dependency – A transformation must be executed before another transformation (3) Inheritance – A transformation extends or overrides another transformation. We defined a simple UML profile to represent the transformation map where a transformation is defined as a class stereotype and it is represented by a circle (Fig. 2). The first transformation shown in the T1 map of Fig. 2 (*SM2IM*) goes from Subsystem Model to Integration Model.

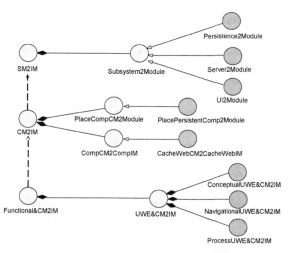

Fig. 2. Transformation MAP of T1

The second transformation (CM2IM) maps from Configuration Model to Integration Model. It is composed by a set of two types of transformations. The first one places components into the modules (PlaceComp2Modules), and the second one transforms each configuration component into one or more integration components (CompCM2Comp IM). The last transformation Functional&CM2IM merges the functional UWE models with the Configuration Model and introduces the functional aspects into the components of the Integration Model.

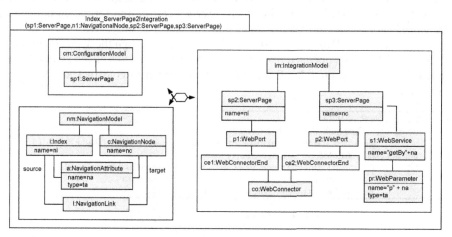

Fig. 3. Example of T1: NavigationalUWE&CM2IM

An example using the QVT-P graphical notation for the transformation *Index-Server Page2Integration*, which merges the navigation and configuration models, is shown in Fig. 3. This transformation specifies how links between index nodes and other navigation nodes in the UWE navigation model are merged into the WebSA configuration model and it results in a corresponding part of the integration model.

A more general transformation which is not depicted here states that every navigation node is merged into a *ServerPage* element. The more specialized transformation of the example additionally generates for every *NavigationAttribute* of an index element a *WebService* element with a *WebParameter* element corresponding to the *Navigation Attribute*. The *ServerPage* elements corresponding to the Index and the *NavigationNode* element are linked by a *WebConnector* element via *Web- ConnectorEnd* and *WebPort* elements, respectively.

4.2 Transformation T2: Transforming from a PIM to a PSM

Once the transformation T1 is completely executed, the functionality is interwoven into the architectural aspects in the Integration Model. Now, we can tackle the final step of the WebSA development process, defining a set of PIM-to-PSM transformations for each target platform such as J2EE, .NET or CORBA from the Integration Model. As is specified in [9], in order to make a transformation from PIM-to-PSM, design decisions must be made. These decisions are specified in the transformation T2 and taken in the context of a specific implementation design. Therefore, T2 is made up by a set of simple transformations in which one Integration Model component is transformed into a platform specific component. To specify T2, it is necessary to have the metamodels of the target platforms (e.g. the J2EE metamodel [10]).

Fig. 4 shows a QVT-P example of transformation T2 for J2EE using the textual notation. It transforms each *ServerPage* component of the Integration Model specified in the first *domain* into a *JavaServerPage* specified in the second *domain*. Furthermore, this *ServerPage* has a set of *WebServices*, each one of them translatable into a Java method, a Javascript method or an HTML form. In this example, we have chosen a translation into an HTML form by the *WebService2Form* transformation defined in the *forall* OCL sentence of the *{when}* part. In the same way, each View element related to the *ServerPage* is translated into a *JavaBean* through the *View2Bean* transformation. The PSMs obtained from the WebSA process are considered an implementation, because they provide all the information needed to construct an executable system.

```
relation ServerPage2J2EE {
    domain {(IM.IntegrationModel) [ (ServerPage) [name=nc,
            services = {(WebService) [name=on, type=ot]}, views = {(View) [name = vn]}]] }
    domain {(JM.J2EEModel) [ (JavaServerPage) [name=nc,
            forms = {(Form) [name=on, type=ot]}, beans = {(JavaClass) [name = vn]}]] }
    when {services -> forAll (s | WebService2Form (s, F1set.toChoice()) )
            views-> forAll (v | View2Bean (v, J1set.toChoice()) )) }}
```

Fig. 4. Example of T2: ServerPage2J2EE

5   Conclusions and Future Work

Using an MDA approach with a transformation component in WebSA we achieve a more automated process for the development of Web applications with a strong focus on architecture modelling. WebSA complements the existing methodologies for the design of Web applications. In this paper we present the development process of WebSA and describe how models are integrated and generated based on model transformations. For the specification of the transformations we choose QVT-P that allows for visual and textual description of the mapping rules. Currently, we are analyzing the possibilities to extend the Web development environments VisualWADE[1] and ArgoUWE[2] to support architectural modelling and model transformations. Further, we plan to test transformation specification and model generation for complex Web applications addressing the scalability of the approach.

References

1. J. Bézivin. In Search of a Basic Principle for Model Driven Engineering, Novática n°1, June 2004, 21-24
2. S. Ceri, P. Fraternali, M. Matera: Conceptual Modeling of Data-Intensive Web Applications, IEEE Internet Computing 6 (4), July/Aug. 2002, 20–30
3. J. Gomez, C. Cachero, O. Pastor: Extending a Conceptual Modelling Approach to Web Application Design. In Proc. 12th CAiSE '00, LNCS 1789, Springer, 2000
4. A. Kleppe, J. Warmer, W. Bast: MDA Explained: The Model Driven Architecture, Practice and Promise, Addison-Wesley, 2003
5. N. Koch, A. Kraus. The expressive Power of UML-based Web Engineering. In 2nd IWWOST02, CYTED, June 2002, 105-119
6. N. Koch, A. Kraus: Towards a Common Metamodel for the Development of Web Applications. In Proc. 3rd ICWE 2003, LNCS 2722, Springer Verlag, July 2003, 497-506
7. S. Meliá, C. Cachero. An MDA Approach for the Development of Web Applications, In Proc. of 4th ICWE'04, LNCS 3140, July 2004, 300-305
8. S. Melía.. The WebSA Composition Model Profile. Technical Report TR-WebSA2, http://www.dlsi.ua.es/~santi/pPublicaciones.htm, Nov. 2004
9. OMG. MDA Guide, OMG doc. ab/2003-05-01
10. OMG. UML Profile for Enterprise Distributed Object Computing Specification. OMG doc. ad/2001-06-09
11. OMG. Request for Proposal. MOF 2.0 Query/Views/Transformations, OMG ad/2002-04-10
12. QVT Partners. Initial Submission for MOF 2.0 Query/View/Transformations RFP, QVT-Partners, http://qvtp.org/downloads/1.1/qvtpartners1.1.pdf, Aug. 2003

---

[1] VisualWADE: http://www.visualwade.com
[2] ArgoUWE: http://www.pst.informatik.uni-muenchen.de/projekte/uwe/argouwe.shtml

Higher-Level Information Aspects of Web Systems: Addressing the Problem of Disconnection*

Farooque Azam**, Zhang Li, and Rashid Ahmad

Software Engineering Institute, Beijing University of Aeronautics and Astronautics
No.37, XueYuan Road, HaiDian District, Beijing 100083, P.R. China
{farooque,lily,r.ahmad}@buaa.edu.cn

Abstract. Current Web modelling languages fail to adequately support higher-level information aspects of Web systems. Researchers have argued that there is a disconnection between *functional architecture* and *information architecture*, and also disconnection between *business models* and *technical architectures*. Addressing the problem; Web Information Exchange Diagram is developed in two flavours, WIED and WIED-UML. WIED-UML is developed to primarily address the problem of disconnection between *functional architecture* and *information architecture*. However, we argue that it, doesn't really address the issue, because WIED-UML is developed on a set of different UML – Unified Modelling Language notations which don't have semantic conformity with current UML metamodel. Creating transformation rules between models not conforming to common metamodel vocabulary, would not lead to an elegant solution. Hence in this paper, we propose a solution, by identifying linkages with two standard UML compliant approaches namely Enterprise Distributed Object Computing (EDOC) Profile and standard UML2.0 notations.

1 Introduction

The ability to reliably and consistently develop systems that utilise Internet and Web technologies has become increasingly important. These systems are typically, both functionally complex and information-rich [1]. In recent years, various approaches have been developed or adapted for representing these complex Web systems with different objectives. For example, the e^3-value™ business modelling method [2] emphasizes a business modelling perspective, UML [3] focuses on functional aspects, and WebML [4] concentrates on the informational aspects of Web systems.

One aspect that has received increasing attention is *information* modelling for these applications, particularly with respect to aspects such as navigation models and their relationships to the underlying content. *Information* modelling approaches, such as RMM [5] and OOHDM [6], and various adaptations of UML, have provided the ability to model the contents of these applications, and the way in which we interact with this information. A good discussion on these modelling approaches is given in [1], where it has been argued that, these models have typically focussed on modelling at a relatively low-level, and have failed to address *higher-level* aspects, such as architectural and even business process modelling.

---

* Supported by Beijing Municipal Science & Technology New Star Plan (H013610270112)
** Corresponding author: Tel: +86-10-82753679

D. Lowe and M. Gaedke (Eds.): ICWE 2005, LNCS 3579, pp. 472–477, 2005.

Several different levels of modelling that might typically occur in representing the design of Web-enabled systems is illustrated in Fig. 1 (from [1]).

– At the *top level* we can model the actual business (business goals, business processes, etc.) by utilising these systems. A typical example is the e³-value™ business modelling notation [2].

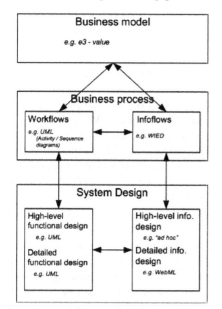

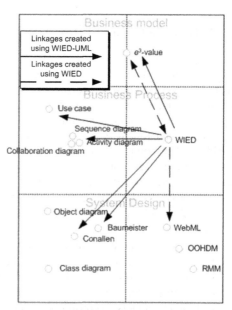

Fig. 1. Evaluation of modelling approaches [1]

Fig. 2. Linkages between WIED-UML and other UML Models [7]

– At the *middle level* in this diagram are models of the high-level system architecture that capture the *domains of functionality* and the *domains of information* that are needed to support the business domains. Functional aspects at this level are well supported by UML as some UML models (such as activity diagrams) can be used to represent the business and operational workflows of a system. However, UML support for *informational* aspects is relatively immature; and to serve this aspect, recently WIED–Web Information Exchange Diagram [1] is developed.
– At the *lowest level* in this diagram are models of the detailed design. These models typically capture design elements that have a direct correspondence to specific implementation artefacts. For example, *functional* elements (such as code modules and communication interfaces) and *information* elements (such as page content and navigational links).

WIED is interesting because, researchers have indicated [8] that there is a disconnection between *functional architecture* and *information architecture*, and also disconnection between *business models* and *technical architectures*, which is the main focus of the WIED concept. However, the WIED concept is still generic and needs more effort to make it a practical companion to existing widely-used UML models and furthermore MDA–Model Driven Architecture [9] compliant approaches.

In this paper, Section2 presents the WIED concept, its allied problems and proposed solutions. Next, moving towards the solution; we briefly present two modelling notations. These notations include, firstly, Object Management Group (OMG)'s Enterprise Distributed Object Computing (EDOC) Profile [10] in Section 3, and secondly, UML 2.0 [11] notations in Section 4. Lastly, Section 5 concludes our work.

2   WIED: Need for Refinement

WIED primarily forms a bridge between two existing modelling languages e^3-value™ (representing business value exchanges) and *WebML* (representing low-level information designs). These are depicted by dashed arrows showing linkages in Fig. 2 (from [7]). Resultantly, it intends to resolve the problem of disconnection between *business models* and *information architectures*. However, WIED-UML [12] has been developed and linked to various UML models and adaptations for addressing the problem of disconnection between *functional architecture* and *information architecture*, because UML comprises well-established notations for representing *functional* aspects. These linkages are depicted by solid arrows in Fig. 2 (see [7] for details). Nevertheless, WIED-UML is associated with a problem:

- *The Problem*: Resolving the problem of disconnection between *functional architecture* and *information architecture*, using WIED-UML doesn't really address the issue, because WIED-UML is developed on a set of different UML like notations as also recognised by the authors [12]. These notations don't have semantic conformity with UML metamodel. Moreover, when moving towards developing automated tools, we need transformations rules between WIED-UML and other models according to identified linkages, which however, will not provide elegant solution because the relevant models don't share the common metamodel vocabulary.
- *Proposed Solution*: The solution to the problem of disconnection, as we perceive, is (1) Finding all possible direct linkages without using WIED-UML; between *generic WIED model* and *notations representing functional architecture*. One possible linkage using EDOC Profile is briefly presented in Section 3. (2) Representing WIED concept in standard UML compliant notations and further linking these notations to various other UML models, adaptations and MDA compliant approaches. In Section 4, we briefly present a possibility of using standard UML 2.0 notations for describing the WIED concept. We argue that, these linkages would allow us to move forward towards integration and interoperability of WIED concept to MDA compliant tools for achieving future goal of full lifecycle Web application development.

3   Linking EDOC Profile and WIED

The vision of the EDOC Profile is to simplify the development of component based EDOC systems by means of a modelling framework, based on UML 1.4, conforming MDA specifications (for details see Part I, Section I–Vision in [10]). EDOC profile comprises various specifications: Among them is the Enterprise Collaboration Architecture (ECA) that is a technology independent profile allowing the definition of PIMs – Platform Independent Models. ECA further comprises a set of five UML profiles: (1) Component Collaboration Architecture (CCA) (2) The Entities profile (3) The Events profile (4) The Business Process Profile (BPP) (5) The Relationships profile. Among these profiles, in the context of WIED, *BPP* is relatively more suitable for mapping because, it specialize CCA, and describes a set of UML extensions those may be used on their own, or in combination with the other EDOC elements, to model system behaviour in the context of the business. Moreover, BPP being specialization of CCA, has inherent capability of modelling the behaviour of the components at varying and mixed levels of granularity.

EDOC Profile is interesting because it is an adopted specification of OMG and most importantly, it comprises the notations for describing PIMs as well as Platform Specific Models (PSMs) encompassing all the three modelling levels as described in Fig. 1. Although being profile of UML it tends to be more expressive of *functional* aspects. Conversely, WIED is also analogous to PIM because it describes *informational aspects* at the business process level without revealing platform specific details.

Linking WIED to BPP notations entails two significant benefits. *Firstly*, we get the ability to form a valuable horizontal linkage at business process level (Fig. 2) between informational and functional flows without using WIED-UML. *Secondly*, once a model is transformed from WIED to BPP notations, subsequently vertical mapping between the models (PIMs and PSMs) can be achieved at all the three levels by means of transformations using various EDOC profiles. Furthermore, EDOC profiles have been developed on the notion of modelling applications according to MDA specification. Hence, we contend that linking WIED to BPP notations can be considered as integration of WIED with MDA compliant approach, which will help to further augment the WIED concept.

This subset of BPP notations used for describing linkage with WIED is depicted in Fig. 3. While creating the linkage, we have defined these mappings in two phases; In Phase-I, we create an *Organisation Collaboration Model* that gives a broader picture of the business process between organisations. In Phase-II, we create *System Collaboration Model* by zooming-in the sub-activities, and subsequently depict internal information flows of the System under consideration. We have carried out a complete analysis of this mapping process and found that it can be depicted elegantly using BPP in a compact form.

4   Using UML 2.0 for Representing the WIED Concept

UML 2.0 Superstructure specifications [11] also provide promising possibility to model informational aspects at higher-level of abstraction. In the context of WIED, the most interesting facility that can be used is the package *InformationFlows* (see Section 17.2 pp. 665 of [11]).The document clearly describes that the *Information-Flows* package provides mechanisms for specifying the exchange of information between entities of a system at a high level of abstraction. They do not specify the nature of the information, nor the mechanisms by which this information is conveyed. Hence InformationFlows package has natural linkage to the WIED concept which models information flows at higher-level of abstraction.

An information flow is represented as a dependency, with the keyword <<flow>> (Fig. 4) conveying *InformationItem* (e.g. product and wage) from source to target (e.g. Company to Customer). Semantically, sources and targets of the information flow can be *kind-of* Actor, Node, UseCase, Artifact, Class, Component, Port, Property, Interface, Package, and InstanceSpecification.

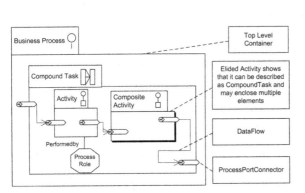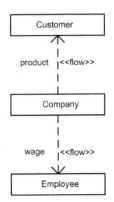

Fig. 3. Subset of EDOC's Business Process Profile notations

Fig. 4. Information flows conveying information items [11]

For representing the WIED concept in UML 2.0 notations, we can map various kinds of *information units* in WIED to appropriately stereotyped Class diagrams on similar rules defined for WIED-UML in [12]. This would also include *Derivation Units* those are mapped in WIED-UML differently. However, WIED-UML depicts, information flows by an arrow (lacking any UML semantics) that has resultantly created new UML diagrams. Instead, by using *InformationFlows* introduced in UML 2.0, we can elegantly map information flows represented in WIED using dependency stereotyped by a keyword <<flow>> as depicted in Fig. 4.

5 Conclusion and Future Work

In this paper, firstly we introduce the WIED and WIED-UML context and highlight the problem associated with WIED-UML. Next we propose the solution. Subsequently, inline with the proposed solution, we identify two methods for representing higher-level information flows, i.e., using (1) EDOC's *Business Process Profile* and (2) *InformationFlows* introduced in UML 2.0. We argue that linking these notations' augments the WIED concept and brings it closer to the MDA vision, allowing a step forward towards integration and interoperability with future MDA compliant tools.

In this paper, we have very briefly presented the proposed solutions. However, we recognize that these linkages should be demonstrated comprehensively so that researchers/practitioners can comfortably adopt these. However, paper size limitation precludes us to do so and therefore we intend to publish it elsewhere.

This paper is the outcome of ongoing work for refining the WIED concept, so that it can further be integrated with ongoing global effort of standardising modelling and model transformation approaches.

References

1. Tongrungrojana, Rachatrin and Lowe, David.: WIED: A Web Modelling Language for Modelling Architectural-Level Information Flows. Journal of Digital Information, Volume 5 Issue 2, Article No. 283, 2004-08-10
   http://jodi.ecs.soton.ac.uk/Articles/v05/i02/ Tongrungrojana/
2. Gordijn, J.: e^3-value in a Nutshell. In Proceedings of International Workshop on E-business Modeling, Lausanne http://www.cs.vu.nl/~gordijn/bmns.pdf
3. Booch, G., Rumbaugh, J. and Jacobson, I.: The Unified Modelling Language User Guide (Addison-Wesley)
4. Ceri, S., Fraternali, P. and Bongio, A.: Web Modeling Language (WebML): a modeling language for designing Web sites. In Proceedings of the ninth International World Wide Web Conference, Amsterdam, May, pp. 137-157 http://www9.org/w9cdrom/177/177.html
5. Isakowitz, T., Stohr, E. and Balasubramanian, P.: RMM: A Methodology for Structured Hypermedia Design. Communications of the ACM, Vol. 38, No. 8, 34-44
6. Schwabe, D. and Rossi, G.: Developing Hypermedia Applications using OOHDM. In Proceedings of Workshop on Hypermedia Development Processes, Methods and Models (Hypertext'98), Pittsburgh
7. Tongrungrojana, R. and Lowe, D.: Forming Linkages from WIED-UML to UML Modeling System. In AusWeb04: The Tenth Australian World Wide Web Conference (Eds, Treloar, A. and Ellis, A.) Southern Cross University, Gold Coast, Australia, 3-7 July 2004, pp. 288-300.
8. Gu, A., B. Henderson-Sellers, et al: Web Modelling Languages: The Gap between Requirements and Current. Exemplars. AusWeb02, Gold Coast, Australia.
9. OMG, Model Driven Architecture, A Technical Perspective, Document ab/21001-02-05, Februray 2001, http://www.omg.org
10. OMG, UML Profile for Enterprise Distributed Object Computing, Document ptc/2001-12-04, December 2001
11. UML 2.0 Superstructure Final Revised Adopted specification
    http://www.omg.org/cgi-bin/doc?ptc/2004-10-02
12. Lowe, D. and R. Tongrungrojana: Web Information Exchange Diagrams for UML. The Fourth International Conference on Web Engineering, Munich, Germany.

As Easy as "Click": End-User Web Engineering

Jochen Rode[1], Yogita Bhardwaj[1], Manuel A. Pérez-Quiñones[1],
Mary Beth Rosson[2], and Jonathan Howarth[1]

[1] Virginia Polytechnic Institute and State University, Center for Human-Computer Interaction
3160 Torgersen Hall, Blacksburg, VA 24061
{jrode,yogitab,jhowarth}@vt.edu, perez@cs.vt.edu
[2] Pennsylvania State University, Information Sciences & Technology,
330 IST Building, University Park, PA 16802
mrosson@ist.psu.edu

Abstract. We are investigating the feasibility of end-user web engineering. The main target audience for this research is webmasters without programming experience – a group likely to be interested in building web applications. Our target domain is web-based data collection and management applications. As an instrument for studying the mental models of our audience and collecting requirements for an end-user web programming tool, we are developing Click, a proof-of-concept prototype. We discuss end-user related aspects of web engineering in general and describe the design rationale for Click. In particular, we elaborate on the need for supporting evolutionary prototyping and opportunistic and ad hoc development goals. We also discuss strategies for making end-user web engineering scalable and for encouraging end-user developers to continually increase their level of sophistication.

1 Introduction

Years after the introduction of CGI-scripting, the creation of a web application is still difficult, requiring a broad range of skills. Professional programmers develop the skills needed to create interactive web applications, but most nonprogrammers engaged in web development are limited to the creation of static websites. We believe that with the right tools and techniques even nonprogrammers may be able to develop web applications. By making web development possible for a wider audience, we may see a greater variety of useful applications being developed, including functionality not yet envisioned. For organizations unable or unwilling to hire professional programmers, end-user development may help streamline work flows and increase productivity and client satisfaction. Indeed, the WWW itself is an excellent example of what happens when technology becomes accessible to "the rest of us". In the words of Deshpande and Hansen [6], it is time for the web engineering community to "devise methods and processes to assist end users" which would help to increase the reliability of applications and "release the creative power of people."

Apart from empowering end users to pursue new goals, the web engineering community should also be considering how best to help novice developers create websites that are more secure, cross-platform-compatible, and universally accessible. User-friendly but "dangerously powerful" web programming languages like PHP [15] are becoming popular even among people who do not have the necessary training and experience to develop web applications of high quality. Harrison [10] calls this the

D. Lowe and M. Gaedke (Eds.): ICWE 2005, LNCS 3579, pp. 478–488, 2005.

"dangers of end-user programming". The web engineering community may advocate abstinence from end-user web development (but see it happen nonetheless) or embrace the needs and motivations of nonprofessional developers and support them as much as possible. We choose the latter.

A good starting point is to focus on the needs and preferences of *sophisticated end users*, people who are experienced with web design in general but not (yet) with the programming required for interactive applications (e.g., input validation, database access, authentication). Our preliminary studies of university webmasters [18] indicates that a substantial fraction of these sophisticated end-users' web application needs are quite simple and similar. For instance, in one survey of Virginia Tech webmasters (n=67) we found that about one third of the applications described by these users are *basic data collection, storage, and retrieval applications* (such as service request forms, searchable publication databases, staff databases, and surveys). Another 40% of the requests could be satisfied through customization of five generic web applications (resource scheduling, shopping cart and payment, message board, content management, and calendar). Research on tailorability demonstrates that customizability is an achievable design goal (e.g., [12]). Diverse requests for more advanced applications comprised the remaining 25%. Based on these analyses, we have focused our efforts on tools for end-user development of web applications (EUDWeb) that revolve around basic data collection and management.

In the balance of this paper we first consider related work in web engineering and end-user development and discuss strategies for making web engineering easier for nonprogrammers. Then, we present our approach to EUDWeb, focusing on features and design rationale for Click (Component-based Lightweight Internet-application Construction Kit), our proof-of-concept EUDWeb tool [20].

2   Related Work

Two complementary domains of research and practice – *web engineering* and *end-user development* – have focused on methods and tools for the creation of web applications. Research in web engineering has concentrated on making web professionals more productive and the websites that they produce more usable, reusable, modularized, scalable, and secure. In contrast, research on end-user development for the web has attempted to empower nonprogrammers to autonomously create websites and web applications. Within the web engineering community, one research focus has been on *model-based approaches* to the design of hypermedia systems (e.g., [23], [5]). While these top-down design approaches address many problems related to productivity, consistency, security, and platform-independence, they normally assume a high-level of abstraction unsuited for nonprofessional web developers. The approach we advocate can be seen as an alternative to model-based, top-down development. Another focus of research and practice is *tools* that assist web developers in becoming more productive. Many powerful CASE/RAD tools have been developed for experienced developers like Web Models' WebRatio [25], IBM's Rational Web Developer for WebSphere Software [11], or Microsoft's Visual Web Developer 2005 [13]. Even though these tools may simplify professionals' web development process by providing wizards and visual tools, none of them have been targeted at nonprogrammer developers, so in general they assume the knowledge, working culture, and expectations of an experienced programmer. In 2004 we reviewed selected state-of-the-art web development tools designed for end users [21] such as Microsoft FrontPage or Macromedia Dreamweaver. Most of the end-user tools that we reviewed do not lack functionality but rather ease of use. For instance, even apparently simple problems such as implementing the intended look and feel become difficult when a novice has to use HTML-flow-based positioning instead of the more intuitive pixel-based positioning. Although most end-user tools offer wizards and other features to simplify particular aspects of development, none of the tools that we reviewed addresses the process of development as a whole, supporting end-user developers at the same level of complexity from start to finish. Fraternali's and Paolini's observation about available web tools [8] seems equally true today as it did five years ago: "...a careful review of their features reveals that most solutions concentrate on implementation, paying little attention to the overall process of designing a Web application."

The possibilities of web application development by end users have only recently become a topic of research. WebFormulate [1] is a tool for building web applications that is itself web-based. FAR [4] combines ideas from spreadsheets and rule-based programming with drag-and-drop web page layout to help end users develop online services. The WebSheets tool [26], although currently limited in power, uses a mix of programming-by-example, query-by-example, and spreadsheet concepts to help nonprogrammers develop fully functional web applications. Although the prior EUDWeb work has investigated many particular aspects and opportunities of web development, we are not aware of any research that has approached the problem in a holistic manner, starting with the needs of developers, analyzing the barriers and then prototyping tools. This is what we strive to provide.

3 Web Engineering for End Users

Web engineering is complex, but many aspects of its current complexity are not inherent to the process. For data management applications, much of what makes web development difficult is what Brooks [3] has termed "accidental complexity"–barriers introduced by the supporting technology rather than the problem at hand. Examples of accidental complexity and corresponding hurdles for web developers include [19]:

- Ensuring security;
- Handling cross-platform compatibility;
- Integrating technologies (e.g., HTML, CSS, JavaScript, Java, SQL); and
- Debugging web applications.

Our empirical studies of nonprogrammers' intuitions about web programming has yielded an even longer list of concerns, for example the stateless nature of HTTP and the necessity for explicit session management, parameter passing between pages or modules of an application, input validation, and establishing and managing database connections [18]. If web development is to become "end-user friendly", *accidental complexity must be eliminated or hidden as much as possible.*.

A common approach to creating processes and tools that better match end users' goals and expectations is to make the tools specific to the users' problem domain [14]. We have adopted this perspective: Rather than looking for an EUDWeb "silver bullet" that is as general and powerful as possible, our approach is to *identify classes of needs and build tools that target these domains specifically*, while at the same time planning for extensibility as users' requirements grow and evolve.

Empirical studies of professional programmers have shown that software developers do not always follow a systematic design approach. Sometimes programmers develop top-down; sometimes they "dive into" details and build parts of an application bottom-up [7]. Furthermore, software developers rarely construct an application in one step but rather perfect it incrementally through evolutionary prototyping [22]. Although there are few if any empirical studies of novice web developers, our informal observations and interviews lead us to believe that this phenomenon extends to these more casual developers just as much (if not more so). Therefore, EUDWeb tools should *support or even encourage opportunistic behavior*.

A critical tradeoff for every end-user development tool is the relationship of usability and expressiveness. Ideally a tool's complexity will be proportional to the problem to be solved: If a developer wants to take the next *small* step, the learning and effort required should be *small* as well. In practice however, most tools' learning curve exhibits large discontinuities (e.g. having to learn many new concepts such as session management, database communication, and encryption before being able to implement a basic authentication feature). One of our EUDWeb design goals is to make the effort required more proportional to the complexity of the problem at hand. We advocate a *"gentle slope of complexity"* [12], arguing for tools that adapt and grow with users' needs in a *layered* fashion. For the Agentsheets simulation tool, Repenning and Ioannidou [16] show how an end-user development tool can offer different layers of functionality that require different degrees of sophistication, in this case ranging from direct manipulation visual construction to a full-fledged programming language. We recommend a similar approach for EUDWeb.

We turn now to a presentation and discussion of the Click prototype, which was built as a demonstration of these EUDWeb requirements and recommendations.

4   Click: A Prototype End-User Web Engineering Tool

We are developing Click [20] as an EUDWeb prototype that is specifically targeted at end users who want to develop web-based data collection, storage and retrieval applications. Before we discuss Click's main contributions in detail, we will briefly illustrate how an end-user developer might use it to create a web application.

4.1   Developing Web Applications with Click

To construct a web application, an end user developer starts with a blank page or a predefined application template (e.g., service request form, online registration, staff database). The construction process is not predetermined; the developer can begin either by placing components on the screen (using drag-and-drop) or by defining a database structure. Figure 1 shows Click being used to define a "Register" button that (ultimately) will save user-entered data into a database and display another web page. Click applications are developed iteratively, with user input mechanisms added and their behavior specified as the developer needs them. Deployment is as easy as "declaring" a web application as public (in response, Click generates a URL that can be used to access the working application).

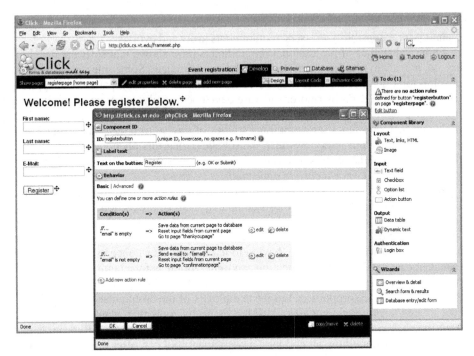

Fig. 1. Defining a "Register" button and associated action using the form-based UI of Click

4.2 Hiding Unnecessary Complexity

Click is an integrated web-based environment that contains visual development tools, code editing features, a preview mode, and a database management interface. No installation or configuration is required by the end-user developer. When the developer instantiates and positions components for a page under construction, Click generates corresponding HTML and component template code (Figure 2).

Separately, Click generates behavioral code that expresses the selected actions via high-level functions (e.g., sendEmail, saveToDatabase, goToPage) that are implemented on top of PHP (Figure 3). These functions are designed to be understandable by novice programmers who want to go beyond the dialog/form-based facilities.

Click's pre-defined components have been selected based on several analyses of both existing web applications and end users' mental models of interactive web programming [18]. The components provide the functionality needed to implement a typical data storage and retrieval application (e.g. a data table, dynamic text output). Click has been designed to make session management, authentication, database management, and so on, relatively automatic and invisible, so that only minimal learning is required. For example, by default, all data entered by a user on a web page persist even after the page has been submitted, so that the web application can continue to refer to and use this data at any point in time (we found that end users assume that once information has been entered, the system should "know" about it).

```
<!DOCTYPE html PUBLIC "-//W3C//DTD XHTML 1.0 Transitional//EN"
"http://www.w3.org/TR/xhtml1DTD/xhtml1-transitional.dtd">
<html>
<head>
  <title>Event registration</title>
  <link rel="stylesheet" type="text/css" href="styles/default.css">
</head>
<body>
<com:Form>
<%include Pages.showOnEveryPage %>
<com:HtmlText ID="htmltext1" X="16" Y="17" Z="61">
  <prop:Text><h1>Welcome! Please register below.</h1></prop:Text>
</com:HtmlText>
<com:InputText ID="firstname" X="14" Y="61" Z="66" Columns="20" Rows="1"
TextMode="SingleLine" DbFieldName="data:firstname" InputRequired="false"    Val-
ueType="Characters" MinValue="1" MaxValue="30">
  <prop:Label><b>First name:</b><br /></prop:Label>
  <prop:ErrorMessage>Please enter between 1-30 characters.</prop:ErrorMessage>
</com:InputText>
<com:InputText ID="lastname" X="14" Y="113" Z="67" Columns="20" Rows="1"
TextMode="SingleLine" DbFieldName="data:lastname" InputRequired="true"
ValueType="Characters" MinValue="1" MaxValue="50">
  <prop:Label><b>Last name:</b><br /></prop:Label>
  <prop:ErrorMessage>Please enter between 1-50 characters.</prop:ErrorMessage>
</com:InputText>
<com:InputText ID="email" X="14" Y="165" Z="68" Columns="20" Rows="1"
TextMode="SingleLine" DbFieldName="data:email" InputRequired="false">
  <prop:Label><b>E-Mail:</b><br /></prop:Label>
  <prop:ErrorMessage>Please enter a valid e-mail address.</prop:ErrorMessage>
  <prop:RegularExpression>\w+([-+.]\w+)*@\w+([-.]\w+)*\.\w+([-
.]\w+)*</prop:RegularExpression>
</com:InputText>
<com:Button ID="registerbutton" Text="Register" X="13" Y="223" Z="70" On-
Click="registerbutton_runActions" />
</com:Form>
</body>
</html>
```

Fig. 2. The "Layout code" view for the screen seen in Fig. 1

```
function registerbutton_runActions($button, $parameter) {
    $condition1 = $this->newCondition('{email}','empty');
    if ($condition1->isTrue())
        {
        $this->runAction('saveToDatabase','registerpage');
        $this->runAction('resetInputFields','registerpage');
        $this->runAction('goToPage','thankyoupage');
        }
    $condition2 = $this->newCondition('{email}','notEmpty');
    if ($condition2->isTrue())
        {
        $this->runAction('saveToDatabase','registerpage');
        $this->runAction('sendEmail','conference@vt.edu','{email}',
          'Conference registration','Dear {firstname} {lastname},
          this confirms your conference registration!');
        $this->runAction('resetInputFields','registerpage');
        $this->runAction('goToPage','confirmationpage');
        }
}
```

Fig. 3. The "Behavior code" view for the screen seen in Fig. 1

A recent review of state-of-the-art web development tools [21] revealed that one problem is that such tools rarely provide "holistic guidance" for developers, instead expecting them to know the exact steps required to implement a web application. Click does not attempt to predict and interrupt a developer's workflow in the way an "intelligent" software agent might do since the risk and costs of false guesses would likely be high [17]. However, Click maintains a non-intrusive "To-do" list (see upper right of Figure 1) that keeps track of the developer's progress and gives recommendations about possible or required future tasks. The messages in the to-do list notify the developer about such undesirable or faulty states as for example:

- pages or input components with generic names (e.g., recalling whether "inputtext4" or "inputtext5" was the input field for the user's first name may be difficult when the developer wants to make references elsewhere),
- a data table component that links to a details page that contains no components to display the details,
- a missing login page in an application that contains pages requiring authentication.

Furthermore, Click is able to automatically create new database fields and web pages if the developer refers to them in a rule (for example in a `saveToDatabase` or `goToPage` action). This eliminates the interruption and distraction caused when a programmer must pause his or her problem-solving process to set up supporting structures.

The layout feature of Click allows developers to place components using drag-and-drop and absolute positioning. This allows for quick prototyping and shields novice web developers from the difficulties of HTML table-based or CSS-based layout. More advanced users can edit the layout code directly and add HTML and CSS code in order to gain more control over the presentation.

Instead of exposing the developer to the page-submit-cycle metaphor typically found in web development tools, Click implements an event-based programming model similar to that found in ASP.NET or Java Server Faces (or programming tools for desktop applications such as Visual Basic). In this model, buttons and links have event handlers whose actions can be defined either by completing a Click form or by using the high-level PHP functions mentioned earlier (`sendEmail`, `goToPage`, etc.) The developer is shielded from the details of passing parameters to a page via HTTP's GET or POST methods, receiving and validating these inputs, and so on.

When the developer selects the *Sitemap* tab, Click automatically generates and displays a graphical representation of the application as it has been defined so far (using AT&T's Graphviz library [2]). Figure 4 shows an example of a sitemap for a "ride board" application. The sitemap is intended to provide an overview of the dynamic relationships between pages, database tables and the authentication system. Color coding is used to differentiate simple hyperlinks (blue) from page transitions or actions initiated by a button (green) or automatic page redirects for pages that require authentication (red). Solid lines show the control flow while dashed lines show the data flow (between pages and database tables). Besides providing a general overview, the sitemap helps developers to discover under-specification such as unreferenced pages or database tables (for example table "users" in Figure 4).

Finally, Click recognizes that EUDWeb will rarely occur solely on an individual level but rather that it is a collaborative process [14]. As a web-based system, Click easily supports multi-user projects. Each web application under development can have one or more "developers". Each of these developers can log into Click and modify the application. Because Click offers different layers of complexity and power (as we will describe later), one possible scenario is that a more novice developer asks an advanced colleague to extend Click by writing a custom component or behavior.

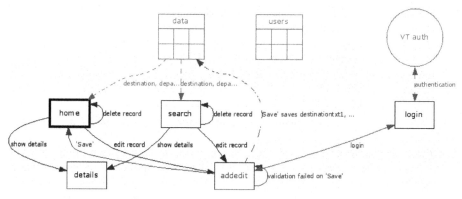

Fig. 4. A sitemap automatically generated by Click

4.3 Evolutionary Prototyping and Opportunistic Development

Supporting iterative and opportunistic development is a key design requirement for Click. Contrary to common code-generation approaches that make late changes to the user interface or behavior expensive to implement, *Click allows modifications to the layout, behavior, and database schema at any point in time.* Moreover, *changes take effect immediately*, thereby facilitating a rapid build-test cycle. We call this paradigm *design-at-runtime.* The design-at-runtime concept builds on the ideas of direct manipulation [24] and on the "debugging into existence" [22] observed for professional programmers working in a prototyping context. In its core it is similar to the automatic recalculation feature of spreadsheets. A critical piece of the concept is that the user is able to develop and use the application without switching back and forth between design and runtime modes (Click additionally provides an explicit preview-only mode; this requirement was discovered through formative usability evaluation). That is, the application is always usable to the fullest extent that it has been programmed. The end-user developer alternates between constructing and "using" the application until he or she tries to use an object whose behavior has not yet been defined. At this point the user is guided through a dialog to define the missing behavior. This interleaving of development and use continues until the whole application has been defined and tested. Of course, the usefulness of working with live data instead of placeholders at design time has been realized before. In Macromedia Dreamweaver MX, developers can switch to the so-called "Live Data View". In this mode live web pages are shown and some adjustments can be made. However, Dreamweaver does not support full use of an application–for example, hyperlinks do not work in this mode.

4.4 A Gentle Slope of Complexity

Tools for end users often have a low ceiling with respect to expressiveness. There is a natural tendency to hide complexity to improve usability, but the cost is often a concomitant loss of power. We hope to make EUDWeb highly expressive, and to provide a gentle learning curve to even greater power and functionality.

Layer 1	Customizing template web applications
Layer 2	Using Wizards to create related sets of components
Layer 3	Designing via WYSIWYG, direct manipulation, parameter forms
Layer 4	Editing layout code (similar to HTML, ASP.NET, JSF)
Layer 5	Editing high-level behavior code
Layer 6	Modifying and extending the underlying component framework
Layer 7	Editing PHP code

Fig. 5. Layers of Click's programming support that illustrate a "gentle slope of complexity"

Click's design provides several layers of programming support (see Figure 5).

At Layer 1, developers may customize existing web applications; ease-of-use is high but trades off with flexibility (assuming that existing applications are not complete matches). At Layer 2, developers may use Click's wizards (e.g. overview-detail page wizard, search form wizard) to create a related set of components. At the next layer, developers can use Click's form-based user interface to insert *new* components, customizing the component behavior through parameterization. If the visual layout tools are too inflexible, at Layer 4 the developer can manually edit the layout code (Figure 2; this is comparable to hand-editing HTML). The predefined high-level functions may be modified by editing the behavioral code (Layer 5; see Figure 3). At this level, developers have the flexibility to define Boolean conditions of nearly unlimited complexity but are not required to write low-level PHP code. At Layer 6 (not yet implemented), developers may access the component-based PRADO framework [27], which like ASP.NET or JSF, abstracts many of the details of web programming. Using PRADO, advanced developers can define new components (by composing existing components or creating new ones from scratch) similar to that supported by WCML [9]. At this level developers can also modify Click's high-level functions (e.g., change `saveToDatabase`) or create a new high-level function (e.g., `receiverRssData`) for use by themselves or other Click users. At the final and most powerful layer 7 (not yet implemented), experienced developers have full access to the capabilities of PHP. To gain ultimate flexibility, Click can export the full application code so that it may be used stand-alone on a separate web server.

We do not expect all users to take advantage of all layers. Rather, we anticipate that novice developers will start with the visual tools, and only explore more advanced features when they become necessary for their work. Indeed many end users may never reach the state of hand-writing code. We also do not see these layers as a "natural progression" for developers as they gain experience. More probably the use of these features will be quite opportunistic and vary on an individual basis.

The layers summarized in Figure 5 are specific to Click but future web development tools may implement similar facilities, perhaps leaving out, changing or introducing new layers. Our intention is for Click to have a *gentle slope of complexity*: offering features and flexibility that grow proportionally with the developer's needs.

4.5 Implementation and Evaluation

Click is implemented in an object-oriented manner using PHP Version 5 [15]. MySQL Version 4 provides the database layer and the PRADO framework [27] provides an underlying extensible component model. PRADO exposes an event-driven programming model similar to that of ASP.NET and JSP and cleanly separates layout from behavior. Click uses many open-source third-party components such as the HTMLArea WYSIWYG editor and a JavaScript-based drag-and-drop library and is itself freely available as open-source software (for references see [20]).

Click is still under development. A series of three formative evaluation sessions (4-6 participants each) has shown that novice web developers can implement a basic 3-page conference registration website within about one hour of time. Although many usability problems are left to be resolved, Click appears to facilitate the first steps into web engineering. However, we still have to evaluate how Click supports the construction of more complex projects. Just now we have begun to evaluate how novice developers manage when asked to autonomously implement non-trivial software (such as an online ride board application) from start to finish.

5 Summary of Contributions and Future Work

We have discussed the opportunities and challenges of EUDWeb and argued that supporting end users in web application development is not only a promising and important opportunity, but also a realistic endeavor. Our Click prototype demonstrates that we can provide high-level functionality that helps even nonprogrammers develop fully functional web-based data collection, storage, and retrieval applications. As an alternative to web engineering approaches that address problems in a top-down, model-based way, we support the natural tendencies of developers to work in a more opportunistic fashion. Also, we recognize that novice developers are likely to handle concrete representations (such as components on screen) more easily than abstract models of an application (e.g., content, navigation, or presentation models). Finally, we advocate web development tools that expose functionality in a layered fashion to facilitate a gentle slope of complexity.

Much work needs to be done before we can claim that end-user web engineering is a reality. We must validate the efficacy of the concepts of design-at-runtime and gradual introduction to layers of functionality. We must also continue to analyze and develop components best suited for the needs and skills of our target audience. The work we have presented here is an early step into the promising future of end user web development and we hope that other research will follow.

References

1. Ambler, A., J. Leopold (1998). Public Programming in a Web World. Visual Languages, Nova Scotia, Canada.
2. AT&T (2005). Graphviz – Graph Visualization Software. http://www.graphviz.org/
3. Brooks, F. (1987). No Silver Bullet: Essence and Accidents of Software Engineering. Computer Magazine. April 1987
4. Burnett, M., S. K. Chekka, R. Pandey (2001). FAR: An End user Language to Support Cottage E-Services. HCC – 2001 IEEE Symposia on Human-Centric Computing Languages and Environments, Stresa, Italy.
5. Ceri, S., P. Fraternali, A. Bongio (2000). Web Modeling Language (WebML): A Modeling Language for Designing Web Sites. Computer Networks 33(1-6): 137-157.
6. Deshpande, Y., S. Hansen (2001). Web Engineering: Creating a Discipline among Disciplines. IEEE MultiMedia 8(2): 82-87.

7. Détienne, F. (2002). Software Design – Cognitive Aspects. Springer.
8. Fraternali, P., and P. Paolini (2000). Model-driven development of web applications: The Autoweb system. ACM Transactions on Information Systems, 28(4): 323–382.
9. Gaedke, M., C. Segor, H.W. Gellersen (2000). WCML: Paving the Way for Reuse in Object-Oriented Web Engineering. 2000 ACM Symposium on Applied Computing (SAC 2000), Villa Olmo, Como, Italy.
10. Harrison, W. (2004). From the Editor: The Dangers of End-User Programming. IEEE Software 21(4): 5-7.
11. IBM (2005). IBM Rational Web Developer for WebSphere Software. http://www.ibm.com/software/awdtools/developer/web/
12. MacLean, A., Carter, K., Lövstrand, L., Moran, T. (1990). User-Tailorable Systems: Pressing Issues with Buttons. ACM. Proceedings of CHI 1990: 175-182.
13. Microsoft (2005). Visual Web Developer. http://lab.msdn.microsoft.com/express/vwd/
14. Nardi, B. (1993). A Small Matter or Programming – Perspectives on End User Computing. MIT Press. Cambridge, Massachusetts, USA, London, England.
15. PHP (2005). PHP: Hypertext Preprocessor. http://www.php.net/
16. Repenning, A. and A. Ioannidou (1997). Behavior Processors: Layers between End-Users and Java Virtual Machine. IEEE VL 1997. Capri, Italy. Sep. 23-26
17. Robertson, T. J., Prabhakararao, S., Burnett, M., Cook, C., Ruthruff, J.R., Beckwith, L., Phalgune, A. (2004). Impact of Interruption Style on End-User Debugging. ACM Conference on Human Factors in Computing Systems, Vienna, Austria, April 2004
18. Rode, J., M. B. Rosson (2003). Programming at Runtime: Requirements & Paradigms for Nonprogrammer Web Application Development. IEEE VL/HCC 2003. Auckland, NZ.
19. Rode, J., M.B. Rosson, M. A. Pérez-Quiñones (2002). The challenges of web engineering and requirements for better tool support. Virginia Tech Computer Science Tech Report #TR-05-01.
20. Rode, J., Y. Bhardwaj, M. Pérez-Quiñones, M.B. Rosson, J. Howarth (2005). Click: Component based Lightweight Internet-application Construction Kit. http://phpclick.sourceforge.net
21. Rode, J., J. Howarth, M. Pérez-Quiñones, M.B. Rosson (2004). An End-User Development Perspective on State-of-the-Art Web Development Tools. Virginia Tech Computer Science Tech Report #TR-05-03.
22. Rosson, M. B. and J. M. Carroll (1996). The reuse of uses in Smalltalk programming. ACM Transactions on Computer-Human Interaction 3(3): 219-253.
23. Schwabe, D., G. Rossi, S.D.J. Barbosa (1996). Systematic Hypermedia Application Design with OOHDM. ACM Hypertext '96, Washington DC, USA.
24. Shneiderman, B. (1983). Direct Manipulation: A Step Beyond Programming Languages. IEEE Computer. 16: 57-69.
25. Web Models (2005). WebRatio. http://www.webratio.com
26. Wolber, D., Y. Su, Y. T. Chiang (2002). Designing Dynamic Web Pages and Persistence in the WYSIWYG Interface. IUI 2002. Jan 13-16. San Francisco, CA, USA.
27. Xue, Q. (2005). The PRADO Framework. http://www.xisc.com

Towards End User Development of Web Applications for SMEs: A Component Based Approach

Jeewani A. Ginige, Buddhima De Silva, and Athula Ginige

University of Western Sydney, Locked Bag 1797,Penrith South DC, 1797, NSW, Australia
{achandra,bdesilva}@cit.uws.edu.au, a.ginige@uws.edu.au

Abstract. 'Garbage in Garbage out!' This is very true when user requirements are not addressed accurately in Web (or any) Application development. Adding fuel to this fire is the ever-changing business requirements that force these web (or any) applications to change and evolve. In order to deliver web applications that meet user requirements, within budget and time constraints, it is important to use appropriate methodologies, tools and techniques suitable for a dynamic environment. Experts in Software Development have been researching and practicing many approaches to over come these issues. However, after a decade into Web application development, only a few of these approaches are effectively used in this domain. This paper discusses use of two such approaches: (a) use of Components and (b) End User development that can be effectively used in combination for Web Application development. In our work in the Small to Medium Enterprise (SME) sector we have developed a set of Components that allow End Users to assemble, deploy and run Web Applications. We have incorporated these Components into a framework that facilitates the deployment of these Components developed by developers.

1 Introduction

With advancements in Web in past decade, businesses have been using Web technologies to make a global presence and/or to enhance internal business processes. Web's ubiquity, simplicity and cost effectiveness have made it a suitable tool especially for Small to Medium Enterprises (SMEs) to be competitive in a global business environment. AeIMS (Advance enterprise Information Management Systems) [1] research group at University of Western Sydney has been working with SMEs in Western Sydney region to investigate how Information and Communication Technologies (ICT) can be used to enhance their business processes to get competitive advantages in global economy[2]. In this work we have identified various issues that SMEs face when trying to implement web based systems to enhance their business processes. These issues vary from not being able to get web applications developed to meet needs of the business in a timely manner to development projects running over budget.

Researches and practitioners in Web domain have been trying to adapt solutions that were initially developed for software engineering [3] .In our research we find that using one approach, method, etc. in isolation does not address all the issues that we have come across in Web Application development in the context of SMEs. Ginige, A. [2] suggests that computers should be viewed as medium to capture knowledge instead of creating specific end products as a way of meeting needs of SMEs in relation to web applications to support their business processes. Fischer, G. also supports this view of End User development as future of software development [2, 4, 5]. IT

D. Lowe and M. Gaedke (Eds.): ICWE 2005, LNCS 3579, pp. 489–499, 2005.

consultants also recommend, "do it your-self", DIY, approach for SMEs [6]. Based on above thinking in this paper we present a solution that enables End Users to develop applications using Components that are developed by web developers.

We have identified two types of basic Components; they are (a) Tools that allow End Users to create and assemble applications and (b) Engines that could be used to run these applications. The concept of Components presents a need for a framework that can support execution of them. Therefore we have extended a web application development and deployment framework, Component Based E-application Deployment Shell, (CBEADS©) which was developed by AeIMS Research group. CBEADS© framework and generic Components allow End Users to assemble, deploy and run applications by themselves. Further more new Components could be added to this extensible framework by developers. End Users can reuse the Components to develop different other applications.

Major findings that we present in this paper are; a discussion of issues in relation to Web Application development for SMEs, combination of Component based approach with End User application assembly and deployment to over come the issues that were identified, a study into finding requirements of aforesaid Components and extension of CBEADS© framework to incorporate Components (Tools and Engines).

2   Solving the Problem at Conceptual Level

In this section we analyse different issues in web application development in SME context followed by an investigation of web application domain to find how other researchers and practitioners have tried to solve similar issues. Then we bring forward a concept of incremental development environment where developers and End Users can work together (not necessarily in the same location) to develop applications to overcome the issues that were identified.

2.1   Web Application Development Issues in SMEs

As a part of our work in SME sector in Western Sydney region of Australia, we have been assisting organisations to eTransform their business activities [7]. In the past three (3) years we have been closely working with fourteen (14) such SMEs. With these companies we have developed seventeen (17) web applications in total, ranging from static public web sites to intranet applications to support their eTransformation process. This work with SMEs provides a test-bed for the three strands of research namely eTransformation, eApplication Development and Emerging Technologies carried out by AeIMS [1] research group. Based on the analysis done on web applications developed so far and also with our previous experiences in software application development we identified the following issues that are related to web application development in the context of SMEs;

- Developers failing to fully understand user requirements.
- Users failing to accurately specify changing requirements in evolving business environment and developers failing to incorporate them successfully into already developed applications.
- Need for incremental addition of new web applications to keep pace with eTransformation stages.

- Keeping up-to-date information in web applications that are visible to a wider audience.
- Web Application development projects failing to deliver on time and within budget.

To address some of the above issues, in past decade experts in web domain have been researching and adapting some concepts used in software engineering into web applications development. In particular researchers such as Li [8], Petkovic et al [9], Gellersen et al [10], Zhao [11] have used Component based approaches for web application development. Also researchers such as Rode et al [12] and Morishima et al [13] have explored suitability of End User computing for web application development. However, we find that use of one approach, methodology, tool or technique in isolation cannot address all the issues of web application development mentioned above.

2.2 Proposed Solution: Combining End User Development with Component Based Development Approach

We studied approaches SMEs have been using to develop different web applications. Applications varied from a simple static web site to an automated internal business process such as a leave approval process, enterprise resource planning etc. Mainly SMEs use one of two methods (Fig 1) in order to develop these applications. First method (see (a) in Fig 1) is to get an analyst to specify application requirements, get designers to design the system and developers to implement it. In reality above tasks are done either by an individual or a group of people, depending on the complexity of applications. Other extreme (see (c) in Fig 1) is to use a tool that allows them to attempt to do this task by themselves. The WYSIWYG type web development tools such as FrontPage and Dreamweaver make it possible for End Users to develop simple web applications without having to do any coding or relying on a developer.

Both above approaches ((a) and (c) in Fig 1) have their own problems. Success of resolving web application development issues in the first method depends on many factors such as how well the users communicate requirements to analyst, skills of design and development team, appropriateness of methodologies used and flexibility of design to incorporate future needs. These factors are beyond the control of SMEs and do not guarantee to solve web development issues outlined in section 2.1 above. On the other hand second option ((c) in Fig 1) makes it possible for users to develop these applications themselves. Hence we can assume issues of communicating user requirements to analysts are eliminated. However, most tools that are available for End User web application development are either not capable of developing complex applications with both front end and back end components or way too complex to be used by nonprogrammers (End Users). Copeland et al's analysis on existing web development tools verifies this observation [14].

Therefore to strike a balance between above two extremes ((a) and (c) in Fig 1) we suggest a hybrid approach. In this approach developers create Components (Tools and Engines), which End Users can use to create and deploy web applications. This hybrid approach also supports incremental development. End users can develop applications when required and also maintain them. Developers can keep adding new Tools and Engines when existing Components cannot meet End User needs.

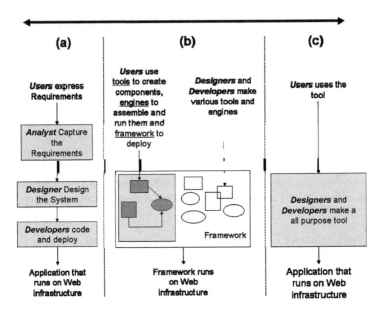

Fig. 1. Possible Approaches for Web Application Development

We believe the use of End User development concept and Component based development approach in combination in an incremental development environment address the issues in web application development in the context of SMEs. Also the reusability aspect of Components (Tools and Engines) makes it possible to rapidly develop web applications within budget. Since these Tools and Engines are agile and supports evolution, End Users themselves could handle change management of applications. Further the incremental development environment allows SMEs to meet new web application needs required in eTransformation [7].

3   Design of Tools and Run Time Engines

In this section first we discuss End User perspective of technical concerns in web application development. This is followed by a discussion on how to encapsulate critical application development know-how instead of application domain knowledge into Components so that End Users can use their application domain knowledge and develop their own web applications. In this approach these Components will be reused across different web applications as we provide generic Components. Further we present implementation of these Components in CBEADS© framework.

3.1   End User Perspective of Technical Concerns of Web Application

In Rode et al's [15] empirical research into 'End Users mental model' they attempted to find functionalities that web application development tools should provide to handle concepts that are critical to web application development. We have extended and categorized their list of critical concerns in web application development (see Table 1 left most column). The concerns critical to web application development are mainly three fold. They are issues in (i) front end development, (ii) back end application development to support the front end and (iii) data layer that supports both backend and front end functionalities. Also in Rode et al's research they have accurately identified that tools provided for End Users to develop web applications should encapsulate issues critical to web domain. Further we argue that it is important to abstract user requirements and develop a set of Components that does not depend on user application domain. This method allows those Components to be used across many application domains to develop applications.

Ginige and Murugesan have researched into categories of web applications and according to their classification they had identified six types of web application categories [16]. We have reorganized this categorization and added few more to it such as web-based application development tools and search tools to bring it up to date.

In Table 1, we have attempted to bring together Rode et al's [15] critical issues of web applications development (left most column of Table 1) with Ginige and Murugesans' [16] types of web applications (top most row of Table 1). Aim of this exercise was to find degree of importance of different concerns with various types of web applications (see Table 1). Then we asked eight (8) experienced web application developers to fill cells in the middle with a rating to identify to what degree each of the critical issues are applicable to different types of web applications. After correlating their input we produced Table 1.

Use of the information gathered in Table 1 is to find different critical concerns that should be supported by a framework and by Components (Tools and Engines). For example a framework should support concerns that are common to all web applications while other issues specific to individual application types need to be addressed by Components. Using this approach we can hide complexities of web application development from End Users and provide a framework that is easy to learn and use. The requirements for Components are found by abstracting different applications, for example if the need for the application is to develop a 'leave application approval process' the Components should be abstracted to a level up (Fig 2). This leads to providing a Tool that can generate forms and attach rules that apply to leave processing and an Engine that can support runtime operation of the form based on the rules.

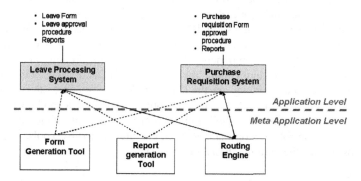

Fig. 2. Meta Level Abstraction of Component Parts of the Application: An example of re using Components (Form Generation Tool, Report Generation Tool and Routing Engine) developed for 'Leave Processing System' in a different application scenario (i.e. to develop a 'Purchase Requisition System')

3.2   Requirements of Components

In creating Components that are suitable for End User application development, developers have to take following requirements into consideration;

- Components should capture domain knowledge of web application development and hide complexities from End User.
- Should not capture application domain specific knowledge into Components. Rather those specific application needs should be abstracted and generic Components (Tools and Engines) should be created that can be used across many application domains (Fig 2).
- Components should be easy to use by End Users, yet they need to be complete so that it aid full capture of all the necessary 'Components parts' of the application such as front end pages, back end processing logic and database information.

3.3   Extensions to CBEADS©

Initial CBEADS© (Component Based E Application Deployment/Development Shell) [2], [17] was created in 1998 with basic functionality of user authentication, role based access control, ability to add more functions and assigning these newly created functions to users. This ability of adding more functions to CBEADS© made it a candidate for it to be the framework that can support incremental development concept. With the extension of CBEADS© with Components that are suitable for End User application development, now it has got four types of modules, as depicted in Fig 3; (a) tools, (b) engines, (c) applications and (d) the shell. Tools and Engines are the Components implemented by developers that can be used by End Users to assemble, deploy and run applications. Applications could be both End User developed or developer implemented applications that are deployed on CBEADS©. However, depending on the need applications could be developed that does not need to run on CBEADS© framework. For example a static web site generated using 'content management system' tools could be deployed with an ISP. The shell contains modules that are common to Tools, Engines and applications to operate smoothly. CBEADS© environment as a whole depend on basic web infrastructure such as operating systems, web servers, etc. for its operation.

When adding new Components to CBEADS© developers need to decide whether it need to be a tool, engine or a module in CBEADS© framework and register them accordingly. Tools are the Components that are needed for creating and assembling 'Component parts' of an application, for example front end pages, business rules, back end databases, etc. Engines are the Components that support runtime operation of the application. If all Tools, Engines or applications need a module it is implemented as a module in the core shell. For example functionalities such as user management, access control, session management, etc. are needed by Tools, Engines and applications. Hence they are in CBEADS© core shell.

4   An Application Scenario

Using Tools and Engines on the extended CBEADS© framework we have enabled SMEs to develop and deploy web applications in an incremental manner. Here we

Table 1. Mapping of Critical Concerns of Web Application Development into different types Web Applications

Critical Concerns in Web App. Dev. \ Type of Web App.	Informational	Search, directory and dictionary look up tools	E-commerce sites and Web portals	Entertainment, interaction and messaging	Workflow or collaborative sites	Service oriented or high end web development tools
Site Structuring and navigation handling	medium-high	medium	high	high	high	high
Page Templates and Form creation	medium	medium	medium – high	medium-high	high	medium-high
Validating inputs	Low-medium	low-medium	Medium-high	Low-medium	high	high
Binding Form inputs with back end databases/tables	low-medium	Low-medium	medium-high	Medium-high	high	high
User authentication and access control	Low-medium	low	Medium-high	Low-medium	high	high
Session Management	Low-medium	low	Medium-high	Low-medium	Medium-high	Medium-high
Representation of business logic (rules) in applications	Low	Low	Medium-high	low	high	Medium
Querying a database and getting conditional outputs	medium-high	high	Medium-high	Medium-high	Medium-high	high
Creation of back end databases and other concerns in DB creation (schema, normalization, indexing, etc.)	low-medium	high	Medium-high	Medium-high	Medium-high	Medium-high
Security of data in storage and transmission	Medium-high	Low-medium	high	low	Medium-high	medium
Handling of multimedia (streaming, etc.)	Low-medium	Low-medium	Low-medium	high	Low-medium	medium

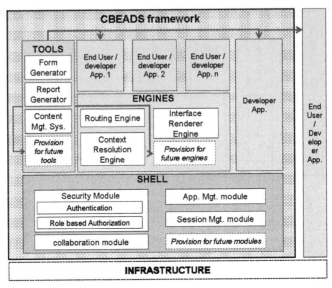

Fig. 3. CBEADS© framework; Tools, Engines, Applications and Shell

Table 2. Tools in CBEADS©

Tools	Critical concept covered	Description
Report Generator	Binding form input with backend database and tables	Use to design reports by defining data and calculations or processing want to apply on data retrieved.
Form Generator	Form Creation & validate inputs	Use to design web forms.
Template Generator	Template creation	Use to design the page templates.

Table 3. Engines in CBEADS©

Engine	Critical concept covered	Description
Routing engine	Representation of business logic (rules) in applications	Use to route a form from one user to another based on business rules.
Context Resolution engine	Querying a database & getting conditional outputs.	Use to resolve the context of artifacts. E.g.: immediate supervisor of given person.
Interface Rendering Engine	Binding form Inputs with backend database tables & validating inputs	Use to render the GUIs with form, report, etc.

elaborate how End Users could use CBEADS©, Form Generator, Report Generator and Routing Engine to develop a leave application. First we have to create a new application and name it as leave application. Through CBEADS© framework we can also assign users or user groups for the applications. Then we have to create a leave form with different fields such as no of days, from to, and leave type, etc. using Form Generator tool and attach rules with the leave form. For example Rules can be routing sequence – from whom to whom the application and result has to be routed and when and what has to be saved to a database etc as shown in Fig 4. Next the leave application should be registered with the routine engine, the run time Component responsible for routine forms. After that report formats and data to be displayed need to be specified. For example the data can be the statistics of leave applications processed with in a given period and the constraint is time period. Finally the reports are registered with the report generator to create the reports dynamically.

This section illustrates how the combination of component approach and end user development address the issues in web application development based on the above Application Scenario.

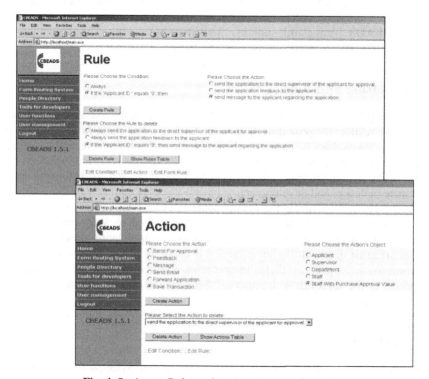

Fig. 4. Setting up Rules and Actions in Form Generator

Possible changes that could be requested after implementation for this leave application would be;

- Changing the initial leave form to add or remove fields
- Variations that could occur due to people (role) changes in the organization structure
- Changing the routing and business rules for example "Form 2005 onwards every leave application that is more than 15 days needs to be approved by the Managing Director"

Since the leave application implementation was abstracted to a level up to allow the changes related to the form itself (fields), its associated business rules and organisational structure to change individually without affecting one another it is easy for the above changes to be implemented to the leave application process.

In the case where there is a need for another leave application form for a sub company (with different organizational structure having changed roles and dissimilar routing and business rules) or a new form (such as purchase requisition form) for the same company, it is easy to implement that system using the same tools that was used for leave application process. Hence it reduces the cost and the time involved in future similar development activities.

As rules can be added through GUI as an expression this allows end users who has got a better understanding of their own application rather than the developers to participate in development. This understanding helps them to improve the applications for their need and to specify requirements for new applications correctly.

The CBEADS© framework supports the incremental addition of applications. We can add, delete, update applications while the framework is in use.

5   Conclusion and Future Work

This paper discusses a Component based End User development approach which is suitable for SMEs. By providing End Users with a set of tools to develop the web applications themselves we can solve the problems with requirement analysis and also reduce the cost and time to develop the applications. However, the mindset of End Users should change for this approach to be successful, as End Users have to actively participate in design and development.

We are currently refining the Components to reduce the effort required by End User when developing applications and providing a feed back mechanism to guide End Users to minimize faults that can happen in web application development. Also another area that needs further investigation is handling of exceptions for an instance of a form (business process) that is in operation. At the same time we are researching on success of the approach with group of SMEs volunteered to develop their applications themselves.

Acknowledgements

The authors wish to thank Dr. Uma Srinivasan of Phi Systems for her invaluable comments and support throughout the writing of this paper.

References

1. AeIMS Research Group Web Site – UWS. last accessed on April, 2005 at http://aeims.uws.edu.au/, Published by Advance enterprise Information Management Systems – University of Western Sydney: Sydney.
2. Ginige, A. Re Engineering Software Development Process for eBusiness Application Development. in Software Engineering and Knowledge Engineering Conference – SEKE02. 2002. San Francisco Bay, USA.
3. Botting, R.J., A Glossary of Software Development methods processes and techniques. 2003, California State University: San Bernardino.
4. Fischer, G. and E. Giaccardi, A framework for the future of end user development, in End User Development: Empowering People to flexibly Employ Advanced Information and Communication Technology, V. Wulf, Editor. 2004, Kluwer Academic Publishers.

5. Fischer, G., et al., Meta Design: A Manifesto for End-User Development, in Communications of the ACM. 2004. p. 33-37.
6. Hason, H., "Cut Price" IT Consultants for SMEs, in Asian Small and Medium Enterprises in the information Age: Asian Perspective. 2001.
7. Arunatileka, S. and A. Ginige, Applying Seven E's in eTransformation to Manufacturing Sector, in eChallenges. 2004.
8. Li, Q., J. Chen, and P. Chen, Developing an E-Commerce Application by Using Content Component Model, in IEEE. 2000.
9. Petkovic, I.M., Component Development of the Client Side of the Web Applications, in TELSIKS 2003. 2003: Serbia and Montenegro.
10. Gellersen, H.W., et al., Patterns and Components: Capturing the Lasting admist the Changes, in Active Web Conference. 1999: UK.
11. Zhao, W. and J. Chen, CoOWA: A Component Oriented Web Application Model, in 31st International Conference on Technology of Object-Oriented Language and Systems. 1999, IEEE: Nanjing, China.
12. Rode, J. and M.B. Rosson, Programing at Runtime: Requirements and Paradigms for Nonprogrammer Web Application Development, in Human Centric Computing Languages and Environments-2003. 2003, IEEE Symposium: Auckland, New Zealand.
13. Morishima, A., et al., Enabling End Users to Construct Data-intensive Web sites from XML repositories: An Example based approach, in 27th VLDB Conference. 2001: Roma, Italy.
14. Copeland, D.R., et al., Which Web Development Tool is Right for You?, in IT Pro. 2000. p. 20-27.
15. Rode, J., M.B. Rosson, and M.A. Perez-Quinones, End-Users' Mental Models of Concepts Critical to Web Application Development, in 2004 IEEE Symposium on Visual Languages and Human Centric Computing (VLHCC'04). 2004, IEEE Computer Society: Roma, Italy.
16. Ginige, A. and S. Murugesan, Web Engineering: An Introduction, in IEEE Multimedia. 2001. p. 14-18.
17. Ginige, A., New Paradigm for Developing Evolutionary Software to Support E-Business, in Handbook of Software Engineering and Knowledge Engineering, S.K. Chang, Editor. 2002, World Scientific Publishing Co. Pte. Ltd.: Singapore. p. pp. 711-725.

Web Applications: A Simple Pluggable Architecture for Business Rich Clients*

Duncan Mac-Vicar and Jaime Navón

Computer Science Department, Pontificia Universidad Católica de Chile
{duncan,jnavon}@ing.puc.cl

Abstract. During the past decade we have been witnesses of the rise of the Web Application with a browser based client. This brought us ubiquitous access and centralized administration and deployment, but the inherent limitations of the approach however, and the availability of new technologies like XML and Web Services has made people start building rich clients as business applications front ends. But very often these applications are tied to the development tools and very hard to extend. We propose a clean and elegant architecture which considers a plugin based approach as a general solution to the extensibility problem. The approach is demonstrated by refactoring a simple application taken from a public forum into the proposed architecture including two new extensions that are implemented as plugins.

1 Introduction

The complexity of today's business information technology infrastructure made Web applications reintroduce the server-based model but with a zero footprint on the client, offering centralized administration and deployment. Users can benefit from ubiquitous access from any internet-connected device using a web browser, which lack the functionality, offline operation, flexibility and performance of desktop applications as a result of a limited user interface technology and multiple round trips to the server to execute trivial tasks.

In the past, rich client and fat client were almost synonyms. Nevertheless in the last few years the emergent technology of Web Services eliminates the need for rich clients to be fat applications. Rich clients can integrate into SOA environments accessing both server located data and local acquired data (hardware devices, etc).

The requirements of next generation rich clients include the ability to use both local and remote resources, offline operation, simple deployment and real time reconfiguration support.

In this paper we will discuss such architectural and extensibility problems and propose an architecture that could be applied to any platform where rich clients are being deployed.

---

* This research is supported in part by the Chilean National Fund for Science and Technology (Fondecyt Project1020733)

D. Lowe and M. Gaedke (Eds.): ICWE 2005, LNCS 3579, pp. 500–505, 2005.

2   Rich Clients Architectural Problems

In rapid application development environments, visual form editors are used to design view components. The editor generates the user interface code as you change it and mixes that code with your event handler.

Once the application has been deployed it may suffer enough change so that it could justify a redeployment, but sometimes, adding a few new small features is all we might want. In the case of mission critical applications that require continuous operation, rebuilding and restarting the application is not an option, and therefore even a good architecture is not enough to ensure extensibility.

Furthermore, we would like that third party vendors or even the user itself be able to build small extensions to the original application as an alternative to wait for a new release from the original vendor.

3   A Proposed Simple Rich Client Architecture

We propose a simple architecture (Figure 1) to build applications which do not suffer the problems described above. For solving the architectural problems we leverage the MVC[1] design pattern splitting the application in three layers in a very clean and elegant manner. But perhaps our main contribution is the way we handle the extensibility problem through the use of plugins managed at the controller layer by a plugin engine.

3.1   The View

A view in our model is represented as a decoupled class containing only visual elements. No event handling is provided at this level. This allows for generating the views from metadata. There are several XML-based technologies like Mozilla XUL[1] and Qt UI[10] schemas that can be used to describe the user interface.

3.2   Controller

There is no single Front Controller[5][2] but as many controllers as view components we have. This kind of micro-controller is modeled as a class inheriting from the view. This allows for simple modeling and decoupling.

The controllers implement event handlers to manage the run-time plugin addition and removal events. Plugins can use the Action (modelled after the command design pattern[5]) pattern to encapsulate GUI commands to avoid coupling.

3.3   The Model

The business model is represented as a set of classes and optionally a database backend used for persistence. In simple scenarios, a service layer to interact with

---

[1] Model View Controller
[2] Front controller pattern is mostly used in the Web application domain

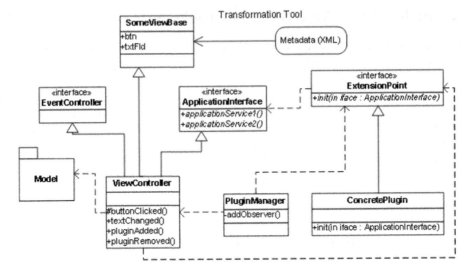

Fig. 1. Proposed Architecture

the database is enough to keep the architecture clean. If there is a complex business model, the Data Access Object pattern[7] is recommended to decouple the data backend handling from the business classes.

3.4   Supporting an Extensible Architecture

Plugins Technology. Plugins are a special type of components that can be optionally added to en existing system at runtime to extend its functionality (relationship between the plugin and the host application is stronger). The system doesn't know about the plugin and all communication happens through well defined interfaces.

Plugins are very popular among modern desktop applications. A good example is the variety of graphic filters and special effects available for Adobe Photoshop.

A plugin architecture avoids the huge monolithic applications as we see them now, allowing real-time deployment, easy maintenance and isolated component development.

Using Plugins in a MVC Architecture. Extension points are explicit holes in the applications where a plugin can plug its functionality a plugin can fill various extension points at the same time). The limits in what a specific plugin can do are set by the host application API and defining a good API for each extension depends a lot of the application context.

Adding plugin support in the application requires some extra code. This could vary from a simple dlopen C function to access a function in a shared library at run-time to a full featured framework to load components dynamically (e.g.:

MagicBeans [3] and JLense [9]). Modern languages like Java support dynamic loading of classes by name, a very handy feature for the needs of building a plugin infrastructure.

We model the plugin engine as a singleton using the observer pattern to generate events (pluginAdded and pluginRemoved) to subscribed controllers. The plugin event is then handled in the controller that manages the view where the plugin might add graphical components.

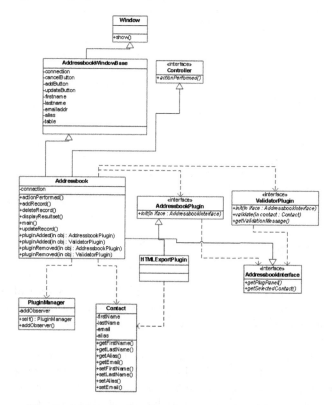

Fig. 2. Addressbook using the proposed architecture

4   An Example Application

As an example of our architecture, we took an addressbook application from a public forum in the Internet and proceed to refactor it to fit our proposed architecture. We set the goal of adding two new features to the application: exporting contacts to HTML and adding arbitrary constraints to new contacts in the entry form.

The original application was coded in Java and used a MySQL database as the backend. The user interface was done using the Swing API[3]. There is a single

---

[3] Application Programming Interface

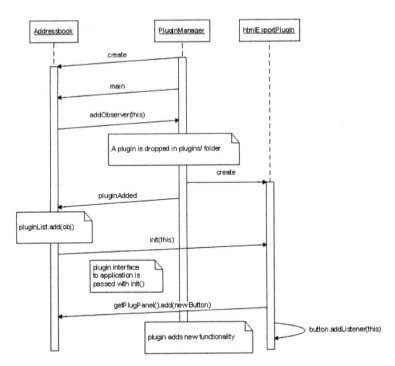

Fig. 3. Sequence diagram of interaction with the plugin manager when a new plugin is found

class which acts as a controller (handling events) and as a view (inheriting from a GUI window), a perfect example of no view/logic separation. Any tool used to assist user interface creation would need to parse the source. There is no model and the business logic is done in the same layer too.

The first step of the refactoring then, was to move all the user interface to a new class called AddresbookWindowBase and keep the existing class as the controller part of the architecture inheriting from the user interface. The new clean controller registers listeners for each user interface controls for each event it wants to handle.

For plugins to communicate with the application, an interface is needed. The interface should provide all the services needed by a plugin in the context. Two services were identified: retrieving contacts and adding actions to the user interface. We created a basic AddressbookInterface which offers a service to retrieve a panel where the plugin can add new actions. This application interface is passed to plugins during loading (Figure 3).

We chose MagicBeans [3] plugin engine because its simple design. Other plugin engine approaches could require wrapping the manager with our model.

The extension points were defined considering the context of the applications. The Validator extension encapsulates a generic algorithm with a contact as input and a boolean as output. Access to the addressbook services are done trough the Application interface see Figure 2).

5   Related Work

Smart Client Model [6] is an architecture proposed by Microsoft to develop thin rich clients. It is tied to the Windows platform and it does not suggest an architectural solution for extensibility.

MagicBeans [3] is a plugin engine developed by Robert Chatley. We use it in our example as the plugin engine.

Eclipse [4] is the most prominent example of a sole plugin based application. As it uses a central plugin registry and relies on XML configuration files, it is too complex and heavyweight for simple applications.

6   Conclusions and Future Work

We have shown here a RAD friendly simple architecture based on the MVC design pattern that allows for easy extensibility of rich clients using a plugin based approach. This gives us many additional benefits:

- New functionality can be quickly added without application redesign .
- Problems are isolated easily (because plugins are separate modules).
- The end user can customize a system without access to the source code.
- Third party developers can add value to the application.

We have built a simple example refactoring an application built using a common bad design to illustrate the level of extensibility that is possible switching to this model. Future work will be focused in generating complete frameworks for various architectures and languages using this concept. Currently we have Java and Qt proof of concepts.

References

1. Xul, the xml user interface language. http://www.mozilla.org/projects/xul/.
2. Robert Chatley, Susan Eisenbach, Jeff Kramer, Jeff Magee, and Sebastian Uchitel. Predictable dynamic plugin systems. In *Proceedings of FASE'04*, 2004.
3. Robert Chatley, Susan Eisenbach, and Jeff Magee. Magicbeans: a platform for deploying plugin components. In *Proceedings of CD'04*, 2004.
4. Eclipse Foundation. Eclipse technical overview. Technical report, Object Technology International, Inc., 2001.
   http://www.eclipse.org/whitepapers/eclipseoverview.pdf.
5. Martin Fowler. *Patterns of Enterprise Application Architecture*. Addison Wesley, 2002.
6. Microsoft. Smart client application model. http://msdn.microsoft.com/netframe work/programming/winforms/smartclient.aspx.
7. Core J2EE Patterns: Best Practices and Design Strategies. Deepak Alur and Dan Malks and John Crupi. Prentice Hall PTR, 2001.
8. Susan Eisenbach Robert Chatley and Jeff Magee. Modelling a framework for plugins. In *Proceedings of the SAVCBS'03 workshop at ESEC/FSE '03*, 2003.
9. Ted Stockwell. Jlense application framework. http://jlense.sourceforge.net, 2001.
10. Trolltech. Ui, the qt toolkit user interface language. http://www.trolltech.com.

From Web Requirements to Navigational Design –
A Transformational Approach

Pedro Valderas, Joan Fons, and Vicente Pelechano

Department of Information System and Computation
46022, Technical University of Valencia, Spain
{pvalderas,jjfons,pele}@dsic.upv.es

Abstract. Although MDA defines each stage for building software from models, it does not specify any concrete technique. In this sense, in the Web applications development, little methodological support is provided to both define and apply model to model transformations. In this work, we present a strategy based on graph transformations in order to define and to automatically apply model to model transformations. This strategy has been used to automate the OOWS CIM to PIM transformation.

1 Introduction

In the MDA [5] development process a *computational independent model* (CIM), a *platform independent model* (PIM) and a *platform specific model* (PSM) are proposed in order to describe the system at different levels of abstraction. Besides the specification of these models, MDA proposes that a set of consecutive transformations should be applied in order to transform these models into code. However, in the Web applications development area, little methodological support is provided to both define and apply model to model transformations

In this work, we introduce a strategy that is based on graph transformations in order to define and to automatically apply model to model transformations. This strategy has been used to automate the OOWS [2] CIM to PIM transformation. This contribution allows us to provide a fully MDA approach that support automatic model transformation.

This paper is organized as follows: Section 2 presents the OOWS method. Section 3 proposes a strategy to automate the CIM to PIM transformation. Finally, conclusions and future work are presented in section 4.

2 OOWS: A MDA-Based Method
for the Web Applications Development

The OOWS [2] development process begins by describing the early requirements of a Web application in the CIM model. Next, the PIM model is obtained by applying a model-to-model transformation. This model describes the Web application with high-level constructs that hide the necessary details for a particular platform. Finally, an automatic transformation is applied to obtain code from the PIM model.

This work focuses on the CIM to PIM transformation. Then, to better understand this transformation, a brief overview of the OOWS CIM and PIM models is next presented.

D. Lowe and M. Gaedke (Eds.): ICWE 2005, LNCS 3579, pp. 506–511, 2005.

2.1 The CIM Model

The OOWS CIM model is defined from: (1) the identification of the tasks that users must achieve and (2) the description of these tasks from the system-user interaction.

2.1.1 Task Identification

To identify tasks, we propose the construction of a task taxonomy. To do this we take a statement of purpose that describes the goal for which the application is being built, as the starting point. The statement of purpose is considered as the most general task. Then, this task is refined into more specific ones until a group of *elementary tasks* are obtained. An *elementary task* is defined as a task that when divided into subtasks involves either the user or the system, but not both. In addition, we propose to enrich this taxonomy by indicating temporal relationships among tasks. To do this, we have used the relationships introduced by the CTT approach (ConcurTaskTree) [6].

Figure 1 shows a partial view of the task taxonomy that we obtain from the statement of purpose of a Web application for the sale of audiovisual and bibliographic products (CDs, DVDs and Books). In order to easily identify the elementary tasks they are circled with a thicker line.

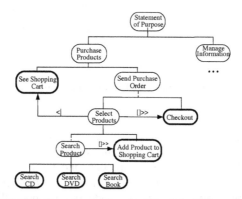

Fig. 1. A Task Taxonomy of an On-Line Sale Web application

2.1.2 Task Description – Activity Diagrams and Interaction Points

To describe elementary tasks we extend traditional description where user and system actions are described by indicating explicitly when (at which exact moment) the interaction between user and system is performed. We introduce the concept of **interaction point (IP)**. In each IP, the system provides the user with information. Moreover, access to operations can also be provided. In this sense, the user can perform several actions with both the information and the operations: he/she can select information (as a result the system provides the user with new information) and he/she can activate an operation (as a result the system carries out an action).

To perform descriptions of this kind, we propose a graphical notation based on UML *activity diagrams* [1] (see Figure 2). Each node (activity) represents an IP (solid line) or a system action (dashed line). Finally, each arc represents (1) a user action (selection of information or operations) if the arc source is an IP or (2) a node sequence if the arc source is a system action.

Figure 2 shows the description of the *Search CD* elementary task. This task starts with an IP where the system provides the user with a list of music categories (1). Next, the user selects a category (2). Next, the task continues with an IP where the system informs about the CDs of the selected category (3). Depending on the user action there are two ways (A and B) to continue with the task: **A)** The user selects a CD (4a) and the task ends with an IP where the system provides the user with a description of the selected CD (5a). **B)** The user selects a search operation (4b). Then, the system performs a system action which searches the CDs of an artist (5b). Finally, since the search result is a list of CDS it is shown in the IP where the full list of CDs is previously shown (6b).

As we can see, details about the information exchanged between the user and the system are not described. To do this, we propose a technique based on information templates such as the CRC Card [9].

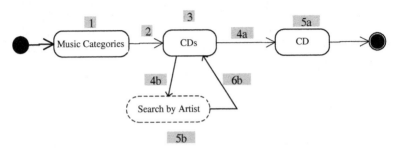

Fig. 2. Search CD Elementary Task

2.2 The PIM Model

The OOWS PIM model describes the different aspects of a Web application at a high level of abstraction. The system static structure and the system behaviour are described in three models (*class diagram* and *dynamic*-and *functional* models) that are borrowed from an object oriented software production method called OO-Method [7]. The navigational aspects of a Web application are described in a *navigational model*.

The navigational model [2] is represented by a directed graph (which defines the navigational structure) whose nodes are *navigational contexts* and its arcs denote *navigational links*. A navigational context (represented by an UML package stereotyped with the *«context»* keyword) defines a view on the class diagram that allows us to specify an information recovery. A navigational link represents navigational context reachability: the user can access a navigational context from a different one if a navigational link between both has been defined.

The navigational context is made up of a set of *navigational classes* that represent class views over the classes of the class diagram (including attributes and operations). Each navigational context has one mandatory navigational class, called *manager class* and optional navigational classes to provide complementary information of the manager class, called *complementary classes*. All navigational classes must be related by unidirectional binary relationships, called *navigational relationships* that are defined upon an existent relationship in the class diagram.

3   From a Task Description to the OOWS Navigational Model: Automating the CIM to PIM Transformation

In this section, we present a strategy based on graph transformations that allow us to automatically derivate the OOWS PIM navigational model from the CIM model. This strategy is divided into two main stages: (1) *Definition of the mapping rules* that transform a model into another model and (2) *Application of the mapping rules.*

3.1 Graph Transformations – Defining the Mapping Rules

In order to define the mapping rules we have chosen a technique based on graph transformations. Graph transformations are specified using transformation systems. Transformation systems rely on the theory of graph grammars [8]. A transformation system is composed of several transformation rules. Technically, a rule is a graph rewriting rule equipped with negative application conditions and attribute conditions. Every rule is composed by a Left Hand Side (LHS), that defines a pattern to be matched in the source graph and a Right Hand Side (RHS) that defines the replacement for the matched subgraph if a Negative Application Condition (NAC) does not matches.

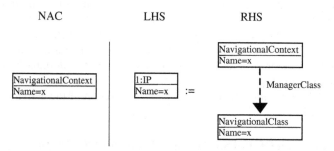

Fig. 3. A Transformation Rule

To define the OOWS CIM to PIM transformation we have defined a set of transformation rules. These rules transform a graph that represents a task description into a graph that represents an OOWS navigational model. Due to space constraints, we only present a representative rule that can be seen in Figure 3. The rest of rules are identified in [3]. The rule of Figure 3 says that when an IP (LHS) is found it must be transformed into a Navigational Context with its Manager Navigational Class (RHS). However, this rule is not applied if the navigational context is already defined (NAC).

3.2 Automatically Applying Graph Transformations

To automatically apply graph transformations we propose the use of the Attribute Graph Grammar (AGG) tool [4]. AGG was chosen because it allows the graphical expression of directed, typed and attributed graphs for expressing rules. It has a powerful library containing notably algorithms for graph transformation, critical pair analysis, consistency checking and the application of positive and negative conditions.

The AGG tool allows us to automatically transform a source *graph* into a target *graph*. However, models are not always defined as *graphs*. In these cases, to fully automate the model-to-model transformation by means of the AGG tool, two additional steps must be fulfilled: (1) The source model must be represented as a correct AGG graph and (2) once the graph transformations are applied into this graph, the obtained graph must be translated into the correct target modelling language.

Next, we present the strategy to achieve these steps in order to automate the OOWS CIM to PIM transformation.

3.2.1 Obtaining an AGG Graph from a Task Description

To automate the transformation of a task description into an AGG graph we propose a strategy based on the translation of XML documents. On one hand, the CIM model is specified in a XML document. This XML specification is built by means of XML elements defined from the task elements presented in section 2.1. On the other hand, the AGG system also uses XML to store its graphs by means of four XML elements: the *NodeType* and *EdgeType* elements that allow us to specify which kind of nodes and edges can be defined in the graph; and the *Node* and *Edge* elements that allow us to define the graph. Then, a translation of XML documents can be easily performed by a XSL Transformation.

The XSL transformation is performed by following the following three steps: (1) We transform the task taxonomy into an AGG graph (tasks are transformed into graph nodes and task relationships define graph edges). (2) Each activity diagram is represented as an AGG graph (IPs and System Actions are transformed into graph nodes while the activity diagrams arcs define graph edges). (3) The defined AGG graphs are joined into a single graph (each node that represents an elementary task is connected to the node that represents the initial IP or System Action of the activity diagram that describe the task).

3.2.2 Obtaining an OOWS Specification from an AGG Graph

When the AGG system transformation is finished we obtain a graph that represents an OOWS navigational model. This graph is made up of a set of nodes and edges defined from the OOWS metamodel elements. These elements have been briefly explained in section 3.2. Figure 4 shows a partial view of the graph that represents the OOWS navigational model of the "Web Sale application". This graph is obtained after applying the full set of transformation rules into the CIM model. According to this figure, two navigational contexts are defined: the *CD* navigational context and the *Cart* navigational context. On one hand, the *CD* navigational context is made up of a manager class (with some attributes and an operation) and a complementary class (with an attribute). On the other hand, the *Cart* navigational context is made up of the manager class with an attribute and an operation (with its parameters). In addition, a link is defined between both contexts.

Following a similar strategy than the previous one, an OOWS specification is obtained from an AGG graph by means of a translation of XML documents. On one hand, the AGG system stores the graph in a XML document. On the other hand, our OOWS case tool stores the OOWS specifications in XML repositories. The transformation between the two XML documents is performed by a XSL transformation.

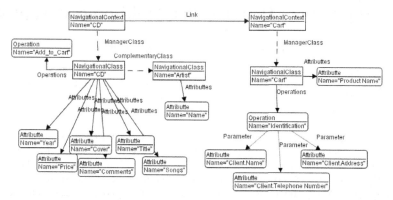

Fig. 4. An OOWS navigational model represented by means of an AGG graph

4 Conclusions and Further Work

We have present a strategy based on graph transformations that allow us to automate model to model transformations following the MDA approach. This strategy has been used to automate the CIM to PIM transformation of the OOWS method. To do this, the CIM and PIM models are represented as graphs by using XML translation based technique. Next, the graph transformations are applied by means of the AGG tool.

References

1. Object Management Group. Unified Modeling Language (UML) Specification Version 2.0 Final Adopted Specification. www.omg.org, 2003.
2. Fons, J., Pelechano, V., Albert, M., and Pastor, O.: Development of Web Applications from Web Enhanced Conceptual Schemas. In ER'03, volume 2813 of LNCS, 2003.
3. Valderas, P.: Capturing Web Application Requirements. Technical report, DSIC, Technical University of Valencia, February 2005. http://oomethod.dsic.upv.es.
4. The Attributed Graph Grammar System v1.2.4. http://tfs.cs.tu-berlin.de/agg/. 2004
5. Object Management Group. Model Driven Architecture (MDA). www.omg.org/mda, 2004.
6. Paternò, F., Mancini, C. and Meniconi, S.: "ConcurTaskTrees: a Diagrammatic Notation for Specifying Task Models", INTERACT'97, Chapman & Hall, 362-369.
7. Pastor, O., Gomez, J., Insfran, E. and Pelechado V.: The OO-Method Approach for Information Systems Modelling: From Object-Oriented Conceptual Modeling to Automated Programming. Information Systems 26 (2001) 507-534
8. Rozenberg, G. (ed.): Handbook of Graph Grammars and Computing by Graph Transformation. World Scientific, Singapore (1997)
9. Wirfs-Brock, Wilkerson, B. and Wiener L.: *Designing Object–Oriented Software*. Prentice–Hall, 1990.

Web Applications Design with a Multi-process Approach

Semia Sonia Selmi, Naoufel Kraiem, and Henda Ben Ghezala

ENSI, National School of Computer Science, 2010 Manouba, Tunisia
Semiasonia.selmi@riadi.rnu.tn, Naoufel.kraiem@ensi.rnu.tn
Henda.BG@cck.rnu.tn

Abstract. This paper deals with a new approach WApDM (Web Applications Design Method) for Web Applications Design. The WApDM is a multi-process approach whish covers all aspects should be considered during design of a Web application. The proposed approach is specified with the MAP formalism. The use of the MAP is three fold: (a) the MAP process meta-model is adapted to the specification of complex methods, (b) MAP introduces more flexibility in the method and (c) implicit information of the method are made explicit during the specification activity.

1 Introduction

Considerable attention has been given to Web engineering: the discipline which is concerned with the establishment and the use of engineering and management principles and disciplined and systematic approaches to the successful development, deployment and maintenance of high quality web-based applications.

In order to manage the overall complexity of development, several methods and models have been proposed. They should provide guidelines for performing activities and suitable models for expressing the results. Our reflection on this issue, which is shared by [8] [6] and others authors, is that the development of a web application should not be an event, but a process. This process will consist of a set of manageable activities. As stressed by [8], it is important to be guided by a sequence of steps to be performed, to know how the different steps co-operate and how they fit into the development process as a whole. Each design activity should address different concerns at the proper stage and at the proper level of abstraction.

However, we have concluded that there is a number of gaps in existing modeling methods, particular with regard to the level of guidance and flexibility provided. In fact, major existing methods do not consider systematically all features should be implied during design of a complex web application such as a Web Information System (WIS) such users profiles or offered services. We argue that the design of a complex web application should comprise the following activities that can not be neglected:

- organization and *presentation* of *information* which form the *navigation* support
- modeling of functional aspect dealing with *services* modeling offered by application
- considering *users* and/or *adaptation* modeling in the purpose to give impression that application is specially developed for user.

In spite of the importance of each of the aforementioned activities, the focus of existing methods is still different, some try to address many aspects in the design process, others try to detail in depth one or two of them.

D. Lowe and M. Gaedke (Eds.): ICWE 2005, LNCS 3579, pp. 512–521, 2005.

Other important issue characterizing existing methods is that they are prescriptive. Their processes specify only what must be done; they are already predefined. However, a design process does not always specify what must be done but contains some specification of what can be done. Therefore, it contains a number of alternative ways of doing a task and a selection of the particular alternative should be done dynamically, depending upon the situation in which designer is placed.

In this context, we consider design process as a decision making one. In fact, at any time a designer is in a situation that he views with some specific intention. His reaction depends on both these factors; i.e. on the context in which he has been involved. Methods should provide designer with the ability to decide how he can proceed according to his evaluation of the situation. Designing a WIS, for instance, requires a number of decisions to be made: what to consider as features?, what technique shall use?, the most appropriate solution?, etc.

In this research, we propose the WApDM method, a meta-approach that covers existing methodologies transparently. It takes as input the application requirements and decides which process to follow. It provides designer with the ability to move through the basic design steps. The work is partially motivated by conclusions derived in both Method Engineering discipline and Web Engineering discipline [4] [10]. It was observed that there is no existing full-featured approach that one can use to develop different kinds of applications with different requirements. Consequently, if one wants to develop more than one application, he might need to use more than one methodology.

Considering the design process as a process of decision taking, the proposed method provides more flexibility since it allows designer to decide in each design process step, and thus, personalize his process.

With regards to purposes to reach, we have opted to adopt the meta-model MAP as modeling formalism, offering different ways to guide achievement of design activities. The MAP provides guidance to a lower level abstraction through associated guidelines.

The remainder of this paper is organized as follows. We provide in the second section an overview of WApDM method, its principle and its components. In the third section, we present the MAP process meta-model used as modeling formalism in section 4. Finally, we summarize our conclusions and future works.

2 Overview of WApDM Method

The WApDM is a multi-process method: it offers panoply of different processes for the design of web applications such as WIS, adaptive applications, e-commerce applications, etc. It supports the most part of design process. Each of activities addresses a particular concern and is accomplished separately.

The WApDM is a meta-approach that covers existing methods transparently. Typically methods consider the design process in terms of process phases and their deliverables, often models.

It is important to note, at this level, that design models should answer the need of formalizing the design of hypermedia applications. They should also help to reason in a structured way on the aspects that are specific to hypermedia design.

A typical web design method has the following phases [5]:

- *Conceptual design:* describes the organization of the information managed by the application, in terms of pieces of content that constitute its information base and their semantic relationships. Modelling aims to construct a *conceptual model* without commitment to any specific detail for navigation paths, presentation and interaction aspects.
- *Navigation design:* concerns the facilities for accessing information and for moving across the application content. The navigation structure should be carefully designed through a *navigation model* by providing the user with the comfortable navigation spaces.
- *Presentation design:* affects the way in which the application content and the navigation commands are presented to the user. This is described in a *presentation model*.
- Besides, and due to the evolution of the web and therefore of web applications, others phases are recognized namely:
- *Requirements analysis:* gathering and forming the specification of users and/or stakeholders requirements. This step delivers a *requirements analysis model*.
- *Adaptation modelling:* the success of web applications is largely dependent on user satisfaction which is achieved by, for example, easy-to-use interface and well structured navigational architectures. The most effective technique to leverage these features is adaptation. It consists on delivering them to the right user at the right time in the right format. This phase presents the objects that participate in the adaptive functionality and describes how this adaptation is performed [9]. It aims to construct an *adaptation model* which is based on a user model.
- *User modelling:* aims to construct a *user model* which contains information that represents the view the system has of the knowledge, goals and/or individual features of user.
- *Business process modelling:* apart from simple web sites, web applications are derived from conventional transaction processing systems. These applications support critical business processes and workflows that are important part of the organisation's core business model. These business functions must be supported and consequently web design methods need to provide the ability to represent these functions and their related design artefacts. It is an important activity in particular for the e-business applications design. It helps designers and developers, for instance, in identifying and understanding the relevant elements in a specific domain and their relationships [15].

The first four phases could be supported during the design process of any web application. However, others are specific to some web applications types.

In fact, adaptation modelling and user modelling phases are both performed when designing adaptive applications as it is defined in [2].

User modelling phase can be also performed in isolation when designing a user-model based application. Designer, in such case, intends to adopt a user-centred approach starting design process with user requirements and characteristics. This has the advantage to solve disorientation and cognitive overload problems.

As for Business process modelling, is particularly recognised for e-commerce applications. As it is referenced by [15] and many others researchers, it helps in identifying and understanding the relevant elements in a specific domain and their relationships. Most existing web design methods fail to address the modelling of functionality in web applications. Their focus has been on the organisation, presentation and navigation aspects while business functions have been consistently overlooked.

Our reflection in this point, that the business process modelling phase should be performed during any web application design. Designer can judge about the domain complexity in term of service complexity. For instance, if services of current domain are of a high complexity, designer should construct the business process model in order to better understand domain. Otherwise, such case of simple web site of very low information complexity, it is useless to perform this step.

As we can notice, design phases mentioned above can be classified according to dependency of their deliverable models on current web application to be designed. In fact, all aspects of organising structure, choosing content or presentation modalities are aspects that totally depend on application. In contrast, others aspects as user modelling or adaptation modelling are considered at a high level of modelling and do not depend directly on application. Besides, the first three activities (structure, navigation and presentation) are typically delivered during web design [5].

Consequently, we have distinguished two models classes: *Application models* class and *Business models* class. The first class comprises application domain model, navigation model and presentation model. The second class is containing requirements analysis model, adaptation model, user model and business process model.

The WApDM method covers all aforementioned design phases and adopt the process meta-model MAP as modeling formalism. In the following section, we present an overview of the MAP and its associated guidelines. In the section IV, the formalization of the WApDM method with MAP is detailed.

3 Overview of MAP

A MAP is a process model which allows designing several processes under a single representation. It is a labelled directed graph with intentions as nodes and strategies as edges between intentions [1]. The directed nature of the graph shows which intentions can follow which ones.

According to the meta-model illustrated in Fig. 1, a Map is composed of one or more sections. A section is a triplet <source intention I, target intention J, strategy Sij> that captures the specific manner to achieve the intention J starting from the intention I with the strategy Sij. An intention is expressed in natural language and is composed of a verb followed by parameters. Each Map has two special intentions "Start" and "Stop" to begin and end the navigation in the Map. Each intention can only appear once in a given Map.

1. A guideline named *"Intention Achievement Guideline"* (IAG) is associated to each section providing an operational mean to satisfy the target intention of the section.
2. *"Strategy Selection Guideline"* (SSG) determines which strategies connect two intentions and helps to choose the most appropriate one according to the given situation. It is applied when more than one strategy exists to satisfy a target intention from a source one.

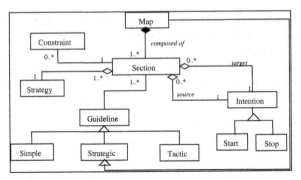

Fig. 1. The MAP process meta-model

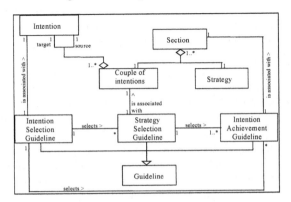

Fig. 2. Guidelines associated with the MAP

3. "*Intention Selection Guideline*" (ISG) determines which intentions follow a given one and helps in the selection of one of them. It results in the selected intention and the corresponding set of either IAGs or SSGs. The former is valid when there is only one section between the source and target intentions, whereas the latter occurs when there are several sections.

Fig. 2 shows that: (1) for a section $<I_i, I_j, S_{ij}>$, there is an IAG, (2) for a couple of intentions $<I_i, I_j>$, there is an SSG, and (3) for an intention I_i, there is an ISG.

4 Formalizing WApDM Method with MAP

Processes identified using the meta-model MAP integrate all main activities of web applications design in different ways that designer can follow in order to achieve design process and, thus, have a web application of quality.

4.1 Presentation of the Generic MAP of Process Model

As shown in Fig. 3, the Map contains two core intentions Define application model and Define Business model in addition to Start and Stop intentions. They correspond to the definition of the different models, deliverables of design activities.

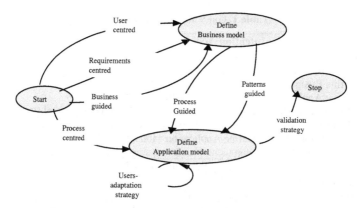

Fig. 3. Generic process model of Web applications design

The generic process model presented in Fig. 3 provides a rich collection of process chunks. These allow identifying several strategies for each of aforementioned intentions.

To achieve the first intention Define Business model, the process model proposes three strategies: the user-centered strategy aims to construct an adaptive application and/or a user-based application. At this level, business model will correspond to user model and/or adaptation model; the Requirements-centered strategy supports users and/or stakeholders requirements analysis. Finally, Business-guided strategy corresponds to the definition of a Business process model. This strategy can be applied during design of any web application and in particular complex applications. These three strategies can be performed alternatively or together.

The second intention can be achieved by using either process-guided strategy or patterns-guided strategy. The patterns-guided strategy is applied when the designer decides to use a catalogue of patterns that helps him during the achievement of Define application model intention. The process-guided strategy is applied when designer decides to follow provided guidelines associated to WApDM method.

Process model generation is under the control of guidelines. Table 1 recapitulates all guidelines associated to the MAP of Fig. 3.

To allow designer navigation in map, WApDM provides a set of factors called *Situational Factors*. These factors help designer to choose the appropriate strategy and appropriate intention among several presented in the MAP. We have identified a number of factors such: the type of the application designer intends to design, complexity of application in term of offered services, similarity of the application with other applications already designed in same domain, degree of user-application adaptation, problem clarification and notation standardization.

In the following section, we present how they can help designer in navigation in map through the choice of the appropriate intention or strategy.

4.2 Example

The sequence of intentions shown in Fig. 4 is an example of a path that could be followed to design a web application. A more in-depth analysis of the process shows that designer is guided in very deep and flexible ways.

Table 1. Guidelines of WApDM Map

Intention Achievement Guidelines
<(Start), Define Business Model using User centred strategy>
<(Start),Define Business Model using Requirements centred strategy>
<(Start), Define Business Model using Buisness guided strategy>
<(Start), Define Application Model using Modelling centred strategy>
<(Define Business Model), Define Application Model using Process guided strategy>
<(Define Business Model), Define Application Model using Patterns guided strategy>
<(Define Application Model), Define Application Model using Users adaptation strategy>
<(Define Application Model), Stop using Validation strategy>
Strategy Selection Guidelines
<(Start), progress to Define Business Model>
<(Define Business Model), progress to Define Application Model>
Intention Selection Guidelines
<(Start), Progress from Start>
<(Define Application Model), Progress from Define application model>

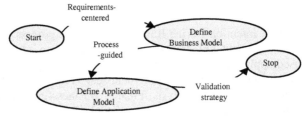

Fig. 4. Example of a web application design path

Sections of WApDM process model are refined to a lower level of abstraction proposing various techniques available to achieve the corresponding intentions.

Guidelines associated to sections included in the path of Fig. 4 namely <Start, Define Business model, Requirements-centred strategy> and <Define Business model, Define Application Model, process-guided strategy> are shown respectively in Fig. 5 and Fig. 6.

Starting from Start intention and by choosing the following section <Start, Define Business model, Requirements-centred strategy>, designer is faced to a cluster providing three alternative strategies to achieve Define requirements analysis model intention. As shown in Fig. 5, designer can either use Goal-driven approaches or Scenario-based approaches or else Goal-Scenario based approaches. Each of these strategies is refined to guide designer in defining a requirements analysis model.

Goal-driven approaches model organizational objectives so as to relate them to the functions of the systems. They aim at the conceptualization of purposeful systems only and represent the Why part of system requirements.

The scenario-based approach is an alternative approach to requirements engineering. By focusing on the users' view points, scenario-based approaches help in modeling purposeful system usage from which useful system functions can be derived.

In order to overcome some of the deficiencies and limitations of both approaches used in isolation, designer can combines goal modeling and scenario authoring through a goal/scenario based approach. For instance, designer can adopt CREWS-L'Ecritoire method [12].

Fig. 5. Cluster associated to <Start, Define Business model, Requirements-centered strategy> section

Once Define Business Model intention is achieved, consisting, during this path, to the definition of a requirements analysis model, designer should realize Define Application Model intention by following the process-guided strategy.

At a lower level of granularity, the following section <Define Business model, Define Application Model, process-guided strategy> is refined with a strategic guideline: MAP as shown in Fig. 6.

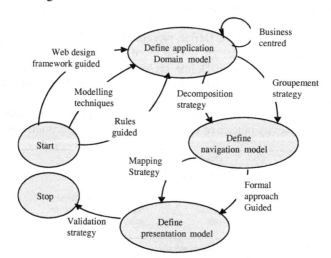

Fig. 6. MAP of <Define Business model, Define Application Model, process-guided strategy> section

The above Map provides panoply of paths and strategies from start and stop intentions. It contains three core intentions Define application domain model, Define navigation model and Define presentation model.

Beginning from the Start intention, designer is faced to three alternatives or manners to achieve Define application domain model intention. This is a Ssg which its body is a hierarchy of contexts. This Ssg is a choice context offering three alternatives.

The Ssg signature <Business model, state (Business model) =defined), progress to Define application domain model> associates the intention of progressing towards the target to define application domain model when the business model has been defined.

Each of these alternatives proposes the selection of an Intention Achievement Guideline to define Application domain model. The modeling techniques strategy is applied when designer decides to start from scratch and to adopt a well known conceptual data model like ER model [3] or any Object-Oriented technique [13] to define application domain model.

By applying web design framework-guided strategy, designer has experience in current domain and has already designed similar applications in similar domain. The third strategy rules-guided strategy is followed when designer has adopted in previous step the user interaction diagram as mean for the analysis requirements. In this case, he can just apply given rules and construct the corresponding application domain model. Arguments (a1, a2 et a3) are proposed to guide the designer in the selection of the appropriate strategy and associated guideline.

The next step in the process, shown in Fig. 6, is the definition of a navigation model. Once the application domain model is defined, designer can progress to achieve Define navigation model intention either by using Decomposition strategy, consisting on following more than one step or Groupement strategy. The both refer to manner that designer can apply to define navigation model. In general, the navigation model design can be achieved following only one step and it is referenced by Groupement strategy or more than one and it is referenced by Decomposition strategy.

Finally, designer can achieve Define presentation model intention. Fig. 7 shows that designer, at this step of design, is also faced to a SsG composed of two alternatives. He can choose to achieve Define presentation model intention using formal approach-guided strategy and so adopt formal approaches such as ADV Charts. Or, he can proceed by only mapping navigational objects to presentation objects, following, so, the mapping strategy. This strategy can be followed in case of simple web site design of low complexity in term of both information and application complexity.

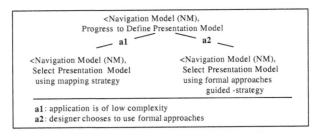

Fig. 7. Details of SSG <(Navigation Model(NM), state(NM=defined), Progress to Define Presentation model>

All these strategies are detailed in a lower level of abstraction in order to provide a more effective guidance to designer. Moreover, designer is guided and directed with respectively guidelines and/or associated arguments which help him to select the best strategy according to its purpose and current situation.

5 Conclusion

The paper has presented the WApDM method for the design of web applications. The proposed method is a multi-process approach. It is formalized with the multi-model process MAP. Although identifying intentions and specially strategies and organising them was not always an easy task, we observed the following additional important benefits:

- specifying web design methods using the map formalism raised details and levels of abstraction,
- the knowledge underlying the web design is made more explicit,
- web design process map specifies explicitly "why", "how" and "when" to use process chunks. Obviously, these qualitative observations have to be validated with more detailed experiments, e.g. empirical studies.

References

1. Benjamen, A.: Une approche multi-démarches pour la modélisation des démarches méthodologiques. PhD Thesis, University Paris 1(1999)
2. Brusilovsky, P.: Methods and Techniques of Adaptive Hypermedia. Int. J. User Modeling and User-Adapted Interaction (1996b). Kluwer Academic Publishers Vol 6, 2-3, 87-129
3. Chen, P.P.: The Entity-Relationship Model: toward a unified view of data. ACM TODS 1 (1976) 1, 9-36
4. Christodoulou, S.P., Styliaras, G.D., Papatheodorou, T.S.: Evaluation of hypermedia application development and management systems. Hypertext'98
5. Fraternali, P.: Tools and Approaches for Developing Data-Intensive web Applications: A Survey. ACM Computing Surveys (1999)
6. Ginige, A.: Web Engineering: Methodologies for Developing Large and Maintainable. Proc IEEE International Conference on Networking the India and the World CNIW-98, Ahmedabad, India
7. Isakowitz, T., Stohr, E.A., Balasubramanian, P.: RMM: a Methodology for Structured Hypermedia Design. ACM Communications (1998) vol. 38, no. 8, 34-44
8. Jacobson, I.: Object-oriented Software Engineering: A Use case driven Approach.Addison Wesley (1992).
9. Koch, N.: Software Engineering for Adaptive Hypermedia Systems-Reference Model. Modelling Techniques and Development Process, Ph.D Thesis (2001), Fakultät der Mathematik und Informatik, Ludwig-Maximilians-Universität München
10. Lee, H., Lee, C., Yoo C.: A Scenario-based Object-Oriented Methodology for Developing Hypermedia Information Systems. Proc of 31st Annual Conference on Systems Science (1998), Sprague R. (Ed.)
11. Rolland, C., Prakash, N.: A proposal for Context-specific Method Engineering. IFIP TC8 Working Conference on Method Engineering (1996), Atlanta, Georgie, USA
12. Rolland, C., Ben Achour, C.: Guiding the Construction of Textual Use Case Specification. In Data & Knowledge Engineering Journal (1998b), Vol 25, No 1-2, 125-160, (ed. P. Chen, R.P. van de Riet), North Holland, Elsevier Science Publishers
13. Rumbaugh, J., Blaha, M., Premerlani, W., Eddy, F., Loresen, W.: Object-oriented modeling and design. Prentice Hall international (1991)
14. Takahashi, K., Lang, E.: Analysis and Design of Web based Information Systems. Sixth International World Wide Web Conference (1997)
15. Ushold, M., King, M.: Toward a Methodology for Building Ontologies. Workshop on Basic Ontological Issues in Knowledge Sharing (1995), held in conjunction with IJCAI-95, Montreal

"Designing for the Web" Revisited:
A Survey of Informal and Experienced Web Developers

Mary Beth Rosson[1], Julie F. Ballin[1], Jochen Rode[2], and Brooke Toward[1]

[1] Pennsylvania State University, Information Sciences & Technology
330 IST Building, University Park, PA 16802
{mrosson,jfb15,bet133}@psu.edu
[2] Virginia Polytechnic Institute and State University, Center for Human-Computer Interaction
3160 Torgersen Hall, Blacksburg, VA 24061
jrode@vt.edu

Abstract. We report a subset of findings from a survey of over 300 web developers – a mixture of professional and more casual developers – targeted at understanding the needs, problems and the processes that developers follow and the tools they use. The prototypical web developer from our sample is meticulous about the quality of the web sites she produces, considers usability issues but neglects accessibility concerns. Web developers have many similar interests regarding web applications or features such as authentication, databases, online surveys or forms. They value ease of use as the most important property of a web development tool but mention many other needs such as integration with other tools, strong code editing features, or WYSIWYG facilities. This report details findings regarding process, tools, quality control, and learning.

1 Introduction

The diversity within the web development community is changing rapidly. For instance the number of end users who build web applications is increasing as general computing skills become more sophisticated (e.g., through use of spreadsheets, CAD, scientific visualization, and so on). Indeed the ubiquity of the web and the resultant ease of publishing content to a huge audience has been an important element in motivating web users to learn more powerful development techniques. The rapidly expanding population of web developers presents a mixture of opportunities and challenges for researchers and engineers building web development tools.

Despite the pervasiveness of the web – and the breadth of the associated developer population – little empirical work has studied web developers as "users". In 1998, Vora [7] surveyed professional web developers to better characterize prototypical professional web development practices. For example, Vora queried web developers about the methods and tools that they use, and the problems that they typically encounter. He summarized a number of technical problems, including web browser interoperability and usability, and lack of standards compliance of WYSIWIG editors.

In this work, we build on the Vora survey, but with the goal of reaching out to the combined population of professional and more casual web developers. The survey is done within the context of a research program aimed at analyzing and supporting the needs, problems, and preferences of "informal web developers" (individuals not explicitly trained in web programming techniques). Our sampling is intentionally biased towards these casual (nonprogrammer) web developers and therefore care should be taken when viewing the results in the context of professional web development.

D. Lowe and M. Gaedke (Eds.): ICWE 2005, LNCS 3579, pp. 522–532, 2005.

2 Related Work

In general, the analysis of web developers' needs has received only little attention in the web engineering literature. In two of our pilot studies (using both survey and interview methods), we analyzed the experiences and concerns of experienced web developers within a university context [3] [4]. These developers reported a number of problems that overlap to some extent with those report by Vora [7] and include security, cross-platform compatibility, integrating technologies (such as HTML, CSS, JavaScript, Java, SQL) and debugging of web applications.

As one phase in their user-centered design of the Denim prototyping tool for web site development, Newman et al. [1] interviewed 11 web development professionals. They found that these experts' design activities comprise many informal stages and artifacts. Expert designers employ multiple site representations to highlight different aspects of their designs and use many different tools to accomplish their work. They concluded that there is a need for informal tools that help in the early stages of design and integrate well with the tools designers already use.

In a study of web development in a community computing context, we interviewed 12 informal web developers about how they came to be doing web development, how they acquired their skills, the kinds of projects and programming issues they encountered in their everyday development, and what concerns, if any, they had about the tools they used [5]. We found that these individuals' development activities are situated in a collaborative context in which they depend on colleagues for content, expert advice, and testing. Their choice of tools was often based on organizational issues such as cost or who else was using the tool, rather than their own preferences or analysis of tools available. They learned new skills in an informal and as-needed fashion, often by tracking down and adapting or modeling the examples of others.

3 A Survey of Web Developers

To develop a broad characterization of the current web developer population – both professional and casual – we conducted an online survey and recruited participants from a variety of web development communities. The survey was based on our prior surveys and interviews of local web developers; it contained questions about web development experiences, including problems encountered; whether and how testing was carried out; desirable features or applications to incorporate in web development (e.g., databases, authentication); development style, including individual working style variations, and basic demographics (for a full list of the 37 questions see [6]).

We took two general approaches in recruiting participants. First, we contacted user groups associated with web tools (e.g., Macromedia, Frontpage); second we searched the web for other organizations that seemed to be oriented towards web use or even computer use in general. We particularly sought out organizations that might rely on *informal* developers (e.g., clubs or community organizations), but our survey invitation was aimed at *both* professional and casual developers.

We initiated contact with 591 organizations: approximately 30% product-centered groups (Coldfusion, Frontpage, etc.), 20% platform-centered (Mac, Linux, etc.), 38% hobby or 'computer club' type groups, and the remaining groups falling into language-oriented (e.g., ASP), professional/networking organizations and specific websites. We sent our email invitation to the listserv contacts, asking them to forward it to their members; the email summarized the study, data security/privacy, and the drawing for cash prizes (10 prizes of $50) used as an incentive for participation.

4 Survey Results

We received 334 responses to the survey. In this report we highlight a subset of the findings that seem especially relevant to the web engineering community (see [6] for additional results). In the following, question numbers refer to the actual position in the survey, so that interested readers may integrate the results reported here with the full survey and summary results available online. Note that percentages reported in this paper are the percentage of respondents who answered a particular question, not the percentage of the entire survey population with missing responses. Many respondents skipped one or more questions, so we follow the norm of including the relevant sample size as each percentage result is reported.

Interestingly, the answer to whether or not a respondent self-identified as a "programmer" was not often a useful grouping variable for the web activities and problems summarized here. For this reason the results discussed use the entire dataset.

4.1 Participants

The survey population included both men and women (70% and 30% respectively); most respondents (86%) reported their race or ethnicity as white/Caucasian. As one would expect, this web developer sample was relatively highly educated: 29% of respondents reported that they had completed an undergraduate degree and an even larger proportion (35%) reported completing at least some post-graduate education.

There was considerable age diversity in our sample (remember the survey's bias towards informal web developers). Interestingly, the single largest group of respondents age-wise was those who identified as age 60 or older (21%). In combing for computer related groups to whom we wanted to promote the survey, we discovered many groups oriented towards or run by senior citizens; this may explain the large proportion of older respondents. Other respondents were spread relatively evenly across age categories of 26-30, 31-35, and so on up through the age group 56-59. Only 6% of the sample reported their age as 25 or younger.

A small majority of respondents (54.7%) reported that "work" was the most common reason for them to develop and maintain websites. This is interesting as it emphasizes that, although considerable web development is being carried out in professional contexts, there is a sizable number of projects underway for other purposes. The two next most common motives were "special interest/hobby" (16.6%) and "civic, volunteer, or community work" (12.4%).

4.2 Perceived Value of Web Functionality

One question aimed at understanding web developers' current needs asked them to rate the perceived value of a number of predefined features (Figure 1; these items were developed through our pilot studies). As indicated in Figure 1, access restrictions, online databases, member registration systems, and online surveys/forms are seen as particularly valuable to our respondents, all being well above the mid-point on a range from 1 (not valuable) to 5 (extremely valuable). Communication-oriented features like discussions and chat are seen as relatively less valuable.

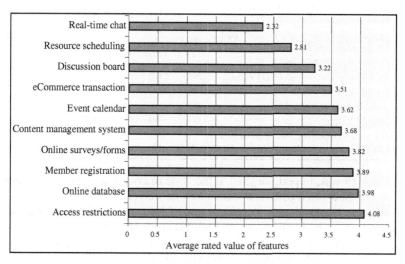

Fig. 1. Results from Question 5: "The following question asks you to judge the value of these same 10 features in your web development projects, regardless of whether you have worked with them yet or not." (N=314 to 318)

4.3 Characterizing the Web Development Process

To gain insight into the typical web development process and attitudes towards web development, question 16 asked the respondents to rate their agreement with a series of statements (1=strongly disagree, 5=strongly agree).

Our respondents tended to agree with the statement: "I spend a lot of time making sure my site's layout, formatting, content, and interactive elements are just right before I "go live"" (mean=4.18, SD=0.93, n=274). They voice similarly strong agreement with: "After my websites "go live", I check back frequently to make sure that everything works like it should (links, images, forms, etc.)" (mean=4.11, SD=1.0, n=274). These responses suggest that attention to the details of a web page is high on these developers' list of concerns.

Respondents tended to disagree with the statement: "When taking on a new web project, I immediately start constructing pages" (mean=2.43, SD=1.25, n=272), implying that they take steps to plan their project before jumping into building web pages. However the statement: "When working on a web site, I have a systematic process I follow" evoked a rather neutral response, only slightly biased towards "agree" (mean=3.56, SD=1.12, n=273). This is an area we hope to further explore in later research.

Most respondents also agreed with the statement: "As I work on a web project, I think about how I might come back later to change or expand it" (mean=4.16, SD=0.96, n=274). This is a promising result as it implies that they are planning for enhancement or other maintenance activities. See Table 1 for details.

Table 1. Question 16: statements ranked from 1 (strongly disagree) to 5 (strongly agree)

	1	2	3	4	5	Average
I spend a lot of time making sure my site's layout, formatting, content, and interactive elements are just right before I "go live"	1% (3)	4% (11)	17% (47)	32% (87)	46% (126)	**4.18** (n=274)
After my websites "go live", I check back frequently to make sure that everything works like it should (links, images, forms, etc.)	0% (1)	7% (20)	20% (56)	24% (67)	47% (130)	**4.11** (n=274)
When taking on a new web project, I immediately start constructing pages	29% (79)	28% (77)	20% (55)	15% (41)	7% (20)	**2.43** (n=272)
When working on a web site, I have a systematic process I follow	2% (5)	18% (50)	28% (77)	26% (70)	26% (71)	**3.56** (n=273)
As I work on a web project, I think about how I might come back later to change or expand it	1% (4)	5% (13)	16% (45)	31% (86)	46% (126)	**4.16** (n=274)

Question 15 was, in part, targeted at the issue of code reuse and participants were asked to rate how often particular statements are true (1=hardly ever; 5=quite often). The statement "I consult and reuse/copy code I have previously written myself" received a relatively high rating (mean=3.90, SD=1.36, n=273). This can be contrasted to their ratings for reusing others' code: "I search the web for snippets of code that I can directly copy, paste and edit" (mean=3.01, SD=1.33, n=273).

4.4 Web Development Tools

Question 6 asked: "What is the primary development tool you use for working on your site(s)?" 42.1% of the respondents cited Macromedia Dreamweaver. Microsoft Frontpage tied with HTML editors (Bbedit, Homesite etc.) at 12-13% each, followed by Text editors such as notepad or vi with 9.7%. No other tool exceeded 3%. Note that the relatively high proportion of Dreamweaver users is likely biased by our recruiting strategy (the Macromedia user groups were large and had good response rate). Of course, this predilection for Dreamweaver should also be considered when interpreting responses to questions concerning tool likes and dislikes.

Question 8 asked: "What are the three things you like MOST about your primary web development tool?" Three open response fields were provided and we received 286 responses for the first, 272 for the second, and 246 the third – a total of 804 individual responses, typically just a few words long. We coded the results by first scanning all responses and establishing categories. Next, we coded all comments according to the previously established categories. Fig. 2 visualizes about 90% of grouped comments (719 responses). 10% of developers' comments were coded as "other" because they were too diverse to be grouped in a meaningful fashion.

Question 9 asked: "What are the three things you like LEAST about your primary web development tool?" Again, three open response fields were provided and we received 259 responses for the first, 193 for the second, and 143 the third, for a total of 547 individual responses (excluding 48 responses such as "nothing" or "n/a").

We used a similar coding strategy, resulting in 16 categories. Not surprisingly, many of the comments made in response to things liked least can be seen as the inverse versions of things liked most (e.g., the number one group in both cases is related to the rather general evaluation of ease of use). Interestingly however, while feature

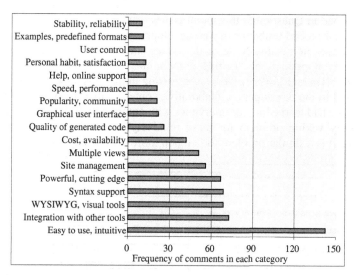

Fig. 2. 90% of responses to question 8 "What are the three things you like MOST about your primary web development tool?" were coded into 17 categories

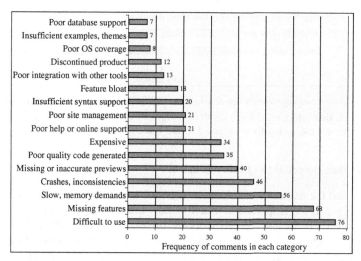

Fig. 3. 88% of responses to question 9 "What are the three things you like LEAST about your primary web development tool?" were coded into 16 categories

coverage was rarely mentioned as a reason to *like* a tool, it was the second most common category for *disliking* a tool.

4.5 Problematic Development Situations

To explore the problems that web developers may encounter we asked our respondents to rate eleven problems according to how frequently they occur. As with the features probed in Question 5, this list of issues was based on our earlier surveys and interviews that probed problems in web development.

Fig. 4 shows the results. None of the issues stands out as a particularly frequent problem, except perhaps of "getting content in a timely manner from others..." (mean=3.32, SD=1.41, n=272). This is interesting in that it is the one issue that is very much related to the developers' collaborative context – that is, to their dependencies on others. We had learned in our interviews with community webmasters that this was a particularly vexing problem for these relatively informal web developers [5]; it appears that it is a similar problem for a much more diverse population.

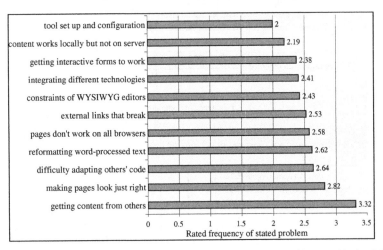

Fig. 4. Responses to Question 14 "How often do you experience problems with the following kinds of issues that sometimes arise in web development work? Please use a scale from 1 (one) to 5 (five) where 1 means hardly ever, and 5 means quite often." (n=267 to 276)

4.6 Attention Directed to Quality Control

To understand the extent to which quality control is a concern for our sample of web developers, we asked respondents to tell us how often they performed certain testing tasks (1=never, 5=always; "When working on websites, how often do you test to make sure..."; Question 12). An overwhelming majority of respondents agreed that they evaluate the general *usability* of their websites always or almost always: "...it is easy for users to do what they want to do on the site and to find what they might be looking for (usability)" (mean=4.33, SD=0.93, n=276). However, they seem to be much less likely to worry about universal access: "Users who might have disabilities will be able to use your site (ADA compliance, section 508, Equal Access, etc.)" (mean=2.75, SD=1.41, n=276).

Although most developers appear to test for platform and browser compatibility, not all of them do so routinely ("It will work across different operating systems and different web browsers such as Internet Explorer, Netscape Navigator, Safari, etc."; mean=3.75, SD=1.26, n=276).

The three items analyzed above represent a relatively superficial assessment of developers' testing processes. To probe more deeply we included an open-ended question "Please briefly describe when and how you test the websites you build or maintain". This generated 514 comments; 415 addressed *how* testing is done and 99 *when*. We coded responses by first scanning all responses and establishing categories and then classifying comments into to these categories. Some respondents did not answer the question and answers from a single respondent often contained multiple codes. 17% of responses were coded as "other" because they were too diverse to be grouped in a single category or were not specific enough. The distribution of the *how* comments is graphed in Fig. 5. The majority of responses related to browser compatibility and operating system concerns (note that we had just raised these concerns in the immediately preceding survey items). These data are also consistent with a small interview study of expert web developers where compatibility was among the most frequently cited challenges in web engineering [4].

Our prior study of community webmasters had indicated that nonprogrammers working in this context often use informal testing mechanisms (e.g., asking friends or coworkers to critique a site, [5]). Similar strategies are apparent in this larger survey: Many respondents said that the main test method they use is to simply "eyeball" the site before going live. We were surprised that only *one* respondent mentioned testing of security. This is particularly interesting given our prior interviews with web development experts who listed this as their primary concern [4]. Perhaps this is indicative of how difficult security testing is for many web developers, even though it is recognized as a central issue.

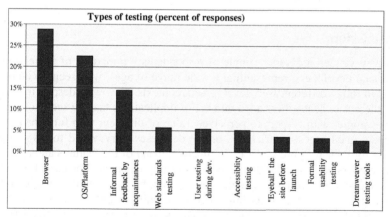

Fig. 5. Nine categories of testing *how* comments account for 83% of responses (N=415)

Our open-ended survey probe also asked for information about *when* website testing is done. We developed and applied a coding scheme (eight categories, see Fig. 6) for the content that described *when* website testing is conducted. Of the 99 responses received, 7% were coded as "other" because they were too diverse to be grouped in a single category or were not specific enough. The most common response (32%) was that testing was carried out after every change or update to the site. An almost identical number (30%) said that testing is simply conducted throughout development. Only a few mentioned a specific time interval at which they test; three respondents did volunteer that they never test their work!

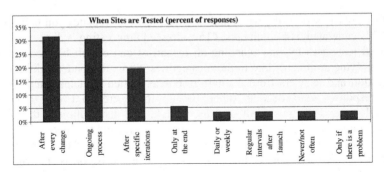

Fig. 6. Eight categories of testing *when* account for 93% of the comments (N=99)

4.7 Learning New Web Development Skills

We asked participants to rate how likely they would be to consult particular resources for assistance in case they needed to learn something new (Question 11; 1=not likely; 5=very likely). "FAQs, books, or tutorials" were rated most highly (mean=4.53, SD=0.88, n=257), followed by "Examples of similar sites from which you can get ideas and copy code" (mean=3.97, SD=1.18, n=259), and "A friend or coworker who knows how to do it" (mean=3.76, SD=1.26, n=259). Respondents indicated that they would be less likely to consult sources such as interactive software wizards, software agents, seminars, or support hotlines.

5 Discussion

Our survey yielded a diverse sample of respondents – a mixture of professional and more casual developers, representing a wide range of ages, who seem to be pursuing projects in rather different web development contexts. However, despite the variation among the respondents, there are a number of implications that we see in our results.

For example, with respect to perceived value of different web functionality, most developers rated access restrictions, online databases, survey and forms as valuable elements for their web presence. Unfortunately, many of the features and applications that developers see as valuable are not easily implemented. For casual or informal web developers, providing access restrictions may be conceptually simple and obvious, but current tools make its implementation quite challenging. One of the other highly valued features–online databases–seems to be even more difficult to implement than access restrictions. Again, although the interactions with databases may be conceptually simple (e.g., consisting of overview and detail pages, a search function and some data input and edit forms), they are typically beyond the implementations skills for casual web developers. Current web development tools do not sufficiently abstract technical concepts such as session management, input validation or URL parameter passing. This requirement underscores an opportunity to develop more powerful web development tools designed for end users, tools that would raise the ceiling on what is achievable for nonprofessionals.

Our analysis of questions about respondents' web development process suggests that – at least in our sample – the prototypical web developer is meticulous and particular about the quality of the web sites she produces and maintains. Also, generally our web developers seem to invest some thought before embarking on a new project rather then implementing web pages ad-hoc, although they may or may not follow a strict process. Web developers also appear to frequently reuse code they wrote earlier but only occasionally search the web for example code to copy and use. These general findings are an encouraging indication that even an increasingly diverse web developer population is attuned to the "traditional" concerns of software engineering such as design and quality assurance.

The responses to the question about features most liked in web development tools show that this sample of web developers value ease of use as the most important property of a web development tool. They also clearly appreciate a tool that integrates well with other tools and provides frequently needed site management features such as integrated file upload. While they highly regard powerful WYSIWYG visual design and code generation features, they also demand support for viewing and *editing*, testing, and previewing the code behind the scenes. They appreciate code auto formatting and tag completion but at the same time expect to have full control over the layout of hand-written code.

At the same time, the responses to the question about what developers least like about their web development tool(s) show that many web developers are still not satisfied with usability aspects of their tools. While many respondents request more powerful features, such as more extensive WYSIWYG support, others complain about feature bloat. Across all comments, concerns about performance problems and faulty behaviors take the lead in complaints about tools. Another common complaint refers to automatically generated code that appears "messy", "bloated", and non-compliant to standards.

Regarding the typical problems that web developers encounter we were not able to detect any major distinctions in developer's experiences. Only the issue of "getting content in a timely manner from others..." was rated above the mid-point on a frequency rating scale. This concern is interesting, as it is much more social in nature (being dependent on a colleague for input) than most of the other concerns. It may be that social problems of this nature plague everyone, whereas the other listed problems are much more dependent on the types of applications or work contexts in which developers operate. Our future research will investigate these problematic aspects of web development more carefully, for example also probing perceived severity of individual problems, connecting problems to developers' working context, and providing an opportunity to describe problems in an open-format question.

Questions about the quality control process show that the vast majority of developers from our sample routinely validate website usability (although we do not know about the procedures they employ and standards they maintain) and sometimes check for cross-platform issues but rarely for accessibility problems. These accessibility checks may be omitted because of lack of awareness and concern, but it may be at least partly due to the relatively tedious and time-consuming tool support for such checks (too verbose, reporting many false positives; lack of automation).

6 Future Work

The results from this survey paint a high-level picture of today's web developers, their needs and habits. In a more detailed fashion we hope to investigate the specific processes that informal and professional web developers follow for planning, development, testing and debugging. Another dimension worthy of investigation is the collaborative aspects of web development – with respect to general problems, the most frequently reported problem was obtaining content from other people, which reinforces the importance of the organizational context in which web work is done.

Another direction for future work is to refine our analysis of professional versus casual developers, so as to better distinguish among their experiences and concerns. Our high-level contrast of developers who do or do not self-identify as a programmer did not prove to be an important categorical factor in their responses. However, there are a number of other issues related to this self-judgment (e.g., the projects a developer undertakes, the context in which a project takes place, the training the person has received); these variables may combine in complex ways to reveal subgroups within this diverse community. If we can identify such distinctions, we may be able to create a more refined picture of the habits and needs – and develop the corresponding tools – for the large and growing population of web developers.

References

1. Newman, M., Lin, J. Hong, J., Landay, J. (2003). DENIM: An Informal Web Site Design Tool Inspired by Observations of Practice. Human-Computer Interaction 18: 259-324.
2. Pitkow, J. and Kehoe, C. (1998). GVU 1998, 10th WWW User Survey. http://www.cc.gatech.edu/gvu/user_surveys/survey-1998-10/.
3. Rode, J. and M.B. Rosson (2003). Programming at Runtime: Requirements & Paradigms for Nonprogrammer Web Application Development. IEEE HCC 2003.
4. Rode, J., M.B. Rosson, M. A. Pérez-Quiñones (2002). The challenges of web engineering and requirements for better tool support. Virginia Tech Computer Science Tech Report #TR-05-01.
5. Rosson, M.B., J. Ballin, H. Nash. (2004). Everyday programming: Challenges and opportunities for informal web development. IEEE VL/HCC 2004: 123-130. New York: IEEE.
6. Rosson, M.B., J.F. Ballin, J. Rode (2005). Survey of Informal and Experienced Web Developers. Results summary. http://eudweb.cs.vt.edu/webdevelopersurvey/summary.html
7. Vora, P. (1998). Designing for the Web. ACM interactions, 13-30.

Web OPEN-Integrated:
Proposed Framework for Web Development*

Rashid Ahmad**, Zhang Li, and Farooque Azam

Software Engineering Institute, Beijing University of Aeronautics and Astronautics
No.37, XueYuan Road, HaiDian District, Beijing 100083, P.R. China
{r.ahmad,lily,farooque}@buaa.edu.cn

Abstract. Most Web applications are designed in an ad-hoc manner. Web applications, due to their peculiar nature, cannot be just developed as conventional software projects. Haire et al advocate Web OPEN [1] [2], extension to OPEN (Object-oriented Process, Environment, and Notation), as suitable model and provide a good study on it. We however, argue Web OPEN does address some of the peculiar issues of Web applications but not all, which we identify in this paper. We then propose a hypothesis that Web OPEN can be augmented in its efficacy with integration of components from other methodologies. In this paper we have investigated such components that could serve our hypothesis. We name the new model as Web OPEN Integrated.

1 Introduction

OPEN (Object-oriented Process, Environment, and Notation) is a process-focused methodological approach to software-intensive systems development useful for both object-oriented and Component-Based Development (CBD). OPEN was developed and is maintained by the not-for-profit OPEN Consortium, an international group of methodologists, CASE tool vendors and developers. It is documented in a series of books, papers (e.g. [1], [2], [3], [4], [5], [6], [7]) and in many journal articles, particularly in the journal JOOP. A unique aspect of OPEN is that it is not merely a process but a configurable family of processes, defined in terms of a metamodel (Fig. 1), known as the OPEN Process Framework (OPF). From these instances of the process fragments, organizationally-specific processes can be readily constructed. The component-based nature of OPEN permits appropriate extensions to support development in new domains. One such set of extensions is those for Web development, called Web OPEN (see Haire et al. [1], [2] for a detailed discussion on Web OPEN).

2 Some Important Issues Not Addressed by Web OPEN

In this section we will briefly discuss few important issues specific to WBA (web based applications) that have not been addressed in the Web OPEN.

- *Quality Assurance for Documentation:* When an engineering manual or the content of the website has an error or foggy expression, the quality is lowered because that manual/content is ultimately read by millions of readers. Good techni-

---

* Supported by Beijing Municipal Science & Technology New Star Plan (H013610270112)
** Corresponding author: Tel: +86-13691144459

D. Lowe and M. Gaedke (Eds.): ICWE 2005, LNCS 3579, pp. 533–538, 2005.

cal documentation can help people avoid common mistakes and errors. Web OPEN does emphasize on documentation but does not say how.

– *Process Variation:* Web applications are software intensive, and for software, process variation can never be eliminated or even reduced below a moderate level. No two modules are the same, so process performance always includes an intrinsic degree of variability. There are large differences in skills and experience from one developer to another. Web OPEN does not address this issue.

– *Increased Importance of "Quality" Attributes and "Security":* We discuss security and quality together because we believe both are interrelated. They address this issue with task *define website testing strategy* which emphasizes on whether the users can see the website concurrently or not. Another task they have "*define website standards*" which emphasize on consistency. We argue that quality and security being the most important issues have not been dealt with effectively.

– *Navigation Design:* Once the WBA architecture has been established and the components of the architecture have been identified, the designer must define Navigation Pathways that enable a user to access WBA contents and services. Web OPEN addresses this with task "create navigation map for website" but we argue that creating this map is broad term and we have to perform many subtasks before we are able to create navigation map for the website. This issue has not been addressed in Web OPEN.

– *Short Time Frames for Initial Delivery:* We believe this is the major driving force behind the ad-hoc ism in website development. This is creating a big gap between the commercial practice in this area and the researcher's direction. Although they say this issue has been indirectly addressed in activity "*Website management*" but we believe this needs to be addressed explicitly so that the clients are convinced they would reach to the market in time.

– *Process Improvement Component:* Room for improvement always exists in software processes. Despite this fact, OPF and Web OPEN do not have any component for improvement of processes.

3   Proposed Hypothesis: Web OPEN-I (Web OPEN Integrated)

Web OPEN which specifically focuses on Web development is handicapped with some limitations and is unable to address some of the peculiar issues associated with Website development. Our hypothesis focuses to cure it by integrating it with another well established methodology. We have selected Six Sigma and we contend that we can augment the efficacy of Web OPEN by integrating it with some components/tools from "six sigma for software".

3.1   Overview of Six Sigma for Software

Originated at Motorola in mid 80's, Six Sigma is a business-driven, multi-faceted approach to process improvement, reduced costs, and increased profits. With a fundamental principle to improve customer satisfaction by reducing defects, its ultimate performance target is virtually defect-free processes and products (3.4 or fewer defective parts per million (ppm) or 99.9997 percent defect free). The Six Sigma methodology, consisting of the steps "Define, Measure, Analyze, Improve, Control

(DMIAC)" is the roadmap to achieving this goal. Within this improvement frame-work, it is the responsibility of the improvement team to identify the process, the definition of defect, and the corresponding measurements. This degree of flexibility enables the Six Sigma method, along with its toolkit, to easily integrate with existing models of software process implementation.

When and how does a DMAIC Project Start? A DMAIC project is an opportunity to improve a process. So it starts when we identify that a business process needs im-provement. How do we know when a business process needs improvement? There can be various sources, for example,

- We have a process that the customer is complaining about very often then resolv-ing the problem, because of which customer is complaining, is a basis to improve our process.
- Our process is not meeting its service level.

3.2 Connecting Web OPEN and Six Sigma

Due to the existing incredible synergy between Web OPEN and Six Sigma, DMIAC can be very well integrated to the metamodel of OPF. Fig. 2 (for clear readability of the figures, please **zoom to 200%**) shows our proposed integrated metamodel of OPF in UML. The producer can invoke DMIAC project anytime when needed. Circum-stances when we invoke DMIAC project, has been explained in section 3.1 above. The out put of this process is the product that has to be delivered.

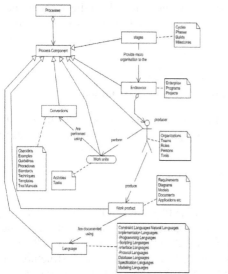

Fig. 1. Original OPF metamodel

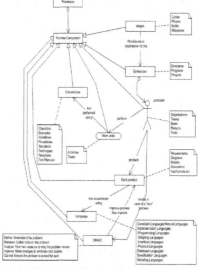

Fig. 2. Proposed OPF metamodel

4 How Web OPEN-I Addresses the Issues Discussed in Section 2

The integration of components from "six sigma for software" enables us to propose new Tasks and Techniques for Web OPEN. In total we have proposed following 3 new tasks, 7 new sub tasks and 1 new technique. Below (in Table 1) we have listed the issues and the proposed tasks, subtasks and techniques that will address them.

Table 1. New Tasks, Subtasks and Techniques

Issues	Addressed by
• Quality assurance for documentation	• *New task* "Do Document" (fig.5) • *New technique* "Controlled Natural Languages" (fig. 6)
• Process Variation	• *New task* "Measure Process Variation"
• Increased importance of "Quality" attributes and "Security"	• *New subtask* "Create CSS standards" • *New subtask* "Validate the web" • *New subtask* "Comply with WAI - The Web Accessibility Initiative" • *New process component* DMIAC concentrates on "Reducing Defects" with a goal of 99.9997 percent defect free system (not only defects from code but also other defects like deign defects etc)
• Navigation Design	• *New subtask* "Identify semantics of navigation" • *New subtask* "Define mechanics (syntax) for navigation" • *New subtask* "Create navigation conventions" • *New subtask* "Deign navigation aids"
• Short time frames for initial delivery	• *New task* "Create 'time to market' plan"
• Process improvement component	• *New process component* (DMAIC) added to the OPF metamodel (see fig. 2)

Due to the limitation of the space we are unable to explain all the new tasks, sub tasks and techniques. We will however (as sample) explain task "Do Document" and technique "Control Natural Language" to show how it will address the issue of "Quality assurance for documentation" in WBA. Explanation of other tasks and subtasks will be published elsewhere.

4.1 Task "Do Document" and Technique "Controlled Natural Languages" Explained

For quality assurance in technical documentation we have proposed one new task "Do Document" (Fig. 3) and one new technique "Controlled Natural Languages" (Fig. 4). Let's have a look at it.

5 Conclusion and Future Work

The *Software Process Engineering Metamodel* (SPEM) recently adopted technology by OMG's, is a metamodel for defining processes and their components. This metamodel is used to describe a concrete software development process or a family of related software development processes. The SPEM specification is structured as a UML profile, and provides a complete MOF-based metamodel. This approach facilitates exchange with both UML tools and MOF-based tools/repositories. The Meta-Object Facility (MOF) is the OMG's adopted technology for defining metadata and representing it as CORBA objects. The deliverables of OPEN can be represented in any notation like OML, UML etc. However there are some aspects of OPEN that can be expressed readily in OML but cannot be expressed or will not be properly expressible within the semantics of UML (e.g. responsibilities, rule sets, exceptions etc) [4].

Task: Do Document	Technique: Controlled Natural Languages
Focus: standardization of documentation and Quality assurance for technical documents. **Typical supportive techniques:** Controlled Natural Languages, Controlled English **Explanation:** The term Six sigma refers to deviations from an ideal level of operation, where a high sigma means fewer defects. Six sigma equates to 3.4 defects per million. If you are making parts, a six sigma level means 999,999.6 flawless parts. If you are writing documentation, six sigma is method to quantify the quality of documentation. "6 sigma" means 99.99966% accuracy and "2 Sigma" i.e. 69.1% accuracy performance is where many non-competitive companies run. When an engineering manual or the content of the website has an error or foggy expression, the quality is lowered because that manual is ultimately read by millions of readers. Good technical documentation can help people avoid common mistakes and errors. One of the ways to write the perfect *manual* is to use a Controlled English vocabulary to reduce ambiguity and improve quality, readability and usability. Controlled English (CE) is the new *lingua franca* (common language) for global product support. CE has approximately 1,500 basic words, plus the terminology for a product or service. **Producers for this task include:** Content Developer, Web Publisher, people involved in documentation. **Preconditions for this task include:** Existence of any of the errors listed in (Table 2). **Post-conditions for this task might include:** an agreed level of sigma	**Focus:** Minimizing errors in documentation, standardization of documentation. **Typical tasks for which this is needed:** Do Document **Technique description:** A controlled natural languages technique can be thought of learning a different language. The aim of the technique is to minimize the errors in written documents and contents. Using this technique is particularly useful in web development as by nature they are content driven. **Typical supportive tools:** Acrocheck (http://www.acrolinx.de), CLAT (Controlled Language Authoring Technology) (http://www.iai.uni-sb.de/iaide/de/clat.htm), MAXit – Controlled English Checker http://www.smartny.com **Technique usage:** This technique can be used by following simple steps for six sigma standard. • Create a CE vocabulary for your company (tools such as SMART Text Miner can be used for the rapid development of a CE vocabulary) • Teach the writers how to use Controlled English. • Use English-to-Metric converter to avoid conversion errors. Use available tools to find the errors in the text • Check currencies, quantities, qualities, sizes, URLs • Use tool metrics to calculate the percentage of error. • Validate signal names, instrument labels and safety warnings. • Consult lawyers for safety compliance (Product Liability). **Deliverables and outputs (post-condition):** A document that demonstrates a high standard of error free and ambiguity free documentation.

Fig. 3. Task "Do Document"

Fig. 4. Technique "Controlled Natural Languages"

Table 2. Common errors in document

• Spelling errors	• Measurements are vague, missed or wrong
• Foggy writing with confused gobbledygook/ jargon	• Use of -ing words that cause English ambiguity
• Long sentences that are more than 21 words	• Wrong metric conversions/omitted dual dimensions
• Key information is missed, confused or omitted	• Obsolete telephone numbers, URLs, product names
• "Failure to Warn" missing or wrong warnings	• Wrong or missing illustrations, graphics, callouts
• Wrong or non-existent page number references	• Invention of terminology for writer convenience
• Incorrect labels/references for instrumentation	• Multiple meanings for the same abbreviation
• Content is nice to know, not need to know	• Acronyms that do not follow global standards
• Wrong/multiple names for parts or nomenclature	• Tools/materials listed are not available worldwide
• Texts written by engineers in "engineering-ese"	• Failure to edit/review texts for technical accuracy

Therefore to comply with the widely accepted OMG's standards, the future work includes: making OPF as MOF compliant, and Mapping between SPEM and OPF/Web OPEN-I.

References

1. B. Haire, B. Henderson-Sellers, and D. Lowe: "Supporting web development in the open process: additional tasks," in COMPSAC'2001: International Computer Software and Applications Conference, Chicago, Illinois, USA, Submitted, IEEE Computer Society
2. Henderson-Sellers, B., Lowe, D., & Haire, B.: OPEN Process Support for Web Development. Annals of Software Engineering, 13, 163-201,2002
3. I. Graham, B. Henderson-Sellers, and H. Younessi: The OPEN Process Specification, Addison-Wesley, 1997
4. B. Henderson-Sellers, A. Simons, and H. Younessi: The OPEN Toolbox of Techniques, Addison-Wesley, UK, 1998
5. D. Firesmith, G. Hendley, S. Krutsch, and M. Stowe: Object-Oriented Development Using OPEN: A Complete Java Application, Addison-Wesley, Harlow, UK, 1998
6. B. Henderson-Sellers and B. Unhelkar: OPEN Modeling with UML, Addison-Wesley, Harlow, UK, 2000
7. D. Firesmith and B. Henderson-Sellers: The OPEN Process Framework. An Introduction, Addison-Wesley, Harlow, UK, 2001

Framework for Collaborative Web Applications

Ioakim Makis Marmaridis and Athula Ginige

AeIMS Research Group, School of Computing and IT,
University of Western Sydney, Sydney, Australia
makis@cit.uws.edu.au, a.ginige@uws.edu.au

Abstract. Traditionally organisations have been collaborating to complement one another's capacity and capability. The nature of these collaborations has been long-term, taking a long time to establish, and leading to fairly rigid IT infrastructure to support these. Now organisations are beginning to collaborate on specific short-term projects, established in a short time and are highly volatile driven by varying degrees of trust and need. A new IT framework for collaborative web applications is needed to support this type of dynamic, short term, opt-in and opt-out approach to collaboration. Building on our previous work on a peer to peer architecture for Dynamic eCollaboration, we propose a framework that allows web applications to be exposed to business partners by enabling selective information and business logic sharing. This information sharing is end-user driven, easy to perform and secure. We believe this framework effectively addresses the needs of Dynamic eCollaboration bringing us closer to realizing its full potential.

1 Introduction

Today's marketplace is extremely competitive, and the survival and growth of an organisation is very much linked to its ability to be agile, to sense and respond to market changes and be able to obtain efficiencies where others fail.

Traditionally, organisations have found that collaborating and building strong business relationships has been an effective way of surviving and growing in the market [1]. We define collaboration as "to work together, especially in a joint intellectual effort" [2]. This is by no means a new term and it is not even directly relevant to information technology. Collaboration has been well known to happen many centuries before computers were invented, or even electricity for that matter. With the advent of computers in businesses, the term eCollaboration was born to mean "the use of internet based technologies to enable continuous automated exchange of information between suppliers, customers and intermediaries" [3].

In the recent past a new type of collaboration has emerged that is now termed as Dynamic eCollaboration. Contrary to eCollaboration as discussed previously, Dynamic eCollaboration involves very flexible relationships between business partners and facilitates common work on typically short to medium term projects. New relationships can be created almost ad-hoc, and taken down just as fast with organisations being able to realise a truly distributed "sense and respond" approach in their business operations.

In the course of working with a group of SME Toolmakers, helping them embrace Dynamic eCollaboration, we have identified the lack of necessary ICT framework

D. Lowe and M. Gaedke (Eds.): ICWE 2005, LNCS 3579, pp. 539–544, 2005.

that can support this and other similar collaborative efforts [4]. We have identified the specific features required by such framework and how Trust and Need influence those features. Based on our experience of working with the Toolmakers, in this paper, we present a new framework that facilitates sharing of information and business logic. It is based on a pure peer to peer (P2P) [5] [6] architecture for Dynamic eCollaboration [7] and it is end-user driven, simple to operate and secure.

2 Drivers and Need for Dynamic eCollaboration

Dynamic eCollaboration depends on and is driven by two distinct factors – Trust and Need. Although these are not new in Dynamic eCollaboration, they greatly influence the degree of information exposure and sharing of applications in collaborative projects. After both Trust and Need are established, a suitable IT infrastructure must also be in place to facilitate the actual sharing process. However what is suitable from an IT point of view to support traditional eCollaboration falls well short of the requirements for supporting Dynamic eCollaboration. Here change is constant while projects are short term and participation to those nearly ad-hoc, the time frames are compressed and therefore the impact of fluctuations in the levels of Trust and Need are exaggerated placing new requirements and demands upon the underlying IT infrastructure supporting the Dynamic eCollaboration effort.

2.1 IT Infrastructure Issues in Dynamic eCollaboration

There are some fundamental differences between eCollaboration and Dynamic eCollaboration projects. They both have different characteristics that put particular requirements upon their respective support IT Infrastructure. The following table summarises those differences.

Table 1. Characteristics of eCollaboration projects versus Dynamic eCollaboration projects

Characteristic	eCollaboration	Dynamic eCollaboration
Project startup time	Significant. Enough to allow infrastructure setup by IT staff and exchange of data formats, applications, access control etc.	Very short. IT infrastructure must be mostly in place ahead of time and used with minimum configuration.
Project duration	Long enough to warrant the involvement of expert IT staff to manage the infrastructure.	Very short term. Impractical to involve IT staff. Low overhead and fast action needed.
Upfront knowledge of sharing requirements	Mostly well known and communicated to IT staff in order to configure systems accordingly.	Not known. They will be influenced by fluctuations in Trust and will be discovered as the project progresses.
Project value ($)	Sufficient to cover IT staff expenses for setting up and managing the infrastructure.	Not very big. Can not justify the ongoing involvement of IT staff.
Timeframe for addressing changes to project needs	Medium to long term. Enough for the supporting rigid IT infrastructure to be adjusted.	Short term. Changes to requirements must be addressed immediately. No room for unproductive time.

As the table above clearly shows, Dynamic eCollaboration has got some very unique characteristics. In traditional eCollaboration IT staff is in charge of establishing and maintaining each project as well as enabling the actual data sharing between parties. They achieve this typically through using a mix of technologies such as VPN, FTP and DB exports or in some cases special purpose frameworks [8-10]. This proves not effective enough to cater for Dynamic eCollaboration however where the continuous involvement of IT staff imposes a large overhead in both time and cost. Therefore, business staff must be enabled to establish and maintain their own projects directly, assisted by an intelligent technology framework that can take care of lower lever issues, such as sharing protocols, enforcing security decisions and more. Section 3 that follows discusses our proposed framework and how we believe it can support Dynamic eCollaboration Projects.

3   A Framework for Dynamic eCollaborative Web Applications

There are four major subsystems that make up the framework that facilitates Dynamic eCollaboration. Figure 1 shows the relationships between these four subsystems.

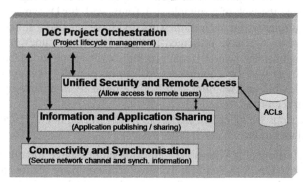

Fig. 1. Subsystems of the framework for Dynamic eCollaboration and their relationships

The functions of these subsystems are as follows:

- Dynamic eCollaboration Project Orchestration – This subsystem is responsible for interfacing with the business users as they initiate, define and setup collaborative projects. It also features fail-safe checks and balances to actions requested by business staff safeguarding the security and integrity of the collaboration.
- Network Connectivity and Synchronisation – This subsystem enables the respective IT systems to establishing a secure communication channel over standard network communication protocols. It is able to transparently handle the distribution and caching of shared information and business logic access. It also has in-built caching mechanisms for better fault-tolerance and can intelligently work across a range of protocols such as SOAP, XML_RPC, HTTP and HTTPS or even integrate to an Enterprise Messaging Bus (EMB).
- Unified Security and Remote Access – This subsystem provides a unified view of the parties and individuals involved in a particular collaborative project for the purposes of security, cross systems access and information flow management.

Through the concept of virtual team mates, all participants to a project can be managed and have access rights to information given or taken from them. It features per project granular role based access control (RBAC) and offers hooks for programmatic access by applications developers.

- Information and Applications Sharing – This subsystem is capable of offering different views of the applications that can be shared throughout the project while supporting ad-hoc changes to the shared views at all times. Business users are thus empowered to expose and share different parts of their applications as this is required by the goals that they are trying to achieve in the project.

The next section describes a typical usage scenario and how the framework makes this possible.

4   A Verification of the Architecture for the Framework

The framework described in this paper has come about as a result of our intense work with several SMEs in the toolmaking industry while attempting to help them embrace Dynamic eCollaboration and increase their competitiveness. Through this work so far we have identified the lack of a suitable ICT framework for Dynamic eCollaboration, defined the requirements for such framework and have created a suitable architecture for it – all of which we have presented in this paper. The framework proposed has been verified against the overall requirements for Dynamic eCollaboration. It also fulfils the processes that the Toolmakers wish to use. Finally, the architecture of this framework is flexible and we think can fulfill similar requirements by other companies in different sectors as well.

Here are the steps we identified as necessary to carrying out a typical project using Dynamic eCollaboration:

- Project establishment – Where the interested parties agree to collaborate and use their respective DeCS to establish a computer to computer secure channel of communication and the virtual team of users for the particular project.
- Sharing a large job amongst the different SMEs – This is where by exposing parts of their web based job management application, the SME that has the relationship with the customer, will be able to facilitate the break-down of the job to its smaller parts. Once the other parties agree on who takes what part, these decisions will be recorded in the job management application and through sharing they will be available to all the parties involved.
- Quoting for each part of the job – Putting a joint or individual quote together still requires collaboration, to ensure the prices quoted are suitable and to get overall agreement for the final price. Through their respective DeCS, each SME will be able to indicate the time and materials charges, markup and final price for their part of the work. Sharing this information with the others means that each will have a complete view of the quote and its constituent parts. A view that will be dynamically updated as parts of it change.
- Tracking the job progress after winning the bid – Each SME through their own DeCS will be able to mark their progress for the part they are responsible for and share that information with the rest of the group. The sharing will be dynamic, so

any changes made to the status will be automatically reflected to the shared copies accessible by the other partners in the collaboration.

5   Conclusions and Future Work

From working with a group of Toolmakers who wanted to share some large toolmaking jobs that they are getting we identified a process that they can use. We also found that the level of information sharing can vary with time depending on the level of trust among the collaborating partners. After studying the process Toolmakers wanted to use to collaborate, we developed a generalised architecture for a Web based system that can support sharing of the information required for this and other similar Dynamic eCollaboration projects. A special feature of this architecture is that each end user can vary the depth and breadth of information they are going to expose to the collaborating partners depending on the need and the level of trust that exist at the time. We defined the four subsystems of the framework and verified the operation of each using some of the collaborative processes the Toolmakers want to use. We are now extending one of our existing technology frameworks into incorporating the ability to server as a platform for Dynamic eCollaboration.

The main contribution made in this research project was to identify the specific features required for a web based Dynamic eCollaboration system and to develop an architecture that can meet the requirements of a group of Toolmakers who want to collaborate with each other to gain a competitive advantage.

Acknowledgements

The authors wish to thank Dr. Uma Srinivasan of Phi Systems for her invaluable comments and support throughout the writing of this paper.

References

1. Ginige, A., Collaborating to Win – Creating an Effective Virtual Organisation, in International Workshop on Business and Information, M. Lee, Editor. 2004: Taipei, Taiwan.
2. The American Heritage® Dictionary of the English Language. 2000, Houghton Mifflin Company.
3. Donnan, D., CEO/Presidents' Forum – Action Plan for Trading Partner e-collaboration. 2002, GMA CEO/Presidents' Forum. p. 8.
4. Schuster, K., Cross-Industry Standard Key to eCollaboration Success, in News Release issued by Ticona. 2002: Philadelphia.
5. Prasad, V. and Y. Lee, A scalable infrastructure for peer-to-peer networks using web service registries and intelligent peer locators, in Cluster Computing and the Grid, 2003. Proceedings. CCGrid 2003. 3rd IEEE/ACM International Symposium on. 2003. p. 216-223.
6. Marmaridis, I., J.A. Ginige, and A. Ginige, Web based architecture for Dynamic eCollaborative work, in International Conference on Software Engineering and Knowledge Engineering. 2004.
7. Marmaridis, I., et al., Architecture for Evolving and Maintainable Web Information Systems. 2004: IRMA04.

8. Dustdar, S. and H. Gall, Architectural concerns in distributed and mobile collaborative systems, in Eleventh Euromicro Conference on Parallel, Distributed and Network-Based Processing, 2003. 2003. p. 475-483.
9. Kawashima, T. and J. Ma, TOMSCOP – a synchronous P2P collaboration platform over JXTA, in 24th International Conference on Distributed Computing Systems Workshops. 2004. p. 85-90.
10. Dustdar, S., H. Gall, and R. Schmidt, Web services for groupware in distributed and mobile collaboration, in Proceedings. 12th Euromicro Conference on Parallel, Distributed and Network-Based Processing, 2004. 2004. p. 241-247.

Discovering Re-usable Design Solutions in Web Conceptual Schemas: Metrics and Methodology

Yannis Panagis[1,2], Evangelos Sakkopoulos[1,2], Spiros Sirmakessis[1],
Athanasios Tsakalidis[1,2], and Giannis Tzimas[1,2]

[1] Research Academic Computer Technology Institute
61 Riga Feraiou str., GR-262 21 Patras, Hellas
{panagis,sakkopul,syrma,tsak,tzimas}@ceid.upatras.gr
[2] University of Patras, Computer Engineering and Informatics Department
GR-26504, Rio Patras, Hellas

Abstract. In the Internet era, the development of Web applications has impressively evolved and is characterized by a large degree of complexity. To this end, software community has proposed a variety of modeling methods and techniques. In this work, we provide a methodology and metrics for mining the conceptual schema of applications, to discover recurrent design solutions in an automatic manner. The mechanism is designed for models based on WebML, a modeling language for designing data-intensive applications. This approach, when applied in an application's conceptual schema, results in effective design solutions, as it facilitates reuse and consistency in the development and maintenance process. Furthermore, when applied to a large number of applications, it enables hypertext architects to identify templates for Web application frameworks for specific domains and to discover new design patterns extending the predefined set of patterns supported by WebML. Finally, we illustrate a validation scenario.

1 Introduction

The unprecedented adoption of Internet is setting new standards to the development of Web applications. Web applications are becoming the de facto underlying engine of any e-service, including e-learning, CSCW, e-business and e-government. Consequently, the hypertext architect has to design the application in such a way, that it can efficiently manage huge amounts of data, integrate complicated functions and sophisticated business logic. At the same time the application must provide access to users with different preferences and needs, who use a variety of access devices including mobile ones.

Novel challenges are therefore posed to developers. As the market needs increase swiftly and the use of a large number of new technologies evolves at a rapid pace, advanced Web application development becomes more and more slow, expensive and error prone, often yielding products with large numbers of defects, thereby causing serious problems of usability, reliability, performance, security and degradation of other quality of service characteristics.

Several Web application modeling methods have been proposed to tackle web development setbacks, primarily based on the key principle of separating data management, site structure and page presentation. Some proposals derive from the area of hypermedia applications like the RMM [16] and HDM [14] which pioneered the model-driven design of hypermedia applications and influenced several subsequent

D. Lowe and M. Gaedke (Eds.): ICWE 2005, LNCS 3579, pp. 545–556, 2005.

proposals like HDM-lite [9], a Web-specific version of HDM, Strudel [8], and OOHDM [20].

Araneus [2] is a proposal for Web design and reverse-engineering, in which the data structure is described by means of the E-R Model and navigation is specified using the Navigation Conceptual Model (NCM). OOHDM (Object-Oriented Hypermedia Design Method) is concerned with the conceptual modeling, navigation design, interface design, and implementation of hypermedia applications. Navigational contexts in OOHDM provide a rich repertoire of fixed navigation options. There also exist several proposals for using UML [4] for modeling the architecture of web applications. Some extensions to the UML notation have been proposed by Conallen [7].

In this work, WebML [5] has been utilized as design platform for the discovery methods proposed, mainly because of the robust CASE tool called WebRatio [22] that it is supported by. In fact, WebML builds on several previous proposals for hypermedia and web design. It provides graphical, yet formal, specifications, incorporated in a complete design process, which can be assisted by visual design tools for expressing a hypertext as a set of pages made up of linked content units and operations, and for binding such content units and operations to the data they refer to. WebML is a visual language for specifying the content structure of a Web application and the organization and presentation of contents in one or more hypertexts. The first step of designing in WebML is to specify the *data schema* of the Web application, in order to express the organization of contents using E-R primitives. The next step is *Hypertext Design*, which produces schemes expressing the composition of content and the invocation of operations within pages, as well as the definition of links between pages. Apart from content publishing, WebML allows specifying data update operations, like the creation, modification and deletion of instances of an entity, or the creation and deletion of instances of a relationship. Special purpose operations, as e-mail, login, and e-payment, can also be specified.

1.1 Motivation

In a plethora of web applications the final outcome is a result of the joint design decisions made by separate groups of experts, often with diverse backgrounds. Typical examples of this practice are e-shops and e-learning environments. Furthermore, even when a modeling method such as the WebML is deployed in the development stage, such is the scale of the development that a large number of coordinated developers are required to deliver the end product. These facts account for inconsistencies, debugging overheads and moderate code and design reusability.

A first approach to face these problems is to apply design patterns during the development/implementation stages aiming at improving application consistency and overall quality. In this respect, Schwabe et al. [19] state: "It is not surprising that good applications apply a set of principles that can be systematized as patterns.". Nevertheless, design patterns are still devised by *experienced software designers*, who study or reverse-engineer a set of successful applications and then define one or more design templates. However, it is implied in [19] that the task of detecting re-usable designs is mainly carried out by a closed group of experts. The authors [19], report that the desired design patterns may be hidden in a particular instantiation of the problem making it hard even for experienced designers to come up with re-usable design examples.

On the other hand, the ability to detect, during the early development stages, similar design snippets or even larger design constructs that perform the same functionalities, can increase implementation consistency, application maintenance and quality. Additionally, a methodology to infer frequent constructs at the design level, when applied to the same application domain, can lead to safe conclusions as for when a specific construct constitutes a *design pattern*. The remainder of this paper is organized as follows: Section 2 presents in detail a methodological approach for identifying reusable design solutions within the conceptual schema of Web Applications, while Section 3 illustrates a validation example of the proposed methodology in an instance of an application scenario. Finally, Section 4 provides concluding remarks and discusses future steps.

2   Methodology and Metrics for Identifying Reusable Designs

The notion of design patterns as tools that describe a piece of design experience and/or expert advice and make it reusable, was initially conceived by the architect C. Alexander, in the context of architecture and urban planning [1]: "... *Each pattern describes a problem which occurs over and over again in our environment, and then describes the core solution to that problem, in such a way that you can use this solution a million of times over...*". Nowadays, the use of patterns has been further extended in a diversity of domains. In the field of software engineering, design patterns are increasingly used to capture expertise in object-oriented programming [12]. More recently, design patterns have been introduced in the Web modeling field as well, for describing the navigation and structure of Web applications [3], [14], [17], [18], [19]. The availability of design patterns, which offer verified solutions to typical page configuration requirements, further facilitates the task of the hypertext architect and enforces a coherent design style over large and complicated applications, augmenting hypertext regularity and usability [11].

2.1   The Notion of Design Patterns Within WebML

A primitive set of design patterns has already been identified in WebML, comprising compact and consistent, one-step solutions, applicable in real-life scenarios of Web applications. Patterns have been discovered for data design, by identifying typical roles of information objects within the data schema (i.e., core concepts, interconnection concepts, access facilitators), and typical data sub-schemas constructed around such roles (i.e., core, interconnection, access, personalization sub-schema) [6]. Patterns have also been defined for hypertext design, by identifying unit compositions representing typical hypertext navigation chains and *content publishing* (cascaded index, filtered index, filtered scrolled index, guided tour, indexed guided tour, object viewpoint, nested data, hierarchical index with alternative sub-pages). Moreover, WebML also introduces patterns for *content management* operations (object creation/deletion/modification, relationship creation/deletion, create/connect pattern, cascaded delete) [5].

A pattern in WebML, typically consists of a *core specification*, representing the invariant WebML unit composition that characterizes the pattern, and a number of *pattern variants*, which extend the core specification with all the valid modalities in which the pattern can start (*starting variants*) or terminate (*termination variants*). Starting variants describe which units can be used for passing the context to the core pattern composition, while termination variants describe how the context generated by the core pattern composition is passed to successive hypertext compositions [11].

2.2 The Methodology

In this section, we present in detail a methodology for mining recurrent design solutions in the conceptual schema of applications modeled using WebML. Our objective is to capture compositions of hypertext elements (pages, units, operations, links) serving several application purposes. Examples could be the arrangement of pages, units, and links for supporting the navigation between a number of core objects, or for accessing a core object via one or more access objects and creating a new object through an operation.

These configurations are captured in the process of (or after) modeling a Web application, are complementary to the WebML predefined set of patterns and can serve as effective design solutions enabling reuse, consistency and quality improvement in the development and maintenance process. The methodology can be applied to a large number of Web applications, in order to assist in the identification of templates for Web application frameworks for specific domains and in the discovery of new design patterns extending the predefined set of patterns supported by WebML, since the process of finding new patterns involves analyzing successful applications and reverse-architecting its underlying design structure [19]. In the remainder of the paper we will refer to these configurations as "candidate patterns" or "design constructs/solutions".

In the sequel we present in detail the seven steps of the extraction mechanism:

Steps 1 & 2: Conceptual Schema Initialization

1. Iteratively, we traverse each site view of the Web application's conceptual schema and search for the existence of predefined WebML patterns (content publishing and content management patterns) taking into account their variants. Every pattern found is stored in a *pattern occurrences repository*, along with its starting and termination variants. The repository also stores the occurrence frequency of each pattern. Fig. 1 depicts the retrieval of a filtered index, within a site view. The above can be achieved using XSL [11]. The XSL language [23] allows writing pattern-matching rules that can be applied to an XML document for generating a new XML document. Each rule contains a matching part for selecting the target XML elements, and an action part to transform the matched elements. The XSL documents serve therefore the purpose of extracting the instances of patterns from the XML specification of the WebML conceptual schema.

2. The purpose of this step is to create a more uniform conceptual schema, thus enabling the easier extraction of design constructs in the steps to follow. Taking into account the various predefined WebML pattern variants, and utilizing XSL rules, we substitute, where possible, the variants found within each site view with a default pattern variant. The default pattern variant is the one having the maximum occurrence frequency (e.g. if we find a modify pattern and its termination variant having the larger occurrence frequency is the same page termination variant, we

use it as the default pattern and substitute all the other variants)[1]. In case that more than one pattern is assigned the maximum frequency, we choose the first found.

Step 3: Design Solutions Extraction

3. We traverse each area, sub-area and page of all the newly generated site views, in order to locate identical configurations of hypertext elements along with their variants, either within a site view or among different site views, using the methodology presented in section 2.3. The configurations retrieved should not already belong to the predefined WebML set of patterns, but may contain one or more of them. The notion of a variant in this case follows the definition of the WebML pattern variants presented in section 2.1. This way, we extract a first set of design constructs. Fig. 1 depicts the retrieval of a design construct within a site view, while Fig. 2 represents the identification of such a design construct retrieved from two distinct site views. The constructs identified are stored in a repository (of candidate patterns), along with their frequency and a list of other parameters described in section 2.5.

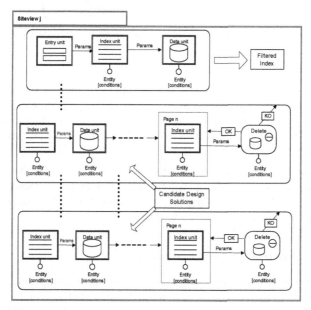

Fig. 1. Retrieval of a predefined WebML pattern and a design construct within a site view

Steps 4, 5 and 6: Extending the Sets of Design Solutions and Their Variants

4. Following the procedure described in step 2 and taking into account the design constructs and variants' definitions stored in the repository, we compute a new XML definition of each site view, by substituting -where possible- the variants with the default construct variant, aiming to create a more canonical schema. We

---

[1] This step requires the designer's intervention to assure that the substitution does not lead to inconsistencies in the conceptual schema

then repeat step 3 in order mine a larger set of hypertext configurations that have not already retrieved in the previous step.

5. Based on the procedure introduced in section 2.4 we try to capture larger – possibly combinations of – design constructs in order to enrich the repository with the maximum number of design solutions.

6. We examine every pattern within the repository and in case it contains a predefined WebML content management pattern, but one or more of the remaining patterns is missing, we add the respective missing ones. For instance, if we locate a design construct containing a create pattern, we complement it by adding the modify and/or delete pattern(s).

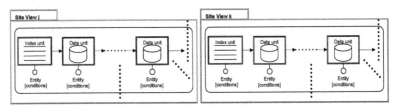

Fig. 2. Retrieval of a design construct from different site views

Step 7: Design Solutions Evaluation and Ranking

7. It is obvious that the number of design solutions obtained by the above methodology can be very large if applied to a complex Web application or even worse to a number of applications. Thus a first evaluation has to be performed in order to decrease their number, and provide a first level of ranking. An analytical method accomplishing that is presented in section 2.5.

Upon the completion of the above steps, the hypertext architect has access to a repository that contains a set of design solutions along with their variants. This library is composed of basic design configurations and combinations of larger ones that can be extended (in terms of usage) by defining new variants.

2.3   Automated Extraction of Design Solutions

In this section we describe a methodology for construct (compositions of hypertext elements) mining in the site views of a WebML fabricated web application. This approach is heavily based on graph mining algorithms. Intuitively, after modeling the site views as directed graphs the task is to detect frequently occurring induced subgraphs. The problem in its general form boils down to finding whether the isomorphic image of a subgraph in a larger graph exists. The latter problem is proved to be NP-complete [13]. However, graph mining appears in many contexts including bioinformatics and chemistry and therefore quite a few heuristics have been proposed to face this problem. The most prominent approaches include *gSpan* [25], *CloseGraph* [24] and *ADI* [21]. In the following we provide some notation prior to reducing the problem to graph mining.

We define a site view as a directed graph, $G(V, E, f_V, f_E)$, comprising of a set of nodes V, a set of edges E, a node-labeling function $f_V: V \rightarrow \Sigma_V$, and an edge-labeling function $f_E: E \rightarrow \Sigma_E$. f_V assigns letters drawn from an alphabet Σ_V to nodes in V, whereas f_E has the same role for edges and the edge alphabet Σ_E. Σ_V has a different letter for each different WebML element, where "element" includes content units, operations, pages, areas, etc. Correspondingly Σ_E comprises of all the different kinds of edges. We demand that units in WebML do not exactly correspond to nodes in V and the same is true for links between units and edges in E.

This choice was dictated by the rather complicated WebML conceptual model. We have to model the fact that a hyperlink can e.g. point to a data unit as well as to a hypertext *containing* several data units. Furthermore, links can also be classified into contextual and non-contextual, not to mention that a design construct can generally span different hypertexts. Therefore, before applying any graph mining technique, we preprocess the site view into its graph representation as follows: We process the WebML application definition and assign each unit and operation a letter according to its type. We install edges between units and label each edge with a 'C' (contextual), or with a 'N' (non-contextual). As a second step we map each page, area, etc. into a separate node. An edge is introduced between e.g. a page-node and the nodes corresponding to elements it contains. This containment edge is labeled with a special letter 'c', to denote containment. Note that arbitrary containment sequences can exist. A transformation example is depicted in Fig. 3.

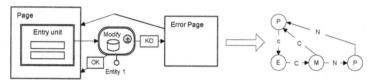

Fig. 3. Transformation of a WebML pattern to its graph equivalent

Once having transformed all site views with the same methodology, design construct identification is reduced to mining frequent subgraphs of the site view database. The latter can be accomplished with any of the methodologies in [21], [24], [25] provided the desired *support*[2] is given.

2.4 A Mechanism to Acquire Larger Design Solutions

A more complex case is the detection of implicitly interconnecting design solutions. It is about the cases of the proposed methodology step 4. The main concept is that new broader design solutions appear when taking into account the intermediate constructs as parts of the already detected variants (see Fig. 4). A minimal approach would be to look for couples of constructs that are interconnected through a single link or unit. However, we broaden the discovery procedure to include any number of constructs within a site view interconnected through intermediate structures. We think of larger design solutions to have identified constructs as a dominating part of them. As a result, we query for interconnection variants that are smaller than any other configuration involved in the larger design solution. Therefore, we utilize these constructs that include, at most, the minimum units among the configurations involved. In this way,

---

[2] The minimum percentage of occurrences in the entire database

we avoid exhaustive iterations or racing conditions. In worst case, a whole site view would be evaluated as candidate design solution, but it will be rejected according to the previous constraints.

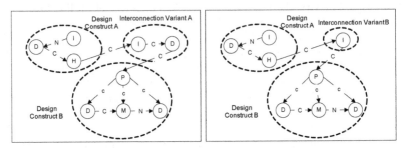

Fig. 4. Acquiring larger design solutions

2.5   Design Solutions Evaluation Metrics

After the completion of the above method, the number of design solutions identified can result very high. In fact this number increases when applying the method to a series of applications. Taking into consideration the occurrence frequency of a design solution can only partially help in distinguishing the most important design solutions. For instance, solutions that consist of two or three WebML elements will probably have the most high frequency. To provide metrics in the design solutions' identification process, a number of evaluation factors are taken into consideration, most of which derived intuitively but in a straightforward sense. These metrics are presented in the sequel.

The first metric has been already mentioned to be the frequency of a design solution. We call this metric *appearance f*. It is comprised by: a) f_o: overall number of appearing instances, b) f_a : number of areas that the solution appears in, c) f_σ: number of site views that the solution appears in and d) f_π: number of pages that the solution appears in.

The volume of the design solution is another important factor. Intuitively, the repetition of a "large" design solution cannot be a random event but rather the result of a detected design pattern. The "larger" be the design solution, the higher is the probability to detect an effective reusable pattern. As a result, we define *population p* that denotes the number of WebML elements involved. This metric is dependant on the following parameters: a) p_δ number of content units, b) p_t number of links, and c) p_{op}: number of operation units (including designer-defined generic operations).

Combining the frequency of appearance and the population of a design solution, the *importance* V_j of the design solution *j* can be computed as follows:

$$V_j = f_j \times p_j . \tag{1}$$

$$\text{where: } f_j = \frac{f_{o,j}}{f_{o,\max}} + \frac{f_{a,j}}{N_\alpha} + \frac{f_{\sigma,j}}{N_\sigma} + \frac{f_{\pi,j}}{N_\pi} , f_j \in [0,4] . \tag{2}$$

The notation f_{max} is the maximum value of the corresponding metric and N is the corresponding sum of areas, site views and pages overall in a specific WebML definition.

$$p_j = \frac{p_{\delta,j}}{p_{\delta,\max}} + \frac{p_{i,j}}{p_{i,\max}} + \frac{p_{op,j}}{p_{op,\max}}, p_j \in [0,3] . \tag{3}$$

One more metric that needs to be taken into consideration is the *complexity* d_j of the design solution j. Complexity depends on the *fragmentation* φ that represents the number of pages hosting the design solution. Complexity is defined as:

$$d_j = \frac{1}{\phi_j} . \tag{4}$$

Finally, the metric *entities involvement (semantic value)* e is introduced. It represents the number of data schema entities that participate in the design solution, when considering their conceptual involvement in the solution. The metric involves: a) e_c: entities belonging to the core sub-schema, b) e_{per}: entities belonging to the personalization sub-schema and c) e_{acc}: entities belonging to the access sub-schema.

The interconnection sub-schema is not taken into consideration, because it refers exclusively to the relationship between entities.

As a result, the semantic value e_j of the design solution j is set as follows:

$$e_j = \frac{e_{c,j}}{e_{c,\max}} + \frac{e_{per,j}}{e_{per,\max}} + \frac{e_{acc,j}}{e_{acc,\max}}, e_j \in [0,3] . \tag{5}$$

Overall, the *impact* I of a design solution j in a WebML conceptual schema combines all above metrics into a single value according to the following computation:

$$I_j = \frac{e_j}{\phi_j} V_j . \tag{6}$$

After estimating the value of the factor I_j for every design solution j in a specific conceptual schema, results are presented in a descending order to depict the most important and effective design solution on the top. This procedure can be applied recursively to site views of different applications in order to detect similar "pattern" implementation behaviors and to formulate groups of resulting design solutions as suggestions.

3 Exemplifying the Methodology

Due to space limitations we will exemplify a fragment of the methodology, referring to an instance of a multinational enterprise-intranet, in which we identify a candidate design solution. The data model of the application is rather simple and is omitted. We exemplify the third and sixth step of the methodology.

In the example depicted in figures 5 and 6, we capture a candidate design solution, by traversing two distinct site views of the intranet application. The first is a fragment of an employee's site view (Fig. 5), depicting a *News* area and the second is a fragment of the manager's site view including a *Forums* area (Fig. 6).

Comparing the two site views, we can easily identify the existence of a candidate design solution. It consists of the entire composition of WebML elements contained in the employees site view. When applying the methodology, this design construct is stored in the repository. Moreover, in the case of the manager's site view, one variant of the previously identified construct can be extracted. This variant extends the design solution with an object creation pattern (as shown in Fig. 6, the "*SelectedItem*" data unit is linked with an entry unit used to supply values to a create unit).

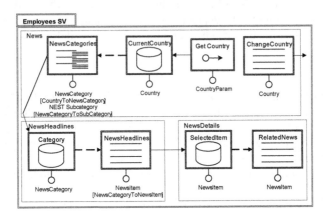

Fig. 5. A fragment of the employees site view depicting the News section[3]

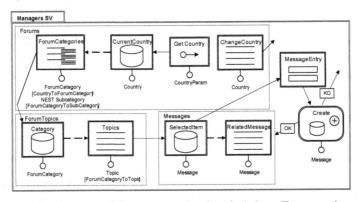

Fig. 6. A fragment of the managers site view depicting a Forum section

Once variants containing content management patterns have been retrieved, we should extend the repository with variants derived by the missing content management patterns. For instance, a variant containing the object deletion pattern in place of the object creation pattern should be stored in the repository, as well as all the possible combinations computed using all the content management patterns.

Thus, although we have retrieved only one common navigation chain, we have constructed and stored in the repository more variants. Moreover, we have possibly identified a candidate design solution for the public information exchange within the enterprise. The presented example only outlines the capabilities of the approach. To depict even more interesting and analytic paradigms multiple instances need to be involved and depicted on numerous figures impossible in the current context.

---

[3] *Get Country* is a *get unit* enabling the retrieval of a global parameter handing the applications multinational support

4 Conclusions and Future Work

This paper illustrated a methodology and provided metrics for discovering recurrent design solutions within an applications conceptual schema modeled using WebML. This methodology when applied to a large number of WebML application schemas can form the basis for the identification of templates in specific domain Web application frameworks and become a valuable tool for hypertext architects for the identification of Web design patterns.

The design solutions extracted can complement WebML predefined patterns in the process of modeling or redesigning an application providing effectiveness, reusability and consistency. Moreover, our methodology extends the quality evaluation framework presented in [10], [11] by means of providing a mechanism for capturing project data about the recurrent use of some design solutions, through the automatic analysis of XML application schemas.

The proposed approach has been designed and based on WebML. The transformation of a conceptual schema into a graph is a key point of the methodology. When this transformation can be achieved in cases of other design languages, then the main concept of the approach can be applied. Nevertheless, the specifics of this applicability need to be further investigated in the future. Moreover, fine-tuning has to be performed, even within WebML models, to support efficiently the transformation, while applying the methodology to a specific application domain and design approach. We currently implement and test several flavors of the methodology on different design solution cases.

In the future, we plan to extend the methodology by providing more precise metrics for the design solutions extraction taking into account a larger number of parameters quantifying the semantic context impact on the design configurations identified. Moreover, we plan to apply the methodology on a large number of Web applications, in order to refine the methodology and fine-tune the design solutions evaluation metrics. Finally as stated above, it is also open to investigate the particular circumstances of applying the methodology to other modeling languages.

References

1. Alexander, C., Ishikawa, S., Silverstein, M., Jacobson, M., Fiksdahl-King, I., Angel, S.: A Pattern Language. Oxford University Press, New York (1997)
2. Atzeni, P., Mecca, G., Merialdo, P.: Design and Maintenance of Data-Intensive Web Sites. Proc. EDBT. (1998) 436-450
3. Bernstein, M.: Patterns of Hypertext, Proc. of HyperText'98. Pittsburgh PA (1998)
4. Booch, G., Jacobson, I., Rumbaugh, J.: The Unified Modeling Language User Guide. The Addison-Wesley Object Technology Series (1998)
5. Ceri, S., Fraternali, P., Bongio, A., Brambilla, M., Comai, S., Matera, M.: Designing Data-Intensive Web Applications. Morgan Kauffmann (2002)
6. Ceri, S., Fraternali, P., Matera, M.: Conceptual Modeling of Data-Intensive Web Applications. IEEE Internet Computing, 6(4), (2004) 20-30
7. Conallen, J.: Building Web Applications with UML. Addison-Wesley, Reading MA (1999)
8. Fernandez, M. F., Florescu, D., Kang, J., Levy, A. Y., & Suciu, D. (1998). Catching the Boat with Strudel: Experiences with a Web-Site Management System. *In the Proceedings of ACM-SIGMOD Conference*, 414-425.

9. Fraternali, P., & Paolini, P. (1998). A Conceptual Model and a Tool Environment for Developing More Scalable, Dynamic, and Customizable Web Applications. *In the Proceedings of EDBT 1998*, 421-435.
10. Fraternali, P., Matera, M., Maurino, A.: Conceptual-Level Log Analysis for the Evaluation of Web Application Quality. Proc. of IEEE LA-Web Conference. Chile (2004)
11. Fraternali, P., Matera, M., Maurino, A.: WQA: an XSL Framework for Analyzing the Quality of Web Applications. Proc. of IWWOST'02. Malaga Spain (2002)
12. Gamma, E., Helm, R., Johnson, R., Vlissedes, J.: Design Patterns - Elements of Reusable Object Oriented Software. Addison Wesley (1995)
13. Garey, M.,R., Johnson, D., S.: Computers and Intractability: A guide to NP-Completeness. Freeman, New York (1979)
14. Garzotto, F., Paolini, P., & Schwabe, D. (1993). HDM - A Model-Based Approach to Hypertext Application Design. *TOIS*, 11 (1), 1-26.
15. Garzotto, F., Paolini, P., Bolchini, D., Valenti, S.: Modeling-by-Patterns of Web Applications. In Proceeding of the ER'99 Workshop "World Wide Web and Conceptual Modeling". Paris France (1999) 293-306
16. Isakowitz, T., Stohr, E., & Balasubramanian, P. (1995). RMM: A Methodology for Structured Hypermedia Design. *Communications of the ACM*, 38 (8), 34-44.
17. Nanard, M., Nanard, J., Kahn, P.: Pushing Reuse in Hypermedia Design: Golden Rules, Design Patterns and Constructive Templates. In Proc. of ACM Hypertext'98. Pittsburgh, PA (1998) 11-20
18. Schwabe, D, Esmeraldo, L., Rossi, G., Lyardet, F.: Engineering Web Applications for Reuse. IEEE Multimedia. Vol. 8, Issue1. (2001) 20-31
19. Schwabe, D., Garrido, A., Rossi, G.: Design Reuse in Hypermedia Applications Development. In Proc. of ACM Hypertext '97. Southampton, UK (1997) 57-66
20. Schwabe, D., Rossi, G.: An Object-Oriented Approach to Web-Based Application Design. Theory and Practice of Object Systems (TAPOS). vol. 4. no. 4, (1998) 207-225
21. Wang, C., Wang, W., Pei, J., Zhu, Y., Shi, B.: Scalable Mining of Large Disk-based Graph Databases. In Proc. ACM KDD04. (2004) 316-325
22. WebRatio: http://www.webratio.com
23. XSL: Extensible Style sheet Language. W3C Recom. http://w3.org/TR/XSL/. (2001)
24. Yan, X., Han, J.: CloseGraph: mining closed frequent graph patterns. In Proc. of KDD03. (2003) 286-295
25. Yan, X., Han, J.: gSpan: Graph-based substructure pattern mining. In Proc. of Int. Conf. on Data Mining (ICDM'02). Maebashi (2002) 721-724

The Role of Visual Tools in a Web Application Design and Verification Framework: A Visual Notation for LTL Formulae

Marco Brambilla[1], Alin Deutsch[2], Liying Sui[2], and Victor Vianu[2]

[1] Dipartimento Elettronica e Informazione, Politecnico di Milano,
Via Ponzio 34/5, 20133 Milano, Italy
mbrambil@elet.polimi.it
[2] Computer Science and Engineering Dept., UC San Diego,
La Jolla, CA 92093-0114, USA
{deutsch,lsui,vianu}@cs.ucsd.edu

Abstract. As the Web becomes a platform for implementing complex B2C and B2B applications, there is a need to extend Web conceptual modeling to process-centric applications. In this context, new problems about process safety and verification arise. Recent work has investigated high-level specification and verification of Web applications. This relies on a formal data-driven model of the application, which can access an underlying database as well as state information updated as the interaction progresses, and a set of user inputs. Properties verified concern the sequences of events, inputs, states, and actions resulting from the interaction. For the purpose of automatic verification, properties are expressed in linear-time or branching-time temporal logics. However, temporal logics properties are difficult to specify and understand by users, which can be a significant obstacle to the practical use of verification tools. In the present paper, we propose two alternative visual notations for specifying temporal properties. One alternative is to restrict the sequences of events using existing workflow specifications, such as BPMN, describing the execution flow of tasks within the application. However, such workflow formalisms have limited ability to express temporal properties. Another alternative is to develop a visual approach for explicitly specifying temporal operators, thus recovering their full expressiveness.

1 Introduction

Since the Web is becoming the most popular implementation platform for complex B2B applications, supporting business processes becomes a priority for Web application design, and development lifecycles should explicitly consider this aspect. The spread of Web applications interacting with users and programs while accessing an underlying database has been accompanied by the emergence of tools for their high-level specification [1, 10]. A representative, successful example is WebML [4, 11], which allows to specify a Web application using a visual interactive variant of the E-R model augmented with a workflow and query formalism. The code for the Web application is automatically generated from the WebML specification. This not only allows fast prototyping and productivity increment, but also provides a new opportunity for the automatic verification of Web applications.

D. Lowe and M. Gaedke (Eds.): ICWE 2005, LNCS 3579, pp. 557–568, 2005.

We focus here on interactive Web applications modeled by WebML, generating Web pages dynamically by queries on an underlying database. The Web application accepts input from external users or programs. It responds by taking some action, updating its internal state database, and navigating to a new Web page determined by yet another query. A run is a sequence of inputs together with the Web pages, states and actions generated by the Web application. We use a WebML-style formalism proposed in [6], which models the queries used in the specification as first-order queries (FO).

As discussed in [6, 7], verification of high-level WebML-like specifications concerns properties of the sequences of events, inputs, states, and actions resulting from the interaction, which range from basic soundness of the specification (e.g. the next Web page to display is always uniquely defined) to semantic properties (e.g. no order is shipped before the payment is received). Of special interest are workflow-based properties, describing the execution flow of the tasks within the application. Those properties can capture activity execution constraints and special process features like pro-activity, exception handling, errors compensation. Such properties can be expressed using an extension of linear-time temporal logic (LTL), called LTL-FO [8]. Properties of runs of a Web application are defined by formulae using temporal operators such as G, F, X, U, and B. For example, Fp means that p eventually holds; and pBq holds if either q always holds, or it eventually fails and p must hold sometime before q becomes false. Classical LTL formulae are built from propositional variables, using temporal and Boolean operators. An LTL-FO formula is obtained by combining FO formulae with temporal and boolean operators (but no further quantifications). The remaining free variables in the resulting formula are universally quantified at the very end. For example, the LTL-FO formula

$$\forall x \forall y \forall id[(pay(id,x,y) \wedge price(x,y))B\neg Ship(id,x)]$$

states that whenever item x is shipped to customer id, a payment for x in the correct amount must have been previously received from customer id. Results in [6] show that it is decidable in PSPACE whether a Web application specification satisfies a LTL-FO formula, under a restriction called input boundedness. Input boundedness requires that all quantified variables range over values from user inputs, in all formulae used in the rules of the specification. And in [7], the authors implemented a verifier for high-level WebML-style specification languages, based on the result in [6].

While the results of [6, 7] on automatic verification are encouraging, describing formal models of applications and temporal logic properties is a very technical task, which many designers may not appreciate, since specifying even simple temporal properties can be complex and error-prone. Indeed, LTL properties are difficult for the average user involved in specification, design, development, and verification of Web applications since he is not a logic expert. To increase the likelihood of acceptance by users, a more user-friendly and easy to understand visual tool for specifying temporal properties is called for.

Existing workflow specification languages already provide a way to specify temporal constraints on the sequence of activities. Thus, they may be an appealing way to specify temporal properties. To investigate this possibility, we focus on BPMN, a well known notation for workflows. We begin by providing semantics to the BPMN notation in terms of LTL formulae. This has a twofold benefit: first, it allows compiling BPMN specifications into LTL formulas, which can then be passed on to a verifier; second, it provides insight into the ability of BPMN diagrams to express LTL properties. In particular, it turns out that BPMN cannot express all LTL properties (for example, BPMN cannot express the X operator, or negation). Given such limitations of BPMN, we next consider an extension of this formalism with explicit temporal operators, which achieves full expressiveness relative to LTL. The extension is consistent with the workflow-oriented visual style of BPMN.

Other works use visual notations for model checking, but with a quite different flavor: in [5] lattices and other graph representations are used for multi-valued modelchecking, useful for analyzing models that contain uncertainty or inconsistency; [9] uses LTL for automatic checking of diagrams representing architectural models.

2 Overall Framework

This section describes the general framework of our investigation, providing a comprehensive approach to the design and verification of workflow-based Web applications. We make use of several existing software tools, techniques and methodologies.

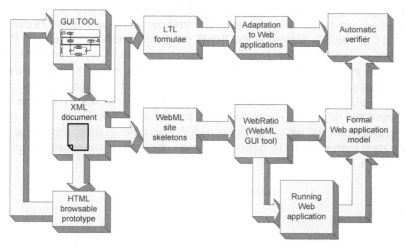

Fig. 1. Overall view of the proposed design and verification framework

The architecture we aim for is represented in Fig. 1: the central element is a visual CASE tool that allows the design of BPMN workflow diagrams and the automatic generation of LTL formulae to be verified on a given formal specification of a Web application. Since the tool produces a XML representation of the workflow, several other translations can be implemented, by simply programming new XSLT transformations.

For example, it is possible to exploit the workflow diagram to generate a browsable HTML or even JSP prototype. Another interesting transformation automatically generates Web application diagrams according to existing modeling languages for the Web. Some of these languages (e.g., WebML [2]), have been recently extended with primitives for business process management. To apply automatic verification, the Web application must be formally specified. This can be done by hand, or by implementing automatic translation. The verification itself can be achieved by using an automatic verifier such as the one described in [7]. The formulae to be checked can be LTL rules, automatically extracted by the BPMN representation of the site.

3 Workflow Notations

Workflow design methods concentrate on notations capable of expressing process specifications. These notations capture activity execution constraints and special process features like pro-activity, exception handling, error compensation. In B2B Web applications, the process must be deployed on the Web, which raises novel issues due to the specific nature of Web interfaces. First, Web interfaces lead to the prevalence of hypertext-based navigation as a mean of user interaction with the process; this navigation has to be well formalized and incorporated in the very design of the process to enact, in order to guarantee correct application behavior. Second, the pull-based nature of Web applications (the HTTP protocol imposes that clients ask the server to perform some computations) lacks convenient means for interactions initiated by the server (typically known as notifications).

Processes can be pictorially represented with the Business Process Management Notation [3], which is adopted by the BPML standard, issued by the Business Process Management Initiative. The BPMN notation allows one to represent all the basic process concepts defined by the WfMC [12] model, and provides further constructs, more powerful conditional gateways, event and exception management, free combination of split/join points, and other minor extensions. BPMN events (messages, exceptions, and so on) can occur during the process execution. Gateways are process flow control elements; typical gateways include decision, splitting, merging and synchronization points. Table 1 briefly summarizes the main visual constructs provided by BPMN.

Table 1. BPMN main constructs

Events

Start	End	Intermediate

Gateways

Or gateway	Xor gateway	And gateway

Activities and Flows

Activity	Pool and Lanes	Sequence flow	Message flow	Data Association

BPMN activities extend WfMC activities, as they can express various behaviors (looping execution, compensation, internal sub-process structuring, event catching, and so on). BPMN activities can be grouped into pools, and one pool contains all activities that are to be enacted by a given process participant. Within a pool, we use BPMN lanes to distinguish different user types that interact with the specific peer. The flow of the process is described by means of arrows, representing either the actual execution flow, or the flow of exchanged messages. Another type of arrows represents the association of data objects to activities; these are meant just as visual cues for the reader, and do not have an executable meaning.

4 BPMN Formalization Using LTL Formulae

BPMN appears to be a good and accepted notation for representing business processes. Since our target consists of verifying properties of process-based Web applications, BPMN is a good candidate as a visual representation of rules to be verified. For the BPMN formalization, we consider a significant subset of the full BPMN notation; indeed, BPMN comprises several particular symbols that are not interesting for the formalization.

The main actor in our solution is the concept of *activity*. An activity is a task to be executed, whose status is of interest. For sake of simplicity, we assume only two possible states for an activity: active and completed. In the following we adopt these abbreviations:

- A1a: $= A1.status=$ *"active"*;
- A1c: $= A1.status=$ *"completed"*.

Obviously, the following holds: $A1a \ B \ \neg A1c$.

This section presents the temporal logic translation of the main BPMN visual primitives. For the translation, we do not consider a single element at time, but significant combinations of elements. In our proposal, we assume that temporal operators are connected through conjunction. This means that it's possible to translate single elements (or simple combinations) and then connect them with AND ($\wedge$) connectors. Table 2 summarizes the proposed notation.

A **sequence** is a combination of two (or more) activities that can be executed only in sequential order. Its semantics can be naturally represented by the B temporal operator. The associated semantics is that activity A1 must complete before activity A2 can start. Because of the operator semantics, we introduce a negation on the second operand. The resulting LTL translation is: $A1c \ B \ \neg A2a$.

AND Split represents the case in which the execution flow is spawn in two (or more) parallel branches, thus enabling mandatory parallel execution of two (or more) activities. The semantics of And split can be represented by saying that both the branches must eventually be executed. Notice that we do not impose any constraint on the actual temporal parallel execution: one of the two activities may start (and finish) before the other, or vice versa, or possibly they may be executed in a real parallel enactment. The important issue here is that both of them must be executed. The resulting LTL is: $F \ A2a \wedge F \ A3a$.

AND Join represents the case in which two (or more) parallel execution flow branches merge into a single flow, after all branches are completed. The semantics is

Table 2. BPMN symbols translation in LTL formulae

BPMN CONCEPT	BPMN VISUAL NOTATION	TEMPORAL LOGIC
Sequence		(A1c B ¬ A2a)
AND split		(F A2a ∧ F A3a)
AND join		(A2c ∧ A3c) B ¬ A4a
OR split		(F A2a ∨ F A3a)
OR join		(A2c ∨ A3c) B ¬ A4a
XOR split		(F A2a xor F A3a)
XOR join		(A2c xor A3c) B ¬ A4a

represented by the fact that both A2 and A3 must complete before the next activity (A4) can start: *(A2c ∧ A3c) B ¬ A4a* .

OR Split represents the case in which the execution flow is spawn in two or more parallel branches, thus enabling possible parallel execution of two (or more) activities. Its semantics is that an arbitrary (non-empty) subset of the branches can be executed. Again, we do not impose any constraint on the actual temporal execution. The resulting LTL translation is: *F A2a ∨ F A3a* .

OR Join represents the case in which two (or more) parallel execution flow branches merge into a single flow. In this case, semantics implies that it is enough that one of the two activities ends for allowing the prosecution of the flow to the next activity (A4): *(A2c ∨ A3c) B ¬ A4a.*

XOR Split represents the case in which the execution flow is spawn in two or more branches, thus enabling the execution of one and only one activity among the available set. The semantics is that one and just one branch can be executed among a set of branches. The resulting LTL translation is: *F A2a xor F A3a.*

XOR Join represents the case in which two (or more) mutually exclusive execution branches merge into a single flow. Its semantics consist in allowing the continuation of the execution once one of the branches ends: *(A2c xor A3c) B ¬ A4a.*

Notice that explicit negation is not allowed for activities within a workflow diagram. This limitation is meant for allowing coherence with the semantics of workflow modeling, in which capability of negating the execution of tasks is not usually provided.

The above specification allows compiling a BPMN specification into an LTL formula, which can then be passed on to a verifier. The translation also points out limitations in the expressive power of BPMN. Indeed, it is clear that BPMN cannot express all LTL properties. For example, the *X* operator cannot be specified, and neither can negation.

5 A Visual Notation for Full LTL Expressive Power

Since BPMN diagrams cannot express all LTL properties, we would like to develop an extension providing a complete visual representation of Linear-time Temporal Logic. For this purpose, we extend the BPMN notation with a few other primitives. We take as the basic building block of the diagram any generic property instead of a process activity. Indeed, at this point we no longer deal explicitly with workflows, but rather with generic temporal formulae. However, the proposal presented next is completely compatible with the BPMN semantics in Section 4. A property is assumed to be a logic proposition that does not contain any temporal operator. In this sense, we suppose that a simple Boolean logic formula does not need to be visually represented. Visual aid becomes fundamental for expressing complex temporal properties.

As mentioned earlier, from the expressive power point of view, the workflow primitives fall short in two main respects relative to full LTL: using BPMN operators (and in general any workflow notation) it is not possible to specify explicit negation and the concept of "next step" in the time scale. Indeed, workflow languages do not need to provide such primitives. We cover these aspects with our extended notation.

For representing generic LTL formulae we adopt the following visual elements: a *property* is represented with a rounded rectangle, which is the same symbol of activities within workflows; *parentheses*, which are essential for specifying evaluation priority in formulae, can be represented by dashed blocks surrounding properties (this choice is coherent with BPMN notation, which introduces the concept of *group* for representing grouping of activities); *Before* is represented with a simple arrow connecting two properties, thus allowing compatibility with the semantics of workflow sequences (for coherence, we impose the arrow symbol to comprise the semantics of *Before Not*); for *Next* operator we propose a symbol that recalls the concept of after/before in BPMN, and then adds the notion of "immediately" after (a double headed arrow, as depicted in Table 3); *Globally* has no direct counterpart in BPMN (although it can be simulated), therefore we propose a symbol represented by a rounded rectangle with two slashes on the sides, ideally representing the fact that the property has no time limitations; *Eventually* is a unary operator, that we represent with a simple arrow, with no starting point, similarly to the Next operator (notice that the before operator has a similar symbol, but the arrow always starts from a property or a group); *Until* is represented by two properties that intersect on one side, to represent the fact that the first property must hold until the second one holds;

Classical Boolean operators *(And, Or, Not, Xor, Implication)* are represented by the diamond symbol of BPMN gateways: depending on the operator, the diamond contains the proper initial letter (e.g., *A* for And, *O* for Or, and so on). We decided to avoid using the symbol of "+" for And (like in BPMN) for coherence with the other symbols and because in Boolean logics the "+" symbol is often associated with the Or operator. In case of binary operators, the diamond directly attaches to the two operands. In case of unary operators *(Not)*, the diamond attaches to the single property the operator applies to.

Again, we assume that temporal operators at the same level of nesting are connected through conjunction. Notice that unary temporal operators, like Eventually *F* and Next *X*, must be represented only by arrows with no starting point, while binary operators can be depicted as arrows with a starting element.

Table 3. Visual translation of LTL operators

OPERATOR	LTL FORMULA	VISUAL NOTATION
Property	Prop	Prop
Before	(Prop1 B ¬ Prop2)	Prop.1 → Prop.2
Next	X Prop	o→ Prop
Always	G Prop	/ Prop /
Eventually	F Prop	o→ Prop
Until	(Prop1 U Prop2)	Prop.1 Prop.2
And	(Prop1 ∧ Prop2)	Prop.1 ⟨A⟩ Prop.2
Or	(Prop1 ∨ Prop2)	Prop.1 ⟨O⟩ Prop.2
Xor	(Prop1 xor Prop2)	Prop.1 ⟨X⟩ Prop.2
Implication	(Prop1 → Prop2)	Prop.1 ⟨→⟩ Prop.2
Not	not Prop1	⟨¬⟩ Prop
Parenthesis	(Prop1 ∧ Prop2)	Prop.1 ⟨A⟩ Prop.2

A shortcut notation can be adopted for unary operators, which allows to connect a starting point of a unary temporal operator directly to a logic connector (And, Or, Xor, Implication), as represented in Fig.2. Notice also that the proper combination of sequence arrows and Boolean diamonds can produce the same effect as BPMN gateways.

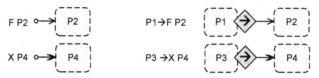

Fig. 2. Visual shortcuts for unary temporal operators

To illustrate the resulting diagrams, we provide some examples of visual notation corresponding to given LTL formulae.

Example 1. *(X P1) → G (P2 ∧ P3)*

Fig. 3. Visual diagram representing the formula of Example 1

Example 2. *((P1 ∧ not P2) U (P3)) ∨ (P4 B P5 ∧ P6 → X P7)*

Evidently, increasing the complexity of formulae results in increasingly complex diagrams. There is a reasonable complexity beyond which the visual notation becomes unpractical.

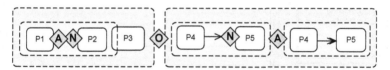

Fig. 4. Visual diagram representing the formula of Example 2

6   Implementation

This section presents the implementation of a prototype tool that allows to design BPMN diagrams and to automatically generate the corresponding LTL formulae. This tool has been developed to automate the generation of LTL formulae and to implement other automatic translations of BPMN diagrams. The implemented prototype allows designing workflow diagrams according to the BPMN standard. The designer can create, save and reload projects. At the moment, each project can contain only a single diagram.

The example shown in Fig. 5 is the BPMN specification of the process for the validation of an online loan request. The process takes place within a single pool, consisting of three parallel lanes, one per type of user. The process starts with an application request issued by an applicant, which is submitted for validation to a manager of the loan company. The manager may either reject it (if the application is not valid), which terminates the process, or assign it in parallel to two distinct employees for checking. After both checks are complete, the manager receives the application back and makes the final decision.

The tool allows top-down design of the application, because it provides also sub-process primitives, according to the BPMN specifications. This allows the designer to specify the workflow schema "in the large", and then he can drill down in the design, by detailing each single activity in more specific sub-processes. This multi-level representation of the workflow, can be automatically flattened in a single level workflow schema, from which the LTL formulae can be extracted.

The user interface of the tool is organized as follows: the *main panel* of the tool consists of a board for drawing, zooming and browsing the diagrams, provided with a set of buttons that enable the user to insert the proper visual primitives; on the top-left corner, a *bird's eye view panel* always shows the complete diagram (this is particularly useful in case of big projects); if the project includes sub-processes, at any level it is possible to have the bird's eye view of any super-level; on the bottom-left corner, a *property panel* provides the description of the currently selected object; the *menu bar* allows to execute automatic transformations of the diagram (e.g., to generate LTL formulae) and to set some preferences.

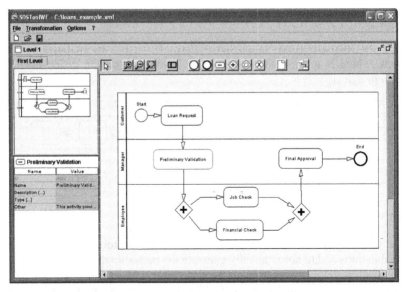

Fig. 5. CASE tool GUI for designing BPMN processes

The tool is designed to be flexible and extensible. It is able to manage user-defined properties of objects, and to dynamically add XSLT diagram transformations. The project is stored as an XML document and LTL formulae are generated using XSLT technology. Generation rules have been built based on the translation table presented in Section 4. To facilitate the translation, some assumptions have been made: gateways are considered as particular activities, thus allowing to insert them within precedence rules; in the transformation, it is enough to consider a pair of BPMN elements at time for defining the basic rules; the rest of the transformation is obtained through composition of such rules. These assumptions do not affect the generality of the transformation approach.

The LTL formula generated from the diagram shown in the picture is the following:

> *(F LoanReq.a)* ∧ *(LoanReq.c **B** ¬PreValid.a)* ∧ *(PreValid.c **B** ¬And1)* ∧ *(And1*
> ***B**¬(JobCheck.a* ∧ *FinCheck.a))* ∧ *((JobCheck.c* ∧ *FinCheck.c) **B** ¬And2)* ∧
> *(And2 **B** ¬FinApp.a)* ∧ *(**F** FinApp.c)*.

Its interpretation is quite straightforward: for each process instantiation, LoanRequest will eventually be active, and it will complete before PreliminaryValidation can start. PreliminaryValidation must complete before the And split is enabled, and the And split will be evaluated before both JobCheck and FinancialCheck can start. These two activities must complete before the And join gateway, which in turn must precede the FinalApproval activity.

7 Conclusions

The proposed approach allows representing temporal formulae in a visual fashion. Our visual notation is inspired by workflow notations and concepts, since they appear to be the visual models that best fit the description of temporal properties. We extended such notations to yield the full expressive power of Linear-time Temporal Logic, thus enabling non-expert designers to tackle the verification of Web applications. We stress that we do not advocate the need of a new approach for verification of Web applications: traditional verification results still apply. The main contribution of this paper stands in the contribution of a visual notation for LTL formulae representation, which dramatically increase acceptance of verification approaches by the Web engineering community.

The implementation of a tool that allows to visually design models and to automatically generate LTL formulae greatly improves the usability of the approach. Future work will address semantic specification of the BPMN multi-level feature (i.e., the capability of structuring processes in sub-processes). The tool currently supports only BPMN the diagrams. The next task is to implement the complete library of symbols proposed in Section 5 for covering full LTL expressive power. Other extensions will include: an XSL transformation towards WebML diagram skeletons for helping the designer to specify the hypertext of the Web application; an XSL transformation towards HTML browsable prototypes, and a more refined automatic JSP prototype generation.

References

1. Atzeni, P., Mecca, G., Merialdo, P.: Design and Maintenance of Data-Intensive Web Sites. EDBT 1998: 436-450.
2. Brambilla, M., Ceri, S., Comai, S., Fraternali, P., Manolescu, I.: Specification and design of workflow-driven hypertexts, Journal of Web Engineering, Vol. 1, No.1 (2002).
3. Business Process Management Language (BPML) and Notation (BPMN): http://www.bpmi.org
4. Ceri, S., Fraternali, P., Bongio, A., Brambilla, M., Comai, S., Matera, M.: Designing Data-Intensive Web Applications, Morgan-Kaufmann, December 2002.
5. Chechik, M., Devereux, B., Easterbrook, S., Gurfinkel, A.: Multi-valued symbolic model-checking. ACM TOSEM, Volume 12, Issue 4 (October 2003), pp. 371 - 408

6. Deutsch A., Sui L. and Vianu V.: Specification and Verification of Data-driven Web Services. PODS 2004: 71-82.
7. Deutsch, A., Marcus, M., Sui, L., Vianu, V., and Zhou, D.: A Verifier for Interactive, Data-Driven Web Applications. SIGMOD 2005, Baltimore, June 13-16,2005.
8. Emerson, E.A.: Temporal and modal logic. In Leeuwen, J.V., editor, Handbook of Theoretical Computer Science, Vol. B, pages 995-1072. North-holland Pub. Co./MIT Press, 1990.
9. Muccini, H.: Software Architecture for Testing, Coordination and Views Model Checking. Ph.D. Thesis, 2002.
10. Schwabe, D., Rossi, G.: An Object Oriented Approach to Web Applications Design. TAPOS 4(4): (1998).
11. WebML Project Homepage: http://www.webml.org
12. Workflow Management Coalition Homepage: http://www.wfmc.org

OOHDMDA – An MDA Approach for OOHDM

Hans Albrecht Schmid and Oliver Donnerhak

University of Applied Sciences Konstanz, Brauneggerstr. 55, D 78462 Konstanz
`schmidha@fh-konstanz.de`

Abstract. The MDA approach "OOHDMDA" generates servlet-based Web applications from OOHDM. An OOHDM application model, built with a UML design tool, is complemented with the recently proposed behavioral OOHDM semantics to serve as a PIM. This paper describes the transformation from a PIM XMI-file into a PSM XMI-file for a servlet-based PSM. It is performed by an XMINavigationalTransformer, which contains an XMI parser and a transformation class for each transformation rule.

1 Introduction and Related Work

The model-driven architecture (MDA) [1] models the business aspects of an application in a platform-independent model (PIM). The technological aspects are added when the PIM is transformed into a platform-specific model (PSM).

The modeling and design method OOHDM [2] describes hypermedia-based Web applications by an object model on three levels: the conceptual level, the navigational level, and the interface level. OOHDM is well-suited as a starting point for MDA since it is a platform-independent model, and it is an object model, so that the object classes may be easily transformed. But it has no well-defined semantics.

Therefore, we use an OOHDM application model only as a base PIM, adding to it the behavioral semantics definition of OOHDM core features and business processes [3]. This semantics derives application-related OOHDM classes from behavioral model classes with a predefined semantics, which is well-defined and executable.

This paper describes the OOHDMDA approach for a servlet-based PSM (see [4] for an overview). It generates from an OOHDM application model and the behavioral semantics model a servlet-based Web application front-end that accesses backend classes. For lack of space, we must restrict the paper to present the transformation of dynamic navigation (which is sufficiently complex) as only example, though OOHDMDA covers currently all core constructs of OOHDM (but no contexts, etc.) together with business processes [5].

Different Web application design methods, like WebML [6], UWE [7], OO-H [7], and OOWS [8], generate code from the Web page design or a design model. OOWS captures functional system requirements formally to construct from them the Web application. [9] compares the annotation approach and the diagram approach for the automatic construction of Web applications.

After an overview on the MDA-process with OOHDM in section 2, we describe the PIM for dynamic navigation with the behavioral semantics definition in section 3. Section 4 presents for dynamic navigation the transformation to a servlet-based PSM as platform-specific model.

D. Lowe and M. Gaedke (Eds.): ICWE 2005, LNCS 3579, pp. 569–574, 2005.

2   MDA Process

A Web application designer designs with a UML-based design tool the OOHDM conceptual and navigational schema of a Web application (without behavioral model classes) as the **Base PIM** for the MDA process (see Fig. 1.). The OOHDM classes are to be marked with a stereotype indicating the model class, from which the OOHDM class is derived

The **Base PIM to PIM transformation** transforms the output XMI-file of the design tool to a modified UML class diagram: it replaces navigational links by model classes; it derives the base PIM classes from the model classes according to the stereotype and adds the model classes; it adds directed associations from nodes to the associated conceptual schema entities; and does further smaller transformations.

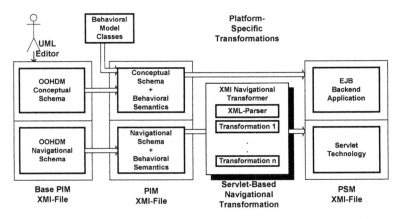

Fig. 1. Conceptual and navigational Base PIM, PIM and transformation to servlet-based Navigational PSM with XMINavigationalTransformer

The OOHDM conceptual and navigational schemas represent two different, relatively independent aspects of a Web application, the Web front-end, and the application backend. Consequently, we partition also the PIM into a **Conceptual PIM** submodel and the **Navigational PIM** sub-model (see Fig. 1.). The Conceptual Transformation and Navigational Transformation (see Fig. 1.) are completely independent, except for the operation invocations of Conceptual PSM objects from the Navigational PSM, where the kind of invocation may vary. Thus, you may select and combine the implementation technology and platform of the Conceptual PSM and the Navigational PSM quite independently, as [4] shows.

This paper focuses on the **Navigational Transformation** from the Navigational PIM into a servlet-based Navigational PSM, both represented by files in XMI format. It is described by transformation rules. Since we could not find a transformation tool to be parameterized with the transformation rules meeting our requirements, we developed an XMINavigationalTransformer, which contains an XMI parser, and for each transformation rule a transformation class. It generates as output an XMI file, from which the PSM to code transformation (not shown in Fig. 1.) generates Java code.

3 Navigational PIM for Dynamic Navigation

The OOHDM behavioral semantics derives the OOHDM application model from behavioral model classes, as e.g. conceptual schema entities, like CD, from a model class, like Entity or subclasses, and navigational schema nodes, like CDNode, from a model class, like Node or subclasses. Model classes collaborate with a Web Application virtual Machine (WAM), which models basic Web-browser characteristics, i.e. HTTP-HTML characteristics, as seen from a Web application. Both model classes and WAM have a well-defined behavioral semantics [3].

Class Node defines the operations: getPage(): Page, getField(n:Name): Value, setField(n: Name, v: Value), getFieldNames(): Name [], which are mainly used by the WAM to display the content of a page. A Node refers to the entity or entities it displays, and contains an array of InteractionElements like Anchor's or Button's, and a Page. Node has subclasses FixedEntityNode and DynEntityNode that represent pages with a fixed content and dynamically generated content.

We distinguish two kinds of navigation, navigation to a Web page with fixed content and dynamic content, i.e. navigation to a FixedEntityNode and DynEntityNode. We present the PIM for the latter one.

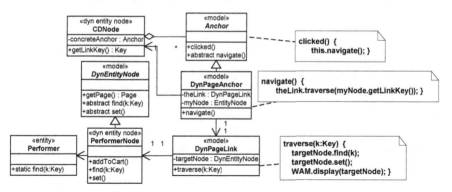

Fig. 2. PIM for dynamic navigation from CDNode to PerformerNode

Fig. 2. shows the PIM for a dynamic link in the navigational schema, like one from (the user-defined classes) CDNode to PerformerNode. The source node, like CDNode, references a DynPageAnchor that references a DynPageLink, which references the target node of the link, a DynEntityNode like PerformerNode. These references are set by a constructor parameter when the model classes are configured to work together.

The WAM has the attribute currentNode, which references the currently displayed Node. When a user clicks at an InteractionElement of the currently displayed Web page, like the anchor of a dynamic link on the CD Web page, the WAM calls the clicked-operation of the corresponding InteractionElement of the currentNode, like that of DynPageAnchor of CDNode, which forwards the call to the navigate operation. The navigate-operation fetches the key of the dynamic content that the target node should display, from the source node CDNode (referenced by attribute myNode), calling its getLinkKey-method that returns a key, like a Performer name. Then it calls the traverse-operation, passing the key as a parameter.

The traverse-operation of DynPageLink calls the find-operation of its target node, like PerformerNode with the key as a parameter, and then its set-operation so that the target node sets its dynamically generated content. Last, traverse calls the display-operation of the WAM with the target node as a parameter. The method display(n: Node) sets that node n as the current node and calls its getPage-operation to display the page.

4   Transformation to Servlet-Based Navigational PSM

A servlet connects the backend application with the Web; it runs on a Web server, receiving an HTTP request as a parameter of a doGet- or similar operation, and sending out a HTTP response as a result of the operation. The doGet-method analyses the user input and creates the new Web page as output.

The processing performed by a servlet is similar to the processing performed by the WAM in the Navigational PIM. The doGet-method of a servlet is triggered by a user interaction and reacts on that interaction by creating a Web page as a response, in the same way, as the OOHDM behavioral model is triggered by the WAM on a user interaction and creates and displays a mask for a Web page on the WAM.

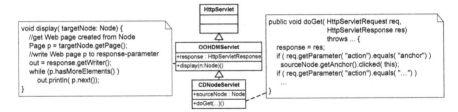

Fig. 3. PSM-classes CDNodeServlet with doGet-method analyzing request parameter and calling clicked-method of the clicked-at InteractionElement, and OOHDMDAServlet

As a consequence, the navigational transformation replaces the WAM by a servlet. The **EntityNodeToServlet** transformation rule generates from each PIM Entity Node class, like CDNode, a PSM servlet class, like CDNodeServlet (see Fig. 4.), that has a reference to the node, like PSM::CDNode, which is not modified from the PIM. When a user presses an interaction element of the Web page, the doGet-method of the generated servlet analyses the response parameter and calls the clicked-method of the pressed InteractionElement of the referenced node (see Fig. 3.).

The navigational transformation modifies also the Navigational PIM classes Anchor, PageAnchor, and Link, such that the new page is not displayed by the WAM, but put into the response-parameter of the doGet-method. Doing that straightforwardly would result in the Navigational PSM being very different from the Navigational PIM, which would make the navigational transformation a complex expenditure. To keep the transformation as simple as possible, we developed the solution that the servlet provides, similarly as the WAM, a display-method which puts the node into the response parameter.

Since that responsibility is identical for all node servlets, we introduce with the **EntityNodeToServlet** transformation rule the PSM class OOHDMDAServlet, extending HttpServlet, as common superclass of all NodeServlet classes (see Fig. 3.). Its method display(targetNode: Node) gets the associated Page from the parameter targetNode; since it has no direct access to the response parameter of doGet, it writes the Page to the member variable "response" that refers to the HttpResponse, after an assignment by the doGet-method (see Fig. 3.). Thus, the page contained in the parameter targetNode is put as content into the response parameter and displayed as Web page at the return from the doGet-method call.

The navigational transformation rules **Anchor**, **PageAnchor**, and **Link** modify the clicked-method of the class Anchor, the navigate-method of the class DynPageAnchor, and traverse-method of DynPageLink so that the traverse-method of DynPageLink can call the display-method provided by the servlet: a reference to the servlet is added as an additional parameter to these methods and forwarded from call to call.

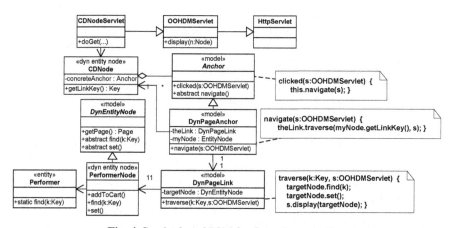

Fig. 4. Servlet-based PSM for dynamic navigation

Fig. 4. shows the resulting Navigational PSM for dynamic navigation. The method doGet of CDNodeServlet, which has a reference to CDNode, calls the clicked-method of DynPageAnchor, passing a reference to the servlet as a parameter. The transformed behavioral model classes collaborate in the same way as described in section 3, passing additionally a reference to CDNodeServlet as a parameter. The traverse-method calls the find- and set-method of the target node so that PerformerNode gets the dynamic page content from the DynEntity Performer, and inserts it into the DynPage that contains already the static HTML page content. Then, traverse calls the display-method of CDNodeServlet with PerformerNode as a parameter.

5 Conclusions

The OOHDMDA approach generates servlet-based Web applications from an OOHDM design model with the behavioral semantics as a PIM. It includes all core constructs of OOHDM and the business process extension [3] though dynamic navigation was given as only example. Based on atomic transformation rules, we have constructed an XMINavigationalTransformer, which transforms the PIM XMI-file into a PSM XMI-file. The trivial PSM-code transformation generates from a PSM

XMI-file executable Java code, which works quite efficiently. Our first experiences with the OOHDMDA approach and tool are very encouraging.

Acknowledgements

Our thanks are due to Gustavo Rossi for hosting Oliver in La plata, the International Bureau of the BMBF, Germany, for the Bilateral Cooperation with Argentina support; and the Ministerium fuer Wissenschaft und Forschung, Baden-Württemberg for a partial support of the project.

References

1. http://www.omg.org/mda/
2. D. Schwabe, G. Rossi: "An object-oriented approach to web-based application design". Theory and Practice of Object Systems (TAPOS), Special Issue on the Internet, v. 4#4, pp.207-225, October, 1998
3. H. A. Schmid, O.Herfort "A Behavioral Semantics of OOHDM Core Features and of its Business Process Extension". In Proceedings ICWE 2004, Springer LNCS, 2004
4. H. A. Schmid: "Model Driven Architecture with OOHDM". Engineering Advanced WebApplications, Proceedings of Workshops in Connection with the 4th ICWE, Munich, Germany, 2004, Rinton Press, Princeton, USA
5. H. A. Schmid, G. Rossi "Modeling and Designing Processes in E-Commerce Applications". IEEE Internet Computing, January 2004
6. S. Ceri, P. Fraternali, S. Paraboschi: "Web Modeling Language (WebML): a modeling language for designing Web sites". Procs 9th. International World Wide Web Conference, Elsevier 2000, pp 137-157
7. N.Koch, A.Kraus, C.Cachero, S.Melia: "Modeling Web Business Processes with OO-H and UWE". Procs. IWWOST 03 Workshop, Oviedo, Spain, 2003
8. O.Pastor, J.Fons, V.Pelechano: "OOWS: A Method to Develop Web Applications from Web-Oriented conceptual Models". Procs. IWWOST 03 Workshop, Oviedo, Spain, 2003
9. M. Taguchi, K. Jamroenderarasame, K. Asami and T. Tokuda "Comparison of Two Approaches for Automatic Construction of Web Applications: Annotation Approach and Diagram Approach" In Procs ICWE 2004, Springer LNCS 3140, Springer, Berlin, 2004

A Service-Centric Architecture for Web Applications

Hans Albrecht Schmid

University of Applied Sciences Konstanz, Brauneggerstr. 55, D 78462 Konstanz
schmidha@fh-konstanz.de

Abstract. Service-centric architectures are gaining more and more importance, due to their benefits over conventional architectures. We propose a service-centric Web application architecture that provides these benefits also for browser-based Web applications. An additional advantage is that B2C Web applications can be used also from B2B-clients. We extend OOHDM and its business process extension for service-centric Web applications architectures.

1 Introduction and Related Work

State-of-the-art Web applications are B2C (business-to-customer) applications where a customer may perform a spectrum of interactions like: navigation, the entering or updating of information, and the execution of business processes; with a business site or a similar site. Web application modeling and design methods (see e.g. [1,2]) mirror that spectrum, but do not reflect to a wide degree areas like business-to-business commerce (B2B) and Web services.

In B2B-commerce, the business processes of business partners communicate, without a person interacting. Web services, defining platform-independent and standardized interfaces for service invocation over the Web (compare [3,4]), are going to be predominantly used for B2B-communication [5]. Web service composition clients proposed for B2C [6] are not browser-based.

B2B-aspects and Web services have so far not really been integrated into browser-based Web applications. Currently proposed is an architecture that provides composed Web services in parallel to the Web application [7]. E.g., Amazon allows external software applications to search and order articles by a parallel Web service interface [8]. [9] introduce Web services as additional data sources for Web applications in WebML.

In this paper, we propose to integrate Web services into Web applications so that we move from a data-centric or object-centric to a service-centric architecture. The objective of that architectural change is to obtain a system structure with well-defined services as interfaces, which are more stable, better suited for internal reuse of services and for system evolution, and also usable in a B2B-environment. The differences to [7] are that the services are not offered in parallel to the Web application, but directly integrated, and that we address problems related to business processes and conversations.

We present in section 2 the service-centric architecture for Web applications, propose a slight extension of OOHDM that allows to model it, and compare it with the state-of-the-art architecture. Section 3 shows how business processes fit into the architecture, and how conversational services are modeled.

D. Lowe and M. Gaedke (Eds.): ICWE 2005, LNCS 3579, pp. 575–580, 2005.

2 Service-Centric Architecture of Web Applications

The **state-of-the-art Web application architecture (SAWAA)**, shown in Fig. 1. (left), is formed by: a browser; a Web front-end that is e.g. a servlet or a Java Server Page; a business object or application backend that is formed e.g. by persistent objects or Enterprise JavaBeans (EJB); and a database.

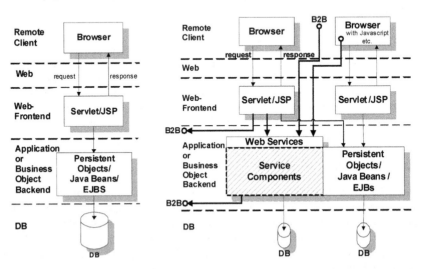

Fig. 1. State-of-the-art (left) and service-centric Web application architecture (right) with service and passive (top middle) and active (top right) HTML page

The interface of the Web front-end towards the browser defines a user request as an HTTP request type. This is a basic disadvantage of the conventional architecture, as the example of a hotel Web application shows. The hotel Web page contains information about the hotel, and a name and address input field and a button, which allow a prospective customer to request a hotel information flyer. The front-end servlet analyses the user input to the hotel page, detects a hotel information request, and processes that request together with the backend.

The problem is the Web front end receives a request for an action, like the hotel-info request, that is defined implicitly by the Web page layout, like that of the hotel page (since the request contains the names and contents of the page input fields, buttons, etc.). If somebody modifies that page, e.g. by splitting the address in city and street address, the application logic code of the front-end must be modified. Further, another Web page of the same application cannot reuse the request. Moreover, no external B2B-application can make a hotel-info request to the Web application.

A **service-centric architecture (SCA)** (compare [6]) that consists of relatively fine-granular (possibly distributed) components with service interfaces may solve these problems. Therefore, we introduce a **service-centric Web application architecture (SCWAA**, see Fig. 1. right) which has a **backend** that provides **business-related services** via a service interface.

Consider the hotel-info example: a SCWAA provides a Web service called *Hotel-Service*, which defines operations like *sendHotelInfo(String customer, String ad-*

dress, Hotel theHotel) sending the hotel information to the customer. A service like *HotelService* is called an **action service**, since it provides independent actions like *sendHotelInfo* as operations. An action service is provided by a service component, which the invoker of the service does not (have to) know.

Operations of a business-related service may be invoked (see Fig. 1. right, thick arrowhead lines), typically without dynamic discovery and binding, either from the Web front-end, or from an active HTML page, or from an external application.

1. The **front-end** is strongly simplified if it invokes an action service, instead of performing the related responsibilities itself. For example, if the hotel-info servlet invokes the *sendHotelInfo*-operation of the *HotelService* on a user hotel information request, its only responsibility is to return the next page as response.
2. An **HTML page** may invoke directly a Web service in a function call of a scripting language, like JavaScript, e.g. with Web Service Behavior libraries from Microsoft. We use that feature to invoke an action service, like *sendHoteInfo* (see Fig. 1., top right) directly from the page, like the hotel page, from which a user triggers the execution of an action. As a consequence, we achieve a clear separation of concerns: the HTML page with the scripting code has the responsibility for data entry and for the invocation of the action; and the front-end has the responsibility for dynamic navigation. Therefore, we prefer this architectural option.
3. An **external B2B-application** may invoke an action service provided by a Web application if it has the access rights. Thus, B2B-interactions may be executed with a browser-driven Web application. For example, a tourist information Web application can request a hotel flyer with a B2B-communication from the Web application of the selected hotel, invoking the provided *HotelService*.

Further, a Web application may invoke externally provided services as additional data sources from the Web front-end or from a backend service component, either public services like train timetable information, or B2B-services from another Web application.

Service Representation by OOHDM

We propose to represent an action service, like the *HotelService*, in the OOHDM **conceptual schema** as an interface with a stereotype like <<*action service interface*>>, which refines the stereotype <<*service interface*>> (see Fig. 2. left).

When a Web application provides and implements a Web service, the OOHDM conceptual schema may represent not only the Web service interface, but also the component implementing it, like the *HotelServiceComponent* that implements the service interface and collaborates with persistent classes like *Hotel* and *Customer* (see Fig. 2. left). When a Web application invokes an external service, it is not concerned about the implementation of the service. Therefore, the conceptual schema represents only the service interface, and does not show how it is implemented.

The OOHDM **navigational schema** (see Fig. 2. right) models the responsibilities of the front-end by nodes, like *HotelInfoNode*, that may have action methods, like *requestHotelInfo*. If a method of a node invokes a Web service, the node has a directed association to the service interface, which is represented by a circle.

Summarizing, a SCWAA provides the business-related services as a well-defined, clear and stable interface to the backend components, which might, as an additional advantage, also be realized by an existing application system in the context of enter-

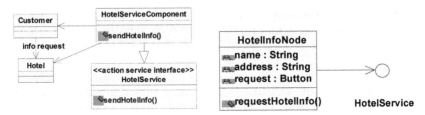

Fig. 2. OOHDM conceptual schema (left) with HotelService provided by HotelServiceComponent, and OOHDM navigational schema (right) with a directed association from the HotelInfoNode to the HotelService

prise application integration (EAI). Moreover, also external B2B-applications may
invoke services that are primarily provided for internal use.

3   Realizing Business Processes with Web Services

A B2C business process [2], like the check-out process of a Web shop, guides a user
in a prescribed order through several activities, like *Login, ConfirmItems, Select-
ShippingAddress*, etc. During each activity, the user enters specific data like the user-
login data; possibly after the activity has shown data from a database as default entries, like a previously entered shipping address.

A Web application with a SCWAA provides a business process service, like a
CheckOutService (see Fig. 3.). The difference to an action service is that a **business
process service** includes a set of interrelated operations, often one per activity of the
business process. For example, *CheckOutService* provides the operations *enterLog-
inData(u: UserData), enterOrderedItems(...)*, etc. The operation *confirmOrder* collects all entered data and creates a valid order. All operations or a subset of them must
be invoked in a particular order, called the conversation protocol, to complete the
business process. Thus, a business process service defines a **conversation**, which has
a state, in contrast to a sequence of stateless invocations. Both the definition of a
"conversational" service, and the interactions between such a service and a client
like the Web front-end are more complex than for single, independent invocations.

The operations of a business process service may be invoked, same as those of an
action service, from an active HTML page, from the front-end (we use the second
option for the reasons described in section 2), or from a B2B-application.

We model a SCWAA for business processes with OOHDM by including the business process service interface into the OOHDM conceptual schema and the invocation of its operations in the OOHDM navigational schema.

We use the check-out process of the Web shop example and present it with a
SCWAA, to allow a comparison with the SAWAA shown in [2]. The **conceptual
schema** (see Fig. 3. left) includes the business process service *CheckOutService* implemented by the component *CheckOut*. A business process like *CheckOutProcess* is
represented by a process class with the stereotype *<<root activity>>* with child activities as attributes. It has as responsibilities the sequencing among the activities, and
providing the pages to be displayed by an activity. A process is light-weight in comparison to the SAWAA, since the process service takes over all responsibilities related to the handling of process-related data entered by the user.

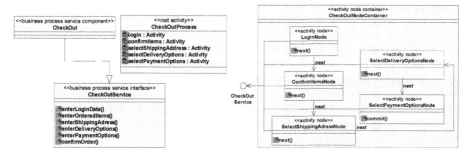

Fig. 3. OOHDM conceptual schema (left) and navigational schema (right) of the check-out process of a CD Webshop

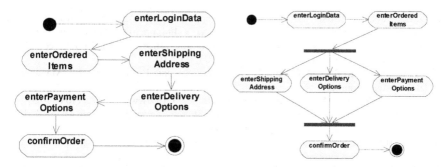

Fig. 4. Activity diagrams for CheckOutService conversation protocol specification

To specify the **conversation protocol**, we add for each business process service interface an UML activity diagram that represents the conversation protocol (see Fig. 4. for two alternative conversation protocols), to the conceptual schema. This is consistent with the OOHDM business process specification [2] that uses an activity diagram to define the correct sequences of activity execution.

The **navigational schema** (see Fig. 3. right) is similar as in the SAWAA, except for the activity nodes with methods invoking services. The differences is that the activity nodes have a reference to a process service, like *CheckoutService*, since their methods invoke an operation of it.

The navigational schema, implemented by the front-end, is designed so that it guides a user through the activities of a business process and presents the Web pages in an order that complies to the protocol specification.

4 Conclusions

We have proposed a service-centric architecture for Web applications that transfers the benefits of service-centric architectures to Web applications. It has been successfully used to implement several Web applications with business processes.

Due to lack of space, we could not address light-weight solutions for problems related to service-centric business process execution, like conversation protocol specification, protocol compliance verification and conversation routing. The light-weight solutions are adapted to the Web application scenarios which are simpler and less general than those for cooperating business process in the Web service community (see [10]).

Acknowledgements

My thanks are due to Marco Pfeifer and Thorsten Schneider for his help with the figures; and to the Ministerium fuer Wissenschaft und Forschung, Baden-Württemberg for a partial support of the project.

References

1. D. Schwabe, G. Rossi: "An object-oriented approach to web-based application design". Theory and Practice of Object Systems (TAPOS), V.4#4, pp.207-225, October, 1998
2. H. A. Schmid, G. Rossi " Modeling and Designing Processes in E-Commerce Applications". IEEE Internet Computing, Jan./Feb. 2004, pp.2-10
3. F.Leymann, D.Roller, M.T.Schmidt: Web Services and Business Process Management; IBM Systems Journal Vol.41, No2, 2002
4. W3C: Web Services Architecture Requirements. see: http://www.w3.org/TR/wsa-reqs
5. T.Andrews et al: Specification of the Business Process Execution Language for Web Services Version 1.1; at: http://ifr.sap.com/bpel4ws/
6. Procs. IEEE International Conference on Services Computing, Shanghai, China, 2004, IEEE Press, Los Alamitos, 2004
7. I.Manolescu, S.Ceri, M.Brambilla, P.Fraternali, S.Comai: "Exploring the combined potential of Web sites and Web services". Poster, Procs World Wide Web 2003
8. Amazon Inc.: Amazon Web Services; http://www.amazon.com/Webservices
9. M.Brambilla, S.Ceri, S.Comai, P.Fraternali, I.Manolescu: "Model-driven Specification of Web Services Composition and Integration with Data-Intensive Web Applications".
10. G.Alonso, F.Casati, H.Kuno, V.Machiraju: Web Services - Concepts, Architectures and Applications; Springer, Berlin, 2004

NavOptim:
On the Possibility of Minimising Navigation Effort

Xiaoying Kong and David Lowe

University of Technology, Sydney, P.O. Box 123, Broadway, NSW, Australia
{xiaoying.kong,david.lowe}@uts.edu.au

Abstract. Web applications have rapidly become critical to the interaction that organisations have with their external stakeholders. A major factor in the effectiveness of this interaction is the ease with which users can locate information and functionality which they are seeking. Effective design is complicated by the multiple purposes and users which Web applications support. In our earlier work we described a model for evaluating the weighted effort required of users. In this paper we describe an approach to minimizing this navigational effort.

1 Introduction

Over the last decade the Web has become a key vehicle for accessing organisational applications. These applications often provide crucial business or government services, and hence the quality of the user interaction and the extent to which users are able to achieve their goals is vital to the success of the systems. Given this, effective design of the web application interface is crucial. This in turn raises the issue of what is actually meant by "effective design"? Effectiveness can be defined in terms of the ability to support the users' goals – yet for Web applications these goals are typically both complex and diverse, with different users having different expectations and objectives. Optimising the design becomes a difficult activity involving trade-offs of multiple constraints. Despite this the design of navigation structures is rarely treated as an optimization problem.

2 Related Work

Numerous approaches have been developed for performing the design of the navigational structure of Web systems. Early approaches in this area tended to emerge from the Hypertext community and evolved out of work on Entity-Relationship modelling (e.g. RMM [1]) or object-oriented modelling (e.g. OOHDM [2]). Other approaches have included EORM [3] and WSDM [4], and more recently WebML [5]. The focus of these approaches is very much on modelling the underlying content, the user viewpoints onto this content, and the navigational structures that interlink the content. They have however usually undertaken the navigation design based on a subjective view of how users are likely to want to interact with the information. In most cases this is not well informed by the underlying requirements that drive this architecture. They do not typically provide any formal way to ensure that the navigation structures are theoretically optimal. There has also been substantial research investigating navi-

D. Lowe and M. Gaedke (Eds.): ICWE 2005, LNCS 3579, pp. 581–584, 2005.

gation design based on either likely usage patterns or an analysis of actual usage –
e.g. user-centred design [6]. Again, however, this does not guarantee a theoretical
optimisation.

3 Minimising Navigational Effort

In each of the above cases the approach is focussing on subjective analysis and refinement of the navigational structure. We argue that this is inappropriate, since the
design subjectivity lies not in the navigational structure, but rather in the significance
of the various information and services that are provided to users and the design
choices about the usage patterns which we wish the system to support. Once this is
known we ought to be able to design the navigational structure which provides the
theoretical minimum navigational effort required by users in accessing these services
and information – assuming we have a reliable measure of navigational effort.

In our earlier work we described a model of the relationship between the intended
user tasks, the navigational structure and the resultant overall navigational effort. The
overall weighted navigational effort for a site can be modelled as:

$$H_{sys} = -\sum_{j=1}^{n} [Sgnf(j) * (\sum_{i=1}^{m} p_i \log p_i)] \qquad p_i = \frac{SmtCoh(V_i, V_{Taskcase})}{\sum_{j=1}^{m} SmtCoh(V_j, V_{Taskcase1})}, i = 1:m \qquad (1)$$

where $Sgnf(j)$ is the significance of a particular task j, and $SmtCoh$ provides a measure
of the semantic cohesion between two information vectors, and V is an information
vector. Details on this model are given in [7]. Whilst this equation provides a basis
for evaluating and comparing designs, it still does not allow us to determine the theoretical optimum structure. We can compare this to data compression algorithms in
information theory: if we have a message "Msg" which consists of M different symbols, each with a given probability of appearing in the message Msg, then we can
then identify the theoretical minimum for the average number of bits to code each
character in the string. Further, techniques such as Huffman coding [8] provide an
algorithm that determines the the coding for each symbol in order to achieve this
minimum.

We would like to be able to identify an equivalent algorithm for determining the
navigational structure which achieves a theoretically minimum navigational effort.
We have however found this problem to be intractable. This is for several reasons.
The first is that whilst the Huffman coding tree is a binary tree, the NavOptim navigation tree is an n-ary tree where n varies in each branch of the tree. Even more problematic is that whilst the characters in the Huffman coding are independent, the same
is not true of the nodes in the NavOptim tree. The individual entropies of each navigational path are related to the location of all nodes within the tree. In other words,
whilst there will indeed be a thoereticaly optimal navigation structure for a given set
of task cases, the algorithmic determination of this structure is an intractable problem.
This then leads to the question of whether we can identify a (sub-optimal) approximation to the theoretically optimal navigation tree?

Given the intractability of finding a navigational design algorithm which can be
mathematical proven to result in the minimization of equation 1, we can turn our

attention to approaches which approximate an optimal design, but which are strongly guided by the underlying theory. We begin by analyzing the mathematical models captured by equation 1. The first observation is that the effort is strongly coupled to the overall navigational depth of specific content. As content is located deeper within the navigational tree, the navigational effort to locate it will typically increase (all other factors being equal). The second is that the effort is strongly related to the semantic cohesion. As we create stronger cohesion within branches of the tree, we enable clearer navigation choices and hence reduced entropy and effort. Figure 1 illustrates this issue graphically for different content clusterings, where the spatial positioning of the pages represents the semantic distance between the pages, and the highlighted page is the target of a given task.

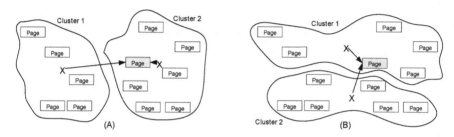

Fig. 1. Example clustering

4   Conclusions

In this paper we have discussed issues in the design of navigational structures based on the optimisation of a navigational effort metric weighted by the task significances. Subsequent work, to be published elsewhere, describes an approach which will lead to a reduction in the average effort required to locate information or services within websites. We are also investigating tools to simulate different websites to see how they are optimised using our approach, followed by subjective evaluation to determine whether this does indeed lead to qualitative improvements.

References

1. T. Isakowitz, E. Stohr, and P. Balasubramanian, "RMM: A Methodology for Structured Hypermedia Design," *Communications of the ACM*, vol. 38, pp. 34-44, 1995.
2. D. Schwabe and G. Rossi, "Developing Hypermedia Applications using OOHDM," presented at Workshop on Hypermedia Development Processes, Methods and Models (Hypertext'98), Pittsburgh, USA, 1998.
3. D. Lange, "An Object-Oriented Design Method for Hypermedia Information Systems," presented at HICSS-27: Proc of the Twenty Seventh Hawaii International Conference on System Sciences, Maui, Hawaii, 1994.
4. O. De Troyer and C. Leune, "WSDM: A user-centered design method for Web sites," presented at 7th International World Wide Web Conference, Brisbane, Aust, 1997.
5. S. Ceri, P. Fraternali, and A. Bongio, "Web Modeling Language (WebML): a modeling language for designing Web sites," presented at Proceedings of WWW9 Conference, Amsterdam, 2000.

6. D. A. Norman and S. W. Draper, *User-Centered Design*. Hillsdale, N.J.: Lawrence Erlbaum Assoc, 1986.
7. D. Lowe and X. Kong, "NavOptim Coding: Supporting Website Navigation Optimisation using Effort Minimisation," presented at 2004 IEEE/WIC/ACM International Conference on Web Intelligence, Beijing, China, 2004.
8. D. A. Huffman, "A method for the construction of minimum redundancy codes," *Proc. IRE*, vol. 40, pp. 1098-1101., 1952.

A First Step Towards the Web Engineering Body of Knowledge

Antonio Navarro, José Luis Sierra,
Alfredo Fernández-Valmayor, and Baltasar Fernández-Manjón

Dpto. Sistemas Informáticos y Programación, Universidad Complutense de Madrid, C/
Profesor José García Santesmases s/n, 28040, Madrid, Spain
{anavarro,jlsierra,alfredo,balta}@sip.ucm.es

Abstract. The *Software Engineering Body of Knowledge* (SWEBOK) is an IEEE-led project that provides an explicit characterization of the boundaries of software engineering. Inspired by SWEBOK, this paper proposes the formulation of a Web *Engineering Body of Knowledge* (WEBOK), an effort similar to SWEBOK for the Web engineering domain. The main goal of WEBOK development will be the explicit characterization of the boundaries of Web engineering. In addition, WEBOK will identify the areas of Web engineering more closely related to software engineering, and others that have evolved from software engineering principles. Finally, WEBOK will identify some areas of Web engineering where further research is necessary. Due to the great effort represented by WEBOK development, this paper presents a limited version of this with two purposes: (i) to serve as a first step towards WEBOK; and (ii) to promote the total development of WEBOK by the Web engineering community.

1 Introduction

The *Software Engineering Body of Knowledge* (SWEBOK) is an IEEE-led project that provides an explicit characterization of the boundaries of software engineering [8]. The body of knowledge is subdivided into ten software engineering *Knowledge Areas* (KAs): software requirements, software design, software construction, software testing, software maintenance, software configuration management, software engineering management, software engineering process, software engineering tools and methods and software quality. The descriptions of KAs are designed to discriminate among the various important concepts, thereby permitting readers to find their way to subjects of interest quickly [8].

The objectives of SWEBOK are: (i) to promote a consistent view of software engineering worldwide; (ii) to clarify the place (and set the boundary) of software engineering with respect to other disciplines; (iii) to characterize the contents of the software engineering discipline; and (iv) to provide a foundation for curriculum development and for individual certification and licensing material.

According to Murugesan et al. [6] *Web engineering* can be defined as the application of a systematic, disciplined, quantifiable approach to development, operation, and maintenance of Web-based applications or the application of engineering to Web-based software. In spite of the similarity between this definition and the IEEE definition of software engineering [3], Ginige, Murugesan and Pressman [2][7] consider Web engineering to be a new emerging discipline in its own right, rather than sub-

D. Lowe and M. Gaedke (Eds.): ICWE 2005, LNCS 3579, pp. 585–587, 2005.

sumed into software engineering. Therefore, we think[1] it is necessary to develop a *Web Engineering Body of Knowledge* (WEBOK), inspired by SWEBOK, but taking into account the special characteristics of Web engineering [1].

The Guide to the SWEBOK[2] [8] has been developed by hundreds of reviewers worldwide. In the same manner, we think that the Guide to the WEBOK should also be developed by a sufficient amount of reviewers in the Web engineering community to assure a body of knowledge agreed upon by consensus. Therefore, this paper is not so much a characterization of a body of knowledge as a seed for such a characterization. In addition, the WEBOK proposed in this paper resembles the KAs identified by the Guide to SWEBOK. We think that these KAs are consistent with the Web engineering domain and do not need to be changed, at least in this first step. Moreover, in SWEBOK, every KA is divided into several *sub-areas*, which are divided into *topics*. Due to the lack of space, in this paper we will focus mainly on these knowledge areas.

2 Conclusions and Future Work

We agree with Ginige, Murugesan and Pressman that Web engineering and software engineering are different disciplines. The great amount of specific literature about Web engineering, and our own experience designing and developing the *Virtual Campus* of the Universidad Complutense de Madrid [9], seems to support this claim. Therefore, we defend the interest of an explicit formulation of the WEBOK as the result of a shared effort by the Web engineering community.

Regarding KAs, software design and software engineering process are the ones that have received more attention from the Web engineering community. In our opinion, this success is due to: (i) the inherent need to organize the development process; and (ii) the need for design notations to characterize the design of a Web application. These *reality-driven* constraints have promoted the rise of these two KAs.

Pushed by software design KA, tools and methods areas have also had a significant impact, providing CASE support to the design notations presented in Web engineering. In our opinion, more feedback is needed about the use of these tools and the design notations that inspire them.

Finally the important KA of software requirements has found less impact in Web engineering than design KA. Work done in this direction is very important, and, in our opinion, more feedback is needed from the industry and the academy. For example, is the IEEE Std. 830 [4] a suitable way of characterizing the requirements of a hypermedia application? We think that this question is well worth further analysis.

The rest of KAs of SWEBOK are tightly related to Web engineering, but, again, we think that more feedback is necessary from industry and academy. In particular, software testing and related disciplines should be explored.

---

[1] We were not aware of the Kappel´s proposal [5] when we proposed the development of the WEBOK, but we agree with her

[2] For the sake of conciseness, in this paper we do not differentiate between a body of knowledge with its guide, although in practice, they are different things

Future work with WEBOK must involve the participation of the overall Web engineering community and should be aimed in two directions. Firstly, to expand and to complete the ideas presented in this paper Secondly, to explore in depth the KAs in order to determine the differences between software engineering and Web engineering. As a main result of this exploration, new KAs could emerge, and existing KAs could be changed or removed.

Acknowledgements

The Spanish Committee of Science and Technology (TIC2001-1462, TIC2002-04067-C03-02 and TIN2004-08367-C02-02) has supported this work.

References

1. Deshpande, Y., Hansen, S. Web Engineering: Creating a Discipline among Disciplines. IEEE Multimedia. 2 (2001) 82-87
2. Ginige, A., Murugesan, S.: The Essence of Web Engineering-Managing the Diversity and Complexity of Web Application Development. IEEE Multimedia. 2 (2001) 22-25
3. IEEE Std. 610.12-1990 IEEE standard glossary of software engineering terminology
4. IEEE Std. 830-1998 IEEE recommended practice for software requirements specification
5. Kappel, G. Web Engineering, Old Wine in New Bottles? International Conference on Web Engineering 2004. Invited Talk. http://www.icwe2004.org/download/ICWE_Kappel.pdf
6. Murugesan, S., Deshpande Y., Hansen, S., Ginige, A.: Web Engineering: A New Discipline for Development of Web-Based Systems. Web Engineering, Software Engineering and Web Application Development. LNCS Vol. 2016 (2001) 3-13.
7. Pressman, R.S.: Software Engineering: A Practitioner's Approach. 5th edition. McGraw-
8. SWEBOK Project Website. Guide to the Software Engineering Book of Knowledge. http://www.swebok.org
9. UCM Virtual Campus. https://campusvirtual1.ucm.es/cv/

Design Considerations
for Web-Based Interactive TV Services*

Meng-Huang Lee and He-Rong Zhong

Department of Information Management, Shih-Chien University, Taipei, 104 Taiwan
`meng@mail.usc.edu.tw`

Abstract. Due to the performance limitation of set-top-box and viewing behavior of TV users, web page design for ITV services is not as same as for Internet. In this paper, we present two practical concerns and their solutions for the web application design for web-based ITV services.

1 Introduction

Current interactive TV (ITV) services adopt web-based and IP based technologies [1]. In web-based ITV services, there is a set-top-box connecting to Internet by ADSL or Cable Modem and using TV monitor as its display device [4]. By these technologies, ITV services are very similar to traditional Internet services except the devices at client's side are set-top-box with TV display. For the technical issues and cost issues, a set-top-box is something like a PC but with limited resources. It also has CPU, RAM, small disk size and MPEG-2 decoder, etc. but the computing power and capacity are far away from the specifications of current off-the-shelf PC [2],[3].

In addition to system resource limitation, ITV user's viewing behavior issue also makes the web page design different from Internet. For computer users, the input or navigation devices are keyboard and mouse. When they click one button or keystroke, they usually watch the response from the computer. But for ITV users, they use controllers as their interactive devices and they are used to the quick response of traditional TV services. In web-based ITV services, the browsing and navigation procedure are similar to Internet web-based services. The system loads the web pages from web servers and the browser in the set-top-box then processes web pages and displays the results on TV screen. For the limited processing power of set-top-box, the response time of web page transition is not as quick as expectation of traditional TV services. Most ITV users do not know these procedures, they just wonder if something wrong in the system. Then a lot of controller presses are issued and finally the set-top-box crashes. Turn-off the set-top-box and turn-on again seems the only way that users can do for the situations.

In this paper, we propose two practical solutions in our system design. In section 2, *key-lock* mechanism is used to disable all the inputs during the web page transition and avoids system crash. In section 3, scrolling mechanism is used to reduce the number of web transition of an ITV service.

---

* This work has been supported in part by Shih-Chien University, Taiwan, under Grant USC 93-05-38804-035 and by Imagetech Co. Ltd, Taipei, Taiwan

D. Lowe and M. Gaedke (Eds.): ICWE 2005, LNCS 3579, pp. 588–590, 2005.

2 *Key-Lock* During Web Page Transition

The web page transition usually occurs when a page is leaving and a new page is loading. During the transition, the system design is to disable all the inputs from users and make sure the transition is safe. To assure the *key-lock* during the transition, *key-lock* mechanism is activated when current page is leaving and the new page is fully loaded. Fig.1 shows the *key-lock* mechanism for the web page transition.

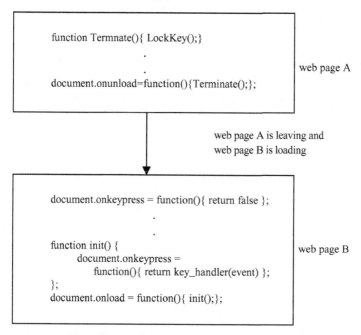

Fig. 1. The *key-lock* mechanism during web page transition

3 Using Scrolling Mechanism to Reduce Number of Web Page Transition

Due to the slow transition of web pages, avoiding lots of web page transition in a service is a key design concept. In traditional web applications, the browser can resize its display window, and if the page presentation exceeds the size, then a scroll bar in horizontal axis or vertical axis will appear such that the user can scroll the presented page. But for ITV services, TV screen resolution is fixed (e.g. NTSC screen is set to 640X480) and it lacks the input devices (e.g. mouse) for a user scrolls the presented page manually so that the exceeded part of the presented page can not be seen on screen by user. This feature gives a good direction for the web page design to avoid lots of web page transition. Fig.2 assumes three menu items and an area on the right side to show the corresponding information page when a menu item is selected. According our design described above, the information pages for Menu-item-1, Menu-item-2, and Menu-item-3 are all loaded in one web page transition. If a user selects Menu-item-2, our web page program just scrolls to the corresponding position of the information page of Menu-item-2. For the TV resolution is fixed, only Menu-item-2 information page can be seen on the screen and information pages of Menu-item-1 and Menu-item-3 are hidden on the screen(even though they are loaded).

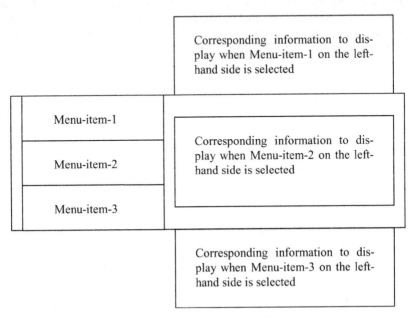

Fig. 2. An example for the menu application using scrolling design

References

1. George Abe: Residential Broadband, Second Edition.Cisco Press, 2000.
2. Browser Development Guide. 2000 Pace Micro Technology plc.
3. Web & Video Application Design's Guide for IP Set-Top-Box (PB03018 Project). Fox-conn, 2004.
4. Meng-Huang Lee: System Architecture for Interactive Home TV Services. 8th IEEE International Symposium on Consumer Electronics, Reading, UK, September 3, 1996.

Web Service Based Integration
of Biological Interaction Databases

Seong Joon Yoo[1], Min Kyung Kim[2], and Seon Hee Park[3]

[1] School of Computer Engineering, Sejong University,
98 Gunja, Gwangjin, Seoul, Korea 143-747
sjyoo@sejong.ac.kr
[2] Department of Computer Science and Engineering, Ewha University,
11-1 Daehyun-dong, Seodaemun-gu, Seoul, 120-750, Korea
minkykim@ewha.ac.kr
[3] Bioinformatics Team, Electronics and Telecommunication Research Institute,
161 Gajeong-Dong, Yuseong-Gu, Daejun, 305-350, Korea
shp@etri.re.kr

Abstract. While designing a web service based integration framework, it is not easy but most important to define API for biological SOAP servers. Therefore, we propose in this paper a web service API especially for the interaction databases: BIND, DIP and MINT. Each biological laboratory can configure their own application systems accessing these three databases transparently. The three databases are mirrored in our local computers on which we have implemented a prototype of SOAP servers for the interaction databases.

1 Introduction

As a part of efforts to solve bio-database integration problem, web services have been deployed in a few biological databases including myGRID[1], BioMoby[2], and KEGG[3]. myGRID is designed for data or service providers who want to build applications for biologist. None of these databases, however, provide web services for interaction information.

Even though the web services have much advantages, this technology is not rapidly introduced into biological field since it is not easy for computer engineers to define practically useful API due to their lack of biological information. System designers should study and know well about the application area – interaction databases in this work – to produce well-designed SOAP objects. We define API for the SOAP servers of interaction databases. The API is practically useful and well designed since it is based on the cooperation between biologists and computer engineers, and the experiences obtained from a datawarehouse design for the interaction databases in the past years. In this paper, we describe the interaction databases that have been spotlighted in terms of its data amount and importance thanks to the introduction of proteomics.

2 Design of the Web Service API for the Interaction Databases

Fig. 1 shows the web service based architecture of the interaction databases and examples of building application systems that are capable of accessing and integrating the three interaction databases. Each interaction database provides web service API with which client systems can implement bioinformatics systems for their own pur-

D. Lowe and M. Gaedke (Eds.): ICWE 2005, LNCS 3579, pp. 591–593, 2005.

poses. The BIND database[1] has three API classes: BindInteractionIF, BindPath-wayIF, and BindComplexIF. The DIP interaction database[5] has defined a single class: DIPInteractionIF. The MINT interaction database[6] provides one class: MINTInteractionIF.

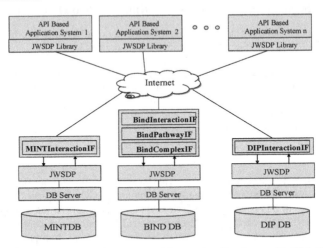

Fig. 1. The Architecture of the Integrated Interaction Database with Web Services

3   An Application Example

Fig. 2 show an example of using the API defined in the previous section for accessing pathways that include a query interaction from the BIND database. Fig. 2 is a SOAP message requesting a pathway ID including the given interaction ID. We have developed a prototype of the SOAP servers and databases in our local systems. Since original sites of the above three interaction databases do not provide their own SOAP servers, we needed to build our own databases by copying the original data in non-relational database format and transforming these into relational database format. We have used three servers with Intel Pentium4 1.9 CPU, Memory 512MB, and the software environment of Windows 2000 Professional, JWSDP 1.3, and Java 1.4.

```
<?xml version="1.0" encoding="UTF-8"?>
<env:Envelope
xmlns:env="http://www.w3.org/2001/06/soap-envelope"
xmlns:xsd"http://www.w3.org/2001/XMLSchema"
xmlns:xsi"http://www.w3.org/2001/XMLSchema-instance"
xmlns:enc"http://schema.xmlsoap.org/soap/encoding/"
xmlns:bind="http://bind.ca"
env:encodingStyle="http://www.w3.org/2001/06/soap-encoding">
        <env:Body>
                <bind:get_PathwayIdByInterId>
                    <Int_1 xsi:type="xsd:string">1653</Int_1>
                </bind:get_PathwayIdByInterId>
        </env:Body>
</env:Envelope>
```

Fig. 2. A SOAP Message Requesting a Pathway ID Including the Given Interaction ID

4 Conclusion

In this paper, we have proposed a practically useful API for SOAP servers of interaction databases. Bioinformaticians may build their own client software that accesses data from those three interaction databases through these objects on the SOAP servers. Once the source databases implement the proposed API on their own databases and SOAP servers, worldwide users can access the interaction databases more easily. Users can use this system with the interaction of gene ontology for semantic integration of interaction databases. We are working on this issue.

References

1. Stevens RD, Robinson AJ, and Goble CA.: myGrid: personalised bioinformatics on the information grid, Bioinformatics. 19, 2003.
2. Wilkinson, M.D. and Links, M.: BioMOBY: an open source biological web services proposal, Brief Bioinform. 3, 2002.
3. Kawashima, S., Katayama, T., Sato, Y. and Kanehisa, M.: A Web Service Using SOAP, WSDL to Access the KEGG System, Genome Informatics, 14, 673-674, 2003
4. Bader, G.D. and Hogue, C.W.: BIND-a data specification for storing and describing biomolecular interactions, molecular complexes and pathways, Bioinformatics 16, 465-477, March 2000.
5. http://dip.doe-mbi.ucla.edu
6. Cesareni, G. and Gimona, M.: MINT: a Molecular INTeraction database, A. Zanzoni et al./FEBS Letters 513, 135-140, December 2001.

Integrating Process Management
and Content Management for Service Industries

Young Gil Kim, Chul Young Kim, and Sang Chan Park

Dept. of Industrial Engineering, Korea Advanced Institute of Science and Technology
(KAIST), 373-1 Gusung-dong, Yusung-gu, Daejeon, Korea
{ttaldul,fezero,sangchanpark}@kaist.ac.kr

Abstract. Content management utilizing Web technologies plays an important role in e-business environment because it enables the seamless flow of information among business participants. In this paper, we present a framework for incorporating content management facilities into a process management system and apply to marketing research processes for demonstrating the feasibility of the proposed framework.

1 Introduction

Competitive pressures of the modern global economy are forcing business participants to continually improve their performances such as quality, speed and cost. Also today's management trends shift from data-centric to process-centric approach [1]. New technologies have become available for adopting this approach. However business executives have struggled to justify continued investments into the systems to reflect the increasing knowledge intensity of all types of work in the organization.

2 Related Works

Process management systems can be used to integrate existing applications and support process change by merely changing the process diagram. Web and Internet tools can support these aspects effectively. Content management (CM) is generally a term that describes the issues around creating, versioning, storing and disseminating information [2], or it is often equated a repository based facility to store contents with some metadata management. While most researches are focused on content management to manage and integrate content-flow itself, we concentrate on content management supporting to process management within organization's workflows.

3 Framework and Implementation

To construct a process management system incorporated with CM facilities, it should be identified firstly what process-related contents is. As depicted in Fig. 1 left, we define process-related contents as that applied in a process. These contents would be bound with XML metadata and stored in repositories. The elements for the metadata consist of three major elements: organization, description, and deployment.

D. Lowe and M. Gaedke (Eds.): ICWE 2005, LNCS 3579, pp. 594–596, 2005.

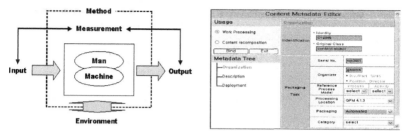

Fig. 1. The entities of process contents and the web interface for content metadata template

For streamlined and effective supports for building mature processes, our idea is to embed the structure of information items into metadata template, which are then filled on the fly doing daily work. The contents used in or produced from multiple sources are registered with automated metadata capturing facilities (See Fig. 1 right).

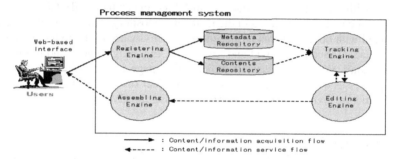

Fig. 2. The framework for content management engines incorporating into process management

The proposed framework has four major engines and two repositories for managing process-related contents (See Fig. 2). The primary role of the CM modules incorporated in a process management system is to bind contents with synthesized metadata and so, to acquire, manage, reused, and service the various types of contents that are produced from a process. The role of each component in process management is:

- **Registering engine:** bind contents with the metadata using XML and register contents and metadata to the repositories. The metadata is whether deployment and processing information of the registered contents or content structure itself;
- **Tracking engine:** with seeking out metadata, retrieval and extract the appropriate contents required by users;
- **Editing engine:** Edit and organize the constitutions of contents, that is, this engine can make various contents needed to a content constitution organized to hierarchical structure or re-composite contents;
- **Assembling engine:** assemble contents using the content constitution information produced by editing engine for visualizing contents;
- **Metadata repository:** store metadata elements using XML and database, also it includes the information of prior content constitutions;
- **Content repository:** store content objects. It can be physical repository or electrical database. It has the information about a physical location of contents.

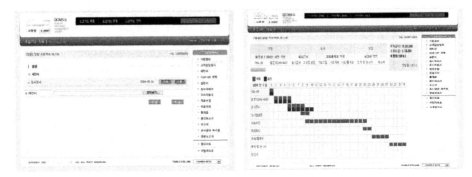

Fig. 3. Snapshots of registering and monitoring interface for a marketing research process

In implementation, a content produced from a process activity is stored in the content repository through the registering engine. In that time, the content is bound and packaged with XML-based metadata having three major part collected by metadata editor, and the metadata is stored in the metadata repository. The stored object content is packaged with other contents produced in the activity according to the organization part of metadata (See Fig. 1 right and Fig. 3 left). Fig. 3 right shows monitoring interface for certain marketing research project. This page includes the key contents of critical processes of the project and shows the project status according to a predefined content structure and deployment information using the CM engines.

4   Conclusion

In this paper, we presented a methodology for developing CM facility-based process management system. The metadata including process entities with 4M1E and content aggregation methods could be used for better understanding a company's processes and easily constructing a web-based process management system. Also the process content metadata consisting of organization, description, and deployment parts could be used for process control and content recomposing and reuse. The proposed framework enables real-time content integration among user's workflow information, organizational knowledge, and a variety of business applications.

References

1. van der Aalst, W.M.P.: Business Process Management: A personal view. BPMJ, Vol. 10. No. 2 (2004) 248-253
2. Stonebraker, M., Hellerstein, J. M.: Content Integration for E-Business. ACM SIGMOD Record, Vol. 30, Issue 2 (2001) 552-560

Service Publishing and Discovering Model in a Web Services Oriented Peer-to-Peer System*

Ruixuan Li, Zhi Zhang, Wei Song, Feng Ke, and Zhengding Lu

College of Computer Science and Technology,
Huazhong University of Science and Technology, Wuhan 430074, Hubei, P.R. China
rxli@public.wh.hb.cn, wustzz@sina.com, sw_cyt@126.com,
michael_ke@163.com, zdlu@mail.hust.edu.cn

Abstract. To enhance the reliability and scalability of the service oriented architecture, this paper introduces a Web Services Oriented Peer-to-peer (WSOP) architecture with a combination of centralized and decentralized characteristics, and gives a framework of service publishing and discovery model based on WSOP architecture.

1 Introduction

Web Services and peer-to-peer technologies widely emerged during the last several years and these two diagrams tend to be polled together in the recent researches. Recent work in content-based search include content-addressable networks – where the content of queries is used to efficiently route messages to the most relevant peers as well as some variations of publish/subscribe networks [1]. These content-based P2P networks place emphasis on locating and distributing the contents rather than on a logical organization of the system architecture and on publishing and discovering Web Services through the peer-to-peer network. Several other projects concern the combination of web services and peer-to-peer networks where [2] gives a general overview and a classification of P2P based web services. This paper introduces Web Services Oriented Peer-to-peer (WSOP) architecture with a combination of centralized and decentralized characteristics, and presents a framework of Web Services publishing and discovery model based on WSOP architecture.

2 Web Services Oriented Peer-to-peer (WSOP) Architecture

We present a Web Services Oriented Peer-to-peer (WSOP) architecture based on the integration of different peer-to-peer systems and Common Web Services (CWS) with the SOAP (Simple Object Access Protocol) connectivity (see Fig. 1). In our approach, peers residing as the neighbors (e.g. with the same interests) on the same P2P network are pulled together to form a peer group. There is at least one super peer in each peer group. It maintains a Local Service Registry Broker (LSRB), providing the fast service registration and invocation in the peer group environment. The CWS, hosted on the SOAP server, consists of service provider, service requestor and Com-

---

* This work was partially supported by National Natural Science Foundation of China under Grant 60403027, National Key Technologies R&D Program of China under Grant 2002BA103A04

D. Lowe and M. Gaedke (Eds.): ICWE 2005, LNCS 3579, pp. 597–599, 2005.

mon Service Registry Broker (CSRB). The CSRB provides access to a P2P network interconnecting nodes (i.e. super peers) in different physical networks using different transport protocols and maintains the mappings of service descriptions between CSRB and LSRB. An important advantage of this architecture would be the flexibility of registering new services to the system via employing the super peers and LSRBs. It will definitely reduce the heavy load of the CSRB when the number of nodes and services in the environment are very large. Another advantage is that service request delivering would not be flooded in the whole systems.

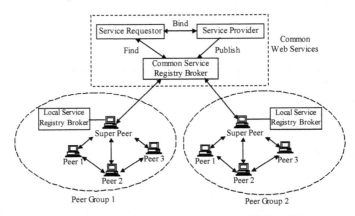

Fig. 1. Web Services oriented peer-to-peer (WSOP) architecture

3   Service Publishing and Discovery Model Based on WSOP Architecture

In traditional manner, the mechanism of service publishing and discovery are centralized through using common UDDI. The WSOP-based architecture will employ the peer-to-peer technologies and decentralize the UDDI service directory. Each peer in the P2P overlay network plays the roles of service provider and service consumer. The super peers in the peer group will take the responsibility for service registry in the group. So, the peer will take most of the work for service publishing and discovery. Fig. 2 illustrates the framework of service publishing and discovery model based on WSOP architecture.

The framework includes several modules, such as P2P System Initialization, Peer Group Discovery, Peer Authentication, Web Services Configuration, WSDL Processing. Service Publishing module uses a service advertisement to publish a service the Export Pipes and the peers can cache the published Web Services advertisements. The Service Discovery module will look up the discovered Web Services advertisements in the local service cache and discover new Web Services advertisements in the WSOP-based system through using static and dynamic discovery methods. It also can cache the discovered valuable Web Services advertisements. Once the services are discovered, the peer can invoke and utilize the service through WSIF (Web Services Invocation Framework) protocol. It uses the same programming model whatever the Web Services are implemented through using WSIF protocol. It can also access the services dynamically generated without stubs.

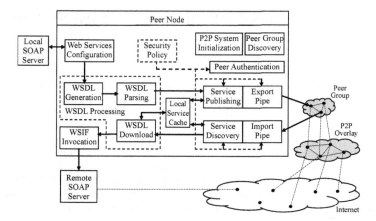

Fig. 2. The framework of service publishing and discovery model based on WSOP architecture

4 Conclusions

In this paper we highlighted key intersect points that enable using Web Services infrastructure and peer-to-peer technologies together and presented an architectural approach and infrastructure towards unifying them. There are several advantages that the service publishing and discovery model based on WSOP architecture offers. These include simplicity and ease of use, openness, reliability, scalability and security.

References

1. Papazoglou, M. P., Kramer, B. J., Yang, J.: Leveraging Web-Services and Peer-to-Peer Networks. In: Proceedings of the 15th International Conference on Advanced Information Systems Engineering(CaiSE2003), Lecture Notes in Computer Science, Vol. 2681. Springer-Verlag, Berlin Heidelberg New York (2003) 485–501
2. Schmidt, C., Parashar, M.: A Peer-to-Peer Approach to Web Service Discovery. World Wide Web archive, Vol. 7(2) (2004) 211–229

A Web Services Method on Embedded Systems

Whe Dar Lin

The Overseas Chinese Institute of Technology, Dept of Information Management,
No. 100, Chiao Kwang Road, Taichung 40721, Taiwan
darlin@ocit.edu.tw

Abstract. An embedded system is driven by the rapid growth of the Internet, communication technologies, pervasive computing, and portable consumer electronics. This paper describes how mobile-based services on embedded systems of Web services can be implemented on low cost ARM microprocessors with reasonable performance. ARM is a high-performance, low-cost, low-power RISC processor. A great deal of attention has focused on simple step. We design a new method using time from which a new required was generated by the home mobile-based server and the visiting network to translate method to protocol in the mobile agents for embedded systems. We can implement mobile devices in mobile-based services where home mobile-based server must reliability connection each other. For our mobile-based service playing an increasingly important role in enhance the reliability, we propose a framework to achieve property for mobile agents of Web services.

1 Introduction

In a mobile web service providing lots of advantages for platform independency, easy personal services communication system, the computation cost and the communication cost are the key factors when a protocol being designed on embedded systems for Web services application.[1]

Web services consist of XML-based system, component based distributed computing technology independent of Web services. Let $K_{h,v}$ be the secret key shared by H and V. Let $K_{h,i}$ be the secret key shared by H and $M(ID_i)$. The $\{m\}_{eh}$ denotes the ciphertext of m encrypted by some public key cryptosystem using public key e_h. The $(m)_k$ denotes the ciphertext of m encrypted using the secret key k of some secure symmetric cryptosystem.

We consider a service network of n agents and an adaptive adversary that can corrupt up to a minority n/2 of mobile agents. The mobile agents have access to a broadcast channel, there are insecure links between each pairs of them. In our system, H has a public key e_h, and the corresponding secret keys p_h and q_h, where p_h and q_h are two large strong primes, and $O_h = p_h*q_h$.

The system has a large prime P, and Q is a prime factor of P-1. Let g be an element of order Q in Z_P*. H has a secret key x_h and a public key y_h. When mobile device MD wants to send a privacy message in the wireless network, M must purchase a privacy ticket from H. This is based on the bound for algebraic curve, the number of point of a curve of g over a finite field for large enough g. To evaluate the proportion of complexity analysis, we consider the number of point of over Fq which is approximatively q. The complexity of our method will be exponential in the size of q, so we will count the number of operations which can be done in polynomial time by addition and mul-

D. Lowe and M. Gaedke (Eds.): ICWE 2005, LNCS 3579, pp. 600–602, 2005.

tiplication and hashing, which can satisfy the requirement of low computational, and communication cost due to the limited power of handset application..

In our system, M randomly selects an integers a and computes respectively A=g^a mod P, A time stamp T, an expire time day T_{expire}, and the certificate $Cert_i$ =(ID_i, A, T)$_{Kh,i}$. V only transfers the received encrypted message send to H. H receiving the message from the visit network, H first decrypts the message and then checks if M's identification is valid by verifying if T is in the content of the certificate $Cert_i$ and if T has not been presented before.

$$S_M = x_h + b * B * A * T_{expire} \bmod P - 1 \tag{1}$$

If yes, H computes, where x_h is the secret key of home domain, y_h ($y_h = g^{x_h} \bmod P$) is the public key of the home domain, a is a random number ($A = g^a \bmod P$)and b is a random number ($B = g^b \bmod P$). And then H deducts a fixed amount of money from M's account. Then he sends the privacy ticket $\{S_M\}_{Kh,i}$ back to V. The mobile device can check the ticket and see if the following equation holds or not.

$$g^{S_M} = y_h B^{BAT_{expire}} \bmod P \quad where$$
$$g^{S_M} = g^{x_h + b*B*A*T_{expire}} = (g^{x_h})(g^b)^{BAT_{expire}} = y_h B^{BAT_{expire}} \tag{2}$$

If the above equation holds, the privacy information (B, T_{expire}, S_M) is validly issued by H (H has secret key x_h and public key y_h).

1.1 Only One Step Service Method

In the service phase, mobile device (MD) uses information (B, T_{expire}, S_M) and sends his Name and time stamp T_{now}, T_{expire}, K and L to V.

MD randomly selects random numbers a, c and y then computes respectively A= g^a mod P, C= g^c mod P, Y= C^y mod P and H has public key y_h.

T_{now} is a real time stamp. The mobile unit computes Name as follows: Name = $y_h\|C\|E$ where E=A*B mod P. And M computes L

$$L = S_M + a * T_{expire} + c*K + c*k*T_{now} \tag{3}$$

V can verify $(Name, T_{now}, T_{expire}, K, L)$ according to the equation (4)

$$g^L = y_h B^{BAT_{expire}} A^{T_{expire}} C^K K^{T_{now}} \bmod P \tag{4}$$

If the above equation holds, then the mobile device (MD) can use the mobile-based service ticket $(Name, T_{now}, T_{expire}, K, L)$.

1.2 Discussion

Proposition: Our proposed protocol can support the Web-based services on mobile EC location.

Proof: Let N be a random variable with probability distribution P and N>0, if K is large enough, then N^K distributed according to independent realization of N. More precisely, the probability of the typically event tends to zero faster than $1/N^2$. We know much weaker than uniformity condition. In the service phase, when MS visits VN nodes $(V_1,V_2,...,V_N)$, Home account management system deducts a fixed amount of money from MS's account, then Home account management agent will broadcasts $(B, T_{expire}, E_M)_{Kh,i}$ to VN nodes $(V_1,V_2,...,V_N)$, where $K_{h,i}$ is the secret key shared with ID_i and home domain, V_j is the visit domain ID number with mobile device M and home domain H. When VN nodes $(V_1,V_2,...,V_N)$ receive the message $(B, T_{expire}, S_M)_{Kh,i}$. There is no information about user ID_i, the secret key $K_{h,i}$ is only known to HMBS and user ID_i. No attacker can get $K_{h,i}$ from $(B, T_{expire}, S_M)_{Kh,i}$ because assumed secure since it is infeasible. The attacker and V_j do not know the cryptographic algorithm key. This is exactly the discrete logarithm problem so the intruder fails. In fact, our proposed scheme, user ID_i is kept unknown to attacker and V_j. Therefore, the MS (ID_i) can use $Name_j$ to roam $VN(V_j)$. The different IDs used in different VNs are that our proposed protocol keeps the Web-based services on mobile EC location. Since B is not uniformly distributed between zero and 2^g. We can provides a heuristic argument to show $P = 2^{hg}$. With $h>1/2$, then with probability greater than $\log(h/1-h)$ for cover application in complexity is $2^{hg+O(1)}$.

2 Conclusion

In this paper, we propose an efficient general service method on embedded system for mobile-based services on Web-based system. Our approach of new scheme can adopt a chaining relationship to prevent some known attacks and provide data integrity and mobile agent. Mobile devices only compute addition, multiplication and hashing, which can satisfy the requirement of low computational, and communication cost due to the limited power of handset application. A great deal of attention has focused on simple step. We design a new method using time from which a new required was generated by the home mobile-based server and the visiting network to translate method to secure protocol in the mobile agents for embedded systems. Our method can face the rapid growth of the Internet, significant number of Web-based information processing has come to rely on services cluster technology to service lots of mobile users.

References

1. Whe Dar Lin, "EC Services Use Different Web-based systems," Lecture Notes in Computer Science, LNCS-2658, pp1059-1068, 2003.

Evaluating Current Testing Processes
of Web-Portal Applications

Harpreet Bajwa, Wenliang Xiong, and Frank Maurer

University of Calgary, Department of Computer Science
Calgary, Alberta, Canada T2N 1N4, Tel. +1 (403) 220-7140
{bajwa,xiongw,maurer}@cpsc.ucalgary.ca

Abstract. Web-portal application development needs to be improved by comprehensive testing processes and practices. Building the initial knowledge by
evaluating and improving the state of the art in testing will steer the future for
better tested portal solutions. In this paper, we present the results of an industrial case study that helped us 1) to understand the testing practices and tools in
use and 2) to identify challenges in testing web portal applications.

1 Introduction

Java-based enterprise portal application [1] and JSR 168[1] based [4] portlet development is growing rapidly. Consequently, identifying practices that improve the testing
of web portal applications become important in increasing the quality and reducing
the time required for the development, deployment and test cycle of these applications. A prerequisite to providing support for better tested applications is an early
assessment of the existing testing process and nature of challenges in the real world.
The inspiration for the empirical study conducted by us came from this need. To our
knowledge, no studies have been undertaken to evaluate how web portal applications
are being tested in the real world. Our paper helps to fill this gap.

The paper reports on the results of the case study and makes two contributions.
First, the results provide empirical evidence on the nature of existing challenges that
impact comprehensive testing of web portal applications and the strategies developers
use to cope with these challenges. Second, the results highlight requirements on tool
support in areas where portal applications cannot be tested automatically.

2 Industrial Case Study Discussions and Results

We conducted an interpretive industrial case study [6] in collaboration with Sandbox
Systems[2] using qualitative methods to explore how developers tested and engineered
portal artifacts. Data collection methods included administration of a questionnaire
[8], interviews, notes we took and numerous discussions with the chief architect responsible for developing portlet-based e-business tools. We relied on the extensive

---

[1] JSR 168 standarizes the interface between portlet container and the portlet
[2] This work was supported under an industrial research grant provided by Sandbox systems

D. Lowe and M. Gaedke (Eds.): ICWE 2005, LNCS 3579, pp. 603–605, 2005.

professional experience of the chief architect at the company to provide deeper insight into the development and testing practices. To gain further understanding on the nature of tests the developer's were writing and running, we inspected an existing web-portal application built by the company.

The challenges in web-portal application testing brought to light are:

Challenge 1: Web portal applications are implemented using the Model-View-Controller (MVC) paradigm. MVC pattern testing for portal applications are automated at the model and controller layers, but it is difficult to test the view layer. Portlets are the chief building block of portal applications forming the view part of the MVC model. Portlet relies extensively on the services provided by the portlet container [1]. Therefore, testing portlets is difficult although important. As reported by the developer's portlets in an application work correctly in the test environment but errors are seen when the same portlets are deployed and executed in the portal server production environment [2]. This is a severe problem as no functionality is available to the end user since the portlet does not display any data. To debug, the portlet is disabled and the logs are examined and analyzed till an eventual fix is determined. This causes the developers a lot of time and effort when deploying the application in the production environment. Existing testing frameworks do not allow a direct fine grained testing of portlets. A testing approach is needed that permits executing the test code inside the container environment and the ability to access and control the environment specific objects. We call this in-container testing (ICT). Although ICT is slow and running tests frequently is infeasible, it might be needed for performing portlet application health checks when the application is deployed on the production environment. Our paper [7] presents a solution to this problem.

Challenge 2: Access to sensitive portlets and pages is controlled by assigning permissions to various user groups. Currently, the administrator setting the permissions must login as a user related to a role and test manually each time the applications are deployed to verify whether the permissions have been correctly assigned. Being able to switch roles quickly is a challenge. Most unit testing of portal applications are done with the current user id for the portal. A framework that allows in setting up a series of ids to use in "role-based" unit testing would be helpful. At this time, this testing needs to be done manually. Our above mentioned paper also addresses this issue.

Challenge 3: As reported by the developers testing frameworks such as HttpUnit [5] geared towards black box testing of web-applications are inconvenient for portal applications because html parsing is slow, there is a lack of detailed control over the environment and constructing an initial state for the HttpUnit tests is time consuming. Portlets unlike servlets are not bound to a single URL which imposes additional problems in using frameworks such as HttpUnit.

Challenge 4: The developers at the company would like to use test driven development (TDD), a practice of agile methods [3], for developing portal applications. TDD encourages that tests must be written first and allowed to fail before the functionality to pass the test is written and testing activities are closely tied in with application development. Unit testing portlets requires the portlet container environment and the ability to access and control the environment specific objects. Consequently, unit tests developed using TDD cannot easily access the functionality in the portlet application code. In the chief architect's words "developing portlet code in a TDD way would be nice". Besides, small changes to the application code can be tested using the mock portlet API reducing the development, deployment and test cycle of portlet applications. Mocking the portlet API is one way of supporting TDD of portlets which is currently being explored by us.

3 Future Work

To gain further insight into the testing practices, we are conducting a qualitative survey and interviews of independent portal developers. In future we will report the results of the survey. Our current efforts are directed towards developing a set of testing practices and tools that aim to meliorate the challenges in automated unit testing of portlets as well as web portal applications. WIT[3] Framework is developed by us to solve one of the testing challenges presented in section 2.

Acknowledgements

We convey our sincere gratitude to Sandbox Systems for their continuous inputs.

References

1. Portal-Introduction-IBM. http://www-106.ibm.com/developerworks/ibm/library/ i-portletintro (Last Visited: February 7, 2005).
2. IBM Websphere Portal Zone http://www7b.software.ibm.com/wsdd/zones/portal/ (Last Visited: February 7, 2005).
3. Test Driven Development-Guide David Astels.;Test Driven Development-A practical Guide, ACM Press (2003).
4. JSR-168 portlet Spec. http://www.jcp.org/aboutJava/communityprocess (Last Visited: February 7, 2005)
5. Client Side Testing using HttpUnit. http://httpunit.sourceforge.net/ (Last Visited: February 7,2005
6. Association For Information Systems, Qualitative research Micheal D Myers http://www.qual.auckland.ac.nz/ (Last Visited: February 7,2005).
7. Wenliang Xiong, Harpreet Bajwa, Frank Maurer: WIT: A Framework For In-Container Testing of Web-Portal Applications. Proc of ICWE 2005.
8. Portlet Testing-EBE. http://ebe.cpsc.ucalgary.ca/ebe/Wiki.jsp?page=Root.Portlettesting (Last Visited: April 15, 2005).

---

[3] WIT-Web Portal In container testing Framework was implemented as a result of this study. Design, implementation and tool usage are reported in the paper published in ICWE 2005 [7]

XML Approach to Communication Design of WebGIS

Yingwei Luo, Xinpeng Liu, Xiaolin Wang, and Zhuoqun Xu

Dept. of Computer Science and Technology, Peking University, Beijing, P.R. China, 100871
lyw@pku.edu.cn

Abstract. XML can describe the concept model of inclusion relationship conveniently. Also, it can directly express the concept model in an understandable way, and the expression format is so flexible that no useless element will be included there. While describing communication protocols by XML, we can not only give a common format for data and control commands, but also reuse the existing XML parsers, so as to facilitate the expansibility and integration of protocols in a system. W3C had proposed Simple Object Access Protocol (SOAP) [1], which is a light weight protocol based on XML used to build information exchange framework under distributed environments. ArcInfo's ArcIMS also used ArcXML as the fundamental command and data transmission protocols to communicate between users' web pages and backend spatial data servers [2]. Our idea of XML based communication protocols for WebGIS benefits from the SOAP model, but we basically focus on the application in WebGIS. With the aid of UML, the typical requiring and responding protocols of WebGIS are analyzed firstly. Then the mechanism of designing communication protocols following W3C's XML Schema specification is illustrated.

1 Analysis of WebGIS Communication Protocols

Interactions between users and WebGIS client determine main contents of the communication protocols for WebGIS: the protocols are mainly responsible for requests and replies of map data. The following two parts show detailed illustrations of client request and server reply protocols as well as formal descriptions by UML diagram.

(1) WebGIS Request Protocols. A map consists of several layers, and the basic request is to ask for a layer. There are different ways to request a layer: (a) Request a layer by providing the layer's name; (b) Request a layer by specifying the layer's redirection address; (c) Request a block of entities in a layer by providing a spatial index sub tree; (d) Request a block of entities in a layer by specifying a spatial range.

Figure 1 presents the UML descriptions of map data request protocols for WebGIS. Each request starts from root class *Requests*, which acts as a container of series of *Request*. Class *Request* should have an *id*, as well as a *time* recording the request time. Class *LayerRequest* derived from *Request* denotes that the current protocols we designed only contain layer request. Every *LayerRequest* should contain a necessary attribute *name*, which indicates the layer name. As described above, there are four classes corresponding to four request ways – *GetLayer*, *GetRedirection*, *GetSpatialIndex* and *GetEntities*, all derived from *LayerRequest*.

(2) WebGIS Reply Protocols. Just like request protocols, replies from server may have a corresponding design: (a) For *GetLayer* request, which is determined only by the layer name, the reply is whole layer data of the layer. (b) For *GetSpatialIndex*

D. Lowe and M. Gaedke (Eds.): ICWE 2005, LNCS 3579, pp. 606–608, 2005.

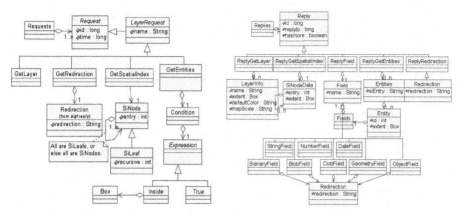

Fig. 1. UML Descriptions of Request Protocols   **Fig. 2.** UML Descriptions of Reply Protocols

request, the reply is corresponding spatial index sub tree with each node carrying with index information; (c) For ***GetEntities*** request, the reply is all information of geometry entities located in the specified spatial range or a redirected address of some fields of those entities; (d) For ***GetRedirection*** request, the reply is simply a redirected address, and redirected data will be retrieved by corresponding disposal modules of server; (e) For the request of getting a single field of geometry entities, the reply is a redirected address of the field of those entities.

Figure 2 illustrates the class hierarchy of the reply protocols in UML diagram. Class ***Replies*** is a container of ***Reply***, which can represent different replies from server. Class ***Reply*** must have an *id* to identify itself, *replyto* to specify the reply-to object, *hasmore* to denote whether the current reply is the last one. There are five concrete classes of replies inherited from class ***Reply***: ***ReplyGetLayer***, ***ReplyGetSpatialIndex***, ***ReplyGetEntities***, ***ReplyRedirection*** and ***ReplyField***.

2   Implementation of XML-Based Communication Protocols

We can conveniently convert class hierarchies in UML to corresponding expressions in XML Schema. The conversion is usually based on the following rules [3] (see http://gis.pku.edu.cn/Projects/WebGIS/protocol/ for detailed XML Schema of request and reply protocols): (a) A class in UML has a counterpoint – a complex type in XML Schema. The classes in UML may be divided into abstract and non-abstract class. In XML Schema, the ***abstract*** attribute is used to identify corresponding complex type of abstract class; (b) Attributes of class in UML is equal to those of corresponding complex types in XML Schema; (c) Class inheritance in UML is denoted by the value of ***base*** attribute, which is an extended mark in XML Schema. The value specifies the type of base class in an inheritance chain; (d) Member class in UML is expressed by nesting sub-element, which is a complex type in XML Schema.

When using XML-based protocols in WebGIS, the protocols should be packed from object set into XML stream as well as parsed from XML stream back into object set at both client and server side. Figure 3 describes a sample for conversation flow of packing and parsing the protocols. A user launches a request of get layer "Traffic

Lines". Firstly, an object tree for the protocol (GetLayer) was constructed. The object tree can be packed into an XML character stream at client side and sent to server side. The stream then is reconstructed to an object tree at server side and be recognized and dispatched to GetLayer-processing module. GetLayer-processing module queries database by attributes of GetLayer to retrieve the layer "Traffic Lines".

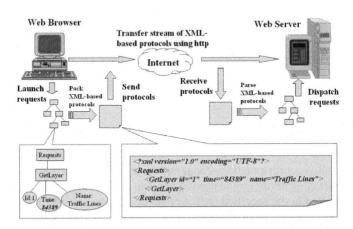

Fig. 3. Packing and Parsing of XML-based Protocols for WebGIS

3   Conclusion

A basic thought to express WebGIS communication protocols using XML is proposed. The XML-based protocols possess favorable scalability because of the usage of class inheritance and composition. The protocols can be used in spatial information exchange among heterogeneous platforms of in distributed environment.

Acknowledgement

This work is supported by the 973 Program under Grant No.2002CB312000; the NSFC under Grant No.60203002; the 863 Program under Grant No. 2004AA131023.

References

1. W3C XML Protocol Working Group, http://www.w3.org/2000/xp/group/.
2. ArcXML Programmer's Reference Guide (ArcIMS 3), PDF on CD only (2001).
3. W3C Extensible Markup Language (XML), http://www.w3.org/xml/ .

Automatic Generation of Client-Server Collaborative Web Applications from Diagrams

Mitsuhisa Taguchi and Takehiro Tokuda

Department of Computer Science, Tokyo Institute of Technology
Meguro, Tokyo 152-8552, Japan
{mtaguchi,tokuda}@tt.cs.titech.ac.jp

Abstract. We have designed and implemented Web application generators based on a diagram approach, which is an approach to generating data-intensive Web applications by using diagrams that represent dataflow relationships among Web components. In this paper, we illustrate how to extend the generator systems to generate client-server collaborative Web applications, in which client-side programs collaborate with server-side programs in performing the whole business logic. The client-side programs contribute toward not only reducing the load on Web servers but improving security and session management of the generated application.

1 Introduction

We have designed and implemented Web application generators to support development of consistent and secure data-intensive Web applications based on a diagram approach [1–4], in which we first compose diagrams to describe overall behavior of the application, select appropriate programs from predefined and general-purpose ones, and then generate an implementation. Although the current implementation focuses on generating server-side programs, the approach is sufficiently flexible to generate *client-server collaborative Web applications*, in which client-side programs collaborate with server-side programs in performing the whole business logic. In this paper, we illustrate how to generate client-server collaborative Web applications based on the diagram approach. The extended generator systems can generate both traditional Web applications and client-server collaborative Web applications from the same diagrams.

2 Client-Server Collaborative Web Applications

As services on the Web become complex, we need client-side programs that are activated by client-side events and collaborate with server-side programs in performing the whole business logic. In this paper, we call such Web applications client-server collaborative Web applications. In general, the behavior of the application is as follows (Fig. 1).

D. Lowe and M. Gaedke (Eds.): ICWE 2005, LNCS 3579, pp. 609–611, 2005.
© Springer-Verlag Berlin Heidelberg 2005

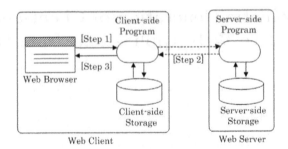

Fig. 1. The architecture of client-server collaborative Web applications

1. A Web client first gets a Web document with client-side programs from Web servers. When the client-side programs are activated, the programs may check the query and change the client-side state.
2. The programs then decide whether a request to a Web server is necessary or not. If there are available data on the client side, the programs process the local data before sending a request.
3. After obtaining the data from the Web server, the client-side programs arrange a Web page to be generated. In addition, the programs may change the client-side state according to the result of the processing.

Client-side programs are expected to contribute toward not only reducing the load on Web servers but improving security and session management of the application. For example, the client-side programs can control the view of Web documents, process the received data before generating a Web page, handle the local data, and manage the client-side state.

3   Extension of T-Web System

T-Web system is a system to generate executable data-intensive Web applications from *Web transition diagrams*, which are special diagrams to describe the behavior of target applications. The nodes and links of the diagrams are (a) a fixed Web page node, (b) an output Web page node, (c) a processing node, (d) a database node, (e) a page transition link, and (f) a data-flow link. The T-Web system has predefined and general-purpose program templates so that it can generate executable Web applications from the diagrams.

Fig. 2 shows an example of the Web transition diagrams and the generation rules for data filtering applications. If we generate the application as a client-server collaborative Web application, the client-side programs interrupt clients' events. When users try to browse a next page or sort the items, the client-side programs process the catalog data that are downloaded on the client side and then embed the result into the Web page template. The client-side programs can be implemented by Java Applet and JavaScript. For each processing node whose processing can be done on the client side, source code of a client-side program

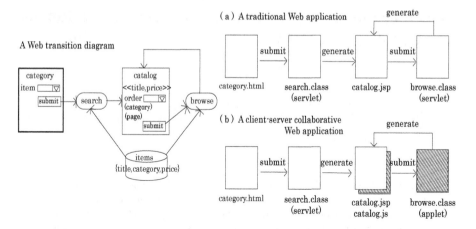

Fig. 2. A Web transition diagram for a Web application with data filtering

such as an applet program is generated. For each fixed/output Web page node whose events activate the above client-side program, a static/dynamic Web page document and a client-side script such as JavaScript are generated.

4 Conclusion

In this paper, we illustrated how to generate client-server collaborative Web applications based on a diagram approach. The extended T-Web system can generate both traditional Web applications and client-server collaborative Web applications from the same diagrams called Web transition diagrams. As future work, we may concentrate on generating a program that dynamically measures the capability of Web clients and invokes appropriate programs, together with programs for a variety of Web clients.

References

1. T. Matsuzaki, T. Suzuki and T. Tokuda. A Pipe/Filter Architecture Based Software Generator PF-Web for Constructing Web Applications. *Computer Software of Japan Society for Software Science and Technology Vol.19 No.4*, pp.266-282, 2002.
2. K. Jamroendararasame, T. Matsuzaki, T. Suzuki and T. Tokuda. Generation of Secure Web Applications from Web Transition Diagrams. *Proc. of the IASTED International Symposia Applied Informatics*, pp.496-501, 2001.
3. M. Taguchi, T. Suzuki and T. Tokuda. A Visual Approach for Generating Server Page Type Web Applications Based on Template Method. *Proc. of the 2003 IEEE Symposium on Visual and Multimedia Software Engineering*, pp.248-250, 2003.
4. M. Taguchi, K. Jamroendararasame, K. Asami and T. Tokuda. Comparison of Two Approaches for Automatic Construction of Web Applications: Annotation Approach and Diagram Approach. *Proc. of the 4th International Conference on Web Engineering*, pp.230-243, 2004.

Web Operational Analysis Through Performance-Related Ontologies in OWL for Intelligent Applications

Isaac Lera, Carlos Juiz, and Ramon Puigjaner

Universtity of Balearic Islands,
Carretera de Valldemossa, km. 7,5, 07122 Palma de Mallorca, Spain
{cjuiz,putxi}@uib.es
http://www.uib.es

Abstract. Web performance engineering techniques are classically based on the augmented description of the model regarding performance annotations. However, these annotations are only related with the syntactical view of the system. The next generation of performance assessment tools for intelligent systems would be capable of acquiring knowledge and even reasoning about performance as the systems will work. The use of ontologies with performance-related information may be used to build on-line performance brokers that assess the performance of the system during its execution. We present the web operational analysis as an example of its future utilization by a framework for building intelligent applications based on semantic web.

1 Performance-Related Ontologies in OWL

There are several issues to be considered when defining a framework for the performance assessment of intelligent applications that seems to be similar to traditional software performance engineering techniques: (i) It must be decided about the way the intelligent system is modelled and therefore, how to add the performance-related information into the software specification with the minimal interference; (ii) Once the performance aspects of the system are depicted in the model, how to transform the architectural options onto performance models and finally; (iii) the way to evaluate every performance model derived from previous steps. This strategy does not consider the semantic representation of the information on the model. On the other hand, an ontology is an explicit formal description of concepts in the domain composed of classes, properties of each class, and restrictions on properties [6]. OWL (Web Ontology Language [2]) ontologies express the set of terms, entities, objects and classes and also the relations among them with formal definitions. Therefore, performance-related information may be also declared through this new web engineering approach, not only for performance evaluation of the different components of the system, but also in scenarios where it is possible to reason about the performance activity in an intelligent application environment and even take actions based on it.

2 Annotation of Performance-Related Information in OWL

An ontology may consider performance-related information as description of a performance view of the application as measurable parameters. However, these performance parameters have been discovered from the relationship among several entities:

D. Lowe and M. Gaedke (Eds.): ICWE 2005, LNCS 3579, pp. 612–614, 2005.

client-web browser utilization or process-cpu demand, etc. This example shows the OWL classes involved in the description of the performance-related information model:

```
<owl:Class rdf:ID="PerformanceMeasure"/>
<owl:Class rdf:ID="Client"/>
<owl:Class rdf:ID="Device"/>
```

Each client or device class member possess different functional or non-functional attributes, however, we are mainly interested on computing certain operational values that are observed during a time interval for the ulterior performance analysis of the application. Clearly, it is possible to reuse existing temporal ontologies which consist on a good example of the ontology information sharing. The response time of a transaction, the service time of a process or even the interval observation time are parameters belonging to the time domain. Therefore, the efficiency of the ontological representation resides on using specific classes for time units, i.e. the OWL-Time ontology in [3] and [5]. This example shows a simple performance object property in OWL, the response time, reusing the time ontology:

```
<owl:FunctionalProperty rdf:ID="ResponseTime">
<rdf:type
rdf:resource="http://www.w3.org/2002/07/owl#ObjectProperty"/>
<rdfs:range rdf:resource="http://www.isi.edu/~pan/damltime/time-
entry.owl#DurationDescription"/>
<rdfs:domain rdf:resource="#PerformanceMeasure"/>
</owl:FunctionalProperty>
...
<ResponseTime>
<time-entry:DurationDescription rdf:ID="BusyTimeID1">
<time-entry:seconds
rdf:datatype="http://www.w3.org/2001/XMLSchema#decimal">
20.0
</time-entry:seconds>
</time-entry:DurationDescription>
</ResponseTime>
```

3 Working with a Performance-Related Ontology in OWL

Once the OWL code has been implemented it is necessary to build some external application (broker) for interpreting, computing and updating performance values on instantiations of clients and devices [7]. Jena [1], is a Java framework for building Semantic Web [4] applications that support inference engines over OWL. We built a tool to operate with the performance-related ontology in order to compute interesting performance magnitudes taken from the operation of web server monitorization. This simple application emulates the future broker implementation which will provide information for ulterior reasoning. Figure 1 shows three instantiations of web clients and two web servers on the ontology. The performance values have been obtained during benchmark operation of the web server *deviceID2*. From this information is possible to compute the throughput of the device applying operational analysis by the broker at any instant. The result of the analysis could be take actions on clients or devices whether the intelligent application design provides this feature. For example, it should be used to compare the computed average throughput with the maximum number of transactions per second (tps) that the device supports and take actions when the application will reach to overload the quality of service required.

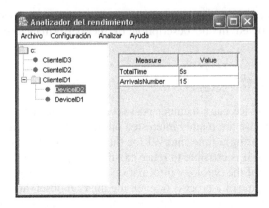

Fig. 1. Performance broker-emulator during operation

References

1. Jena, Java framework for building Semantic Web applications http://jena.sourceforge.net/
2. OWL, Web Ontology language, http://www.w3.org/TR/owl-features/
3. DAML Ontology of Time, http://www.cs.rochester.edu/~ferguson/daml/
4. Berners-Lee, T., Hendler, J. and Lassila, O.: The Semantic Web. Scientific American, May (2001)
5. Hobbs, J.R., Pan, F.: An Ontology of Time for the Semantic Web. ACM Transactions on Asian Language Information Processing, Vol. 3, No. 1, March (2004) 66-85
6. Mesina, E.R., Meystel, A.M. (eds.): What is the Role of Ontology in Performance Evaluation? Panel discussion in Proceedings of 2002 PerMIS Workshop (2002)
7. Haring, G., Juiz, C., Kurz, C., Puigjaner, R., Zottl, J.: Framework for the Performance Assessment of Architectural Options on Intelligent Distributed Applications. In Proceedings of the Conference on Performance Metrics for Intelligent Systems, Gaithersburg (2005)

WCAG Formalization with W3C Techniques

Vicente Luque Centeno[1], Carlos Delgado Kloos[1],
Martin Gaedke[2], and Martin Nussbaumer[2]

[1] Carlos III University of Madrid
{vlc,cdk}@it.uc3m.es
[2] University of Karlsruhe
{gaedke,nussbaumer}@tm.uni-karlsruhe.de

Abstract. Web accessibility consists of a set of restrictions that Web pages should follow in order to be functional for different devices and users. These restrictions, which are quite heterogeneous and rather expensive to evaluate, unless relayed to human judgement, are usually expressed within a program's code. Different solutions have recently emerged to express these restrictions in a more declarative way. We present a comparison of some of them and propose some W3C techniques for expressing these constraints. Using W3C technologies, the evaluation cost can be clearly minimized.

1 Accessibility

WAI (Web Accessibility Initiative)'s WCAG (Web Content Accessibility Guidelines) 1.0 [1,2] is an important contribution to Web accessibility, focusing not only on eliminating barriers for disabled people, but also a major step towards device independence, allowing Web interoperability to be independent from devices, browsers or operating systems. WCAG 1.0 have become an important reference for Web accessibility in the Web community. However the set of the 65 WCAG's checkpoints that accessible documents have to pass is a very heterogeneous set of conditions whose evaluation and repair is difficult to evaluate. WCAG 1.0 specification is written in a high abstraction level which is frequently quite far away from the low level technical detail of the HTML format. Many of those checkpoints are also open to subjective interpretation, including implicit conditions or, simply, containing conditions whose detection can not be automated.

2 WCAG Evaluability

Several rules can not be evaluated automatically by a program with an acceptable degree of trust because they require human judgement. However, there are some automatable rules that can be automatically evaluated with a computer's program. Typical evaluation tools [8,9,10] automate the evaluation of these restrictions **with their own program's code**. XML-based APIs like DOM [5],

D. Lowe and M. Gaedke (Eds.): ICWE 2005, LNCS 3579, pp. 615–617, 2005.

SAX [6] or JDOM [7] can be used in programming languages like Java or Haskell as long as Web pages get a similar aspect as a XML file. However, this involves several difficulties and differences on how their programmers interpret this set of rules. As a result, tools really implement their own set of constraints which are based on the original from W3C, but having important differences from each other that result on different evaluation results, even for the same document, depending on which tool is being used.

The need for a declarative set of restrictions for expressing constraints within Web documents has been recently addressed by some previous work. Taw [8] has had an attempt to express this rule in an internal XML file based on regular expressions that should match document's markup, but the expresivity power was really poor and regular expressions maintainability was not very cost effective. Kwaresmi [11] recently used a self-developed XML-based language for expressing accessibility constraints. It was based on the document's structure (not the document's markup itself), so things like the order of the attributes within a tag, uppercase or lowercase sensitivity or white-spaces became properly treated, among others. However, this XML-based language results rather verbose and is no more than a *ad-hoc* developed format specifically devoted to express accessibility constraints. More generic approaches can be achieved with generic XML-based restriction languages like Xlinkit [12] which is a first-order logic XML-based language for generic restrictions on XML documents. This language could effectively be used to express declarative rules that are automatically checked by a generic validation tool that spots all XML nodes that do not follow the declared restrictions. Each failing node is spotted with a unique XPath locator that facilitates where accessibility barriers may be found. Xlinkit provides evaluating constructors for first-order logic operators including conditional, comparison and quantified expressions. Though this solution is generic and powerful, tools incorporating Xlinkit should use their implementor's platform.

In front of these related works, we have found that XPath 1.0 [3] and XQuery 1.0 [4] may be used to express accessibility restrictions. Table 1 shows several XPath locators for nodes breaking some WCAG checkpoints. Other XQuery 1.0 based expressions can be found at [13].

Table 1. XPath 1.0 locators for nodes breaking accessibility constrains

WCAG #	XPath 1.0 rule
1.1b	//input[@type="image"][not(@alt)]
1.1e	//frameset[not(noframes)]
3.5a	//h2[not(preceding::h1)]
4.3	//html[not(@xml:lang)]
6.4a	//*[@onmouseover != @onfocus]
7.4, 7.5	//meta[@http-equiv="refresh"]
9.2a	//*[@onmousedown != @onkeydown]
9.2c	//*[@onclick != @onkeypress]
10.4b	//textarea[normalize-space(text())=""]
12.1	//frame[not(@title)]

Acknowledgements

The work reported in this paper has been partially funded by the projects IN-FOFLEX *TIC2003-07208* and SIEMPRE *TIC2002-03635* of the Spanish Ministry of Science and Research.

References

1. W3C *Web Content Accessibility Guidelines 1.0*
   www.w3.org/TR/WCAG10
2. W3C *Techniques For Accessibility Evaluation And Repair Tools W3C Working Draft, 26 April 2000*
   www.w3.org/TR/AERT
3. W3C *XML Path Language (XPath) Version 1.0 W3C Recommendation 16 November 1999*
   www.w3.org/TR/xpath
4. W3C *XQuery 1.0: An XML Query Language W3C Working Draft 29 October 2004*
   www.w3.org/TR/xquery
5. W3C *Document Object Model (DOM) Level 3 Core Specification, W3C Recommendation 07 April 2004*
   www.w3.org/TR/2004/REC-DOM-Level-3-Core-20040407/
6. Megginson Technologies Ltd *SAX: The Simple API for XML*
   www.megginson.com/SAX
7. Hunter J. and McLaughlin B *The JDOM Project*
   www.jdom.org
8. Fondazione Ugo Bordoni *Torquemada, Web for all*
   www.webxtutti.it/testa_en.htm
9. Watchfire *Bobby Accessibility tool*
   bobby.watchfire.com/bobby/html/en/index.jsp
10. CEAPAT, Fundación CTIC, Spanish Ministry of Employment and Social Affairs (IMSERSO) *Online Web accessibility test*
    www.tawdis.net
11. Jean Vanderdonckt, Abdo Beirekdar, Monique Noirhomme-Fraiture *Automated Evaluation of Web Usability and Accessibility by Guideline Review*
    Proc. of 4th International Conference on Web Engineering (ICWE 2004), Munich, July 2004, N. Koch, P. Fraternali, M. Wirsing (Eds.), Lecture Notes in Computer Science, Springer-Verlag
12. C. Nentwich, L. Capra, W. Emmerich, and A. Finkelstein *xlinkit: A Consistency Checking and Smart Link Generation Service*
    ACM Transactions on Internet Technology, 2(2):151–185, 2002.
13. Vicente Luque Centeno, Carlos Delgado Kloos, Martin Gaedke, Martin Nussbaumer *WCAG Formalization with W3C Standards*
    WWW2005 conference, May 2005, Chiba, Japan, accepted poster

Analyzing Time-to-Market and Reliability Trade-Offs with Bayesian Belief Networks

Jianyun Zhou and Tor Stålhane

Department of Computer and Information Science,
Norwegian University of Science and Technology, 7491 Trondheim, Norway
{jianyun,stalhane}@idi.ntnu.no

1 Introduction

Web-based systems are software systems with a Web interface. In recent years it has successfully penetrated into our everyday life. Development of such systems has also opened a new area in software engineering: Web engineering. Many studies found that Web development often experiences much shorter cycle time than traditional software development. It conflicts with some non-functional requirements, such as system reliability. When they can not be simultaneously satisfied, trade-off decisions must be made. Such decisions are typically difficult in software development due to the complexity and uncertainty of the development process. They are usually decided in an ad hoc manner. The purpose of this paper is to propose a new methodology for conducting trade-off analysis. Bayesian Belief Networks (BBNs) is used to offer this opportunity. By capturing and modelling the cause-effect relationships between time and reliability in BBN models, it provides a systematic way for doing comprehensive trade-off analysis throughout the whole development process.

2 Why Bayesian Belief Network (BBN)

A BBN is a directed graph, together with an associated set of probability tables to express cause-effect relationships between linked nodes. The use of BBN in software engineering concerns mostly software quality. Recently its application extends to other areas, such as process modeling and cost estimation. Our objective is to use it as a tool to conduct trade-off analysis for time-to-market and reliability. Analyzing the relationships between time-to-market and reliability in the development process is not an easy task: (1) their relationship is not explicit and can not be directly identified. It is transferred by the development process and activities in the process; (2) their relationship is uncertain. There are a lot of confounding factors existing in the process; (3) their relationship is not easy to be evidenced. Different kinds of data from difference sources are difficult to be combined together.

Regarding the advantages of BBNs, the above mentioned problems can be solved because: (1) BBNs are able to model the development process and activities in the process by depicting the cause-effect relationship between the attributes of process components; (2) BBNs identify probabilistic relationships among nodes. They enable

D. Lowe and M. Gaedke (Eds.): ICWE 2005, LNCS 3579, pp. 618–620, 2005.

to reason with uncertain and incomplete information by adding a probability to both the input and output information; (3) BBNs can collect evidence from many different sources, such as expert knowledge, historical data, and so on.

In general, with BBNs we can capture direct and indirect, explicit and implicit relationships between time-to-market and reliability throughout the development process. Such models will support trade-off analysis to be performed in a process scale.

3   Trade-Off Analysis Model for Web-Based System Development

The overall goal of the model is to facilitate trade-off analysis for time-to-market and reliability. Particularly, the model is supposed to address how the total development time and time allocation will affect the reliability of the final system. It will help decision makers choose appropriate time strategies for achieving reliability requirements, and provide a foundation for schedule planning and progress control.

Developing such a model involves three steps: (1) Identify process components, that is, main activities involved in the development; (2) Identifying attributes of the process components, which are relevant to trade-off analysis; (3) Identifying probabilistic dependencies between attributes and draw cause-effect diagram.

For the purpose of illustration, we develop a generic model based on a general understanding of activities involved in the Web development process. At first we define that any Web-based system development consists of the following activities: Requirements and analysis; Architecture design; System development; and Testing. Each of activities has two sub-phases: initial work and rework. The purpose of this decomposition is closely related to the goal of trade-off analysis as how the time is allocated to these activities will affect the system reliability. In addition, reliability is not only affected by the development process, it is also a property of the system. Web-based system is usually constructed using multiple modules. The activity component *system development* can therefore be further decomposed into sub-activities for developing presentation layer, business logic layer, and data management layer. How the time is allocated to develop these layers will have effects on the system reliability.

The full model is illustrated in Figure 1. It consists of fragments that represent different process components. In requirements and analysis fragment, the node *Problem complexity* represents the degree of complexity inherent in the new system to be developed. It influences the actual time used in the requirements initiative and the serious defects introduced in the initial requirements documents. During requirements rework, a number of the serious defects are found and fixed. The node *defects remained after requirements* contains the total number of defects inherent at the end of the phase. Fragments architecture design, development and testing follow the same principle. The node *Technical risk* is defined as level of difficulty under development. It influences both the time attribute and the introduced defects attribute. Finally, the reliability level of the system is directly influenced by *Defects in presentation layer*, *Defects in business logic layer*, *Defects in data management layer*, and *Defects delivered*.

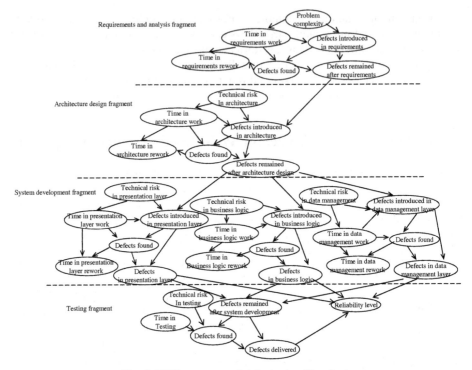

Fig. 1. BBN process model for trade-off analysis

4 Discussion

The effect of time allocation on reliability is transferred by variables in the model. It provides us an opportunity to perform trade-off analysis for time-to-market and reliability and gives decision makers an objective basis for assessing different time strategies, predicting reliability, and controlling progress. We do not make any claims about this model being correct for all situations. In particular, we have not taken into account some typical features of the process, such as iteration, increments, and parallelism. As these properties influence development time and introduced defects, they should be captured in proper variables. The detailed level of attributes in the model is also very limited. Many other attributes might be included in the topology. The exact process variables and topology are context-dependent.

Although a BBN model is easy to build, the real difficulty lies in the validation, that is, determining whether the model correctly represent the relationships in a real process. At the heart of the problem lies a lack of quantitative data. It seems that we have little choice but to rely on information from domain experts. How to collect and treat with this information is therefore a critical issue for the refinement of the BBN analysis model. It is also one of our main research interests in the future.

A UI-Driven Lightweight Framework
for Developing Web Applications*

Keeyoull Lee[1], Sanghyun Park[1], Chunwoo Lee[1], Woosung Jung[1],
Wookjin Lee[1], Byungjeong Lee[2,**], Heechern Kim[3], and Chisu Wu[1]

[1] School of Computer Science and Engineering, Seoul National University, Korea
{kylee,zez4shy,oniguni,wsjung,duri96,wuchisu}@selab.snu.ac.kr
[2] School of Computer Science, University of Seoul, Korea
bjlee@venus.uos.ac.kr
[3] Department of Computer Science, Korea National Open University, Korea
hckim@knou.ac.kr

Abstract. Due to the increasing complexity of Web applications, systematic processes and supporting tools are required for the development of Web applications. In this paper, we propose a UI-driven lightweight framework for building Web applications. This framework is based on an incremental and iterative process that covers the whole development phases. Each identified stakeholder carries out their activities in a collaborative and parallel manner. In the proposed framework, a UI prototype and a conceptual model are produced in the early phase of the development.

1 Introduction

As Web applications are becoming larger in size and complexity, ad-hoc Web development methods are not suitable for developing high quality Web applications. Therefore, several Web application development methods and processes have been proposed [1, 2, 3, 4]. These methods, however, define too many artifacts or focus on only design phase of the whole development lifecycle. In this paper, we propose a systematic and practical framework for developing Web applications.

2 UI-Driven Development Framework

Our framework is based on an incremental and iterative process that covers each and every development phase and supports quick development processes. The process is lightweight rather than heavyweight such as RUP. Our framework supports reuse of components identified in component identification activity. Also, it supports parallel and collaborative development of Web applications. The stakeholders of Web applications include domain experts, software analyzers, UI designers, component developers, DB developers, resource managers, testers and project managers. UI designer builds user interface of Web applications and writes Web pages.

---

* This work was supported by grant No. R01-2002-000-00135-0 from the Basic Research Program of the Korea Science & Engineering Foundation
** Corresponding author

D. Lowe and M. Gaedke (Eds.): ICWE 2005, LNCS 3579, pp. 621–623, 2005.

The overall process of the proposed framework can be summarized as follows: Given the problem statements of the client, the stakeholders first perform Preliminary Analysis. Then, a Detailed Analysis and UI prototyping is performed, following by the Design and UI refinement, Implementation and Validation which are executed iteratively and incrementally (see Fig. 1).

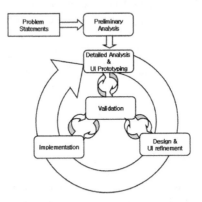

Fig. 1. Web Application development process

The basic elements of a UI are identified and refined from the early phase of a development lifecycle. The navigational structure and the interaction between the UI and clients can be designed with the UI prototype relatively early in the process. Clients effectively communicate with other stakeholders by using the UI prototype. So it reduces waste of developer's resources, times, and efforts invested in the project.

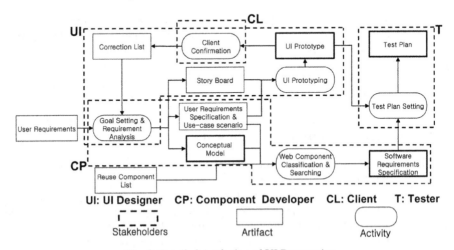

Fig. 2. Detailed Analysis and UI Prototyping

Figure 2 shows the activities and related artifacts of the Detailed Analysis and UI Prototyping phase. In this phase, a goal of the current development cycle is set. Then Requirement Analysis, UI Prototyping, Web Component Classification and Searching, Client Confirmation and Test Plan Setting are executed.

The UI designer develops a UI prototype by using the storyboard from Requirements Analysis. This UI prototype shows the decision hold in the storyboard, and continues to evolve and becomes an actual UI of Web application. In Web component classification and searching activity, the reusable components and components to be developed are identified based on conceptual model, user requirements, and the list of reusable components.

Figure 3 shows the activities and related artifacts of the Design and UI Refinement phase. Due to the limitation of the page length, we have omitted the details of the phase.

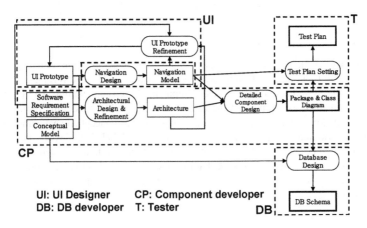

Fig. 3. Design and UI Refinement

3 Conclusion

In this paper, we have proposed a UI-driven lightweight framework for developing applications. In the future we plan to refine the models and processes in our framework and develop supporting tools. Finally, we will perform empirical studies.

References

1. Ceri, S., Franternali, P., Bongio, A.: Web Modeling Language (WebML): a modeling language for designing Web sites. Computer Networks, Vol. 33 (2000) 137-157
2. Conallen, J.: Building Web Applications with UML. 2nd edn. Addison Wesley (2002)
3. Hennicker, R., Koch, N.: A UML-Based Methodology for Hypermedia Design. In Proceedings of UML 2000 Conference (2000)
4. Schwabe, D., Rossi, G., Esmeraldo, L., Lyardet, F.: Engineering Web Applications for Reuse. IEEE Multimedia, Vol. 8. (2001) 2-12

624

Modelling the Behaviour of Web Applications with ArgoUWE*

Alexander Knapp[1], Nora Koch[1,2], and Gefei Zhang[1]

[1] Ludwig-Maximilians-Universität München
{knapp,kochn,zhangg}@pst.ifi.lmu.de
[2] F.A.S.T. GmbH, Germany
koch@fast.de

Abstract. A methodology needs to be empowered by appropriate tool support. The CASE tool ArgoUWE supports designers in the use of the UWE methodology for the systematic, UML-based development of Web applications. ArgoUWE is implemented as a plugin of the open source ArgoUML modelling tool. Besides extending ArgoUML by features for modelling conceptual, navigational, and presentation structures, the new version of ArgoUWE includes support for modelling the behavioural aspects of workflow-driven Web applications. Moreover, ArgoUML's design critic mechanism has been extended to give continuous feedback of deficiencies and inconsistencies in UWE models during the modelling process.

Web applications have evolved from Web information systems to workflow-driven software systems supporting business processes. Therefore, models of Web applications had evolved, too, to explictly support the business process view. The UWE methodology [6] allows for the specification of conceptual, navigation, and presentation models for Web applications following the clear separation of the three structural Web-inherent aspects: content, hypertext, and layout. Additionally, UWE integrates a business process view by offering models for specifying the process structure and behaviour of business workflows, such as those used for the design of reservation systems (e.g., for flights or hotels) or e-commerce applications such as online book shops, and combining processes into the conceptual, navigation, and presentation structure.

We present a new version of the ArgoUWE [4, 5] CASE tool[1] which includes modelling facilities to support the UWE-based design of process-driven Web applications. A business process model and new stereotyped classes are included as well as a set of additional constraints that are used for consistency checks and semi-automatic generation of process models. In contrast to older versions of ArgoUWE, consistency of models is now checked in the background during modelling. This way the developer is supported but not constrained in his modelling activities with suggestions for corrections and improvements.

---

* This research has been partially sponsored by the EC 5th Framework project AGILE (IST-2001-32747) and Deutsche Forschungsgemeinschaft (DFG) within the project MAEWA (WI 841/7-1)
[1] http://www.pst.ifi.lmu.de/projekte/argouwe

D. Lowe and M. Gaedke (Eds.): ICWE 2005, LNCS 3579, pp. 624–626, 2005.
© Springer-Verlag Berlin Heidelberg 2005

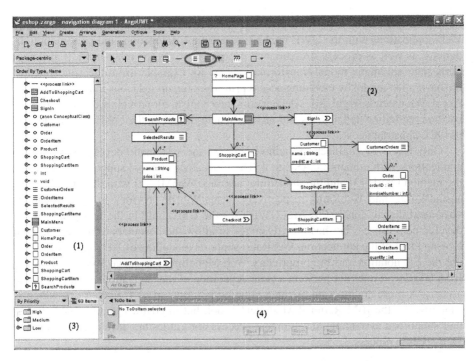

Fig. 1. Navigation model after integration of process nodes

In ArgoUWE, business process modelling is integrated in the design on the levels of use case modelling, process structure and process flow modelling, and navigation modelling. On the use case level, separation of ≪navigational≫ use cases and process use cases is offered. Both kinds of use cases are combined into a navigation structure model (see Fig.1): ArgoUWE generates a ≪process node≫ (visualised by an arrow symbol) in the navigation model for each (non-navigational) use case that is manually selected by the modeller. Thereby, a ≪process class≫ is generated for the ≪process node≫ of the selected use case and automatically included in the process structure model. A process structure model is represented by a UML class diagram and describes the relationship of a ≪process node≫ and other ≪process class≫es whose instances are used to support this business process. The logic of the business process is described by a process flow model visualised as a UML activity diagram.

ArgoUWE is implemented as a plugin of the open-source UML-CASE tool Ar-goUML[2]. ArgoUWE makes use of ArgoUML's general graphical user interface (see Fig. 1) and thus is intuitive to ArgoUML users. In particular, the *explorer pane* (1) provides a tree structure of all diagrams and model elements of the current project. A single UWE diagram is edited in the *editing pane* (2). Issues of design critics are listed in the *to-do pane* (3), sorted by several possible criteria like priority or the model element causing the critique. The *details pane* (4) comprises several panels for showing and editing details of the currently selected model element or to-do item.

---

[2] http://www.argouml.org

On the one hand, ArgoUWE provides the necessary diagram types for modelling Web-applications with the UWE method: conceptual, navigation, and presentation diagrams, as well as process structure and process flow. On the other hand, it also supports semi-automatic model transformations as, for example, from the conceptual to the navigation model by including access primitives (encircled icons in Fig. 1). Finally, ArgoUWE extends ArgoUML's design critic mechanism for providing continuous feedback on modelling deficiencies and inconsistencies based on the UWE metamodel and its OCL constraints.

Only few Web engineering methods support the systematic development of Web applications with a mature CASE tool. The most advanced tool support is offered for the method OO-H [3] and the modelling language WebML [1] with their CASE tools VisualWADE and WebRatio, respectively. VisualWADE provides an operational environment that in contrast to ArgoUWE uses the UML only in the first phase of the development process but has the advantage to allow the designers to render the final look and feel of the application. WebRatio supports modelling of Web applications using the ER notation and the proprietary Web Modelling Language WebML differing from UWE as it does not perform a clear separation of the navigation and presentation aspects. A more architecture-oriented notation is proposed by Conallen [2], which is supported by the IBM Rational Modeller™ tool, but in contrast to ArgoUWE it neither supports a systematic development process nor guides the developer through the Web-specific process.

References

1. Stefano Ceri, Pietro Fraternali, Aldo Bongio, Marco Brambilla, Sara Comai, and Maristella Matera. *Designing Data-Intensive Web Applications*. Morgan-Kaufmann, San Francisco, 2002.
2. Jim Conallen. *Building Web Applications with UML*. Addison-Wesley, Reading, Mass., &c., 2nd edition, 2003.
3. Jaime Gómez, Cristina Cachero, and Oscar Pastor. On Conceptual Modeling of Device-Independent Web Applications: Towards a Web-Engineering Approach. *IEEE Multimedia*, 8(2):26–39, 2001.
4. Alexander Knapp, Nora Koch, and Gefei Zhang. Modeling the Structure of Web Applications with ArgoUWE. In Nora Koch, Piero Fraternali, and Martin Wirsing, editors, *Proc. 4th Int. Conf. Web Engineering (ICWE'04)*, volume 3140 of *Lect. Notes Comp. Sci.*, pages 615–616. Springer, Berlin, 2004.
5. Alexander Knapp, Nora Koch, Gefei Zhang, and Hanns-Martin Hassler. Modeling Business Processes in Web Applications with ArgoUWE. In Thomas Baar, Alfred Strohmeier, Ana M. D. Moreira, and Stephen J. Mellor, editors, *Proc. 7th Int. Conf. Unified Modeling Language (UML'04)*, volume 3273 of *Lect. Notes Comp. Sci.*, pages 69–83. Springer, Berlin, 2004.
6. Nora Koch and Andreas Kraus. The Expressive Power of UML-based Web Engineering. In Daniel Schwabe, Oscar Pastor, Gustavo Rossi, and Luis Olsina, editors, *Proc. 2nd Int. Wsh. Web-Oriented Software Technology (IWWOST'02)*, pages 105–119. CYTED, 2002.

Simulating Web Applications Design Models

Pedro Peixoto

Faculty of Engineering
University of Technology, Sydney
Broadway, PO Box 123
Sydney, NSW 2007, Australia

Abstract. In the last decade several design models have been proposed and efficiently used for the developing of highly complex Web applications. Their suitability to deal with the Web design intricacies have result in a wide acceptance from the Web developer community. There has however been little consideration given to the simulation of the resulting design models. Simulation of the models would provide developers with the means for an in-depth analysis and assessment of the design, contributing for the reduction of both length and cost of the testing phase of the software life cycle. This paper presents a simulation tool that has been developed for the evaluation of Web application design models.

1 Introduction

Web application design has reached a point where only with specialized modeling techniques are developers able to tackle its complexity. To cope with that, several design models have been proposed and a few have gained wide acceptance for their suitability for addressing complex design issues. Design models such as UML [3], WebML [4] and OOHDM [5] are commonly used by developers in the Web application design field. However, developers still have to undertake some coding in order to test and assess specific aspects of the applications, namely presentation, navigation, functionality, and data access and content issues.

Simulation of Web design models has several notable advantages - developers may more accurately and almost instantaneously evaluate the design requirements by observing its response to a set of well known stimulus. Presently, however, simulation of the design model itself has been almost entirely neglected. This paper argues that simulating Web application design models is a not only a desirable but an attainable objective.

2 The WDL Simulation Model

To be able to simulate the several heterogeneous existent Web application design models with a single simulation tool, a new description language was developed – the Web Description Language (WDL) [1, 2]. Essentially, the design model written in languages such as UML or WebML, is mapped into a WDL design

D. Lowe and M. Gaedke (Eds.): ICWE 2005, LNCS 3579, pp. 627–629, 2005.

using four basic entities: Page, Link, Script, and Data, each encompassing a description of its structure and behavior. These basic WDL entities may be further extended and combined to form more intricate components. The resulting WDL model is then loaded by the simulator tool and the system awaits for stimuli to process and proceed.

The WDL simulation model revolves around a four layer concept, namely: Presentation, Navigation, Functional, and Content. It is from these layers perspective that simulation is performed, processed, displayed, and evaluated. A more thorough description of each layer objectives and implementation can be found in [2].

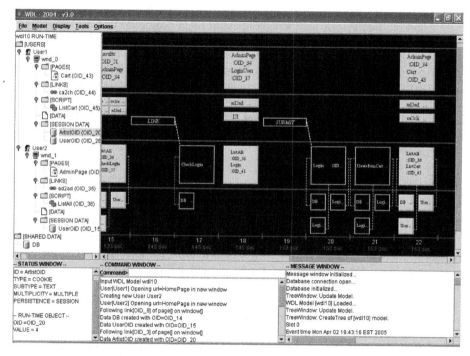

Fig. 1. A snapshot of the WDL Simulation Tool

3   Implementation and Example

The WDL Simulation Tool was implemented using Java and has been progressively refined to maximize its analysis capabilities. Simulation is driven by the input events which act upon the design's constituents, each of which is capable of processing the stimuli and reacting accordingly. The graphics module renders the stimulus and outcome of the simulator engine into a suitable and convenient format for a straightforward and meaningful analysis.

The simulator entails support for multi-session and multi-user processing, contributing to an even more powerful and complete analysis tool. Distinct users may be simultaneously simulated, each with their own private and shared data space, and concurrent access issues to shared resources such as files or databases may be promptly assessed. These features lead to significantly broaden the scope of the simulation analysis, by not only simulating the design itself but by also taking in consideration the concurrent and distributed nature of a Web application implementation.

Figure 1 shows a snapshot of part of a simulation of an online music store Web application, in which two users are simultaneously accessing the application. The simulator enables a meaningful evaluation of the impact that each user's followed path has on the application's state from the above-mentioned four layers perspective. The Web application state resulting from a specific stimulus may be observed and verification of its correctness may be easily performed.

At each instant access to the Web application state is possible, namely the content being displayed to the user, the value of the variables of the executed scripts, and the content of each data entity. This enables a more thorough, flexible and automatic testing phase, leading to a faster error identification and, consequently, to a higher quality of the final product.

4   Future Work

Future work will focus on improving the analysis capabilities of the simulator, such as a requirements assessment module that will automatically evaluate the Web model state looking for a set of specific conditions to be met.

References

1. Pedro Peixoto and KK Fung and David Lowe, *A Framework for the Simulation of Web Applications*, ICWE'04, Munich, Germany, 2004.
2. Pedro Peixoto and KK Fung and David Lowe, *A Framework for the Simulation of Web Applications - Technical Report*, Technical report, University of Technology, Sydney, Australia, 2004.
3. Conallen, Jim, Addison-Wesley, *Building Web Applications with UML*, Addison Wesley Object Technology Series, 1999
4. Ceri, S. and Fraternali, P. and Bongio, A., *Web Modeling Language (WebML): a modeling language for designing Web sites*, Proceedings of WWW9 Conference, Amsterdam, 2000
5. Schwabe, Daniel and Rossi, Gustavo, *The Object-Oriented Hypermedia Design Model*, Communications of the ACM, vol. 38, number 8, pp. 45-46, 1995
6. Ashenden, P., *The Designer's Guide to VHDL*, Morgan Kaufmann Publishers, 1st Ed. 2002

Author Index

Acuña, César J.   334
Ahmad, Rashid   472, 533
Akanda, Mohammed Abul Khayes   136
Almeida, Virgilio A.F.   3
Aouf, Rashad   232
Ardagna, Claudio   363
Atterer, Richard   36
Azam, Farooque   472, 533

Bae, Hae-Young   142
Bajwa, Harpreet   87, 603
Balasubramanian Appiah,
   Venkatakrishnan   435
Ballin, Julie F.   522
Baresi, Luciano   75
Baumeister, Hubert   406
Beckers, Tom   394
Bhardwaj, Yogita   478
Brambilla, Marco   557
Breu, Michael   8
Breu, Ruth   8
Bustos, Pablo   185

Caldera, Amithalal   63
Calvo, Rafael A.   243, 328
Cameron, Mark A.   173
Carroll, Nicholas L.   328
Castelluccia, Daniela   69
Ceri, Stefano   417
Chung, Kyoil   191
Chávez-Gutiérrez, Francisco   237
Clemente, Pedro J.   98
Comai, Sara   209
Coninx, Karin   197
Counsell, Steve   110

Damiani, Ernesto   363
Daniel, Florian   417
Davis, Al   1
De Capitani di Vimercati, Sabrina   363
Delort, Jean-Yves   161
Demaldé, Vera   417
Deshpande, Yogesh   63
De Silva, Buddhima   489
Deutsch, Alin   557
Di Sciascio, Eugenio   69

Donini, Francesco M.   69
Donnerhak, Oliver   569

Errey, Craig   5

Facca, Federico M.   417
Fernández-Manjón, Baltasar   585
Fernández-Valmayor, Alfredo   585
Fons, Joan   506
Fraternali, Piero   75
Fugazza, Cristiano   363

Gaedke, Martin   203, 615
García-Sánchez, Francisco   334
German, Daniel M.   136
Ghezala, Henda Ben   19, 512
Ghose, Aditya K.   104
Ginige, Athula   489, 539
Ginige, Jeewani A.   489
Goh, Angela   302
Golovin, Nick   375
Gómez, Juan Miguel   334
Goodyear, Peter   243
Guan, Ying   104

Hafner, Michael   8
Han, Ingoo   387
Han, Minmin   221
Hansen, Steve   232
Hendrickx, Filip   394
Hernández, Juan   98
Hofmeister, Christine   221
Hong, Gye Hang   263, 267
Honkala, Mikko   340
Houben, Geert-Jan   453
Howarth, Jonathan   478

Jang, Dong Sik   263
Jarzabek, Stan   30, 252
Juiz, Carlos   612
Jung, Woosung   318, 621

Ke, Feng   597
Kim, Chul Young   594
Kim, Heechern   318, 621
Kim, Min Kyung   591

Kim, Sungrim   167
Kim, Tae Hyun   263
Kim, Woo-Hun   352
Kim, Young Gil   594
Kinno, Akira   296
Kloos, Carlos Delgado   615
Knapp, Alexander   406, 624
Koch, Nora   406, 465, 624
Kong, Xiaoying   581
Kraiem, Naoufel   19, 512
Kraus, Andreas   465
Kuo, Zhang   429
Kwon, Joonhee   167

Lee, Byungjeong   318, 621
Lee, Chunwoo   621
Lee, Eunjoo   318
Lee, Jae-Dong   142
Lee, Jang Hee   263, 267
Lee, Keeyoull   621
Lee, Meng-Huang   588
Lee, Wookjin   318, 621
Lera, Isaac   612
Li, Ruixuan   597
Li, Xing   152
Li, Zhang   472, 533
Lin, Whe Dar   130, 600
Liu, Xinpeng   606
Lowe, David   581
Lu, Jianguo   273
Lu, Zhengding   597
Luo, Yingwei   606
Luque Centeno, Vicente   615
Luyten, Kris   197

Mac-Vicar, Duncan   500
Marmaridis, Ioakim Makis   539
Maurer, Frank   87, 603
Meinecke, Johannes   203
Meliá, Santiago   465
Mendes, Emilia   53, 110
Min, Sung-Hwan   387
Molina, Hernán   42
Mongiello, Marina   69
Moon, Kiyoung   191
Morasca, Sandro   75
Moreno, Nathalie   441
Mosley, Nile   110
Murugesan, San   435

Nakayama, Takehiro   296
Navarro, Antonio   585
Navón, Jaime   185, 500
Neuneier, Ralph   308
Ngan, Le Duy   302
Nowak, Andrea   8
Nussbaumer, Martin   203, 615

Olsina, Luis   42
Oorts, Nico   394
Ortiz, Guadalupe   98

Panagis, Yannis   545
Papa, Fernanda   42
Park, Namje   191
Park, Sang Chan   263, 594
Park, Sanghyun   621
Park, Seon Hee   591
Park, Soon-Young   142
Park, Youngjoo   318
Peixoto, Pedro   627
Pelechano, Vicente   506
Pérez-Quiñones, Manuel A.   478
Puigjaner, Ramon   612

Rahm, Erhard   375
Rajapakse, Damith C.   30, 252
Rasmussen, Lars   7
Rho, Hyung Min   263
Rico, Mariano   334
Rode, Jochen   478, 522
Rosson, Mary Beth   478, 522

Sakkopoulos, Evangelos   545
Samarati, Pierangela   363
Sánchez-Nielsen, Elena   237
Schmid, Hans Albrecht   569, 575
Schmidt, Albrecht   36
Selmi, Semia Sonia   19, 512
Senellart, Pierre   124
Sierra, José Luis   585
Sirmakessis, Spiros   545
Skubacz, Michal   308
Song, Wei   597
Stålhane, Tor   618
Stolz, Carsten   308
Sui, Liying   557
Szczepaniak, Piotr S.   400

Taguchi, Mitsuhisa   609
Takeshita, Atsushi   296

Taylor, Kerry   173
Tisi, Massimo   75
Tokuda, Takehiro   609
Totaro, Rodolfo   69
Toward, Brooke   522
Tsakalidis, Athanasios   545
Turani, Aiman   243
Tzimas, Giannis   545

Valderas, Pedro   506
Vallecillo, Antonio   441
Vanderhulst, Geert   197
Vandervelpen, Chris   197
Van De Walle, Rik   394
Vdovjak, Richard   453
Veres, Csaba   285
Vianu, Victor   557
Viermetz, Maximilian   308
Vuorimaa, Petri   340

Wang, Ju   273
Wang, Shengrui   273
Wang, Xiaolin   606
Wegrzyn-Wolska, Katarzyna   400

Won, Dongho   191
Wu, Chisu   318, 621

Xiaoge, Wang   429
Xiong, Wenliang   87, 603
Xu, Jingfang   152
Xu, Zhuoqun   606

Yanni, Wu   429
Yip, Michael Chun Long   53
Yoo, Kee-Young   352
Yoo, Seong Joon   591
Yoon, Eun-Jun   352
Yu, Chen   429
Yukitomo, Hideki   296

Zhang, Gefei   406, 624
Zhang, Zhi   597
Zheng, Yuliang   191
Zhenkun, Zheng   429
Zhong, He-Rong   588
Zhou, Jianyun   618
Zhu, Yangbo   152

Lecture Notes in Computer Science

For information about Vols. 1–3501

please contact your bookseller or Springer

Vol. 3626: B. Ganter, G. Stumme, R. Wille (Eds.), Formal Concept Analysis. X, 349 pages. 2005. (Subseries LNAI).

Vol. 3615: B. Ludäscher, L. Raschid (Eds.), Data Integration in the Life Sciences. XII, 344 pages. 2005. (Subseries LNBI).

Vol. 3607: J.-D. Zucker, L. Saitta (Eds.), Abstraction, Reformulation and Approximation. XII, 376 pages. 2005. (Subseries LNAI).

Vol. 3598: H. Murakami, H. Nakashima, H. Tokuda, M. Yasumura, Ubiquitous Computing Systems. XIII, 275 pages. 2005.

Vol. 3597: S. Shimojo, S. Ichii, T.W. Ling, K.-H. Song (Eds.), Web and Communication Technologies and Internet-Related Social Issues - HSI 2005. XIX, 368 pages. 2005.

Vol. 3596: F. Dau, M.-L. Mugnier, G. Stumme (Eds.), Conceptual Structures: Common Semantics for Sharing Knowledge. XI, 467 pages. 2005. (Subseries LNAI).

Vol. 3587: P. Perner, A. Imiya (Eds.), Machine Learning and Data Mining in Pattern Recognition. XVII, 695 pages. 2005. (Subseries LNAI).

Vol. 3586: A.P. Black (Ed.), ECOOP 2005 - Object-Oriented Programming. XVII, 631 pages. 2005.

Vol. 3584: X. Li, S. Wang, Z.Y. Dong (Eds.), Advanced Data Mining and Applications. XIX, 835 pages. 2005. (Subseries LNAI).

Vol. 3582: J. Fitzgerald, I.J. Hayes, A. Tarlecki (Eds.), FM 2005: Formal Methods. XIV, 558 pages. 2005.

Vol. 3580: L. Caires, G.F. Italiano, L. Monteiro, C. Palamidessi, M. Yung (Eds.), Automata, Languages and Programming. XXV, 1477 pages. 2005.

Vol. 3579: D. Lowe, M. Gaedke (Eds.), Web Engineering. XXII, 633 pages. 2005.

Vol. 3578: M. Gallagher, J. Hogan, F. Maire (Eds.), Intelligent Data Engineering and Automated Learning - IDEAL 2005. XVI, 599 pages. 2005.

Vol. 3576: K. Etessami, S.K. Rajamani (Eds.), Computer Aided Verification. XV, 564 pages. 2005.

Vol. 3575: S. Wermter, G. Palm, M. Elshaw (Eds.), Biomimetic Neural Learning for Intelligent Robots. IX, 383 pages. 2005. (Subseries LNAI).

Vol. 3574: C. Boyd, J.M. González Nieto (Eds.), Information Security and Privacy. XIII, 586 pages. 2005.

Vol. 3573: S. Etalle (Ed.), Logic Based Program Synthesis and Transformation. VIII, 279 pages. 2005.

Vol. 3572: C. De Felice, A. Restivo (Eds.), Developments in Language Theory. XI, 409 pages. 2005.

Vol. 3571: L. Godo (Ed.), Symbolic and Quantitative Approaches to Reasoning with Uncertainty. XVI, 1028 pages. 2005. (Subseries LNAI).

Vol. 3570: A. S. Patrick, M. Yung (Eds.), Financial Cryptography and Data Security. XII, 376 pages. 2005.

Vol. 3569: F. Bacchus, T. Walsh (Eds.), Theory and Applications of Satisfiability Testing. XII, 492 pages. 2005.

Vol. 3568: W.-K. Leow, M.S. Lew, T.-S. Chua, W.-Y. Ma, L. Chaisorn, E.M. Bakker (Eds.), Image and Video Retrieval. XVII, 672 pages. 2005.

Vol. 3567: M. Jackson, D. Nelson, S. Stirk (Eds.), Database: Enterprise, Skills and Innovation. XII, 185 pages. 2005.

Vol. 3566: J.-P. Banâtre, P. Fradet, J.-L. Giavitto, O. Michel (Eds.), Unconventional Programming Paradigms. XI, 367 pages. 2005.

Vol. 3565: G.E. Christensen, M. Sonka (Eds.), Information Processing in Medical Imaging. XXI, 777 pages. 2005.

Vol. 3564: N. Eisinger, J. Małuszyński (Eds.), Reasoning Web. IX, 319 pages. 2005.

Vol. 3562: J. Mira, J.R. Álvarez (Eds.), Artificial Intelligence and Knowledge Engineering Applications: A Bioinspired Approach, Part II. XXIV, 636 pages. 2005.

Vol. 3561: J. Mira, J.R. Álvarez (Eds.), Mechanisms, Symbols, and Models Underlying Cognition, Part I. XXIV, 532 pages. 2005.

Vol. 3560: V.K. Prasanna, S. Iyengar, P.G. Spirakis, M. Welsh (Eds.), Distributed Computing in Sensor Systems. XV, 423 pages. 2005.

Vol. 3559: P. Auer, R. Meir (Eds.), Learning Theory. XI, 692 pages. 2005. (Subseries LNAI).

Vol. 3558: V. Torra, Y. Narukawa, S. Miyamoto (Eds.), Modeling Decisions for Artificial Intelligence. XII, 470 pages. 2005. (Subseries LNAI).

Vol. 3557: H. Gilbert, H. Handschuh (Eds.), Fast Software Encryption. XI, 443 pages. 2005.

Vol. 3556: H. Baumeister, M. Marchesi, M. Holcombe (Eds.), Extreme Programming and Agile Processes in Software Engineering. XIV, 332 pages. 2005.

Vol. 3555: T. Vardanega, A.J. Wellings (Eds.), Reliable Software Technology – Ada-Europe 2005. XV, 273 pages. 2005.

Vol. 3554: A. Dey, B. Kokinov, D. Leake, R. Turner (Eds.), Modeling and Using Context. XIV, 572 pages. 2005. (Subseries LNAI).

Vol. 3553: T.D. Hämäläinen, A.D. Pimentel, J. Takala, S. Vassiliadis (Eds.), Embedded Computer Systems: Architectures, Modeling, and Simulation. XV, 476 pages. 2005.

Vol. 3552: H. de Meer, N. Bhatti (Eds.), Quality of Service – IWQoS 2005. XVIII, 400 pages. 2005.

Vol. 3551: T. Härder, W. Lehner (Eds.), Data Management in a Connected World. XIX, 371 pages. 2005.

Vol. 3548: K. Julisch, C. Kruegel (Eds.), Intrusion and Malware Detection and Vulnerability Assessment. X, 241 pages. 2005.

Vol. 3547: F. Bomarius, S. Komi-Sirviö (Eds.), Product Focused Software Process Improvement. XIII, 588 pages. 2005.

Vol. 3546: T. Kanade, A. Jain, N.K. Ratha (Eds.), Audio-and Video-Based Biometric Person Authentication. XX, 1134 pages. 2005.

Vol. 3544: T. Higashino (Ed.), Principles of Distributed Systems. XII, 460 pages. 2005.

Vol. 3543: L. Kutvonen, N. Alonistioti (Eds.), Distributed Applications and Interoperable Systems. XI, 235 pages. 2005.

Vol. 3542: H.H. Hoos, D.G. Mitchell (Eds.), Theory and Applications of Satisfiability Testing. XIII, 393 pages. 2005.

Vol. 3541: N.C. Oza, R. Polikar, J. Kittler, F. Roli (Eds.), Multiple Classifier Systems. XII, 430 pages. 2005.

Vol. 3540: H. Kalviainen, J. Parkkinen, A. Kaarna (Eds.), Image Analysis. XXII, 1270 pages. 2005.

Vol. 3539: K. Morik, J.-F. Boulicaut, A. Siebes (Eds.), Local Pattern Detection. XI, 233 pages. 2005. (Subseries LNAI).

Vol. 3538: L. Ardissono, P. Brna, A. Mitrovic (Eds.), User Modeling 2005. XVI, 533 pages. 2005. (Subseries LNAI).

Vol. 3537: A. Apostolico, M. Crochemore, K. Park (Eds.), Combinatorial Pattern Matching. XI, 444 pages. 2005.

Vol. 3536: G. Ciardo, P. Darondeau (Eds.), Applications and Theory of Petri Nets 2005. XI, 470 pages. 2005.

Vol. 3535: M. Steffen, G. Zavattaro (Eds.), Formal Methods for Open Object-Based Distributed Systems. X, 323 pages. 2005.

Vol. 3534: S. Spaccapietra, E. Zimányi (Eds.), Journal on Data Semantics III. XI, 213 pages. 2005.

Vol. 3533: M. Ali, F. Esposito (Eds.), Innovations in Applied Artificial Intelligence. XX, 858 pages. 2005. (Subseries LNAI).

Vol. 3532: A. Gómez-Pérez, J. Euzenat (Eds.), The Semantic Web: Research and Applications. XV, 728 pages. 2005.

Vol. 3531: J. Ioannidis, A. Keromytis, M. Yung (Eds.), Applied Cryptography and Network Security. XI, 530 pages. 2005.

Vol. 3530: A. Prinz, R. Reed, J. Reed (Eds.), SDL 2005: Model Driven. XI, 361 pages. 2005.

Vol. 3528: P.S. Szczepaniak, J. Kacprzyk, A. Niewiadomski (Eds.), Advances in Web Intelligence. XVII, 513 pages. 2005. (Subseries LNAI).

Vol. 3527: R. Morrison, F. Oquendo (Eds.), Software Architecture. XII, 263 pages. 2005.

Vol. 3526: S. B. Cooper, B. Löwe, L. Torenvliet (Eds.), New Computational Paradigms. XVII, 574 pages. 2005.

Vol. 3525: A.E. Abdallah, C.B. Jones, J.W. Sanders (Eds.), Communicating Sequential Processes. XIV, 321 pages. 2005.

Vol. 3524: R. Barták, M. Milano (Eds.), Integration of AI and OR Techniques in Constraint Programming for Combinatorial Optimization Problems. XI, 320 pages. 2005.

Vol. 3523: J.S. Marques, N. Pérez de la Blanca, P. Pina (Eds.), Pattern Recognition and Image Analysis, Part II. XXVI, 733 pages. 2005.

Vol. 3522: J.S. Marques, N. Pérez de la Blanca, P. Pina (Eds.), Pattern Recognition and Image Analysis, Part I. XXVI, 703 pages. 2005.

Vol. 3521: N. Megiddo, Y. Xu, B. Zhu (Eds.), Algorithmic Applications in Management. XIII, 484 pages. 2005.

Vol. 3520: O. Pastor, J. Falcão e Cunha (Eds.), Advanced Information Systems Engineering. XVI, 584 pages. 2005.

Vol. 3519: H. Li, P. J. Olver, G. Sommer (Eds.), Computer Algebra and Geometric Algebra with Applications. IX, 449 pages. 2005.

Vol. 3518: T.B. Ho, D. Cheung, H. Liu (Eds.), Advances in Knowledge Discovery and Data Mining. XXI, 864 pages. 2005. (Subseries LNAI).

Vol. 3517: H.S. Baird, D.P. Lopresti (Eds.), Human Interactive Proofs. IX, 143 pages. 2005.

Vol. 3516: V.S. Sunderam, G.D.v. Albada, P.M.A. Sloot, J.J. Dongarra (Eds.), Computational Science – ICCS 2005, Part III. LXIII, 1143 pages. 2005.

Vol. 3515: V.S. Sunderam, G.D.v. Albada, P.M.A. Sloot, J.J. Dongarra (Eds.), Computational Science – ICCS 2005, Part II. LXIII, 1101 pages. 2005.

Vol. 3514: V.S. Sunderam, G.D.v. Albada, P.M.A. Sloot, J.J. Dongarra (Eds.), Computational Science – ICCS 2005, Part I. LXIII, 1089 pages. 2005.

Vol. 3513: A. Montoyo, R. Muñoz, E. Métais (Eds.), Natural Language Processing and Information Systems. XII, 408 pages. 2005.

Vol. 3512: J. Cabestany, A. Prieto, F. Sandoval (Eds.), Computational Intelligence and Bioinspired Systems. XXV, 1260 pages. 2005.

Vol. 3511: U.K. Wiil (Ed.), Metainformatics. VIII, 221 pages. 2005.

Vol. 3510: T. Braun, G. Carle, Y. Koucheryavy, V. Tsaousidis (Eds.), Wired/Wireless Internet Communications. XIV, 366 pages. 2005.

Vol. 3509: M. Jünger, V. Kaibel (Eds.), Integer Programming and Combinatorial Optimization. XI, 484 pages. 2005.

Vol. 3508: P. Bresciani, P. Giorgini, B. Henderson-Sellers, G. Low, M. Winikoff (Eds.), Agent-Oriented Information Systems II. X, 227 pages. 2005. (Subseries LNAI).

Vol. 3507: F. Crestani, I. Ruthven (Eds.), Information Context: Nature, Impact, and Role. XIII, 253 pages. 2005.

Vol. 3506: C. Park, S. Chee (Eds.), Information Security and Cryptology – ICISC 2004. XIV, 490 pages. 2005.

Vol. 3505: V. Gorodetsky, J. Liu, V. A. Skormin (Eds.), Autonomous Intelligent Systems: Agents and Data Mining. XIII, 303 pages. 2005. (Subseries LNAI).

Vol. 3504: A.F. Frangi, P.I. Radeva, A. Santos, M. Hernandez (Eds.), Functional Imaging and Modeling of the Heart. XV, 489 pages. 2005.

Vol. 3503: S.E. Nikoletseas (Ed.), Experimental and Efficient Algorithms. XV, 624 pages. 2005.

Vol. 3502: F. Khendek, R. Dssouli (Eds.), Testing of Communicating Systems. X, 381 pages. 2005.